# Handbook of Doing Business in South East Europe

# Handbook of Doing Business in South East Europe

Edited by

Dietmar Sternad and Thomas Döring

palgrave
macmillan

First published 2012 by
PALGRAVE MACMILLAN

Palgrave Macmillan in the UK is an imprint of Macmillan Publishers Limited,
registered in England, company number 785998, of Houndmills, Basingstoke,
Hampshire RG21 6XS.

Palgrave Macmillan in the US is a division of St Martin's Press LLC,
175 Fifth Avenue, New York, NY 10010.

Palgrave Macmillan is the global academic imprint of the above companies
and has companies and representatives throughout the world.

Palgrave® and Macmillan® are registered trademarks in the United States,
the United Kingdom, Europe and other countries.

ISBN 978–0–230–27865–3

This book is printed on paper suitable for recycling and made from fully
managed and sustained forest sources. Logging, pulping and manufacturing
processes are expected to conform to the environmental regulations of the
country of origin.

A catalogue record for this book is available from the British Library.

Library of Congress Cataloging-in-Publication Data
Handbook of doing business in South East Europe / edited by Dietmar
    Sternad and Thomas Döring.
        p.    cm.
    Includes bibliographical references and index.
    ISBN 978–0–230–27865–3 (alk. paper)
    1. Balkan Peninsula—Economic conditions—Regional disparities.
    2. Balkan Peninsula—Economic integration. 3. Balkan Peninsula—
    Economic policy.    4. Economic development—Balkan peninsula.
    5. Political culture—Balkan Peninsula.    I. Sternad, Dietmar.
    II. Döring, Thomas.
    HC401.H36 2011
    330.9496—dc22                                        2011012471

10    9    8    7    6    5    4    3    2    1
21   20   19   18   17   16   15   14   13   12

Printed and bound in Great Britain by
CPI Antony Rowe, Chippenham and Eastbourne

This product includes Intellectual Property from the European National Mapping
and Cadastral Agencies and licensed on behalf of these by EuroGeographics

# Contents

## Part I Political and Legal Perspectives on South East Europe

## Part II Perspectives on Economic Developments in South East Europe

## Part III Social and Cultural Perspectives on South East Europe

# Tables

# Figures

# Abbreviations

## Countries

| | |
|---|---|
| AL | Albania |
| AT | Austria |
| BG | Bulgaria |
| BIH | Bosnia and Herzegovina |
| CN | China |
| FR | France |
| GER | Germany |
| GR | Greece |
| HR | Croatia |
| HU | Hungary |
| IT | Italy |
| KOS | Kosovo |
| MD | Moldova |
| MK | The Former Yugoslav Republic of Macedonia |
| MN | Montenegro |
| RO | Romania |
| RU | Russia |
| SLO | Slovenia |
| SRB | Serbia |
| TR | Turkey |
| UA | Ukraine |
| UK | United Kingdom |
| US | United States |

## Other abbreviations

| | |
|---|---|
| AIC | Akaike information criterion |
| ALMP | Active labour market policies |
| ANI | (Romanian) National Anticorruption Directorate |
| ATAKA | Attack Politic Party |
| ATP | Autonomous Trade Preference |
| bn | Billion |
| BSP | Bulgarian Socialist Party |
| BTI | Bertelsmann Transformation Index |
| CCEE | Countries of Central and Eastern Europe |

| | |
|---|---|
| CDR | Democratic Convention of Romania |
| CEE | Central and Eastern Europe |
| CEEC | Central and Eastern European countries |
| CEEPUS | Central European Exchange Program for University Studies |
| CEO | Chief Executive Officer |
| CE | Council of Europe |
| CF | Conflict area |
| CIT | Corporate income tax |
| CMS | Corruption Monitoring Systems |
| CoE | Council of Europe representative |
| COMECON | Council for Mutual Economic Assistance |
| CPESSEC | Centre of Public Employment Services of Southeast European Countries |
| CPI | Corruption Perception Index |
| CPSU | Communist Party of the Soviet Union |
| CSD | Center for the Study of Democracy |
| CVM | Cooperation and Verification Mechanism |
| DACI | Directorate for Anti-Corruption Initiatives (Montenegro) |
| DCFTA | Deep and comprehensive free trade area |
| DEMOS | Demokratična opozicija Slovenije (Democratic opposition of Slovenia) |
| DIACA | Department for Internal Administrative Control and Anti-Corruption |
| DO | Donor representative |
| DSB | Democrats for a Strong Bulgaria |
| EA | Europe Agreement |
| EATR | Effective average tax rate |
| EBRD | European Bank for Reconstruction and Development |
| EC | European Commission, European Community |
| ECTS | European Credit Transfer System |
| EEA | European Environment Agency |
| EFTA | European Free Trade Association |
| EHEA | European Higher Education Area |
| EIB | European Investment Bank |
| EIS | European Innovation Scoreboard |
| EMAC | European Marketing Academy |
| ENP | European Neighbourhood Policy |
| EPL | Employment Protection Legislation |
| EPO | European Patent Office |

| | |
|---|---|
| ER | Elected representative |
| ESS | European Social Survey |
| EU | European Union |
| EULEX | European Union Rule of Law Mission in Kosovo |
| EUR | Euro (European currency) |
| EVS | European Values Study |
| FDI | Foreign direct investment |
| FDSN | Democratic National Salvation Front (*Romanian political party*) |
| FED | Federation |
| FELU | Faculty of Economics, University of Ljubljana |
| FMCG | Fast-moving consumer goods |
| FP7 | Seventh Framework Programme |
| FSN | National Salvation Front (*Romanian political party*) |
| FYR | Former Yugoslav Republic |
| GDP | Gross domestic product |
| GDPpc PPP | Gross domestic product per capita at purchasing power parity |
| GERB | Citizens for the European Development of Bulgaria (*Bulgarian political party*) |
| GERD | Gross domestic expenditure on research and Development |
| GRP | Gross regional product |
| GO | Government official |
| HBS | Household budget survey |
| HDI | Human Development Index |
| HDZ | Croatian Democratic Union (*Croatian political party*) |
| HIDAA | High Inspectorate for Declaration and Audit of Assets |
| ICT | Information and communication technology |
| ICTY | International Criminal Tribunal for the Former Yugoslavia |
| IDA | International Development Assistance |
| IDI | In-depth interviews |
| IFC | The International Financial Corporation |
| IFN | Informal network |
| IFC | International Finance Corporation |
| ILO | International Labour Organization |
| IMF | International Monetary Fund |
| IPF | Infrastructure Projects Facility in the Western Balkans |
| ISO | International Organization for Standardization |
| JIU | (Albanian) Joint Investigative Unit |

| JU | Judge/prosecutor |
| INGO | International non-governmental organization representative |
| ISCED | International Standard Classification of Education |
| ISPA | Instrument for Structural Policies for Pre-Accession |
| ISSP | International Social Survey Programme |
| KFOR | Kosovo Force |
| KLA | Kosovo Liberation Army |
| LB | Representative of local business |
| LFS | Labour Force Survey |
| ME | Media representative |
| MMR | Maximum to minimum ratio |
| mn | Million |
| MNC | Multinational company |
| MNE | Multinational enterprise |
| MRF | Movement for Rights and Freedoms |
| n.a. | Not available |
| NATO | North Atlantic Treaty Organization |
| NGO | Non-Governmental Organization |
| NIC | National innovation capacity |
| NIS | National innovation system |
| NMS | National Movement Simeon II (*Chapter 3*); New EU member states (*other chapters*) |
| NS | National Socialism |
| NUTS | Nomenclature des unités territoriales statistiques |
| OECD | Organisation for Economic Co-operation and Development |
| OSCE | Organization for Security and Cooperation in Europe |
| PC | Personal computer |
| PD | Democratic Party (*Romanian political party*) |
| PDSR | Party of Social Democracy of Romania |
| PHARE | Poland and Hungary: Aid for Restructuring of the Economies |
| Pkm | Passenger kilometers |
| PNL | National Liberal Party (*Romanian political party*) |
| PNUSKOK | National Police Office for the Fight Against Corruption and Organized Crime (Croatia) |
| pp | Percentage points |
| PP | Political party representative |
| PPP | Purchasing power parity |

| | |
|---|---|
| PR | Public procurement official |
| PRM | Greater Romania Party (*Romanian political party*) |
| PSM | Socialist Labour Party (*Romanian political party*) |
| R&D | Research and development |
| RS | Republika Srpska |
| RZS | Order, Law, Justice (*Bugarian political party*) |
| SAA | Stabilization and Association Agreement |
| SAP | Stabilization and Association Process |
| SCPC | State Commission for Prevention of Corruption (Macedonia) |
| SDA | Party of Democratic Action (*Political party in Bosnia and Herzegovina*) |
| SDS | Serbian Democratic Party (*Political party in Bosnia and Herzegovina*) |
| SDP | Stranka demokratskih promjena (Party for Democratic Change) (*Croatian political party*) |
| SDR | Special Drawing Rights |
| SEE | South East Europe |
| SEEC | South East European countries |
| SEESSP | South-East European Social Survey Project |
| SELDI | Southeast European Legal Development Initiative |
| SFR | Socialist Federal Republic |
| SII | Summary Innovation Index |
| SME | Small and medium-sized enterprise |
| SPS | Socialist Party of Serbia |
| SSEES | School of Slavonic and East European Studies |
| ST | State level |
| S&T | Science and technology |
| TEN-T | Trans-European Transport Network |
| TFP | Total factor productivity |
| Tkm | Freight tonne kilometers |
| UDF | Union of Democratic Forces |
| UDMR | Democratic Alliance of Hungarians in Romania |
| UN | United Nations |
| UNCTAD | United Nations Conference on Trade and Development |
| UNDP | United Nations Development Programme |
| UNMIK | United Nations Interim Administration Mission in Kosovo |
| UNO | United Nations Organization |

| | |
|---|---|
| UNPR | National Union for the Advancement of Romania (*Romanian political party*) |
| USKOK | Office for the Fight Against Corruption and Organized Crime (Croatia) |
| USPTO | United States Patent and Trademark Office |
| WBIF | Western Balkans Investment Framework |
| WBS | Western Balkan countries |
| WDI | World Development Indicator |
| WEF | World Economic Forum |
| WHO | World Health Organization |
| WIIW | Wiener Institut für internationale Wirtschaftsvergleiche |
| WVS | World Values Survey |

# Acknowledgements

We would like to acknowledge the great support of our colleagues at Carinthia University of Applied Sciences, in particular of our Dean, Dietmar Brodel; of Andrea Adametz and Eithne Knappitsch for their very valuable language editing; of Marika Gruber, Christina Kucher and Anja Prochiner for preparing the SEE country profiles; and of Natascha Nagele for her help during the editing process. We would also like to thank our Senior Commissioning Editor at Palgrave Macmillan, Virgina Thorp, as well as Paul Milner, for their trust, assistance and advice. We are very grateful also to our students in the International Business Management Master's course at Carinthia University of Applied Sciences for the inspiration they have given us during invaluable discussions. A special thank you goes to our families, to Katja, Jakob, Franziska, Nikitas and Aljoscha, for their patience and understanding during the process of editing this book.

*Dietmar Sternad and Thomas Döring*
*Villach/Austria, December 2010*

# Notes on Contributors

**Will Bartlett** is Senior Research Fellow in the Political Economy of South East Europe at the London School of Economics, and Honorary Professor at both the London School of Hygiene and Tropical Medicine and the University of Bristol. He has an MA in economics from the University of Cambridge, an MSc from the University of London and a PhD from the University of Liverpool. He has been Lecturer in Economics at the universities of Southampton, Bath and Bristol, and Research Fellow at the European University Institute in Florence. His research interests lie in the field of economic and social development and in the field of comparative economic systems, with a focus on South East Europe. His book *Europe's Troubled Region: Economic Development, Institutional Reform, and Social Welfare* was published in 2008.

**Christian Bellak** is Associate Professor of Economics in the Department of Economics, University of Economics and Business, Vienna, Austria. His research interests include international factor flows (foreign direct investment; migration) and economic policy. He has published several contributions in multi-author volumes and is the author of several articles published in international scientific journals. He is a consultant to UNCTAD and other international bodies and has been a visiting lecturer at several universities.

**Ágnes Borgulya** is Associate Professor for Corporate and International Communication at the University of Pecs, Faculty of Business and Economics, Hungary. Her main research fields are corporate communication and culture, as well as cross-cultural and international communication of enterprises. She is the author and editor of several books and research articles in Hungarian and English.

**David Crosier** is an education system and policy analyst at Eurydice, the EU information network on education. He is responsible for the network's higher education activities, leading work on monitoring higher education reforms across Europe. Between 2002 and 2008 he worked for the European University Association, where he managed the Trends in European Higher Education project and co-authored the Trends V report. Prior to that, he worked for the Council of Europe in Strasbourg and was responsible for education action programmes in post-conflict South Eastern European countries.

**Danica Fink-Hafner** is a professor and Head of the Centre for Political Science Research at the Faculty of Social Sciences, University of Ljubljana, Slovenia. She has been a Fulbright scholar in Portland, Oregon, and a visiting researcher at the University of Strathclyde and at the University of Warwick (PECO grant). She has published widely, including articles in journals such as the *Journal of European Public Policy*, *Public Administration*, *Europe-Asia Studies* and the *Czech Sociological Review*.

**Åse B. Grødeland** is Senior Researcher at the Chr. Michelsen Institute, Bergen, Norway. Her research interests include civil society, corruption-related issues and legal culture in post-Communist Europe. She is currently directing international research projects on European legal cultures, and on legal culture and anti-corruption reform in the Western Balkans. She has published extensively on these issues; her most recent publications include 'Elite Perceptions of Anti-Corruption Efforts in Ukraine' (*Global Crime*, 2010).

**Elizabeth Heath** is Education Programme Manager at SPARK, a Dutch NGO specializing in higher education development in post-conflict areas. She is responsible for a number of the organization's education project activities, many in South East Europe. These include working with universities to develop their international strategy and integration into the European Higher Education Area. Before joining SPARK, she researched opportunities for change at the University of Mitrovica in relation to its political environment. Between 2004 and 2006, she was based in central administration and management at the University of Warwick, UK, and worked for the UKGRAD network to develop a network of universities in the region to share their skills training provision for PhD students.

**Dobromir Hristov** is a research fellow at the Economic Programme of the Center for the Study of Democracy, Sofia, Bulgaria. He has been a Japanese Government grantee at the Osaka School of International Public Policy. After finishing his PhD, he pursued a career as one of the core young researchers of the CSD, conducting research in the field of good governance, grey economy and corruption.

He has been one of the leading researchers in a recently commissioned project by the European Commission's Directorate General Justice, Liberty and Security, concerning the cooperation of border agencies at the external borders of the EU.

**Valentin Inzko** is the High Representative and EU Special Representative in Bosnia and Herzegovina. A lawyer and linguist (Russian and Serbo-Croat) by training, he has been involved in South East European diplomacy since joining the Austrian Foreign Ministry in 1981. His extensive experience in the region includes appointments in Belgrade (1982–86), Sarajevo (1996–99) and Ljubljana (2005–09). From 1999 to 2005, he headed the Austrian Foreign Ministry's department responsible for Central, Eastern and Southern Europe.

**Daniela Ivanova** is Associate Professor at the Department of Natural Resource Economics, University of National and World Economy in Sofia, Bulgaria, where she lectures on commodity science and quality management. Her research is focused on sustainable production and consumption, consumer attitude and behaviour in Bulgaria. She participates in numerous national and international projects in this area. She is also President of the Bulgarian National Consumers Association.

**Reinhold Kosfeld** is Professor at the Institute of Economics at the University of Kassel, Germany, where he lectures on statistics, econometrics and economic growth. His research interest is focused on regional economics and spatial econometrics. He is co-author of several books on empirical research methods and applied econometrics.

**Đuro Kutlača** is Head of S&T Policy Research Center, Scientific Counsellor at the 'Mihajlo Pupin' Institute and Professor at the Faculty of Information Technology in Belgrade, where he teaches project and innovation management. He was formerly a visiting researcher at the Fraunhofer-Institut für Systemtechnik und Innovationsforschung, Karlsruhe, Germany, and at the Science Policy Research Unit, University of Sussex, UK, and a member of the National Experts for S&T Indicators group at the OECD. He has also been a member of several research teams and has presented and published numerous scientific papers and books. His research interests include science and technology and industry development and policy, metrics in science and technology, and innovation and innovation theory and practice.

**Damjan Lajh** is Assistant Professor of policy analysis in the Faculty of Social Sciences, University of Ljubljana, Slovenia, and a researcher at the Centre for Political Science Research at the same faculty. His research interests are focused on EU policy-making processes, Europeanization processes and comparative analysis of democratic transition in the post-Yugoslav region. As author or co-author, he has published five books and many scholarly articles in edited volumes and scientific journals.

**Markus Leibrecht** is Senior Economist at the Vienna University of Economics and Business, Austria, where he received his doctoral degree and his habilitation (post-doctoral degree). His research is focused on public economics, foreign direct investment and economic policy. He has published in international journals such as *Public Choice, World Economy, Applied Economics, Economics of Transition, Finanzarchiv, Open Economies Review, Structural Change and Economic Dynamics* and *Empirica*. He is also the author of several chapters in multi-author volumes.

**Mario Liebensteiner** is Research Assistant at the Vienna University of Economics and Business, Austria. He gained his first research experience contributing to projects about migration in the EU-15 and about consumer and business confidence.

**Karin Liebhart** is Lecturer at the Department of Political Science, University of Vienna, Austria, and Visiting Fellow at the Institute of European Studies and International Relations, Jean Monnet Chair, Comenius University Bratislava, Slovakia. Previously she worked as a visiting professor at the Institute of Government and Politics, University of Tartu, Estonia, and as a researcher at the Institute of East and Southeast European Studies, Vienna, Austria. Her research is focused on European integration and the enlargement process, European neighbourhood policy, political, economic, social and cultural transformation processes, political cultures, memory politics and the visual representations of politics.

**Maja Makovec Brenčič** is Associate Professor of International Business and Marketing and Vice Dean for Development at the Faculty of Economics, University of Ljubljana, Slovenia. Her main research areas are the internationalization of firms, international marketing, B2B and relationship marketing. She is one of the leading marketing and international business academics in Slovenia, involved with various professional associations (EMAC, President of Slovenian Marketing Association and Vice-Chair of the Slovenian Advertising Arbitration Board). She is a vice-president of the supervisory board of Gorenje. Her activities are also dedicated to the area of quality assurance in higher education in Slovenia.

**Reinhard Neck** has been Full Professor of Economics at Klagenfurt University, Austria, since 1997. He finished his PhD *sub auspiciis praesidentis* (with special distinctions), was Assistant Professor at the University of Fribourg, Switzerland, and at the Vienna University of Economics and Business Administration, Austria, Joseph Schumpeter Research Fellow at Harvard University from 1991 to 1992 and Austrian Visiting Professor at Stanford University in 2001. He was a professor at the German universities of Bielefeld and Osnabrück from 1992 to 1997. His numerous publications in scientific journals and books deal with issues of economic policy, macro-economics, applied econometrics, public economics and European integration (among other subjects).

**Alexander Patsch** is a practising lawyer and partner of Graf Patsch Taucher Rechtsanwälte, Vienna, Austria. He is also a lecturer at the universities of Graz and Vienna on issues related to the law of foreign direct investments in East and South East Europe.

**Christian Promitzer** is Assistant Professor at the Centre for South Eastern European History at the University of Graz, Austria. His research interests include ethnic minorities in Central and South Eastern Europe, civil societies in the Balkans, post-Communist historiography in South East Europe, symbolic geographies, and eugenics and the social history of medicine in South East Europe. He has published widely on these topics and has also headed a research project entitled 'Hidden Minorities between Central Europe and the Balkans'.

**Slavo Radosevic** is Professor of Industry and Innovation Studies at University College London (School of Slavonic and East European Studies – SSEES). He is also Deputy Director of SSEES and Director of the Centre for Comparative Economics. His research interests are in the areas of science, technology, industrial change and foreign direct investments in countries of Central and Eastern Europe, and he continues to be involved in international projects in this area. Slavo Radosevic has published extensively in international journals on issues of innovation policy and innovation in CEE, and he has edited several books in this field. He is author of *International Technology Transfer and Catch Up in Economic Development* (1999). He has acted as an expert for the various director generals of the European Commission, and as consultant to UNESCO, OECD, UN ECE, UNIDO, World Bank and Asian Development Bank, as well as to several CEE governments. He is a member of the Management Committee of the ERAWatch network.

**Albert Simkus** is Professor of Sociology at the Department of Sociology and Political Science at the Norwegian University of Science and Technology in Trondheim and a senior researcher at the Center for the Study of Civil War at PRIO in Oslo. His publications include various articles in international journals, such as the *American Sociological Review* and the *International Journal of Sociology* (*IJS*). He has edited special issues of *IJS* on Eastern Europe and the Western Balkans, was director of the South East European Social Survey Project (SEESSP) and is co-editing, with Kristen Ringdal, a book about the SEESSP.

**Dimitrina Spencer** obtained her doctorate in social anthropology at the Institute for Social and Cultural Anthropology and Linacre College, University of Oxford. She works at the Department of Education, University of Oxford, teaching anthropology and conducting research on scientific pedagogy, affect and technology. Previously she conducted fieldwork in Bulgaria, Greece, Turkey, Macedonia, Nigeria and the UK on social capital, migration and social networks, well-being, European Islam and post-socialist transition. She is co-editor of *Anthropological Fieldwork: A Relational Process* (2010) and *Emotions in the Field: the Psychology and Anthropology of Fieldwork Experience* (2010).

**Ruslan Stefanov** is Director of the Economic Programme of the Center for the Study of Democracy. For eight years he has been the coordinator of an expert group on the hidden economy and corruption in Bulgaria. Currently he is studying the mechanisms of good governance and anti-corruption in the energy sector in Bulgaria. He is an expert on, and closely follows, Bulgaria's progress on fighting corruption and organized crime under the Cooperation and Verification Mechanism of the European Commission.

**Elka Vasileva** is Associate Professor at the Department of Economy of Natural Resources, University of National and World Economy, Bulgaria, where she lectures on commodity science and on quality and environmental management. Her research is focused on sustainable production and consumption and consumer policy. She is co-author of several books and of a multitude of publications in Bulgarian and English, the most recent being on consumer education for sustainable consumption. She has participated in international, European and national projects in the area of sustainable policy and consumer behaviour. She has also been involved in Environment National Contact Point for the Seventh Framework Programme for Research and Technological Development (FP7).

**Hermine Vidovic** is Senior Economist at the Vienna Institute for International Economic Studies, Austria, where she works as an expert on labour markets in the new EU member states and in the Western Balkan countries, as well as on the economies of Slovenia and Croatia.

**Alexander Werner** is Research Assistant at the Institute of Economics at the University of Kassel, Germany, where he lectures on statistics and econometrics. His research interest lies in the fields of econometrics and regional economics. Currently he is working on his doctoral thesis on spatial quantile regression.

**Vesna Žabkar** is Full Professor of Marketing and Head of the Institute for Marketing at the Faculty of Economics, University of Ljubljana. Before her affiliation with the Slovenian university, she worked in the marketing department of BOSCH GmbH, Karlsruhe, Germany. She was a Fulbright visiting scholar in a doctoral programme at the J. L. Kellogg Graduate School of Management, Northwestern University, Evanston, Illinois, and Visiting Professor at the Chair of International Marketing, Betriebswirtschaftliches Zentrum, University of Vienna. She is the author and co-author of several articles published in professional and scientific journals in Slovenia and internationally. Her research interests involve marketing relationships, marketing communications and business-to-business marketing. She is one of the editors of the *Economic and Business Review*.

# Foreword: South East Europe Means Business

*Valentin Inzko*

*The High Representative and EU Special Representative in Bosnia and Herzegovina*

I am particularly pleased to introduce this useful and timely book as it originates from the University of Applied Sciences in Carinthia, which is my home state in Austria and which, because of its geography and its historical, cultural and commercial links to the wider region, offers a unique vantage point from which to view South East Europe.

I believe this handbook can play an important role in realizing the hitherto untapped potential of South East European economies, including the economy of Bosnia and Herzegovina, where I have served as Austrian ambassador, the International Community's High Representative and the European Union's Special Representative.

Today we are seeing all across our part of Europe – in those countries that are already EU member states and in those that are working steadily to become member states – a rediscovery of the cultural and economic synergies that have always existed among the states of this region but which have been disrupted by history.

History is being helpful again, and that means that South East Europe – a vibrant market of 55 million people – can systematically and profitably reintegrate in the wider continental and global economy.

The region's industrial and transport infrastructure has been substantially upgraded and now needs significant investment for further development. At the same time, competitive education and training standards and competitive labour costs make for an optimal production base, right next to the major European markets.

For much of the 1990s, South East Europe – the Western Balkans in particular – was generally viewed through a prism of social and political crises. That prism has long been obsolete, and it is time that the region came to be seen and understood in a more positive, more accurate and more up-to-date light.

I hope that this handbook will help to *re-brand* South East Europe – because that is a process that will benefit not just those in the region but all those who invest in and trade with the region.

My central message to you, after nearly three decades of working on and/or living in that region, is that South East Europe means business.

The ways of doing business in this part of the continent are, as elsewhere, distinctive, but they are certainly not obscure or impenetrable. For centuries, businesspeople in these countries have thrived on a sophisticated and pragmatic understanding of different cultures and different markets.

At the same time, the region as a whole is well advanced along the road to European integration, which involves, among other things, establishing a business environment that is both recognizable to prospective investors and welcoming to inward investment.

This handbook incorporates information that will be invaluable for doing business in South East Europe. It is being published at a time when such information is at a premium, because the region is set to grow exponentially. Those who enter this market stand to benefit significantly, and they will do so against a backdrop of rising living standards and greater prosperity, something that all of us who care about South East Europe and its people will welcome unreservedly.

# Introduction

## South East Europe: A Diversity of Perspectives on a Diverse Region

*Dietmar Sternad and Thomas Döring*

When teaching economics and management courses in our university's International Business Management master's programme, which has a special focus also on the specifics of doing business in South East Europe (SEE), we found that the literature on the business context in the region is limited. Most of the existing literature about the emerging markets in Europe focuses on Central and Eastern Europe (CEE) but does not specifically address the particularities of what was formerly known as the 'Balkans' and is now increasingly referred to as 'South East Europe'. The use of the phrase 'South East Europe', however, is not new. According to Hösch et al. (2004), it dates back to the nineteenth-century Albania expert Johann Georg von Hahn (1811–69). This more comprehensive designation for the region is also a less emotionally loaded one, as 'in the historical and literary imagination, the Balkans loom large as a frightening but ill-defined space' (Wachtel, 2008, p. 1). This, according to Maria Todorova (1994), is due to developments at the beginning of the twentieth century, when 'Balkanization' was added to Europe's repertoire of *Schimpfwörter* ('disparaging words'), as she called them – becoming a synonym for the backward and primitive, or for Europe's 'dark side within' (p. 482). Thus most people in the region do not refer to themselves as living in the Balkans, which leads to a widely cited saying that, wherever you go in SEE, the Balkans always begins in the next village.

Our intention is not to show the Balkans of the past, nor to fuel any prejudices. We intend to provide different perspectives on the SEE of today – a region which is characterized by rapid economic and social changes after the fall of communism, with a significant rise in foreign direct investments and in privatization, as well as with evolving political and legislative systems. SEE has become a region that is already partly integrated into European systems and structures, other parts being on their way towards integration. It is a region that is both distinct and tremendously diverse.

As the individual chapters of this book will show, diversity is one of the major characteristics of SEE – diversity in ethnicities, diversity in religions, diversity in languages, and diversity in economic and technological development, to name just a few areas. We are well aware that no book could ever do justice to this diversity, which is both a blessing and a curse, as the long history of conflicts in the region shows. We acknowledge that there is not one SEE and that, according to the perspective you take, things will always look a bit different. Our approach, therefore, was to invite a wide variety of academics, some living and working in the region, others originally from the region but working abroad, and others still who are experts on the region without having their origins there. Furthermore, we include colleagues from a variety of disciplines: historians, economists, social scientists, higher education experts, jurists and management researchers (among others) who apply the distinctive approaches of their individual fields to analysing developments that are relevant to doing business in SEE, thus painting a rich picture of the region.

Allowing variety always means compromising on standardization. The individual chapters therefore vary in their approach. Although many of them are mainly based on the analysis of empirical data, we think that the critical perspective that some of our authors have taken, as well as commentary-like expert contributions, add to a more comprehensive understanding of the complexities of this very diverse region. The common denominator of all the chapters in the book is that they individually, but especially taken together, shed light on the key developments, trends and processes that shape the business environment in SEE.

We hope that businesspeople already working, or planning to work or invest, in the region, as well as scholars and students from different disciplines researching and studying in and about the SEE region, will find this volume a useful resource of concise and scientifically well-grounded information on the region, which in our definition includes Croatia (HR), Bosnia and Herzegovina (BiH), Serbia (SRB), Kosovo (KOS), Albania (AL), the former Yugoslav Republic of Macedonia (MK), Montenegro (MN), Moldova (MD) and the EU member states Slovenia (SLO), Hungary (HU), Romania (RO) and Bulgaria (BG). There is no standard as to how to determine which countries belong to SEE. We restricted ourselves to the former Communist countries of the region – that is why Greece and Turkey, which are geographically part of the region, are left out (though sometimes are included in the analyses as a means of better comparison). Some of the countries, such as Hungary, Slovenia and Croatia, are historically as well as today also seen as primarily Central European. We included them, however, because of their close historical and present-day ties with other countries of the region.

Not every chapter will address all the countries of the region, partly for reasons of different data availability, and partly because some chapters take an in-depth look into phenomena by using a qualified subset of the region's countries. Overall, this book aims to cover the whole variety of factors that can have an influence when doing business in SEE. Against this background, we organized it into three main sections.

**Part I** of this handbook is devoted to historical developments as well as to the political and legal environment in SEE.

The first chapter, 'South East Europe 1980–2010: A Short Historical Overview', is distinct from the others insofar as it consists of an introduction to the historical developments in SEE during the last 30 years. The particularities of the region cannot be properly appraised without a basic understanding of its recent history, including the Wars of Yugoslav Succession and the transition from communism to democracy and market economy. Christian Promitzer, a historian specializing in SEE history, also provides insight into mature socialism, nationalistic tendencies and socialist legacies. The historical background sets the stage for the subsequent chapters in the book.

The development of SEE is very closely tied to the interests of the European Union (EU) in the region and to the efforts of individual SEE countries to integrate into the EU. Danica Fink-Hafner and Damjan Lajh in 'Europeanization in South East Europe' review the domestic impact of the EU's policy towards the region, also taking its geopolitical interests in SEE into account. The chapter also covers trends in the attitude of the EU towards the region's countries and changing conditions for their acceptance, membership negotiations and subsequent full membership.

A closer look at the political environment in two selected SEE countries is offered by Austrian political scientist Karin Liebhart in 'Political Culture in South East Europe: The Examples of Bulgaria and Romania'. The author traces many of the prevailing political phenomena back to historical developments and gives an in-depth account of changing political systems and how they are perceived by the local population.

A culture of corruption and law-breaking is also often associated with informal networks. Corruption is a widespread phenomenon in the region. We therefore dedicate a full chapter to it, 'Corruption in

South East Europe', by Ruslan Stefanov and Dobromir Hristov, anti-corruption experts from the Center for the Study of Democracy in Sofia. They provide an overview of different measures of corruption, of the current situation and of anti-corruption policies and achievements on a country-by-country basis. They further show how corruption is linked with economic development, international trade, organized crime and the grey economy, and they identify further necessary steps in combating corruption at EU and country government level.

Åse Berit Grødeland, in her chapter, 'Networks and Informal Power Structures in South East Europe', reports on the results of extensive qualitative and quantitative studies investigating informal practices in selected countries in both politics and business across the region, providing the reader with comprehensive data, as well as individual accounts of the power and influence of informal networks. According to the author, informal networks can be traced back to national history, the socialist experience and national culture, and are used as mechanisms to cope with ineffective legislative and judiciary systems, thus playing an outstandingly important role in SEE in both business and politics.

Doing business without having a supportive legal environment is hard to envisage. In 'Legal Certainty and the Rule of Law in South East Europe', therefore, Alexander Patsch describes how the phrases 'legal certainty' and 'rule of law' originate in two different legal traditions (the Anglo-Saxon and the German legal systems), and reports on several attempts to quantify these concepts. Drawing on quantification efforts by different international institutions, the author presents an overview of the current status of the development of legal certainty and the rule of law respectively in individual countries in SEE.

**Part II** of our handbook provides perspectives on major factors that are influencing economic developments in the region.

The region of SEE is experiencing an economic catching-up process compared with the EU. SEE itself is characterized by large regional disparities in economic development that are attributable to various reasons. In particular, the differences in economic performance were intensified by political and military conflicts in the 1990s. Reinhold Kosfeld and Alexander Werner, both spatial economists from the University of Kassel (Germany), in their chapter 'Regional Disparities and Economic Convergence in South East Europe', provide information about whether the existing economic disparities are beginning to abate. For this, they investigate the development of economic disparity and convergence since 2001 on the basis of inequality measures and growth equations. It is shown that differences in the economic situation across the regions in SEE between 2001 and 2007 have diminished. Compared with the EU, the entire region is catching up.

Although the majority of SEE countries will probably not become members of the EU within the next few years, it still makes sense to start thinking about the consequences of that event already. In the chapter entitled 'Macroeconomic Consequences of the Integration of the SEE Area into the Eurozone', Reinhard Neck, economist at the University of Klagenfurt (Austria), attempts to gather information relevant for assessing possible membership of (some or all of) SEE in the Euro Area – that is, their full participation in EU integration. His analysis is concentrated on the macro-economic aspects of such a change, special emphasis being given to issues relating to fiscal and monetary policies. Most of this evidence is highly speculative, but may still contribute to assessing the macro-economic consequences of integrating SEE into the Eurozone.

Đuro Kutlača and Slavo Radosevic, in 'Innovation Capacity in the SEE Region', propose a multi-dimensional framework for measuring national innovation capacity (NIC), and they apply this framework to SEE countries. The individual countries vary widely in the four NIC indicators – absorptive capacity, R&D supply, diffusion and demand – thus revealing different challenges for each of them in the process of catching up.

Will Bartlett of the London School of Economics, in his chapter, 'Small Firms as a Development Factor in South East Europe', looks at the important role that entrepreneurial small firms play in creating jobs and economic growth in the region. Determining a relationship between the density of small firms in a country and the level of economic development, he focuses on the barriers to entry that small businesses are faced with, suggesting different policies of removing barriers to entry and growth, among them the need to establish a supportive institutional framework.

Christian Bellak and Mario Liebensteiner, both from the Vienna University of Economics and Business, in their chapter, 'Direct Taxation of Business in SEE Countries' assess the substantial changes in direct taxation of business and in tax policy in SEE countries, and their role in the location choice of foreign firms in particular. After describing some major changes in tax rates and tax policy, they show the recent development of foreign direct investment (FDI) in SEE and they discuss the likely relationships between these two important indicators, taxes and FDI. Taken together, the tax policy in the field of direct taxation of business in SEE is characterized by the authors as 'tax competition for FDI'. In addition, the policy challenge ahead for governments in SEE trying to stimulate domestic and foreign investment is described as managing complex relationships between the location factor 'taxes' and 'regulations and the other business environment', where finding the right balance is, however, difficult.

The democratization of SEE countries and their impending accession to the EU brought about profound changes in people's lives and a transformation of consumption patterns and consumer behaviour. The transition to a market economy has turned the region into a kind of laboratory for research on the nature of consumer transformation. Against this background, Elka Vasileva and Daniela Ivanova, consumer behaviour experts at the University of National and World Economy in Sofia (Bulgaria), in their chapter, 'Consumer Behaviour and Food Consumption Patterns in South East Europe', summarize and analyse the findings of existing economic literature and research studies dealing with this issue. They describe emerging consumer cultures, ethnic aspects of consumer behaviour and the relevance of social class as an explanation of given consumption patterns in SEE in general, with emphasis on both national and regional characteristics and with an outline of similarities with European and global consumers.

Markus Leibrecht and Mario Liebensteiner are economists at the Vienna University of Economics and Business. In their chapter 'The Transport and IT Infrastructure in South East European Countries' they provide an overview of the current state of the infrastructure endowment in eight SEE countries, placing a focus on two types of production-related material infrastructure: the transport and the information and communication (IT) infrastructure. Their descriptive analysis implies that the current state of the infrastructure endowment in SEE still is of relatively low quality and quantity, particularly in the transport sector and in the least developed countries of the region. However, the authors point out that some progress has been made in recent years, especially in the IT sector. Moreover, due to the financial involvement of European and international institutions, further improvements will probably be achieved in the transport sector in the near future.

**Part III** of this handbook is devoted to social and cultural perspectives on SEE, with a particular emphasis on developments in this domain that have an influence on doing business in the region.

Dimitrina Spencer from the University of Oxford takes a critical perspective on the ' "Social Capital" in Central, Eastern and South East

Europe'. Specifically, the author assesses critically the instrumentalization of a one-dimensional interpretation of the concept of 'social capital' by the World Bank. Referring to studies on and from the region, she reviews the work on social capital in a wider sense, including networks, trust, culture and socialist legacies, thereby advocating an interdisciplinary approach to the study of societal phenomena and also taking into account the findings of other disciplines, for instance anthropology.

Labour markets in SEE differ significantly from those in most EU member states. Employment rates are very low compared with EU averages, and unemployment and labour migration (including brain drain) have been much higher. Hermine Vidovic, a labour market expert at the Vienna Institute for International Economic Studies, in her chapter 'Trends in the Western Balkan Labour Markets', provides an overview of the current situation, particularly in some of the successor states of the former SFR of Yugoslavia. Beside an analysis of some structural features of Western Balkan labour markets (for instance long-term unemployment, supply of and demand for skills, informal labour markets and labour protection legislation among others), the major characteristics of labour market policies in the Western Balkan countries are described briefly.

Higher education experts David Crosier and Elizabeth Heath, in their chapter 'Higher Education in Former Yugoslav Countries: Impact of the Bologna Process', take a critical and distinctly European perspective when commenting on the challenges of aligning the higher education systems in the former Yugoslav countries with European standards. Being advocates of the Bologna Process, the authors identify obstacles to reforms and major steps still to be taken on the way to fully integrating the educational systems in the region into a single European Higher Education Area.

Albert Simkus, in 'Cultural Diversity in SEE', demonstrates that generalizations made about 'the Balkans' are very problematic, as SEE comprises a very heterogeneous mix of ethnic groups, language groups and religions. The diversity is made explicit through the use of survey-based comparisons of cultural variables, which, remarkably, reveal that differences within the region can be as salient as differences between countries from all parts of Europe. We are thus faced both with a picture of variety and with interesting idiosyncrasies of individual SEE cultures and subcultures.

In 'Work-Related Attitudes in the SEE Region', Ágnes Borgulya reveals fundamental shifts in the status of work during the transition from communism to free market economies, with differences still to be determined between the older and younger generations. The author suggests a general model of determinants of work-related values and attitudes and identifies four main categories of work-related values and attitudes that are of high importance for people in SEE financial security, supporting working atmosphere, self-fulfilment and family components and comforts and social perspectives. The reader also finds a detailed analysis of the status of work in individual countries in the region, on the basis of the 2008 European Values Survey.

In 'Values and Trust in Business Relationships in Former Yugoslav Markets', Maja Makovec Brenčič and Vesna Žabkar explore the attitudes and values that managers in selected South Eastern European countries hold regarding the relationship with their business partners. Specifically, they also show that, despite the wars and turbulent political situation after the break-up of Yugoslavia, business has found a way to continue relationships, with common values and mutual trust being key elements in successful cooperations.

As an appendix to this Handbook, as a means of reference, we provide country profiles with some basic structural data – also on a timeline – for the individual countries of SEE.

With around 70 million inhabitants, SEE is an important market – even more so, if we take into account the further perspective of stronger integration of the region into the EU. We hope that our book can contribute to a better understanding of the specifics of the business environment in SEE, and that by taking different perspectives it provides some insight into the diversity of this vibrant and integral part of the continent.

## References

Hösch, E., Nehring, K., Sundhausen, H. (eds) (2004) *Lexikon zur Geschichte Südosteuropas* (Wien/Köln/Weimar: Böhlau).

Todorova, M. (1994) 'The Balkans: From Discovery to Invention', *Slavic Review*, 53, 453–482.

Wachtel, A. B. (2008) *The Balkans in World History* (Oxford: Oxford University Press).

# Part I

# Political and Legal Perspectives on South East Europe

# 1
# South East Europe 1980–2010: A Short Historical Overview

*Christian Promitzer*

## Introduction

In South East Europe the three decades between the early 1980s and the present day have been marked by a historical caesura, which can be roughly described as the transition from a system of 'real Socialism' towards a concept that can be subsumed under the terms of 'democracy' and 'free market economy'. The 1990s were characterized by the onset of war, 'ethnic cleansing', mass rape and destruction for a considerable part of the region. In the last decade we can finally observe the accession to the European Union (EU) of three of the region's countries – Slovenia in 2004, and Romania as well as Bulgaria in 2007. There is also the promise of accession for other candidates – Croatia, Montenegro and probably Serbia. Simultaneously we can also observe a shared disillusionment among the population about the achievements of the last 20 years. In the so-called 'Western Balkans' (Petrović, 2009), state borders and the number of states did not remain the same during this period. From 1991 to 1992, the Socialist Federative Republic of Yugoslavia was dismembered through the recognition of Slovenia, Croatia, Bosnia and Herzegovina and Macedonia (officially called the 'Former Yugoslav Republic of Macedonia') as independent states. The two remaining republics, those of Serbia and Montenegro, formed the 'Federal Republic of Yugoslavia' in 1992, which was renamed as 'Serbia and Montenegro' in 2003. In 2006 Montenegro became independent, while the Autonomous Province of Kosovo officially seceded from Serbia by declaring its independence in 2008. Since 1995, after the end of the war on its territory, Bosnia and Herzegovina has been an international protectorate of the United Nations (UN) and of the EU. Likewise, since the end of the war between Serbia and NATO in 1999, Kosovo has become the second international protectorate under the auspices of both the UN and the EU.

At first sight, this summary of the succession of processes and events does not allow one to see interconnections between the development paths that the region of South East Europe has taken during the last three decades. Therefore it is necessary to structure this short historical survey into several sections, in order to shed some light on important aspects of the course of events. All of the countries under consideration shared a common system called 'real Socialism'; therefore we will have to deal with the character of this system, which in the 1980s was already in a state of maturity, not to say close to decay in terms of economy. Thereafter we will discuss the process of transition to multi-party systems in the individual countries. Two sections will briefly describe the Wars of Yugoslav Succession of 1991–95 and the Kosovo War of 1999. The final section will deal with the legacies of real Socialism in the first decade of the twenty-first century.

## Real Socialism in South East Europe

Socialism, a once powerful economic and social system that controlled one-third of the world, has, within two decades, been transfigured under a mist of oblivion. Out of the arena of the bipolar world, the Western model of free market economy and democracy emerged victorious in a grudge match, which had allegedly wound up in the 'end of history'. Forgetfulness about the once powerful reality of real socialism may also be connected with the caesura of 9/11. It seems that the once strong memory of the apprehension caused by mutually assured destruction has faded away under the impression of the events of 2001; the latter brought along a new fear of terrorist assaults on institutions of the triumphant Western model, a fear that is still determining the relationship of the so-called Western world with Muslims, a small fraction of whom also lives as an autochthonous population in the Balkans.

Real socialism claimed to have achieved ultimate social equity and to be on the way to a classless society. In practice, the people's democracies were under the ideological hegemony of single-ruling communist parties that availed themselves of a powerful state security apparatus in each case; thus we have to speak of different nuances of police states that sensibly narrowed the freedom of action of their citizens. The Yugoslav model was the least intolerable in South East Europe, while the Albanian and Romanian people's democracies had the harshest regimes.

The people's democracies had many features in common – single-party rule; the prominence role of the state security; the transfer of private ownership of the means of production in industry, trade and banking sector to the public sector. But their concrete manifestations could differ from each other in fundamental respects. For example, while in Albania, Bulgaria and Romania agriculture was solely organized on the base of state and cooperative property, in Yugoslavia private individuals could own plots up to an area of ten, and in certain cases even fifteen hectares.

The reasons for these differences can primarily be sought in the way communist parties came to power in the countries of South East Europe. In Romania, the establishment of the People's Republic of Romania in 1948 was a consequence of the Soviet occupation of the country in August 1944. Real socialism, therefore, was introduced with the bayonets of the Red Army. The case of Bulgaria was similar. Soviet occupation of the country took place in the first half of September 1944. Here it is also important to mention the overthrow of the government on 9 September 1944 by the communist-led Fatherland's Front in Sofia, several days before the Soviet troops reached the Bulgarian capital. In retrospect, the Bulgarian Communists would call this event the 'socialist revolution' in Bulgaria. Consequently, Romania up to the mid-1960s and Bulgaria even up to Mikhail Gorbachev's advent to power as General Secretary of the Communist Party of the Soviet Union (CPSU) in 1985 were the closest allies of the Soviet Union in South East Europe, and Bulgaria in particular followed literally all the provisions issued by Moscow.

The course of events was quite different in Yugoslavia and Albania. In these two countries, which had been occupied by 'Axis Powers' since 1941, communist-led partisan movements gained strength over bourgeois or monarchist resistance groups at an early stage. There were no communist cadres flown in from Moscow, such as Giorgi Dimitrov (1882–1949), the former leader of the Moscow-based Communist International, in the case of Bulgaria – just to name the most striking example. Also, the communist takeovers, both in Yugoslavia and Albania, were different from those in Bulgaria and Romania; they happened by way of popular uprisings, though led by totally Stalinist parties. Consequently the new rulers in Yugoslavia and Albania felt more self-confident towards Moscow than their comrades in Bulgaria and Romania, and they abolished the façade of the multi-party system earlier than was the case there. At different stages of history, the communist elites of Yugoslavia and Albania developed self-styled policies independent from advice from Moscow, although, ideologically, the two countries would run in totally different ways. Stalin's failed attempt to subdue the victorious partisan leader Josip Broz Tito (1892–1980) led to an ideological split in 1948, which would set Yugoslavia on the track of socialist self-management, through which the already nationalized means of production were transferred into 'social property'. At least in theory, social property was controlled by worker's councils in the individual enterprises. This new system led to the partial abandonment of central planning and to the introduction of market elements. The Communist Party renamed itself the 'League of the Communists' in order to signal its return to authentic Marxism, since this was the name of the organization in whose name Karl Marx and Friedrich Engels had written their *Communist Manifesto* in 1848. The Yugoslav League of Communists claimed to have abandoned the classical role of communist parties with respect to their identity as power-holders within the framework of single-party systems and to have adopted the role of 'an active participant during the deepening and implementation of socialist democracy' (Popović, 1980, p. 76). Simultaneously, the role of the central power was increasingly reduced in favour of those of the five Republics (Macedonia, Serbia, Montenegro, Bosnia and Herzegovina, Croatia and Slovenia) and of the two autonomous regions of Vojvodina and Kosovo. Due to the constitution of 1974, Yugoslavia – still a federation by name – became a confederation in practice. The country was mainly kept together by the still powerful ideology of the Titoist variant of socialism and by the charismatic figure of Josip Broz himself.

Albania, whose partisan detachments during the war had profited from supplies of their Yugoslav comrades, would stay devotedly on the path of Stalinism, however. For the Albanian communist leader Enver Hoxha (1908–85), Tito's split with Stalin offered a welcomed opportunity to liberate himself from Yugoslav paternalism, and the same was the case with the Soviet Union more than a decade later, after Nikita Sergeyevich Krushchev (1894–1971), then General Secretary of the CPSU, had openly turned away from the adoration of his predecessor, Joseph Stalin (1878–1953).

Regardless of their concrete manifestations, all these variants of real socialism in South East Europe can be termed developmental dictatorships. By their brutal policies of investment in heavy industries and of transforming the dominant rural population into a working class, the ruling elites wanted to rocket these predominantly agricultural countries (with the exception of Slovenia) to the level of mature industrial societies, even if consumption and demands for a better living standard of the masses had to suffer during this period. The people's republics of South East Europe indeed achieved high rates of economic growth in the 1950s, and even partly in the 1960s. In the 1970s it was considered necessary to transform extensive economic growth into intensive growth, in order to stabilize these economic achievements. At that time the additional build-up of consumer industries, which had been neglected for a long time, was increasingly financed by credits from the capitalist world. Attempts to adjust to the standards of the latter, however, not to mention exceeding them, were far from satisfactory. In the case of Albania, it was the autarkic strategy that led to stagnation and to intensified isolation, particularly after the country cut its links with China, its last ally, in 1978.

## Mature socialism

If we want to understand the underpinnings of mature socialism in the 1980s, we have to proceed from the fact that popular support for its individual variants differed from country to country. With the exception of Croatia, where a mass movement for greater autonomy at the expense of the federation had taken place in 1971, the Yugoslav variant of real socialism – at least until the death of Tito – enjoyed relatively wide support among the population under its rule. In Bulgaria, too, communist rule was accepted by the broad masses as long as the modest promise of improvement in living standards could be credibly upheld. If we put aside the special case of Yugoslavia, it is interesting to note that the phenomenon of dissidence, which could otherwise be observed in the case of the people's republics of Central Europe and in the Soviet Union, did not very prominently occur in South East Europe. The lack of intellectual opposition was therefore one of the reasons why the harsh regime of Nicolae Ceauşescu (1918–89) in Romania and of Enver Hoxha in Albania could go on unimpeded even in the 1980s. In this period, the Romanian population suffered deeply from the austerity measures imposed by Ceauşescu, who wanted to assure the repayment of loans granted by the International Monetary Fund. In Albania, on the other hand, the last years of Hoxha's personal regime became increasingly weird. Among his legacies were more than 700,000 bunkers scattered across the country – a vivid symbol of his paranoid fear that Albania could be overrun by its neighbours.

In a widely read article, the American anthropologist Katherine Verdery (1996) described the main features in real socialism's way of functioning. For Verdery, the bargaining of managers within the framework of central planning led to the 'padding of budgets and hoarding of materials', therefore the main traits of real socialism were those of economies of shortage (Verdery, 1996, p. 21). Since 'the system's mode of operation tended to sacrifice consumption in favor of production and controlling the products', the population was engaged in acquiring consumer goods on grey markets (p. 27). The regimes tried to eliminate the informal economy by means of Western loans, which were to be invested into consumer industries. But informality became more and more influential and undermined the pillars of the system after 'the 1979–80 decision of the Western banking establishment not to lend more money to socialist countries', so that those factions within the communist elites – mostly the managers – who were in favour of economic reform gradually gained preponderance (p. 32).

Verdery does not see the fall of real socialism as a necessary consequence of built-in flaws, but of its incapability to keep pace with the developments in capitalism. Real socialism was prepared to match itself with the Fordist mode of capitalist regulation, but since the 1970s this mode was bit by bit replaced by a more flexible regime of accumulation, which relied on new developments in telecommunications and in computer engineering, as well as on the reduction of costs for 'human capital' through the weakening of trade unions and on the increasing role of financial markets and financial speculation. This mode of regulation is often called neo-liberalism or post-Fordism. If the socialist debtor countries had united in a boycott of debt repayment, Verdery maintains, they could have avoided their own demise and 'they might well have brought down the world financial system' (p. 37) This assertion is not unreasonable, if we bear in mind the major dimensions of the financial crisis of 2007–10. But at that time the ideological aplomb of the communist elites was already shaken to a degree that made concerted action impossible.

## Nationalism – from surrogate to leverage

Due to their increasing ideological weakness, communist power holders increasingly began to rely on different variants of what James F. Brown (2001) called 'surrogate nationalism' (p. 38). Originally, real socialism had claimed that it had overcome ethnic tensions that had characterized the modern states of South East Europe since their foundation. The relationship of the communists towards nation and nationalism was not really consistent; they maintained that national liberation had ended with the creation of people's republics, but in principle they never put into question the concept of nation as they had inherited it from the bourgeois period. This principle was based on the German idea of the nation as a genetic community with a common origin (Sundhaussen, 1992). Throughout the last one and half centuries, this idea was much more prone to be (mis-)used by nationalist movements than the more inclusive French model of a nation of citizens (although the latter also has its weaknesses, as the recent uprisings in the Parisian sub-urbs have shown). Even the multiethnic Socialist Federative Republic of Yugoslavia was not immune to nationalist unrest, all the more as the fed-eration increasingly became an agglomeration of six nation-states (the six Yugoslav republics) together with a seventh one – the Autonomous Province of Kosovo, an embryonic second Albanian nation-state. It was therefore only logical that the ruling bureaucracies of Romania, Bulgaria and of some of the Yugoslav republics resorted to nationalism in order to safeguard their retaining power after they had realized that their ideological hegemony was decreasing.

Beyond Albania, where the communists already practised national-ism by isolating the country from its neighbours, the ruling elites in other South East European states either stirred nationalist emotions among the population against other ethnic groups in their own polity or were engaged in assimilation programmes. Already in 1968, Romania's Ceauşescu had abolished the remnants of the Hungarian Autonomous Region in Transylvania. His ensuing policies of de-Magyarization even led to a harsh protest of the 'brotherly' Communist Party of Hungary in 1985. In Bulgaria, attempts to merge the Turkish minority with the 'uni-fied Bulgarian Socialist Nation' can be observed since the second half of the 1950s. In 1984 the communist leader of Bulgaria, Todor Zhivkov (1911–98), launched an anti-Turkish campaign of particular intensity. It was planned that all Muslims of the country should change their names to Slavic ones, in addition to a prohibition of Turkish clothing and a ban of the use of Turkish language. In order to guarantee the sup-port of the Bulgarian population, the campaign was termed a measure of national 'revival'. In practice this 'revival' led to resistance from the Turkish minority and to the brutal use of police force. Finally, in May 1989, when the clashes reached a climax and resulted in casualties, the Communist Party organized the exodus of 300,000 Turks to Turkey, of whom only a small fraction would return after the fall of the Zhivkov regime several months later.

In 1981, one year after Tito's death, the guiding principle of social-ist Yugoslavia, 'Brotherhood and Unity', was severely shaken; Albanian protestors in the city of Prishtina unsuccessfully asked for the constitutional advancement of the Autonomous Province of Kosovo to the status of a formal republic under their control, since nine-tenths of the population of Kosovo was Albanian. Several years later, the alleged endangerment of the Serbian minority in Kosovo formed the main argument for the rise of the Serbian Party leader Slobodan Milošević (1941–2006) as the national leader of the Serbs across Yugoslavia. Due to the ample use of nationalist populism, Milošević's claim would go undisputed by a major part of the Serbs for a long time. Milošević found his ideological base in the *Memorandum of the Serbian Academy of Sciences and Arts* of 1986, which denounced the discrimination of Serbs and Serbia not only in Kosovo, but also in other parts of Yugoslavia. In 1988 and 1989 Milošević launched what was known as the 'Anti-Bureaucratic Revolution', a series of mass protests against the governments of the Autonomous Region of Vojvodina, of the Socialist Republic of Montenegro and finally of Kosovo. This move enabled Milošević to replace the local leaderships with politicians who were dependent on him. In the case of Kosovo, this strategy meant the dismissal of Albanian politicians and the suppression of the Albanian majority for more than a decade.

The only adversary of Milošević's advance was the League of Communists in Slovenia, which in turn had to cope with a democratic movement similar to the simultaneous green and pacifist movements in Western countries. This movement intensified in 1988, when a political trial by the Yugoslav People's Army was held against four journalists, on a charge of 'betraying military secrets'. Within a short period, the cause of the four became a national one. The show trial itself shook the pro-Yugoslav attitude of the Slovene communists and brought the democratic opposition into a more nationalist wake against the Yugoslav federalism. Milošević's strive for the control of the Yugoslav state presidency, now made possible by the changed power relations as a consequence of the 'anti-Bureaucratic Revolution', his handling of Albanians in general and quarrels about the distribution of the resources between the republics in the ailing federation even resulted in an economic warfare between Serbia and Slovenia. The break-up of Yugoslavia became, all of a sudden, a realistic scenario.

## The transition to multi-party systems (1989–91)

In retrospect, the demise of communist rule in Central and South East Europe appears to have been consequent. Contemporaries, however, were taken aback by the rapidity of the transition to multi-party systems. The repercusssions of the careful steps of political and economic reform taken in Hungary and Poland in the late 1980s, Mikhail Gorbachev's will to release the East Central European countries from the Soviet grip and the prospective economic collapse put a sudden end to nearly half a century of communist rule in this part of the world.

In South East Europe the first ground was broken in Bulgaria, and not – as one would have thought – in Yugoslavia, the least authoritarian polity under communist rule. After Tadeusz Mazowiecki had become the first non-communist premier in Poland and Erich Honecker (1912–94) had been dismissed as General Secretary of the Socialist Unity Party of Germany, the Central Committee of the Communist Party of Bulgaria, in its meeting on 10 November 1989, relieved Todor Zhivkov from his post as General Secretary, which he had held for 33 years. Eight days later, the first informal organizations – the trade union Podkrepa and the civic organization Ekoglasnost – organized the first public demonstration. The parliament consequently removed the leading role of the Communist Party from the text of the constitution. In early 1990 the first round table between the government and the opposition took place. In the first multi-party elections of June 1990, the Communist Party – then figuring as the Bulgarian Socialist Party – gained the absolute majority of votes.

In contrast to the change in Bulgaria, transition in Romania took a violent path. In mid-November 1989 Ceauşescu was re-elected as General Secretary of the Communist Party. Although the people's republics around Romania were falling apart and public protests in the country itself could only be suppressed by ample use of the Securitate, Ceauşescu managed to stay in power, at least for the moment, by referring to his policy of severe rationing, which had resulted in the successful repayment of the external debts. Beneath the surface, however, Ceauşescu's harsh economic policy had caused widespread discontent even within the Communist Party. In mid-December, public protests and riots broke out in the western Romanian town of Timişoara; they were brutally suppressed by the police, which resulted in several casualties. Ensuing protests in Bucharest were supported by dissenters among the ruling elite. Thus, in the bloody revolution the protest had grown into, a National Salvation Front under the deviant communist cadre Ion Iliescu emerged as a *deus ex machina*. Ceauşescu and his wife were arrested and executed after a summary judgment. The Salvation Front established itself as the new power holder and would consequently prepare the path to a multi-party system under its tutelage.

The development in Yugoslavia needs to be considered separately for each republic. Although the country was not part of the Warsaw Pact, the crumbling of the other people's republics did not leave the ruling elites untainted, especially as economic crisis, national tensions and Slobodan Milošević's control of Serbia, Montenegro, Vojvodina and Kosovo had already been discussed at length in the mass media of the country. Economic transition towards a fully fledged marked economy, the introduction of a multi-party system and aspirations to transform the Yugoslav federation into a confederation formed an inextricable knot. This knot would be unravelled by military force.

When the Congress of the League of Communists of Yugoslavia met in Belgrade in January 1990, it came to a showdown between the already belligerent factions of the Slovene Communists, who demanded far-reaching reforms of the political and economical system with respect to a further decentralization of the country, and their Serbian 'comrades', who argued for the status quo, in which they hoped to secure a majority for themselves. The Slovene delegates, who were outvoted, left the congress, while the remaining majority adjourned it indefinitely. The League of Communists of Yugoslavia had ceased to exist. Multi-party elections were organized separately by each Yugoslav republic. Slovenia and Croatia organized the first elections in April 1990. The reformist Communists competed in the two countries under the new names of Party of Democratic Renewal and Party of Democratic Change, respectively. The acronym SDP should announce their defection to social–democratic ideology. In both cases, these formations were defeated by the still embryonic opposition – DEMOS in Slovenia and the openly nationalist party Croatian Democratic Union (HDZ) under Franjo Tuđman (1922–99) in Croatia. The latter would stay in power for a decade. DEMOS started to steer a stricter course with respect to Slovenian autonomy, and eventual independence. Tuđman's HDZ did so, too, but apart from that it also reduced the constitutional and practical role of the autochthonous Serbian minority in Croatia, which in turn caused an uprising among them and eventually paved the way for war in this republic.

In Bosnia and Herzegovina the first multi-party parliamentary and presidential elections were held in November 1990. They led to a national assembly, which was dominated by three ethnically based parties: the Muslim or Bosniak Party of Democratic Action (SDA), the Serbian Democratic Party (SDS) and the Croatian Democratic Union (HDZ) – which was a local branch of the party now governing in Croatia. These parties, whose ringleaders had simultaneously won seats in the republic's presidency, would form a loose coalition in order to overcome the vestiges of communist rule and to divide the country into ethnic portions under their respective influence. Since two of the three parties – the SDS and HDZ – were prone to directives from their respective 'mother republics', Bosnia and Herzegovina would soon be a bone of contention between Serbia and Croatia, whereby the Muslim population would become the main victim.

Likewise, in November 1990 parliamentary and presidential elections were held in the Republic of Macedonia. Here the nationalist Internal Macedonian Revolutionary Organization – Democratic Party for Macedonian National Unity (VMRO–DPMNE) gained the relative majority, while the League of Communists of Macedonia – Party of Democratic Change and the Union of Reformist Forces (which would later become the Liberal Party of Macedonia), together, held the absolute majority and consequently formed a coalition government that would pave the way for independence of the country. The main issue of the country – as the future would show – was not so much the issue of Yugoslav succession, but the threatening of its national identity from the side of Greece. It is important to notice here that the foundation of Macedonia as a separate nation was the result of a compromise between Bulgarian and Yugoslav communists during the Second World War in order to dampen aspirations on both sides for controlling the area. But this compromise would prove to be viable, and the local Slavic population of the Republic of Macedonia accepted it very soon. The novelty of Macedonian nation-building was, furthermore, the reason for provocative moves of Macedonian nationalists of the 1990s against the Greek part of the historical region of Macedonia, which in turn provoked Greek nationalism. The conflict resulted in a Greek plea, in response which Macedonia was internationally recognized only under the clumsy name of Former Yugoslav Republic of Macedonia.

But let us return to the developments of 1990: Slobodan Milošević, seeing that he himself could not avoid facing multi-party elections, secured the parameters for his eventual victory. He merged his League of Communists of Serbia with the Socialist Alliance, a mass organization that had hitherto been responsible for the organization of elections within the single-party system, and dubbed the new formation the Socialist Party of Serbia (SPS). By trimming the electoral system as his last move, Milošević was able to outmanoeuvre the emerging non-communist opposition in the parliamentary and presidential elections of December 1990. But with respect to further elections in the 1990s, it was mainly the boycott of the Albanian voters from Kosovo who would grant Milošević preponderance over his adversaries in the inner-Serbian rally until his final downfall.

In Montenegro, finally, Milošević's adherents in the local League of Communists won the December elections of 1990. This party changed its name to the Democratic Party of Socialists of Montenegro in 1991. Under Milo Đukanović, who seized the reins in 1997, the party became more flexible with respect to UN and EU demands; it consequently started to distance itself from Milošević's Serbia. This independent orientation, an elastic, not totally transparent handling of black market structures in the country, lucrative dealings with foreign investors in the field of tourism and the inclusion of representatives of ethnic minorities into power structures have secured this party a firm and unrelenting grip on power since the end of the Second World War until the present day.

Due to its isolation, Albania was the late-comer in the process of transition to a multi-party system. Demonstrations against the regime started in early 1990 and went on throughout the year, despite brutal police encroachments. In autumn the regime had to accede to negotiations with the demonstrators. In December the Democratic Party was founded. Due to the deteriorating economic situation, the collective emigration which had started in mid-1990 increased rapidly. Supported mainly by the rural population, the regime could have won the first, elections of April 1991. But already in summer, due to a general strike, it had to accept the inclusion of the Democratic Party into government, and it also signed the Decalogue of the Helsinki Accords. Several months later, the Democratic Party left the unstable government and were in a position to easily defeat the incumbent Socialist Party of Albania (as the former Communists called themselves at the time) in the hasty elections of March 1992. Under their leader Sali Berisha, a Democrats formed a new government. However due to the poor economic starting position of the country, Berisha could not stop further emigration of the population. His rule became more and more authoritarian, which was symbolized by the imprisonment of Fatos Nano, the popular leader of the Socialist Party. Finally, due to the failure of then prominent Ponzi schemes, the 'Lottery uprising' in 1997 led to Berisha's fall and to the socialists' return to power under Nano.

## The Wars of Yugoslav succession (1991–95)

The most prominent event in 1990s in South East Europe was undoubtedly the Wars of Yugoslav Succession. The number of casualties has still not been finally assessed. For Bosnia and Herzegovina alone the official number of casualties ranges between slightly above 100,000, as estimated by the International Criminal Tribunal for the former Yugoslavia in the Hague, and about 200,000, as estimated by the Bosnian government. A major part of the infrastructure was destroyed or damaged in the affected countries. The war also touched the neighbouring countries of former Yugoslavia and seriously interfered with their further development.

After the demise of the League of Communists of Yugoslavia, none of the newly elected republican presidents or parliaments was interested in creating a new, democratically legitimated institution at the federal level. In the first six months of 1991, the republican presidents decided to discuss the future of the federation in informal talks within their own ranks. But, due to their different concepts – the notion of federation promoted by the presidents of Serbia and Montenegro, that of a confederation, proposed by the Slovenian and Croat presidents, and that of a compromise, an 'asymmetric federation', presented by Macedonia and Bosnia and Herzegovina – it was not possible to reach a common standpoint.

On 25 June 1991 Slovenia and Croatia declared independence. Two days later the Yugoslav People's Army attempted to seize the border checkpoints in Slovenia but could not overcome the resistance of the units of the Slovene Territorial Defence. After ten days, the first, rather low-key war was over. In the following weeks and months the Yugoslav People's Army retreated from Slovene territory, so that Slovenia became de facto independent.

Croatia was the next site of military conflict. The Serbian uprising of 1990 had led to the foundation of the Serbian Autonomous Region of Krajina on its territory. In spring of 1991, the first military clashes between Croatian special police and Serbian paramilitary forces took place in Plitvice and eastern Slavonia. The Yugoslav People's Army first imposed itself as an arbitrator between the warring sides, but in the course of summer 1991 it went over to open support for the Serbian side. In autumn there was already regular warfare between the Yugoslav People's Army and Serbian irregular forces on the one hand, and the Croatian National Guard (the later Croatian Army) and Croatian irregular forces on the other hand. Serbians in the other parts of Croatia were put under pressure because of their nationality and many of them left the country; in the occupied territories the local Croatian population in turn became victim to Serbian oppressors and was overwhelmingly expelled. Towards the end of 1991 combat operations abated, since a major part of the Serbian war aims – the military conquest of an essential part of the Serbian areas of settlement in Croatia and the foundation of the 'Republic of Serbian Krajina' – had been achieved. At this moment Germany single-handedly recognized Croatia and Slovenia as independent states; on 15 January 1992 the other member states of the European Community followed suit.

During the following years the demarcation lines were supervised by UN peacekeeping troops, the UNPROFOR. In spite of a general arms embargo for states on the territory of former Yugoslavia, the Croatian government managed to obtain weapons via illegal channels and to train their own army with tacit help from the USA. In May 1995 the Croatian Army recaptured western Slavonia, and in early August the major part of the 'Republic of Serbian Krajina'. The recapture led to a mass exodus of the Serbian population from the affected territories, only a minor part of which has returned since.

The third war on the territory of former Yugoslavia took place in Bosnia and Herzegovina in the years of 1992–95. In early 1992, the Bosniak (Muslim) and Croat parties supported a referendum for independence, which was accepted by two-thirds of the population. The Serbs, however, who constituted the last third of the population, at the behest of their SDS party, were in favour of the retention of Bosnia and Herzegovina within the remains of Yugoslavia. On 6 April 1992 the European Community recognized Bosnia and Herzegovina as an independent state. Against benevolent expectations, this move did not result in ending the fighting that had already broken out. At least visibly, Slobodan Milošević wanted to avoid a connection of Serbia with the developments in Bosnia and arranged the proclamation of the Federal Republic of Yugoslavia, consisting of Serbia and Montenegro alone, on 27 April 1992. Consequently, all officers of the Yugoslav People's Army who were born in Serbia and Montenegro were asked to leave Bosnia. This move did not prevent the new Yugoslav state, however, from becoming subject to severe economic and political sanctions proclaimed by the UN, which also did not accept the claim of the Federal Republic of Yugoslavia to be the legal successor of the Socialist Federative Republic of Yugoslavia. Nor did it accept the new state as a member. In the meanwhile, the bulk of the Yugoslav People's Army's weaponry was handed over to the newly established Army of the Serbian Republic of Bosnia and Herzegovina, later known as Republika Srpska. With this logistic aid, the military forces of the Bosnian Serbs, together with irregular forces from Serbia, were able to consolidate their territorial conquest of about 70 per cent of the territory of Bosnia and Herzegovina. Mainly the Bosniak, but also the Croat population living in these regions, underwent immediate expulsion at best, detention, torture and murder in camps at worst. Many women became victims of mass rapes. This made Bosnia and Herzegovina the major venue of war crimes in Europe after the Second World War, even before the events in Srebrenica.

In 1993, plans by representatives of the EU and the UN as to how to divide ethnically Bosnia and Herzegovina resulted in further clashes between Croat and Bosniak military forces, which had been hitherto united in their fight against the military forces of the Bosnian Serbs. In this year, the only result that would have a longlasting impact was the establishment of the International Criminal Tribunal for the former Yugoslavia. Until 2010 the court that had its seat in The Hague had indicted 161 persons from various ethnic backgrounds. In Bosnia – after months of mutual fighting and deportation of civil population – a peace agreement between the two warring parties was achieved with the help of the USA in February 1994. The Washington Accord not only stipulated a ceasefire, but also a viable federation of Bosniak and Croat territories.

In July 1995 the Army of the Republika Srpska conquered Bosniak enclaves in Eastern Bosnia that had been proclaimed 'save havens' under the protection of the UN. Much of the male population of Srebrenica was executed. Shortly thereafter heavy Serbian shelling of Sarajevo finally provoked an air war of NATO forces under the auspices of the UN against positions of the Army of Republika Srpska. This enabled the Bosniak and Croat ground forces, together with the Croatian Army, to recapture a considerable part of Serbian-held territories, which dwindled down to about 50 per cent. Thereafter NATO immediately terminated bombing from the air. This status quo formed the base for the Dayton Peace Accord, which once more stipulated the independence of Bosnia and Herzegovina. It was declared a polity consisting of two entities, one of which was the Bosniak–Croat Federation of Bosnia and Herzegovina due to the 1994 Washington Accord, while the other part was the territorially essentially reduced Republika Srpska.

Since the Dayton Accord, Bosnia and Herzegovina has become a protectorate of both the UN and the EU; the main institution of this protectorate is the Office of the High Representative, which has far-reaching competencies. Despite many partial successes with respect to overcoming various consequences of war, the return of refugees is still not fully implemented. Those nationalist parties that started the war are still in power, or have been replaced by similar political networks. The most problematic ones are those in the Republika Srpska, because they know that they would lose influence if the central powers of Bosnia and Herzegovina were strengthened in order to make the country a viable state. In any case, Bosnia's main problem consists in the fact that clandestine groups manipulate the ethnic segmentation of the population as a shield for hiding their own material interests.

## The Kosovo War of 1999 and its repercussions for the whole region

The last military conflict of high intensity was the Kosovo War of 1999. It was preceded by the already mentioned suspension of the autonomy status of the Province of Kosovo in 1989 by Slobodan Milošević. During a decade of peaceful protests, which were organized by the Democratic League of Kosovo under Ibrahim Rugova (1944–2006), the Albanian majority boycotted the Serbian elections and, relying on their own resources and on those of Albanian migrants in Western and Central Europe, managed to build up a parallel underground state that operated in the fields of education, medical care and taxation. But the power relations on the ground had not been changed essentially, and the road to independence was not paved by this approach. Such an assessment established the basis for the creation of the KLA, the Kosovo Liberation Army, which appeared on the scene in 1996. The KLA profited from the far-reaching disintegration of the Albanian state in the wake of the Lottery uprising of 1997, which opened the possibility to acquire weapons from the stocks of the Army of Albania. Also other 'dark' and criminal channels were tapped in order to organize armaments for the freedom fighters. Subsequently, major actions of the KLA against the Serbian occupation took place in 1998. As an act of reprisal, the Yugoslav Army and units of the Serbian Ministry of Interior Affairs burnt to the ground Albanian villages that were considered to be strongholds of the KLA and proceeded in various ways against the Albanian civil population, which had to take shelter in the forests and mountains. This activated a cycle of violence and counter-violence, which in early 1999 led to negotiations under international supervision. The Serbian side rejected the conditions of a treaty that provided for the deployment of foreign troops. Consequently, on 24 March 1999 NATO – without being authorized by the UN – started air raids against Yugoslavia. Meanwhile the Serbian forces organized the expulsion of several hundred thousand Albanians from Kosovo. The ceasefire of 9 June 1999 initiated the retreat of Yugoslav forces from Kosovo. Serbia's defeat heralded the start of Milošević's downfall. He was toppled by popular protests during his failed re-election as president of Yugoslavia in October 2000; some months later he was handed over to the International Criminal Tribunal for the former Yugoslavia for war crimes in Croatia, Bosnia and Herzegovina and Kosovo. In early 2006, amidst the court proceedings, Milošević died of a heart disease. Political change in Serbia itself was once more threatened by the assassination of its prime minister, the philosopher Zoran Đinđić (1952–2003), by members of criminal networks whom he had declared war on. But even this incident did not cause a change of the pro-Western course that Đinđić had pursued immediately after the fall of Slobodan Milošević.

In Kosovo, military protection was taken over by the multinational Kosovo Force (KFOR) immediately after the ceasefire, while the civilian administration fell under the competencies of the United Nations Interim Administration Mission in Kosovo (UNMIK). The ceasefire opened the possibility for the return of both the Albanian refugees and the KLA. A considerable part of Kosovo's Serbian minority as well as members of other ethnic groups – in particular Roma – felt endangered by these developments and fled from Kosovo. In March 2004 the conflict between the dominant Albanians and the Serbs of Kosovo flared up for a short period, resulting in encroachments from both sides. Since then, the Serbian communities are even more isolated in their enclaves throughout the country.

Due to UN-Resolution 1244, Kosovo was recognized as part of the Federal Republic of Yugoslavia. The transformation of the latter into the confederation of Serbia–Montenegro in 2003 did not change this status; nor did the declaration of independence of Montenegro in 2006, which simply transferred the affiliation of Kosovo to the newly independent Republic of Serbia. Negotiations about the future status of the province continued, but no solution could be found that was viable for both sides, since Serbia claimed Kosovo as an essential part of its territory, while the Albanian side – backed by the majority of the population – strove for full independence, which was finally declared by Kosovo's parliament in early 2008. A division of the province that would annex to Serbia a small part in the north, mainly inhabited by Serbs, was not seriously considered. Since the end of 2008 major competencies of the UNMIK were transferred to the European Union Rule of Law Mission in Kosovo (EULEX). Since then, the manpower of KFOR, which had amounted to 50,000 soldiers in the beginning, was also reduced to 10,000 men in 2010.

In retrospect, one can safely say that the Kosovo War has changed the further development of the whole region. It motivated the foundation of the Stability Pact for South Eastern Europe, which in the years of 1999–2008 stimulated developments towards the strengthening of peace, democracy, human rights, market economy and private sector business in this part of Europe. Among the representatives of the international community, one has to name the World Bank, the European Investment Bank and the European Bank for Reconstruction and Development, as well as the International Monetary Fund. Another spin-off effect of the Kosovo War was the advancement of the Montenegrin attempts for independence, and – due to their official compliance with respect to the international sanctions against the Federal Republic of Yugoslavia and during the NATO air raids of 1999 – the accession of Serbia's Eastern neighbours, Romania and Bulgaria, to NATO in 2004 and to the EU in 2007.

The clashes of 2001 between Albanian insurgents who had been formed after the example of the KLA and military and police forces of the Republic of Macedonia ended with the Ohrid Agreement, which improved the constitutional position of Macedonia's Albanian citizens. Thus dreams of a 'Greater Kosovo' as a second Albanian nation-state that, beyond Kosovo, would also comprise parts of Montenegro, Southern Serbia and Macedonia had to be shelved.

## Socialist legacies at the beginning of the early twenty-first century: a conclusion

With the end of the Yugoslav Wars of Succession of 1991–95 and of the Kosovo War of 1999, the brutal dynamics of the recent history of South East Europe have, at least temporarily, exhausted themselves. With this development, shared structural contexts are going to be more and more discernible for the region's countries. A possible approach to assess the common situation in these countries in the early twenty-first century is the concept of socialist legacies or – to use another term – the notion of 'post-socialism', as developed by the political scientist Dieter Segert. Due to Segert, the use of the terms 'transformation' or 'transition' is misleading, since these concepts are based on the assumption that the lethal crisis of real socialism created a *tabula rasa*, which would have enabled energetic agents of the new post-communist elites to rebuild certain institutional contexts of the West – namely democracy and a market economy. By way of contrast, the notion of post-socialism refers to the manifold bridges between the socialist past and the present situation. Continuities are the focus of this approach – continuities in social expectations, as well as in other contexts and spheres of everyday life.

And, what is more, even if the aim of creating market economies was met, one has to admit that these new market economies function in a different way from those of the West. In this respect one has to consider the peripheral status of the countries of South East Europe within a symbolic and practical geography of capitalist power relations, the nucleus of which is shaped by the EU. Or, to put it in the words of Dieter Segert (2007): 'Until now, at least, the East has not arrived in the West' (p. 3).

Today three countries of the region are members of the EU, although only one of them, Slovenia, has fully met the requirements on the base of its own economic power. The accession of Romania and Bulgaria was conditioned by political reasoning, as already indicated. This is the reason why these two states are regularly under scrutiny of the European Commission with respect to corruption and the rule of law. Croatia is the only other state of the region that could immediately meet most of the requirements of the EU; it would have already been a member state if there had not been longlasting negative consequences to Franjo Tuđman's authoritarian regime of the 1990s, which until 2004 prevented the country from becoming a candidate for EU accession. In the meantime, 2009, Croatia, as well as Albania, became member of the NATO. But there is still a considerable distance between Croatia, which is already far in EU-membership negotiations, and the Republic of Macedonia, which was granted the status of candidate just one year later. Montenegro applied for EU membership in 2008 and was granted the status of candidate in late 2010; Serbia applied in 2009. Albania, Bosnia and Herzegovina and Kosovo are listed as *potential* candidate countries.

Membership or prospective membership pf the EU is, however, not a yardstick for the well-being of the population of the polities in question. In the territory of former Yugoslavia the consequences of warfare have caused immense economic damage, Bosnia and Herzegovina being the most affected country. Due to longlasting international sanctions and to the Kosovo War, the economic power of Serbia and Kosovo is also severely weakened. For the whole region one can, furthermore, observe a debilitation of state authority. A major part of the economic life is now taking place outside state control. This process already started under mature socialism, when the informal economy had grown into an increasingly important sector. Its consequences are corruption and private appropriation of the commons by the ruling political and economic elites, and in addition by nepotistic, criminal and nationalist networks. In former Yugoslavia these networks have come to power due to their 'merits' in warfare and the war economy. But in the whole region such networks are continuously produced by the underlying conditions of post-socialism. The Austrian political scientist Vedran Džihić (2007) claims that in the successor states of former Yugoslavia – with the exception of Slovenia – 'rentier economies' (p. 176) are at stake. Such economies consist of distorted market relations, which are characterized by corruption, informal networks, oligopolies, unequal starting conditions for individual players and a weak state, which in certain economic sectors may partly profit by assuming the role of a 'rentier state'. 'Rentier economies' find their highest expression in the protectorates of Bosnia–Herzegovina and Kosovo, where high amounts of aid money circulate; similar structures are also present beyond the former Yugoslav territory, namely in Albania, Bulgaria and Romania. But we should not turn a blind eye to the investment policies of the member states of the EU either, which are mostly based upon neo-liberal logics and often concentrate themselves on the financial services industry, without paying attention to small- and medium-sized businesses (Džihić, 2007). On the other hand, foreign investment in South East Europe in privatized communal services often results in palpable price increases for consumers. Nor should we forget that foreign investments tend to use South East Europe as an extended work bench in order to reduce production costs, as the examples of Renault and Nokia in Romania show.

The lack of redistribution of wealth in the face of accelerated growth, low wages, high working hours and the continued poverty of large portions of the population are the main reasons for emigration and for the ongoing brain drain from the states of South East Europe. This general situation features apathy, disillusionment and fears for the future as general concomitants of everyday life; it also creates two other phenomena that are widely disseminated in the region: nostalgia for socialism and right-wing populism. As for nostalgia, this cannot be interpreted as a political programme. Left-wing organizations with convincing programmes are hardly present on the political scene; and the former communist parties, which have given themselves social democratic programmes, belong to the right wing within the Socialist International. When in power, their social and economic policies do not differ much from those of the other parties. Idealization of the socialist past is therefore mostly an expression of a vague demand for social security, combined with the recollection of one's own youth in socialism. In the absence of left-wing options, populism from the moderate or far right of the spectre has gained ground in several countries of South East Europe. Therefore, if we want to understand fully the undaunted popularity of ethnic nationalism, we also have to consider that it is still fuelled by right-wing populists who are exploiting a situation of permanent social crisis in order to find scapegoats among ethnic minorities and marginal groups.

An assessment of the changes in South East Europe since 1989–91 necessarily needs to be ambiguous. The new freedom of movement, which was yearned for under communist rule, was soon restricted by the harsh visa regimes of the EU member countries in the 1990s. Only since December 2009 has the EU abolished visa requirements for Serbia and Macedonia; Bosnia and Herzegovina, then Albania following by the end of 2010. The introduction of a market economy only partly fulfilled the expectations of large portions of the population with respect to welfare and consumption. Democracy opened the chance for voting for different options, but at the same time South East Europe has become a focal point for post-democratic structures: the ideologies and practice of the competing political groups do not differ much from each other, and parliamentary decisions have lost their importance due to informal decision structures within the ruling elites, the influence of foreign investors and provisions from the European Commission, which have to be fulfilled even by non-member states in order to secure their future accession to the EU. Most of the governments in the region advocate an idiosyncratic ideology, which consists of nationalism, a neo-liberal approach in economic affairs and lip-service to 'European values'. At the same time, people increasingly turn away from political participation; many tend to idealize the socialist period, although this cannot be of practical help. What remains is an uncertain future in the backyard of the EU.

# References

Brown, J. F. (2001) *The Grooves of Change: Eastern Europe at the Turn of the Millennium* (Durham and London: Duke University Press).

Džihić, V. (2007) 'Spurensuche im jugoslawischen Postsozialismus – Was bleibt?' in Segert, D. (ed.), *Postsozialismus: Hinterlassenschaften des Staatssozialismus und neue Kapitalismen in Europa* (Vienna: Braumüller), 165–183.

Petrović, T. (2009) *A Long Way Home: Representations of the Western Balkans in Political and Media Discourses* (Ljubljana: Peace Institute), http://mediawatch. mirovni-institut.si/eng/a_long_way_home.pdf, accessed 20 December 2010.

Popović, M. (1980) 'Bund der Kommunisten Jugoslawiens (BdKJ)', in Trifunović, B. (ed.), *Die sozialistische Selbstverwaltung in Jugoslawien. Grundbegriffe* (Belgrade: Sozialistische Theorie und Praxis), 75–78.

Segert, D. (2007) 'Postsozialismus-Spätsozialismus-Staatssozialismus: Grundlinien und Grundbegriffe einer politikwissenschaftlichen Postsozialismus-Forschung', in Segert, D. (ed.), *Postsozialismus: Hinterlassenschaften des Staatssozialismus und neue Kapitalismen in Europa* (Vienna: Braumüller), 1–23.

Sundhaussen, H. (1992) 'Nationsbildung und Nationalismus im Donau-Balkan-Raum', *Forschungen zur osteuropäischen Geschichte*, 48, 223–258.
Verdery, K. (1996) *What Was Socialism, and What Comes Next?* (Princeton, NJ: Princeton University Press).

## Further reading

Aligică, P. D. and Evans, A. J. (2009) *The Neoliberal Revolution in Eastern Europe: Economic Ideas in the Transition from Communism* (Cheltenham: Edward Elgar).
Böröcz, J. (2009) *The European Union and Global Social Change: A Critical Geopolitical–Economic Analysis* (London: Routledge).
Brunnbauer, U. (2007) *'Die sozialistische Lebensweise': Ideologie, Gesellschaft, Familie und Politik in Bulgarien (1944–1989)* (Köln/Wien/Weimar: Böhlau).
Breda Luthar, B. and Pušnik, M. (eds) (2010) *Remembering Utopia: The Culture of Everyday Life in Socialist Yugoslavia* (Washington: New Academia).
Ramet, S. P. (2002) *Balkan Babel: The Disintegration of Yugoslavia from the Death of Tito to the Fall of Milošević*, 4th edn (Boulder, Colorado: Westview Press).
Ramet, S. P. (ed.) (2010) *Central and Southeast European Politics since 1989* (Cambridge: Cambridge University Press).
Todorova, M. (2009) *Imagining the Balkans*, 2nd edn (New York: Oxford University Press).

# 2
# Europeanization in South East Europe

*Danica Fink-Hafner and Damjan Lajh*

## Introduction

During the last two decades, Europeanization has become an attractive research area and an integral part of the study of European Union (EU) politics. It has become a fashionable and yet contested concept, especially since the turn of the twenty-first century (Olsen, 2003), and as such it has developed many different faces. It can be said that, in the context of the development of the EU as a predominantly Western political community, Europeanization has been defined in many ways, but without any clear boundaries.[1] According to Börzel and Risse (2006, pp. 484–485), Europeanization is understood in at least three different ways: (1) it is perceived as a bottom-up process and refers to a somewhat broader understanding of European integration; (2) it is a top-down process by which EU-level institutions and decisions shape and transform the domestic politics, policies and institutions of individual states (both member and non-member states); and (3) it encompasses both of the above-mentioned definitions, being conceived as a combination of a bottom-up and a top-down process.

Europeanization processes are not just limited to EU member states; they also encompass those states expressing an interest in integration with the EU. This has been especially the case for countries negotiating full EU membership (Goetz, 2001). In fact, in the EU enlargement processes that affect post-communist countries, the concept of Europeanization has gained a rather narrow political definition, as well as a rather narrow research focus, which adopts a top-down approach to prospective candidates in terms of their adaptation to European pressures. Initially the EU indirectly influenced national political systems and their practices by evaluating and estimating the level of democracy achieved, as well as other aspects of social, and especially economy-related, transformations. In this respect, the EU has often been seen as an important catalyst and facilitator of transition towards democracy (Grabbe, 2001). Only recently have analysts been (increasingly) stressing the fact that Europeanization is not only closely linked to the European Community (EC)/EU's proclaimed aim of *democracy promotion*, but has also been adding its weight behind other international organizations that have been pushing for a *neoliberal model of capitalism* (see for instance Bohle and Greskovits, 2007; Scharpf, 2010). Indeed, looking at the conditions of EU membership set since the beginning of the 1990s, the pressure to transform property (privatization) and many other aspects of economic systems that are important for the EC/EU from an economic point of view (they open up new markets for Western European capital and goods), as well as from a security point of view, has been rather evident.

Europeanization literature has to a large extent overlooked the global picture of the Europeanization processes. However, it is increasingly difficult to understand these processes without taking into account the *geopolitical* dimension of the EC/EU's positioning and its changing role following the collapse of the military–political division of Europe at the end of the Cold War (Lajh and Fink Hafner, 2002). At the end of the twentieth and the beginning of the twenty-first centuries, the EU had to redefine its relations with the other world powers, both at the global level and on its eastern and south-eastern borders. On the one hand, the EC/EU had to position itself in relation to the former (Russian-dominated) Soviet Union by determining the EC/EU's treatment of the Baltic countries (the former Soviet republics) and of those countries that were formerly members of the 'Soviet bloc', being economically (the Comecon countries) and militarily (the Warsaw Pact countries) integrated under the Soviet leadership. On the other hand, on its south-eastern border, the EC/EU had to Edefine its new relationship not only with Russia, but also with other political and military forces involved in halting the war and stabilizing the former Yugoslav region (with the exception of Slovenia, which joined the EU integration process along with other post-communist East Central European countries) – foremost among these being the USA, NATO and the United Nations (UN).

The *war* in the former Yugoslav region also interfered with the process of Europeanization. In fact the war had three consequences that made the South East Europe (SEE) region rather special: it delayed and disrupted the democratization processes; it created the problem of having to deal with war criminals; and it fostered illegal economic activities (smuggling and corruption). The EU responded to these problems by introducing special preconditions for most of the countries in the region, as well as specific conditions for individual countries, in addition to the general criteria determined for the first (the 2004) round of the EU enlargement process, which involved the post-communist countries.

Since this chapter is focused on the Europeanization of SEE,[2] we take into account the above-described idiosyncrasies. Following Radaelli's (2000) suggestion of 'unpacking' the broad concept of Europeanization, for the purposes of this chapter we understand the Europeanization process in SEE as *the domestic impact of Europe aiming at promoting democracy while taking into account the EU's interest in security and the geopolitical positioning of the EU in this region.* However, we believe that domestic factors (first of all the characteristics of democracy-building and of domestic political mechanics) filter the transfer of Europeanization pressures into domestic political adaptations, while we also note the changes and (especially when viewed from the perspective of the potential candidate states) inconsistencies in the EU's enlargement policy.

*The main thesis of our chapter is as follows.* The countries in the SEE region compose four different clusters, both in terms of characteristics of multiple transitions and in terms of their relationships with the EC/EU: (1) Slovenia and Hungary, with their socio-economic and political characteristics belonging to the Central European cluster of post-communist countries, which joined the EU in 2004; (2) Romania and Bulgaria, having difficulties fulfilling the Copenhagen Criteria and being set additional conditions (both joined the EU in 2007); (3) Croatia, Bosnia and Herzegovina, Serbia (Kosovo as a former part of it), Montenegro (also a former part of the Serbian–Montenegrin federation) and the Former Yugoslav Republic (FYR) of Macedonia – all having difficulties with the transition to democracy, and whose direct or indirect involvement in the Yugoslav War has resulted in their being treated with less evident prospects of full EU membership than the first two clusters (Croatia being somewhat of an exception); and (4) Moldova – having problems with the transition to democracy and problems breaking free of the Russian geopolitical interest zone, and having been included in the newly developing European Neighbourhood Policy (ENP)[3] without any clear prospect of full EU membership. The countries investigated have not only experienced different trajectories as they abandoned communism, but have also achieved various levels of democratic political system functioning as well as very different levels of involvement in a war and its consequences. Also, as a dynamically changing entity, the EC/EU's policy towards countries that have expressed an interest in participating in the European integration processes has become increasingly inconsistent. The variations in EU policy correlate with the democratization characteristics of the country in question, and also with its level of association with the consequences of the Yugoslav War; however, these variations are mediated by global geopolitical factors. Due to variations in the EU's policy towards a particular country's integration into the EU and to the simultaneous presence of other (non-EU) international forces in the SEE region, the EU has been losing its credibility as the primary association option for post-communist countries in the region.

This chapter is structured as follows. Firstly, the idiosyncrasies of the Europeanization of post-communist countries will be analysed; this will be followed by a section on the EC/EU as a dynamically changing regional factor. The various domestic dynamics that are characteristic of the several clusters of post-communist countries that expressed an interest in joining the EU at the various stages of the EU enlargement processes will be compared, together with their domestic political mechanics as they relate to the European integration processes. In a separate section, the relevance of other international factors for particular countries will be considered, taking into account their geopolitical positioning. In the concluding section, the main findings will be brought together in a synthesis.

## Europeanization

The democratization of former communist countries, the collapse of the military–political division of Europe and the divisions between politically defined 'blocs' and economic borders during the Cold War created pressure on the EU to open up to new members. In the past 15 years, the majority of post-communist countries have been confronted by multiple political–institutional challenges. All of the countries have gone through the processes of: (a) building the institutions and practices of a democratic political system and market economy; and (b) institutional adaptation to the processes of Europeanization. Some of them have also been building an independent state, including the establishment of institutions that had previously been located in the political centres of the former multinational states they used to belong to. In other words, even in the early stages, the integration of post-communist countries into the EU started to interfere with the national political systems of those countries.

While investigating Europeanization processes, Börzel and Risse (2006, p. 485) proposed the term 'Europeanization', to indicate a focus on the dimensions, mechanisms and outcomes by which EU-level institutions and processes affect domestic-level institutions and processes. They believe that, even when we focus on a top-down process of Europeanization, Europeanization does not necessarily impact directly on the domestic sphere. In addition, it is not even necessary that EU-level actors actively seek the domestic transformation of a political system in accession countries in order to be able to discern evidence of Europeanization. Therefore we must also take into account domestic factors that may either trigger or inhibit Europeanization processes. Domestic factors hold special importance in post-communist countries, since these countries followed various (historical and institutional) trajectories in their transition from communism to democracy. These domestic factors include, among others, the key characteristics of the political and electoral system, socio-economic conditions, the development of civil society, media freedom, ethnic division and involvement in war. Finally, since the EU lacks rules in many areas of political conditionality, it demanded compliance with the rules of international organizations such as the Council of Europe, the Organization for Security and Cooperation in Europe or the International Criminal Tribunal for the Former Yugoslavia (ICTY) (Sedelmeier, 2010).

In the case of EU accession states or (potential) candidate states, the impact of Europeanization on the different domains of their political systems varies considerably with respect to the level of their institutional relations with the EU. In this context, Lippert et al. (2001) identify five steps in the Europeanization of accession states. In the pre-phase of Europeanization, the first contacts between applicant states and the EU are re-established. The first phase of Europeanization begins with the candidate country's signature to an agreement with the EU (the Europe Agreement or Stabilization–Accession Agreement), which represents the backbone of (future) institutional relations. The second phase of Europeanization embraces the pre-accession period, which leads to the first elementary institutional adaptations. The third phase includes the negotiation process, in which either incremental or radical changes in individual policy fields occur. Finally, the last phase of Europeanization is the period of full membership (Lippert et al., 2001). In terms of both the pre-phase and the first phase of Europeanization, Ágh (2003) discusses 'anticipatory Europeanization' (p. 117), which in the case of Central and Eastern European post-communist states applied in the first half of the 1990s and was combined with the processes of democratization and modernization that occurred under the supervision of various international organizations – not only the EC/EU, but also, for example, the World Bank or the International Monetary Fund (IMF) – which acted as 'institutional mentors'. From the second phase of Europeanization, according to Lippert et al. (2001), Ágh talks about 'adaptive Europeanization'.

The Europeanization stages described above have not been theoretically or politically predefined. In fact they have developed gradually, as the dynamically changing EC/EU has responded to the increasing pressures from these nations to join the club of the democratic and prosperous world region. In order to keep these pressures under control, the EC/EU has taken to inventing *ad hoc* policies for applicants from post-communist sub-regions as they have come knocking at the EU's doors. This has usually happened after watershed elections. On the one hand, the outcome of the EU's policy towards particular countries (sub-regional clusters of countries) has been a result of the EU's political, economic and security interests, and of their development in the context of the dynamically changing post-Cold War international community. On the other hand, the policy has depended on domestic factors of the applicant countries, which have determined the scope and dynamics of their adaptation to European pressures. In cases in which veto players appear to be stronger and non-governmental actors weaker and/or poorly informed about European integration processes, and in particular about the conditions of EU membership, domestic factors have acted as a brake on the process. The EU, however, tends to intervene in domestic political mechanics more directly.

## The EU's policy towards South East Europe: variability and inconsistency of the EU factor

Straightforward European adaptational pressures are a rather recent phenomenon. They are closely linked to the most recent sub-wave of transitions to democracy in the context of the third global wave of democratization. Unlike the cases of Portugal, Spain and Greece (also belonging to the third global democratization wave), post-communist countries that longed to 'return to Europe' were faced with clearly determined criteria that had to be fulfilled before they could gain EU membership. The Central European EU enlargement wave (2004) was soon followed by the EU's further enlargement with two additional countries (Bulgaria and Romania) from the South Eastern European periphery (2007). This was followed by a significantly different treatment of those countries (with the exception of Slovenia) that emerged from former Yugoslavia with a delayed expression of interest in joining the European integration process after the end of the Yugoslav War; there is an even more circumspect treatment of Moldova within the framework of the EU's Neighbourhood Policy and of the EU's Eastern Partnership (see Table 2.1).

For those countries that had been involved in the war of 1991–95 in former Yugoslavia (Croatia, Bosnia and Herzegovina, Serbia, Kosovo, Montenegro and indirectly the FYR of Macedonia), a new regime of conditions was established, including additional preconditions to be fulfilled in order to proceed with further steps towards integration with the EU – albeit without any clear and straightforward prospect of full EU membership. When countries emerging from the former Soviet Union began to express their interest in integration with the EU (as for instance in the case of Moldova), the EU started pursuing the European Neighbourhood Policy, allowing the countries to develop economic and social ties with the EU, but without any mention of EU membership prospects. In May 2009 the EU launched the Eastern Partnership (EaP) to enhance relations with six countries in Eastern Europe and the Caucasus, including Moldova.[4]

### The conditions of the Central European enlargement (the 2004 EU enlargement wave)

At the beginning of the 1990s, when the Central East European countries (including Hungary and Slovenia) started clearly expressing their wish to join democratic and rich Western Europe, the European Community was neither sure of the long-term success of transitions from communism nor institutionally prepared for such a major and complex enlargement. While it intensified its response to the need to adapt its political systems and develop its institutions, it also set the criteria to be fulfilled by countries aiming to become full EC/EU members.

The Copenhagen Criteria not only involved clearly determined economic criteria but also political criteria. The latter, in fact, followed the theoretically determined preconditions for a liberal–democratic model of governance, as presented most clearly by Dahl (1971). The political criteria were developed in the context of numerous transitions to

*Table 2.1* Key milestones in the Europeanization processes in Central East and South East Europe (Moldova has so far been excluded from these processes)

| | Anticipatory Europeanization | | Adaptive Europeanization | | |
|---|---|---|---|---|---|
| | Signature of Europe agreement/Stabilization–accession agreement | Membership application | Start of accession negotiations | End of accession negotiations | Full membership |
| Albania | June 2006 | April 2009 | | | |
| Bosnia and Herzegovina | June 2008 | | | | |
| Bulgaria | March 1993 | December 1995 | February 2000 | December 2004 | January 2007 |
| Croatia | October 2001 | February 2003 | October 2005* | December 2002 | May 2004 |
| Czech Republic | October 1993 | January 1996 | March 1998 | December 2002 | May 2004 |
| FYR of Macedonia | April 2001 | March 2004 | | | |
| Hungary | December 1991 | April 1994 | March 1998 | December 2002 | May 2004 |
| Montenegro | October 2007 | December 2008 | | | |
| Poland | December 1991 | April 1994 | March 1998 | December 2002 | May 2004 |
| Romania | June 1995 | June 1995 | February 2000 | December 2004 | January 2007 |
| Serbia | May 2008 | December 2009 | | | |
| Slovakia | October 1993 | June 1995 | February 2000 | December 2002 | May 2004 |
| Slovenia | June 1996 | June 1996 | March 1998 | December 2002 | May 2004 |

* Croatia has twenty-five provisionally closed chapters, and negotiations have been opened in thirty-three chapters (status on 5 November 2010).

*Source:* Sedelmeier (2010, pp. 404–405).

democracy in the environment of the European Community (as it was known at the time). By their adoption, the selection of possible candidates was narrowed down to those post-communist countries in which not only had the transition to democracy been temporarily successful, but it had also been consolidated successfully, while at the same time they had introduced a capitalist economy and opened their national markets to Western companies via the process of privatization. The first post-communist enlargement wave (the 2004 'big-bang' enlargement) integrated the most Westernized post-communist countries with the EU. In fact it can be said that the Europeanization processes were closely linked to the processes of modernization.[5]

With respect to anticipatory Europeanization and in accordance with Article 2 of the Lisbon Treaty, principles of human dignity, freedom, democracy, equality, the rule of law and respect for human rights, including the rights of persons belonging to minorities, became the main preconditions for full EU membership. In this way, to become part of the EU,[6] the respective country had to fulfil the economic and political conditions known as the Copenhagen Criteria[7] (Jacobsen, 1997). The Copenhagen Criteria set accession conditionality as follows:

> Membership requires that the candidate country has achieved stability of institutions guaranteeing democracy, the rule of law, human rights and respect for and protection of minorities, the existence of a functioning market economy as well as the capacity to cope with competitive pressure and market forces within the Union. Membership presupposes the candidate's ability to take on the obligations of membership including adherence to the aims of political, economic and monetary union. The Union's capacity to absorb new members, while maintaining the momentum of European integration, is also an important consideration in the general interest of both the Union and the candidate countries.
>
> (European Council in Copenhagen, 1993)

Two years later, the European Council in Madrid added the condition of 'administrative capacity':

> The European Council also confirms the need to make sound preparation for enlargement on the basis of the criteria established in Copenhagen and in the context of the pre-accession strategy defined in Essen for the CCEE; that strategy will have to be intensified in

order to create the conditions for the gradual, harmonious integration of those States, particularly through the development of the market economy, the adjustment of their administrative structures and the creation of a stable economic and monetary environment.

(Madrid European Council, 1995)

In 1990 the European Council in Dublin agreed to create a template for establishing relations between the EU and individual countries; this was known as the Europe Agreements (EAs). The EA, as a new type of association agreement, part of the new pattern of relationships in Europe, was first offered to the leading reformers Hungary, Poland and Czechoslovakia. These EAs consisted mainly of the gradual establishment of a free trade area for industrial products, supplemented by political dialogue on foreign policy and backed by technical and financial assistance through PHARE (Poland and Hungary: Aid for Restructuring of the Economies) and through economic and cultural cooperation (Sedelmeier, 2010). EAs were also concluded with Slovenia, Bulgaria and Romania.

### The 2007 EU enlargement

The 2007 enlargement involved the less prepared post-communist countries Romania and Bulgaria. The political conditions laid down in Madrid became particularly important for these two accessions (Sedelmeier, 2010). Nevertheless, it was agreed that Romania's and Bulgaria's geopolitical location supported the decision in favour of their accession to the EU (Phinnemore, 2006).

Bulgaria and Romania had already been exposed to tighter EU conditions during the negotiation of their association agreements in 1992. Upon the insistence of the EU, the Bulgarian and Romanian Europe Agreements included in their preamble a specific 'human rights clause' that made explicit reference to the protection of minority rights (Papadimitriou and Gativa, 2009). Later on, the Commission's opinion on the membership applications of the ten Central Eastern and South Eastern countries, published in July 1997 in Agenda 2000, confirmed that the pace of reform in Bulgaria and Romania had fallen behind that of the region's frontrunners. Indicative of this was the fact that both Bulgaria and Romania were judged to have failed the economic criteria set in Copenhagen, whereas Romania and Slovakia were the only candidate countries to have failed to meet the political criteria fully (Papadimitriou and Gativa, 2009). Calls for enhanced conditionality and more robust mechanisms of EU monitoring grew louder in Brussels as Bulgaria's and Romania's membership prospects became more real. Evidence of suspicion regarding the pace of domestic reform can be detected in most of the regular reports published by the Commission since 1997, as well as in almost all European Parliament reports on the two countries (Papadimitriou and Gativa, 2009). By 2003, both countries had opened all of the remaining 31 *acquis communautaire* chapters. However, European Commission officials again signalled that, in order to complete successfully their preparations for accession, both countries would need to increase their efforts to meet the EU economic criteria and to implement and enforce the *acquis communautaire* as opposed to simply transposing it. In particular, they also needed to continue their reforms of the public administration and judiciary sectors (Spendzharova, 2003). Despite the emerging discussions on the EU's 'absorption capacity' and despite a growing enlargement fatigue, the two countries were allowed to accede to the EU on 1 January 2007, although with the provision that stricter conditions would apply to them than to any other candidate country previously. Specifically, following Romania's and Bulgaria's accession, the Commission preserved the right to monitor their judicial systems and the steps being taken to fight corruption and organized crime. The Commission also reserved the right to invoke 'safeguard measures'[8] against the two countries (Trauner, 2009b, p. 2).

## EU conditions for the Western Balkans

The development of the EU's conditionality for the Western Balkan countries can be regarded as an accumulation of the conditions developed for the 2004 round of enlargement, enriched with the lessons drawn from the 2007 enlargement (with Romania and Bulgaria having experienced problems in implementing in practice preconditions that had formally already been achieved) and with the responses to particularities of the region, especially its involvement in the 1991–95 Yugoslav Wars and in several other armed conflicts. In fact the EU has increasingly set the following: (1) additional stages in EU integration; (2) special, additional preconditions for the region; and (3) additional, particular preconditions for individual countries.

The number of stages that interested countries have to go through has grown with each additional wave of enlargement (see more in Vachudova, 2006). The eight post-communist countries that joined the 2004 enlargement wave went through four main stages: (1) initial screening; (2) opening negotiations based on the Copenhagen Criteria; (3) the successful closing of particular negotiation chapters; and

(4) completion of the negotiations and accession. Bulgaria and Romania had to go through the additional evaluation stage of determining their readiness to join the EU, which implied the possibility of postponing their accession. The Western Balkan countries have been required to go through an additional three stages before any possibility of succeeding in the initial screening was open to them: (1) a feasibility study for opening negotiations on a special kind of association agreement – the Stabilization and Association Agreement (SAA); (2) the start of negotiations on the SAA; and (3) the signing of the SAA.

The *political conditions* were also expanded for this cluster of countries and, further, they included issues relating to the violent break-up of socialist Yugoslavia, such as the return of refugees and the obligation to cooperate with the ICTY. A new and special template for relations between the EU and the countries of the Western Balkans was determined in the shape of the SAA. Following the violent break-up of Yugoslavia and the US-brokered Dayton peace agreement that ended the war in Bosnia and Herzegovina, the EU agreed on a 'regional approach' towards the countries of SEE in February 1996 (Sedelmeier, 2010). In June 1999 the European Council in Cologne endorsed an initiative taken by the German presidency for a Stability Pact for SEE (see Lajh, 2000). At the same time, the Commission elaborated proposals for a Stabilization and Association Process (SAP). The key element of the SAP was a specific type of agreement – the SAA. SAAs were largely modelled on the EAs, but included much more detailed political conditions (Sedelmeier, 2010).

Additional particular preconditions were set *for individual countries.* In the Commission's document 'The Western Balkans: Enhancing the European Perspective' (Communication from the Commission to the European Parliament and the Council, 2008), the criteria for individual countries were expanded as follows:

- *Croatia*: cooperation with the ICTY, judicial and administrative reforms, fighting corruption, minority rights, return of refugees, restructuring of the shipbuilding sector and solving open questions with its neighbours (including, for example, the issue of the Ecological and Fisheries Protection Zone).
- *FYR of Macedonia*: the implementation of the SAA, dialogue between political parties, the implementation of the law regulating the police force and anti-corruption legislation, reform of the judiciary and public administration and employment policy measures to enhance a business-friendly environment.

- *Albania*: electoral reform (particularly in view of the 2009 parliamentary elections), strengthening the rule of law, reform of the judicial system and the fight against corruption and organized crime.
- *Montenegro*: cooperation with the ICTY, judicial independence and accountability, the fight against corruption and organized crime, the continuation of administrative reform and the strengthening of administrative capacity.
- *Bosnia and Herzegovina*: cooperation with the ICTY, the reform of the constitutional framework, the fight against corruption and organized crime and functional and effective institutions.
- *Serbia*: cooperation with the ICTY, the fight against corruption and organized crime, regional cooperation and good neighbourly relations.

In addition, the EU began to interfere more directly in domestic affairs, especially at critical instances prior to general elections and referenda.

## Moldova

When countries emerging from the former Soviet Union started expressing their interest in EU integration (the Ukraine and Georgia as well as Moldova), the EU initiated the European Neighbourhood Policy allowing selected neighbouring countries to develop economic and social ties with the EU, but without mentioning any prospects of EU membership. As Moldova had shown progress in fulfilling its own programme of democratic and economic reform as set out in the 2005 Action Plan, it earned the EU's approval to expand the Partnership and Cooperation Agreement by the addition of policies such as the 2008 additional Autonomous Trade Preferences (ATPs), a twinning project (beginning in 2008) between the Moldovan, French and Hungarian parliaments, designed to strengthen the role of parliament in the reform process, development of a Pilot Mobility Partnership for strengthening legal migration channels and migration management for preventing illegal migration. All of these processes have also been backed by an increase in financial assistance during the period 2007–10, an examination of the feasibility of establishing a deep and comprehensive free trade area (DCFTA) and, more recently, the opening of a dialogue on the possibility of allowing visa-free travel within the EU for Moldovan citizens. In January 2010 Moldova also signed a three-year arrangement with the IMF as part of the Extended Credit Facility and of the Extended Fund Facility – Special Drawing Rights (SDR) 369.6 mn euros (Commission of the European Communities, 2010a).

## Summary of trends

The EU has increasingly developed strategies and policy instruments that allow it to keep the new European periphery 'at arm's length', while at the same time expecting that more and more neighbouring countries will Europeanize (incorporate EU norms and expectations into their domestic environments) without being given any clear indication of whether they might one day be included within EU borders. These trends have been mirrored in changes in the EU's discourse (see, for instance, Phinnemore, 2006). The change in discourse began when the EU designated Turkey as being 'destined to join' the Union (the Helsinki European Council in December 1999), while some countries (in particular Austria, Germany and France) proposed a 'privileged partnership' for Turkey instead of membership. The Feira European Council in June 2000, which focused on the Western Balkans, introduced the phrase 'potential candidate status', whilst the 2003 Thessaloniki European Council referred to the countries of the Western Balkans as becoming 'an integral part of the EU', but without clearly noting their accession or membership. The 2004 Brussels European Council talked about the EU's engagement with candidate countries, which thus made the EU contribute to Europe's prosperity, stability, security and unity.

Over time it has become clear that the EC/EU has been moving from a more general membership conditionality towards a growing policy conditionality, while at the same time expecting the latecomers to adapt to EU law without closer formal integration (Trauner, 2009a). For Sedelmeier (2010), the EU's main instrument for making the prospect of membership credible in the context of its eastern enlargement is the opening of accession negotiations. It is only Croatia that currently enjoys the realistic possibility of becoming a full member within the next few years. Additionally, the EU's internal differences in dealing with particular issues, and the unequal treatment of certain ethnic groups by both the EU and individual EU members,[9] have proved to be increasingly damaging to the EU's image.

## Domestic factors

SEE countries belong to three quite different social worlds. While Slovenia and Hungary rank in the category of 'very high human development' in the Human Development Index ranking, together with the most developed countries in the world, Montenegro, Croatia, Serbia and Albania are found in the cluster rated as 'high human development', together with countries like Chile, Argentina and Turkey; Moldova is the only SEE country in the cluster with a 'medium human development' rating (UNDP, 2010). The SEE region is also composed of a variety of political regimes – from full democracies to illiberal regimes (Table 2.2). Additionally, the SEE countries not only differ in the characteristics of their multiple transitions and nation-building, but they also differ in the timing of their clear orientation towards Western Europe. Their domestic political mechanics relating to European orientation vary accordingly.

As a rule, a pro-European orientation among domestic elites corresponds to watershed elections (Vachudova, 2006). While the Central East European post-communist countries had experienced watershed elections at the end of the 1980s and beginning of the 1990s (the exception being Slovakia, with watershed elections in 1998), many SEE countries (except Slovenia and Hungary, which follow the Central European transition pattern) followed with a delay, and in some cases are still awaiting such elections. It is possible to note watershed elections in Romania (1996), Bulgaria (1997), Croatia (2000) and Serbia (2000). Exceptions to the rule are Montenegro (the only country in the region where post-communists in fact maintain power), Bosnia and Herzegovina (with no real watershed elections so far, as power remains divided among the three main ethnic parties)[10] and Moldova (see, for instance, Munteanu, 2009).

The EU's mechanisms for promoting democracy were first used in Slovakia and go hand in hand with domestic support for pro-democratic political reformers (see e.g. Vachudova, 2006; Fink-Hafner, 2008). They have also been used in Romania, Croatia and Serbia, as well as – in a particular form, namely by supporting an alliance among less nationalist parties – in Bosnia and Herzegovina (here in fact the competing alternative options involve a conflict between a pro-EU-oriented movement and a political struggle attempting to maintain the status quo). While these mechanisms proved to be particularly successful in the case of Slovakia and, in the long term, also in Croatia, they function only weakly in countries like Serbia or Bosnia and Herzegovina. In fact, in Serbia the externally encouraged reformers were brutally stopped in the early stages (Prime Minister Zoran Djindjić was assassinated in March 2003) and the process could continue only very slowly. Also, Serbia has so far been the only post-communist country whose political leaders stress that they see their country and the EU as 'equal partners'. In addition, the lack of a common position, among EU member states, on evaluating and promoting the process of Serbia's integration into the EU has fed the nationalist anti-European political forces within Serbia,

## 40

*Table 2.2* Institutional characteristics, political system functioning, and the characteristics of civil society in SEE compared with selected countries

| | EU member (2004) | Constitutional system | Fish-Kroenig parliamentary powers index (2009)* | Democracy index 2008** | Political participation (Democracy Index 2008)** | Civil liberties (Democracy Index 2008)** | Corruption perceptions index 2008*** | Management index 2008 (part of the Bertelsmann Transformation Index)**** |
|---|---|---|---|---|---|---|---|---|
| AL | N | Parliamentary | 0.75 (PAR) | Hybrid regime (5.91) | 4.44 | 7.06 | 3.4 | Successful with weaknesses (5.60) |
| BIH | N | Parliamentary (with a collective presidency consisting of three members) | 0.63 | Hybrid regime (5.70) | 4.44 | 7.94 | 3.2 | Moderate (4.59) |
| BU | Y | Parliamentary | 0.78 (PAR) | Flawed democracy (7.02) | 6.11 | 8.82 | 3.6 | Successful (6.73) |
| HR | N | Semi-presidential parliamentary | 0.78 (PAR) | Flawed democracy (7.04) | 6.11 | 8.24 | 4.4 | Successful (6.87) |
| CZ | Y | Parliamentary | 0.81 (PAR) | Full democracy (8.19) | 6.67 | 9.41 | 5.2 | Successful (6.62) |
| FYROM | N | Semi-presidential parliamentary | 0.81 (PAR) | Flawed democracy (6.21) | 6.67 | 8.24 | 3.6 | Successful (6.52) |
| HU | Y | Parliamentary | 0.75 (PAR) | Flawed democracy (7.44) | 5.56 | 9.12 | 5.1 | Successful (6.67) |

| | | | | | | | | |
|---|---|---|---|---|---|---|---|---|
| MD | N | Parliamentary Semi-presidential parliamentary | 0.75 (PAR) | Flawed democracy (6.50) | 6.11 | 7.94 | 2.9 | Moderate (4.48) |
| MN | N | Semi-presidential parliamentary | N.A. | Flawed democracy (6.43) | 5.00 | 7.35 | 3.4 | Successful with weaknesses (6.13) |
| PO | Y | Semi-presidential parliamentary | 0.75 (PAR) | Flawed democracy (7.30) | 6.11 | 9.12 | 4.6 | Successful with weaknesses (5.27) |
| RO | Y | Semi-presidential | 0.72 (HYB) | Flawed democracy (7.06) | 6.11 | 8.53 | 3.8 | Successful (6.49) |
| RU | N | Presidential | 0.44 (PRE) | Hybrid regime (4.48) | 5.56 | 5.00 | 2.1 | Moderate/close to weak (3.84) |
| SRB | N | Semi-presidential parliamentary | 0.69 (PAR) | Flawed democracy (6.49) | 5.00 | 7.65 | 3.4 | Successful with weaknesses (5.41) |
| SLO | Y | Parliamentary | 0.75 (PAR) | Full democracy (7.96) | 6.67 | 8.82 | 6.7 | Successful (6.83) |
| UA | N | Semi-presidential | 0.59 (HYB) | Flawed democracy (6.94) | 5.56 | 7.94 | 2.5 | Successful with weaknesses (5.21) |

*Notes*: PAR = parliamentary, HYB = hybrid, PRE = presidential; 10 shows the highest development in democratic structures in the Democracy Index, 0 the lowest development; 0 on the Corruption Perception Index means 'highly corrupt', 10 means 'highly clean'.

*Sources*: * Fish and Kroenig (2009); ** Transparency International (2008); *** Economist Intelligence Unit (2008); **** Bertelsmann Stiftung (2008).

which argue that a complex and heterogeneous EU can be compared to the former Yugoslavia and will not be able to survive as a viable entity. Furthermore, the idiosyncratic political mechanics within Serbia signify that the competition is not simply bipolar (pro-EU *vs.* anti-EU), but also includes other geopolitical alternatives – first of all pro-Russia, and occasionally also pro-China. On the issue of Kosovo (for Serbs, 'the question of all questions'), Russia in fact openly presented itself as Serbia's ally and an interested geopolitical party in the region. Moldova stands out with an even more clear-cut domestic bipolarity: pro-EU versus pro-Russia, which is reminiscent of the Cold War.

## The role of the (extra-EU) international community

Non-EU actors from the international community have entered the region in several ways, most crucially militarily, as the region had been experiencing several armed conflicts (see Appendix A.1). The US helped to change the military power relationships by empowering the Croatian army and thereby ending the Yugoslav War (1991–95). In the period between March and June 1999, NATO bombing prevented the spillover of Serbian-led military activities to the other neighbouring countries not yet involved in the Yugoslav War.

It was not until the end of the Yugoslav War that the EU started developing assistance programmes for the Western Balkans. The EU has played a rather important role in peacekeeping and conflict operations; significant operations first began in the former Yugoslav Republic of Macedonia in March 2003, being followed by operations in Bosnia and Herzegovina in 2004 that led to the transfer of responsibility for peacekeeping activities from NATO to the EU since December 2005 (Timmins and Jović, 2006). The EU has also been playing an active role in the negotiation process on the final status of Kosovo. Its direct involvement in solving the Macedonian crisis in 2001 has in fact led to national institutional adaptation, which in turn has led to the recognition of two nations (Macedonians and former ethnic minority Albanians). Nevertheless, many open border issues in the former Yugoslav region remain to be resolved satisfactorily.[11]

The role of the EU in the Western Balkans has been co-determined by various factors. First of all, it has been the result of global geopolitical factors, especially the EC/EU's lack of capacity to play a more decisive role in the prevention, and later in the halting, of the Yugoslav War. The weakness of the EC/EU has been embedded in the underdevelopment of a common foreign policy and of a common military capacity. Even the recent establishment of a common EU diplomacy reflects the EU's confederal rather than federal capacities. Moreover, the EU's policy towards the Western Balkans has been deliberately linked to the activities of other international organizations in the region. This means that, in practice, the pressure on domestic elites in the region to satisfy the EU's expectations has been to some extent transferred to organizations such as the Organization for Security and Cooperation in Europe (OSCE), the Council of Europe (CE) or the ICTY. The EU's 'outsourcing' of international influence is obvious in processes such as the finalizing of individual reports on a particular country's progress in fulfilling the EU's conditions for advancement along the track to European integration. When it comes to economic issues, the European Commission has consulted the evaluations and analyses of the World Bank, the IMF and the Economic Commission for Europe of the UN. When evaluating the fulfilment of the Copenhagen Criteria and any additional political criteria, the Commission tends to incorporate the findings of the most recent reports of the OSCE, the Council of Europe and particularly the ICTY. Negative reports from the ICTY concerning a particular country's failure to cooperate with the court in locating war criminals can carry decisive weight in the EU's policy decisions towards that particular country.

In the context of managing armed conflicts in the former Yugoslav region, the EU's responses are usually evaluated as a string of failures (Elbasani, 2008). The EU generally seems to continue to rely on the USA and on NATO for military power, while combining a reactive and proactive approach of its own to securing its primary security and economic interests in the Yugoslav region. By contrast, it seems that the EU has become more proactive on its eastern borders, challenging Russia's geopolitical interests, particularly those involving its recently developed Eastern Partnership (2009) and a strategy for the Baltic Sea Region (2009),[12] which aims at developing macro-regional cooperation in the fields of economy, transport, security and the environment (see, for instance, Michalski 2009; Haukkala, 2009).

## Conclusion

If we consider the SEE region as a whole, only Slovenia, Hungary, Bulgaria and Romania more or less followed the Central and Eastern European 'natural' pattern and passed the test, according to Ágh (2003), of both anticipatory and adaptational Europeanization. With the 2007 EU enlargement, the overlap between the EU and NATO enlargements has largely been achieved. Other parts of South East Europe have only recently entered the phase of anticipatory Europeanization, while Croatia has started the adaptive Europeanization phase. For most of the countries in the SEE region, advancement along the path to European integration has remained a rather vague aim, or has not been clearly established at all. European enlargement processes seem to have been increasingly replaced by policies allowing selected neighbouring countries to integrate economically and, to some extent, socially, while they are expected to adopt European norms into their domestic environment without any clear promise of future full EU membership. With the economic and financial crisis, the EU's limited capacity for further enlargement, and also the socio-economic and political vulnerability of many countries in the SEE region, appears to have added both to the EU's enlargement reticence and to at least some SEE countries' re-evaluation of their economic and political options when they take into account the particular mechanics of domestic politics. The atmosphere of unpredictability, augmented by the increasing domination of EU member states' national agendas (Hillion, 2010), is damaging for the EU's credibility, as well as for the security of the EU's neighbouring countries.

## Appendix A.1: Armed conflicts in the SEE region after 1990

| 1991 | Ten-Day War in Slovenia | The Slovenian war of independence, a brief military conflict between the Slovenian Territorial Defence and the Yugoslav People's Army. The conflict was formally ended with the 'Brioni Accord'. |
| --- | --- | --- |
| 1991–95 | Homeland War in Croatia | The Croatian war of independence was fought between Croatian forces on one side, and the Serbia-controlled Yugoslav People's Army together with local Serb forces on the other. The fighting in Croatia ended in mid-1995, after the Croatian Army launched two rapid military operations, codenamed 'Operation Flash' and 'Operation Storm'. The war formally ended with the negotiation of the Dayton Peace Agreement, which was signed in Paris in December 1995. |
| 1992–95 | War in Bosnia-Herzegovina | The war in Bosnia and Herzegovina was an international armed conflict that took place between April 1992 and December 1995. The |

|  |  | war involved the armed forces of the Republic of Bosnia and Herzegovina and those of the self-proclaimed Bosnian Serb and Bosnian Croat entities within Bosnia and Herzegovina (the Republics of Srpska and Herzeg-Bosnia); the Republics of Srpska and Herzeg-Bosnia enjoyed substantial political and military support from Serbia and Croatia respectively; the war formally ended with the negotiation of the Dayton Peace Agreement, which was signed in Paris in December 1995. |
| 1998–99 | Kosovo conflict and NATO intervention | The Kosovo conflict was an armed conflict between the army of the Federal Republic of Yugoslavia and the Kosovo Liberation Army that started in early 1998. The conflict ended with NATO bombing of Yugoslavia between 24 March and 11 June 1999. The bombing (which had proceeded without the approval of the UN Assembly) led to the withdrawal of Yugoslav forces from Kosovo and the establishment of UNMIK (UN mission in Kosovo). |
| 2001 | Insurgency in the Former Yugoslav Republic of Macedonia (FYROM) | The insurgency in the FYROM was an armed conflict between the ethnic Albanian National Liberation Army and the security forces of the FYROM that lasted from January to November 2001. The conflict ended with the signature of the Ohrid Agreement, by which Albanian rebels agreed to disarm in exchange for greater ethnic rights. |

*Source:* The authors.

## Notes

1. Radaelli (2000) not only observed a lack of definition of what Europeanization is *not*, but also that the concept is being stretched over a rather broad range of fields and social aspects, while at the same time also becoming blurred with other concepts, such as harmonization, political integration and EU policy process.
2. The phrase 'South East Europe' is used in this chapter for the following countries: Albania, Bosnia and Herzegovina, Croatia, Serbia, Kosovo, FYR of Macedonia, Montenegro, Moldova and the EU member states Slovenia, Hungary, Romania and Bulgaria.
3. The European Neighbourhood Policy (ENP), established in 2004, is focused on the EU's neighbouring countries that emerged after the last wave of EU enlargement. Its main goal is to strengthen prosperity, stability and security. Sixteen of the EU's closest neighbours have been included in the ENP: Algeria, Armenia, Azerbaijan, Belarus, Egypt, Georgia, Israel, Jordan,

Lebanon, Libya, Moldova, Morocco, the Occupied Palestinian Territories, Syria, Tunisia and Ukraine. More details available at http://ec.europa.eu/world/enp/policy_en.htm.

4. The EaP countries are Moldova, Ukraine (Eastern Europe) and Georgia, Azerbaijan and Armenia (the Causasus). For more see Michalski (2009).

5. Similarly, Hix and Goetz (2001) argue that the processes of Europeanization interlock with the processes of democratization, liberalization and privatization in the post-communist countries.

6. Article 49 of the Lisbon Treaty states:

> Any European State which respects the values referred to in Article 2 and is committed to promoting them may apply to become a member of the Union. The European Parliament and national Parliaments shall be notified of this application. The Applicant State shall address its application to the Council, which shall act unanimously after consulting the Commission and after receiving the consent of the European Parliament, which shall act by a majority of its component members. The conditions of eligibility agreed upon by the European Council shall be taken into account. The conditions of admission and the adjustments to the Treaties on which the Union is founded, which such admission entails, shall be the subject of an agreement between the Member States and the Applicant State. This agreement shall be submitted for ratification by all the contracting States in accordance with their respective constitutional requirements.

7. Before the Commission and the European Council set direct statements of accession conditions, the EU used conditionality as part of its external relations. For example, during the 1990s, PHARE aid was provided only to countries that had made progress in their democratic transition. Consequently the EU suspended aid to Romania in 1990, after the government violently repressed the post-election demonstrations; it suspended aid to Yugoslavia in 1991, after the outbreak of war following the secession of Slovenia and Croatia; and it suspended aid to Croatia in 1995, after the military offensive to establish government control over the Serb-held Krajina region (Sedelmeier, 2010).

8. The Accession Treaties with Bulgaria and Romania, signed on 25 April 2005, codified the safeguard clauses, which meant that the Commission was given the right to invoke safeguard measures for up to three years after accession if serious shortcomings were observed in three areas of the *acquis*: the economy; the internal market; and justice and home affairs. The activation of the safeguard measures may result in the suspension of EU funds or in bans on the export of food (Trauner, 2009b).

9. Besides the largely anti-Islamic attitudes towards the closer integration of Turkey, the unequal treatment of ethnic groups living in Bosnia and Herzegovina also became apparent during the EU's decision on the liberalization of the visa regime. The act of delaying visa liberalization for Bosnia and Herzegovina effectively penalized the Bosniaks, since the Croats and Serbs living within Bosnia and Herzegovina have been able to obtain Croatian and Serbian passports. Similarly discriminatory is also the EU's

treatment of Kosovars in the context of the EU's visa policy (depend-ing on whether they are Kosovo Albanians, Kosovo Serbs, Kosovo Roma, Kosovo Bosniaks, Kosovo Ashkali or Egyptians). Furthermore, while the EU is having a 'visa dialogue' with Russia, Ukraine and Moldova, it recently declared that Kosovo is not ready for such a dialogue. Among the most recent cases of differential treatment of ethnic minority groups is the treat-ment of the Roma, who have collectively been returned from France to Romania.

10. Nationalist, ethnically based parties have more or less kept the predominant positions, while at the same time not having the capacity to lead the country through multiple transitions.

11. As borders between the former Yugoslav Republic were not determined in detail, the process of creating newly independent states between 1991 and 2010 (the latest being the recognition of Kosovo – formerly an autonomous entity of Serbia – as an independent state by several European nations) has led to an ever-growing number of open border issues between them. Croatia is involved in the greatest number of border disputes (with Slovenia, Bosnia and Herzegovina, Serbia and Montenegro); it is followed by Kosovo (with Serbia, FYR of Macedonia and Montenegro), Bosnia and Herzegovina (with Croatia and Serbia), Montenegro (with Croatia and Kosovo), FYR of Macedonia (with Kosovo and Serbia) and Slovenia (with Croatia). Croatia and Montenegro agreed to submit their border issue to the International Court of Justice in The Hague and both countries have agreed to respect the court's decision. In 2010, Slovenia and Croatia also agreed to solve their border dispute by means of international arbitration.

12. For more on the EU's strategy in the Baltic Sea Region, see Commission of the European Communities (2010) and Bengston (2009).

# References

Ágh, A. (2003) *Anticipatory and Adaptive Europeanization in Hungary* (Budapest: Hungarian Centre for Democracy Studies).

Bengston, R. (2009) 'An EU Strategy for the Baltic Sea Region: Good Intentions Meet Complex Challenges', *European Policy Analysis*, 9, http://www.sieps.se/en/publications/european-policy-analysis/an-eu-strategy-for-the-baltic-sea-region-good-intentions-meet-complex-challenges-20099epa.html, accessed 4 December 2010.

Bertelsmann Stiftung (2008) 'Management Index' (as part of the Bertelsmann Transformation Index), http://bti2008.bertelsmann-transformation-index.de/fileadmin/pdf/Anlagen_BTI_2008/BTI_2008_Ranking_EN.pdf, accessed 10 December 2010.

Bohle, D. and Greskovits, B. (2007) 'The State, Internationalization, and Capital-ist Diversity in Eastern Europe', *Competition and Change*, 11, 89–115.

Börzel, T. A. and Risse, T. (2006) 'Europeanization: The Domestic Impact of European Union Politics', in Jørgensen, K. E., Pollack, M. A. and Rosamond, B. (eds), *Handbook of European Union Politics* (London, Thousand Oaks, New Delhi: SAGE Publications), 483–504.

Commission of the European Communities (2008) *Western Balkans: Enhancing the European Perspective*, Communication from the Commission to the European Parliament and the Council, COM (2008) 127 final (Brussels: Commission of the European Communities).

Commission of the European Communities (2010) 'EU Strategy for the Baltic Sea Region', http://ec.europa.eu/regional_policy/cooperation/baltic/, accessed 4 December 2010.

Commission of the European Communities (2010a) *Implementation of the European Neighbourhood Policy in 2009*, Progress Report, Republic of Moldova, Commission Staff Working Document accompanying the Communication from the Commission to the European Parliament and the Council (Brussels: Commission of the European Communities), http://ec.europa.eu/world/enp/pdf/progress2010/sec10_523_en.pdf, accessed 4 December 2010.

Dahl, R. (1971) *Polyarchy: Participation and Opposition* (New Haven and London: Yale University Press).

Economist Intelligence Unit (2008) *The Economist Intelligence Unit's Democracy 2008*, http://graphics.eiu.com/PDF/Democracy%20Index%202008.pdf, accessed 10 December 2010.

Elbasani, A. (2008) 'EU Enlargement in the Western Balkans: Strategies of Borrowing and Inventing', *Journal of Southern Europe and the Balkans*, 10, 293–307.

European Council in Copenhagen (1993) *Presidency Conclusions*, 21–22 June 1993.

Fink-Hafner, D. (2008) 'Europeanization and Party System Mechanics: Comparing Croatia, Serbia and Montenegro', *Journal of Southern Europe and the Balkans*, 10, 167–181.

Fish, S. M. and Kroenig, M. (2009) *The Handbook of National Legislatures: A Global Survey* (New York: Cambridge University Press).

Goetz, H. K. (2001) 'Making Sense of Post-Communist Central Administration: Modernization, Europeanization or Latinization?', *Journal of European Public Policy*, 8, 1032–1051.

Grabbe, H. (2001) 'How Does Europeanization Affect CEE Governance? Conditionality, Diffusion and Diversity', *Journal of European Public Policy*, 8, 1013–1031.

Haukkala, H. (2009) 'From Zero-Sum to Win-Win? The Russian Challenge to the EU's Eastern Neighbourhood Policies', *European Policy Analysis*, 12, http://www.sieps.se/en/publications/european-policy-analysis/from-zero-sum-to-win-win-the-russian-challenge-to-the-eus-eastern-neighbourhood-policies-200912e.html, accessed 4 December 2010.

Hillion, C. (2010) *The Creeping Nationalisation of the EU Enlargement Policy*, Report No. 6 (Stockholm: Swedish Institute for European Policy Studies), http://www.sieps.se/en/publications/rapporter/the-creeping-nationalisation-of-the-eu-enlargement-policy-20106.html, accessed 4 December 2010.

Hix, S. and Goetz, H. K. (2001) 'Introduction: European Integration and National Political Systems', in Hix, S. and Goetz, H. K. (eds), *Europeanised Politics? European Integration and National Political Systems* (London, Portland: Frank Cass), 1–26.

Jacobsen, D. H. (1997) 'The European Union's Eastward Enlargement', *European Integration Online Papers*, 1 (14).

Lajh, D. (2000) *Stability Pact: Slovenia – NGOs* (Ljubljana: Peace Institute).

Lajh, D. and Fink Hafner, D. (2002) 'Institucionalno prilagajanje slovenske izvršne oblasti povezovanju Slovenije z ES/EU: mednarodno primerjalni pogled', *Teorija in praksa*, 39, 970–999.

Lippert, B., Umbach, G. and Wessels, W. (2001) 'Europeanization of CEE Executives: EU Membership Negotiations as a Shaping Power', *Journal of European Public Policy*, 8, 980–1012.

Madrid European Council (1995) *Presidency Conclusions*, 15–16 December 1995.

Michalski, A. (2009) 'The Eastern Partnership: Time for an Eastern Policy of the EU?', *European Policy Analysis*,14, December 2009, http://www.sieps.se/en/publications/european-policy-analysis/the-eastern-partnership-time-for-an-eastern-policy-of-the-eu-200914epa.html, accessed 4 December 2010.

Munteanu, I. (2009) 'Post-Electoral Moldova in the Search for Legitimacy', *South-East Europe Review*, 12, 7–19.

Olsen, P. J. (2003) 'Europeanization', in Cini, M. (ed.), *European Union Politics* (Oxford, New York: Oxford University Press), 333–348.

Papadimitriou, D. and Gativa, E. (2009) *Between Enlargement-Led Europeanisation and Balkan Exceptionalism: An Appraisal of Bulgaria and Romania's Entry into the European Union*, Hellenic Observatory Papers on Greece and Southeast Europe, GreeSE Paper No. 25 (London: The Hellenic Observatory, London School of Economics and Political Science).

Phinnemore, D. (2006) 'Beyond 25 – The Changing Face of EU Enlargement: Commitment, Conditionality and the Constitutional Treaty', *Journal of Southern Europe and the Balkans*, 8, 7–26.

Radaelli, M. C. (2000) 'Whither Europeanization? Concept Streching and Substantive Change', *European Integration Online Papers*, 4 (8), at http://eiop.or.at/eiop/texte/2000-008.htm, accessed 15 September 2010.

Scharpf, F. W. (2010) 'The Socio-Economic Asymmetries of European Integration or Why the EU cannot be "Social Market Economy" ', *European Policy Analysis*, 10 (October), http://www.sieps.se/en/publications/european-policy-analysis/the-socio-economic-asymmetries-of-european-integration-201010epa.html, accessed 4 December 2010.

Sedelmeier, U. (2010) 'Enlargement: From Rules for Accession to a Policy towards Europe', in Wallace, H., Pollack, M. A. and Young, A. R. (eds), *Policy-Making in the European Union*, 6th edn (Oxford, New York: Oxford University Press), 401–430.

Spendzharova, A. B. (2003) 'Bringing Europe In? The Impact of EU Conditionality on Bulgarian and Romanian Politics', *Southeast European Politics*, 4, 141–156.

Timmins, G. and Jović, D. (2006) 'Introduction: The Next Wave of Enlargement', *Journal of Southern Europe and the Balkans*, 8, 1–5.

Transparency International (2008) '2008 Corruption Perceptions Index', http://www.transparency.org/news_room/in_focus/2008/cpi2008/cpi_2008_table, accessed 25 October 2010.

Trauner, Florian (2009a) 'From Membership Conditionality to Policy Conditionality: EU External Governance in South Eastern Europe', *Journal of European Public Policy*, 16, 774–790.

Trauner, F. (2009b) 'Post-Accession Compliance with EU Law in Bulgaria and Romania: A Comparative Perspective', in Schimmelfennig, F. and Trauner, F.

(eds), 'Post-Accession Compliance in the EU's New Member States', *European Integration online Papers (EIoP)*, Special Issue 2, Vol. 13, Art. 21, http://eiop.or.at/eiop/texte/2009-021a.htm, accessed 10 December 2010.

UNDP (2010) 'Human Development Index 2010', http://hdr.undp.org/en/statistics/, accessed 4 December 2010.

Vachudova, M. A. (2006) *Democratization in Postcommunist Europe: Illiberal Regimes and the Leverage of International Actors*, CDDRL Working Papers, No. 69 (Stanford: Center for Democracy, Development and the Rule of Law, Freeman Spogli Institute for International Studies), at http://cddrl.stanford.edu, accessed 14 August 2010.

# 3
# Political Culture in South East Europe: The Examples of Bulgaria and Romania

*Karin Liebhart*

## Introduction

The end of the bipolar bloc system and the proximate reshaping of the post-1945 European political landscape have resulted in the eastern and south-eastern enlargement of the European Union (EU) and NATO. Both processes have not reached their limits yet. The related issues are central topics of ambivalent, or even conflicting, public and political discourses.

Wolfgang Merkel (2004), drawing on the Bertelsmann Transformation Index, declared the transition countries belonging to the 2004 enlargement round, as well as the candidate countries at the time – Bulgaria, Romania and Croatia – to be stable but deficient democracies 'with some transitory features' (cf. Ágh, 2008, p. 47). After the accession of eight Central and East European (CEE) countries, Malta and Cyprus, the debate on democratic deficits focused on the two remaining members of the so-called 'Helsinki Group',[1] the South East European states Bulgaria and Romania (Olteanu and Autengruber, 2007). Both eventually became members of the EU in 2007.

From the perspective of these two nations, the accession process of Bulgaria and Romania was seen as their 'return to Europe' (Cemrek, 2004, p. 3) and 'as a tool for catching up with economically developed countries' (Malová and Lisonová, 2010, p. 177). It was subject to even more controversial discussion than the accession process of the eight transition countries that joined the EU in 2004. The capacity of Bulgaria and Romania to meet the Copenhagen Criteria and to synchronize their legislative systems with the EU *acquis communautaire* (Cemrek, 2004) was seriously doubted. This is especially true in such fields as democratic quality, institutional and administrative capacities, efficiency of the legal system, corruption, social and minority rights (particularly regarding child protection, living conditions of disabled persons and anti-discrimination policies), trafficking in human beings and, not least, the economic performance of the two states (European Commission, 2006a, 2006b; Cemrek, 2004). However, Bulgaria and Romania became EU members, though a lot of the problems mentioned were not solved prior to their accession, mostly due to a deficient implementation of the agreed measures. The impact of the EU on democratic consolidation and on the reshaping of political cultures in both countries during the pre-accession period should nevertheless not be underestimated. It certainly helped to speed up reforms (Cemrek, 2004).[2]

Against this background, this chapter seeks to portray major features of the political cultures in the South East European states of Bulgaria and Romania.

## Analytical concept: political culture

There are a variety of approaches to the concept of political culture – a concept that plays a key role in the interpretation of current political, economic and social developments. Political culture research in the tradition of Gabriel Almond and Sydney Verba's classical study (1963, revisited 1989),[3] which was mainly oriented towards a typology of the political system and its characteristics, experienced a renaissance in the 1990s, especially in regard to the so-called 'third wave' of democratization (Huntington, 1991; Fuchs and Roller, 1998). The new democracies of Central, East and South East Europe were considered to be a part of this wave (Rose and Haerpfer, 1992, 1998; Schmitter, 1995; Plasser et al., 1997; Barnes and Simon, 1998; Whitehead, 2001).[4]

The 'classic' concept of political culture was critically reviewed and refined several times from a broader perspective of political anthropology and cultural studies (Thompson et al., 1990; Ellis and Thompson, 1997; Dörner, 1999).[5] The anthropologist Mary Douglas and the political scientist Aaron Wildavsky (1983), for instance, conceived of political culture as part of an overarching culture of social groups, which develop political preferences and patterns of orientation within this cultural framework in order to create specific arrangements for their social life. Political culture can thus be described as an organizational framework of reference, emerging in the discursive process of meaning ascription (Horak and Spitaler, 2002).[6] This new type of political culture research comprehends culture as a shared universe of interpretation and as a generator of meaning (Schirmer, 2002). This approach provides an additional perspective on political phenomena.

Regarding the analysis of transition processes, this broader concept of political culture seeks to challenge what was traditionally supposed to be a linear evolution of system change, leading to stable democracies and market economies. The cases under investigation can rather be seen to be the result of a combination of contextual factors. Moreover, such an approach suggests that transformation need not be limited to the change of political institutions and economic framework conditions, but is also connected to cultural processes and affected by underlying symbolic structures: 'culture matters' (Ellis and Thompson, 1997; Harrison and Huntington, 2000). Additionally, concepts of political culture allow for a more differentiated analysis of national identity constructions, which play a key role in the new democracies. After the system change, transition countries face the challenge of repositioning themselves in the new political surroundings and of reconstructing their identities. Following cultural studies approaches, identity is seen as a narrative, a meaningful story offering various forms of identification for the members of a collective. The 'blueprints' of identity are contained in the memories and traditions that link the present and the past, as well as in the notions shaped around them. At the same time, they also appear in political relations and institutions, social practices and expressions of everyday culture (Hall, 1994). Against this backdrop, nations cannot be described only as institutional configurations, but should also be regarded as systems of cultural representations or of discourse formation, construing meanings and producing identities.

This chapter takes these approaches into consideration. It focuses on selected results of the 'traditional' political culture research, while adding alternative analytical perspectives. Its objective is to provide a more differentiated description of the restructured political sphere in parts of the South East European region. For this purpose, the analysis also focuses on current debates regarding political memories and identity constructions, as well as on cultural patterns. The latter also comprise expressions outside the political field that can be seen as symbolic representations of political orientations that are influencing political views and perspectives.

## Survey data relating to political culture in Bulgaria and Romania

Analyses of political culture in the tradition of Almond and Verba (1963) basically rely on survey data. Therefore selected figures that capture characteristic aspects of political culture in Bulgaria and Romania are presented in this section. The data refer to opinion polls conducted during the last two decades and concentrate on the early 1990s on the one hand, and on recent surveys on the other hand.

According to the Eurobarometer survey 70/2010, a majority of respondents in both Bulgaria (60 per cent) and Romania (51 per cent) are dissatisfied with the lives they lead, in contrast to the average of 76 per cent satisfied EU citizens (European Commission, 2010a).[7] Regarding the personal financial situation in times of economic and financial crisis, 64 per cent of EU citizens are positive about their household's financial situation and 56 per cent also consider their current job situation as good. In contrast, 62 per cent of Bulgarians and 53 per cent of Romanians state that the financial situation of their households is poor. Only 41 per cent of Bulgarians and 40 per cent of Romanians believe that their job situation is good. Moreover, 75 per cent of respondents in Bulgaria and 58 per cent of respondents in Romania indicate that they have difficulties in paying all their bills at the end of the month, the EU average lying at 46 per cent. The data show not only worse than average results for inhabitants of both these South East European countries but also that Bulgarians rate their personal economic and financial situations worse than Romanians.

At the same time, 47 per cent of Bulgarian and 46 per cent of Romanian respondents assess the current situation regarding the cost of living in their countries as very bad. Ninety-two per cent of Bulgarian respondents and 85 per cent of Romanian respondents also consider the situation in their countries regarding living costs as worse than the European average. Eighty per cent of the interviewees in Bulgaria and 77 per cent in Romania are dissatisfied with the quality of the healthcare services in their countries, compared with a 43 per cent EU average. The current situation regarding the way in which public administration is run in their countries is valued fairly negatively by the Bulgarian (78 per cent) and Romanian (84 per cent) population. The environmental situation is also considered bad in Bulgaria (64 per cent) and in Romania (70 per cent). Such data suggest that the population in both countries is not at all satisfied with the performance of the political system.

The poor evaluation of the political systems' performance in both countries goes hand in hand with the assumption that the situation of the national economy is generally worse than the situation of the European economy: only 14 per cent of the respondents in Bulgaria and 22 per cent of those in Romania share the opinion that the situation of the national economy is very good, or fairly good (compared with a European average of 29 per cent). At the same time, 54 per cent of

Bulgarians and 52 per cent of Romanians assess the European economy as good, a remarkably high percentage compared with the European average of 33 per cent.

Answers to questions about whether things are generally going in the right (or wrong) direction in the EU show the following pattern: 55 per cent of the respondents in Bulgaria and 57 per cent in Romania consider things to be on the right track (EU average 35 per cent). When it comes to their own countries, the picture is quite different: only 23 per cent of Bulgarians and 39 per cent of Romanians state that things are going in the right direction. It has to be mentioned, though, that the EU average is also rather low (28 per cent) regarding this item.

Community commitment to democratic values (Fuchs and Roller, 1998), as well as trust in institutions and in political actors, are indicators that are considered to be of special importance for the assessment of political culture, particularly regarding the issue of democratic consolidation. Thus it is critical that only 8 per cent of Bulgarians and 19 per cent of Romanians currently trust the national parliament (EU average 34 per cent). A slightly better picture emerges regarding the level of trust in the national government: 15 per cent of Bulgarians and 25 per cent of Romanians trust this institution (EU average 35 per cent). Political parties are generally not trusted by the Europeans (average value: 75 per cent do not trust them). This share increases to 86 per cent in Bulgaria and 82 per cent in Romania (European Commission, 2010a). Seventy-three per cent of Bulgarian and 69 per cent of Romanian respondents are also critical of their judicial systems (European Commission, 2010a).[8] Local or regional public authorities are trusted by 31 per cent of Bulgarians and by 39 per cent of Romanians (the EU average being as high as 50 per cent). Especially in Bulgaria, supra-national and international institutions are trusted more than national ones by the majority of people (Schüler, 2008).

According to a survey conducted in 1990–91, trust in the government was also at a rather low level (44 per cent in Bulgaria and 48 per cent in Romania) right after the system change (Wessels and Klingemann, 1998). Nevertheless, citizens of Bulgaria and Romania have generally supported democracy from the outset, with principled support of elections in Bulgaria at 97 per cent and in Romania at 94 per cent; support of the parliament as an institution of representation in Bulgaria at 96 per cent, and in Romania at 94 per cent; and of the multi-party system in Bulgaria at 93 per cent and in Romania at 86 per cent (Fuchs and Roller, 1998). Though the performance of democracy was not assessed as good by the respondents in 1990–91 (22 per cent in Bulgaria and

35 per cent in Romania), the political structure of democracy in principle was evaluated as being particularly good: in Bulgaria 92.3 per cent, in Romania 96 per cent (Fuchs and Roller, 1998). As Barnes (1998) noted: 'The populations are committed to democratic ideals, at least in the sense that there are no other visions of the good life that seem to have any hold on the imaginations of [...] citizens' (p. 123). Oscar W. Gabriel (2008) characterizes this type of political culture as 'distant' (p. 207): though citizens in principle support democracy, they are dissatisfied with the concrete performance of the democratic system and are lacking trust in the rule of law and in political institutions.

The evaluation of the transparency of the national public administration is a key criterion concerning the issue of corruption. As this question was left out in Eurobarometer 70/2010, we refer to the relevant data from Eurobarometer 69/2008, because they show a rather interesting result. While only 8 per cent of interviewees in Bulgaria consider the public administration in their country as being transparent, the figure goes up to 20 per cent in Romania, which is much closer to the EU average of 24 per cent (European Commission, 2008). The Transparency International Corruption Perceptions Index 2002 (Transparency International, 2002), using a scale from 0 (highly corrupt) to 10 (highly clean), showed the following results: Bulgaria ranked 45th (4.0) and Romania 77th (2.6). According to a recent special Eurobarometer, 97 per cent of respondents in Bulgaria and 93 per cent of respondents in Romania agreed that corruption – primarily caused by close links between business and politics – is a major national problem, as compared with the 78 per cent European average (European Commission, 2009b).[9] Moreover, the interviewees see corruption at all levels of the political system (local, regional and national). In Bulgaria, 76 per cent of respondents consider national politicians to be corrupt, compared with 60 per cent for regional politicians and 58 per cent for local politicians. The corresponding figures for Romania are 53 per cent (national), 40 per cent (regional) and 40 per cent (local), the European average being 57 per cent (national), 49 per cent (regional) and 48 per cent (local). The police service is considered corrupt by 80 per cent of respondents in Bulgaria, compared with 82 per cent for the judicial services and 87 per cent for customs services. The data for Romania show 68 per cent (police), 60 per cent (judicial) and 57 per cent (customs), the European average being 39 per cent (police), 37 per cent (judicial) and 36 per cent (customs). Persons who are in charge of awarding public tenders or issuing building permits, inspectors in fields such as health, construction or food equality, persons in charge of issuing business permits and people working in the health or in the education sector were named as major categories susceptible to corruption. With the exception of the educational sector, all other groups show values above 60 per cent in Bulgaria. The Romanian values are remarkably lower, at between 30 per cent for those working in the field of education and 57 per cent for people acting in the healthcare sector. Regarding the responsibility for fighting corruption, 36 per cent of Bulgarians and 22 per cent of Romanians (European average 24 per cent) declare that not only national institutions but also the EU are responsible.

How can these data, as well as the differences between the two countries, be explained? Bulgaria and Romania have numerous historical and political commonalities, such as the shared history in the Ottoman Empire, their location in the communist-dominated part of Europe from the end of the Second World War until 1989 and, currently, their membership in both the EU and NATO. Nevertheless, they also show remarkable differences due to particular patterns that refer to political and economic, as well as cultural and societal, developments. Differences regarding the type of system change may serve as an example: Romania is sometimes said 'to have suffered a coup rather than a systemic revolution' (Barnes, 1998, p. 126). The following chapters explore such similarities as well as national particularities.

## Parameters and patterns of political culture in Bulgaria

Bulgaria is located in South East Europe, also known as the Balkans region (Cemrek, 2004, p. 3), and borders Turkey and Greece to the south, Macedonia and Serbia to the west, Romania to the north and the Black Sea to the east. According to a survey made in 2001, about 84 per cent of the population belongs to the ethnic Bulgarian majority, about 9.4 per cent to the Turkish minority,[10] and about 4.7 per cent to the Roma minority. Approximately 2 per cent are of Macedonian, Armenian or Tatar origins. Nonetheless, 'multiculturalism [...] does not grow on Bulgarian soil' (Ditchev, 2004). The dominant religion is the Bulgarian Orthodox Church. For Bulgaria, Christianity has become an important symbolic issue, particularly in the wake of '1989'. Since the 'national revival' in the nineteenth century, Christianity has been used as a symbol for the 'true Bulgarian spirit', monasteries having been presented as relating symbols. Until now no one has tried to distinguish the religious from the national (or ethnic) side of Bulgarian identity. Nowadays Orthodox Christianity is not only a mark of being Bulgarian but also of 'the choice of civilization'. It is a way to inscribe Bulgaria into the European context while preserving its particularity. After 1989 monasteries, churches and holy places have therefore been promoted as outstanding tourist destinations. In connection with Christianity, it is part of the identity construction of Bulgaria to have stopped the advance of the Arabs and slowed down the onslaught of the Turks, and thus saved Western Europe by sacrificing itself. The times of the 'Turkish yoke' from 1396 to 1878, when Bulgarians were living under Ottoman domination, also contributed to this particular relationship between religion and national identity. Communist experience added 'We have been sold to the Soviets at Yalta' to an old tradition of victimization discourse.

The Bulgarian narrative of national identity starts in ancient Thracia, which was partially located on the territory of modern Bulgaria (Crampton, 2005). A lot of archaeological excavations still constitute an asset for the tourism industry today. The emergence of a unified Bulgarian state dates back to the seventh century. About 200 years later Bulgaria adopted Orthodox Christianity. The First Bulgarian Empire (681–1018), especially under the reign of Tsar Simeon the First, at the turn of the ninth to the tenth century, is currently widely considered to be Bulgaria's 'Golden Age', in which the arts and literature flourished and the Cyrillic alphabet was developed there by followers of the Saints Cyril and Methodius. At its peak, the First Bulgarian Empire covered large parts of the Balkans and became a Slavic cultural centre in the Middle Ages (Crampton, 2005). In 1018 the Byzantine Empire conquered the Bulgarian Empire, subsequently ruling its territory until 1185, when Bulgaria broke free and established the Second Bulgarian Empire (1185–1396). Many of Bulgaria's famous monasteries were founded during this period. With the decline of this realm, Bulgarian territories were conquered by the Ottoman Empire, which held sway from the end of the fourteenth century for nearly 500 years. Bulgaria shares this experience of Ottoman dominance with almost the whole Balkan Peninsula (Crampton, 2005).

The eighteenth and nineteenth centuries were characterized by the 'Bulgarian cultural revival' (Daskalov, 2004), by the struggle for independence and by several uprisings, mainly borne by the movement of the 'awakeners' (Crampton, 2005). Eventually the Russo-Turkish War led to the defeat of the Ottoman troops by the Tsarist army, which was supported by Bulgarian and Romanian volunteers, and to the Treaty of San Stefano. As a result, an autonomous Bulgarian principality was established in 1878. The principality won a war against Serbia and gained full sovereignty as a kingdom in 1908, while incorporating the Ottoman territory of Rumelia (Crampton, 2005). Bulgaria actively participated in the Balkan Wars in 1912–13; it was victorious at the beginning but was heavily defeated in the end. In the First World War, Bulgaria sided with the Central Powers and thus with the vanquished, and lost a great part of its territory (Bulgarian Government, 2005). Tsar Boris III (in power from 1918 to 1943) established an authoritarian royal dictatorship (Berend, 2001). This was legitimized by referring to severe social and economic problems, political unrest and communist uprisings.

Bulgaria entered the Second World War as an ally of the Axis Powers in 1941 (Berend, 2001), but never declared war on the Soviet Union (USSR). It is noteworthy that the authoritarian tsarist regime, supported in this matter by prominent politicians as well as by the Orthodox Church and by the general public, saved Bulgaria's Jewish population from deportation to National Socialist (NS) concentration camps, thus not complying with National Socialist Germany's demands (Chary, 2009). During the EU accession process, former Foreign Minister Nadejda Mihailova recalled the story of the salvation of Bulgarian Jews in the Second World War as proof that the country was a role model for Europe. She emphasized that, 'today more than ever, South East Europe needs a successful model. Bulgaria proposed such a model [...] [and] in such way Bulgaria best shows that it shares the European values and supports the European community' (OSI, 2002).

Towards the end of the war Bulgaria changed sides and aligned itself with the Soviets and the Allied Forces. In 1944 the Red Army entered the country, and the Fatherland Front Government came to power (Crampton, 2005), following strikes and riots after the death of Tsar Boris III in 1943. After the Second World War Bulgaria became a communist state, Georgi Dimitrov being the most prominent political leader from 1946 to 1949. A planned economy was established, and some market-oriented experiments were included later on. From the outside Bulgaria was seen as 'the most obedient of the Soviet allies' (Brunwasser, 2009). Todor Zhivkov, the longest-serving leader in the Eastern bloc, ruled communist Bulgaria for three and a half decades, from 1954 to 1989 (Crampton, 2005). The beginning of his era had been marked by the successful de-Stalinization process in Bulgaria.

In the year in which the bipolar world system came to an end, the Bulgarian Communist Party gave up its political monopoly, too. In November 1989 Todor Zhivkov was removed[11] and Bulgaria undertook a transition to parliamentary democracy as well as towards a free market economy.[12] The first multi-party elections were held in 1990. The Communist Party changed its name to that of 'Bulgarian Socialist Party' (BSP) and won elections with a small majority. The BSP government was brought down by a general strike in late 1990 and replaced by a transitional coalition government.

In 1991 a new constitution was adopted. The first democratic direct presidential elections also took place in 1991. Zhelyu Zhelev, a communist-era dissident, became president, having been elected by the national assembly. Zhelev served until early 1997. The parliamentary elections of 1991 were won by the Union of Democratic Forces (UDF) under the slogan 'back to normality' (Kiossev, 2008). The UDF formed a coalition government with the Turkish party Movement for Rights and Freedoms (MRF). This coalition collapsed in 1992 and was succeeded by a technocratic government installed by the MRF.

The 1990s were characterized by political and economic unrest. Bulgaria had to demonstrate conformity with requested criteria of political and economic stability under difficult conditions (Schüler, 2008). From 1993 onwards Bulgarian society faced a mass privatization programme, but the government did not manage to improve living standards nor to provide for economic growth. In 1994 the Socialist Party returned to power, but again could not solve the crucial problems of the country.

> During the first years after the 1989 change people were badly off, but they were confident that things would become better soon. There was much talk about a new departure, about a difficult period ahead, an interim low. Nobody suspected that the descent would continue and the anticlimax would be reached by the end of the century
>
> (Trojanov, 2006, p. 17).[13]

In late 1994 the BSP won pre-term elections and remained in power till the beginning of 1997.[14] The sustained economic and financial crisis eventually led to mass protests in the winter of 1996–97, when even the parliament was stormed by the crowd. These events, in turn, led to the return of a UDF government under Prime Minister Ivan Kostov. Crampton (2005) calls the period starting with the Kostov government in 1997 'the real transition', as opposed to the 'incomplete transition' between 1989 and 1997. The government introduced a reform package that helped to stabilize the country's economy, but at the same time led to a further increase of social inequality. In foreign policy, Kostov put Bulgaria on the Euro-Atlantic path. 'We are taking the time machine' (24 Tchasa, 10.12.1999), he declared at the opening of negotiations to join the EU in 2000.

In July 2001 Bulgaria's former tsar, Simeon Sakskoburggotski,[15] became prime minister as the leading candidate of his personal party, the National Movement Simeon II (NMS). He succeeded in the election campaign with the popular promise to increase the standard of living within 800 days (Schüler, 2008), a promise that he eventually could not keep (Riedel, 2010). During the election campaign it was fairly easy for the NMS 'to use the common dissatisfaction with politics and the politicians and the widespread disappointment with the performance of the political elites' (Riedel, 2010). Simeon II won due to a mistrust of parliamentary practices and parties in general. The elections of 2001 were a protest vote, for the third time after 1995 and 1997 (Deimel, 2002):

> For a society such as the Bulgarian one, which has undergone painful reforms causing hardship, deprivation, loss of status of large groups of people, dramatic social mobility and a series of other processes foreign to the communist regime in the 1980s, populism seems unavoidable. The combination of weak democratic institutions and poor living standards gives rise to social discontent, which naturally fuels the need for populist rhetoric.
>
> (Malinov, 2008)

The victory of the NMS was nevertheless a surprise, because the party had been founded just two months earlier. More than 70 per cent of the voters decided to elect representatives who were unknown to them. Though the outgoing UDF government had succeeded in the field of financial stability and had also started negotiations with the EU, it was punished by the majority of voters on account of increasing unemployment rates caused by the economic reforms. Additionally, the UDF was blamed for corrupt practices, especially in the process of privatization. Due to the bad image of Bulgarian political parties, the NMS declared that it was not a party, but would try to unite all experts for the good of the country.[16] The general public perceived Simeon Sakskoburggotski as a personification of national interest and as a highly symbolic figure. He did not want to abandon his 'transcendent' royal position and thus left decision-making to his deputy prime ministers. As to foreign policy, Simeon Sakskoburggotski's government continued to pursue Euro-Atlantic integration. Bulgaria joined the North Atlantic Treaty Organization in 2004.[17]

As a result of the 2005 parliamentary elections, Sergei Stanishev of the BSP became the new prime minister, heading a coalition government with NMS and the MRF. He continued Bulgaria's integration with the Euro-Atlantic world.[18] In 2006 Georgi Parvanov, the former leader of the Bulgarian Socialist Party, was re-elected president as an independent candidate in a run-off against Volen Siderov, the leader of the extreme nationalist party (ATAKA). Parvanov also played an important role in Bulgaria's EU and NATO integration process, supporting a consistent, pro-Western foreign policy.

At the beginning of 2007 Bulgaria became a member of the EU. In the Comprehensive Monitoring Report undertaken two years before accession, the European Commission (2005) confirmed that Bulgaria continued to fulfil the political criteria for membership and had, in principle, reached compliance with the EU requirements. Nevertheless, with reference to the White Paper on the Modernization of the Administration, adopted by the Bulgarian government in 2004, it was underscored that further action was needed, particularly regarding public administration reform – including decentralization, which was designed to foster local and regional governance. Improving the legal system (especially in matters of efficiency and accountability), combating high-level corruption, implementing minority rights (mainly the effective integration of the Roma minority, see NDI, 2003a, 2003b; Popkostadinova, 2008; Freedomhouse, 2010a), protecting children and people with disabilities and fighting the traffic in human beings also continued to pose problems of concern (Spirova, 2007).

In a way, Bulgaria can be called a country of extremes: urban centres and highly developed coastal regions contrast with poor and partly depopulated rural areas with almost no infrastructure (Schüler, 2008). For the greater part of the population, the desired advancement of the living standard has not yet come true.[19] In contrast, prices of food, energy and rents have increased steadily.[20] Thus it is remarkable that more than half of the Bulgarians had optimistic expectations in 2007 regarding the future (Schüler, 2008).

In 2006 the parliament passed legislation on the fiscal decentralization of municipalities, granting them authority over the collection and administration of some taxes in order to enhance local economic stability. In 2007 the Bulgarian government lowered corporate tax rates to 10 per cent, to attract additional foreign investment. A flat tax rate of 10 per cent for personal income was introduced in 2008. Against the backdrop of the global financial and economic crisis, Bulgaria's economy fell into recession after ten years of economic growth. At the same time, unemployment and household debt increased.

In the 2009 parliamentary elections Bulgarian voters punished the socialist-led government for corruption scandals and for the related freeze of EU funds.[21] However, the new government, too, 'has failed to address the underlying causes of corruption' (Emerging Europe Monitor, 2010). A new party, Citizens for the European Development of Bulgaria (GERB), gathered around 40 per cent of the votes and took nearly half of the seats in parliament.[22] The party's (informal) leader, the former mayor of Sofia, Boyko Borissov, became prime minister. The minority government he installed was supported by ATAKA, by Order, Law, Justice (RZS) and by the 'Blue Coalition'. The latter comprised the UDF, the Democrats for a Strong Bulgaria (DSB) and a few more centre-right parties. As mentioned above, ATAKA can be called a nationalist and right-wing populist, if not right-wing extremist, party. It is led by the journalist Volen Siderov. ATAKA had already managed to gain parliamentary representation in 2005. On the occasion of the 2009 elections, the party campaigned with the slogan 'Let us fetch back Bulgaria!' ATAKA combines nationalism, hostility against minorities, an anti-US attitude and a critical position towards the EU (Sommerbauer and Lötzsch, 2007; Schüler, 2008; Riedel, 2010).

Bulgarian society and political life are still mainly characterized by clientelism, patriarchy,[23] personal loyalties, corruption and opportunism (Schüler, 2008; Riedel, 2010). Members of the former nomenklatura and of the secret service played a key role in the founding process of the political parties in the 1990s and have kept their influence. Almost all parties are closely connected with economic interest groups – a fact that is especially true at the local level of politics (Schüler, 2008). 'The dominant understanding of the essence of politics in Bulgaria today can be formulated as a struggle for power; politics is understood as a process of imposing private interests on the public' (Malinov, 2008). Though 'transition in Bulgaria is essentially conceived as a plan for bringing Bulgarian society closer to EU standards' (Todorov, 1999, p. 10), political parties remain particularly elite-centred and lack transparency regarding internal structures and decision-making processes (Schüler, 2008). Such issues have loomed large over all governments after the system change. During the last two decades, this problem has not been solved. Thus some speak of a crisis of political elites and legitimization deficits, because the state is perceived as unable, on the one hand, to satisfy societal needs and, on the other hand, to fight against criminality and corruption in the economy, politics, the judiciary and the police, despite the existence of all relevant judicial and institutional mechanisms (Schüler, 2008).[24] A further implication of this phenomenon is that most people describe themselves as apolitical and not interested in participating in political processes. Many of those who state they are principally interested in politics are, at the same time, disappointed and dismissive when it comes to political parties (Schüler, 2008).

National protest emerged in early 2009, organized by students in concert with environmental and farmer organizations. They demanded a change of the system – not just of the faces – as well as transparent governance, direct public control and improved possibilities for citizens' participation. The protest movement used the slogan 'United we stand to bring about change' and made reference to the low level of living and social standards, organized crime, corruption and amnesia regarding the communist past (Guineva, 2009).

The debate on politically organized amnesia concerning the communist past overshadowed the final weeks before EU accession; this was due to the parliament's decision to release only a limited number of former State Security files (Sommerbauer and Lötzsch, 2007). Though the question of how to ensure a proper commemoration for the victims of communist crimes had already become a central topic of public discussion in the first decade after 1989 (Vukov, 2007), Bulgarian society and politics had not yet come to terms sufficiently with the past. The memory of the socialist period has oscillated 'between allergy and nostalgia' since the system change (Vukov, 2007, p. 80; cf. also Baeva et al., 2010). This manifested itself in debates on the retention or replacement of monuments of the socialist period (Vukov, 2007) as well as in the question of whether a 'post-socialist approach to "national history" should include or exclude the socialist times' (Vukov, 2007, p. 77). The problem has not yet been solved.

## Parameters and patterns of political culture in Romania

Romania borders the Black Sea, Hungary, Serbia, Bulgaria, Moldova and Ukraine. Lucian Boia (2006) considers Romania to be 'part of a different Europe' on account of rural structures prevailing until recently, political authoritarianism and paternalistic mindsets.

The greater part of the country's population lives in rural and agricultural areas, but besides the capital Bucharest, which has about 2 million inhabitants, there are some cities with populations of about 300,000 or more – such as Constanţa, Iaşi, Timişoara, Cluj-Napoca, Galaţi and Brasov.

Regarding ethnic groups, in 2010 89 per cent of the population indicated they were ethnic Romanians and thus traced themselves back to Latin-speaking Romans. Another 7.1 per cent identified themselves as Hungarians. Hungarians and Roma (2.5 per cent) are the primary minority groups. The latter face prejudice from parts of the majority population (Nicolae, 2006) and are quite marginalized – many of them living under severe conditions, on the fringes of society, and being 'economically, socially and culturally disadvantaged' (Boia, 2006; cf. NDI, 2003b). Furthermore, there are also 0.5 per cent Germans and other small minorities such as Ukrainians, Serbs, Croats, Russians, Greeks, Armenians and Turks (European Commission, 2007b).[25] The very small number of Jews living in Romania nowadays is due to the participation of Romanian troops in the murder of the Jewish population of Bessarabia, Transnistria (regions that nowadays belong to the Republic of Moldova) and Bukovina (which is now part of Ukraine) during the Second World War. Jews who lived in the territory that now comprises Romania had a slightly better chance of surviving the Holocaust, but the Romanian government at that time supported pogroms, which resulted in more than 130,000 Romanian Jews being killed by the pro-Nazi Hungarian authorities in Transylvania (Heinen, 2007).

As to religion, Christianity prevails. The Orthodox Church (86.8 per cent) dominates, being followed by the Roman Catholic Church (5 per cent), the Reformed Protestant Church, the Baptists and Pentecostals (5 per cent altogether), the Uniate Greek Catholic Church (1 per cent to 3 per cent, especially ethnic Hungarians and Germans) and Islam (0.2 per cent). Less than 0.1 per cent belong to the Jewish religion (European Commission, 2007b). The famous Romanian Orthodox monasteries, with their medieval pieces of art, and the wooden Transylvanian Christian churches do not function only as religious sites. The buildings and the sacral artistic works they contain are frequently used as reference points in the process of national identity construction:[26] 'The Romanians like to portray themselves as the defenders of Europe and Christianity against the Ottoman Empire' (Boia, 2006). What is more, religious sites also play a key role in the tourism industry (Hannover, 2007).

Romanian history reaches back to some 200 years BC, when the territory was settled by the Dacians, a Thracian tribe. In 106 AD, after a series of conquests, the region was incorporated into the Roman Empire under the name of Dacia Province; however, the Romans withdrew from it between 271 and 274 AD (Pop, 2000). The historical myth of Romanian ethnogenesis tells that Romanian people evolved when the local Dacians were mixed with the legions of Emperor Trajan and the Roman colonists brought there by the conquerors. Thus the

Romanian people lay claim both to the 'noble' Roman tradition and to the autochthonous tradition, which stands for ethnic continuity and 'originality' (OSI, 2002). During the Middle Ages the principalities of Moldavia and Wallachia, both of them administered by the Ottoman Empire, formed a region out of which the later Romanian state emerged in the nineteenth century. Moldavia and Wallachia were unified in 1859 by Prince Alexandru Ioan Cuza and gained full independence about two decades later, as a result of the Treaty of Berlin (1878). In 1881 the first Romanian king was crowned: Carol of Hohenzollern-Sigmaringen. The new state was encircled by the Ottoman Empire, the Austro-Hungarian Empire and tsarist Russia (Boia, 2006). Intellectual and political elites were Western-oriented.[27] They particularly looked to France as a model for cultural, educational and administrative development (Scharr and Graf 2008). Modernization was inspired by the French model, but this was also viewed critically by relevant members of the intellectual elite, who evaluated the 'social representation of modernization as a violation of the traditional self' (Mungiu-Pippidi, 2007, p. 122). Those intellectuals and artists idealized traditional, rural, peasant society and conceived 'the state as an expression of the peasant society' in the form of 'direct links between the ruler and the ruled [...] modernization meant therefore a denial of the Romanian self' (Mungiu-Pippidi, 2007, pp. 123–125).[28] Apart from the legacy of economic underdevelopment, Alina Mungiu-Pippidi (2007) describes this unfinished modernization process of the society as the major determinant of contemporary political culture in Romania.[29]

Romania was an ally of the Entente Powers and the USA in the First World War and was granted large territories with Romanian populations, notably Transylvania, Bessarabia and Bukovina, after the war (Pop, 2000). During the interwar period most Romanian governments, although maintaining the form of a liberal constitutional monarchy, tended to adopt authoritarian characteristics. A main political player and influential force was the fascist Iron Guard movement. The Iron Guard combined nationalism, fear of communism, xenophobia and anti-Semitism and acted as a key destabilizing factor. King Carol II established a royal dictatorship in 1938, but in 1940 the authoritarian General Ion Antonescu took over control.

Romania belongs to the part of the world where foreign influence is the most important agent of political change. In 1940 the constitutional monarchy was reversed by domestic fascism due less to the strength of the Iron Guard than to the Molotov-Ribbentrop

Pact. The pact deprived Romania of important territories, which dealt a mortal blow to the legitimacy of the monarch.

(Mungiu-Pippidi, 2007, p. 119)

In 1941, Romania entered the Second World War on the side of the Axis Powers. Antonescu aimed, *inter alia*, at recovering the regions of Bessarabia and Bukovina, which had been annexed by the Soviet Union in 1940. He was eventually overturned by a coup led by King Mihai, who was supported by the army and opposition politicians. Subsequently Romania changed sides and fought with the Allies against the National Socialists. After the end of the war the Soviet annexation of Bessarabia and of parts of Bukovina was confirmed in the Treaty of Paris in 1947, while northern Transylvania – handed over to Hungary by the NS German Reich in 1940 – was returned to Romania (Scharr and Graf, 2008).[30]

The Soviets strongly supported the inclusion of Romania's negligible Communist Party in the post-war government, while non-communist political leaders were steadily removed from political life. Eventually, at the end of 1947, King Mihai resigned under pressure and left Romania. The former monarchy became the 'People's Republic of Romania'. As early as the late 1950s, the communist government started to seek some independence from the influence of the Soviet Union. In the mid-1960s Nicolae Ceauşescu became the head of the Communist Party (1965) and subsequently also head of state (1967). The particularity of the Ceauşescu regime was a specific type of power structure, which relied on nepotism, personal loyalties, arbitrariness and corruption. The outcome was some kind of 'dynastic Socialism' (Olteanu, 2007a, p. 70), with 'almost complete lack of an opposition' (Boia, 2006). Ceauşescu denounced the 1968 Soviet invasion of Czechoslovakia and, due to his independent foreign policy course, gained a positive image in the West. Western political leaders thus overlooked the internal repression, arbitrariness and violation of human rights, which had characterized the Ceauşescu regime since at least the late 1970s, accompanied by severe austerity. At the same time, Ceauşescu developed a personality cult in 'North Korean style' that was 'much stronger than in other countries' (Boia, 2006).[31]

In 1989 Romania was the last country of the East and South East European single-party states to get rid of communism. In December of that year people protested in Timişoara against the forced relocation of a pastor belonging to the Hungarian minority. Local unrest fuelled a countrywide protest against the Ceauşescu regime (Oschlies, 1998).

About 1,500 people died in street fighting, but eventually the army sided with the protestors and dispossessed the dictator. Ceauşescu and his wife were executed on the basis of an illegitimate and cursory military trial. The National Salvation Front (FSN) led by Ion Iliescu, a former Communist Party official demoted by Ceauşescu in the 1970s, installed itself as the new government, dissolved the Communist Party and proclaimed the restoration of democracy in Romania (Gabanyi 1998).[32]

The first free presidential elections were held in 1990. Iliescu won, earning 85 per cent of the vote. The FSN also captured about two-thirds of the seats in the parliamentary elections held in the same year (Gabanyi, 1990). The FSN got 66.3 per cent of the votes and put forward Petre Roman as prime minister. The most successful opposition parties were the Democratic Alliance of Hungarians in Romania (UDMR) (7.2 per cent) and the National Liberal Party (PNL) (6.4 per cent). The new government cautiously introduced economic reforms, while the opposition parties favoured quick and more fundamental reforms, such as immediate privatization. In April 1990 protests against the continuous influence of Ceauşescu-era elites (Oschlies, 1998) in politics were dispersed by coal miners from the Jiu Valley, to whom President Iliescu expressed thanks. Moreover, the miners attacked private houses and offices of opposition politicians. Petre Roman's government fell in 1991, when the miners returned to Bucharest and demanded higher salaries as well as better living conditions. Theodor Stolojan became the head of an interim government (Olteanu, 2007b). A new constitution was adopted in 1991 and approved by a popular referendum (77.3 per cent) in the same year.[33]

In March 1992 the FSN split into two groups: the Democratic National Salvation Front (FDSN), led by Ion Iliescu, and the FSN, led by Petre Roman. The latter party subsequently changed its name to the Democratic Party (PD). The FDSN became the Party of Social Democracy of Romania (PDSR) in 1993. Presidential elections in 1992 resulted in the re-election of Ion Iliescu by a clear majority. The FDSN also won the majority of seats in both chambers of parliament. The political divide between urban centres and the countryside became marked: rural voters were in favour of President Ion Iliescu and his FDSN party, urban voters favoured the Democratic Convention of Romania (CDR). The CDR coalition was made up of a colourful range of parties and civic organizations, which opted for quicker reforms and gained second place. Following the elections, the FDSN and the CDR formed a government mainly consisting of technocrats. Nicolae Văcăroiu became prime minister. An economist by profession, he was supported by the nationalist

Party of Romanian National Unity (PUNR), by the nationalist Greater Romania Party (PRM) as well as by the former Communist Socialist Labour Party (PSM). All three parties had been anti-Hungarian, anti-gypsy and anti-Semitic, as well as anti-democratic. In 1992 Romania also signed an association agreement with the EU, which was followed by a free trade agreement with the European Free Trade Association (EFTA) in 1993. Thus the basic framework for further economic integration was created (Gabanyi 1998).

The 1996 local elections indicated a major shift in the political orientation of Romanians. Opposition parties won the elections in Bucharest and in many of the larger cities. They repeated their success in the national parliamentary elections in the same year: the opposition did not only dominate the cities, but also won remarkable numbers of votes in rural areas, while the PDSR lost a lot of voters in its traditional strongholds, and thus its majority standing. The fight against corruption and economic reform were the two topics the opposition had focused on in the pre-election campaign. Victor Ciorbea, trade union leader and former mayor of the capital, became prime minister. Emil Constantinescu became president. The new coalition invited the Democratic Union of Hungarians in Romania (UDMR) into the government. In spite of internal frictions and a triple change of prime minister, this coalition retained power for the whole election period (Gabanyi, 1998).

The government, however, did not manage to fight corruption and improve the standard of living (Light and Phinnemore, 2001), for which it was punished by the electorate in the 2000 elections. These elections mark a watershed in Romanian political life: the communist versus anti-communist divide (Tismăneanu, 1998) lost its key role, while socio-economic and regional divides became more important (Gabanyi, 2010). The PDSR won the elections and formed a minority government. Although the Greater Romania Party (PRM) was successful in the parliamentary elections, former president Ion Iliescu defeated his opponent Corneliu Vadim Tudor, leader of the extreme nationalist PRM, in the second round of the presidential election. The PDSR changed its name to PSD (Social Democratic Party) in 2001, after a merger with the Romanian Social Democratic Party. The PSD government, led by Prime Minister Adrian Năstase, acted on the basis of a de facto coalition with the ethnic Hungarian UDMR. Năstase continued the pro-Western policy and partially succeeded in creating political and economic growth. Romania achieved greater macroeconomic stability,[34] while corruption remained a key problem. The government stayed in power for four years.

In 2003 the centre-right National Liberal Party (PNL) and the centrist Democratic Party (PD) formed an alliance for the 2004 elections, a move that brought Romania closer to a political system dominated by two large political blocs (Autengruber, 2006).

Romania became a NATO member in 2004[35] and signed the EU accession treaty in 2005. In 2004 parliamentary and presidential elections also took place. The latter were won by the former mayor of Bucharest, Traian Băsescu, the candidate of the centre-right PNL/PD alliance, who defeated the PSD candidate Adrian Năstase. Băsescu appointed PNL leader Calin Popescu-Tăriceanu as prime minister. Shortly before EU accession,[36] the government coalition collapsed after the Conservatives left the four-party coalition (Sommerbauer and Lötzsch, 2007). Former prime minister Tăriceanu's PNL ran an ultra-minority government, in coalition with the UDMR and with the tacit support of the PSD, until the parliamentary elections in 2008.[37] In April 2007 Băsescu became the first Romanian president to be officially suspended from office on charges of unconstitutional conduct, but he was reinstated a month later, in a national referendum on his impeachment, which failed. Such political developments also indicate some instability of the Romanian political system (Sturdza and Zaragiu, 2009).

After the elections in 2008 the PDL and the PSD formed a new government, with the PDL as the leading partner.[38] Prime Minister Emil Boc – who saw the government's top priorities as addressing the effects of the global economic turmoil on Romania's economic development and coping with significant fiscal and budgetary challenges – faced a no-confidence motion in October 2009. However, difficulties in nominating and approving a new cabinet allowed Boc to remain in power. The PDL ruled as a caretaker government, until a new coalition government was formed in December 2009, consisting of the PDL, the UDMR, some members of the National Union for the Advancement of Romania (UNPR) and independents (Gabanyi, 2010). Economic concerns also dominated the November 2009 presidential elections. No candidate gained a majority of the votes, but President Traian Băsescu narrowly succeeded in the second-round run-off. Despite charges of irregularities, the Constitutional Court certified Băsescu as the winner. He asked acting prime minister Boc to form a new cabinet, which after two months of instability was eventually approved by parliament.

The global financial crisis aggravated Romania's economic contraction. Thus the government agreed to a financial assistance package with the IMF, the European Commission and the World Bank in March 2009. This resulted in budget cuts in the public sector in order to reduce the budget deficit. Nevertheless, the agreement had to be renegotiated several times. As the economy continued to contract in 2010, Prime Minister Boc proposed austerity measures such as a 25 per cent cut in public sector salaries and a 15 per cent reduction in pensions, to meet the IMF's requirements. These measures caused the protest of some 40,000 people in Bucharest. Nevertheless, parliament passed the austerity package.

The protest seems to be contrary to the appraisal of Romanian political culture as somehow 'fatalistic', characterized by apathy and resignation and 'dominated by distrust on all levels. The individual citizen sees no point in exercising his "free will", nor does he have enough trust in his fellow citizens to be open to collective action' (Mungiu-Pippidi, 2007, p. 119). However, the majority of Romanians believe that citizens' needs 'aren't taken into consideration when political decisions are made' (Soros, 2010). Such an attitude eventually leads to the erosion of the credibility of the country's democratic institutions: 'The political spectacle of the last four years has undermined not just the credibility of the main democratic protagonists [...] but also that of the system as a whole [...] the benefits of democracy have not materialized for most Romanians', as Grigore Pop-Eleches wrote in 2001 (p. 167). The transformation process is allegedly seen as a life of suffering (Gabanyi, 2010), not least due to the 'obstruction of free and fair access to resources and services by a narrow group of transition winners' (Savin, 2003), many of whom are members of the pre-1989 nomenklatura and therefore able to transform traditional informal networks into a modified 'informal, but efficient, structure that monopolizes resources [...] and nurtures corruption' (Savin, 2003). Corruption, in turn, delegitimizes democratic political regimes and constrains political participation (Olteanu, 2007a). Though political power has become pluralistic after the system change, political recruitment has still a lot to do with patronage, clientelism and donations. Moreover, there is no clear division between the political arena, respectively the political parties, and the administrative arena (Olteanu, 2007b). Similar phenomena can be observed when it comes to alliances between politics and business, especially at the regional level (Olteanu, 2007b).

Another key problem in Romanian politics after 1989 has been the role of the former communist elite and the legacy of more than four decades of communist rule, especially regarding the extensive internal security apparatus. Political representatives of all parties across the political spectrum were members of the Communist Party before the system change – a source of ongoing controversy.[39] Petrescu and Petrescu

(2010) call this controversy a fight for memory against amnesia: 'After the fall of the communist regime, the interest of the public on the communist period was driven by the desire to understand why Romania experienced such a deviant form of national-communism and why only its exit from communism was accompanied by violence and bloodshed' (Petrescu and Petrescu, 2010, p. 571). In 2003 President Iliescu established an international commission, which was in charge of investigating the Holocaust in Romania. The respective report was issued in 2004 and did not fit into the traditional Romanian mainstream historiography as described by Müller (2007), which, for instance, saw Ion Antonescu mainly as a patriot who fought against the Soviets, while forgetting that Antonescu especially was responsible for Romanian participation in the Holocaust. The Commission for the Analysis of Communist Dictatorship in Romania issued its final report at the end of 2006. In addition to a detailed description of the different phases of Romanian communism and related injustices and crimes, the report criticized the insufficient way in which post-communist Romanian officials dealt with the communist past. Moreover, it suggested that prominent politicians such as Ion Iliescu and Corneliu Vladim Tudor are responsible for having supported an 'illegitimate and criminal regime' (Sommerbauer and Lötzsch, 2007). The authors emphasize that the crimes of the communist era have enjoyed impunity (Trappe, 2008). The commission called this phenomenon 'systematically supported amnesia' (Trappe, 2008, p. 194) and stated that it has hampered democratic consolidation and caused feelings of disappointment and frustration (Trappe, 2008). Compared with other East European states, Romania has lagged behind. Until 2006 – when the Romanian president Băsescu eventually gave a speech on this issue – there was no official statement from the side of state institutions condemning the previous communist regime (Trappe, 2008). The presidential speech marks a break in the official Romanian politics of memory, which can be seen as a result of the political change in 2004.[40]

## Conclusion

Though 1989 marks a break in historical continuity, political, economic and societal transformation processes in Bulgaria and Romania should not be interpreted as an immediate consequence of the system change only. In some cases their roots lay in pre-1989 developments, as has been shown, for instance, in the example of late modernization, due to long-lasting rural socio-economic structures, or the impact of paternalistic patterns of society.

Though the two states experienced different types of system change, they share the political phenomenon of elite continuity after 1989. In Bulgaria, the negotiated system change was conducive to further political influence of the pre-1989 communist elites. Romanian politics, in spite of a violent system change, is also characterized by a continuity of elites.

Regarding the party systems of both countries, there are commonalities and, at the same time, differences. The political and societal contradictions in Bulgaria, between those in favour of democracy and market reforms on the one hand and the old nomenklatura on the other hand, characterized the bipolar party system until the 2001 elections. These elections marked a decisive break. Since the beginning of the new century, differentiation between the respective parties has become more difficult, due to a lack of distinctness when it comes to ideological and political positions and to a general increase in populist-style politics (see Simeon II or GERB as examples; Autengruber, 2008). Romania has developed a relatively stable party system. Regular changes in government testify to the functioning of pluralistic political competition. However, the relevant parties lack clear and steady ideological, programmatic boundary lines. This often leads to surprising coalitions between parties that, at first glance, represent opposite political positions. The Romanian party system is characterized by programmatic volatility and by a problematic trend towards the commercialization of the political sphere, following the interests of relevant groups. Citizens therefore perceive politics as a 'pabulum' in which they cannot see any significant difference between the governing elites (Olteanu, 2008).

At the same time, civic society is said to be underdeveloped in former single-party states, especially those located in South East Europe. Before the system change, Bulgaria and Romania experienced 'patrimonial socialism', characterized by patronage, clientelism and personal dependencies, state bureaucracy being less developed and institutionalized (Tiemann, 2007). Civic engagement is considered to be particularly low in Romania and Moldova, where 'less than 3 percent, possibly as low as 1 per cent, in each country belong to civic groups' (Bădescu et al., 2004, p. 340). However, positive effects of the increasing role of civic society engagement and of NGOs in fighting against corruption can also be found in Romania (Olteanu, 2007a). In particular, universities (students) and churches are important sources for civic society activism in both countries (Bădescu et al., 2004).

Corruption is a key issue not only for the European Commission, but also for the ordinary citizens in Bulgaria and Romania: surveys in former

East and South East European single-party states indicate that citizens believe that corruption has increased since the system change (Olteanu, 2007a). The Freedom House Report confirms this assumption: 'Romania was ranked 71 out of 180 countries surveyed in Transparency International's 2009 Corruption Perceptions Index, tying Greece and Bulgaria for the worst performance in the EU' (Freedom House, 2010a). It goes without saying that fighting corruption in Romania and Bulgaria will remain an 'uphill struggle' (Emerging Europe Monitor, 2010).

What is more, the social gap between the poor and the rich is increasing in Bulgaria (Autengruber, 2008). The same is true for Romania. In a survey conducted in 2007, 69.5 per cent of Bulgarian respondents and 54.5 per cent of Romanian respondents consider the economic situation of their household worse compared with 1989 (Segert, 2009). While 73 per cent of European citizens consider poverty to be widespread in their countries, the rates for Romania (92 per cent) and Bulgaria (90 per cent) are much higher (European Commission, 2010c). Eighty-three per cent of Bulgarians and 82 per cent of Romanians also believe that poverty levels in their respective countries have increased in the last three years (EU average 89 per cent; European Commission, 2010c). The transformation process, especially in Bulgaria and Romania, was accompanied by recession, increasing unemployment rates, hyperinflation and general worsening of living conditions (Hackfurth, 2005; de Nève and Olteanu 2006; European Commission, 2010c). On the other hand, 69 per cent of Romanians and 68 per cent of Bulgarians agree with the statement that '[f]ree competition is the best guarantee for economic property' (European Commission, 2008), the EU average being at 61 per cent. At the same time, 75 per cent of Romanians and 69 per cent of Bulgarians are in favour of more equality and justice, even if this means less freedom for the individual (European Commission, 2008).[41]

Knowledge about how the EU works is not widespread in Bulgaria (41 per cent) and Romania (42 per cent), but only slightly below the EU average (44 per cent; European Commission, 2009a). Furthermore, only 30 per cent of respondents in Bulgaria and Romania know what their rights as EU citizens are (EU average 42 per cent; European Commission, 2010b).[42] The same trend could be observed in the pre-accession phase: the average person did not know much about EU matters. However, pro-European or pro-Western orientations dominated before accession in both countries – even though Bulgaria 'has less a tradition of identifying as European' (Sommerbauer and Lötzsch, 2007). Although in Romania and in Bulgaria – as in the case of almost all countries of the 1995 and 2004 enlargement rounds – fears were expressed regarding the loss of local traditions that could be destroyed by EU regulations, in principle the EU meant economic upturn, higher salaries, freedom of travel and a better life in the future.[43] There was a general EU euphoria, although concrete plans for the post-entry phase did not exist; thus optimism tended to turn into disappointment after accession (Sommerbauer and Lötzsch, 2007).

## Notes

1. The 'Helsinki-Group' comprised Bulgaria, Latvia, Lithuania, Malta, Romania and Slovakia. EU accession negotiations with these countries started in 2000, whereas negotiations with the Czech Republic, Estonia, Hungary, Poland, Slovenia and Cyprus (the 'Luxembourg Group') had already begun two years earlier in 1998.

2. Besides the enlargement process, the EU implemented an additional tool in 2002–03, the 'European Neighbourhood Policy' (ENP). Its purpose has been to enhance stability and security beyond the EU borders. Compared with the current candidate countries Croatia, FYROM, Montenegro, Turkey and Iceland – as well as with the Western Balkan states, which were also granted a membership perspective in the long run – the ENP aims to bring closer to the EU a number of other East European, South East European and Mediterranean states, without offering a membership option. Nonetheless, cooperation within the frame of ENP seems to be sufficiently attractive for the respective countries to comply with democratic standards, security requests and economic reforms stipulated by the EU (Vobruba, 2007). Collaboration within the ENP tool allows for participation in various EU programmes (particularly in the fields of education, science, culture, environmental policy, infrastructure or youth policy). Conversely, broad technical and financial support and customized measures fostering economic integration are offered. One of the countries taking part in the European Neighbourhood Policy, as well as in the Eastern Partnership Initiative, is the Republic of Moldova (European Commission, 2007a). This country – formerly part of the USSR – only reached a higher level of perception among citizens of EU member states after Romania's EU accession. Meanwhile, the country is not only known on account of its particular but complicated relations with Romania; Moldova is also one of those EU neighbouring countries that face a secession conflict: Transnistria separated in 1990 and formed a de facto state within the borders of the Republic of Moldova. This process led to a civil war in 1992, which was ended by Russian intervention and a forced armistice. Though Transnistria finally reached autonomy in 1997, the tensions between the two parts of Moldova persist. In an internationally unacknowledged referendum organized in 2006, 97.1 per cent of the polled citizens of Transnistria voted for independence (Die Welt, 14.6.2008). The status quo can be described as 'frozen conflict'. Although negotiations are regularly conducted, they have not yet led to a real improvement of the stand-off.

3. The 'civic culture' concept refers to input and output categories as well as to behavioural patterns that are said to influence directly the political system and its sub-systems (such as parties, lobbies, elites and so on) or the areas immediately influencing the political system (such as mass media). Respective studies are mainly based on survey research and concentrate on measuring attitudes and mindsets by means of quantitative methods. Almond's and Verba's approach finally aimed at contributing to the predictability of democratic developments.

4. The scope of available literature covers country case studies as well as comparative analysis. The authors mainly follow proven concepts of transition, which before '1989' had concentrated on the system change of South European and Latin American states (Diamond et al., 1989; Pridham and Vanhanen, 1994). These studies focus on the issue of the consolidation of democracy and the formal interplay of institutions such as parliaments, political parties, elites or media, among others (Ágh, 1998), as well as on subjective views of the citizens towards democratic institutions and processes (Dawisha and Parrot, 1997; Segert et al., 1997; Ágh, 1991, 2005).

5. Contrary to other disciplines such as the humanities or sociology, a cultural science perspective on social phenomena has been accepted only hesitantly in political science (Schwelling, 2004).

6. Culture as such is understood as a set of control mechanisms designed to regulate behaviour (Geertz, 1973), or as a system of rules for the construction of social reality (Patzelt, 1987).

7. All the data in this and the following three paragraphs are also taken from European Commission (2010a).

8. The Candidate Countries Eurobarometer 2001 showed 26 per cent trust in institutions for Bulgaria and identified the most trusted institutions, such as the army (58 per cent), the Church (48 per cent) and the police (37 per cent). The corresponding figure for Romania was 30 per cent trust, and in this case, too, the Church (83 per cent), the army (72 per cent) and the police (35 per cent) were more trusted. The military enjoys such popular acceptance in Romania partly because of its role in supporting the December 1989 revolution.

9. All the further data in this paragraph are also based on European Commission (2009b).

10. An assimilation campaign under Communist Party leader and head of state Todor Zhivkov in the late 1980s, directed against ethnic Turks, forced some 300,000 Bulgarian Turks to leave the country for Turkey.

11. In 1992 he was sentenced to seven years in prison for corruption in office, but the sentence was later overturned (BBC, 2005).

12. Bulgaria is a parliamentary democracy. The unicameral parliament, the National Assembly (240 members), is elected for a four-year term on the basis of proportional representation and by means of a mixed electoral system. Parties and political coalitions need 4 per cent of the popular vote to qualify. Votes belonging to parties not passing the 4 per cent threshold are distributed to other parties by using the method of the smallest remainder. The president is directly elected every five years for a maximum of two terms. Each of the 28 provinces (including the capital region of Sofia) is headed by a regional governor. More than 260 municipalities form

the basis for administrative self-government. The Constitutional Court, which is separate from the rest of the judiciary, interprets the constitution and constitutionality of laws and treaties (Riedel 2010).

13. *'In den ersten Jahren nach der Wende ging es den Menschen schlecht, sie waren aber sicher, dass es ihnen bald besser gehen würde. Es war viel von Aufbruch die Rede, von einem Tal, das durchschritten werden muss, von einem Zwischentief. Keiner vermutete, dass der Abstieg andauern, dass zum Ende des Jahrhunderts der bisherige Tiefpunkt erreicht werden würde'* (Trojanov, 2006, p. 17, translation by the author).

14. Petur Stoyanov, the candidate of the UDF, won a decisive victory in the 1996 presidential elections and assumed the presidency at the beginning of 1997.

15. Tsar Simeon II took the throne in 1943, at the age of six, following the death of his father Boris III. He was forced into exile in 1946.

16. To some extent, such an attitude is a reminder of the 1930s, when the father of Simeon, Boris III, abolished the party system; some say he did so to the profit of the country.

17. In February 1994 Bulgaria joined NATO's Partnership for Peace. Bulgaria is a leader in the multilateral peacekeeping force for South East Europe.

18. In May and August that year Bulgaria was hit by a series of heavy rains, which caused floods in large parts of the country. The floods in turn caused serious infrastructural damage, especially concerning roads, railway lines and bridges.

19. See indicators such as GDP $48.7 billion (2009, est.); real GDP growth −5.0 per cent (2009 est.), per capita GDP $6,423 (2009, est.), inflation rate 1.6 per cent (2009), unemployment rate 9.1 per cent (2009). Bulgaria's economy contracted dramatically after the collapse of the COMECON system because it had been closely linked with the Soviet market. The standard of living fell constantly, and eventually the economy collapsed in the mid-1990s, as was mentioned above (http://earthtrends.wri.org/pdf).

20. Pensioners, handicapped people, single mothers and minority group members especially face high risks of poverty. Young and educated Bulgarians often see few chances to succeed in their own country and look for work abroad (Schüler, 2008). In 2008 the monthly minimum wage in Bulgaria was 92 euros, 14 times lower than in France (Wirtén, 2008).

21. In 2008, the European Commission again blocked the payment of grants on the grounds of evidence of fraud and corruption (Schüler, 2008).

22. Results were as follows: GERB 39.7 per cent, BSP 17.7 per cent, MRF 14.4 per cent, ATAKA 9.4 per cent, Blue Coalition 6.8 per cent, RZS 4.1 per cent, other 7.9 per cent; seats by party were GERB 116, BSP 40, MRF 38, ATAKA 21, Blue Coalition 15, RZS 10 (U.S. Department of State, 2010). Results of the 2009 European Parliament elections were GERB 24.36 per cent, 5 seats; BSP 18.5 per cent, 4 seats; DPS 14.14 per cent, 3 seats; ATAKA 11.96 per cent, 2 seats; NDSV 7.96 per cent, 2 seats; Blue Coalition (SDS-DSB and other right-wing parties) 7.95 per cent, 1 seat (turnout: 37.49 per cent) (U.S. Department of State, 2010). As to European Parliament elections, see European Commission (2010a).

23. Traditional Bulgarian familial and societal relations survived the post-war wave of modernization. To introduce an example: though the communist regimes promoted the emancipation of women, paternalism and traditional female roles remained strong in Bulgarian society (Liebhart et al., 2003).

24. On the occasion of the local elections in 2007, the buying of votes was a phenomenon broadly discussed in the media for the first time (Schüler, 2008).

25. In principle, minorities have far-reaching rights. Each minority, for example, has the right automatically to send a representative to the national parliament (Boia, 2006).

26. Church-related schools developed as early as the eleventh century. The oldest known school in Romania came into being in a monastery (Hannover, 2007).

27. The feeling of isolation and lack of an audience generated by the marginal position of the Romanian language exacerbated the sense of lack of traditional roots: Romanian intellectuals have always assumed the mission of recovering the cultural delay and of covering the gaps that separated them from other countries. This is why intellectuals were often motivated to be in the avant-garde of Westernization. But they also faced the compensatory reaction of promoting anti-Westernizing attitudes and 'Romanianism' against 'foreign' influences. Ruralism and (partly) religious orthodoxy were the basic traits of the intellectual conservatism that shaped mainly the interwar period (OSI, 2002). Boia (2006) speaks of a 'simultaneous desire for Western Europe and for national isolation'.

28. From this point of view, the West as well as Catholicism are 'alien to the Orthodox spirit' (Nae Ionescu: Mungiu-Pippidi, 2007, p. 124).

29. The pattern described above eventually led to a 'culture of omitting laws', which according to Mungiu-Pippidi (2007) was 'later to help the Romanians endure the communist institutional revolution, but nowadays [...] seriously hinders the process of adjusting to the new European institutions' (p. 124).

30. The treaty also forced Romania to pay massive war reparations to the Soviet Union.

31. Lucien Boia considers that the fact that the 'memory of Romanians is dominated by personalities' helped a lot. Personality cult was also implemented by Ceaușescu's predecessor, Gheorghe Gheorghiu-Dej (Boia, 2006).

32. Since the violent system change, Romania has been a parliamentary democracy with a strong presidential character (semi-presidential system), a bicameral parliament (consisting of the Chamber of Deputies/*Camera Deputaților* and the Senate/*Senat*). Deputies and senators are elected for four-year terms by means of a mixed election system (majority and proportional). The president (elected by popular vote for five-year terms and a maximum of two terms), the mayors and the county council presidents are elected individually. In the wake of the system change, more than 200 new political parties arose, most of them centred round personalities rather than political programmes. Their 'behaviour does not always correspond to their names', and it often happens that politicians change sides (Gabanyi 2010). Nevertheless, all major parties kept up democratic values, as well as

market reforms. Not all of the parties were new. Some of them, such as the Liberals and the Peasant Party, were revivals of their pre-war predecessors. Romania comprises 41 counties (*judeţe*) and the capital Bucharest. The central government appoints a prefect for each county and for the Bucharest municipality. A prefect may block the action of a local authority if he/she considers it unlawful or unconstitutional. Since 1999 local councils have had control over the spending of their allocations from the central government budget (ibid.).

33. The constitution was amended in 2003, also by popular referendum (89.7 per cent voted in favour), to bring Romania's law into compliance with EU legal standards. Articles were introduced on EU integration and NATO accession, to ensure that both could take place by parliamentary vote alone. A further article grants minorities the right to use their native language in courts and regarding issues of local administration. The president's term was extended to five years, and foreigners were allowed to own land in Romania (Gabanyi 2010).

34. Recent economic data show a GDP of $161.1 billion (2009), and an annual GDP growth rate of 7.1 per cent. Romania's inflation rate in 2010 was 4.4 per cent. Unemployment reached 7.8 per cent in 2009. (http://earthtrends.wri.org/pdf/).

35. Romania also hosted a NATO Summit in April 2008.

36. In December 2004 pre-accession negotiations with Romania were concluded.

37. In July 2005 Prime Minister Tăriceanu expressed plans to resign so as to prompt new elections, but then he recanted due to severe problems caused by the summer floods.

38. Results of the 2008 parliamentary elections (*Biroul Electoral Central*, 2008): Democratic Liberal Party 32.4 per cent; PSD-PC Alliance/Social Democratic Party and Conservative Party 33.1 per cent; National Liberal Party 18.6 per cent; Hungarian Democratic Union of Romania 6.2 per cent; ethnic minorities parties 3.6 per cent; Greater Romania Party 3.2 per cent.

39. See, for instance, the controversy regarding history textbooks for higher schools in the late 1990s (Olteanu, 2007a).

40. Prime Minister Tăriceanu, for instance, founded an Institute for the Investigation of Communist Crimes in Romania in 2005 (Trappe, 2008). See also the establishment of the Sighet Memorial and Museum to commemorate the victims of communism (Petrescu and Petrescu, 2010).

41. In this regard both countries are close to some South European states, for instance Italy (78 per cent), Portugal (78 per cent) and Spain (71 per cent).

42. Only France ranks lower (28 per cent; European Commission, 2010b).

43. Accession negotiations with Bulgaria and Romania were opened in the early 1990s, but the two South East European countries have been perceived as lagging behind the East Central European states, which joined the EU in 2004. Especially, the first Enlargement Progress Report made it clear that Bulgaria as well as Romania will be counted among the less advanced group of candidate countries (Andreev, 2007; Leiße, 2007). Within the next few years it became obvious that Bulgaria and Romania faced severe problems, particularly in their economies and judiciary systems, and thus would be left out from the 2004 enlargement round (Andreev, 2007; Leiße, 2007).

Moreover, both countries showed clear deficits concerning minority rights and support: But, beyond issuing critical reports, Brussels did not bring about much change in the status or prospects of the Roma. On paper, both Romania and Bulgaria now comply with EU standards on human rights, employment, housing and education. While the Commission's Katharina von Schnurbein describes how Brussels 'worked closely with Bulgaria and Romania to set up various support programmes which aim at improving the housing, education and health situation of Roma,' Radu Motoc says that the EU approach was deficient. 'There were sectors that were totally left out [in the Romanian accession process], such as the social sector. Like the Bulgarians, we focused on anti-corruption and on reform of the judiciary' (Popkostadinova, 2008, p. 7).

# References

24 Tchasa (10.12.1999), Newspaper edition of 10 December 1999.

Ágh, A. (1991) 'The Transition to Democracy in Central Europe: A Comparative View', *Journal of Public Policy*, 11, 133–151.

Ágh, A. (1998) *The Social and Political Actors of Democratic Transition, Budapest Papers on Democratic Transition No. 75* (Budapest: Hungarian Center for Democracy Studies).

Ágh, A. (2005) *Institutional Design and Regional Capacity Building in the Post-Accession Period* (Budapest: Hungarian Centre for Democracy Studies).

Ágh, A. (2008) 'Democratization and Europeanization of the ECE Countries: Post-Accession Crisis and Catching-Up Process in the New Member States', Paper for the CEPSA Annual Conference, Opatija.

Almond, G. and Verba, S. (1963) *The Civic Culture: Political Attitudes and Democracy in Five Nations* (Princeton: Princeton University Press).

Andreev, S. A. (2007) 'Path Dependence During the EU's Fifth Enlargement: Comparing East-Central and Southeast Europe', in Ágh, A. and Ferencz, A. (eds), *Overcoming the EU Crisis: EU Perspectives after the Eastern Enlargement* (Budapest: 'Together for Europe' Research Center), 132–157.

Autengruber, C. (2006) *Die politischen Parteien in Bulgarien und Rumänien: Eine vergleichende Analyse seit Beginn der 90er Jahre* (Hannover: Ibidem).

Autengruber, C. (2008) 'Bulgarien: Zwischen anfänglichen Konsolidierungstendenzen und aktuellen Umbrüchen', in Bos, E. and Segert, D. (eds), *Osteuropäische Demokratien als Trendsetter? Parteien und Parteiensysteme nach dem Ende des Übergangsjahrzehnts* (Opladen: Verlag Barbara Budrich), 133–146.

Badescu, G., Sum, P. and Uslaner, E. M. (2004) 'Civil Society Development and Democratic Values in Romania and Moldova', *East European Politics and Societies*, 18, 316–341.

Baeva, I., Kalinova, E. and Poppetrov, N. (2010) 'Die kommunistische Ära im kollektiven Gedächtnis der Bulgaren', in Troebst, S. (ed.), *Postdiktatorische Geschichtskulturen im Süden und Osten Europas* (Göttingen: Wallstein Verlag), 405–501.

Barnes, S. H. (1998) 'The Mobilization of Political Identity in New Democracies', in Barnes, S. H. and Simon, J. (eds) *The Postcommunist Citizen* (Budapest: Erasmus Foundation and Institute of Political Science of the Hungarian Academy of Sciences 1998), 117–137.

BBC (2005) *BBC News Timeline Bulgaria*, 26 April 2005.

Berend, I. T. (2001) *Decades of Crisis: Central and Eastern Europe before World War II* (California: University of California Press).

Biroul Electoral Central (2008) 'Alegeri pentru autoritatile administratiei publice locale iunie 2008', http://www.beclocale2008.ro, accessed 6 December 2010.

Boia, L. (2006) 'Historische Wurzeln der politischen Kultur Rumäniens', http://www.eurotopics.net/en/archiv/magazin/gesellschaft-verteilerseite/beit ritt_rumaenien_bulgarien_01_2007/apuz_historische_wurzeln_120207/

Brunwasser, M. (2009) 'Bulgaria Still Stuck in Trauma of Transition', *The New York Times*, 10 November 2010.

Bulgarian Government (2005) 'About Bulgaria: History', http://www.government.bg/cgi-bin/e-cms/vis/vis.pl?s=001&p=0159&n=000002&g=, published 27 September 2005, accessed 20 December 2010.

Cemrek, M. (2004) 'The EU Impact on the Political Culture of Bulgaria, Romania and Turkey', *euro Journal of Foreign Policy of Moldova*, 7, http://www.ceeol.com, accessed 6 December 2010.

Chary, F. B. (2009) *The Bulgarian Jews and the Final Solution 1940–1944* (Pittsburgh: University of Pittsburgh).

Crampton, R. J. (2005) *A Concise History of Bulgaria* (Cambridge: Cambridge University Press).

Daskalov, R. (2004) *Building a Balkan Nation and More: Interpreting the Bulgarian Revival* (Budapest: Central European University Press).

Dawisha, K. and Parrott, B. (1997) *The Consolidation of Democracy in East-Central Europe* (Cambridge: Cambridge University Press).

Deimel, J. (2002) 'Quo vadis Bulgaria? Parteien und politische Kultur nach zehn Jahren Transformation', *Europäische Rundschau*, 30, 79–88.

Diamond, L., Linz, J. J. and Lipset, S. M. (1989) *Politics in Developing Countries: Comparing Experiences with Democracy* (Boulder/Colorado: Lynne Rienner Publishers).

Die Welt (14.6.2008) 'Die Patrioten von Transnistrien', http://www.welt.de/welt_print/article2102593/Die_Patrioten_von_Transnistrien.html, accessed 6 December 2010.

Ditchev, I. (2004) 'Monoculturalism as Prevailing Culture', http://www.eurozine.com, accessed 6 December 2010.

Douglas, M. and Wildavsky, A. 1983) *Risk and Culture* (Berkeley: Los Angeles).

Ellis, R. and Thompson, M. (ed.) (1997) *Culture Matters: Essays in Memory of Aaron Wildavsky* (Boulder/Colorado: Westview Press).

Emerging Europe Monitor (2010) *Emerging Europe Monitor South East Europe Monitor*, 17 (7).

European Commission (2006a) *Monitoring Report on the State of Preparedness for EU Membership of Bulgaria and Romania*, presented by the Commission on 16 May 2006, http://www.europarl.europa.eu/sides/getDoc.do?pubRef=-//EP//TEXT+TA+P6-TA-2006-0262+0+DOC+XML+V0//EN&language=EN, accessed 6 December 2010.

European Commission (2006b) *Monitoring Report on the Preparedness for EU Membership of Bulgaria and Romania*, COM (2006) 549 final (Brussels: Commission of the European Communities), 26 September 2006.

European Commission (2007a) *European Neighbourhood and Partnership Instrument: Republic of Moldova Country Strategy Paper 2007–2013* (Brussels: Commission of the European Communities).

European Commission (2007b) 'Romania – Country Profile', http://ec.europa. eu/enlargement/archives/romania/index_en.htm, page archived on 1 January 2007, accessed 9 December 2010.

European Commission (2008) *Eurobarometer 69: Values of Europeans* (Brussels: Commission of the European Communities).

European Commission (2009a) *Eurobarometer 71: Europeans and the 2009 European Elections* (Brussels: Commission of the European Communities).

European Commission (2009b) *Special Eurobarometer 325: Attitudes of Europeans towards Corruption* (Brussels: Commission of the European Communities).

European Commission (2010a) *Eurobarometer 70* (Brussels: Commission of the European Communities).

European Commission (2010b) *Eurobarometer 73 First Results* (Brussels: Commission of the European Communities).

European Commission (2010c) *Special Eurobarometer 321: Poverty and Social Exclusion* (Brussels: Commission of the European Communities).

Freedom house (2010a) 'Freedom in the World – Bulgaria', http://freedomhouse. org, accessed 9 December 2010.

Fuchs, D. and Roller, E. (1998) 'Cultural Conditions of Transition to Liberal Democracy in Central and Eastern Europe', in Barnes, S. H. and Simon, J. (eds), *The Postcommunist Citizen* (Budapest: Erasmus Foundation and Institute of Political Science of the Hungarian Academy of Sciences), 35–77.

Gabanyi, A. U. (1990) *Die unvollendete Revolution: Rumänien zwischen Diktatur und Demokratie* (München: Piper).

Gabanyi, A. U. (1998) *Systemwechsel in Rumänien: Von der Revolution zur Transformation* (München: R. Oldenbourg Verlag).

Gabanyi, A. U. (2010) 'Das Politische System Rumäniens', in Ismayr, W. (ed.), *Die politischen Systeme Osteuropas*, 3, Auflage (Wiesbaden: Vs Verlag und GWV Fachverlag), 627–676.

Gabriel, O. W. (2008) 'Politische Einstellungen und politische Kultur', in Gabriel, O. W. and Knopp, S. (eds), *Die EU-Staaten im Vergleich: Strukturen, Prozesse, Politikinhalte*, 3, Auflage (Wiesbaden: VS Verlag für Sozialwissenschaften), 181–214.

Geertz, C. (1973) *The Interpretation of Cultures* (New York).

Guineva, S. (2009) '1368 Views', http://www.sofiaecho.com/, accessed 6 July 2010.

Hackfurth, O. M. (2005) *Die zweite Transformationskrise in Rumänien: Gesamtwirtschaftliche, regionale und sektorale Auswirkungen* (München: Ravensburg).

Hall, St. (1994) Die Frage der kulturellen Identität, In: Hall, St. (ed.), *Rassismus und kulturelle Identität: Ausgewählte Schriften 2*. Argument Sonderband 226 (Hamburg-Berlin), 180–222.

Hannover, B. G. (2007) *Rumänien entdecken: Kunstschätze und Naturschönheiten* (Berlin: Trescher-Reihe Reisen).

Harrison, L. E. and Huntington, S. P. (ed.) (2000) *Culture Matters. How Values Shape Human Progress* (New York).

Heinen, A. (2007) *Rumänien, der Holocaust und die Logik der Gewalt* (München: Oldenbourg).

Horak, R. and Spitaler, G. (2002) 'Das Politische' im Feld: Über Ethnographie und die Möglichkeiten politikwissenschaftlicher Kulturstudien. In: Österreichische Zeitschrift für Politikwissenschaft 31, 2, 191–204.

Huntington, S. (1991) *The Third Wave: Democratization in the Late Twentieth Century* (Oklahoma: University of Oklahoma Press).

Kiossev, A. (2008) 'The Oxymoron of Normality', http://www.eurozine.com/ articles/2008-01-04-kiossev-en.html, accessed 6 December 2010.

Leiße, O. (2007) 'Romania and Bulgaria before EU Accession', http:// www.eurotopics.net/en/archiv/magazin/gesellschaft-verteilerseite/beitritt_ rumaenien_bulgarien_01_2007/apuz_vor_eubeitritt_120207/, date accessed 6 December 2010.

Liebhart, K., Pető, A., Schiffbänker, A. and Stoilova, R. (2003) 'Familienpolitische Maßnahmen in Österreich, Bulgarien und Ungarn', *Österreichische Zeitschrift für Politikwissenschaft*, 2003/04, 417–427.

Light, D. and Phinnemore, D. (2001) *Post-Communist Romania: Coming to Terms with Transition* (Houndsmills: Palgrave Macmillan).

Malinov, S. (2008) 'Radical Demophilia: Reflections on Bulgarian Populism', http://www.eurozine.com, date accessed 6 December 2010.

Malová, D. and Lisonová, Z. (2010) 'Conclusion: Political Culture and Style in the New Member States', in Malová, D., Rybar, M., Bilcik, V., Lastic, E., Lisonova, Z., Misik, M. and Pasiak, M. (eds), *From Listening to Action? New Member States in the European Union* (Bratislava: Political Science Department, Comenius University).

Merkel, W. (2004) 'Embedded and Defective Democracies', *Democratization*, 11, 33–58.

Müller, D. (2007) 'Strategien des öffentlichen Erinnerns in Rumänien nach 1989: Postkommunisten und postkommunistische Antikommunisten', in Brunnbauer, U. and Troebst, S. (eds), *Zwischen Amnesie und Nostalgie: Die Erinnerung an den Kommunismus in Südosteuropa* (Köln/Weimar/Wien: Böhlau Verlag), 47–69.

Mungiu-Pippidi, A. (2007) 'Hijacked Modernization: Romanian Political Culture in the 20th Century', *Südosteuropa*, 55, 118–144.

de Nève, D. and Olteanu, T. (2006) 'Die rumänische Gesellschaft in der Transformation', in Kahl, T., Metzeltin, M. and Ungureanu, M. (eds), *Rumänien: Raum und Bevölkerung, Geschichte und Geschichtsbilder, Kultur, Gesellschaft und Politik heute, Wirtschaft, Recht und Verfassung, Historische Regionen* (Wien: Österreichische Osthefte), 510–525.

NDI (2003a) *Roma Political Participation in Bulgaria* (Washington: National Democratic Institute for International Affairs).

NDI (2003b) *Roma Political Participation in Bulgaria, Romania, and Slovakia* (Washington: National Democratic Institute for International Affairs).

Nicolae, V. (2006) 'Fourth Arm of the Atate: Romania's Press Becomes a Willing Partner in Prejudice', http://www.eurozine.com, accessed 6 December 2010.

Olteanu, T. (2007a) 'Korruption in Rumänien – ein Erbe des Staatssozialismus?', in Segert, D. (ed.), *Postsozialismus: Hinterlassenschaft des Staatssozialismus und neue Kapitalismen* (Wien: Braumüller), 65–85.

Olteanu, T. (2007b) 'Demokratie auf Rumänisch', in Werndl, K. (ed.), *Rumänien nach der Revolution: Eine kulturelle Gegenwartsbestimmung* (Wien: Braumüller), 71–80.

Olteanu T. (2008) 'Rumänien: Vom Einparteiensystem zum Einheitsbrei?', in Bos, E. and Segert, D. (eds), *Osteuropäische Demokratien als Trendsetter? Parteien und Parteiensysteme nach dem Ende des Übergangsjahrzehnts* (Opladen: Verlag Barbara Budrich), 147–166.

Olteanu, T. and Autengruber, C. (2007) 'Wie ernst meint es die EU mit der Demokratie? Standardsetzung am Beispiel der EU-Beitrittsvorbereitungen mit Bulgarien und Rumänien', *Österreichische Zeitschrift für Politikwissenschaften*, 36, 81–94.

Oschlies, W. (1998) *Ceaușescus Schatten verschwindet: Politische Geschichte Rumäniens 1988–1998* (Köln: Böhlau).

OSI (2002) *Nationale Identitäten und Europäische Identität im Prozess der EU-Erweiterung, Projektbericht für das BMBWK* (Wien: Österreichisches Ost- und Südosteuropainstitut/Abteilung Sozialwissenschaften).

Petrescu, C. and Petrescu, D. (2010) 'The Pitesti Syndrom: A Romanian Vergangenheitsbewältigung', in Troebst, S. (ed.), *Postdiktatorische Geschichtskulturen im Süden und Osten Europas* (Göttingen: Wallstein Verlag), 502–618.

Plasser, F., Ulram, P. A. and Waldrauch, H. (1997) *Politscher Kulturwandel und demokratische Konsolidierung in Ost-Mitteleuropa: Theorien und Trends* (Opladen: Leske + Budrich Verlag).

Pop, I. A. (2000), *Romanians and Romania: A Brief History (East European Monographs)* (Columbia University Press).

Popkostadinova, N. (2008): 'No Maths and No Water in Stolipinovo: The jobs Boom in Bulgaria Has Left the Roma Behind', http://www.eurozine.com, accessed 6 December 2010.

Pridham, G. and Vanhanen, T. (1994) *Democratization in Eastern Europe: Domestic and International Perspectives* (New York: Routledge).

Riedel, S. (2010) 'Das Politische System Bulgariens', in Ismayr, W. (ed.), *Die politischen Systeme Osteuropas*, 3, Auflage (Wiesbaden: VS Verlag/GWV Fachverlage), 677–728.

Rose, R. and Haerpfer, C. (1992) *New Democracies Between State and Market: A Baseline Report of Public Opinion, Studies in Public Policy no. 204* (Glasgow: Centre for the Study if Public Policy, University of Strathclyde).

Rose, R. and Haerpfer, C. (1998) *New Democracies Barometer V: A 12-Nation Study* (Glasgow: Centre for the Study if Public Policy, University of Strathclyde).

Savin, A. (2003) 'The Political Economy of Corruption in Transition and the Pressures of Globalization', http://www.sar.org.ro/polsci/?p_376, accessed 6 December 2010.

Scharr, K. and Graf, R. (2008) *Rumänien: Geschichte und Geografie* (Wien/Köln/Weimar: Böhlau Verlag).

Schirmer, D. (2002) Vom schwierigen Verhältnis von Kultur" und Politikwissenschaft, In Rossade, W. et al. (ed.), *Politik und Bedeutung: Studien zu den kulturellen Grundlagen politischen Handelns und politischer Institutionen* (Wiesbaden), 17–26.

Schmitter, P. C. (1995) 'The Consolidation of Political Democracies: Processes, Rhythms, Sequences and Types', in Pridham, G. (ed.), *Transition to Democracy*.

*Comparative Perspectives from Southern Europe, Latin America and Eastern Europe* (Aldershot: Dartmouth).

Schüler, S. (2008) 'Zur politischen Kultur im heutigen Bulgarien', *Südosteuropa Mitteilungen*, 48 (2), 82–98, http://www.ceeol.com, accessed 6 December 2010.

Schwelling, B. (2007) *Politikwissenschaft als Kulturwissenschaft: Theorien, Methoden, Problemstellungen* (Wiesbaden: VS Verlag).

Segert, D., Stöss, R. and Niedermayer, O. (1997) *Parteiensysteme in postkommunistischen Gesellschaften Osteuropas* (Opladen: Westdeutscher Verlag).

Segert, Dieter (2007) *Postsozialismus: Hinterlassenschaft des Staatssozialismus und neue Kapitalismen in Europa* (Wien: Braumüller).

Segert, Dieter (2009) 'Sozialer Wandel in Osteuropa nach 1989 und staatssozialistisches Erbe', *Berliner Debatte Initial*, 20, 114–29.

Sommerbauer, J. and Lötzsch, K. (2007) 'In the Union of the Insane', http://www.eurotopics.net/en/archiv/magazin/gesellschaft-verteilerseite/ beitritt_rumaenien_bulgarien_01/2007/hintergrundtext_beitritt_rumaenien_ bulgarien-01_2007/, accessed 6 December 2010.

Soros (2010) http://www.soros.ro/eu/communicate_detaliu.php?comunicat=79, accessed 1 November 2010.

Spirova, M. (2007) *Political Parties in Post-Communist Societies: Formation, Persistence and Change* (Basingstoke: Palgrave Macmillan).

Sturdza, A. and Zaragiu, G. (2009) 'Romanian Presidential Elections Deepen the Political Crisis: News Analysis', *TheEpochTimes e-Newsletter*, 9 December 2009, http://www.theepochtimes.com/n2/content/view/2650/, accessed 6 December 2010.

Thompson, M., Ellis, R. and Wildavsky, A. (1990) *Cultural Theory* (Boulder/San Francisco/Oxford: Westview Press).

Tiemann, G. (2007) ' "Cleavages" oder "Legacies"? Die Institutionalisierung und Struktur des politischen Wettbewerbs im postsozialistischen Osteuropa', in Bos, E. and Segert, D. (eds), *Osteuropäische Demokratien als Trendsetter? Parteien und Parteiensysteme nach dem Ende des Übergangsjahrzehnts* (Opladen: Verlag Barbara Budrich), 33–53.

Tismăneanu, V. (1998) *Communism and Post-Communism in Romania: Challenges to Democratic Transition* (Washington: National Council for Eurasian and East European Research).

Todorov, A. (1999) *The Role of Political Parties in the Bulgaria's Accession to the EU* (Sofia: Center for the Study of Democracy).

Trappe, J. (2008) 'Kollektive Unschuld und die Rückkehr nach Europa – Rumäniens Umgang mit dem Unrecht der kommunistischen Vergangenheit', in Fritz, R., Sachse, C. and Wolfrum, E. (eds), *Nationen und ihre Selbstbilder: Postdiktatorische Gesellschaften in Europa* (Göttingen: Wallstein), 193–210.

Transparency International (2002) 'The Global Coalition against Corruption', http://www.transparency.org/pressreleases_archive/2002/2002.08.28.cpi. de.html, accessed 9 December 2010.

Trojanov, I. (2006) *Die fingierte Revolution: Bulgarien, eine exemplarische Geschichte* (München: Deutscher Taschenbuch Verlag).

U.S. Department of State (2010) http://www.state.gov/, accessed 9 December 2010.

Vobruba, G.(2007) 'Expansion ohne Erweiterung. Die EU-Nachbarschaftspolitik in der Dynamik Europas', http://www.eurozine.com, accessed 6 December 2010.

Vukov, N. (2007) 'Refigured Memories, Unchanged Representations: Post-Socialist Monumental Discourse in Bulgaria', in Brunnbauer, U. and Troebst, S. (eds), *Zwischen Amnesie und Nostalgie: Die Erinnerung an den Kommunismus in Südosteuropa* (Köln/Weimar/Wien: Böhlau Verlag), 71–86.

Wessels, B. and Klingemann, H. D. (1998) 'Transformation and the Prerequisites of Democratic Opposition in Central and Eastern Europe', in Barnes, S. H. and Simon, J. (eds), *The Postcommunist Citizen* (Budapest: Erasmus Foundation and Institute of Political Science of the Hungarian Academy of Sciences), 1–34.

Whitehead, Laurence (2001) 'The Enlargement of the European Union: A "Risky" Form of Democracy Promotion', in Whitehead, Laurence (ed.), *International Dimensions of Democratization: Europe and the Americas* (Oxford: Oxford University Press), 415–444.

Wirtén, P. (2008) 'Unacknowledged, Unseen, Unmentioned: Poverty in Europe', http://www.eurozine.com, accessed 6 December 2010.

# 4
# Corruption in South East Europe

*Ruslan Stefanov and Dobromir Hristov*

## Introduction

Regardless of the wide range of anti-corruption measures proposed across the region during the past decade, corruption in South East Europe (SEE) is still endemic, including in the new EU member states Bulgaria and Romania. Corruption remains one of the major obstacles for sustainable development in the South East European countries. Together with the related malfunctioning of the judicial systems, it is seen as a significant obstructive factor for the accession and integration of the region into the European Union (EU) and into its system of rule-of-law institutions.

Although no clear empirical link has yet been established, corruption was identified as one of the main impediments to sound and smooth recovery from the 2008–09 global economic and financial crisis. The levels of corruption uncovered in the popular media in Greece following the country's near default in 2010 exemplify the role that corrupt practices are assumed to play in the gradual deterioration of economic and social cohesion. Left unrepaired during booms, malfunctions in governance seem to aggravate in subsequent economic downturns.

The perspective of EU membership has been a driving force for anti-corruption efforts in SEE for the past decade. The decisive freeze of considerable amounts of EU funds allocated for Bulgaria's cohesion into the EU due to a misuse of funds and a lack of progress in anti-corruption and judicial reform in 2008 seems to have strengthened the European Commission's leverage in its demands for reforms in SEE (Transparency International, 2009a). The precedent of Bulgaria has given a clear signal to candidate countries in the region that EU membership is not an automatic transfer of money from rich fellow members, but requires consistent compliance with rules and a high degree of responsible behaviour. It can be expected that the experience of the EU with the two waves of expansion in 2004 and 2007 will result in the application of stricter rule-of-law and anti-corruption criteria for the accession of future members. The politically nuanced decision for the accession of Bulgaria and Romania in 2007 will possibly pave the way for an even more stringent bureaucratic scrutiny of candidates during upcoming EU accession negotiations and eventual accession.

The experience from previous waves of enlargement has demonstrated that EU membership does not automatically result in a reduction of political corruption. The financial and economic stability guaranteed by EU membership generates a huge inflow of financial resources to the poorest member states. This trend reinforces corruption pressures on the governments to redistribute resources to local businesses, which are politically connected and non-competitive on the European market, through public procurement, concessions, real estate and land swaps (CSD, 2007a). The same trend can be found regarding the huge inflow of pre-accession funds (pre-accession instruments) to not yet fully stabilized candidate countries. The misuse of funds in Bulgaria was first detected in an audit of the former pre-accession funds of Poland and Hungary: Aid for Restructuring of the Economies (PHARE) and Instrument for Structural Policies for Pre-Accession (ISPA).[1]

## Methodological approach for corruption measurement in SEE

Various methodological tools have been employed in the past decade for monitoring corruption trends in SEE. Transparency International's Annual Corruption Perception Index (CPI) is one of the well-recognized instruments for measuring a country's susceptibility to bribery as well as to compromised governance processes. It measures the perceived level of public sector corruption in 180 countries and territories around the world. The CPI is a 'survey of surveys', based on 13 different expert and business surveys (Transparency International, 2009b).[2]

The Governance Indicator tool of the World Bank is another instrument for measuring corruption perceptions. It provides a broad range of opportunities to correlate various governance parameters and economic indicators into a more comprehensive picture for every country in the world (World Bank, 2010).

The European Commission uses a standard matrix for assessing each candidate country's progress in the area of anti-corruption. Though based on a list of measures, it can be seen as the most subjective instrument for monitoring progress. After the accession of Bulgaria and Romania, 'benchmarks' were introduced as part of a cooperation and verification mechanism aimed at assessing the progress of the two countries in countering organized crime and corruption. However, these benchmarks employed by the Commission are also greatly subjective (CSD, 2007b). As a result, each progress report is preceded by lengthy and heated informal discussions between governments and the Commission on the true value of the benchmarks.

Some tools for measuring the extent of corruption were also developed in the region itself. The Corruption Monitoring Systems (CMS) developed by the Center for the Study of Democracy (Sofia) uses indices based on population and business surveys to measure different aspects of corruption, including corruption victimization (as opposed to perceptions of corruption). The CMS has been employed in Bulgaria since 1998. In 2001 and 2002, the Southeast European Legal Development Initiative (SELDI)[3] employed the CMS survey methodology for corruption diagnostics in seven SEE countries – Albania, Bosnia and Herzegovina, Bulgaria, Croatia, Macedonia, Romania and Serbia and Montenegro – and conducted a unique corruption assessment in SEE countries in 2001 (CSD, 2010a).

## The current situation of corruption in South East Europe

The 2009 CPI demonstrated that corruption remains a serious challenge for the entire SEE region. Almost all the countries register scores below 5 out of 10 (no corruption at all) – indicating that they are facing perceived high levels of domestic public sector corruption. Nevertheless, the region displays a wide variation between countries in corruption index performance, Slovenia ranking 27th in the world, with an index of 6.6, while Bosnia and Herzegovina ranked 99th, with an index of 3.0 (Transparency International, 2009c). The different results in the control of corruption performance adequately mirror the disparities of socio-economic development in the region (see Figure 4.1). To a certain degree, they resemble the ranking of countries by gross domestic product (GDP).

A comprehensive review of the latest reports by the European Commission on corruption in SEE reveals that most of the countries face common challenges in fighting corruption and in trying to implement effective anti-corruption policies (Table 4.1). Despite disparities in the socio-economic development of the various countries in the region, the common past and the legacy of the centralized economy

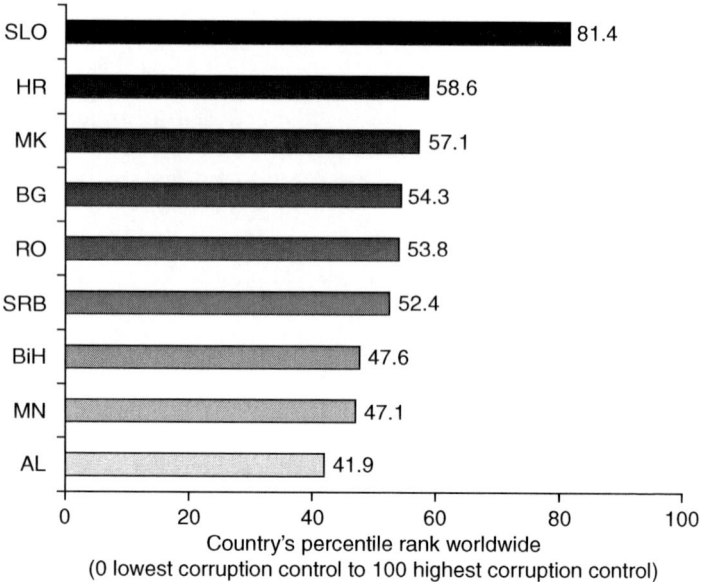

*Figure 4.1* Control of corruption in South East Europe in 2008
*Source*: World Bank (2010).

*Table 4.1* Common issues in fighting corruption in SEE

| Trends | HR | BG | RO | SRB | MN | MK | BIH | AL |
|---|---|---|---|---|---|---|---|---|
| Few sanctioned and prosecuted cases of conflict of interest | ● | ● | ● | | ● | | | |
| Ineffective conflict of interest detection system | | ● | ● | | ● | | | ● |
| 'Tolerance' to dignitaries and high-level officials in public office | ● | | ● | | ● | | ● | |
| Weak public procurement legislation and law enforcement | ● | ● | ● | ● | | | ● | |
| Frequent irregularities with public procurement procedures and tendering | ● | ● | | ● | | | | |
| Low administrative capacity of public procurement agency | ● | ● | | | | | | |

| | | | | | | | | |
|---|---|---|---|---|---|---|---|---|
| Low administrative capacity of public financial inspection agency | • | • | | • | | | | • |
| Dissatisfactory or problematic cooperation and coordination between institutions | | • | • | | • | | • | • |
| Lengthy or suspended trials, few final judgments, inconsistent or dissatisfactory sentences | • | | • | | • | • | • | |
| Weak monitoring mechanisms for anti-corruption policies | • | | • | • | • | | | |
| Legislation on financing of parties not arranged/no impact | • | | | • | • | • | • | • |
| Culture of impunity | • | | | | | | | • |
| Low investigative capacity and weak prosecution | | | | • | • | • | • | • |
| Threats to civil society organizations and media | | | | | | | • | |
| Limited or no data on corruption made publicly available | • | | | | | | • | |
| Lack of trust in public institutions | | | | | | • | | |
| Insufficient protection of corruption whistleblowers | | | | • | | | | |

*Source*: Created by CSD on the basis of European Commission's Progress Reports.

have predetermined the patterns of corruption in the region. The combination of weak administrative capacity, lack of transparency and overburdening in the SEE public sectors constitutes a fertile ground for both petty and large-scale corrupt practices.

The slow pace of reforms in the judicial system and the insufficient capacity of state institutions to enforce the law and deter bad governance practices have entrenched a traditional mistrust of the population in state institutions, complemented by a sense of impunity among high-rank politicians and administrators across the region. Detailed legal frameworks and regulations have not necessarily been followed by effective policy implementation in fighting corruption, which can largely be blamed on the low administrative capacity of state ministries and control agencies, as well as on a continuous lack of political will for reform.

Proper and functioning mechanisms for monitoring and the detection of corruption are seldom in place in SEE countries.

The wave of privatization that followed the democratization in SEE countries triggered two major parallel instruments for political corruption – the management of public property (including land and buildings) and the awarding of public procurement contracts and concessions. Because of the concentration of economic and financial resources and the level of discretion involved in it, public procurement remains the most significant risk factor and source of large-scale corruption in the region, involving unfair appropriation of state and European funds.

The following sections outline the major findings of the most recent EU Commission reports on corruption and on anti-corruption policies in SEE countries, thus providing a basis for deriving common patterns of development and outlining appropriate anti-corruption measures.

## Corruption in EU member states

When joining the EU on 1 January 2007, Romania and Bulgaria still had to make progress in the fields of judicial reform, corruption and organized crime. To smooth the entry of both countries and at the same time safeguard the functioning of its own policies and institutions, the EU decided to establish a special 'cooperation and verification mechanism' (CVM)[5] to help the two countries in addressing these shortcomings. The CVM reports annually review the level of implementation of policies and the achievements in the aforementioned areas according to six 'benchmarks' – three on the legal system, two on corruption and one on organized crime. CVM reports are published each summer and are followed up each winter by technical updates on the progress made on key recommendations (Markov, 2010).

### Bulgaria

Bulgaria scored 3.6 in Transparency International's CPI for 2010, thus ranking 73rd in the world on perceived corruption levels. Recently the country has stepped up its efforts to fight organized crime and corruption, which has been commended both locally and by the country's international partners (Table 4.2). The European Commission's analysis in the 2010 CVM progress report (European Commission, 2010a), however, underlined that the country has suffered from continuing shortcomings regarding the prevention of corruption and protection against conflict of interest. Effective implementation of the

*Table 4.2* Anti-corruption policies and achievements in Bulgaria (2009–10)

| Area | Policy |
| --- | --- |
| Administration | Increased number of inspections and disciplinary sanctions in the central administration |
| Legislation | National Anti-Corruption Strategy and action plan adopted (November 2009) |
| Prosecution and Investigation | Highest level corruption cases (acting and former minister and deputies, high-level officials and mayors) |
| Audit | Strengthened capacity of the EU fraud joint team (two emblematic cases regarding fraud with EU funds and money laundering) |

*Source*: European Commission (2010a).

new national anti-corruption strategy adopted in November 2009 has not yet started, and the implementation of the conflict of interest law has still been insufficiently effective. Shortcomings in the implementation of public procurement procedures and the misuse and mismanagement of state resources and taxpayers' money were so widespread that it could be assumed that corruption had permeated even the lowest levels of the state's supply chain.

To foster the prevention of corruption and conflict of interest, the European Commission advised Bulgaria to pursue plans to create a special and independent commission for protection against conflict of interest, to accelerate the implementation of the action plan for the national anti-corruption strategy and to strengthen legislation on asset forfeiture. Bulgaria has not yet addressed the Commission's recommendations regarding the strengthening of inspectorates and has not yet been able to report results in reinforcing the regional anti-corruption councils (European Commission, 2010a).

*Romania*

Romania scored 3.7 on Transparency International's CPI, thus ranking 69th in the world in 2010. The country has recently improved its track record in the fight against corruption (Table 4.3). An indisputable achievement has been the establishment and functioning of the National Anticorruption Directorate (ANI). These achievements, however, have been weakened substantially by the changes to the law on ANI, which were adopted in 2009 as a reaction to a decision by the

*Table 4.3*   Anti-corruption policies and achievements in Romania (2009–10)

| Area | Policy |
| --- | --- |
| Administration | Detailed guidelines for training in several institutions, developed by the Bucharest Court of Appeal |
| Prosecution and Investigation | Good and stable track record in the investigation of high-level corruption, and increased capacity of the National Anticorruption Directorate (ANI) |
| | Investing in local prosecution offices' efforts |
| | Stricter and fewer suspended sentences in ANI cases |
| | More indictments with a greater focus on public officials and more complex investigations |
| Transparency | Asset and interest declarations posted on the website of ANI |

*Source*: European Commission (2010b).

Romanian Constitutional Court. The Constitutional Court ruled that ANI had taken the character of a quasi-judicial institution, in violation of the Constitution, and that the publication of asset and interest declarations breached the right to private life. It further stated that the unfounded confiscation of assets breached the presumption of innocence. The corresponding amendments introduced in parliament reduced the effectiveness of ANI's investigations and the transparency of assets of high-ranking officials (European Commission, 2010b).

Similarly to Bulgaria, Romania suffers from suspected fraud and misuse of public and EU funds. Public procurement is the main channel for siphoning state-owned resources. The Commission has already made a number of specific suggestions to improve public procurement practices in the management of EU funds in Romania in order to prevent cases like the suspension of EU funding in Bulgaria (European Commission, 2010b).

## Corruption in EU candidate and potential candidate countries

### Albania

Albania scored 3.3 on CPI in 2010, thus ranking 89th in the world. Corruption is prevalent in many areas, despite a judicial reform and prioritized measures in the fight against organized crime and corruption by the government (Table 4.4). An Inter-Sectoral Strategy on the Prevention and Combating of Corruption 2008–2013 was adopted in October 2008. This was followed by the adoption of an action plan in January 2009. However, realistic implementation mechanisms

*Table 4.4*  Anti-corruption policies and achievements in Albania (2009–10)

| Area | Policy |
| --- | --- |
| Links between Administration and the Private Sector | Measures for reducing face-to-face contacts with officials |
| | Reduction of bureaucracy |
| | Reform of procedures (e-procurement, e-taxation, one-stop shop for registration and licensing of businesses and e-government) |
| | Internal administrative control by the Department for Internal Administrative Control and Anti-Corruption (DIACA) |
| Education | Anonymous system for university entrance exams |
| Legislation | Measures under the Council of Europe Civil Convention against Corruption |
| Economy | The multi-disciplinary Joint Investigative Unit (JIU) on economic crime and corruption |
| Audit | Publication of an annual report by the High Inspectorate for Declaration and Audit of Assets (HIDAA) |

*Source*: European Commission (2009a).

and timeframes were missing, together with indicators for monitoring and adequate resources for implementation. In many areas the efforts of the government to tackle corruption are already stalling at the strategy stage, or are only selectively applied. The legal framework and inter-agency structures to counter corruption are in place, but implementation remains uneven. The commitment of the authorities to combating corruption has not been backed by a consistent implementation of legislation (European Commission, 2009a).

### Bosnia and Herzegovina

Bosnia and Herzegovina scored 3.2 on CPI in 2010, thus ranking 91st in the world. The country has made little progress in fighting corruption. Corruption in Bosnia and Herzegovina is prevalent in many areas and continues to be a serious problem, especially within government and in other state structures linked to public procurement, business licensing or in the health, energy, transportation infrastructure and education sectors. Private sector corruption is also prevalent (European Commission, 2009b).

The implementation of the corruption-related aspects of the 2006–09 Strategy for the Fight Against Organized Crime and Corruption has shown very limited results. This overshadowed the adoption of a new Strategy for the Fight Against Corruption 2009–14 and the related action plan. Furthermore, Bosnia and Herzegovina has not yet signed the Additional Protocol to the Council of Europe Criminal Law Convention on Corruption and the OECD Convention on Combating Bribery of Foreign Public Officials in International Business Transactions (European Commission, 2009b).

## Croatia

Croatia scored 4.1 on CPI in 2010, thus ranking 62nd in the world and therefore doing better than the two EU member states Bulgaria and Romania. The country has made comparatively good progress in the fight against corruption (Table 4.5). Implementation of the anti-corruption strategy and related action plan has continued. Additionally, the legal framework to combat organized crime and corruption has been improved. Anti-corruption efforts continue and are producing initial results, but corruption remains prevalent in many areas and the tools are not being deployed with sufficient vigour, especially in the field of political corruption (European Commission, 2009c).

## Former Yugoslav Republic of Macedonia

Macedonia scored 4.1 in CPI in 2010, thus also ranking 62nd in the world, together with Croatia. Good progress has been made in strengthening and implementing the anti-corruption framework in Macedonia (Table 4.6). Nevertheless, corruption remains prevalent and continues to be a serious problem in many areas. Although plenty of

*Table 4.5*   Anti-corruption policies and achievements in Croatia (2009–10)

| Area | Policy |
| --- | --- |
| Legislation | Amendments to the Criminal Code that introduced new rules on the confiscation of assets from persons convicted of organized crime or corruption offences |
| | Proactive National Council regarding the monitoring of the anti-corruption strategy (hearings, public debates, national anti-corruption campaign) |
| | Re-established Committee for the Prevention of Conflicts of Interest (CPCI) |
| Investigation and Prosecution | Operational National Police Office for the Fight Against Corruption and Organized Crime (PNUSKOK) |
| | Office for the Fight Against Corruption and Organized Crime (USKOK) (high level corruption cases) |

*Source*: European Commission (2009c).

*Table 4.6* Anti-corruption policies and achievements in FYR Macedonia (2009–10)

| Area | Policy |
| --- | --- |
| Monitoring | Frequent meetings of the Government Council to monitor the implementation of the anti-corruption action plan |
| Legislation | Transparency provisions in the Electoral Code concerning election campaign financing |
| | Amendments to the Law on Financing of Political Parties |
| | Provisions on extended confiscation of proceeds of crime, illicit enrichment and criminal liability of legal persons for trading influence to the Criminal Code |
| | Amendments to the Law on Conflict of Interest |
| Investigation and Prosecution | Move towards the establishment of a national intelligence database |
| | Interconnection of the databases of the State Commission for Prevention of Corruption (SCPC) and of the Public Revenue Office |
| | High level cases (former prime ministers, deputy ministers, and so on) |
| Audit | Strengthened efforts of the Public Revenue Office and of the State Audit Office |

*Source*: European Commission (2009d).

legal provisions and amendments to legislation have been adopted, the fragmented legal system continues to generate difficulties when it comes to implementation (European Commission, 2009d).

*Montenegro*

Montenegro scored 3.7 on CPI in 2010, thus ranking 69th in the world. There has been progress in the fight against corruption, but corruption continues to be a cause for concern in Montenegro (Table 4.7). The strategic framework for fighting it has been fine-tuned to place greater emphasis on monitoring the implementation of the anti-corruption measures included in the action plan against organized crime and corruption. However, corruption remains prevalent in many areas and continues to be a particularly serious problem. The commitment of the authorities has not yet been backed by consistent implementation of anti-corruption legislation. While there is a positive trend, investigation capacities and the degree of coordination of law-enforcement agencies remain weak. There is insufficient supervision in the areas

*Table 4.7*   Anti-corruption policies and achievements in Montenegro (2009–10)

| Area | Policy |
|---|---|
| Administration | Intensive training for administrative bodies |
| Civil Society Participation | Participation of NGOs in public awareness raising |
| | Participation of NGOs in the work of the national commission for fighting corruption and organized crime |
| | Screening of legislation |
| Legislation | New Criminal Procedure Code (July 2009) |
| | Law on Prevention of Conflicts of Interest in Performing Public Functions |
| | Law on Internal Financial Control |
| | Law on Financing the Election Campaigns for the President, Mayors and Presidents of Municipalities of Montenegro |
| Investigation and Prosecution | Enhancing preventive and investigative anti-corruption bodies – Directorate for Anti-Corruption Initiatives (DACI); high court units for organized crime and corruption |
| | Increased human resources and equipment of the special prosecutor's office for fighting organized crime, corruption, terrorism and war crimes |
| | Anticorruption training for the police, border police, customs officers, prosecutors and judges |
| | Internal investigations and charges against policemen and judges |

*Source*: European Commission (2009d).

of financing of political parties and conflict of interests (European Commission, 2009e).

*Serbia*

Serbia scored 3.5 on CPI in 2010, thus ranking 78th in the world. The country made progress on improving the institutional framework for the fight against corruption (Table 4.8). However, corruption remains prevalent in many areas and continues to be a serious problem. There are major obstacles to rooting out systemic corruption. The effectiveness of law enforcement and judicial authorities remains low. The setting-up of the anti-corruption agency has been slow and the relevant legislation needs further improvement. Political party financing

*Table 4.8* Anti-corruption policies and achievements in Serbia (2009–10)

| Area | Policy |
| --- | --- |
| Administration | • Anti-corruption agency inauguration |
| Investigation and Prosecution | • High-profile corruption cases |

*Source*: European Commission (2009f).

and conflicts of interest remain serious causes for concern (European Commission, 2009f).

## The link between economic development and corruption in SEE

Corruption is often linked to the socio-economic development of a country. As Johann Graf Lambsdorff put it, 'corruption clearly goes along with a low GDP, inequality of income, inflation, increased crime, policy distortions and lack of competition [...]' (Graf Lambsdorff, 2010, p. 26). The direction of causation between these indicators, however, remains controversial, as corruption may cause these characteristics in a country but is at the same time likely to be their consequence as well. SEE countries share similar characteristics – relatively high levels of corruption and low levels of GDP per capita. As the case of Greece in the 2008–09 financial and economic crisis has demonstrated, corruption hurts economic development even at substantially higher levels of income than the ones currently prevalent in most SEE countries.

Socio-economic factors with a possible influence on corruption include the wealth of a country, the distribution of national income and the way in which public revenues are invested in the overall structure of the state, which fundamentally shapes the quality of life of the population. It comes as no surprise that higher levels of national income and development are associated with lower levels of both street-level and high-level corruption. On the other hand, evidence suggests that tax and customs administrations are usually among the most corruption-prone government agencies, especially in developing countries (Buscaglia and Van Dijk, 2003). Hence, it can be expected that the countries in SEE are more affected by corruption than others, given their comparatively low levels of national income. Most SEE economies are fairly small economies (far less than 1 per cent of EU's GDP), and very open ones (the sum of exports and the sum of imports are almost equal to, or higher than, their annual GDP). When around 40 per cent of GDP is redistributed by the national government, it comes as no surprise that national customs and public procurement administrations are seen as endemically corrupt.

In 2007 Jan Van Dijk argued that corruption has a negative correlation with the Human Development Index, and an even stronger negative correlation with the GDP per capita. By carrying out a multiple regression analysis and taking GDP as a dependent variable, the author found that corruption was the most significant factor negatively affecting GDP (Van Dijk, 2007). State capture has been identified by various analyses of the World Bank Institute as a major cause of institutional failure and as an obstacle to development.

The juxtaposition of 2009 CPI scores to GDP easily verifies the link between economic development and corruption in SEE (Figure 4.2). The fact that the 2009 CPI scores of Turkey and Croatia (both EU candidate countries), 4.4 and 4.1 respectively, are higher than those of the

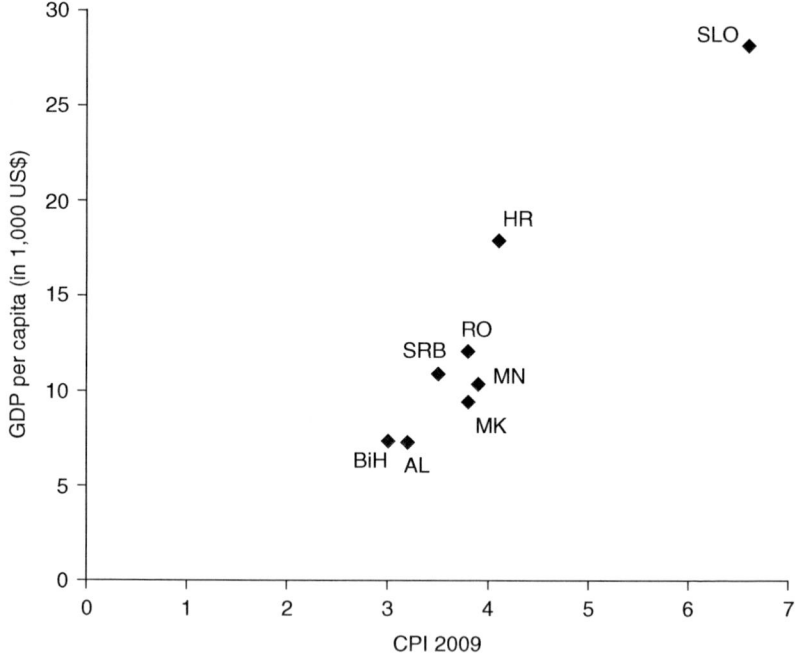

*Figure 4.2* The link between corruption and economic development
*Source*: Created by the authors on the basis of data sources from Transparency International (2009b) and of GDP estimations of the International Monetary Fund, April 2010.

newest EU members Bulgaria and Romania, both at 3.8, is yet another indication of this link.

Generally, the higher the level of GDP, the lower the level of corruption in SEE countries. Furthermore, parallel to the economic development, it can be observed that the level of corruption declines faster than income levels with the introduction of political and economic reforms and innovative policies, which are expected of new EU member states such as Bulgaria, Slovenia and Romania.

## The link between corruption, organized crime and the grey economy in SEE

The existence of strong links between corruption, on the one hand, and the grey economy and organized crime, on the other hand, is now broadly recognized. As corruption tends to be an integral part of organized crime's modus operandi, it is reasonable to assume that a high prevalence of organized crime may result in higher levels of corruption in a given country. Over the last decade a number of studies have tested and examined various hypotheses concerning this assumed link. In a study published by van Dijk in 2007, for instance, a proxy indicator of 'high-level corruption' derived from the World Bank governance indicators was found to be strongly positively correlated to the Organized Crime Perception Index.

The basis for this assumed link is the argument that organized crime uses corruption as a tool in achieving its goals. Criminal organizations tend to target and infiltrate legitimate state structures in order to sustain and expand their lucrative activities – to ensure the circulation of illicit goods, facilitate money laundering and minimize the risks of successful prosecution. Thus corruption of public officials, including law enforcement and court officers, is a common feature of organized crime that allows criminal groups to secure the survival of their structures (Chêne, 2008). The spread of organized crime and its manipulation of corrupt practices are among the strongest impediments to the development of South East Europe (CSD, 2003).

On the other hand, the grey economy could also influence levels of corruption and organized crime, as it provides a nourishing environment for both (Belev, 2003). Schneider (2006) and Schneider and Dreher (2005) argue that the grey economy influences corruption in two ways: through tax corruption, when companies try to hide revenues by corrupting tax inspectors; or through administrative corruption, when companies in the grey economy try to corrupt various administrative units (for example, industry control institutions, including labour control) in order to avoid regulations or sanctions for using illegal workers. Various types of illegal markets entail different kinds of corruption and different targets for organized crime in law enforcement or in public institutions (CSD, 2010b).

Goev (2009) suggested a reverse causal link between corruption and grey economy in the case of Bulgaria. He claimed that the presence of corruption is the principal reason for the existence of a hidden economy (a majority of 58.9 per cent of the survey respondents supported this hypothesis). Respondents of the same survey pointed out that the reduction of corruption could be a principal measure for limiting the hidden economy (65.1 per cent). Regardless of the direction of causation, it is clear that corruption and the hidden economy are closely interconnected.

Countries in SEE are particularly prone to the triple threat of a hidden economy, corruption and organized crime due to multiple factors in their development – not least to their heritage of central planning and to the series of wars in the 1990s. The weak institutional set-up and the insufficient levels of administrative capacity and state control have unleashed such phenomena in significant proportions in SEE. The large profits generated by criminal activities such as the smuggling of embargoed goods, the drugs trade, prostitution and human trafficking (amongst others) make organized criminals powerful actors in these countries, allowing them to gain influence both in politics and in business. Bribery of top officials may be a relatively straightforward way to penetrate government structures, but contributions to the financial campaigns of political candidates are also one of the regular methods used by wealthy criminals to gain influence over elected officials. The most dangerous form of corruption, which destabilizes both internal and regional security in SEE, however, is the symbiosis between organized crime and the former communist security sector in the Balkan countries, both of which can have the same representatives (CSD, 2004).

Criminal networks endanger the stability of democratic institutions in SEE by capturing governments through systemic corruption. The impact of dirty money in politics is especially negative through the financing of political parties and of their election campaigns, both at national and at local levels. This has a negative impact on the public's trust in the emerging democratic and market economy institutions in SEE and has caused disillusionment with reforms in general, which is clearly reflected in persistently low scores in CPI and other perception-based corruption measurements (CSD, 2007c).

The situation in Bulgaria in the years of transition, and even after its accession to the EU, exemplifies the links between organized crime, the grey economy and corruption in SEE countries:

> In Bulgaria, the borderline between the legal and the illegal economies is much less clear than most of the EU MS [member states]. Organized crime generating wealth from drugs, smuggling and prostitution has merged with corporations and groups that own privatized state-owned assets and has transformed its accumulated wealth into political and administrative power. This influence in the political and administrative structures allows companies to use corruption to win public tenders, avoid taxes, and systematically break laws to gain competitive advantages. Organized crime networks have infiltrated most public institutions, including the police, customs and prosecutors' offices. Organized crime highly influences the political elite and political parties at the local level, while some criminal structures have been able to influence MPs or national level politicians.
>
> (CSD, 2010b, p. 19)

## The link between corruption and trade in SEE

Corruption and organized crime disrupt the transition to a market economy by destroying fair competition and the potential for free private initiative. Corruption is a structural factor for international trade and investment, and there are a couple of principles already proven by empirical studies. There is, for instance, a statistically significant correlation between the levels of corruption in importing and exporting countries and their trade portfolios and investment decisions. Trading countries prefer markets with features similar to those of their own business environment, thus maintaining the status quo in the country they deal with. Therefore the level of corruption and the state of the business environment determine the quality of the investment and trade projects that are implemented by a given state (CSD, 2007a).

On the other hand, the potential impact of the anti-corruption reforms on each individual member state is dependent on, and constrained by, the average levels of corruption of its major trade and investment partners. In the case of Bulgaria, for instance, in 2006 some 40 per cent of foreign trade was generated with more corrupt countries (Russia, China) or with countries with a similar CPI level (Turkey, Greece and Italy), which probably resulted in the spillover of bad business practices into the country and restricted the potential impact of the anti-corruption reforms pursued by the Bulgarian government. A short overview of the main trading partners of SEE countries gives an idea of the tendency towards corruption persistence in the region (see Table 4.9).

Unlike trade, foreign direct investments hold the potential to produce a positive anti-corruption effect; but, again, this depends on the origin of the biggest investors in the country.

The degree of economic freedom of a country is another major factor linked to the spread of corruption. Economic freedom means fewer contacts between private economic operators and state institutions; hence fewer opportunities for corruption arise. Greater economic freedom also means greater competition and fewer barriers applied to the economic interaction among physical and legal persons, thus making it harder to build privileged relations on the basis of vested interests. The amount of protectionism and the levels of foreign direct investment were also examined, and the results showed that a more open domestic market was linked to less street-level and high-level corruption (Buscaglia and Van Dijk, 2003).

Although competition on the single European market is expected to reduce the administrative barriers to business, lack of sufficient political accountability in some new democracies leads to the monopolization of certain lucrative business activities through legal corruption. Yet, as in the case of Bulgaria, the reduction of the level of the hidden economy

*Table 4.9*   Main trading partners of SEE countries

| SEE Countries (with 2009 CPI) | Main Trading Partner (with CPI) | |
| --- | --- | --- |
| | Export | Import |
| SLO (6.6) | GER (8.0), IT (4.3), HU (4.1) | GER (8.0), IT (4.3), AT (7.9) |
| HR (4.1) | IT (4.3), BIH (3.0), GER (8.0) | IT (4,3), GER (8.0), RU (2.2) |
| BG (3.8) | GR (3.8), GER (8.0), TR (4.4) | GER (8.0), IT (4.3), UA (2.2) |
| RO (3.8) | GER (8.0), IT (4.3), FR (6.9) | GER (8.0), IT (4.3), HU (5.1) |
| SRB (3.5) | BIH (3.0), MN (3.9), GER (8.0) | RU (2.2), GER (8.0), IT (4.3) |
| MN (3.9) | – | – |
| MK (3.8) | – | RU (2.2), GER (8.0), SRB (3.5) |
| AL (3.2) | IT (4.3), GR (3.8), SRB (3.5) | IT (4.3), GR (3.8), CN (3.6) |
| BIH (3.0) | HU (4.1), SRB (3.5), GER (8.0) | HU (4.1), GER (8.0), SRB (3.5) |

*Note*: AT-Austria, BIH-Bosnia and Herzegovina, CN-China, FR-France, GER-Germany, GR-Greece, HU-Hungary, IT-Italy, MN-Montenegro, RO-Romania, RU-Russia, SRB-Serbia, TR-Turkey, UA-Ukraine
*Source*: Transparency International (2009b), UN data (2010).

and corruption in Bulgaria's business sector in 2006 and 2007 was a sign of an improved business environment in the country and of broader opportunities for market development, to become available to Bulgarian entrepreneurs after the country's accession to the EU. This trend could also be traced in the reduced susceptibility of Bulgarian businesses to corrupt practices (CSD, 2007a).

## Conclusion

Regardless of the success of national anti-corruption policies so far, both the governments in SEE and the EU institutions have to continue their efforts to curb corrupt practices in the region. Financial support for reforms from the EU should not be discontinued and/or discouraged, but a functioning system of monitoring and a verification mechanism designed to counter the misuse and appropriation of funds should be established for candidate countries on the same basis as for Bulgaria and Romania. Revitalizing investment, notably towards small and medium enterprises that compete against politically linked companies, would have significant anti-corruption effects on the SEE economy.

More specifically, the EU should envision and give its full political and financial support for:

- government efforts in the fight against corruption in both member states and candidate countries;
- the application of greater scrutiny and stricter criteria when evaluating the results achieved in the fight against corruption, on the basis of an EU-wide corruption monitoring instrument;
- the adoption of an EU-wide anti-corruption instrument that would initiate and support cooperation between member states and candidate countries on the basis of twinning, knowledge exchange, trainings and so on.

The governments of SEE should:

- increase the capacity of administrative and law enforcement institutions, as well as the level of control;
- continue with the implementation of anti-corruption policies and national strategies;
- activate various mechanisms for incentives for judicial and law-enforcement authorities (acceleration of career promotion, trainings

and study trips abroad, higher salaries corresponding to levels of risk of job and corruption pressure);
- continue judicial reforms and guarantee the rule of law through the increased prosecution of cases of corruption;
- guarantee fixed legal provisions and transparent procedures for public procurement;
- strive for better facilitation of a liberal market, where competitiveness and innovation prevail – rather than political connections and bribery;
- provide for a new type of public–private partnership necessary to secure public backing for the measures against organized crime and corruption. This partnership should seek to include civil society as well as private sector institutions as stakeholders in the process of prevention and enforcement.

## Notes

1. The PHARE programme and the ISPA are two of the pre-accession instruments financed by the EU to assist candidate countries in the Central and Eastern European region in their efforts to prepare for EU accession.
2. Transparency International's CPI uses a reversed 10-degree scale, 10 meaning 'the least corrupted' and 1 'the most corrupted'.
3. http://www.seldi.net.
4. Control of corruption is a perception measure, and it provides an aggregate view on the quality of governance in the area of corruption control. The data are gathered from a number of enterprise, citizen and expert surveys (World Bank, 2010).
5. European Commission Decision 2006/929/EC of 13 December 2006.

## References

Belev, B. (2003) *The Informal Economy in the EU Accession Countries: Size, Scope, Trends and Challenges in the Process of EU Enlargement* (Sofia: Center for the Study of Democracy).

Buscaglia, E. and Van Dijk, J. (2003) 'Controlling Organized Crime and Corruption in the Public Sector', *Forum on Crime and Society*, 3, 1, 2, 3–34.

Chêne, M. (2008) *Organised Crime and Corruption*, Transparency International/U4 (U4 Helpdesk query 171), Chr. Michelsen Institute, Bergen, Norway, http://www.u4.no/helpdesk/helpdesk/query.cfm?id=171, accessed 2 October 2010.

CSD (2003) *Contraband and Organized Crime in Southeast Europe* (Sofia: Center for the Study of Democracy).

CSD (2004) *Partners in Crime: The Risk of Symbiosis between the Security Sector and the Organized Crime in Southeast Europe* (Sofia: Center for the Study of Democracy).

CSD (2007a) *Anti-Corruption Reforms in Bulgaria: Key Results and Risks* (Sofia: Center for the Study of Democracy).

CSD (2007b) *The Future of Corruption Benchmarking in the EU*, Policy Brief 11 (Sofia: Center for the Study of Democracy).

CSD (2007c) *Organized Crime in Bulgaria: Markets and Trends* (Sofia: Center for the Study of Democracy).

CSD (2010a) 'Corruption Monitoring System of the Center for the Study of Democracy', http://www.anticorruption.bg/index.php?id=777, accessed 30 August 2010.

CSD (2010b) *Examining the Link between Organized Crime and Corruption*, Report of the study to examine the links between organized crime and corruption commissioned by the Directorate General Justice, Freedom, and Security of the EU (Sofia: Center for the Study of Democracy).

European Commission (2009a) *Albania 2009 Progress Report*, SEC (2009) 1337 (Brussels: European Commission).

European Commission (2009b) *Bosnia and Herzegovina 2009 Progress Report*, SEC (2009) 1338 (Brussels: European Commission).

European Commission (2009c) *Croatia 2009 Progress Report*, SEC (2009) 1333 (Brussels: European Commission).

European Commission (2009d) *The Former Yugoslav Republic of Macedonia 2009 Progress Report*, SEC (2009) 1335 (Brussels: European Commission).

European Commission (2009e) *Montenegro 2009 Progress Report*, SEC (2009) 1336 (Brussels: European Commission).

European Commission (2009f) *Serbia 2009 Progress Report*, SEC (2009) 1339 (Brussels: European Commission).

European Commission (2010a) *Report on Progress in Bulgaria under the Co-Operation and Verification Mechanism*, COM (2010) 400 (Brussels: European Commission).

European Commission (2010b) *Report on Progress in Romania under the Co-Operation and Verification Mechanism*, COM (2010) 401 (Brussels: European Commission).

Goev, V. (2009) 'Estimating the Hidden Economy in Bulgaria', *South-East Europe Review*, 12, 77–93.

Graf Lambsdorff, J. (2010) 'Consequences and Causes of Corruption – What Do We Know from a Cross-Section of Countries?', Diskussionsbeitrag Nr. V-34-05, *Volkswirtschaftliche Reihe*, University of Passau, http://www.icgg.org/downloads/Causes%20and%20Consequences%20of%20Corruption%20-%20Cross-Section.pdf, accessed 27 August 2010.

Markov D. (2010) *The Cooperation and Verification Mechanism Three Years Later: What Has Been Done and What Is Yet to Come*, Bulgaria Reports 1/2010 (Sofia: Friedrich Ebert Stiftung).

Schneider, F. (2006) 'Shadow Economies and Corruption All Over the World: What Do We Really Know?', Working paper No. 0617, Department of Economics, Johannes Kepler University Linz, September 2006.

Schneider, F. and Dreher, A. (2005) 'Corruption and the Shadow Economy – Substitutes or Comlements?' In Kreutner, M. (ed.), *The Corruption Monster: Ethik: Politik und Korruption* (Wien: Czernin Verlag), 363–370.

Transparency International (2009a) 'Regional Highlights: South Eastern Europe, Eastern Europe and Central Asia', Corruption Perceptions Index, http://

www.transparency.org/policy_research/surveys_indices/cpi/2009/regional_
highlights, accessed 30 September 2010.

Transparency International (2009b) 'Corruption Perceptions Index 2009', http://
www.transparency.org/policy_research/surveys_indices/cpi/2009,    accessed
25 August 2010.

UN    data    (2010)    http://data.un.org/CountryProfile.aspx?crName=,    accessed
2 September 2010.

Van Dijk, J. (2007). Mafia Markers: Assessing Organized Crime and Its Impact on
Societies, *Trends in Organized Crime*, 10 (4), 39–56.

World Bank (2010) 'Worldwide Governance Indicators Data 1996–2008', http://
info.worldbank.org/governance/wgi/sc_country.asp, accessed 28 August 2010.

# 5
# Networks and Informal Power Structures in South East Europe

*Åse Berit Grødeland*

## Introduction

Business culture in the Balkans is characterized by 'instrumental friend-ships' (Chavdarova, 2007). Due to high levels of distrust in society (Karklins, 2002), business people prefer to deal with people they know and consequently trust, rather than with strangers. Informal rela-tions are also widespread in politics: lobbying tends to be conducted informally – often through relatives and friends of the politicians – and outside the institutions in which the politicians operate (Grødeland, 2010a). The café culture, which is so widespread in the Balkans, is con-ducive to this informal decision-making: decisions tend to be made over a cup of coffee rather than in more formal settings.

Evidence of informal networks[1] in post-communist[2] states is mostly anecdotal or based on corruption scandals exposed by the local media. This chapter investigates the nature of informal networks, their posi-tive as well as their negative sides, and the manner in which they are used, both in politics and in business. More specifically, the chapter looks at informal networks in Bulgaria, Romania, Slovenia, Bosnia and Herzegovina,[3] Macedonia and Serbia. It draws on extensive qualita-tive and quantitative data collected amongst politicians and business representatives in these countries between 2003 and 2009.

The main thesis of the chapter is that informal networks – though largely used in response to problems caused by, and opportunities cre-ated by, transition – are effectively a product of national culture and of the socialist past (Grødeland, 2007). While their overall impact on Balkan society is mixed, the negative effects appear to outweigh the positive ones. Further, there is evidence to suggest that informal net-works curb competition and 'privatize' the political process (Grødeland,

2007). In doing so, they slow down the impact of political and economic reform and thus the potential for economic growth and prosperity.

## Methodological approach

This chapter presents findings from two projects, both of them funded by the Research Council of Norway, which address the use of informal practice and corruption in post-communist states. The first project (2003–06) investigated informal practice and corruption in East Central Europe (Czech Republic, Slovenia) and in South East Europe (Bulgaria, Romania). The second project (2006–10) extended this research into the Western Balkans (Bosnia and Herzegovina, Macedonia, Serbia).[4] Data were collected by means of structured, open-ended elite in-depth interviews (IDIs) and quantitative quota-based elite surveys.[5] In 2003–04 we conducted 360 IDIs in East Central and South East Europe. Another 414 interviews were carried out in the Western Balkans in 2007–08. The IDIs were followed by quantitative elite surveys (N = 600 × 7) undertaken in 2005 and in 2008–09.[6]

The two projects focused on elites working in three areas considered by the European Union (EU) to be particularly vulnerable to corruption: politics (elected representatives; political party representatives), the judiciary (judges; prosecutors) and public procurement (public procurement officials; representatives of local business; representatives of foreign business).[7] In addition to this, our study also investigated the use of informal practice within civil society (media; NGOs), given its role as corruption watchdog.[8] As post-conflict reconstruction is susceptible to corruption, a limited number of IDIs were also conducted amongst local elites working for the international donor community in the Western Balkans.

Sampling for the qualitative and quantitative surveys was conducted by local pollsters according to a detailed sampling scheme prepared at the Norwegian Institute for Urban and Regional Research (the project owner). The IDIs were conduced face to face, according to a detailed list of structured, open-ended questions. Interviews for our quantitative surveys were also conducted face to face, through a structured and close-ended questionnaire. The average length of the IDIs was forty-five minutes, whereas the survey interviews lasted approximately one hour.[9]

In all countries IDIs were conducted in capitals, both at national and at capital level. In Bosnia and Herzegovina (BiH), Macedonia and Serbia, a limited number of interviews were also carried out in areas particularly badly affected by conflict – more specifically in Mostar (BiH), Tetovo (Macedonia) and Novi Pazar (Serbia). As for the quantitative surveys, one-third of the interviews were carried out in the capital (two-thirds at national, one-third at capital level), while the remaining two-thirds were conducted in large cities and towns at the level of Nomenclature des unités territoriales statistiques (NUTS) II[10] (for details, see Appendix A.1).

Given the gap in time between the first and the second project, some caution is called for when comparing data from the two projects. This being said, data were collected in all countries at a time when the latter were either aspiring to EU membership and making political, administrative, judicial and other adjustments to qualify for such membership (qualitative data for all projects, quantitative surveys from the second project), or had just joined the EU (quantitative surveys from the first project). In this sense, it could be argued that comparing data collected in all countries when they were actively pursuing EU membership is more appropriate than comparing data from these countries at a time when some of them were actively pursuing EU membership whereas others were at a fairly early stage of recovering from war (BiH, Serbia) or from domestic conflict (Macedonia).

Surveying elites is more complicated than surveying members of the general public, in that refusal rates tend to be higher and organizing the interviews is more difficult from a logistical point of view, due to time constraints on the part of the respondents. On top of this, the topic of our qualitative and quantitative surveys – informal practice, for our purposes defined as 'behavior not in line with formal procedures stipulated for the solution of a given problem and/or behavior aimed at solving problems for which there are no formal procedures' – is rather sensitive. In all countries except Bulgaria and Macedonia refusal rates were therefore high.[11] Still, given the relatively large number of respondents interviewed within each country as well as the geographical spread of the sample, we have reason to believe that our survey design is sufficiently robust and that the views expressed by the respondents are likely to be fairly representative of the types of elites they themselves represent. However, we can of course not rule out the possibility of a systematic failure to answer questions honestly on the part of certain categories of respondents, or the possibility of specific types of people within categories declining systematically invitations for an interview.

The total number of interviews conducted in some countries slightly exceeded the figure of 600 aimed for, while the sample from BiH is one respondent short. Those national samples in which the number of respondents either exceeded or fell short of the planned number of interviews were therefore weighted down or up to N = 600 (that is, 75 respondents × 8 categories) before the actual analysis was conducted.[12]

This chapter presents quantitative and qualitative findings from Bulgaria, Romania, Slovenia, BiH, Macedonia and Serbia – all of which are collectively referred to as 'the Balkans' in what follows. Quantitative findings are in some places complemented by qualitative findings and in some places illustrated by verbatims from our IDIs.[13]

## Elite perceptions of informal networks

It could be argued that – although largely applied in response to problems caused by transition – informal networks have their roots in national history and national culture (Grødeland and Aasland, 2007). Europe's post-communist states have all been parts of larger empires. Slovenia was ruled by the Habsburgs for a considerable period of time. Bulgaria, Serbia and Macedonia endured more than 500 years of Ottoman rule. BiH, for its part, was mostly ruled by the Ottomans but came under Habsburg rule during the final stage of the Austro-Hungarian Empire. Present-day Romania, too, has been ruled by several empires: the Ottoman Empire, the Austro-Hungarian Empire and the Russian Empire.

Our previous research on post-communist states suggests that ethnic and/or other minorities who resided in these empires were disadvantaged by comparison with the ethnic titular group and that they may therefore have felt compelled to 'try harder' to compensate for their perceived and/or real disadvantages (Grødeland and Aasland, 2007). To gain access to officials with a view to obtaining rights as well as favours, they applied a wide range of informal coping strategies, including informal contacts. The use of informal coping strategies continued during communism – though primarily as a means by which to cope with shortages (DiFranceisco and Gitelman, 1984).

The introduction of democracy, of the rule of law and of the market has not eradicated such mechanisms. Evidence suggests that informal practices are still used to cope with government – and that they are more widespread and also used for less benign purposes in post-communist states whose GDP per capita is low than in states with a high GDP per capita (Grødeland, 2010b).

Table 5.1 suggests that post-communist citizens primarily solve problems informally out of habit rather than out of need. Only a small percentage of the respondents to our quantitative surveys suggested that it is not possible to solve problems in their countries through formal channels. However, in the view of some of them, it is easier and also quicker to apply informal strategies than to follow formal

*Table 5.1* What would you say is the main reason for solving problems (IN COUNTRY) in an informal rather than a formal manner?

|  | SLO % | BG % | RO % | BiH % | MK % | SRB % |
|---|---|---|---|---|---|---|
| It is not possible to solve them formally | 7 | 7 | 3 | 14 | 9 | 8 |
| It is easier to secure a favourable outcome this way | 29 | 28 | 25 | 29 | 25 | 22 |
| Solving problems informally has become a habit | 19 | 27 | 37 | 36 | 44 | 38 |
| It is quicker | 32 | 18 | 19 | 15 | 12 | 18 |
| None of these | 12 | 16 | 13 | 3 | 8 | 11 |
| Depends/difficult to say | 1 | 2 | 2 | 0 | 2 | 3 |
| Don't know | 1 | 1 | 3 | 1 | 1 | 1 |
| N= | 600 | 600 | 600 | 600 | 600 | 600 |

*Note*: Decimals are rounded up or down to the nearest whole number. The numbers in the columns therefore do not always add up to 100.
*Source*: Author.

procedures. The academic literature on transition states lends support to our findings: extensive political and economic reform has caused a certain amount of chaos and insecurity amongst citizens (see, for instance, Aslund, 2007, 2010). Besides, official information is still sometimes difficult to get, and formal legislation is frequently amended and/or changed altogether.

Preferring to solve problems informally is one thing. Not being able to solve them formally, quite another. Table 5.2 suggests that citizens in Romania, BiH and Macedonia primarily seek informal solutions to their problems out of habit rather than because it is not possible to solve problems in a formal manner. In Slovenia informal solutions are sought primarily because they are considered to yield faster results. Citizens in Bulgaria and Serbia, for their part, primarily opt for such solutions as they have no faith in formal procedures. Widespread lack of trust in official institutions probably explains why citizens in post-communist states simply do not believe that their problems may find a formal solution. The lack of trust in state institutions, which was so widespread during communism, appears to have been carried over into post-communist society. Large corruption scandals and negative media coverage of post-communist politicians probably contribute to maintaining the distrust (see, for instance, Mishler and Rose, 1997; Kornai and Rose-Ackerman, 2004a, 2004b; Markova, 2004; Karklins, 2005). In

*Table 5.2*　And what would you say is the main reason for solving problems informally when it is possible to solve them formally?

| | SLO % | BG % | RO % | BiH % | MK % | SRB % |
|---|---|---|---|---|---|---|
| It is easier to secure a favourable outcome this way | 14 | 15 | 14 | 21 | 17 | 15 |
| Solving problems informally has become a habit | 11 | 15 | 31 | 31 | 34 | 26 |
| It is quicker | 31 | 23 | 23 | 18 | 15 | 20 |
| People don't believe that their problems can be solved in a formal way | 29 | 31 | 17 | 26 | 26 | 29 |
| A combination of/none of these | 12 | 13 | 12 | 3 | 7 | 7 |
| Depends/difficult to say | 1 | 2 | 1 | 0 | 1 | 2 |
| Don't know | 1 | 1 | 2 | 1 | 1 | 1 |
| N | 600 | 600 | 600 | 600 | 600 | 600 |

*Note*: Decimals are rounded up or down to the nearest whole number. The numbers in the columns therefore do not always add up to 100.
*Source*: Author.

addition, citizens may simply be poorly informed about their rights and about formal rules and procedures more generally (Miller et al., 2001). Our research into informal practice in Ukraine suggests that the majority of citizens primarily equate democracy with freedom – including the freedom to ignore formal rules and regulations (Grødeland, 2009). Knowing the 'right' people is therefore more important than knowing – and applying – the rules. Added to this, cumbersome administrative procedures cause citizens to seek informal solutions to their problems: solving problems through contacts generally provides quicker solutions than abiding by formal procedures (Miller et al., 2001).

While much is generally known about the use of contacts in post-communist society (see, for instance, Ledeneva, 1998), less is known about informal networks. We applied a fairly general understanding of informal networks, defining them as loosely connected groups of people who are able and willing to help each other.[14] Such networks – as opposed to contacts[15] – tend to bring together, over time, people who share similar characteristics and/or interests. While contacts may be used on a one-off basis, those linked together through an informal network tend to keep in touch more regularly. For this reason, lack of willingness and/or ability to comply with the requests of other network members is likely to be met with sanctions of some kind (Grødeland, 2007).

To establish what elites in Europe's post-communist states think about informal networks, we asked our respondents to assess a number of positive and negative statements about them. Table 5.3 suggests that post-communist citizens primarily view informal networks in instrumental terms, that is, as tools for interest representation. As such, informal networks provide mutual support and protection, thus compensating for general lack of trust in post-communist society. Paradoxically, however, by compensating for lack of trust, informal networks may effectively hinder the emergence of public trust in society. Informal networks are also – though to a lesser extent – perceived as a source of corruption. Only a very limited percentage of our respondents believed

*Table 5.3* Percentage of respondents that (strongly) agree that informal networks ...

|  | SLO % | BG % | RO % | BiH % | MK % | SRB % |
|---|---|---|---|---|---|---|
| Are an inherent feature of the market economy | 42 | 29 | 34 | 39 | 36 | 33 |
| Are a tool for interest representation | 65 | 70 | 60 | 62 | 60 | 64 |
| Promote professionalism in society | 13 | 14 | 11 | 9 | 13 | 7 |
| Compensate for the shortcomings of formal structures in (COUNTRY) | 34 | 45 | 36 | 52 | 29 | 33 |
| Provide mutual support and protection | 35 | 44 | 46 | 50 | 50 | 54 |
| Hinder public trust in society | 38 | 37 | 44 | 56 | 41 | 46 |
| Run counter to democratic principles | 26 | 27 | 38 | 45 | 31 | 41 |
| Render competition meaningless | 16 | 28 | 36 | 42 | 37 | 42 |
| Undermine the rule of law | 24 | 38 | 45 | 50 | 39 | 44 |
| Cause corruption | 35 | 38 | 53 | 57 | 42 | 51 |
| Contributed to (CONFLICT) in (COUNTRY) | n.a. | n.a. | n.a. | 21 | 15 | 23 |
| Helped to promote peace in (COUNTRY) | n.a. | n.a. | n.a. | 10 | 12 | 8 |

*Note*: The last two questions were only asked in BiH, Macedonia and Serbia. Decimals are rounded up or down to the nearest whole number.
*Source*: Author.

that informal networks have a positive impact on post-communist society, for instance by promoting professionalism.

Contacts in post-communist societies are primarily perceived as a result of national culture – though citizens in Romania primarily view them as a result of their country's socialist past. This is perhaps not so surprising, given the animosity Romanians generally feel for the Ceauşescu period. In contrast, informal networks are perceived as a result of national culture and of the transition to a market economy, roughly to the same extent and in all countries (Table 5.4). To some extent, the lack of political stability caused by the collapse of communism – as well as by the new political, administrative and economic structures that have emerged as a result of transition – may have forced people partly to expand, partly to replace their existing circle of contacts. Besides, weak state structures have opened opportunities for financial benefit. This is likely to have caused people sharing certain characteristics to join forces with a view to personal profit. The various types of informal networks that exist in the Balkans will be discussed in more detail below.

Only a very small minority of elites in the Balkans believe that informal networks have a positive impact on public life in their respective countries (Table 5.5). The impact of informal networks is either perceived as limited (Slovenia, Bulgaria and Macedonia) or mostly as negative (Romania, BiH and Serbia). This being said, our data suggest that the phrase 'informal network' is more readily understood by elites in East Central and South East Europe than in the Western Balkans – though

*Table 5.4*   Would you say that informal networks are a result of ...

|  | SLO % | BG % | RO % | BiH % | MK % | SRB % |
|---|---|---|---|---|---|---|
| (COUNTRY's) culture | 28 | 22 | 22 | 31 | 31 | 32 |
| (COUNTRY's) socialist past | 10 | 12 | 27 | 11 | 18 | 16 |
| Transition to the market | 30 | 20 | 23 | 34 | 32 | 12 |
| (CONFLICT) | – | – | – | 12 | 1 | 5 |
| A combination of these | 15 | 31 | 18 | 10 | 13 | 26 |
| Neither of them | 14 | 7 | 6 | 1 | 3 | 4 |
| Don't know | 3 | 7 | 5 | 1 | 3 | 4 |
| N | 600 | 600 | 600 | 600 | 600 | 600 |

*Note*: The question on conflict was only asked in BiH, Macedonia and Serbia. Decimals rounded up or down to the nearest whole number. The numbers in the columns therefore do not always add up to 100.
*Source*: Author.

*Table 5.5*  Do you think that informal networks have primarily a positive or primarily a negative impact on public life in (COUNTRY)?

|  | SLO % | BG % | RO % | BiH % | MK % | SRB % |
|---|---|---|---|---|---|---|
| Primarily a positive impact | 13 | 12 | 9 | 9 | 16 | 6 |
| Primarily a negative impact | 24 | 26 | 46 | 48 | 30 | 50 |
| The impact of informal networks on public life in (COUNTRY) is limited | 57 | 48 | 35 | 38 | 42 | 37 |
| Informal networks have neither a positive, nor a negative impact on public life in (COUNTRY) | 6 | 4 | 2 | 3 | 7 | 6 |
| Depends/don't know | 2 | 10 | 7 | 2 | 5 | 6 |
| N | 600 | 600 | 600 | 600 | 600 | 600 |

*Note*: Decimals are rounded up or down to the nearest whole number. The numbers in the columns therefore do not always add up to 100.
*Source*: Author.

in all three areas the phrase is predominantly understood in a negative sense. Further, a fairly large share of the IDI respondents used the expressions 'contact' and 'informal network' more or less interchangeably. Elites in the Balkans predominantly consider contacts to be a necessary evil. These two factors provide some explanation for our findings.

Post-communist elites believe that informal networks are used (very) successfully in both politics and business. More specifically, they are used (very) successfully for political lobbying, for political party funding and for gaining business preferences. And they are also used (very) successfully for gaining public procurement contracts and – with the exception of Slovenia – for getting the desired outcome in court. Informal networks are used successfully for post-conflict reconstruction to a considerably greater extent in BiH than in Macedonia and Serbia – which is understandable, given that much larger foreign resources have been used for such purposes in the former than in the latter (Table 5.6).

Our IDIs shed some light on the types of informal networks that are used in politics and business – as well as on the reasons why they are used. Elites in the Balkans frequently explain the existence of informal networks in terms of trust and in terms of personal enrichment. As trust is largely absent in post-communist society, informal networks allow people to work with those they know well, feel comfortable with and know they can rely on. The downside of this phenomenon is that

*Table 5.6*   Informal networks are used . . .

| . . . (very) successfully for . . . | SLO % | BG % | RO % | BiH % | MK % | SRB % |
|---|---|---|---|---|---|---|
| Political lobbying | 85 | 76 | 82 | 87 | 81 | 83 |
| Political party-funding | 77 | 74 | 81 | 83 | 78 | 81 |
| Getting the desired outcome in court | 28 | 54 | 52 | 58 | 68 | 53 |
| Gaining business preferences | 74 | 73 | 77 | 85 | 80 | 72 |
| Gaining public procurement contracts | 56 | 68 | 64 | 72 | 68 | 62 |
| Post-conflict reconstruction | n.a. | n.a. | n.a. | 58 | 39 | 34 |
| N | 600 | 600 | 600 | 600 | 600 | 600 |

*Note*: Decimals are rounded up or down to the nearest whole number.
*Source*: Author.

the people engaged in politics or business are not necessarily those who are best qualified for the job. Personal enrichment is primarily sought at the state's expense. In post-communist states there is a notion that public property is the property of the citizens. Consequently, acquiring a part of this property is not necessarily considered to be unethical, even though the manner in which such property is acquired is not quite above board. Violating moral norms, on the other hand – for instance by stealing the private property of other individuals – is perceived in much more negative terms:

[P]oliticians form networks. They have mayors and through them they are influential at the local level. They also influence the economy, mainly big companies. They need money from the big firms for political elections.

(GO-5, SLO[16])

[Informal networks are used] because business is a matter of trust. And it is natural to look for people you could trust on some occasion. And that makes businessmen surround (themselves) by acquaintances, who are not going to compromise them. The same (goes for) politics.

(GO-1, BG)

Parliament is vulnerable to the networks of friends and family members, as well as to locality networks.

(NGO-5, BG)

[I]n politics [...] very little value is placed on merit, competence or professionalism. Here you need to be part of the gang, need to come with important resources – in terms of influence and money – to be accepted. These resources must be doubled by loyalty and you have to be recommended by someone else from the group [...].

(FB-5, RO)

[When I say informal networks are influential] in politics, I am referring to members of political parties, not necessarily to the party leaders, but to the party members who use contacts to access government positions [...].

(FB-5-FED, BiH)

[T]he political parties are (essentially) informal networks [...] (in Macedonia) we have transformed our political parties into an employment agency. You have become a member. You have a political party booklet, and what is this for? The party will employ you.

(PP-4-CF, MK)

[I]t's in one's business interests to have a good political basis so that one can force one's attitudes and personal interests onto official politics. I primarily have in mind the legislative activity. It's very important that your interest can become legalized through a law.

(PR-1, SRB)

Elites suggested that political networks are the most influential kind of informal networks in the Balkans; they are followed by business/economic networks. However, 'low-key' informal networks – composed of family members or friends – also received a high score, as did criminal networks (Table 5.7). Our qualitative data provide some insight into the various types of informal networks that exist, as well as into the manner in which they are referred to. Although the phrase 'informal network' was understood by most respondents, some of them suggested that, locally, such networks are usually referred to as 'circles', 'lobbies', 'clubs' or even 'brotherhoods'. Some respondents hinted that the typical low-key network consists of four to five people who get together with a view to helping each other to achieve specific goals:

Such networks exist in Bulgaria, too. But here they are rather 'friendly circles'. I, for instance, have a circle of friends with whom I go skiing in Italy every year. We're completely different – two doctors, one district governor, three businessmen, two police officers, that is we are people related solely by friendship, and skiing is what brought us together [...].

(ER-10, BG)

[T]he officers of the Securitate, ex-employees of the state apparatus during the communist period [...] form private clubs and provide each other with different advantages [...].

(NGO-5, RO)

[W]e use [the term] network as a euphemism for lobby [...] the hometown lobbies, prison lobbies [...].

(NGO-2-CF, BiH)

I would call them not networks, but lobby groups [...].

(ER-3, MK)

I know about connections based on brotherhood [...] [they] are now appearing as business associations of entrepreneurs and small businessmen [...].

(DO-6, SRB)

*Table 5.7*  Informal networks by type of influence

| % (very) influential | SLO % | BG % | RO % | BiH % | MK % | SRB % |
|---|---|---|---|---|---|---|
| Family-based IFNs | 59 | 56 | 70 | 73 | 83 | 65 |
| IFNs of friends | 66 | 65 | 64 | 74 | 75 | 67 |
| IFNs of acquaintances | 35 | 24 | 42 | 37 | 41 | 25 |
| IFNs of former/current colleagues | 36 | 39 | 33 | 37 | 35 | 35 |
| IFNs of people who went to school/ studied together | 17 | 24 | 20 | 25 | 21 | 15 |
| Regionally based IFNs | 32 | 18 | 23 | 38 | 31 | 32 |
| Ethnically based IFNs | 30 | 46 | 40 | 63 | 56 | 52 |
| IFNs of people who served together in the army | 6 | 14 | 9 | 32 | 9 | 8 |
| Business/economic IFNs | 87 | 78 | 77 | 78 | 65 | 80 |
| Political IFNs | 88 | 79 | 84 | 86 | 79 | 89 |
| IFNs established to secure EU funds | 47 | 62 | 54 | 45 | 49 | 49 |
| IFNs of the former nomenklatura | 42 | 57 | 45 | 48 | 34 | 38 |
| IFNs of former Komsomol members | 18 | 42 | 25 | 11 | 17 | 15 |
| IFNs of former national security staff | 30 | 60 | 50 | 43 | 35 | 62 |
| Religious IFNs | 49 | 32 | 47 | 70 | 37 | 52 |
| Criminal IFNs | 54 | 69 | 50 | 78 | 52 | 77 |
| IFNs uniting people from different areas/branches | 44 | 39 | 32 | 32 | 37 | 32 |

*Note*: For practical purposes the youth organisations of the Socialist Party (Former Yugoslavia) and the Communist Party (Bulgaria and Romania) are referred to as "Komsomol" in this table and also in the main text. Decimals are rounded up or down to the nearest whole number. *Source*: Author.

Elites in Bulgaria frequently equate political networks with political parties and/or factions within them. Factions tend to be organized around one or a few key politicians such as the former president of Slovenia, Milan Kuèan, and the Macedonian politician Branko Crvenkovski.[17] In the view of some respondents, post-communist political parties are not parties in the classical sense, but rather organizations providing their members with various material and other privileges. Respondents in Macedonia, for instance, suggest that in their country political parties are primarily employment organizations: both high-ranking and regular positions in public administration are earmarked for party members and for people who are on good terms with the ruling party:

> [The political party] [...] is a tool for helping you and your family. The rest, the ideology, is pure crap. The real interests are: material incentives, access to public money, avoiding the IRS.
>
> (ME-6, RO)

> [I]n the country I think the informal has been turned into the formal [...] I'd say that Branko Crvenkovski, Buchkovski[18] and all those were members of that Komsomol in Macedonia, they are the Socialist Youth of Macedonia, that later on appeared as a political party.
>
> (DO-4, MK)

> [Y]es, there are such networks and we usually call these networks underground (networks) that control the entire policy. They are particularly engaged in the security spheres and they influence the politicians who are their marionettes. They control the politicians according to those family ties. What are you saying about Mijalkov's[19] family and the present Prime Minister? It is known that Mijalkov's family influences the entire politics of Macedonia. Nobody else. This refers to the economics, the security, the personnel and even who will marry whom.
>
> (JU-2, MK)

Such networks may also be more extensive, including people who are working together with the politicians. To quote a respondent from Bulgaria:

> I divide networks into several strata. The first stratum includes politicians charged with the responsibility of lobbying before the three branches of powers in favour of certain internal and external interests. The second stratum covers people appointed on the orders

of politicians; these include bankers, entrepreneurs and financiers whose task is to provide the financing of the representative model and cover the expenses of the lobbying politicians. The third group, servicing the above two circles, comprises editors, journalists, sociologists, political analysts and other manipulators of public opinion. The fourth stratum, an auxiliary stratum as I call it, includes small armed bands of security guards, underground power groupings and racketeers who not only guard what has been seized by the elites, but also acquire more riches at their own risk and under the protection of the three powers by resorting to blackmail, pressure and murder. Such informal networks were first created in Bulgaria after 1989 and gradually took shape during the years of transition.

(ER-2, BG)

Balkan elites believe that informal networks are also influential in business. Amongst the most influential networks are those of the 'red directors' – that is, people who were directors of former state companies and were able to benefit handsomely from the privatization process. Such directors have later established their own private businesses and they continue to benefit from the connections they formed during socialism. Former members of the Socialist Youth Organizations have also become successful businessmen, especially in Bulgaria. In Macedonia, informal business networks often have an ethnic basis. Several of our IDI respondents singled out the 'Vlach network' as being particularly influential. They claimed that this network controls all the major businesses in Macedonia and that it employs mostly its own family and kin. A fourth type of informal network in the business sphere is the network of so-called 'nouveaux riches'. Respondents in all countries noted that informal networks operating in the business sector are based on trust:

[T]he network of so-called 'red directors' [ . . . ].

(NGO-2, SLO)

[I]n the economy, for example, we talk about the 'old boys' network', which consists of managers who have been running companies dating back to the old system, this is a very powerful network which is even connected to taking over companies. Some have even linked this network with our former president.

(ME-5, SLO)

[P]eople who formerly had positions of responsibility in the Komsomol went into business, concentrated economic means and

financial interests either independently or in carrying out procurement demands, and they formed such an informal network. In my
opinion, such an informal network was perhaps formed by people dismissed from the Ministry of the Interior, the units fighting
organized crime [...].

(JU-6, BG)

[O]ne business network is close to the Vlach lobby – a community
in Macedonia which is very small, but very strong economically.
In their firms, which are pretty strong, the employees are either
mostly relatives or members of their ethnic community [...].

(INGO-5, MK)

[T]hrough various types of business clubs, nouveaux riches and
business people are trying to create networks and their own systems
of values and connections [...].

(ER-5, SRB)

As noted above, our findings on informal practice in the Western
Balkans suggest that low levels of trust in society cause people in need
of help or assistance to turn to those who are close to them. Such people are not only highly trustworthy. They also help each other without
requesting unreasonable or impossible favours or payments in return.
In contrast, while contacts tend to be very willing to help people to
achieve their goals, they often request in return favours that exceed the
request provided – be it in terms of extent, in terms of effort or in terms
of the risk involved. For this reason, some elites are reluctant to seek, or
abstain from seeking, the help of contacts, even when they are unable
to sort out their problems on their own (Grødeland, 2010c). All these
factors help to explain why low-key, or low-level, informal networks are
so widespread in the Balkans.

This might extend to informal networks in the sense that citizens prefer to seek the help of people whom they are close to and they trust.
However, one should not exclude the possibility of political networks or
business networks being composed of people who share a strong affinity
with each other. It is of course also possible that people who are joined
together in political and/or business networks are in a better position to
provide 'unreasonable' requests than others:

In Bulgaria there are several types of networks: neighbourly [net-
works], [networks] from kindergarten, from school ('we graduated
from the English High School'), from university ('we used to be in the
same class at university') [...] when [someone] has to decide whether

or not to hire a given person to work for them, people usually prefer someone they know. And ours is a small country, so that's how we end up with the ever-present extended family connections.

(ME-10, BG)

I think that the godmother and godfather phenomenon is much more important than [networks].

(ER-7, RO)

[T]he strongest [informal networks] are family networks, or those of ethnic affiliation that operate and help one another. I think that informal networks of this kind are necessary as people need to know where what is, how to get things done.

(DO-3-FED, BiH)

[I]t is much easier for you to share your frustrations and dilemmas with [...] your closest circle, that is the circle of relatives and friends, the closest family.

(DO-11, MK)

[I]n Serbia, these are primarily connections with relatives and people that come from the same town. I know someone, you know someone and therefore I will help you and you will help a person close to me so that tomorrow I can help your child and your child will help my child [...].

(ME-6, SRB)

The influence of informal networks composed by people who held leading positions during communism appears to be more significant in Bulgaria than elsewhere. Informal networks of the former nomenklatura, networks of former national security staff and networks of former Komsomol members are perceived as being more influential there than elsewhere. One reason for this could be that Bulgaria was one of the most orthodox communist countries in Eastern Europe. Unlike the case in countries like the Czech Republic, former members of the communist/socialist parties in the Balkans have not been forced out of their positions as a result of lustration.[20] Many of them have, since the collapse of communism, ventured into private business.

Informal networks composed of members of the former nomenklatura are thought to be generally more influential than networks of former national security staff and Komsomol members – though in Romania and Serbia it is the other way round. In Serbia national security staff from the Milošević period are still holding influential positions in society. They are even alleged to have organized the murder of former prime minister Zoran Djindjic (see Zoran Djindjic Fund, 2010). In Romania, members of the former Securitate staff are believed to have largely retained their powers. Slovenian elites who took part in our IDIs referred to former communist businessmen as 'red bosses' and to former communist members as the 'red Mob'. One of the Romanian respondents pointed out that one important feature of the former communist and Securitate networks is that family relations are given high importance within them:

[T]he Red Mob was one of the known networks (ex-party officials).

(PR-7, SLO)

I would say there are two main networks: that of the former Securitate officers and that of the former communists.

(EU-2, RO)

[T]he network of the former communists who are now holding high positions within the state institutions [...] they trust each other [...] the mutual trust amongst these persons is used only to cover the illegalities that someone does for his own benefit.

(PR-6, RO)

[T]he former big company managers [that is, the managers of state-owned companies] who now become company owners, use their connections for private purposes.

(LB-7-SRB)

[T]he most important (networks) are the networks established by people who used to work, or (who) still work, in the secret services. This is similar to other East-European countries. Secret services were the first to understand what transition was and ventured into business. When it comes to business, the network functions amongst the people who used to work in the army, in state security and if they have entered into a private business they will rather employ someone or cooperate with someone who has a similar background, rather than with someone else.

(PP-10, SRB)

Ethnic networks are considered to be very influential in the Western Balkans in general – and in BiH in particular – though they are also considered to be fairly influential in South East Europe. In Slovenia, which is ethnically more homogeneous than the other countries included in this study, ethnically based informal networks appear to be less influential. However, informal religious networks are much more influential in BiH than in the other countries covered by our research. This is not surprising, given that ethnicity and religion in BiH largely overlap.

Although ethnic networks do not appear to be significantly more influential in Macedonia than in other post-communist states, such networks were frequently referred to by the respondents who took part in our IDIs. The ethnic network most frequently referred to was the 'Vlach network'. The Vlachs constitute one of the smallest ethnic groups in Macedonia (see, for instance, Winnifrith, 2010); but, as noted above, members of this community have established themselves as successful businessmen. Some respondents also referred to the ethnic Albanian and ethnic Turk communities as informal networks. Regional networks, notably the 'Galichnik lobby', which was particularly influential during the socialist period, were also frequently referred to:

[T]he Vlach lobby or the Vlach network support each other and now they are directors, he is a director of that company and he is a Vlach, he is a director of that bank and he is a Vlach, and when you look carefully all of them are Vlachs and they support each other and simply protect each other.

(PR-5, MK)

[T]he Vlach network is one of the most important. Apart from the Vlach [network] there is another network, we call them oligarchs. They form the second network in which the Vlachs are an integral part.

(FB-5, MK)

[T]he Vlach lobby, or Vlach community, controls all the more serious businesses in Macedonia [...] they are a tight community and they help each other. Furthermore, there exists a lobby by town of origin, or the origin of others – parents, grandparents, great-grandparents [...].

(ER-7, MK)

[O]ne of the reasons why the political party DUI [Democratic Union for Integration] is not very much liked is because the citizens of Tetovo are very influential [in the party]. In the case of the Turks, we are speaking about Gostivar and Vrapciste; the Turks from Skopje don't like the citizens of Gostivar because they are influential everywhere in the Turkish establishment. In the case of Macedonians,

I think that the citizens of Stip are influential. Let's take the example of the Prime Minister and the other Prime Ministers as well [...].

(DO-3, MK)

## Business representatives and politicians on exposure to informal networks

As noted above, elites in the Balkans hold the view that informal networks are used (very) successfully in lobbying, political party funding, business and public procurement (Table 5.6). To find out how politicians and business representatives perceive the use of informal networks in their respective sectors, we asked them how common it is for people to seek informal outcomes there.

Table 5.8 suggests that informal networks are frequently used at elite level in the Balkans – though to a lesser extent in Slovenia, possibly as the transition process in this country has been smoother and progressed much more rapidly than elsewhere in this region. In Bulgaria and Romania informal networks are more commonly used in politics than in business. In BiH and Macedonia they appear to be more common amongst elected representatives and foreign business representatives than among political party representatives and local business representatives.

Serbia stands out, in that local business representatives appear to engage more in informal practice than other groups of elites. It is possible that this ideology – that is, the division between the West-leaning and the East-leaning elites – is a more important feature of political life in Serbia than elsewhere in the Balkans. Besides, the political situation

*Table 5.8* Percentage of respondents who think it is (very) common for people to seek outcomes in (RESPONDENT'S SECTOR) informally

| % (very) common | SLO % | BG % | RO % | BiH % | MK % | SRB % |
|---|---|---|---|---|---|---|
| Average – other elites | 31 | 71 | 64 | 48 | 58 | 63 |
| Elected representatives | 48 | 77 | 81 | 56 | 75 | 68 |
| Political party representatives | 52 | 72 | 80 | 49 | 59 | 71 |
| Representatives of local business | 49 | 69 | 74 | 43 | 61 | 83 |
| Representatives of foreign business | 46 | 60 | 63 | 56 | 73 | 64 |

*Note*: Decimals are rounded up or down to the nearest whole number.
*Source*: Author.

in Serbia has been rather chaotic in recent years, with frequent elections and frequent changes of government. For this reason local businesses in Serbia may have felt a greater need to establish good terms with a larger number of political parties than local businesses elsewhere in the Balkans.

In terms of influence, informal networks are generally highly influential in the sectors covered by our project – though slightly less so in Slovenia than elsewhere (Table 5.9). At the time of our survey, Bulgaria was preparing for EU membership. At that time both the EU and domestic media paid considerable attention to numerous corruption scandals. This may explain why elites in Bulgaria were rather more inclined to believe that informal networks are (very) influential in their respective sectors. Elected representatives – as a group – were more prone to believe that informal networks are influential in their sector than political party representatives were (BiH and Macedonia being exceptions) and than business representatives (with the exception of local business representatives in Serbia) were. This is not such a surprising finding, given that non-regulated lobbying is widespread throughout post-communist Europe (Grødeland, 2007) and that, to some extent, businesses in the Balkans seek to 'legalize' established business practices and business preferences by lobbying for the adoption of new legislation in parliament.

Our IDIs suggest that informal networks are simply (very) influential in politics and business – though some respondents provided more insight into how they exert their influence. The most interesting finding, however, is that the networks that are able to exert influence in politics and in business are best referred to as 'low-key', in that they link people who went to school together, friends or family members. Some

*Table 5.9*  Would you say that informal networks in (RESPONDENT'S SECTOR) are ...

| % (very) influential | SLO % | BG % | RO % | BiH % | MK % | SRB % |
|---|---|---|---|---|---|---|
| Average – other elites | 36 | 57 | 45 | 43 | 48 | 50 |
| Elected representatives | 53 | 55 | 64 | 56 | 56 | 56 |
| Political party representatives | 52 | 47 | 59 | 57 | 59 | 59 |
| Representatives of local business | 43 | 47 | 56 | 36 | 49 | 71 |
| Representatives of foreign business | 40 | 44 | 43 | 43 | 47 | 52 |

*Note*: Decimals are rounded up or down to the nearest whole number.
*Source*: Author.

respondents pointed out that networks that were established during the communist period still exert considerable influence in society. The latter view was frequently expressed by respondents in Romania and Serbia. Throughout the Balkans, informal networks in business are frequently used to secure public procurement contracts. Some respondents referred to 'Western-style' informal networks such as business networks and commercial networks, though references to such networks and to the influence they exert in business and politics were rarer than references to 'low-key' networks:

> [T]hose networks of friends [...] there is the least of that. It is either schoolmates who studied together, people who met in business, or political relations.
>
> (FB-4, SLO)

> [T]hey [the informal networks] go from the basic acquaintances to economic interests. If you only have an economic interest it is not enough. You also have to know someone.
>
> (LB-2, SLO)

> [I]n our field of work we quite often consult colleagues, most often when we know them from school or from university.
>
> (FB-3, BG)

> [In Romania] there is also the principle of 'the friend of your friend is my friend, too' [...] the principle 'one hand washes the other' is inherently necessary [in this regard].
>
> (FB-7, RO)

> [T]he representative of a foreign company managed to meet with the Prime Minister. To see how things can be done [here]. He had been introduced through some contacts.
>
> (FB-3-FED, BiH)

> [I]f everything was regulated as it should, if everything was normal, the need for some 'defensive' networks would be gone and maybe just (their) positive side [...] would remain [...].
>
> (FB-10, MK)

> [Y]es, they're influential. Just see how many judges that have been arrested. Everything is connected with business. The Commercial Court sold the property of (some) companies and you need just one paper to enable someone to benefit in an illegal way and achieve some gain.
>
> (LB-10, SRB)

Average values for elites in all countries suggest that the impact of informal networks on their respective sectors is negative more than positive – though the net difference in percentage is small for Slovenia and Macedonia (Table 5.10). An interesting pattern emerges when we compare the net difference between positive and negative impact for elected representatives, political party representatives and representatives of local and foreign businesses respectively. Politicians to a greater extent than business people (in all countries except Macedonia) hold the view that informal networks influence their sectors in a negative more than in a positive manner. What is more, the net negative influence is greater in BiH and Serbia than elsewhere, and higher amongst elected representatives than amongst political party representatives. The difference between the two groups is smaller in Slovenia, Bulgaria and Romania.

It could be argued that both politicians and business people have high 'bargaining powers': they control resources and make decisions that are important to a lot of people. In relative terms, politicians – and especially elected representatives at national level – probably have higher 'bargaining powers' than business people. Even though our data suggest a symbiosis between the two groups – in that politicians depend on business for funding election campaigns and for personal economic benefit, while business people depend on politicians for legislation that is beneficial to their business and for other business and personal benefit (for instance public procurement contracts) – the relative importance of the services provided by the former is likely to exceed that of the latter. The (negative) pressure accompanying requests directed at politicians may therefore be greater.

Figure 5.1 shows that political and business elites in post-communist states are frequently approached informally with various types of requests. While politicians in Romania, BiH and Macedonia are approached (very) often with such requests to a greater extent than business representatives, the net difference between those who have been approached – be it (very) often or sometimes – and those who have not (rarely/never) is fairly small, regardless of the respondent category. Added to this, no clear country differences emerge. Our findings thus appear to corroborate those presented in Table 5.1 – that is, that informal practice in post-communist states is, first and foremost, a result of habit and of a lack of faith in the transition rather than an expression of real need. The fact that informal approaches are widespread, however, does not suggest that such approaches are similar throughout the Balkans. They may be used predominantly for benign purposes in one country – and predominantly for non-benign purposes in another.

*Table 5.10* Would you say that informal networks influence (RESPONDENT'S SECTOR) in a positive or negative way?

| | SLO % | BG % | RO % | BiH % | MK % | SRB % |
|---|---|---|---|---|---|---|
| **In a positive way** | | | | | | |
| Average – other elites | 25 | 15 | 20 | 24 | 26 | 14 |
| Elected representatives | 31 | 19 | 27 | 21 | 32 | 15 |
| Political party representatives | 32 | 18 | 22 | 23 | 39 | 12 |
| Representatives of local business | 35 | 16 | 35 | 29 | 33 | 19 |
| Representatives of foreign business | 25 | 23 | 38 | 25 | 31 | 12 |
| **In a negative way** | | | | | | |
| Average – other elites | 28 | 34 | 39 | 43 | 30 | 44 |
| Elected representatives | 37 | 23 | 35 | 51 | 27 | 51 |
| Political party representatives | 36 | 26 | 32 | 41 | 24 | 40 |
| Representatives of local business | 13 | 17 | 28 | 31 | 17 | 40 |
| Representatives of foreign business | 19 | 13 | 24 | 41 | 25 | 39 |
| **They do not influence it at all** | | | | | | |
| Average – other elites | 17 | 7 | 11 | 17 | 17 | 8 |
| Elected representatives | 5 | 9 | 9 | 7 | 19 | 3 |
| Political party representatives | 5 | 5 | 13 | 16 | 15 | 16 |
| Representatives of local business | 19 | 17 | 10 | 13 | 31 | 7 |
| Representatives of foreign business | 20 | 9 | 15 | 15 | 23 | 13 |
| **There are no influential networks in (RESPONDENT'S SECTOR)** | | | | | | |
| Average – other elites | 15 | 6 | 8 | 8 | 11 | 12 |
| Elected representatives | 7 | 4 | 3 | 1 | 7 | 9 |
| Political party representatives | 4 | 12 | 5 | 8 | 12 | 8 |
| Representatives of local business | 11 | 13 | 6 | 9 | 4 | 4 |
| Representatives of foreign business | 10 | 7 | 7 | 7 | 4 | 5 |

*Note*: Decimals are rounded up or down to the nearest whole number.
*Source*: Author.

Informal approaches may take a number of different forms. We therefore asked our respondents whether they ever got the impression that those approaching them for assistance represented an informal network. Our quantitative findings show that close to, or just over, half of those of our respondents who do not work in politics or business believed they had been approached by informal networks (Table 5.11). Further, in all countries except Bulgaria, politicians believed this to be the case to a greater extent than business representatives did.

132

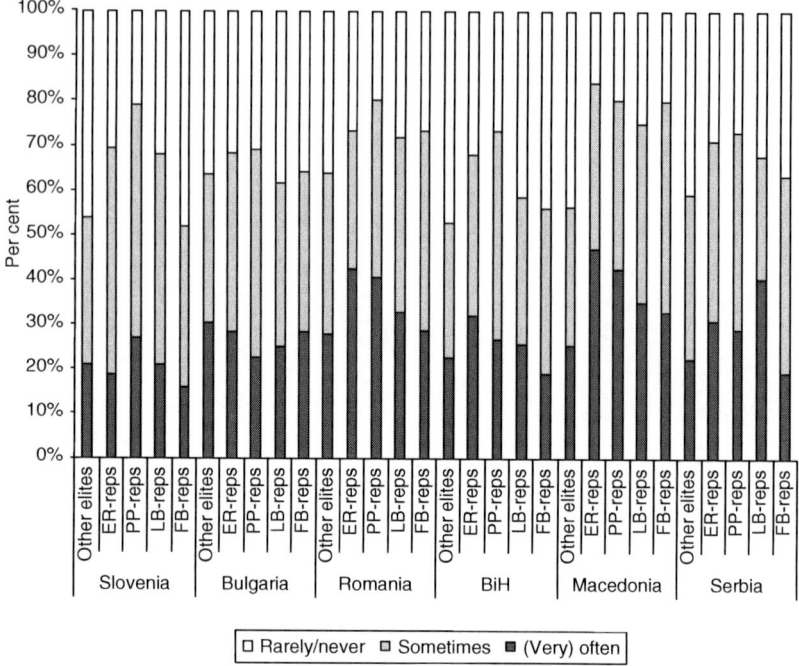

Figure 5.1 How often are you approached by people requesting your help to solve problems informally?
Source: Author.

Table 5.11 Did you ever get the impression that someone who contacted you with a request represented an informal network – i.e. that they belonged to an informal circle of people able and willing to help each other?

| % yes | SLO % | BG % | RO % | BiH % | MK % | SRB % |
|---|---|---|---|---|---|---|
| Average – other elites | 44 | 43 | 47 | 56 | 55 | 44 |
| Elected representatives | 60 | 40 | 51 | 59 | 72 | 65 |
| Political party representatives | 65 | 49 | 49 | 65 | 65 | 52 |
| Representatives of local business | 43 | 37 | 36 | 49 | 55 | 40 |
| Representatives of foreign business | 43 | 35 | 32 | 53 | 47 | 41 |

Note: Decimals are rounded up or down to the nearest whole number.
Source: Author.

Our qualitative data suggest that the respondents often knew in advance that the people approaching them represented informal networks, or that the network representatives made this clear to them. Signs suggesting that those who made the request represented informal networks included the manner of speech and references to other people, either whose support had been secured or whom they claimed to represent:

[M]aybe their attitude (makes me realize) and if you know a person at least a little, you know if there is a group of people behind them who are supporting their person.

(FB-10, SLO)

[T]he main thing is that such a person emphasizes that he knows so-and-so, with whom he/she was a fellow student, and that they have some other schoolmate of theirs, etc [...].

(ER-4, BG)

I either knew that the person asking a favour was part of an informal network or I could understand it from the way in which that person would act or by the way in which he/she would speak.

(FB-6, RO)

[I]n most cases each informal network has a leader, someone influential and powerful, so the members of such informal leagues always resort to the protection and help of the leader and mention his name whenever they can benefit from all the positive aspects of mentioning their leader.

(LB-9, BG)

[T]here isn't a group whose bosses I don't know, including the dead ones [...].

(PP-10, BG)

I believe that they demand rather than asking, that they ask for more than individual people do.

(DO-1-FED, BiH)

Their requests are more substantial, more sophisticated.

(ER-5-ST, BiH)

## Business representatives and politicians on their personal use of informal networks

Academic studies of corruption show that there is a rather big gap between perceptions of corruption, on the one hand, and exposure to corruption, on the other. In post-communist states the general public perceives corruption to be widespread, though its members' own personal exposure to corrupt officials is considerably more limited (Miller et al., 2001). Could there also be a discrepancy between elite perceptions of informal networks and their own personal exposure to, affiliation with and/or use of, such networks?

Table 5.12 shows that the percentage of business representatives and politicians who said that they themselves belong to informal networks is considerably smaller than the percentage of those who say they have been approached by informal networks (see also Table 5.11). Given that the phrase 'informal network' primarily has negative connotations amongst post-communist elites, it could be that Bulgarian elites are reluctant to admit to being part of such networks. On the contrary, those who tend to use the expressions 'contacts' and 'informal networks' interchangeably may perceive the people they turn to as 'contacts' rather than as people who are members of informal networks. Finally, as elites primarily depend on 'low-level' informal networks – that is, networks composed of family, friends or other people considered to be close – they may simply not perceive these people as representing informal networks in the first place.

Belonging to informal networks appears to be more common in Macedonia than in the other countries – and also more common amongst politicians than amongst business representatives. Macedonia, just like Slovenia and BiH, is a small country both in terms of population and in terms of size. Elites in Slovenia and Macedonia often claim that their respective countries are so small that everybody knows everybody. Slovenia is one of the post-communist 'success stories' in terms of economic development and political stability. The economic situation in Macedonia is far worse – and society is much more poorly organized – than in Slovenia, which may explain why being part of informal

*Table 5.12*   Would you say that you yourself belong to any informal networks?

| % yes | SLO % | BG % | RO % | BiH % | MK % | SRB % |
|---|---|---|---|---|---|---|
| Average – other elites | 27 | 26 | 21 | 26 | 36 | 19 |
| Elected representatives | 31 | 26 | 27 | 22 | 40 | 32 |
| Political party representatives | 43 | 24 | 28 | 26 | 45 | 38 |
| Local business representatives | 25 | 20 | 26 | 24 | 37 | 18 |
| Foreign business representatives | 20 | 16 | 30 | 26 | 30 | 23 |

*Note*: Decimals are rounded up or down to the nearest whole number.
*Source*: Author.

networks is more common there. The historical legacy of Macedonia might also have something to do with it: as noted above, Macedonia was part of the Ottoman Empire for some 500 years. In contrast, Slovenia belonged to the Austro-Hungarian Empire, which was generally more orderly. BiH, for its part, differs, in that the country has been ruled both by the Ottoman Empire and by the Austro-Hungarian Empire. More importantly, however, the recent war effectively destroyed existing social structures, including people's social networks.

Our IDIs suggest that elites in the Balkans primarily belong to 'low-level' informal networks composed of friends, former classmates or fellow students and/or family members – though business representatives also admitted to belonging to various poorly defined 'business networks'.[21] Respondents sometimes questioned whether the 'circles' they belonged to could be referred to as informal networks.[22] Given that the phrase 'informal network' has negative associations with the elites in the Balkans, this is to some extent understandable. The purpose of the informal networks to which politicians and business representatives said they belonged is predominantly to obtain information or to gain access to 'useful people':

I belong to this network of closely connected people. People who work in jobs where they can get information about places where something will be built.

(FB-4-CF-BiH)

[I]f the people I went to school with can be called a network, then I do (belong to one).

(LB-1-FED, BiH)

I belong to [a network of] my childhood friends, my friends from the city.

(FB-1, MK)

I belong [to the network] of old Skopje families.

(FB-2, MK)

[I]f you mean my friends from the neighbourhoods, then I do belong to such networks.

(LB-10, MK)

[I]f an informal network is a network of friends from childhood – (then) yes.

(LB-8, MK)

> [Y]ou sometimes belong to these networks whether you want to or
> not [...] [I belong to networks] of my friends who went to the same
> primary school and grew up in the same neighbourhood [...].
>
> (FB-2, SRB)

Politicians and business representatives make frequent use of informal networks to solve work-related problems. Such practice is most
widespread amongst politicians in Macedonia and Serbia – but also
common amongst business representatives in these countries. Informal networks are used less frequently to solve personal problems
(Table 5.13). One explanation may be that people volunteer their assistance to politicians and business people in the hope of gaining some
benefit at some point in the future.[23] It is also possible that the types
of networks politicians and business people turn to in order to solve
their personal problems are low-key networks – that is, networks largely
composed of family and/or friends. Even though family members and
friends of politicians and business representatives may hold high offices
or important positions themselves, they are emotionally close to the
latter. Turning to them may therefore be considered low risk in terms
of reciprocity: one favour cancels out another over time. Consequently
there is less of a need for return of favours in general, and, in particular,
of favours that are either more difficult or more expensive to provide in

*Table 5.13*  How often do you solve ... (% very often/often/sometimes)

|  | SLO % | BG % | RO % | BiH % | MK % | SRB % |
|---|---|---|---|---|---|---|
| **Work-related problems with the help of informal networks?** | | | | | | |
| Average – other elites | 28 | 32 | 24 | 28 | 36 | 27 |
| Elected representatives | 22 | 43 | 36 | 27 | 44 | 44 |
| Political party representatives | 34 | 33 | 26 | 32 | 47 | 39 |
| Local business representatives | 30 | 30 | 34 | 23 | 37 | 37 |
| Foreign business representatives | 15 | 31 | 35 | 16 | 40 | 35 |
| **Personal problem with the help of informal networks** | | | | | | |
| Average – other elites | 23 | 25 | 25 | 22 | 22 | 22 |
| Elected representatives | 11 | 20 | 32 | 24 | 23 | 28 |
| Political party representatives | 9 | 22 | 28 | 28 | 28 | 33 |
| Local business representatives | 16 | 28 | 39 | 33 | 26 | 37 |
| Foreign business representatives | 18 | 34 | 43 | 23 | 20 | 31 |

*Note*: Decimals are rounded up or down to the nearest whole number.
*Source*: Author.

*Table 5.14* How willing are informal networks to help you?

| % (very) willing | SLO % | BG % | RO % | BiH % | MK % | SRB % |
|---|---|---|---|---|---|---|
| Average – other elites | 51 | 41 | 36 | 44 | 54 | 51 |
| Elected representatives | 59 | 55 | 66 | 41 | 66 | 73 |
| Political party representatives | 78 | 52 | 57 | 41 | 71 | 67 |
| Local business representatives | 66 | 47 | 56 | 53 | 71 | 63 |
| Foreign business representatives | 58 | 51 | 55 | 40 | 72 | 63 |

*Note*: Decimals are rounded up or down to the nearest whole number.
*Source*: Author.

terms of cost/value. Besides – as already noted – elites may simply not think of people who one way or another are close to them as an informal network.

Informal networks are remarkably willing to help politicians and business people to solve their problems (Table 5.14). The willingness to help is greatest in Macedonia, but it is also high in Serbia, Slovenia and Romania. In contrast, informal networks appear less ready to help these groups in BiH and Bulgaria. Country size may have something to do with this, as may the level of mobility and/or of migration. During the war in BiH whole communities were uprooted: many people ended up as refugees or as internally displaced people. While some people may have been successful in re-establishing their old networks or in forming new ones, others may have been less successful. Politicians in BiH may also be perceived as less useful to other people in that decisions made by them may be – and often have been – overturned by the High Representative for Bosnia and Herzegovina.[24] For this reason citizens may feel that the potential benefit of providing favours to politicians may not be all that great. The international community has cleaned the ranks of the judiciary in BiH by removing corrupt members of staff (Bergling, 2008). Considerable efforts are also undertaken to reform public administration.[25] Locally elected politicians may therefore be relatively less able to manipulate other sectors of society than they are in other parts of the Balkans.

One might expect business representatives to feel more obliged to return favours rendered by informal networks than politicians do – given that the former are largely dependent on state institutions for the running of their businesses. Table 5.15 shows that the majority of both local and foreign business representatives in all countries felt an obligation towards their informal networks. A fairly strong obligation was also felt on the part of the elected representatives and political party

*Table 5.15*  When you get help from informal networks, do you feel obliged to return the favour?

| | SLO % | BG % | RO % | BiH % | MK % | SRB % |
|---|---|---|---|---|---|---|
| **Elected representatives** | | | | | | |
| Obliged | 25 | 25 | 34 | 43 | 42 | 45 |
| Not obliged | 48 | 35 | 38 | 31 | 42 | 29 |
| Never been helped by informal networks | 27 | 40 | 29 | 26 | 16 | 27 |
| **Political party representatives** | | | | | | |
| Obliged | 30 | 42 | 25 | 47 | 51 | 55 |
| Not obliged | 51 | 21 | 48 | 19 | 31 | 12 |
| Never been helped by informal networks | 19 | 37 | 27 | 34 | 18 | 32 |
| **Local business representatives** | | | | | | |
| Obliged | 55 | 42 | 40 | 48 | 54 | 54 |
| Not obliged | 21 | 21 | 27 | 22 | 27 | 15 |
| Never been helped by informal networks | 24 | 37 | 33 | 30 | 19 | 31 |
| **Foreign business representatives** | | | | | | |
| Obliged | 34 | 37 | 49 | 40 | 58 | 46 |
| Not obliged | 31 | 21 | 25 | 28 | 30 | 26 |
| Never been helped by informal networks | 34 | 42 | 26 | 32 | 12 | 28 |

*Note*: Decimals are rounded up or down to the nearest whole number.
*Source*: Author.

representatives. Elected representatives in Slovenia and Bulgaria felt 'not obliged' to a greater extent than 'obliged' to return such favours, as did political party representatives in Romania. The sense of obligation was felt more strongly by politicians in BiH, Macedonia and Serbia than by politicians in Slovenia, Bulgaria and Romania.

In Macedonia, in particular, political parties are not only political parties in the traditional sense. They are also important employers in the sense that the ruling party at any given time controls a large number of administrative positions. Such positions tend to be distributed amongst people loyal to the party rather than to those who are best qualified for the job. Consequently, political party representatives in Macedonia may feel rather more obliged to others for their positions than corresponding elites do elsewhere. Our previous study of informal networks in politics suggests that Bulgarian political parties are heavily influenced by certain families and/or groups (Grødeland, 2007). This may also be the case in other post-communist states.

As already noted, a fairly large share of the business representatives and politicians whom we interviewed in the Balkans admitted that they belong to informal networks (Table 5.12) and that they make use of informal networks to solve work-related and/or personal problems (Table 5.13). Still, as Table 5.16 shows, the large majority of them (in all countries) believed that it is perfectly possible to resolve work-related as well as personal problems *without* contacts or informal networks. Differences across countries are not all that great.

The general reason why business representatives and politicians still make use of informal networks may therefore have quite a bit to do with habit: citizens in the Balkans are used to sorting out their problems through go-betweens. Their use is historically conditioned and reflects low levels of trust in society more generally, and in state institutions in particular. What is more, even though state institutions undergo administrative reform and the need to use informal networks subsides, citizens may be reluctant to give up their habit. One specific reason for this may be that they would not be as successful without the assistance of informal networks. Another reason may be that turning away from informal networks makes them feel uncomfortable. Speed may also

*Table 5.16*  Is it possible for you to resolve ... (% yes)

|  | SLO % | BG % | RO % | BiH % | MK % | SRB % |
|---|---|---|---|---|---|---|
| **Work-related problems without contacts or informal networks?** | | | | | | |
| Average – other elites | 82 | 76 | 82 | 84 | 71 | 78 |
| Elected representatives | 78 | 81 | 87 | 81 | 72 | 78 |
| Political party representatives | 77 | 81 | 86 | 83 | 78 | 83 |
| Local business representatives | 78 | 87 | 96 | 81 | 70 | 80 |
| Foreign business representatives | 84 | 87 | 88 | 85 | 78 | 86 |
| **Personal problems without contacts or informal networks?** | | | | | | |
| Average – other elites | 85 | 82 | 85 | 90 | 81 | 80 |
| Local business representatives | 80 | 85 | 95 | 88 | 81 | 91 |
| Foreign business representatives | 88 | 88 | 86 | 91 | 91 | 91 |
| Elected representatives | 88 | 80 | 93 | 89 | 86 | 87 |
| Political party representatives | 81 | 83 | 88 | 86 | 86 | 88 |

*Note*: Decimals are rounded up or down to the nearest whole number.
*Source*: Author.

have something to do with it: approaching state institutions through a go-between usually generates a swifter outcome than if one approaches such institutions oneself (Miller et al., 2001). Thus informal networks may in part be used as a result of inertia, and in part for opportunistic reasons.

## Conclusions

Informal networks should not be perceived as a mere response to the phenomenon of transition, but more as a product of national culture and of the socialist experience. In post-communist societies such networks are used to fund political parties, to entice politicians to pass favourable legislation and to obtain specific outcomes. They are also used actively for recruiting people to positions in politics and government administration. In business, informal networks curb competition and facilitate the recruitment of less qualified people. In both politics and business sectors informal networks are used to promote illegitimate, or even illegal, outcomes – including corrupt ones (Grødeland, 2006, 2007).

The findings presented above suggest that politicians and business representatives in the Balkans believe informal networks to be influential in their sectors and that their impact is predominantly negative. What is more, politicians and business people are not only exposed to such networks through their work, they also make use of them for both work-related and private purposes. These circumstances give rise to the question of how to reduce the negative impact of informal networks. The majority of our respondents (in all countries) believed that the most effective way to achieve such an outcome would be to change people's mentality and values through education, to strengthen the rule of law, to strengthen public trust in the state and to strengthen law enforcement (Table 5.17).

Internationally 'informed' anti-corruption efforts tend to focus on the short term. The measures identified by our respondents as the most effective ones in terms of reducing the negative impact of informal networks – which, by elites, is primarily equated with corruption – require a more long-term perspective. Elites interviewed for our previous project on corruption and anti-corruption reform in Ukraine suggested that corruption is very much a part of the Ukrainian mentality. It is not only a feature that developed during communism, but has its roots in national culture (Grødeland, 2009). Consequently, a real reduction in corruption levels can only be achieved by changing people's mentality. Ukrainian

*Table 5.17* Most efficient measure by which to limit the negative impact of informal networks (%)

|  | SLO % | BG % | RO % | BiH % | MK % | SRB % |
|---|---|---|---|---|---|---|
| Change people's mentality and values through education | 19 | 24 | 34 | 24 | 24 | 26 |
| Strengthen the rule of law | 28 | 23 | 20 | 30 | 27 | 30 |
| Strengthen public trust in the state | 14 | 12 | 4 | 7 | 8 | 9 |
| Expose the negative aspects of IFNs in the media | 5 | 5 | 1 | 3 | 2 | 3 |
| Introduce new and better legislation | 6 | 8 | 6 | 6 | 4 | 5 |
| Strengthen law enforcement in (COUNTRY) | 4 | 11 |  | 8 | 13 | 8 |
| Properly regulate political party funding | 0 | 0 | 0 | 1 | 1 | 1 |
| Properly regulate lobbying | 2 | 1 | 2 | 2 | 1 | 0 |
| Better regulate public procurement | 2 |  | 0 | 1 | 1 | 0 |
| Make (COUNTRY's) state administration more open, transparent and efficient | 5 | 4 | 3 | 3 | 4 | 4 |
| Strengthen the accountability of (COUNTRY's) politicians | 4 | 1 | 3 | 4 | 6 | 3 |
| Enhance the efficiency and independence of the judiciary | 3 | 3 | 5 | 4 | 5 | 3 |
| Strengthen (COUNTRY's) anti-corruption bodies and anti-corruption legislation | 4 | 3 | 6 | 5 | 1 | 3 |
| Introduce codes of ethics and professional codes both in the public and in the private sector | 5 | 1 | 1 | 1 | 1 | 1 |
| Limit the influence of the former nomenklatura through lustration | – | 1 | 1 | 1 | 0 | 0 |
| Comply with EU's conditionality requirements | – | 2 | 3 |  |  |  |
| Prepare for EU membership | n.a. | n.a. | n.a. | 2 | 2 | 2 |
| Depends/Difficult to say | – | 2 | 0 | – | 1 | 0 |
| Don't know | – | 4 | 1 | – | 1 | 1 |
| N | 600 | 600 | 600 | 600 | 600 | 600 |

*Note*: Decimals are rounded up or down to the nearest whole number. The numbers in the columns therefore do not always add up to 100.
*Source*: Author.

elites suggested that, at best, this would take a generation or two to achieve, at worst, up to 100 years or more – if it is at all achievable (Grødeland, 2010d). It seems unlikely that the time perspective would be any different in the Balkans.

Other countries that have suffered from extensive corruption, such as Singapore and Hong Kong, have succeeded in eradicating corruption in a fairly short time span. One of the reasons why anti-corruption efforts in Singapore have been such a success is that the rule of law has functioned properly: anti-corruption legislation is effective, the legal apparatus is functioning properly and official anti-corruption efforts are undertaken in an anti-corruption climate that has fostered a strong anti-corruption culture (Ali, 2010).

In contrast, it is a well-known fact that in the majority of Europe's post-communist states legislation is not effective and the judiciary is largely ineffective, even corrupt. One reason for this may be that these states have moved from 'rule by law' to 'rule of law' in a fairly short time frame (Ajani, 2005). A second reason is that transition has largely been brought about by means of legal transfers – that is, by copying and applying legislation designed by, and used in, Western countries.[26] The process of adapting legislation from other countries has tended to be fairly chaotic.[27] A third reason is to be found in public perceptions of, and behaviour towards, law in post-communist states. Our research suggests that, as far as attitudes towards the law are concerned, two different positions appear to coexist in Europe's post-communist states: on the one hand, there appears to be a 'culture of law-breaking'. This culture is to some extent historically 'informed': elites in the Czech Republic and Slovenia, for instance, claim that in their countries breaking the law is considered 'a national sport'. In contrast, violating generally accepted social norms is considered to be widely unacceptable. To some extent the 'culture of law-breaking' is also a result of people's inadequate understanding of what concepts such as 'democracy' and 'rule of law' actually entail. In Ukraine, for instance, elites suggest that citizens largely equate 'democracy' with 'the right to break laws' (Grødeland, 2009).

Further, throughout post-communist Europe laws are largely perceived as illegitimate, in that they are passed by politicians intent on serving their own private interest or those of 'their' people, rather than those of the public as such. Politicians not only pass poor-quality or bad laws, they also fail to comply with the laws they pass. In doing so, they provide the general public with little or no incentive to follow the law.

Recent experiences from Romania suggest that it is possible to investigate and prosecute corrupt people, including high-ranking politicians and government officials, given adequate political will. While such will appears to exist in a formal sense (most politicians in post-communist Europe pay lip service to the anti-corruption position of the EU and other international organizations), it is largely lacking in practice. A good example in this regard is that of the anti-corruption efforts undertaken by Romania in the run-up to EU membership in 2007. To ensure her country's inclusion in the EU, then Minister of Justice in Romania, Monica Macovei, was given wide powers to investigate and prosecute instances of corruption. She did so in a fairly successful manner. However, shortly after Romania had secured EU membership, Macovei was removed from office – apparently on the grounds that her efforts had ruffled the feathers of too many influential people (Ciobanu, 2007).[28]

Given the present political situation in post-communist Europe, it seems unlikely that the negative impact of informal networks will disappear in the foreseeable future. For this to happen, the general economic and political environment in which such networks operate – and which to a great extent facilitates them – needs to change. That requires responsible politicians, who have their country's best interests at heart rather than limited private interest. What is more, it requires responsible citizens.[29]

## Appendix to Chapter 5: Survey design

| Czech Republic | Slovenia | Bulgaria | Romania | BiH | Macedonia | Serbia |
|---|---|---|---|---|---|---|
| **National/capital level** | **National/capital level** | **National/capital level** | **National/capital level** | **National/entity level** | **National/capital level** | **National/capital level** |
| Prague – 200 | Ljubljana – 200 | Sofia – 200 | Bucureşti – 200 | National level – 84 | Skopje – 200 | Belgrade – 200 |
| | | | | FED (Sarajevo) – 73 | | |
| | | | | RS (Banja Luka) – 43 | | |
| **Regional level** | **Regional level** | **Regional level** | **Regional level** | **Regional level** | **Regional level** | **Regional level** |
| Mladá Boleslav – 57 | Maribor – 67 | Pernik – 50 | Iaşi – 57 | Sarajevo – 50 | Kumanovo – 56 | Subotica – 56 |
| Plzeň – 57 | Celje – 67 | Bourgas – 50 | Constanţa – 57 | Banja Luka – 50 | Tetovo – 64 | Novi Sad – 56 |
| Ústí nad Labem – 58 | Novo Mesto – 67 | Varna – 50 | Ploieşti – 57 | Brcko – 50 | Ohrid – 56 | Uzice – 56 |
| Hradec Králové – 57 | Kranj – 66 | Pleven – 50 | Craiova – 57 | Mostar – 50 | Bitola – 56 | Novi Pazar – 56 |
| Brno – 57 | Koper – 67 | Vratsa – 50 | Timişoara – 57 | Tuzla – 50 | Strumica – 56 | Vranje/Bujanovac – 64 |
| Olomouc – 57 | Nova Gorica – 66 | Plovdiv – 50 | Cluj Napoca – 58 | Bihac – 50 | Veles – 56 | Nis – 56 |
| Ostrava – 57 | | Rousse – 50 | Braşov – 57 | Zvornik – 50 | Stip – 56 | Kragujevac – 56 |
| | | Haskovo – 50 | | Trebinje – 50 | | |

*Notes:* (1) Surveys were carried out by GfK-Prague under the direction of Klára Trávníčková, by CATI in Slovenia under the direction of Tomaž Hohkraut and Renata Rakusa, by Vitosha Research in Sofia under the direction of Alexander Stoyanov, by Gallup Romania under the direction of Alexandru Toth, by GfK Bosnia under the direction of Josip Tvrtkovic, by Pro Media in Macedonia under the direction of Klime Babunski and by Argument in Serbia under the direction of Zdenka Milivojevic. Surveys in the Czech Republic, Slovenia, Bulgaria and Romania were carried out in 2005, whereas surveys in BiH, Macedonia and Serbia were carried out in 2007–08. (2) We conducted 200 interviews at national and capital level (in BiH interviews were conducted at national level and at entity level – Federation, Republika Srpska) and 400 interviews at regional level. In Serbia and Macedonia the number of interviews in areas of ethnic conflict (Tetovo in Macedonia, Vranje/Bujanovac in Serbia) slightly exceeded the number of interviews in the other regions.

# Notes

1.  For our purposes, we define an informal network as 'a circle of people who are willing and able to help each other'.
2.  For practical purposes, the term 'post-communist' is used in reference to all countries covered by our research, even though it could be argued that it would be more appropriate to refer to BiH, Macedonia, Serbia and Slovenia as 'post-socialist' rather than as 'post-communist' states.
3.  For practical purposes, Bosnia and Herzegovina will be referred to as BiH in the following.
4.  The project investigates informal practice in three countries that were affected by war or conflict – but to different extents and in different manners.
5.  In East Central and South East Europe, we also conducted one round table in each country.
6.  For an account of the methodology applied for the two projects, see Grødeland (2007) and Grødeland and Aasland (2007).
7.  For our purposes, we define elites as people holding positions in these sectors. These are, as a rule, highly educated people.
8.  Finally, we also interviewed government officials working in the area of anti-corruption, EU and Council of Europe staff (East Central and South East Europe only) and representatives of the foreign donor community (Western Balkans only). For practical reasons, these four categories were not recruited to take part in the quantitative surveys.
9.  The questionnaire contained a total of 308 questions. It was translated from English into Czech, Slovenian, Bulgarian and Romanian respectively, and then translated back into English. Translations and back-translations were checked for accuracy both by native speakers (social scientists) not affiliated with the project and by the Norwegian project team.
10. NUTS (nomenclature of territorial units) II is the main analytical level used in EU regional policy analysis.
11. The average refusal rate for all categories of respondents was 71 per cent in Slovenia, 59 per cent in the Czech Republic and in Serbia, 55 per cent in Romania, 23 per cent in BiH, 17 per cent in Bulgaria and 15 per cent in Macedonia.
12. Findings presented in this chapter have not been weighted by category of elites – that is, by the potential number of respondents for each elite category – as (a) it is not possible to construct accurate weights for all of them; (b) quota samples are fairly small; and (c) not all respondents answered the most sensitive questions on contacts and informal networks. However, we have compared weighted and non-weighted findings for those categories of elites for which we were able to create approximate weights. Weights were calculated on the basis of the discrepancy between the probability of selection and the actual number of respondents for each category. Such data were available for six categories in Bulgaria, five in Slovenia and four in Romania. We did not have access to such data for the Czech Republic. Differences between weighted and non-weighted results were checked for those categories of respondents whose actual or estimated weights were different from/other than 1. At the aggregate level (cross-country comparison), results

differed only by a few percentages (0–2). Weighted and non-weighted find-ings were not compared at the more disaggregated level, as the number of respondents was small, and consequently differences in weights would have a big impact on results. Weighting of the data was done by Dr Aadne Aasland.

13. For a description of how the qualitative data were analysed, see Grøde-land (2007).
14. While no definition of informal network was given to our IDI respondents (the intention with the IDIs was to explore how respondents themselves understood the phrase 'informal network'), respondents who took part in our quantitative surveys were provided with the definition given in endnote 1.
15. We defined a contact as 'a person who is willing and able to help someone'.
16. Respondents are referred to as follows: GO = government official; ER = elected representative; PP = political party representative; JU = judge/prosecutor; PR = public procurement official; LB = representative of local business; FB = representative of foreign business; ME = media represen-tative; NGO = NGO representative; INGO = International NGO represen-tative; DO = donor representative; EU = EU representative; CoE = Council of Europe representative. The country the respondent is from is indi-cated as follows: SLO = Slovenia, BG = Bulgaria; RO = Romania; BiH = Bosnia and Herzegovina; MK = Macedonia; SRB = Serbia. Conflict areas in BiH, Macedonia and Serbia are referred to as CF. The administrative level at which IDIs in BiH were conducted is indicated as follows: ST = state level; FED = Federation; RS = Republika Srpska. Thus GO-5, SLO refers to govern-ment official respondent number 5 from Slovenia.
17. Crvenkovski was president of Macedonia from May 2004 to May 2009. Before that he was prime minister of Macedonia from August 1992 to November 1998 and November 2002 to May 2004. For background, see SETimes.com (2010a).
18. The respondent refers to Vlado Buchkovski, former prime minister of Macedonia. See SETimes.com (2010a).
19. The respondent probably refers to Jordan Mijalkov, former Macedonian politician and former minister of the interior representing VMRO-DPMNE, who died in a mysterious car accident a few years ago, on his way to Serbia.
20. For a discussion of lustration in post-communist Europe, see Bertschi (1994).
21. IDI respondents interviewed for our first project were not asked whether they themselves belonged to informal networks. This question was only asked during IDIs carried out as part of our second project – that is, in BiH, Macedonia and Serbia.
22. It is therefore interesting that they – when discussing the existence of infor-mal networks in their respective countries – referred to these as 'circles', 'clubs' and 'brotherhoods'.
23. Judges and prosecutors in post-communist states are often approached with offers of assistance from people they suspect would like to trade such assistance for other favours in the future. See Grødeland (2010a).
24. The powers of the High Representative are discussed in Szewczyk (2010). For an example of a clash between the High Representative and Bosnian Serbs, see earthtimes.org (2009).

25. See, for instance, an overview of UNDP's efforts to promote democratic governance in BiH, at http://www.undp.ba/index.aspx?PID= 25&RID=27, accessed 15 November 2010.
26. As part of their adjustment and accession to the EU, countries in East Central Europe have had to adopt a large number of legislative measures. In areas such as public procurement, which were non-existent during communism, EU legislation has largely been adopted without prior adjustment to the administrative and political context into which it has been introduced.
27. Czapliński notes that the introduction of EU directives in his native Poland was far from trouble-free. Such directives were simply translated into Polish without proper adjustments being made: 'their nomenclature is often translated word for word, thereby introducing concepts which are not known to the Polish legal system' (Czapliński, 2001 quoted in Kühn, 2006, pp. 228–229). A legally educated person from Romania, involved in supervising the adjustment to the EU and interviewed for our project, indicated that many of the terms used in legislation and borrowed from other countries are simply not understood by the people responsible for introducing such legislation in the Romanian context.
28. Macovei was later removed, though in 2009 she made a comeback by being elected to the European Parliament.
29. It should be noted that members of the general public in post-communist states cannot simply be referred to as victims of corruption. They are at the same time accomplices of corruption – that is, although they largely condemn corrupt politicians and government officials, they are happy to give bribes in order to speed up administrative procedures or to obtain various services or goods to which they are not necessarily entitled by law (Miller et al., 2001).

# References

Ajani, G. (2005) *Das Recht der Länder Osteuropas* (Berlin: Berliner Wissenschafts-Verlag).

Ali, M. (2010) 'Eradicating Corruption – the Singapore Experience', http://www.tdri.or.th/reports/unpublished/os_paper/ali.pdf, accessed 15 November 2010.

Aslund, A. (2007) *How Capitalism Was Built: The Transformation of Central and Eastern Europe, Russia and Central Asia* (Cambridge: Cambridge University Press).

Aslund, A. (2010) *The Last Shall Be the First: The East European Financial Crisis* (Washington, DC: Peterson Institute for International Economics).

Bergling, P. (2008) 'Adaptation, Compensation and Imposition: Paradigms for Purging the Bosnian Judiciary', *International Peacekeeping*, 15, 362–372.

Bertschi, C. C. (1994) 'Lustration and the Transition to Democracy: The Cases of Poland and Bulgaria', *East European Quarterly*, 28, 435–452.

Czapliński, W. A. (2001), 'Harmonisation of Laws in the European Community and Approximation of Polish Legislation to Community Law', 25. *Polish Yearbook of International Law*, 45–54.

Chavdarova, T. (2007) 'Business Relations as Trusting Relations: The Case of Bulgarian Small Business', in Klaus Roth (ed.), *Soziale Netzwerke und soziales*

*Vertrauen in den Transformationsländern. Social Networks and Social Trust in the Transformation Countries* (Vienna/Zürich/Berlin: LIT Verlag), 277–302.

Ciobanu, C. (2007) 'Reformist Minister under Fire in Romania', *Inter Press Service*, March 15, 2007, http://ipsnews.net/news.asp?idnews=36933, accessed 15 November 2010.

DiFranceisco, W. and Gitelman, Z. (1984) 'Soviet Political Culture and "Covert Participation" in Policy Implementation', *American Political Science Review*, 78, 603–621.

Earthtimes.org (2009) 'High Representative and Serbs Clash again in Bosnia', *Earth Times*, Saturday 20 June 2009, http://www.earthtimes.org/articles/news/274131,high-representative-and-serbs-clash-again-in-bosnia.html, accessed 15 November 2010.

Grødeland, Å. B. (2006) 'Informality, Corruption and Public Procurement in the Czech Republic, Slovenia, Bulgaria and Romania', *KICES (Koszalin Institute of Comparative European Studies) Working Papers*, No. 6, 2006, 25–36.

Grødeland, Å. B. (2007) ' "Red Mobs", "Yuppies" and "Lamb Heads": Informal Networks and Politics in the Czech Republic, Slovenia, Bulgaria and Romania', *Europe–Asia Studies*, 59, 217–252.

Grødeland, Å. B. (2009) 'Culture, Corruption and the Orange Revolution', in Besters-Dilger, J. (ed.), *Ukraine on Its Way to Europe? Interim Results of the Orange Revolution* (Frankfurt am Main: Peter Lang), 79–102.

Grødeland, Å. B. (2010a) 'Political Lobbying in Post-Communist Europe', Unpublished manuscript available from the author upon request.

Grødeland, Å. B. (2010b) 'Informal Relations in Public Procurement', in Yasin, E. G. (ed.), *Sbornik dokladov "X Mezhdunarodnaia nauchnaia konferentsia po problemam razvitia ekonomiki i obshchestva"*. Volume 1 (Moskva: Izd.dom. Gos.universiteta – Vyshchei shkoly ekonomiki), 460–473.

Grødeland, Å. B. (2010c). 'Informal Practice in the Judiciary: A Comparison of East Central Europe, South East Europe and the Western Balkans', Paper presented at the VIII ICCEES (International Council for Central and East European Studies) World Congress, Stockholm, July 2010, Panel XII.15: Corruption and Law in Post-Communist Europe.

Grødeland, Å. B. (2010d) 'Elite Perceptions of Anti-Corruption Efforts in Ukraine', *Global Crime*, 11 (Special Issue: Anti-Corruption for Eastern Europe, edited by Diana Schmidt-Pfister and Holger Moroff), 237–260.

Grødeland, Å. B. and Aasland, A. (2007) *Informality and Informal Practices in East Central and South East Europe*, CERC (Contemporary Europe Research Centre, University of Melbourne) Working Papers Series, No. 3/2007.

Karklins, R. (2002) 'Typology of Post-Communist Corruption', *Problems of Post-Communism*, 49, July/August, 22–32, http://www.colbud.hu/honesty-trust/karklins/pub02.pdf, accessed 15 November 2010.

Karklins, R. (2005) *The System Made Me Do It. Corruption in Post-Communist Societies* (Armonk, NY: M.E.Sharpe).

Kornai, J. and Rose-Ackerman, S. (eds) (2004a) *Building a Trustworthy State in Post-Socialist Transition* (Basingstoke: Palgrave Macmillan).

Kornai, J. and Rose-Ackerman, S. (2004b) (eds) *Trust in Post-Socialist Transition* (Basingstoke: Palgrave Macmillan).

Kühn Z. (2006) 'Development of Comparative Law in Eastern Europe', in Zimmerman R. and Reimann M. (eds), *The Oxford Handbook of Comparative Law* (Oxford: Oxford University Press), 215–236.

Ledeneva, A. (1998) *Russia's Economy of Favors: Blat, Networking, and Informal Exchange* (Cambridge and New York: Cambridge University Press).

Markova, I. (ed.) (2004) *Trust as a Pre-Condition to Communication, Social Thinking and Social Practices during Democratic Transition in Post-Communist Europe* (Oxford: Oxford University Press/Proceedings of the British Academy, vol. 123).

Miller, W. L., Grødeland, Å. B. and Koshechkina. T. Y. (2001) *A Culture of Corruption? Coping with Government in Postcommunist Europe* (Budapest: Central European University Press).

Mishler, W. and Rose, R. (1997) 'Trust, Distrust, and Scepticism: Popular Evaluations of Civil and Political Institutions in Post-Communist Societies' *Journal of Politics*, 59, 418–451.

SETimes.com (2010a) 'Branko Crvenkovski', http://www.setimes.com/cocoon/setimes/xhtml/en_GB/infoBios/setimes/resource_centre/bio-archive/crvenkovski_branko, accessed 15 November 2010.

SETimes.com (2010b) 'Vlado Buckovski', http://www.setimes.com/cocoon/setimes/xhtml/en_GB/infoBios/setimes/resource_centre/bio-archive/buckovski_vlado, accessed 15 November 2010.

Szewczyk, B. M. J. (2010) 'The EU in Bosnia and Herzegovina: Powers, Decisions and Legitimacy', Brussels: European Union Institute for Security Studies, Occasional Paper, 83, March 2010, http://www.iss.europa.eu/uploads/media/OccasionalPaper83.pdf, accessed 15 November 2010.

Winnifrith, T. J. (2010) 'The Vlachs of Macedonia', http://www.farsarotul.org/nl20_1.htm, accessed 15 November 2010.

Zoran Djindjic Fund (2010) 'Biography of Zoran Djindjic', http://www.fond-djindjic.org/   en/index.php?option=com_content&task=blogcategory&id=18&Itemid=32, accessed 15 November 2010.

# 6
# Legal Certainty and the Rule of Law in South East Europe

*Alexander Patsch*

## Introduction

In international investor studies on whether or not to choose the region of South East Europe (SEE) as a business location, the concepts of *legal certainty* and of *rule of law* constantly figure prominently. Which of the two concepts is used mainly depends on whether the authors come from the Anglo-Saxon (rule of law) or Central European (legal certainty) legal system. A rigid classification is not possible, however, and the concepts are also increasingly intermingled.

This chapter has four objectives: (1) to show very briefly what lawyers mean or should mean when they speak of legal certainty or the rule of law; (2) to assess to what extent the existence or non-existence of legal certainty/the rule of law is quantifiable in a given country; (3) to show what concepts of quantification exist and which ones apply particularly to South East Europe; and (4) to outline the progress already achieved by countries in the South East Europe region on the way to greater legal certainty and rule of law.

## The concepts of legal certainty and rule of law

### Rule of law

The phrase 'rule of law' describes the general principle that all citizens are equally subject to the law – regardless of whether they are rulers or 'ordinary citizens' – and that everyone has the same and equal right to be protected by law (Pincione, 2009). Where common law prevails, the concept of rule of law is often built on Dicey's (1915) famous definition, which is classically paraphrased as follows: (a) government is not allowed to act against its citizens arbitrarily or with discretionary power, but only in accordance with, and authorized by, the law; (b) everyone, regardless of rank, origin or descent is subject to the ordinary law and to the jurisdiction of ordinary courts; and (c) constitutional rights are determined as a result of court decisions rather than being the result of legislation derived from abstract principles.

Raz (1979 (pp. 214–218)) has specified the requirements or general principles of the rule of law as follows:

'(1)  All laws should be prospective, open and clear. [...]
(2)  Laws should be relatively stable. [...]
(3)  The making of particular laws (particular legal orders) should be guided by open, stable, clear and general rules. [...]
(4)  The independence of the judiciary must be guaranteed. [...]
(5)  The principles of natural justice must be guaranteed. [...]
(6)  The courts should have review powers over the implementation of other principles. [...]
(7)  The courts should be easily accessible. [...]
(8)  The discretion of crime-preventing agencies should not be allowed to perver t the law'.

### Legal certainty

While the origin of the concept of the rule of law lies in the Anglo-Saxon legal system (Alder, 2002), German law, in particular, has developed the criteria for forming the concept of legal certainty. Even though law and certainty have also always been naturally associated with each other in the English, French and Italian legal systems, the specific link between both concepts in *legal certainty, securité juridique* or *certezza del diritto* nevertheless seems to have been influenced by the German term *Rechtssicherheit* ('certainty of the law').

Essential structural elements of German jurisprudential research in connection with the concept of legal certainty are the *reliability, predictability* and *recognizability* of law (Arnauld, 2006). According to Scholz (1955), legal certainty is the possibility of having 'guaranteed confidence in the existence of law and in its impartial and just operation' (p. 3).

In contemporary international legal theory research, the German concept has been widely accepted. Above all, European Community legislation is playing a decisive role in the practical – and also judicial – implementation of such acceptance at a supranational level. In the case of jurisdiction of the European Court of Justice, legal certainty is particularly associated with the following principles, which Arnauld sees as a reflection of his three structural elements of reliability, predictability and recognizability: (1) the obligation to publish legal acts; (2) the requirement of definiteness and clarity; (3) the adoption of court rulings; (4) the finality of rulings; (5) the limitation of retroactivity; (6) the self-binding rules of community institutions; and (7) the protection of confidence (Mertens de Wilmars and Steenbergen, 1985; Arnauld, 2006).

As a result of the acceptance of the legal principle of legal certainty, which is, in accordance with the jurisdiction of the European Court of Justice, an element of the primary law of the European Communities, legal certainty is gaining importance for South East Europe in two ways: (1) the requirement of legal certainty to a certain extent confronts the countries in South East Europe with a joint principle of law of the EU member states; and (2) legal certainty can therefore – also in a conceptual sense – be formulated by the European Commission as a principle that needs to be adhered to and implemented as a prerequisite for joining the EU, and subsequently also to be guaranteed on a permanent basis.

In contrast, the concept of rule of law is not particularly accentuated in the jurisdiction of the European Court of Justice. It is also not established as a specific legal principle, although its importance is undoubted. However, it may be seen as a political principle of the EU (Wennerström, 2007).

## Quantification of legal certainty or rule of law in South East Europe

### Approaches to legal certainty or rule of law quantification

As the aforementioned remarks show, at least in legal theory, there is a well-established opinion of what is to be understood by 'rule of law' and 'legal certainty'. However, whereas it has hitherto been of little concern to legal theory and jurisprudence to quantify the degree of legal certainty in individual legal systems or countries and to compare it with that of other states, such a need has increasingly been expressed by politicians, international organizations or NGOs in the past few years. Three starting points for quantification can be discerned:

(i) *An approach based on fundamental rights*: the aspect of ensuring fundamental rights by the state is a priority above all for NGOs and institutions such as the European Court of Human Rights. Quantifying the progress made by individual states is intended to expose and measure failures and to add extra weight to demands to make improvements.

(ii) *Commercial law quantification*: institutions such as the World Bank, the European Bank for Reconstruction and Development or a few think tanks are exploring the extent to which individual states are making efforts to create sound government.

(iii) *Progress in transition*: this involves the concept of quantifying progress in transition, that is, of developing towards democratic structures and a market economy. Here we can particularly refer to already existing concepts of theories of transition in the field of political science (see for example Von Beyme, 1994).

Quantification of progress and the description of change processes in the countries of South East Europe have been of particular significance in the struggle for rule of law and legal certainty for the EU. Particularly in connection with the efforts of countries in South East Europe to join the EU (which have already succeeded for Romania and Bulgaria), issues related to legal certainty and rule of law have been transformed from theoretical concepts into highly charged actual problems. Quantification was a means to objectify reservations that South East European countries were not – or not completely – meeting the EU's standards for the rule of law. The method employed by the European Commission in the process includes all three approaches discussed above.

Selected attempts to quantify the progress made by particular countries in the struggle for rule of law and legal certainty are presented in the following section.

### Quantification efforts by the World Bank and the IMF

International organizations like the World Bank and the International Monetary Fund (IMF) have developed sophisticated documentation on the progress towards political and economical stability for almost all the countries in the world, including all SEE countries. Both organizations publish country reports and up-to-date surveys for all SEE countries on a regular basis.[1] In addition to this basic and rather neutral information, the World Bank publishes the *Doing Business* ranking, which quantifies selected practical areas of commercial law, for instance the estimated average time (in days) required for certain typical business procedures. Table 6.1 provides an overview of the SEE countries' performance in the 2010 *Doing Business* ranking.

Table 6.1 *Doing business* ranking of the World Bank – selected issues

| | Starting a business | Dealing with construction permits | Registering property | Protecting investors | Trading across borders | Enforcing contracts | Closing a business |
|---|---|---|---|---|---|---|---|
| Albania | 45 | 170 | 72 | 15 | 75 | 89 | 183 |
| Bosnia and Herzegovina | 160 | 139 | 103 | 93 | 71 | 124 | 73 |
| Bulgaria | 43 | 119 | 62 | 44 | 108 | 87 | 83 |
| Croatia | 56 | 132 | 110 | 132 | 98 | 47 | 89 |
| Hungary | 35 | 86 | 41 | 120 | 73 | 22 | 62 |
| Kosovo | 163 | 173 | 65 | 173 | 130 | 155 | 31 |
| Macedonia, FYR | 5 | 136 | 69 | 20 | 66 | 65 | 116 |
| Moldova | 94 | 159 | 18 | 109 | 141 | 20 | 92 |
| Montenegro | 51 | 161 | 116 | 28 | 34 | 135 | 47 |
| Romania | 44 | 84 | 92 | 44 | 47 | 54 | 102 |
| Serbia | 83 | 176 | 100 | 74 | 74 | 94 | 86 |
| Slovenia | 28 | 63 | 97 | 20 | 56 | 60 | 38 |

*Notes:* The figures show the ranks of the SEE economies among 183 economies worldwide.
*Source:* World Bank (2010).

## Quantification efforts by the EBRD

The European Bank for Reconstruction and Development (EBRD) was founded in 1991 to support the development of market economies mainly in the former communist countries of Eastern and South East Europe. Since its founding, the EBRD has put substantial efforts into the documentation of the progress of the respective countries on their way to the rule of law. The idea behind such documentation and scientific research subsidized by the EBRD is (a) to ensure that granting credit to improve the justice and administration infrastructure is justified; and (b) to determine what demands for improving certain standards of rule of law can be made of member states before credit is granted. The EBRD has a very practical approach and puts its emphasis on the documentation of the standards of legislation and of the application of business law legislation (both 'law in the books' and 'law in practice'). From a business perspective, the most comprehensive series of such documentation published by the EBRD is that of the so-called 'country law assessments'. Country law assessments evaluate the process of individual countries in bringing their commercial law to internationally acceptable levels. For this purpose, international standards are used as a benchmark. Local lawyers working in private practice are surveyed as part of these assessments, in order to determine how laws work in practice (EBRD, 2010).

In addition to, and as a summary of, the individual country law assessments, the EBRD publishes its 'Transition Report' on a regular basis. This report contains comprehensive charts comparing the performance of commercial and financial laws as well as the stage of transition of the countries in the SEE region.

## EU monitoring

During the accession process for the candidate countries of the 2007 round of EU enlargement, considerable deficiencies were located in the areas of judicial reform and the fight against corruption in Romania and Bulgaria. As there were still doubts about the readiness of the two countries regarding these two issues shortly before the accession date, a special mechanism for cooperation and the verification of progress (CVM)[2] was introduced – also in order to avoid the use of Article 39 of the Accession Treaty, which would have allowed the postponement of accession by one year (Primatarova, 2010). As part of this mechanism, the European Commission examines the progress made by both countries in the areas of judicial reform and the fight against corruption on an annual basis and publishes appropriate reports.[3] In 2010 the fourth such report was published, and the methodology employed in the process has won wide recognition in the meantime.

Of similar value are the progress reports on the other SEE countries, which are published with equal regularity by the European Commission. These reports differ only slightly, depending on the status of a particular SEE country vis-à-vis the EU. The progress reports on the candidate countries Croatia and Macedonia[4] are the most detailed and most structured. In these cases – as previously in the cases of Romania and Bulgaria – the Commission has particularly examined the progress made in the individual negotiation chapters. For all other states (potential candidates) in the region, a coarser classification into political criteria, economic criteria and the ability to assume the obligations of EU membership is employed. The latter includes, for example, internal market issues, sectoral policies, justice, freedom and security. In the context of the topic of this article, it is interesting to note that the reports, on the one hand, devote a separate section in the political criteria chapter to the subject of the rule of law, while, on the other hand, one must again take a deeper look at the justice, freedom and security chapters to answer the question of how far the rule of law predominates in a given country.

All in all, however, the progress reports are a more than fit method of getting one's bearings with regard to the progress made on legal certainty and rule of law in the SEE countries.

## The Bertelsmann Transformation Index

A specific study on transition countries, with a notable methodology, is published annually by the German Bertelsmann Foundation. The Bertelsmann Transformation Index (BTI) evaluates and assesses a total of 17 categories, which – in the opinion of the authors – measure the progress in the transformation process for a total of 128 countries that may be regarded as transition countries (Bertelsmann Stiftung, 2009a). It is possible at least to make a comparison between the countries documented in the study. The three areas of (1) political transformation, (2) economic transformation and (3) management performance are examined. The method is based on standardized questions being answered by an external expert – that is, an expert from outside the country under examination. These answers are compared with the answers that a second expert – this time from the country in question – gives to the same questions. One question concerning the rule of law/legal certainty is asked within the framework of political transformation. Annual

*Table 6.2* Compilation of the results of the BTI country reports – rule of law

| Country | Separation of powers | Independent judiciary | Prosecution of office abuse | Civil rights | Total |
|---|---|---|---|---|---|
| Albania | 7 | 5 | 5 | 8 | 6.3 |
| Bosnia and Herzegovina | 8 | 6 | 6 | 7 | 6.8 |
| Bulgaria | 9 | 8 | 7 | 9 | 8.3 |
| Croatia | 9 | 7 | 7 | 8 | 7.8 |
| Hungary | 10 | 9 | 8 | 9 | 9.0 |
| Kosovo | 6 | 5 | 5 | 6 | 5.5 |
| Macedonia, FYR | 8 | 7 | 6 | 8 | 7.3 |
| Moldova | 5 | 6 | 6 | 6 | 5.8 |
| Montenegro | 7 | 6 | 5 | 8 | 6.5 |
| Romania | 9 | 8 | 7 | 9 | 8.3 |
| Serbia | 8 | 6 | 6 | 7 | 6.8 |
| Slovenia | 10 | 10 | 9 | 10 | 9.8 |

*Source*: Bertelsmann Stiftung (2010).

country reports are published in which the quality of progress regarding the question of the rule of law is also assessed. On the basis of the individual reports, the Bertelsmann Institute publishes annually an updated quantification of the progress regarding the rule of law for each country.

Table 6.2 provides a comparative overview of the results from the BTI country reports for the SEE region for 2010.

## Status of individual countries

As a result of evaluating the aforementioned attempts to quantify the rule of law or legal certainty respectively for individual countries, we summarize the results for each SEE country in the following sections.

The author abides by his opinion, which has already been presented in Patsch (2005), that legal certainty cannot only be limited to considering the enforceability of the law before state courts, but must always refer to all three levels of state authority – that is, to legislature, execution and justice. The prerequisite for legal certainty and rule of law is always that the state as such is firmly established, to the extent that it has a stable state authority and a stable territory. Whereas in many transition countries such issues are not even raised, they are essential in the case of some countries in South East Europe such as Bosnia and Herzegovina, as there are numerous direct effects on issues concerning law enforcement before courts and administrative authorities if the authority of the courts and authorities itself is questioned.

Critically, it should be noted here that the authors of the various publications that were examined shy away from addressing certain – sociologically and historically undisputed – regional problems, such as the still existing system of patronage (Kaser, 2005) and the often critical and uncooperative attitude of the citizens towards the state and its authorities. In the case of globally active organizations such as the World Bank, or of globally applied studies such as that of the Bertelsmann Institute, this is not surprising, as there are probably numerous regions in the world where such phenomena are even more apparent. There is, however, a specifically South East European characteristic of patronage and scepticism towards the state, which clearly has one of its origins in the historical context of the centuries-long heteronomy from the Ottoman Empire, on the one hand, and from the Habsburg monarchy, on the other hand (Patsch, 2005). As the example of Greece proves best of all, it is much too simplistic to attribute the patronage and scepticism towards the state simply to the decades of communist rule. One must admit that there are also complex connections, which cannot really be dealt with in analyses based, primarily and methodically, on questionnaires.

## The current status of European Union member states

### The situation in Slovenia

Slovenia has been a member of the EU since 2004 and a member of the European Monetary Union since 2007. In contrast to Bulgaria and Romania, no reservations leading to the special 'observation' of the country after accession were voiced with regard to its joining the EU, since the implementation of the principles of the rule of law in the country has been and continues to be beyond dispute.

Paradoxically, it is precisely Slovenia that has a hitherto unresolved issue on the question of statehood, in connection with demarcating the border with Croatia in the Bay of Piran. In this case, however, as a result of massive pressure applied by the EU, an agreement was finally set in motion, which was confirmed – even if only just – in a referendum held in Slovenia that paved the way for a decision made by an arbitration commission.

The last few years have been marked by numerous disputes between the president and the government (or parliamentary majority), which raises questions about how consistently the separation of public powers is being implemented. The independence of the judiciary, however, is evident, and significant progress has been made lately regarding the duration of court proceedings.

## The situation in Bulgaria

Bulgaria has been a member of the EU since 2007, but has – just like its neighbour Romania – been kept under close observation on account of apparent deficiencies in implementing European standards in the field of judicial reform and in the fight against corruption with regard to their further implementation under the cooperation and verification mechanism. Like Romania, prior to accession Bulgaria complied with its obligations to implement the *acquis communautaire* by way of extensive amendments and codification of legislation, to such an extent that the Commission, despite evident defects in the structure and in the implementation of the new laws, could not fail to recommend accession. Already at that stage, the inefficiency of the judicial system and the phenomenon of corruption at all levels of administration were mentioned as weak points. These two problem areas are also at the heart of the European Commission's current criticism.

Above all, however, Bulgaria has incurred the Commission's displeasure with its lack of success in the fight against high-level corruption and organized crime. Several spectacular cases of misusing EU subsidies, which found their way into the pockets of senior officials, have led to a temporary freezing of subsidies for Bulgaria. To address the concerns of the EU, Bulgaria's parliament adopted a new Law on the Conflict of Interests on 16 October 2008, which aims to prevent fraud, including incidents related to EU funds, by requiring that all public administration officials declare themselves to be free from influence peddling.

If we compare the structural progress of particular SEE countries with regard to implementing the rule of law, we must bear in mind that the European Commission's harsh criticism is measured by a postulated European benchmark that has not yet been applied to other South East European states.

## The situation in Romania

Almost everything stated in the case of Bulgaria also applies to Romania: great efforts and success can be noted in implementing the *acquis communautaire* prior to the EU accession, which was granted 'under conditions', due to the weaknesses of the judicial system and the obvious problem of corruption, with continuing ramifications in those areas.

In addition, the conflict between parliament and the government on the one hand, and the country's president on the other hand, has been constantly deteriorating in a worrying manner, with essential aspects of the separation of powers being crushed in the process.

The progress report of the European Commission (2010b) noted that Romania has achieved only limited progress in judicial process efficiency improvements – slow judicial proceedings and imbalances in the workload among courts and prosecution offices were pointed out specifically. In addition, a lack of consistency in jurisprudence was determined. Although some initial steps towards a structural reorganization of courts and prosecutors' offices, and towards redistributing the workload, have been taken by the leadership of the judiciary, these measures are too limited in scope to produce a significant impact. In order to improve the coherence of judicial decisions, the report recommends that Romania should pursue a reform of the High Court of Cassation and Justice and systematically publish the motivations for all court judgements. Suggestions for necessary improvements voiced in the progress report include a reform of the disciplinary system and improvements in the accountability of the judiciary (European Commission, 2010b).

## The current status of non-members of the European Union

### The situation in Croatia

Croatia is also under the scrutiny of the EU due to its candidate status. Both the Commission's comprehensive 'screening' in 2006 and the progress reports, which were subsequently published (the last one dating from 2008), contain findings on the status and development of the rule of law in Croatia.

The Bertelsmann Stiftung (2009c) reports that, while the division between the legislative, executive and judicial branches is basically functioning, the judiciary cannot be viewed as fully independent from political influence. As an example, court presidents (with exceptions only for the Supreme Court and the Constitutional Court) could be appointed as well as dismissed by the minister of justice. Furthermore, 'the State Judicial Council has been criticized for being a politicized and insufficiently competent body and responsible for the "lustration" of judges in 1992, when a number of politically unsuitable judges were replaced by politically suitable ones, who have been blamed for the courts' inadequacy and inefficiency' (Bertelsmann Stiftung, 2009c, p. 8).

The European Commission's (2010a) progress report for Croatia acknowledges that there are continuous efforts to reform the judiciary, the impacts of which, however, still have to face the test of practice. Considerable challenges are still seen in the areas of (a) judicial independence; (b) transparent selection of both judges and prosecutors; and (c) efficiency in the judicial system, especially regarding the length of court proceedings and the enforcement of decisions (European Commission, 2010a). As in the case of Serbia, the hostilities of the 1990s are still showing repercussions today, in the sense that there are still mafia-like structures existing in the country, which have their origins in the war and which are undermining the credibility of the judicial and political systems by means of corruption, and even by physical attacks on state and judicial representatives.

### The situation in Bosnia and Herzegovina

The Bertelsmann Stiftung's (2009b) transformation report on Bosnia and Herzegovina points out that there is no constitutional monopoly over the use of force at country level, as lower levels of government share competences in this area, which go together with overlapping responsibilities and overlapping jurisdictions. There is no clear hierarchy of functions and division of competences between the several layers of government.

Other weaknesses pointed out in the report are inadequate public administration structures, a weak executive function, complex parliamentary decision-making processes with multiple veto possibilities – even for entities at state level – and the ongoing necessity of international intervention, even in day-to-day matters (Bertelsmann Stiftung, 2009b).

The judicial system often ends at the borders of the ethnic entities, or even cantons, and it is not foreseeable at what point in time the country will have a Supreme Court at national level, the decisions of which can be implemented in all parts of the country without exception. It is also proving difficult to combat corruption efficiently, particularly as every accusation made against a politician or senior official of an ethnic group leads to a reaction of solidarity and wholesale rejection.

### The situation in Montenegro

Although some progress in the area of judicial reform – also at a constitutional level – can be noted, trust of the population of Montenegro in its judiciary is still low. Factors that contribute to this are (a) the extremely long duration of court proceedings, combined with a large backlog of court cases; and (b) public perception that politicians still have considerable influence on the judiciary (Bertelsmann Stiftung, 2009e).

Another problem still evident in Montenegro is corruption in administration at the local level. This problem was noted especially in coastal regions, where corruption is seen 'as a result of booming development, privatization and public procurement' (Bertelsmann Stiftung, 2009e, p. 9).

### The situation in Serbia

For Serbia, statehood is a basic issue and the matter of legal and actual control over the entire territory remains unresolved. However, it seems highly probable that, after Kosovo's factual independence, and the recognition of its legal autonomy by Serbia sooner or later, corresponding guarantees of security for predominantly Serbian regions will play an essential role in the process. It is obvious to every foreign investor that the Serbian authorities are no longer points of contact for dealing with legal issues in Kosovo.

Serbia, like Croatia, has been trying to guarantee an independent and efficient judicial system in recent years by implementing several legislative measures. Independent observers are voicing criticism that the existing complicated process of appointing judges allows the parliamentary majority to exert too much influence on the appointment process. The government is also attempting to subject judges appointed in the Milošević era to a verification procedure, which naturally opens up an area of tension with regard to the independence of the judicial system.

Parallels with Croatia can also be discerned in the fight against corruption and against the criminal mafia-like structures that were formed as a direct or indirect result of the wars in Croatia and Bosnia or which benefited from them. As in Croatia, links obviously exist right into the highest political spheres, to the extent that decisions made by administrative authorities and courts could also be subject to political influence. Acts of violence committed against politicians and officials who try to combat this system naturally weaken the progress made.

This is favoured not least by the fact that a considerable share of the economy is still in the hands of state-owned companies, where influence through informal structures is considerable. Also, upcoming privatization processes as well as those already implemented naturally create incentives to wield political influence.

In recent years, foreign investors repeatedly have had to resort to international legal mechanisms to protect their investments in Serbia in cases where promises connected with selling public enterprises to foreign investors have not been respected.

### The situation in Albania

Of all the countries in the region, Albania undoubtedly has the longest way to go towards becoming a functioning state under the rule of law. Atypically for what is ethnically a largely homogeneous state, Albania is unable or unwilling to assert its power monopoly on all its territory.

The relevant political powers hardly seem to identify with the principle of separation of public powers. With each change of government there are regular attempts to replace important posts in the judicial system, particularly with regard to the prosecuting authorities. Brutish political and legislative attempts to dismiss judges with a problematic past, dating back to the time of the communist dictatorship, and to do so relatively easily and without respecting their constitutional rights are particularly disputed and also criticized by the outside world.

The duration of court and administrative proceedings is considerable and the population has even less confidence in the judicial and administrative system than those in other countries of the region. In addition, there are no noteworthy examples of proceedings against corrupt officials, judges or politicians. Although there is a legal basis, the political will has so far been lacking.

### The situation in Macedonia

Like Croatia, the Former Yugoslav Republic of Macedonia has been granted the official status of a candidate country by the EU, a fact that therefore documents the progress made by the country with regard to the Copenhagen criteria.

The EU and other observers basically confirm that the ethnic disputes between the Macedonian majority and the Albanian minority seem to have been overcome to such an extent that the government can, in principle, assert its monopoly on power throughout the country.

In contrast to the situation in several neighbouring states, the court system suffers less from political pressure than from a chronic lack of money and resultant shortages of personnel and resources, which lead to a considerable backlog of decisions to be taken. The Macedonian judicial system is also – again, in comparison with neighbouring states – proceeding quite briskly against corruption in politics and administration. Several senior public officials, among them the former governor of the National Bank and the former director of the Public Revenue Office, have been convicted in court trials (Bertelsmann Stiftung, 2009d).

## Conclusion

Although legal theory distinguishes clearly between the concepts of rule of law and of legal certainty, both concepts are increasingly mixed up in practice and are employed rather arbitrarily. International investors investing in South East Europe are likely to be especially interested in legal certainty – in the sense of predictability in the decisions taken by courts and authorities as well as by the legislator in a particular local legal system. International investors, in particular, naturally place trust in appraisals of the situation *from the outside* – especially through independent international institutions – rather than in tendentiously over-optimistic analyses by local governments or local research facilities. International reports and quantifications are particularly useful if they examine all the countries in the region and if they are also compiled as regularly as possible – usually on an annual basis. These criteria are met especially by publications produced by the World Bank (*Doing Business* ranking), the EBRD (*EBRD Transition Report*), the European Commission (progress reports and reports on progress under the Cooperation and Verification Mechanism) and private think tanks such as the Bertelsmann Institute (BTI country reports). Interestingly, however, all these publications use the umbrella term 'rule of law' rather than 'legal certainty' to summarize the specific aspects they are examining, which nevertheless does not affect the final result.

A glance at the current situation in individual states of South East Europe based on these publications reveals many common problems, but also some which are very clearly specific to particular countries. While countries such as Bosnia and Herzegovina are still struggling to achieve a fundamental consolidation of sovereignty, in other countries (such as Albania) this only applies to some regions. What all these countries have in common is the struggle against the inefficiency of the judicial system and against ubiquitous corruption. In Croatia and Serbia in particular, the credibility of the judicial system and of the executive power is at stake in the fight against mafia-like parallel structures that originated in wartime.

The role of the EU cannot be overemphasized. Despite the considerable formal implementation of the *acquis communautaire* in

Romania and Bulgaria, there has been continuing pressure to monitor these countries on a permanent basis, above all with regard to judicial reform and to fighting corruption. The EU is using considerable resources to describe this progress (or the lack of it) and to evaluate it objectively. In the same way, annual progress reports are drawn up for all other SEE countries, thereby very clearly addressing any misadministration. However, we should take critical note – with regard to the documents of the European Commission and the other attempts at quantification described – of the fact that people shy away from addressing negative regional phenomena, such as the continuing dominant patronage of and the fundamentally critical attitude towards state power. Both have devastating effects (a) on the internalization of the concept of the rule of law and (b) on the citizens of the countries in South East Europe and their desire for legal certainty.

## Notes

1. See http://www.worldbank.org/countries and http://www.imf.org/external/country/index.htm, both websites accessed 15 November 2010.
2. Commission Decision 2006/928/EC of 13 December 2006 establishing a mechanism for cooperation and verification of progress in Romania to address specific benchmarks in the areas of judicial reform and the fight against corruption (OJ L 354, 14.12.2006, p. 56).
3. See http://ec.europa.eu/dgs/secretariat_general/cvm/progress_reports_en.htm.
4. See http://ec.europa.eu/enlargement/press_corner/key-documents/reports_oct_2009_en.htm, accessed 15 November 2010.

## References

Alder, J. (2002) *General Principles of Constitutional and Administrative Law* (Basingstoke and New York: Palgrave Macmillan).

Arnauld, A. (2006) *Rechtssicherheit* (Tübingen: Mohr Siebeck).

Bertelsmann Stiftung (ed.) (2009a) *Transformation Index 2010: Politische Gestaltung im Internationalen Vergleich* (Gütersloh: Bertelsmann Stiftung).

Bertelsmann Stiftung (ed.) (2009b) *BTI 2010 – Bosnia and Herzegovina Country Report* (Gütersloh: Bertelsmann Stiftung).

Bertelsmann Stiftung (ed.) (2009c) *BTI 2010 – Croatia Country Report* (Gütersloh: Bertelsmann Stiftung).

Bertelsmann Stiftung (ed.) (2009d) *BTI 2010 – Macedonia Country Report* (Gütersloh: Bertelsmann Stiftung).

Bertelsmann Stiftung (ed.) (2009e) *BTI 2010 – Montenegro Country Report* (Gütersloh: Bertelsmann Stiftung).

Bertelsmann Stiftung (2010) *Bertelsmann Transformation Index Ranking*, http://www.bertelsmann-transformation-index.de/en/bti/ranking/, accessed 15 November 2010.

Dicey, A. V. (1915) *Introduction to the Study of the Law of the Constitution*, 8th edn (London: Macmillan).

EBRD (2010) *European Bank for Reconstruction and Development Country Law Assessments*, http://www.ebrd.com/pages/sector/legal/cla.shtml, accessed 4 October 2010.

European Commission (2010a) *Croatia 2010 Progress Report*, http://ec.europa.eu/enlargement/pdf/key_documents/2010/package/hr_rapport_2010_en.pdf, accessed 15 November 2010.

European Commission (2010b) *Press Release on the Report on Progress under the Cooperation and Verification Mechanism in Romania*, http://europa.eu/rapid/pressReleasesAction.do?reference=MEMO/10/347& format=HTML& aged=0& language=EN, accessed 15 November 2010.

Kaser, K. (2005) 'Klientelismus: Positive Potentiale und Risiken eines traditionellen Modells sozialer Beziehungen', in Daxner, M., Jordan, P., Leifer, P., Roth, K. and Vyslonzil, E. (eds), *Bilanz Balkan*, Schriftenreihe des Österreichischen Ost- und Südosteuropa-Instituts (Wien: Verlag für Geschichte und Politik), 54–67.

Mertens de Wilmar, J. and Steenbergen, J. (1985) 'La Notion de sécurité juridique dans la jurisprudence de la cour de Justice des Communautés Européennes', in Vander Elst, R. (ed.), (Brussels: Editions de l'Université de Bruxelles), 449–456.

Patsch, A. (2005) 'Rechtssicherheit in den Balkanländern', in Daxner, M., Jordan, P., Leifer, P., Roth, K. and Vyslonzil, E. (eds), *Bilanz Balkan*, Schriftenreihe des Österreichischen Ost- und Südosteuropa-Instituts (Wien: Verlag für Geschichte und Politik), 14–23.

Pincione, G. (2009) *Rule of Law – Philosophical Perspectives*, IVR Encyclopaedia of Jurisprudence, Legal Theory and Philosophy of Law, http://ivr-enc.info/index.php?title= Rule_of_Law_-_Philosophical_Perspectives, accessed 8 October 2010.

Primatarova, A. (2010) 'On High Stakes, Stakeholders and Bulgaria's EU Membership', *EPIN Working Paper 27*, http://aei.pitt.edu/14445/01/EPIN_WP27_Primatorova.pdf, accessed 15 November 2010.

Raz, J. (1979) *The Authority of Law* (Oxford: Oxford University Press).

Scholz, F. (1955) *Die Rechtssicherheit* (Berlin: Walter de Gruyter).

Von Beyme, K. (1994) *Systemwechsel in Osteuropa* (Frankfurt am Main: Suhrkamp).

Wennerström, E. O. (2007) *The Rule of Law and the European Union* (Uppsala: Iustus Förlag).

World Bank (2010) *Doing Business 2011 Report*, http://www.doingbusiness.org, accessed 15 November 2010.

# Part II

# Perspectives on Economic Developments in South East Europe

# 7
# Regional Disparities and Economic Convergence in South East Europe

*Reinhold Kosfeld and Alexander Werner*

## Introduction

The recent history of South East Europe (SEE) is marked by massive changes in the economic situation of the region. Starting with the fall of the Soviet Union, since 1989 there has been a transition process from a communist-influenced economic system with centralized planning to a market economy (Jackson, 1999). In addition there have been military conflicts, resulting in the fall of states accompanied by crucial social, political and economic instability. These conflicts have not yet been resolved and are still the source of potential unrest (Müller and Büchsenschütz, 2009).

In this chapter only the development of the economic situation of SEE is to be analysed. In particular, the development of disparities in the economic situation of SEE regions will be highlighted. Generally speaking, dismantling economic disparities is seen as an important criterion for creating social and political stability. The European Union (EU), to which a few countries in the region already belong, is also pursuing an important political goal in harmonizing the economic and social conditions within its member states (Türck, 2007).

For the period 2001 to 2007 the development of the average gross regional product (GRP) per capita in the SEE regions is taken into consideration. The analysis is carried out using the GRP in original euro values and the GRP in purchasing power parities (PPP), which make it possible to record regional differences in purchasing power. The econometric analysis is twofold. In a first descriptive step the development of traditional methods for measuring economic inequality over time is considered. In the second step the presence of $\beta$ convergence in SEE is analysed by estimating growth equations.

169

## Measuring economic disparities, growth and convergence

The aim of this chapter is to analyse the regional differences in the economic development of the SEE regions. The core question here is whether the economic differences in the SEE regions are becoming stronger or weaker. To answer this question, measures of economic disparity for the years of the period under investigation (2001–07) are compared with each other. Furthermore, growth equations will be estimated in order to investigate whether economic convergence or divergence between the regions can be proved.

To judge the temporal development of economic differences between individual SEE regions, the most important disparity measurements are calculated. For this we will use the GRP per capita in euros and in PPP. In order to gain a first impression, the maximum to minimum ratio (MMR) will be used. The ratio between the GRP per capita of the region with the highest and the region with the lowest GRP per capita provides information about the maximum differences. If the MMR is near 1, the two regions with the extreme values in GRP per capita are similar. The result is that all regions display only small differences with regard to GRP per capita. If the MMR takes large values, it must be considered whether this is caused merely by individual outliers or whether there are really great disparities between all regional units (Shankar and Shah, 2003).

In contrast to the exclusive consideration of the extreme values in the MMR, the deviation of all observation units around the mean is quantified by the unweighted and weighted coefficient of variation. The unweighted coefficient of variation ($CV_u$) is given by the ratio of the standard deviation of the GRP per capita to the mean of the GRP per capita. In contrast to the unweighted coefficient of variation ($CV_u$), the squared deviation in the weighted coefficient of variation ($CV_w$) is multiplied with the shares of the population $q_i = p_i/P$ of the regions. P represents the total population of all regions, $p_i$ the population in region i. Both coefficients of variation take the value zero if all regions have the same GRP per capita. The maximum value occurs if a region incorporates the entire GRP per capita. It is given by $\sqrt{N-1}$ for $CV_u$, with N as the number of regions and $\sqrt{(P - p_{max})/p_{max}}$ for $CV_w$, and with $p_{max}$ as population of the region with the maximum GRP per capita (Shankar and Shah, 2003).

Because the CV reacts sensitively to outliers through the calculation of squared deviations, the relative mean deviation ($R_w$) as an alternative measure is suggested. The $R_w$ reacts less sensitively to outliers, because here, instead of squared deviations, the absolute deviations from the arithmetic mean are considered. The $R_w$ lies between 0 at even distribution and 2 if the entire GRP falls in one region (Shankar and Shah, 2003).

Another frequently used statistic to measure disparities is the Gini index. Here too we differentiate between an unweighted ($G_u$) and a weighted ($G_w$) index. If all regions display the same GRP per capita, both Gini indices take the value 0. If GRP is concentrated completely in one region, the value 1 at $G_u$ and $1 - (p_{max}/P)$ at $G_w$ is achieved (for details see Shankar and Shah, 2003).

Finally the Theil index (T), which takes into account the share of the GRP in a region in the total GRP, is used to record regional disparity distribution of the GRP per capita. With a uniform distribution, the Theil index takes the value 0; its maximum value is calculated by $\log(1/q_{max})$, with $q_{max}$ as population share of the region with the maximum GRP per capita (for details see Shankar and Shah, 2003).

The measures described are calculated for each year of the period under investigation and compared with each other. This descriptive analysis gives early indications as to whether the GRP per capita is converging or whether the disparities are increasing. In addition to these comparative–static measures of disparity across regions, a dynamic analysis of the development of disparities, using regional growth equations, is performed. An overview of the underlying growth theory can be found in Barro and Sala-i-Martin (2004).

The economic growth of regions is measured by the average growth rate of GRP per capita over the survey period. With respect to regional differences, the question of the existence of convergence and divergence is decisive. Convergence appears when regions with a lower GRP in the start period record greater growth rates (Barro and Sala-i-Martin, 2004). The various economic growth theories do not agree on convergence and divergence. The neoclassic Solow–Swan model forecasts convergence, the endogenous growth theory and New Economic Geography provide arguments for both convergence and divergence, while Post-Keynesianism and polarization theory expect divergence (Eckey, 2008). The most important arguments are summarized in Table 7.1.

For an econometric investigation of the convergence process, the concept of $\beta$ convergence is employed. Here we additionally differentiate between absolute and relative $\beta$ convergence.

In the model of absolute $\beta$ convergence, the average growth rate of the GRP per capita of the region in a linear regression model is explained exclusively by the natural logarithm of the GRP per capita in the first year of the period of investigation. Within this model potential

*Table 7.1* Economic growth theory reasons for divergence and convergence

| Theory | Reasons for divergence | Reasons for convergence |
|---|---|---|
| Neoclassic | | Falling marginal yields on capital |
| Post-Keynesianism | Spatially mobile demand and external shocks | |
| Polarization Theory | Dominating centripetal forces | |
| Endogenous Growth Theory | Positive external effects lead to growth and can also trigger divergence. | |
| New Economic Geography (NEG) | Transport costs are the main determining factor for regional development. Depending on their design, transport possibilities lead to convergence or divergence. | |

*Source*: Türck (2007) and Eckey (2008).

exogenous impact factors are represented by residual variables, which are assumed to follow the usual assumptions of the linear regression model (for more details see Le Gallo et al., 2003). If the regression coefficient $\beta_2$ is significantly lower than zero, there is absolute convergence between the regions. The result is that all regions are approaching a common state of equilibrium (Barro and Sala-i-Martin, 2004).

In the case of relative $\beta$ convergence the model is supplemented by p-2 growth-relevant exogenous variables. Through the additional variables a statement about the relative convergence can be made. On the appearance of relative $\beta$ convergence the regions are approaching different states of equilibrium, depending on the levels of the other explanatory variables (Barro and Sala-i-Martin, 2004). Because the levels of the explanatory variables can be very different and also remain stable over time, relative $\beta$ convergence can appear simultaneously with great differences between the regions as a whole (Le Gallo et al., 2003).

Finally, there is a further problem to be considered in the construction of the linear regression models. As we perform a cross-sectional analysis with regional data, whether spatial effects are present must be tested. Because of exchange processes between regions, there is a plausible supposition of reciprocal influences in the growth process. The intensity of the mutual connection increases with spatial proximity. The theoretical foundation for this is provided by the Jacobs- and MAR-externalities. Jacobs-externalities occur when, for example, knowledge spillovers appear because of the spatial proximity of various industries, while MAR-externalities describe this process within an industry (Döring and Schnellenbach, 2006; Türck, 2007).

In order to integrate spatial effects into the regression model, several stages are necessary. In the first step a suitable form has to be selected for representing spatial proximity. Here the usual procedure is followed by creating a standardized neighbourhood matrix W. The elements of the neighbourhood matrix are determined by assigning, in the first step, a 1 to the regions j, which have a common border with region i, or alternatively a 0. This assignment corresponds to the so-called 'rook criterion' (Upton and Fingleton, 1985). In a second step, the elements of the neighbourhood matrix are standardized by being divided by the number of all the neighbours of region i (Türck, 2007). With the help of the neighbourhood matrix W, the regressions of absolute and relative β convergence can be tested for spatial effects. The null hypothesis of missing spatial autocorrelation (that is, spatial randomness) is tested with the help of Moran's I value (for details see Anselin, 1988).

If spatial autocorrelation in the model is established on the basis of the Moran test, three different model extensions are considered. First, in the spatial cross-regressive model, an exogenous variable $X_k$ of surrounding regions can affect growth in the region i. In this case a spatial lag of variable $X_k$, $L \cdot X_k$, is calculated with the neighbourhood matrix and inserted into the regression equation as a further explanatory variable (Le Gallo et al., 2003). To calculate the spatial lag, the lag operator L has to be replaced by the spatial weight matrix W.

Another possibility is that the nature of the dependent variable $y$ (GRP per capita) in the surrounding regions affects growth in region i. In this case the spatial lag of the $y$ variable, $L \cdot Y$, is taken up as another explanatory variable in the model equation. Because of the endogeneity that occurs as a result, this spatial lag model can no longer be estimated consistently with the ordinary least square procedure, so that recourse is made to the maximum likelihood method (Le Gallo et al., 2003).

Finally, it is possible that the residuals of the surrounding regions affect growth in region i. Because the error term of the surrounding regions and region i affect each other, a modification of the least square criterion is necessary, and the maximum likelihood method can be used for the spatial error model (Le Gallo et al., 2003).

In order to be able to choose the most suitable model in the cases of spatial lag and spatial error, four test procedures are used, which will not be explained here in detail (Anselin et al., 1996). Depending on whether the LM(lag) or LM(err) test produces significant results, either the spatial lag model or the spatial error model is used. If both tests are significant, the robust LM(lag) and LM(err) tests are carried out. In these tests the influence of the other components is taken into account and thereby clear differences emerge in the test results. If there is any significance, that model is used in which the test results achieve a higher significance (Türck, 2007).

## Data and regional system

To analyse the economic differences within the SEE region data from the eleven countries–Albania, Bosnia–Herzegovina, Bulgaria, Croatia, Hungary, Macedonia, Moldova, Montenegro, Romania, Serbia and Slovenia – are used as a basis. The EU member states Bulgaria, Hungary, Romania and Slovenia, as well as the EU candidate Croatia, are divided into Nomenclature des unités territoriales statistiques (NUTS)-2 regions in such a way that the observation units comprise six states and twenty-six NUTS-2 regions.[1] The regional subdivision of the six states is to some extent unnecessary, because they correspond in terms of size to the NUTS-2 regions; but to some extent this subdivision cannot be carried out either, because data are not available. In particular, attention has to be drawn to Kosovo, which cannot be considered as an observation unit of its own in the analysis and so has been recorded together with Serbia.

The time dimension of the survey covers the period 2001–07. This period has been selected because, compared with the 1990s, it is marked by more stable conditions. The 1990s, for example, witnessed the Balkan wars and the crisis of the Russian ruble. In addition, the substantially different experiences of countries in accomplishing the transition process from the communist economic system to a market economy have led to major irregularities in economic development (Jackson, 1999). Nevertheless, it must be noted that decisive events have taken place in the time period selected, for example the struggle for independence from Serbia in Montenegro and Kosovo (Müller and Büchsenschütz, 2009).

The most important data sources for the survey are the databases of the EU Statistics Office and of the United Nations Statistics Division – which in turn contain data of other international organizations such as the World Bank. Information on the individual data sets is listed in Appendix A.1.

Table 7.2 gives an overview of the data used in the following analysis. For all the variables, the arithmetic mean, the standard deviation and the maximum and minimum value are specified. In addition, the average of the variables for the EU-27 countries taken as a whole is reported. In the comparison it should be noted that, in the case of SEE regions,

*Table 7.2* Descriptive statistics of the variables in 2001[2]

| Variable | Mean | Standard Deviation | Minimum | Maximum | EU27 Average |
|---|---|---|---|---|---|
| Average growth rate 2001–07 GRP/capita in euros | 0.09580 | 0.03478 | 0.05641 | 0.16264 | 0.01422 |
| Average growth rate 2001–07 GRP/capita in PPP | 0.06208 | 0.02286 | 0.02822 | 0.10280 | 0.01422 |
| GRP/Capita 2001 in euros | 3,573 | 2,916 | 455 | 13,600 | 19,800 |
| GRP/Capita 2001 in PPP | 7,518 | 4,052 | 1,332 | 18,800 | 19,800 |
| GRP/Capita 2007 in euros | 6,619 | 4,489 | 900 | 20,600 | 24,900 |
| GRP/Capita 2007 in PPP | 11,422 | 5,746 | 2,483 | 26,600 | 24,900 |
| Population | 2,105,707 | 1,354,686 | 654,274 | 7,527,952 | 483,797,218 |
| Population density | 133.9 | 220.4 | 44.5 | 1,291.4 | 109.9 |
| Fertility indicator 2000 | 1.38 | 0.22 | 0.98 | 1.88 | 1.45 (2002) |
| Index of economic freedom 2002 | 54.85 | 6.86 | 46.6 | 64.5 | n.a. |
| Number of hotel rooms | 10,698 | 13,458 | 1,344 | 70,770 | n.a. |
| Rate of employees in primary sector (A–B) | 22.65 | 19.61 | 1.85 | 62.62 | 7.53 |

*Source*: Authors' calculations.

the unweighted means are calculated, while for the EU-27 figures the basis is the aggregated variables.

The average annual growth rate of GRP per capita is 9.5 per cent (in euros) or 6.2 per cent (in PPP). However, the rate clearly fluctuates between the regions, the standard deviation being 3.5 per cent (in euros) and 2.3 per cent (in PPP). In addition, the large difference between the minimum and the maximum growth rate shows the substantial heterogeneity of the regions in their economic development. Compared with the EU-27 average it can be seen that SEE altogether is a strong growth region. Growth for the EU-27 states is at an average of 1.4 per cent (both in euros and in PPP), which is clearly still below the minimum values in SEE.

Stronger growth means that SEE is economically catching up on the EU-27 countries, which becomes clear in the figures for GRP per capita in euros and PPP from the beginning of 2001 to the end of 2007. The arithmetic median of the GRP per capita in SEE rose between 2001 and 2007 from 3,573 to 6,619 euros – by 85 per cent. Measured in PPP, the GRP per capita rose from 7,518 to 11,422 – by 52 per cent; whereas the GRP per capita in the EU-27 only increased from 19,800 to 24,900 (in euros and PPP) – by 26 per cent. The figures, however, show the still quite substantial differences between the EU-27 and the SEE region, because the average GRP per capita in SEE is clearly below the average for the EU-27.

To assess the different size of the regions analysed, the population as of 1 January 2001 is specified. Serbia, which cannot be subdivided into regions because of the data situation, is the largest region, with 7.5 million inhabitants. The SEE region comprises 68.1 million inhabitants altogether. In contrast, the population of the EU-27 states in 2001 was 483.8 million. The population density is on average 134 per km². This variable is marked by strong fluctuations between 44.5 and 1,291.4 inhabitants per km². Finally, descriptive data on further variables are specified, and these are taken up in the later analysis of the growth processes. They include the fertility indicator, an index of economic freedom, the number of hotel rooms and the proportion of persons employed in the primary sector. These factors reflect the socio-economic starting position of the regions.

## Empirical analysis

### Graphical analysis of regional disparities

Before a dynamic survey of the regional differences in SEE can be made on the basis of growth equations, a graphical analysis is performed using statistical variables and disparity measures. In this we first consider the geographical distribution of the GRP per capita in 2001 and the average growth rates of the regions.

Figure 7.1 shows the regions of SEE. The map at the top portrays the average growth rate of the GRP per capita in euros in the period 2001–07. The darker the shading, the weaker the growth in the regions concerned, differentiated by quintiles. The map at the bottom shows the logarithmized GRP per capita in 2001, also differentiated by quintiles. The darker the areas, the higher the GRP per capita in the starting period.

Figure 7.2 shows the same conditions for the case where the GRP per capita is measured in PPP. In both diagrams a certain tendency to convergence is detectable. The regions with relatively high GRP per capita in the starting period, such as Slovenia and Croatia, display lower growth rates. On the other hand, regions with a low GRP per capita in the start year 2001, for example in Romania, exhibit particularly strong growth. However, there are also regions that run counter to this convergence behaviour, for example the region of Bucharest (RO32) – which, despite a high starting level of GRP per capita, exhibits strong growth.

To conclude the descriptive analysis of the economic differences in the region of SEE, we turn to the usual disparity measures. All indices of disparity introduced in the methodical part are calculated for GRP per capita, in euros and in PPP. The courses of the resulting curves are shown in Figures 7.3 and 7.4. The falling curves indicate that the disparity diminishes over time and that the regions converge. This tendency is more marked in the measurement of GRP per capita in euros. Various disparity measures hardly point to convergence in the GRP per capita in PPP.

The ratio of maximum to minimum GRP per capita (MMR) in euros increases slightly in the first sample years, but falls altogether from 30 in 2001 to 23 in 2007. For all additional indices, the scale on the left of the diagrams (Figs. 7.3 and 7.4) is used. The relative dispersion around the arithmetic mean declines, because the unweighted coefficient of variation $C_u$ falls from 0.8 to 0.67 and the weighted coefficient of variation $C_w$ falls from 0.85 to 0.7. The relative mean deviation $R_w$ is less sensitive to outliers than the coefficient of variation, because for this measure absolute deviations from the arithmetic mean are determined. It falls from 0.62 to 0.51. The unweighted and the weighted Gini index are almost identical in their values, which fall from 0.403 and 0.388 to 0.369 and 0.363 respectively. Finally, a tendency towards convergence is indicated by the Theil index falling from 0.121 to 0.098.

On the other hand, the indications of a reduction of disparities within the GRP per capita in PPP are not so clear in the analysis of the indices.

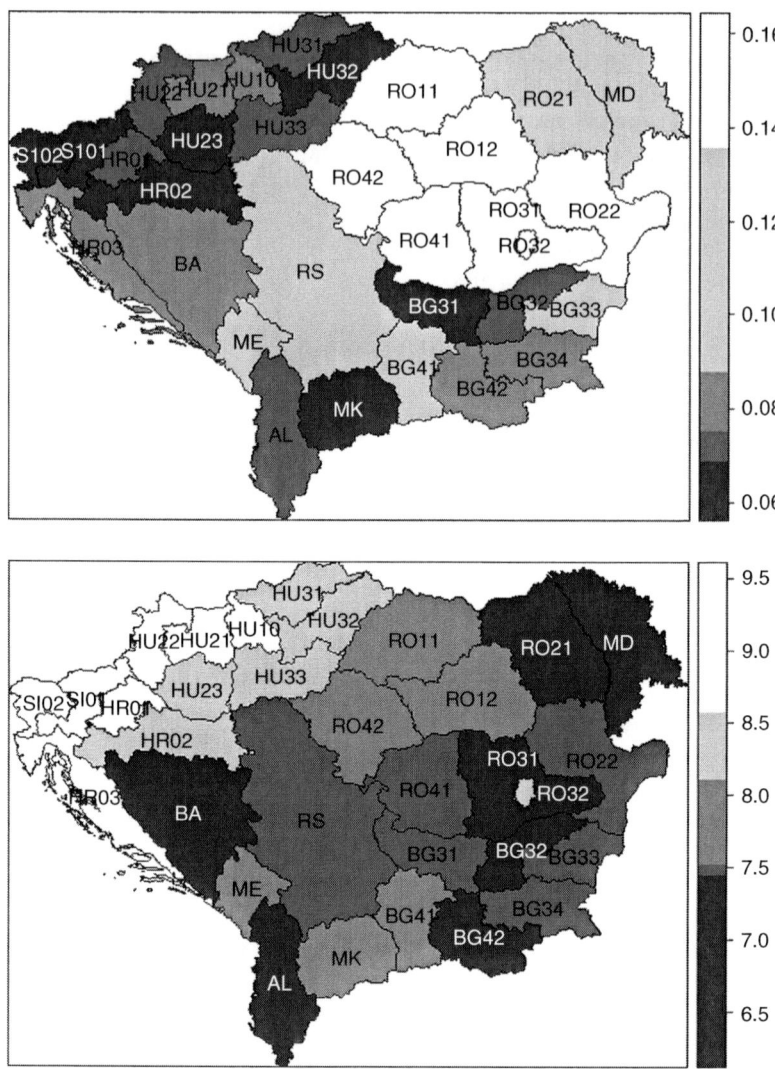

*Figure 7.1* Quintiles of average growth rate of GRP per capita from 2001 to 2007 and of log GRP per capita 2001 in euros

*Source*: Authors' calculations; for data source, see Appendix © EuroGeographics for the administrative boundaries.

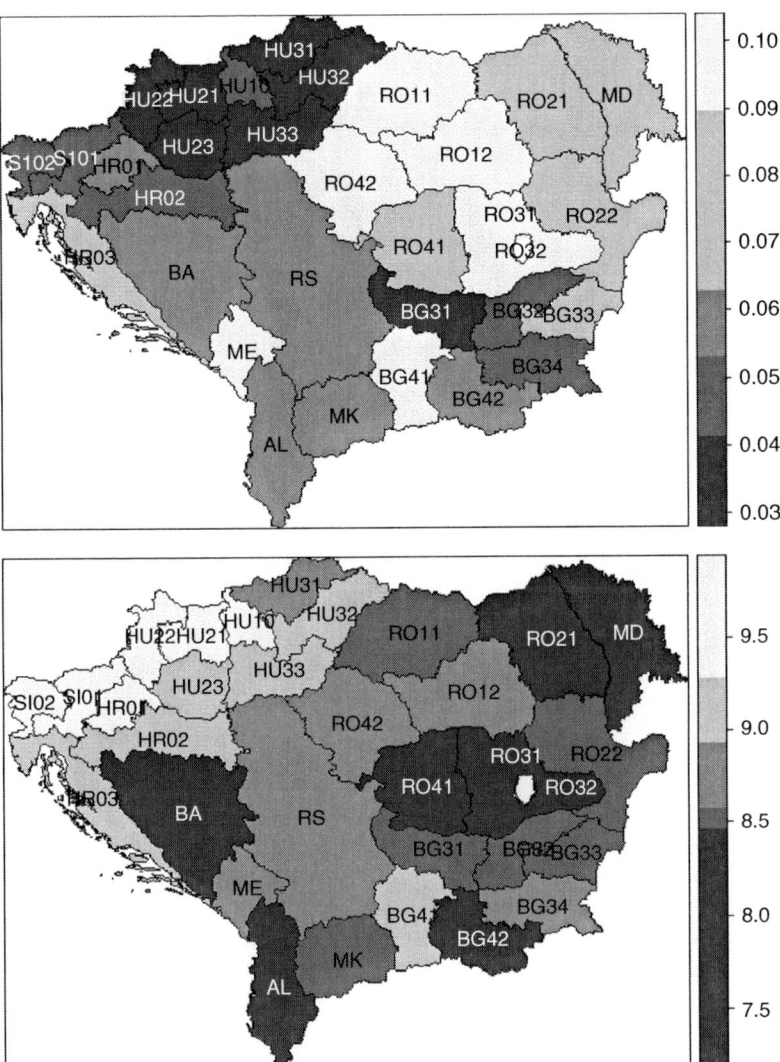

*Figure 7.2*  Quintiles of average growth rate of GRP per capita from 2001 to 2007 and of log GRP per capita 2001 in PPP

*Source*: Authors' calculations; for data source, see Appendix © euro geographics for the administrative boundaries.

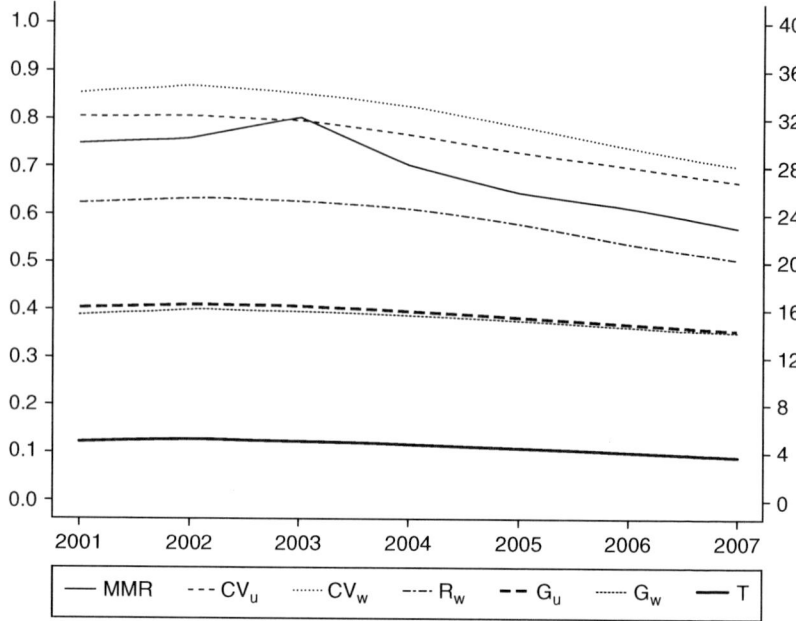

*Figure 7.3*   Disparity indices for GRP per capita from 2001 to 2007 in euros
*Source*: Authors' calculations; for data source, see Appendix.

The ratio of maximum to minimum falls from 14 to 11. The unweighted coefficient of variation falls from 0.53 to 0.5, while the weighted coefficient of variation falls from 0.58 to 0.55. The relative mean deviation falls from 0.43 to 0.4. The unweighted and weighted Gini coefficients in 2001 take the value 0.28; in 2007 they are slightly below with 0.268 and 0.276 respectively. The Theil index decreases from 0.064 to 0.058 during the period under investigation.

### Absolute β convergence

With the aid of indices for economic disparity, it was shown that the disparities within SEE are abating. This indication of convergence is confirmed by the estimation of absolute β convergence. In Table 7.3 the results of the model estimation using the GRP per capita are given both in euros and in PPP.

Absolute β convergence using the GRP per capita both in euros and in PPP can be proved significantly. The convergence is slightly stronger if the GRP per capita is measured in euros. The convergence speed is

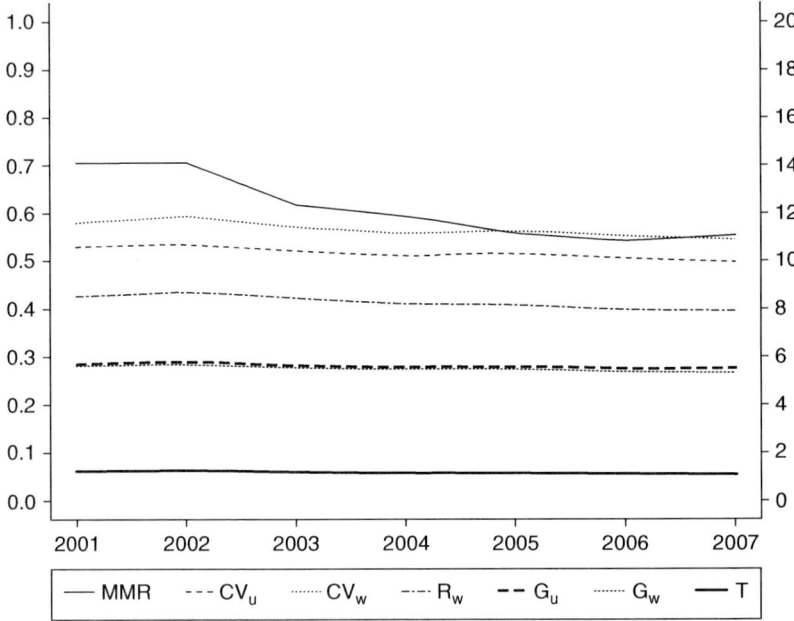

*Figure 7.4* Disparity indices for GRP per capita from 2001 to 2007 in PPP
*Source*: Authors' calculations; for data source, see Appendix A.1.

*Table 7.3* Regression results of the absolute β-convergence model

|  | GRP per capita in euros | GRP per capita in PPP |
| --- | --- | --- |
| const. | 0.2435*** | 0.2091*** |
| log $y_{2001,i}$ | −0.0186** | −0.0167** |
| Adj. R-squared | 0.1195 | 0.1177 |
| F-statistic | 5.206** | 5.135** |
| AIC | −124.28 | −151.08 |

* (**,***): significant at the 0.1 (0.05, 0.01) level.
*Source*: Authors' calculations.

calculated at 0.01997 (1.997 per cent in euros) and at 0.01778 (1.778 per cent in PPP). Thus the convergence rates are very close to 2 per cent, a value that is described from time to time as a 'natural constant' (Abreu et al., 2005). The half-life specifies the number of years after which a region has halved its distance from the state of equilibrium in terms of GRP per capita (Türck, 2007). It is 34.71 (euros) and 38.98 (PPP) years.

Although the regression coefficients are highly significant, the adjusted R-squared value is only at 0.12 in both models. This low explanatory power of the growth equation indicates that the models are underspecified. As an extension of the model, the integration of further explanatory variables and therewith an associated change to the model of conditional β convergence (see next sub-section) is indicated. Alongside this, the following analysis of existence and subsequent integration of spatial effects provides the possibility of estimating a more realistic growth model.

First, the regression results are to be tested for significant spatial effects. The results of the test procedure are reproduced in Table 7.4. In both models there is significantly positive spatial autocorrelation in the residuals. Moran's I value of the euro model is 0.3478, which is significant at the 0.01 level; in the PPP model it is 0.2353, and significant at the 0.05 level. It is therefore necessary to examine which model best integrates the spatial effects. Because in both models the LM(err) and LM(lag) tests produce significant results, a differentiation has to be made between the models using the robust tests. Because the significance level of the robust LM(lag) test is clearly higher than that of the robust LM(err) test, the spatial lag model is chosen. This result is valid for both the euro and the PPP models.

Table 7.5 shows the estimation results for the spatial lag model. In both models, only the autoregressive coefficient ρ is significant. The higher the growth in the regions surrounding region i, the stronger the growth in region i itself. The regression coefficient of the GRP per capita in the start period 2001 now no longer differs significantly from zero, so that there is no indication of either convergence or divergence. As a means of comparing the model with and the model without spatial effects, the Akaike information criterion (AIC) is given in Tables 7.3

*Table 7.4*  Spatial regression diagnostics of the absolute β-convergence model

|  | GRP per capita in euros | GRP per capita in PPP |
| --- | --- | --- |
| Moran's I | 0.3478*** | 0.2353** |
| LM(err) | 7.828*** | 3.5823* |
| LM(lag) | 11.3599*** | 6.9381*** |
| Robust LM(err) | 3.7771* | 5.6172** |
| Robust LM(lag) | 7.309*** | 8.973*** |

*(**,*** ): significant at the 0.1 (0.05, 0.01) level.
*Source*: Authors' calculations.

*Table 7.5* Regression results of the spatial lag model

|  | GRP per capita in euros | GRP per capita in PPP |
| --- | --- | --- |
| const. | 0.0560 | 0.0928 |
| $\log y_{2001,i}$ | −0.0035 | −0.0075 |
| $\rho$ | 0.6981*** | 0.5836*** |
| AIC | −134.62 | −156.53 |

* (**,***): significant at the 0.1 (0.05, 0.01) level.
*Source*: Authors' calculations.

and 7.5. By means of this criterion the models improve to a certain degree when considering a spatial lag of the growth model, because the AIC falls slightly. The spatial autocorrelation may be due to the fact that some of the countries surveyed are divided into regions. Accordingly, in the next section country dummies that record country-specific effects of growth are introduced when calculating the relative β convergence in addition to exogenous growth-relevant variables.

## Relative β convergence

The model of relative β convergence takes into account the fact that the level of the GRP per capita at the beginning of the sample period is not the only explanatory variable for economic growth. Many other explanatory variables, such as sectoral structure and education level, have been investigated as potential influences. Because of missing data it has not been possible to draw on all the variables suggested in the present study.

The adoption of additional explanatory variables leads to various challenges regarding the interpretation of the regression results. Significant β convergence can no longer be adduced automatically to explain the reduction of regional disparities as a whole. The regions are approaching different equilibrium states when convergence is present, and these states depend on the levels of the other explanatory variables. In addition, the multi-collinearity of the variables has to be taken into account, because many variables are indicators of economic potential and thus correspond to the GRP per capita in the starting period.

Table 7.6 shows the estimation results for the model of relative β convergence. In our analysis we confine ourselves to the PPP model. For comparative purposes, the estimation results are given also for the data of GRP per capita in euro. It should be noted that all corresponding regression coefficients have the same sign, but only a few regression coefficients are significant with the euro model.

*Table 7.6*   Regression results of the relative β-convergence model

|  | GRP per capita in euros | GRP per capita in PPP |
|---|---|---|
| const. | 0.1009 | −0.0215 |
| $\log y_{2001,i}$ | −0.0158 | −0.0205* |
| Capital | 0.0255* | 0.0304*** |
| Hungary | −0.0186 | −0.0482*** |
| Slovenia | −0.0241 | −0.0269 |
| Bulgaria | −0.0132 | −0.0241* |
| Croatia | −0.013 | −0.0135 |
| Romania | 0.0666*** | 0.0321** |
| log(Economic freedom) | 0.0353 | 0.0827* |
| log(Population density) | −0.0114 | −0.0137* |
| log(Fertility rate) | −0.0408 | −0.0342 |
| log(Hotel rooms) | 0.0059* | 0.0039 |
| log(Rate AB) | −0.0073 | −0.0089* |
| Adj. R-squared | 0.8682 | 0.7791 |
| F-statistic | 18.02 | 10.11 |
| AIC | −177.68 | −188.01 |

*(**,*** ): significant at the 0.1 (0.05, 0.01) level.
*Source*: Authors' calculations.

For Albania, Bosnia-Herzegovina, Macedonia, Moldova, Montenegro and Serbia, data are available only at the national level. For areas in regional subdivisions, country dummies have been inserted in order to absorb possible country effects. It is evident here that Romania exhibits significantly higher growth than the SEE average, while Hungary, Croatia, Bulgaria and Slovenia have negative country effects. It may be noted that only Hungary and Bulgaria show significant deviations from zero, which can be attributed to some extent to the larger number of regions in these countries. An additional dummy variable is characteristic to those regions where the capital of the country is located. This has a strongly positive influence on the growth rate of the GRP per capita and agrees with the usual observation that economic growth in SEE countries is initially confined to the metropolitan areas in particular (Goschin et al., 2008).

Five more explanatory variables have been taken up into the model in logarithmized form. The variable 'Economic freedom' expresses values of the economic freedom indicator of the Heritage Foundation. It may be noted that this indicator takes the same value for all regions of a country. The indicator is between 0 (zero freedom) and 100 (maximum economic freedom). It is evident that, with increasing freedom, the average economic growth of a region also rises. The positive effect here is that greater economic freedom is accompanied by mutual exchange with larger markets, such as those of the EU (Vukotić and Bácović, 2006). The openness of the regions is measured by the number of hotel rooms in a region. Here, too, the average growth of the GRP per capita rises with the increasing number of hotel rooms, but significantly only with the measurement in euro.

The population variables used are population density and fertility rate. The regression coefficient for the fertility rate is not significantly different from zero. Increase of the population density surprisingly lowers the growth of GRP per capita. This does not fit in with the usual idea, because agglomeration areas are considered to be rather growth-promoting (Eckey, 2008). In this study, this effect is definitely connected with the fact that positive agglomeration effects are already included as a result of capital city dummies. For more rural regions and states, the control is made by means of the proportion of persons employed in sectors A and B ('Rate AB'). Strongly agricultural areas exhibit relatively lower growth rates.

The coefficient of conditional $\beta$ convergence takes a value of $-0.0205$. It is of slight significance, with the result that it can be assumed that the regions are approaching their respective equilibrium states. Moran's I values of the residuals of these regression models prove to be insignificant. In this model no further spatial autocorrelation can be proved, with the result that it can be assumed that spatial dependency in the absolute $\beta$-convergence models is triggered by missing country dummies and by neglected spatially correlated variables (LeSage and Pace, 2009).

## Conclusions

The convergence of living conditions in various regions is a pronounced aim of many international and national institutions. Similar living conditions are considered to be an important factor for good social solidarity and peaceful coexistence. A significant indicator for the evaluation of living conditions is consideration of the economic situation, and for this the average GRP per capita of various regions are frequently compared with each other.

Regarding the SEE region, it is shown in the present survey that differences in the economic situation across the regions have diminished between 2001 and 2007. Accordingly, an economic convergence for the regions can be shown. Compared with the EU, the entire region is catching up, so that the economic disparities between the SEE region and the EU are diminishing.

To promote the SEE region, it is important that these proven positive development trends are continued. A necessary condition for this is the continuing stabilization, especially of political conditions, and the resolution of conflicts such as border disputes. In particular, the closer ties to the EU with corollary use of the entire European market will certainly promote economic growth.

Future analyses will have to ask how the SEE region is dealing with the challenges of the current financial crisis and with the associated dislocations in the world economy. It remains to be seen whether the positive developments of the period from 2001 to 2007 will continue unabated or whether there will be a clear turning point.

## Appendix A.1: Description of model variables

| Variable | Description | Source |
|---|---|---|
| $logy_{t,i}$ in euros | Natural logarithm of GRP per capita in euros | Eurostat |
| $logy_{t,i}$ in PPP | Natural logarithm of GRP per capita in PPP | Eurostat, own estimations for Albania, Bosnia-Herzegovina, Moldova, Montenegro and Serbia – on the basis of gross national income in PPP of the World Bank |
| Capital | Dummy variable, 1 if the region contains the capital city of the country, 0 otherwise (non-capital city regions and all national states) | |
| Hungary | Dummy variable, 1 if the region is Hungarian, 0 otherwise | |
| Slovenia | Dummy variable, 1 if the region is Slovenian, 0 otherwise | |
| Bulgaria | Dummy variable, 1 if the region is Bulgarian, 0 otherwise | |
| Croatia | Dummy variable, 1 if the region is Croatian, 0 otherwise | |
| Romania | Dummy variable, 1 if the region is Romanian, 0 otherwise | |

| | | |
|---|---|---|
| log(Economic freedom) | Natural logarithm of the Economic Freedom Index in the year 2002, which lies between 0 (no freedom) and 100 (maximal freedom) | The Heritage Foundation in 2001; no data are available for Macedonia, Montenegro and Serbia |
| log(Population density) | Natural logarithm of population density in 2001 | Eurostat, Worldbank for Albania, Bosnia-Herzegovina, Moldova, Montenegro and Serbia |
| log(Fertility rate) | Natural logarithm of fertility rate in 2000 | Eurostat, UNO for Albania, Bosnia-Herzegovina, Moldova, Montenegro and Serbia |
| log(Hotel rooms) | Natural logarithm of number of hotel rooms in 2001 | Eurostat, Websites of statistic offices of Albania, Bosnia-Herzegovina and Moldova. Serbia and Montenegro; own estimations on the basis of 2004 Serbia data |
| log(Rate AB) | Natural logarithm of rate of employees in sector A and B in 2001 | Eurostat, Websites of statistic offices of Albania, Bosnia-Herzegovina (data 2006), Moldova, Serbia (data 2006) and Montenegro (data 2004) |

## Notes

1. NUTS (Nomenclature des unités territoriales statistiques) is a system of administrative territorial units used by the EU Statistics Office (Eurostat).
2. The cases are marked if data availability required data of other years. In a few cases our own estimations are required, because of missing data.

## References

Abreu, M., de Groot, H. and Florax, R. (2005) 'A Meta-Analysis of Beta-Convergence. The Legendary 2%', *Journal of Economic Surveys*, 19, 389–420.

Anselin, L. (1988) *Spatial Econometrics: Methods and Models* (Dordrecht: Kluwer).

Anselin, L., Bera, A. K., Florax, R. and Yoon, M. J. (1996) 'Simple Diagnostic Tests for Spatial Dependence', *Regional Science and Urban Economics*, 26, 77–104.

Barro, J. and Sala-i-Martin, X. (2004) *Economic Growth*, 2nd edn (Cambridge: MIT Press), 46–462.

Döring, T. and Schnellenbach, J. (2006) 'What do we know about Geographical Knowledge Spillovers and Regional Growth? – A Survey of the Literature', *Regional Studies*, 40, 375–395.

Eckey, H. (2008) *Regionalökonomie* (Wiesbaden: Gabler).

Goschin, Z., Constantin, D.-L., Roman, M. and Ileanu, B. (2008) 'The Current State and Dynamics of Regional Disparities in Romania', *Romanian Journal of regional Science*, 2, 80–105.

Jackson, M. (1999) 'Transition: Institutioneller und struktureller Wandel', in Hatschikjan, Magarditsch and Troebst, Stefan (eds), *Südosteuropa, Gesellschaft, Politik, Kultur* (München: C. H. Beck Verlag), 303–324.

Le Gallo, J., Ertur, C. and Baumont, C. (2003) 'A Spatial Econometric Analysis of Convergence Across European Regions, 1980–1995', in Fingleton, Bernard (ed.) *European Regional Growth* (Berlin, Heidelberg: Springer), 99–129.

LeSage, J. and Pace, R. (2009) *Introduction to Spatial Econometrics* (Boca Raton: Chapman & Hall/CRC).

Müller, D. and Büchsenschütz, U. (2009) 'Südosteuropa', in Roth, Harald (ed.), *Studienhandbuch Östliches Europa*, vol. 1: Geschichte Ostmittel- und Südosteuropas, 2nd edn (Köln: Böhlau), 80–95.

Shankar, R. and Shah, A. (2003) 'Bridging the Economic Divide within Countries: A Scorecard on the Performance of Regional Policies in Reducing Regional Income Disparities', *World Development*, 31, 1421–1441.

Türck, M. (2007) *European Regional Convergence: An Empirical Analysis of the Enlarged European Union* (Hamburg: Kovac).

Upton, G. and Fingleton, B. (1985) *Spatial Data Analysis by Example 2: Point Pattern and Quantitative Data* (Chichester: Wiley).

Vukotić, V. and Bácović, M. (2006) 'Economic Freedom and Economic Growth in South East Europe', *Transition Studies Review*, 13, 81–91.

# 8
# Macro-Economic Consequences of the Integration of the SEE Area into the Eurozone

*Reinhard Neck*

## Introduction

As a result of the two Eastern enlargements, the European Union (EU) now consists of 27 countries, 17 of which will be members of the euro Area (EA) as of 1 January 2011. Except for Bulgaria, Romania and Slovenia, the South East European (SEE) countries still lack full integration into the EU, although some of them have already obtained, or will soon obtain, candidate status. Because of the EU's internal problems, but also because of the slow progress these countries have made so far towards functional economic and political structures, it cannot be assumed that they will be admitted to the EU, or even to the EA, fairly soon. Fears have been expressed that the accession of SEE countries might increase economic divergence within the EU and might result in more asymmetric shocks acting on European economies. In particular, some observers regard the membership of these former communist countries as a threat to the macro-economic stability of the EU, as some of their political systems appear to have but a weak tradition of macro-economic policies for stability and high growth.

Nevertheless, these countries indisputably belong to Europe and must not be denied participation in the historical project of European integration, or even unification. Therefore it makes sense to consider the effects of their membership in the EU and in the EA, even if this is but a remote possibility or project. Few authors have dealt with these problems so far (Mooslechner, 2004; Horvath, 2005; Uvalic, 2008); thus in the present chapter we discuss some possible consequences of the membership of SEE countries in the EA on the design and effects of macro-economic policies in Europe. Of course, such a scenario presumes that these countries will have become members of the EU before, or at least simultaneously with, their entry into the EA. As this will not happen within a short time (one or two years, say) from now, such an analysis must necessarily be highly speculative. But we hope to be able to contribute at least some pieces to the puzzle of assessing this major step towards European integration.

This chapter is structured as follows. In a first step, possible effects of introducing the euro in the SEE countries are discussed from a theoretical point of view. Next, some tentative conclusions from experiments are drawn, investigating macro-economic scenarios with and without a group of countries (to be interpreted as those of SEE) included in the EA with the help of a model of the global economy. Then the results of a case study for Slovenia are reported – Slovenia being the only SEE country already in the EA. In a further step, an attempt is made to evaluate the scanty evidence on the macro-economic effects of joining the Eurozone for the SEE countries. Finally, the main findings are summarized and conclusions are drawn.

## Theoretical arguments on macro-economic effects of EMU accession

Integrating SEE countries into the EA will have both benefits and costs for the countries involved and for the present members. In this section, the potential costs and benefits for the SEE economies arising from these countries' joining the EA are briefly discussed. As is usual in the literature, a differentiation will be made between possible demand and supply side effects of introducing the common currency. Analytically, the former refer to shifts in the aggregate demand curve (mainly affecting fiscal, monetary and exchange rate policies) and the latter refer to shifts in the aggregate supply curve (mainly affecting the determinants of long-term growth) in a conventional macro-economic model.

*Demand-side effects* arise from changes in the institutional structure of monetary (and, to some extent, fiscal) policy associated with membership in the EA. These affect stabilization, and hence macro-economic policies on the demand side. Some costs arise from abandoning an independent monetary policy and thus foregoing one policy instrument. In the euro System, monetary policy is conducted by the European System of Central Banks (ESCB), and by the European Central Bank (ECB) in particular. Therefore monetary policy and the exchange rate can no longer be used for internal stabilization purposes in member countries. Whether this change entails more costs or more benefits is an open question, however. Apart from political considerations (loss of an element of sovereignty by the acceding country), the main argument on the costs of joining the EA relates to the optimum currency area (OCA) theory, which can be traced back to the seminal contribution of Nobel Laureate Robert Mundell (1961). According to his original OCA theory, countries benefit from a common currency only if factor mobility between the countries is high and if their exposure to asymmetric shocks is low. In the case of the SEE economies these criteria will be only partially fulfilled, even after their accession to the EU and the so-called Exchange Rate Mechanism II (ERM-II). While almost all barriers to international trade and factor movements will have been removed upon EU accession, it cannot be expected that their business cycles will be totally synchronized with that of the EA. Should a SEE country be exposed to major idiosyncratic shocks, the loss of an independent monetary policy may result in increasing output variability.

On the other hand, more recent contributions point to the endogeneity of the OCA criteria (Frenkel and Rose 1998). According to this variant on the theory, deeper trade integration in a currency union leads to increasing business cycle synchronization. If countries form a currency union, the likelihood of fulfilling the OCA criteria increases. This hypothesis is based, among other things, on the assumption that trade among European countries is typically intra-industry trade, due to economies of scale and imperfect competition. As a result, forming a currency union need not result in increasing specialization of the countries; a high degree of sector-specific specialization renders a country vulnerable to asymmetric, sector-specific shocks. Moreover, as evidence from the new EU members from 2004 shows (Bohnec, 2003; Breuss et al., 2004), these countries largely adjusted their economic policies to prepare for membership of the EA; hence the same may be expected of SEE countries after their entry into the EU.

There is little serious literature on the SEE countries' ability to fulfil the OCA criteria. Most observers point out their current failure to fulfil conditions of entry to the EU, in particular in terms of dealing with corruption and other crimes, and of ensuring independent jurisdiction and human rights. Structural convergence towards the incumbent EA member countries has made some progress since the demise of communism but may well be insufficient. However, once these countries have been admitted to the EU, it is likely that idiosyncratic shocks will have been diminished, and therefore the costs of losing an independent monetary policy might well be smaller than the benefits of trade intensification and the expected further synchronization of the business cycle.

In general it is not clear whether pursuing independent demand-side macro-economic policies provides advantages at all. It may well be that subjecting oneself to the discipline of a stability-oriented monetary and fiscal policy reduces policy-driven shocks and thus enhances domestic macro-economic stability. As most of the founding EA countries have a long tradition of aversion to inflation, and thus monetary discipline (Alesina et al., 2003) – which is not the case for most of the SEE countries – the latter may be expected to benefit from importing low inflation from these countries. In fact this may be the main argument for their joining the Eurozone on the basis of credibility enhancement, obtained through these countries' 'tying their hands' and leaving monetary policy up to a stability-oriented institution such as the ECB. Of course, this presumes that the euro System will be able to overcome the difficulties arising from the debt crisis of some of its members.

The macro-economic literature generally agrees that numerous *supply-side* benefits can be expected from joining a common currency. These have already been analysed and used as main arguments in favour of a common currency when assessing the effects of creating the European Economic and Monetary Union (EMU) (Emerson et al., 1992). Of course, the same arguments also apply, *mutatis mutandis*, to the accession of SEE countries to the EA. They refer in particular to transaction cost savings resulting from the elimination of bilateral exchange rates with the incumbent EA members, to trade expansion due to the removal of exchange rate uncertainty and to reductions in the country risk premium contained in the interest rates.

It is clear that, upon Eurozone accession, the bilateral exchange rate of the respective SEE country vis-à-vis the incumbent EA countries disappears. Eliminating exchange rates saves transaction costs incurred by the private sector. These costs can be divided into two groups. The first comprises costs paid by private households and enterprises when they exchange domestic into foreign currency and vice versa, as well as costs for hedging against exchange rate risks. Exchange rate risks occur when the exchange rate changes in the time span between concluding and settling a contract that involves payments in a foreign currency. The second group of transaction costs associated with the existence of bilateral exchange rates consists of the resources used by companies for handling foreign exchange operations, additional accounting activities and lengthier money transfers involving different currencies.

In order to be quantified, these savings on transaction costs and their macro-economic effects have to be included in a theoretical framework. Usually this is done in the context of the neoclassical growth model, where they shift the production function upwards. Total factor productivity (TFP) increases because eliminating transaction costs raises the efficiency with which the factors of production are used in the economy. With a constant savings rate, the resulting rise in income raises the amount of savings. These are used to finance additional capital formation, thereby further increasing the growth rate. In sum, the one-off productivity increase brought about by the transaction cost savings leads to dynamic productivity gains initiated by increasing fixed capital formation (Borowski, 2003).

All SEE countries have small, open economies, whose domestic prices are largely determined by prices on the world market. This does not only pertain to prices for goods and services traded on international markets, but also to imported raw materials and intermediate goods. Therefore the exchange rate is an important determinant of prices in the local currency. Eliminating exchange rate uncertainty thus reduces price uncertainty. This may increase the international competitiveness of the SEE economies and improve their position on international markets.

Perhaps a more important effect of introducing the euro in the SEE countries relates to interest rates: the exchange rate risk premium in the interest rate can be expected to decline. First, if future output prices become less volatile, future revenues from investment projects also become more certain. If investors are risk-averse, diminishing price uncertainty can be expected to boost investment. If the uncertainty regarding future revenues from investment projects in a certain country is higher than in a benchmark country or region, this is reflected in a higher long-term interest rate. Thus the risk premium partly reflects the difference between long-term interest rates in the SEE countries and in the EA. Moreover, in countries with a higher risk of public sector insolvency, not only do the interest rates for government loans exceed those in less indebted countries, but also interest rates on private loans are higher, due to the term structure of interest rates. To the extent that the EA is still regarded as less prone to excessive public and private debt than the SEE countries, EA accession should reduce the long-term interest rate in the SEE countries, entailing a positive effect on fixed capital formation.

In addition, by eliminating exchange rate uncertainty, one abolishes a constraint on foreign direct investment. Gross fixed capital formation is an important source of long-run growth potential. Eliminating the currency risk premium embedded in the long-term interest rate is thus another channel through which EA accession will boost potential output and total factor productivity in the SEE countries. This effect is reinforced by the overall macro-economic advantages of eliminating exchange risk and the need to hedge against exchange rate fluctuations in international trade.

Thus an important TFP-enhancing channel of euro adoption is to be expected from an increase in foreign trade and in foreign direct investment (FDI). Exchange rate uncertainty arising from possible movements of the exchange rate between the conclusion and the settlement of a trade contract renders profits from international trade uncertain, too. Assuming that utility is a positive function of expected profits and a negative function of profit volatility, risk-averse firms will reduce their engagement in foreign trade. Removing exchange rate uncertainty should therefore be beneficial for international trade. In addition, a currency union goes beyond fixing the exchange rate between two currencies. Thus trade among EA members benefits not only from eliminating exchange rate uncertainty but also from sharing a common currency. Empirical studies (Rose and van Wincoop, 2001; Rose and Engel, 2002) confirm these theoretical considerations, although the quantitative importance of the resulting macro-economic effects is still under debate.

Another argument in favour of the growth effects of increased international trade comes from the new trade theory. According to this theory, the growth effects of international trade are not limited to effects from international specialization due to comparative advantages and economies of scale. In addition, and possibly more importantly, foreign trade is likely to induce knowledge spillover effects from technologically more advanced to less advanced economies. Such spillover effects may serve as an engine for total factor productivity growth (Edwards, 1997). Given the still wide technological gap between the EA and the SEE countries, this effect may be of considerable significance, although gaining access to the common EU market will be more important in this respect than adopting the euro.

Several more aspects of EA accession may be relevant for the SEE countries. For instance, higher price transparency can be expected to boost competition. This is particularly relevant for a small, open economy that is also small in geographical terms, which holds true at least for Macedonia, Montenegro and Kosovo. Moreover, the SEE countries have only underdeveloped capital markets. The intensifying capital market integration brought about by joining the EA may entail efficiency gains. By removing the transaction costs incurred by international investors, a currency union affects asset pricing, thus improving capital allocation. In addition, adopting the euro removes the risk of a currency crisis, inducing more FDI and portfolio capital inflows.

## Analysis of Euro Area enlargement with a global macro-economic model

Many studies have investigated macro-economic aspects of monetary unions in general and of the EMU in particular. Some studies are specifically devoted to assessing the effects of enlarging the EA (for instance Fidrmuc, 2004; Dabrowski and Rostowski, 2006). In earlier work we analysed a variety of scenarios, focusing on the results of different policy arrangements after an EA enlargement (Neck et al., 2004, 2005; Haber and Neck, 2005). For these calculations we used the European version MSGR44A of the MSG2 Model (McKibbin-Sachs Global Model). This is a dynamic, intertemporal, general-equilibrium model of a multi-region world economy. It exhibits a mixture of classical and Keynesian properties: partly rational expectations, in combination with various rigidities, allow for deviations from fully optimizing behaviour. In particular, nominal wages are assumed to adjust slowly in the major industrial economies. Nevertheless, the model solves for a full intertemporal equilibrium. The model is described in full detail in McKibbin and Sachs (1991).[1]

The MSGR44A version of the MSG2 Model consists of models of the following countries and regions: the USA, Japan, Germany, the UK, France, Italy, Austria, the rest of the EA (REA), the rest of the Organisation for Economic Co-operation and Development (OECD), Central and Eastern European (CEE) economies (including the SEE economies), non-oil developing countries, oil-exporting countries and the former Soviet Union. For the last three regions, only foreign trade and external financial aspects are modelled, whereas the industrial countries and regions are fully modelled with an internal macro-economic structure. The basic theoretical structure for all industrial regions is the same but institutional differences are taken into account, especially when modelling labour markets.

Although it would be possible to examine the isolated effects of an increase in TFP of the CEE economies and its feedback on the global economy, this cannot be done for the SEE economies only, as they form a block with the other economies of CEE in the model. Moreover, due to the small economic size of the SEE countries, in the context of a global model the macro-economic effects would be near zero. Instead, we can make some indirect inferences by comparing some scenarios we ran with the model, emphasizing the welfare effects of different institutional arrangements, including some with and some without the CEE countries as members of the EA. Qualitative conclusions regarding differences between these two sets of scenarios may be tentatively presumed to hold for the SEE countries *mutatis mutandis*. Otherwise the scenarios differ with respect to the policy rules of the fiscal and monetary policy-makers involved.

In our view, the following results from these investigations also hold for the SEE economies: in the case of a transitory asymmetric negative demand shock affecting only the SEE countries, membership in the EA reduces the ability of the SEE countries to counteract their domestic shock, as it abolishes the possibility of adjusting exchange rates between the SEE countries and the euro. Therefore scenarios with an enlarged EA show higher welfare losses for the acceding countries than for their counterparts with the present EA. The difference is most notable if no other accommodating policy instruments are available that might be substituted for the protective effects of adjustable exchange rates.

If a negative demand shock that is limited to the present EA is assumed, the spillover effects to the acceding countries are not negligible. In this case non-cooperative scenarios dominate cooperative scenarios. This can be attributed to the fact that the SEE countries can use their fiscal instruments to pursue their own objectives in the non-cooperative case, while cooperation causes this instrument to be used for optimizing some joint target of the EA (analytically: a joint welfare loss function) in which the SEE countries' objectives enter with a small weight only.

Under a symmetric demand shock affecting the present EA and SEE economies, on the other hand, cooperation dominates non-cooperation for the present EA countries, and the enlarged EA always produces better results for them than the original one. For the SEE countries enlargement is advantageous in most cases, but no general judgement can be made for them on the issue of cooperation. The best results for both the EA incumbents and the SEE countries can be expected if the monetary policy of the EA targets price stability and fiscal policies are fully cooperative. The qualitative results for a global demand shock are the same as those for the symmetric European shock.

The results are different for transitory negative supply shocks. In this case, results are mixed with respect to the advantages or disadvantages of cooperation versus non-cooperation and with respect to the present versus the enlarged EA for the present EA members. The only general result we could find was the superiority of a rules-based fiscal and monetary policy neglecting the impact of the shock over fiscal or monetary activism.

To summarize, the analyses showed that the advantages and disadvantages of different institutional set-ups strongly depended on the nature of the shock the economies were faced with. Fixed rules can be recommended as an answer to supply shocks, more active (flexible) policy rules as a reaction to demand shocks. In most of the scenarios, EA enlargement did not lead to significant welfare effects on EA's present members. Thus additional macro-economic noise resulting from the SEE countries' membership does not seem to be too much of a problem for the EA incumbents. On the other hand, no significant advantages can be identified for them either. For the new EA members, introducing the euro might cause reductions in macro-economic welfare losses in some cases, but the contrary may also be true.

Again, different results are obtained if the USA is introduced as an active policy-maker. If all the international spillover and feedback effects of shocks and policies are taken into consideration, the results on the advantages of fixed rules in the case of supply shocks and more activist policies for demand shocks are supported for the European countries but not for the USA. Cooperation is not necessarily better than non-cooperative activist policy-making, and, in most cases, cooperation comes at the expense of the 'smaller' player and favours the 'larger' one (at a global level, the USA). Again, in most of the scenarios, EA enlargement does not lead to significant welfare effects for the present members of the EA. For the SEE countries, EA membership generally does not provide significant reductions in macro-economic welfare losses. The results for the scenarios involving the USA can lead to conjecturing that the global effects of EA enlargement will be minor. It remains to be seen how robust these results are with respect to variations in the model used and to assumptions about the objective functions. At present, these results seem to indicate that the decision about countries like those from the SEE area participating in the EA need not primarily be influenced by macro-economic policy considerations.

## A case study for Slovenia

Slovenia was the first of the ten states that entered the EU in May 2004 to join the EA at the beginning of 2007. So far, it is the only SEE country to become a member of the EA. The actual introduction of the euro in Slovenia at the beginning of 2007 took place quickly and without serious technical problems. Due to these facts, Slovenia may be considered to be a role model for an SEE country entering the EA. For obtaining an estimate of the macro-economic consequences of Slovenia's accession to the EA it is, however, not sufficient to compare the performance of the Slovenian economy before and after this move, as differences between these two phases might be due to a variety of influences. Instead, we look at the results of a study we carried out before the event, using a model of the Slovenian economy, and we modify them in the light of recent experience.

In several papers (Weyerstrass and Neck, 2008a, 2008b, 2008c), we aimed to estimate the macro-economic effects of the costs and benefits of EA accession on the Slovenian economy. To do so, simulations with several variants of a macro-econometric model of the Slovenian economy were performed. The macro-economic effects of EA accession were estimated first by contrasting model simulations with and without an independent monetary policy. Further benefits were evaluated by their impact on total factor productivity (TFP). We concentrate here on the last of these exercises, performed with the SLOPOL7 version of the model (for an explanation of this version of the model, see the remarks below).

We proceeded in two steps, distinguishing again between demand-side and supply-side effects. When investigating the former, we concentrated on the implications of linking interest rates to those in the EA. Supply-side effects of joining the EA were evaluated in terms of their impact on the economy's long-run growth potential. Effects on the production possibility frontier can, in particular, be expected from transaction cost savings, from the reduction in the country risk premium in the interest rates and from productivity effects brought about by increasing international trade and FDI.

In order to investigate these possible causal chains empirically, their impact on TFP has to be quantified. For the simulations reported here, we assumed that EA accession raised TFP in Slovenia by 1.5 per cent. Previous estimations for the EA concluded that reductions in the mark-up of prices over marginal costs due to structural reforms on the goods and factor markets could raise TFP in the EA as a whole by 0.57 per cent. At the level of member states, the maximum effect amounts to 0.75 per cent according to van Aarle and Weyerstrass (2008). The effects of introducing the euro in Slovenia can be compared with effects from reforms in the goods and factor markets. As Slovenia still lags behind the 'old' EA countries in terms of capital stock, there is potential for higher productivity gains. Thus, at 1.5 per cent, a slightly higher TFP impact was assumed. This figure is comparable with the estimate of the effect of the EMU on its members in the initial analysis of the macro-economic consequences of the common currency (Emerson et al., 1992).

SLOPOL7 is a medium-sized macro-econometric model of the small open economy of Slovenia. It consists of 60 equations, of which

23 are behavioural equations and 37 are identities. The former were estimated by ordinary least squares (OLS), by using quarterly data for the period from the first quarter of 1995 to the last quarter of 2006. The model combines Keynesian and neoclassical elements. The former determine the short- and medium-term solutions in the sense that the model is demand-driven, and persistent disequilibria in the goods and labour markets are possible. The supply side incorporates neoclassical features. Almost all behavioural equations are specified in error correction form. A detailed description of an earlier version can be found in Weyerstrass and Neck (2007).

Positive macro-economic supply-side effects from EA accession were simulated by an exogenous one-time upward shift of technical progress, which is equivalent to a TFP shift. In particular, it was assumed that the level of total factor productivity was permanently raised by 1.5 per cent.

Upon adoption of the euro, monetary policy in Slovenia is no longer available as an independent policy instrument. Instead the ECB monetary policy, which is oriented towards EA-wide developments, is relevant for Slovenia. In order to explore the macro-economic implications of this institutional change, a version in which the short-term interest rate is available as a policy instrument and another one in which this is not the case have been constructed. In a previous study (Weyerstrass and Neck, 2008b), we also specified a model assuming flexible exchange rates for the Slovenian tolar in a scenario with autonomous Slovenian monetary policy, but at the time of Slovenia's entry into the EA such a policy was of no practical interest, given Slovenia's membership in the ERM-II since 2004 pegging its currency to the euro.

In the version with an independent monetary policy, the short-term interest rate is determined by a Taylor-rule type equation; in other words, it depends on domestic inflation and output gap – that is, on the difference between actual and potential GDP growth. In addition, the short-term interest rate in the EA exerts some influence. In the EA regime, monetary policy cannot be used as an active policy instrument. In this case the short-term interest rate is entirely determined by the three-month interest rate in the EA. In both versions of the model, the long-term interest rate is linked to the short-term rate in a term structure equation. In addition, the long-term interest rate in Slovenia depends on its EA counterpart, reflecting Slovenia's integration in the European capital market.

Several model simulations with SLOPOL7 served to assess the likely macro-economic effects of Slovenia's entry into the EA *a priori*. For the exogenous variables of the model we used recent forecasts and extrapolations. First a baseline simulation without EA accession was performed. Next, the isolated effects of replacing independent monetary policy in Slovenia with the common monetary policy conducted by the ECB – that is, the effects of foregoing an independent monetary policy – were simulated. The isolated effects arising from higher total factor productivity, but with an independent Slovene monetary policy following a Taylor rule as in the baseline simulation, were also determined, in order to give an estimate of the supply-side effects of introducing the common currency. Finally, the combined effects arising from EA accession were obtained. It should be noted that these are not simply the sums of the effects of the two previous simulations, as they arise from a scenario containing both a parameter shift and an institutional change reflected in the substitution of some equations by others.

The baseline simulation already provides a fairly optimistic picture, reflecting the successful transition of the Slovenian economy from a centrally planned to a market economy. According to the forecasts, real GDP growth reaches 4.4 per cent on average from 2007 to 2011, and the rate of unemployment is almost halved. Over the entire simulation horizon, the government runs a small budget deficit in the range of 0.6–1 per cent of GDP. Until 2010, the current account exhibits a declining deficit before entering marginally positive terrain in the final year. Of course, these estimates could not take into account the financial and economic crisis (the 'Great Recession') that occurred in the meantime, making these optimistic forecasts obsolete; but, for our purpose, they are useful in providing us with a standard of reference that is independent from events that have nothing to do with the issue of EA accession.

Abandoning the independent monetary policy conducted by the Bank of Slovenia and adopting the common ECB monetary policy exerts positive effects on the Slovene economy. Due to the de facto hard peg of the Slovene tolar in the ERM-II, interest rates had already converged to a large extent to the EA average. Nevertheless, some room for further convergence was still left to be exploited after the euro was actually introduced in Slovenia. In addition, abandoning an independent monetary policy removes one factor that, in itself, may destabilize the domestic economy, especially in the case of a small open economy like Slovenia. On the other hand, the loss of the monetary policy instrument and of the exchange rate as buffers against idiosyncratic shocks may affect the Slovene economy negatively. According to the simulation results obtained with the SLOPOL7 model, the positive effects of adopting the common monetary policy of the ECB more than compensate for these costs, although by a small amount only.

The favourable isolated effects from increased total factor productivity are stronger than those from abandoning the monetary policy instrument. From 2007 – the year in which the euro is introduced in Slovenia – onwards, positive macro-economic effects can be observed. The growth rate of real GDP increases, additional employment is created and the rate of unemployment is lower than in the baseline run. Public finances are positively affected, but only marginally. Due to higher real GDP, imports rise, but exports are almost unaffected; hence the current account deteriorates slightly. Towards the end of the simulation horizon the levels of the macro-economic indicators considered here return towards their baseline values.

The combined effects of abandoning an independent monetary policy and of the assumed TFP shift are characterized by positive growth over two years. In the final year of the time horizon considered, real GDP exceeds the baseline level by nearly 1 per cent. Inflation is significantly lower in 2007 and 2008 than in the baseline, but, due to the favourable development of the labour market, additional price pressures can be observed in 2010 and 2011. From 2008 onwards, the rate of unemployment remains below baseline values. This development is due to more dynamic employment creation. The overall effect on public finances is slightly positive. Higher income and public consumption create additional tax revenues, and the favourable labour market development results in lower spending on unemployment benefits, together with higher revenues from social security contributions. On the other hand, the current account deteriorates. Higher domestic demand results in increasing imports, while real exports are almost identical to those in the baseline run.

Summing up, introducing the euro in Slovenia brings about temporarily higher real GDP growth, a permanently higher GDP level, more employment, temporarily lower inflation and a permanently lower price level. Public finances are positively affected. On the other hand, the current account deteriorates. The benefits are primarily due to the supply-side productivity increasing and, to a minor extent, to the adoption of the common monetary policy of the ECB, which leads to further reductions in the long-term interest rate in Slovenia.

## An attempt at quantification

Neither the comparison of scenarios without and with the CEE European countries within the global macro-model MSG2 nor the simulations with the Slovenian model SLOPOL7 can answer the question as to how the accession of SEE countries like Albania or Macedonia, for instance, to the EA will affect their macro-economic performance. However, we can take some information from these studies and combine it with specific information about each of the SEE countries to arrive at individual estimates. From this we may attempt to estimate the average or the total macro-economic effects for all of them. It must be stressed that the results of such an exercise are, of necessity, extremely uncertain, as the political conditions, the time schedule of accession of these countries to the EU and (probably several years afterwards) to the EA and even the possibility of any of these countries acceding at all, are completely unknown at present.

Nevertheless, such an attempt should be made. The results for the CEE countries reported in the section on the analysis of the euro Area enlargement with the global macro-economic model, and those for Slovenia, reported in the previous section, give some basic information. Their quantitative results are shown in the relevant columns of Table 8.1. For Slovenia, we already have additional information from the actual introduction of the euro. This information indicates that we underestimated the (one-time) effect of introducing the euro on the price level, which led to a transitory increase in inflation. The reason for this increase is the less than perfect competition, which enables firms to take the opportunity offered by a change in the medium of exchange to raise prices on that occasion. A similar effect can also be expected for

*Table 8.1*  Overall macro-economic effects of EMU integration

| | CEE total | Slovenia | Bosnia and Herzegovina | Serbia | SEE |
|---|---|---|---|---|---|
| GDP at constant prices | 0.2 | 0.9 | 0.0 | 1.3 | 1.0 |
| CPI inflation rate | −0.6 | −1.2 | 0.0 | 0.1 | 0.1 |
| Unemployment rate | −0.3 | −0.2 | 0.0 | −0.1 | −0.1 |
| Employment (1,000 persons) | n. a. | 3.6 | 0.0 | 1.7 | 5.0 |
| Budget balance (% of GDP) | 0.1 | 0.0 | 1.0 | 1.8 | 1.0 |
| Debt level (% of GDP) | −0.1 | 0.2 | −2.2 | −3.9 | −2.0 |

*Note*: Macro-economic effects are measured as deviations from baseline in percentage points – GDP: per cent, employment: 1,000 employees; 2nd year of EA membership: 2008 for Slovenia, 2012 for Bosnia and Herzegovina and for Serbia.

*Source*: CEE total: Neck et al. (2004, 2005); Slovenia: Weyerstrass and Neck (2008c); Bosnia and Herzegovina: Weyerstrass and Neck (2011a); Serbia: Weyerstrass and Neck (2011b); SEE: own 'guesstimates'.

the other SEE countries, hence it should be taken into account when estimating the accession effects.

For Bosnia and Herzegovina and for Serbia we conducted a similar analysis as for Slovenia. The simulations for Bosnia and Herzegovina are reported in Weyerstrass and Neck (2011a). We used the macro-econometric model for Bosnia developed by Weyerstrass (2009). As in the study for Slovenia, we assumed that TFP will increase by 0.75 per cent above the baseline solution from the year of introducing the euro onward. To take account of the price level effect mentioned above, we assumed that inflation would increase by 1.2 percentage points during the first year in the EA. Moreover, in view of the still high rate of interest in Bosnia and Herzegovina, we assumed that introducing the euro would result in a decrease of the risk premium in the rate of interest. We assumed therefore that the long-term interest rate would be lower by 1 percentage point starting with the first year in the EA. On the other hand, no specific change was made with respect to monetary policy proper, as Bosnia and Herzegovina already has a currency board with the euro now.

The problem of when to assume EA entry was solved by taking 1 January 2011 as the starting point. Of course, this scenario is counterfactual, but any such assumption must be arbitrary, and for 2011 and the following years we can build a plausible baseline solution and assume that the model provides a reasonable picture of the macro-economic relations in Bosnia and Herzegovina, which will probably not be the case when the event actually occurs. The same consideration determined our choice of the starting year for Serbia (also 2011).

To analyse the consequences of EA accession in Serbia, we used the macro-econometric model for that country estimated by Berrer et al. (2009). The simulation assumptions were similar to those made for Bosnia and Herzegovina: a permanent shift upwards of TFP by 0.75 per cent, a temporary increase in the rate of inflation by 1.2 percentage points and a permanent decrease in the long-term interest rate by 1 percentage point. As Serbia at present follows its own monetary policy instead of pegging its currency to the euro, we used a Taylor rule for the independent monetary policy in the baseline simulation and a link of Serbia's short-term interest rate to that of the EA, to simulate EA membership.

The results for some key macro-economic variables in both countries are shown in Table 8.1. The lower values for Bosnia and Herzegovina are due to the fact that introducing the euro as legal tender will involve a smaller policy change there than in Serbia, for example; the same will be true for Euroized countries such as Montenegro and Kosovo (Winkler, 2005). On the basis of these estimates, a rough guess is made for the total of the SEE countries in the last column of Table 8.1, and its subjective and preliminary character has to be emphasized. The most important aspect of this 'guesstimate' (and the one that we consider to be fairly well established) is the low effect of integrating the SEE countries into the Eurozone on their 'real' sector, such as on employment and output or real income. These variables will certainly be strongly affected by the countries' membership in the EU (which is assumed to have occurred already before their entry into the EA), but only marginally affected by the introduction of the euro as legal tender.

## Conclusion

Slovenia was the first – and so far the only – SEE country to become a member of the EA, and it is not clear whether and, if so, when other SEE countries will follow. Despite the uncertainties surrounding these integration processes, in this chapter we used information obtained from simulation studies for the total of the CEE countries, for Slovenia, for Bosnia and Herzegovina and for Serbia, to obtain initial estimates of the consequences of possible membership of the SEE countries in the Eurozone. The most prominent result is the small size of the effect on output, income and employment. On the one hand, this may be regarded as disappointing, since these countries hope that introducing the euro will help them towards increased prosperity; this will possibly be associated with their entry into the EU and with its consequences for opening up their markets, but much less so with the introduction of the euro. On the other hand, it is reassuring that the loss of monetary sovereignty associated with the introduction of the euro will probably not cause major problems for these countries.

## Acknowledgements

The author gratefully acknowledges financial support from the EU Commission through MRTN-CT-2006-034270 COMISEF and from the Jubiläumsfonds of the Oesterreichische Nationalbank (project no. 12166). Thanks are due to Klaus Weyerstrass and Gottfried Haber for the joint work on which this chapter is based.

## Note

1. Additional resources are available on the web (http://www.msgpl.com.au/).

# References

Aarle, B. van and Weyerstrass, K. (eds) (2008) *Economic Spillovers, Structural Reforms and Policy Coordination in the Euro Area* (Heidelberg: Springer).

Alesina, A., Barro, R. J. and Tenreyro, S. (2003) 'Optimal Currency Areas', *NBER Macroeconomics Annual 2002*, 301–345.

Berrer, H., Grozea-Helmenstein, D., and Weyerstrass, K. (2009) *A Macroeconomic Model for Serbia: Data, Estimation and Evaluation*, Research Report, ECONOMICA and IHS, Vienna.

Bohnec, D. (2003) 'Impact of EU Enlargement: Challenges for Slovenia's Monetary and Exchange Rate Policies', *Atlantic Economic Journal*, 31, 303–308.

Borowski, J. (2003) 'Potential Benefits of Poland's EMU Accession', *Focus on Transition*, 1, 148–173.

Breuss, F., Fink, G. and Haiss, P. (2004) 'How Well Prepared Are the New Member States for the European Monetary Union?', *Journal of Policy Modeling*, 26, 769–791.

Dabrowski, M. and Rostowski, J. (eds) (2006) *The Eastern Enlargement of the Eurozone* (Dordrecht: Springer).

Edwards, S. (1997) 'Openness, Productivity and Growth: What Do We Really Know?', *Economic Journal*, 108, 383–398.

Emerson, M., Gros, D., Italianer, A., Pisany-Ferry, J. and Reichenbach, H. (1992) *One Market, One Money: An Evaluation of the Potential Benefits and Costs of Forming an Economic and Monetary Union* (Oxford: Oxford University Press).

Fidrmuc, J. (2004) 'The Endogeneity of the Optimum Currency Area Criteria, Intra-Industry Trade, and EMU Enlargement', *Contemporary Economic Policy*, 22, 1–12.

Frenkel, J. A. and Rose, A. K. (1998) 'The Endogeneity of the Optimum Currency Criteria', *Economic Journal*, 108, 1009–1025.

Haber, G. and Neck, R. (2005) 'Shall the New EU Members Introduce the Euro? Some Macroeconomic Policy Effects', *Atlantic Economic Journal*, 33, 139–149.

Horvath, J. (2005) 'Choice of Exchange Rate Regime: Implications for South–East Europe', in Liebscher, K., Christl, J., Mooslechner, P. and Ritzberger-Grünwald, D. (eds), *European Economic Integration and South–East Europe: Challenges and Prospects* (Cheltenham, UK and Northampton, MA, USA: Edward Elgar), 145–154.

McKibbin, W. J. and Sachs, J. D. (1991) *Global Linkages* (Washington, DC: Brookings Institution).

Mooslechner, P. (2004) 'EU Enlargement and Monetary Integration – The Next Steps: ERM II and beyond', in Liebscher, K., Christl, J., Mooslechner, P. and Ritzberger-Grünwald, D. (eds), *The Economic Potential of a Larger Europe* (Cheltenham, UK and Northampton, MA, USA: Edward Elgar), 161–175.

Mundell, R. (1961) 'A Theory of Optimum Currency Areas', *American Economic Review*, 51, 657–665.

Neck, R., Haber, G. and McKibbin, W. J. (2004) 'European Monetary and Fiscal Policies after the EU Enlargement', *Empirica*, 31, 229–245.

Neck, R., Haber, G. and McKibbin, W. J. (2005) 'Global Macroeconomic Policy Implications of an Enlarged EMU', in Breuss, F. and Hochreiter, E. (eds), *Challenges for Central Banks in an Enlarged EMU* (Vienna and New York: Springer), 235–257.

Rose, A. K. and Engel, C. (2002) 'Currency Unions and International Integration', *Journal of Money, Credit, and Banking*, 34, 1067–1087.

Rose, A. K. and Wincoop, E. van (2001) 'National Money as a Barrier to International Trade: The Real Case for Currency Union', *American Economic Review*, 91 (2), 386–390.

Uvalic, M. (2008) 'Integrating the Balkans with the European Union', in Quadrio Curzio, A. and Fortis, M. (eds), *The EU and the Economies of the Eastern European Enlargement* (Berlin and Heidelberg: Physica-Verlag), 85–94.

Weyerstrass, K. (2009) 'A Macroeconometric Model for Bosnia and Herzegovina', *Eastern European Economics*, 47 (4), 61–90.

Weyerstrass, K. and Neck, R. (2007) 'SLOPOL6: A Macroeconometric Model for Slovenia', *International Business and Economics Research Journal*, 6(11), 81–94.

Weyerstrass, K. and Neck, R. (2008a) 'Macroeconomic Consequences of the Adoption of the Euro: The Case of Slovenia', *International Advances in Economic Research*, 14, 1–10.

Weyerstrass, K. and Neck, R. (2008b) 'Macroeconomic Effects of Slovenia's Integration in the Euro Area', *Empirica*, 35, 391–403.

Weyerstrass, K. and Neck, R. (2008c) 'On the Macroeconomic Effects of Introducing the Euro: A Case Study for Slovenia', in Welfe, W. and Welfe, A. (eds), *MACROMODELS 2007* (Lodz: University of Lodz), 85–100.

Weyerstrass, K. and Neck, R. (2011a) *Macroeconomic Effects of the Adoption of the Euro in Bosnia and Herzegovina*, Unpublished manuscript, Klagenfurt University.

Weyerstrass, K. and Neck, R. (2011b) *Macroeconomic Effects of the Adoption of the Euro in Serbia*, Unpublished manuscript, Klagenfurt University.

Winkler, A. (2005) 'Lessons from Sustained Cases of Official Dollarization/ Euroization', in Liebscher, K., Christl, J., Mooslechner, P. and Ritzberger-Grünwald, D. (eds), *European Economic Integration and South–East Europe: Challenges and Prospects* (Cheltenham, UK and Northampton, MA, USA: Edward Elgar), 77–96.

# 9
# Innovation Capacity in the SEE Region

*Đuro Kutlača and Slavo Radosevic*

## Introduction

A majority of the countries of SEE are so-called 'catching-up' economies.[1] This basically means that their enterprises operate largely behind the technological frontier, by using the best available foreign technologies and by competing on the basis of production capability. However, catching up is not a process of mere imitation; it requires adaptation and innovation (Fagerberg and Verspagen, 2003; Fagerberg and Godhino, 2005). The capability to innovate remains essential, as no nation can 'free-ride' on the world scientific system (Salter and Martin, 2001). Economic catch-up in the twenty-first century places greater demands on the knowledge-related capabilities of the catching-up economies (Mowery, 2005, p. 30). The changing conditions surrounding the catching-up process make 'the role of indigenous public research more important today than it was in the 20th century' (Nelson, 2005, p. 19). Accordingly, assessing the innovation capacity of South East Europe is not an exercise in studying the future, but a quite important element for our understanding of the growth potential of this region in the medium and long term.

With the end of the Cold War, South East Europe became a new European periphery in terms of research and development (R&D) and innovation. At the same time, it is a quite diverse periphery, which encompasses mainly catching-up economies (most of the countries in the region), two moderate innovators (Hungary and Greece) and one innovation follower (Slovenia; see below).[2] Although complete data are not available for many Western Balkan countries, it seems that differences between countries at different stages of catching up are substantial. This diversity is an important structural feature of the region and should have its advantages in terms of doing business. Differences in innovation capacities should enable multinational companies – including those from the region – to combine different levels of labour costs and technology into bundles of competitive products and services (Zysman and Schwartz, 1998). In addition, differences in technological levels and innovation capacities should represent some advantage for those lagging behind, as they can catch up through technical assistance and close interaction with their partners in more developed parts of the region. The question we want to address is whether these potential advantages have been exploited so far, and what SEE countries have done to exploit these opportunities. Competition is a dynamic process; enterprises and industries need to upgrade continually. So the issue is the level of innovation capacity in SEE countries and whether this level is improving. With this perspective in mind, the present chapter aims to assess the innovation capacity of SEE and its individual components, as well as issues pertaining to the integration of technology in SEE. First, we briefly explain the concept of national innovation capacity (NIC), which serves as our conceptual framework, and this is followed by an analysis of the position of the SEE countries in terms of their innovation capacity. The analysis will then be extended to cover issues of technology integration, distinguishing between upstream integration (R&D cooperation) and downstream integration – foreign direct investment (FDI) and production networks.

## National innovation capacity, growth and industrial upgrading in SEE

There is a general consensus among economists that technological innovation plays a central role in the process of long-term economic growth. However, there is a wide variety of approaches when it comes to understanding the underlying drivers of growth and the innovation process itself. Aggregate presentations of technology innovation such as total factor productivity (TFP), or the part of growth which cannot be attributed to labour and capital, are not very useful, due to the overly aggregate nature of these indicators. In addition, it is not appropriate to consider physical capital, human capital and technology as separate factors. To think of them as separate from each other is a highly unrealistic assumption.

Innovation studies show that innovation does not result solely from one specific factor, for instance supply of R&D (see Freeman and Soete,

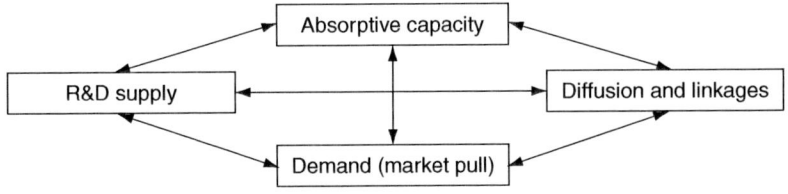

*Figure 9.1*   The concept of national innovation capacity
*Source*: Radosevic (2004).

1997 for an overview). In order to understand the key issues behind country differences in growth and technology, our analysis must be placed within a multi-dimensional framework – that is, one that captures several important dimensions, all of which determine innovation capacity (see Figure 9.1).

The development of an economy reflects the accumulation of its knowledge capital from micro-level (firm) to macro-level (national economy), as well as the institutional structuring of that capital through its national innovation system (NIS) (Lundvall, 1992). In this chapter, metrics are applied to identify potentials for development, which we conceptualize as national innovation capacity (NIC). A reader should be aware that any attempt to capture a highly multi-dimensional concept such as 'innovation capacity' into one composite indicator is inevitably subject to numerous objections.[3] However, we think that, in spite of the problems with this approach, the latter is still a useful and insightful exercise. SEE countries are at different stages of development insofar as technology and innovation are concerned, and these play quite diverse roles in growth and industrial upgrading. An overview of the different stages of technological development as well as of the factors by which they are determined should offer new insights, which are of relevance both for business and for policy-makers.

The NIC approach enables us to look beyond R&D to understand innovation capacity. In keeping with the national innovation system approach, the NIC approach measures indicators of innovation capacity organized into four groups: R&D supply, absorptive capacity, diffusion and demand (see Table 9.1) – following the idea that the growth and innovation capacity of an economy depends not only on the supply of R&D, but also on the capability of the country to absorb and diffuse technology, as well as on the demand for its generation and utilization.

*Table 9.1*  Indicators of innovation capacity

| Name of indicator | Abbreviation | Year | Source |
|---|---|---|---|
| **Absorptive capacity** | | | |
| Expenditures in education in % of GDP | eductgdp | 2007 | Eurostat |
| Science and engineering graduates (% 20–29 population) | segrdpop | 2007 | EIS |
| Population with 3rd-level education | pop3educ | 2008 | EIS |
| Participation in life-long learning (% of working-age population) | llearng | 2008 | EIS |
| Employment in high-tech manufacturing | emplmdhtec | 2008 | EIS |
| Employment in high-tech services | emphsrvc | 2008 | EIS |
| **R&D supply** | | | |
| Public R&D expenditures (% of GDP) | pubrd | 2008 | EIS |
| Business R&D expenditures (% of GDP) | besrd | 2008 | EIS |
| R&D personnel per labour force | rdpsnlab | 2008 | Eurostat |
| EPO patent applications (per million population) | epopc | 2008 | EPO |
| USPTO patent grants (per million population) | usptopc | 2008 | USPTO |
| Resident patents per capita | respat | 2008 | WIPO |
| **Diffusion** | | | |
| Training enterprises as % of all enterprises | trainent | 2005 | Eurostat |
| CVT in % of labour costs of all enterprises | cvtlabct | 2005 | Eurostat |
| ISO 900 certifications per capita | iso9kpc | 2008 | ISO |
| Internet users per 10,000 inhabitants | internet | 2008 | ITU |
| Fixed broadband Internet subscribers (per 100 people) | fbbint | 2008 | ITU |
| ICT expenditures (% of GDP) | ictgdp | 2006 | Trendchart |
| **Demand** | | | |
| Stock market capitalization in % of GDP | stockmkt | 2008 | World Bank |
| Domestic credit provided by banking sector (% of GDP) | domcredi | 2008 | World Bank |
| Share of FDI stock in GDP | fdigdp | 2008 | UNCTAD |
| Share of trade in GDP | tradegdp | 2008 | World Bank |
| Index of patent rights | iprindex | 2005 | Pack (2008) |
| Registered unemployment | unempl | 2008 | UNECE |
| Consumer price index | cpi | 2008 | UNECE |

*Note*: CVT = Continuous Vocational Training; EPO = European Patent Office; FDI = Foreign Direct Investment; GDP = Gross Domestic Product; ICT = Information and Communication Technology; ISO = International Organization for Standardization; R&D = Research & Development; USPTO = US Patent and Trademark Office.
*Source*: The authors.

Individual elements of the framework are interrelated. In aggregation, they produce the national innovation capacity (Radosevic, 2004).

In the following sections of this chapter we analyse the position of SEE countries with respect to each of the four major components of their NIC.

### Absorptive capacity for industrial upgrading

Absorptive capacity is the ability to absorb new knowledge and to adapt imported technologies. This capability is essential if catching-up economies are to grow and innovate. Indicators that measure absorptive capacity are expenditures in education as a per cent of GDP; science and engineering graduates (percentage of population 20–29 years old); population with third-level education; participation in life long learning; employment in medium/high-tech industries; and employment in high-tech services industries. Table 9.2 shows where SEE countries stand in relation to the EU-27 average. Percentages highlighted in bold indicate areas above EU average, while percentages highlighted in grey indicate those areas where SEE countries are significantly (more than 50 per cent) below EU average.

The absorptive capacity of South East Europe is clearly not an area of advantage when compared with the EU average. Only Slovenia has absorptive capacity indicators that are either above or close to the EU average. The majority of other countries are ranked below the EU average. The most pronounced differences are evident in life long learning activities, where all SEE countries (except Slovenia) lag behind the EU average by more than 50 per cent. In terms of absorptive capacity, Greece does not differ from the rest of the region; this includes the low participation of its population in life long learning. Also, the structure of its economy shows only a very small share of medium- and high-tech industries, with the share of high-tech service industries still at the levels of Slovenia and Hungary. As will become evident later on, weak life long learning activities are accompanied by very weak firm-level training activities in most of the SEE economies.

### R&D and innovation activities

R&D capability is important not only in generating new knowledge, but also as a mechanism to absorb it. Indicators that measure R&D capability are public R&D expenditures (in per cent of GDP); business R&D expenditures (in per cent of GDP); R&D personnel per labour force; European Patents Office patent applications (per million population);

Table 9.2 Indicators of absorptive capacity, SEE countries as % of EU average

| | SI | HU | GR | TR | BG | RO | HR | SRB | MK | AL | MN | BIH |
|---|---|---|---|---|---|---|---|---|---|---|---|---|
| Expenditures in education as a % of GDP | **104.6** | **104.8** | 80.6 | 57.7 | 83.3 | 85.7 | 82.1 | 82.3 | 94.8 | 57.8 | 86.2 | – |
| S&E graduates (% of 20–29 population) | **102.4** | 72.60 | 61.4 | 54.4 | 85.2 | 118.3 | 56.7 | 85.2 | – | – | – | – |
| Population with 3rd-level education | 93.2 | 79.1 | 93.2 | *42.8* | 93.7 | 52.9 | 68.4 | 51.3 | 60.1 | 83.4 | 62.6 | 56.9 |
| Participation in life-long learning | **144.8** | *32.3* | *30.2* | *18.8* | *14.6* | *15.6* | *22.9* | *13.0* | – | – | – | – |
| Employment in medium/ high-tech industries | **137.9** | **140.4** | *31.1* | 58.5 | 77.8 | 84.9 | 70.1 | 58.7 | – | – | – | – |
| Employment in high-tech services industries | 73.0 | 81.6 | 79.6 | *39.8* | 56.0 | *37.9* | 65.3 | **226.7** | – | – | – | – |

Source: European Innovation Scoreboard (EIS) 2009; World Bank Development Indicators database (2009).

US Patent and Trademark Office patent grants (per million population); and resident patents per capita.

As indicated by the large number of shaded (grey) areas in Table 9.3, knowledge generation capacity is a very weak component of SEE innovation capacity. SEE lies more than 50 per cent below the EU average in all factors except public funding of R&D. The biggest gap is in patent activities – not only in world frontier technology patenting (EPO and USPTO patents), but also in terms of resident patenting per capita. With the exception of Slovenia, resident patenting per capita is below 50 per cent of the EU average in all other SEE economies. The business sector (again, with the exception of Slovenia) does not make a significant investment in R&D either; here the gap also reveals that figures for SEE countries are more than 50 per cent below EU average. In terms of R&D employment, Slovenia lies above the EU average, while Hungary, Greece, Croatia and Serbia are below the EU average. This gap, however, is much lower than in the case of outputs of R&D activity. This suggests that the effectiveness of the R&D systems of these economies is an issue that deserves further attention.

### Diffusion of innovation

Diffusion is the key mechanism for reaping economic rewards from investment in R&D and for increasing absorptive capacity. Indicators that measure diffusion include: training enterprises as a percentage of all enterprises; continuous vocational training (CVT) (in per cent of labour costs of all enterprises); ISO 9000 certifications per capita; Internet users per 10,000 inhabitants; fixed broadband Internet subscribers (per 100 people); and information and communication technology (ICT) expenditures (in per cent of GDP). Here the gap between the EU average and SEE is the smallest (see Table 9.4). This is to be expected for economies where the economic growth should be based on importing and on the diffusion of foreign technologies and knowledge. Also, this is an area where, at least in some indicators, several SEE economies are above the EU average. Slovenia and Hungary respectively rank best in the region in terms of diffusion capacity. Again, Greece ranks quite low, none of the indicators being above the EU average. SEE countries seem to lag least in ICT expenditures as a per cent of GDP (though data are not available for half of the countries). The difference is biggest in terms of fixed broadband Internet subscribers, which also reflects, partly, the low-income levels.

*Table 9.3* Indicators of R&D capability, SEE countries as % of EU average

| | SI | HU | GR | TR | BG | RO | HR | SRB | MK | AL | MN | BIH |
|---|---|---|---|---|---|---|---|---|---|---|---|---|
| Public R&D expenditures (% of GDP) | 86.6 | 67.2 | 61.2 | 64.2 | 49.3 | 61.2 | 74.6 | 64.2 | 7.0 | – | 12.4 | – |
| Business R&D expenditures (% of GDP) | 88.4 | 43.8 | 13.2 | 24.8 | 12.4 | 14.9 | 33.1 | 5.4 | 3.3 | – | 1.1 | – |
| R&D personnel per labour force | 107.8 | 63.1 | 69.9 | 26.2 | 46.6 | 30.1 | 53.4 | 57.4 | 67.1 | – | 53.7 | – |
| EPO patent applications (per million population) | 47.4 | 8.2 | 6.2 | 2.1 | 1.5 | 0.6 | 4.3 | 0.4 | 0.0 | 0.0 | 0.0 | 0.2 |
| USPTO patent grants (per million population) | 13.8 | 13.6 | 4.3 | 0.9 | 4.4 | 1.0 | 7.5 | 1.0 | 0.9 | 0.0 | 0.0 | 0.5 |
| Resident patents per capita | 64.5 | 30.1 | 32.4 | 13.9 | 14.2 | 20.1 | 34.0 | 22.9 | 7.3 | – | – | 6.8 |

*Note:* EPO = European Patent Office; GDP = Gross Domestic Product; USPTO = US Patent and Trademark Office.
*Sources:* European Innovation Scoreboard (EIS) (2009); EUROSTAT (2010); EPO (2010); USPTO (2010).

*Table 9.4* Indicators of diffusion of innovation, SEE countries as % of EU average

| | SI | HU | GR | TR | BG | RO | HR | SRB | MK | AL | MN | BIH |
|---|---|---|---|---|---|---|---|---|---|---|---|---|
| Training enterprises as % of all enterprises | 121.7 | 81.7 | 35.0 | 47.9 | 48.3 | 66.7 | 143.3 | 60.9 | 31.6 | 33.2 | 42.0 | 110.8 |
| CVT (continuous vocational training) in % of labour costs of all enterprises | 125.0 | 118.8 | 37.5 | – | 68.8 | 68.8 | 81.3 | – | – | – | – | – |
| ISO 9000 certifications per capita | 116.8 | 125.8 | 76.4 | 23.1 | 85.1 | 60.9 | 66.5 | 34.7 | 16.2 | 1.7 | 31.4 | 26.3 |
| Internet users per 10,000 inhabitants | 88.9 | 93.4 | 68.9 | 54.9 | 55.5 | 46.0 | 80.6 | 71.7 | 66.3 | 38.1 | 75.5 | 55.4 |
| Fixed broadband Internet subscribers (per 100 people) | 88.1 | 72.8 | 55.9 | 32.5 | 46.2 | 48.6 | 49.4 | 25.6 | 37.0 | 8.5 | 41.7 | 20.8 |
| ICT expenditures (% GDP) | 90.0 | 169.5 | 83.0 | 77.3 | 120.1 | 93.6 | – | – | – | – | – | – |

*Sources*: European Innovation Scoreboard (EIS) 2009; EUROSTAT (2010); ISO (2010); World Bank Development Indicators database (2010).

## Demand for innovation

Demand for R&D and innovation is the key economic mechanism that initiates value creation through R&D, absorption and diffusion activities. Indicators that measure demand for R&D and innovation are the availability of finance (stock market capitalization in per cent of GDP); domestic credit provided by the banking sector; share of FDI (in GDP); competition (share of trade in GDP; index of patent rights); and macro-economic stability (registered unemployment; consumer price index). We assume that the more developed the financial system, the better it can articulate demand for innovation, given equality of technological opportunities. Share of trade and foreign direct investments (FDI) in GDP are used as proxies for the intensity of competition, together with the index of patent rights.[4] We assume that macro-economic stability through extending the horizon for entrepreneurs promotes demand for innovation.

The overall picture in terms of demand (see Table 9.5) is not so favourable as it is in terms of diffusion or absorption capacity, but it is better than it is in terms of knowledge generation capacity. Financial indicators (except FDI) show an undeveloped financial system, which does not generate pull for innovation. The situation is best in terms of FDI, as SEE economies have attracted FDI from developed EU countries, in particular from Germany, Austria and Italy. However, there is an issue as to whether FDI contributes to technology transfer, which we will address below. SEE economies are small and open economies, which have made attempts to attract foreign investors and hence have reformed their intellectual property rights regimes for both domestic and foreign innovators. A high FDI and trade openness further reinforce the importance of national innovation systems, generating synergies with trade and FDI partners (see below). On the demand side, macro-economic stability is generally much better than it used to be in the period of early transition. However, in comparison with the EU average, the SEE economies (except Slovenia) show higher unemployment rates and higher levels of inflation. These are indicators for economies that operate below full capacity and with significant cost pressures. Both of these factors are incentives for improving production capacity through new investments rather than innovation capability.

Overall, the analysis of the four components of innovation capacity shows that SEE lies far behind the EU average – with the exception of Slovenia, which ranks very close to or at EU average. The countries in the region that perform worse than the EU average in the generation of new knowledge, are better in terms of diffusion and are best in terms

Table 9.5  Indicators of demand for R&D and innovation, SEE countries as % of EU average

| | SI | HU | GR | TR | BG | RO | HR | SRB | MK | AL | MN | BIH |
|---|---|---|---|---|---|---|---|---|---|---|---|---|
| Stock market capitalization in % of GDP | 56.8 | 31.7 | 67.0 | 42.3 | 46.8 | 26.3 | 101.9 | 64.1 | 22.8 | – | 154.3 | – |
| Domestic credit provided by banking sector | 61.3 | 56.5 | 76.4 | 36.8 | 46.8 | 28.7 | 52.6 | 26.9 | 29.9 | 47.3 | 57.0 | 41.0 |
| Share of FDI in GDP | 84.5 | 116.5 | 29.1 | 36.0 | 261.1 | 106.8 | 144.8 | 95.0 | 135.4 | 58.8 | 201.8 | 123.2 |
| Share of trade in GDP | 174.8 | 199.5 | 67.9 | 64.5 | 177.3 | 86.7 | 113.8 | 101.3 | 161.8 | 111.7 | 141.9 | 90.8 |
| Index of patent rights | 98.6 | 103.2 | 98.6 | 92.0 | 104.1 | 95.6 | 98.4 | 98.2 | 98.2 | – | 98.3 | – |
| Registered unemployment | 62.9 | 111.4 | 110.0 | 138.6 | 80.0 | 82.9 | 120.0 | 194.3 | 482.9 | 185.7 | 240.0 | 334.3 |
| Consumer price index | 103.4 | 109.5 | 101.9 | 122.2 | 120.3 | 111.0 | 103.7 | 121.9 | 104.8 | 100.3 | 107.9 | 106.6 |

*Sources*: UNECE-EUROSTAT; UNCTAD; World Bank.

of absorptive capacities. A better ranking in terms of absorptive capacities is expected for catching-up economies, and it seems that policymakers should focus on significantly improving diffusion and demand capacities, both of which are essential for employing absorptive capacities. Knowledge generation capacities cannot improve without positive reinforcements from the other three components. Factors of demand for innovation and R&D are, relatively speaking, better than knowledge generation, but still below absorptive and diffusion capacities. Current policies in the majority of SEE countries are largely focused on R&D capacities, while neglecting the other components. However, our framework suggests that the effects of R&D policies will ultimately fail unless they are supported by positive signals from the other three components. This calls for new approaches to policy that are primarily concerned with interactions in innovation system and which therefore go beyond narrowly defined R&D policies.

## Assessing national innovation capacity in SEE

So far we have shown a cross-section picture of innovation capacity in the SEE region. Following a procedure based on that developed by Zinnes et al. (2001) and Porter et al. (2002), we continue with standardizing the data, multiplying them by assigned weights and adding together all the resulting products. In this way we construct aggregate values for each of the four components of national innovation capacity. By summing up the values of the four components we calculate the aggregate national innovation capacity index. We assign equal weights to all indicators, except for a few cases where indicators measure similar aspects of components – in those cases we reduce the weight of individual indicators. In measuring absorptive capacity, each of the six indicators carries one-sixth of the weight. For R&D supply we assign one-fifth to each of the indicators, since we treat US and European patent office patents as one single indicator, with half a weight assigned to each of them. We adopt the same procedure to calculate diffusion capacity. We assign one-fifth to each of the five indicators, since we treat Internet use and personal computers (PCs) per capita as one single indicator, with half a weight assigned to each. Unemployment and consumer price indices are inversely proportional to the NIC index. We change the signs of these two indicators to make them, like other indicators, positively proportional. The summary innovation capacity index is the simple summation of the four components. Table 9.6 and Figure 9.2 show aggregate values of the NIC index based on this methodology.

*Table 9.6*  National innovation capacity, SEE countries

|  | SI | HU | HR | BG | GR | SRB | RO | MK | TR |
|---|---|---|---|---|---|---|---|---|---|
| Aggregate NIC | 4.552 | 2.613 | 0.751 | 0.053 | −0.682 | −0.936 | −1.333 | −1.850 | −3.167 |
| Absorptive capacity | 1.309 | 0.504 | −0.434 | 0.010 | −0.309 | 0.055 | −0.069 | 0.067 | −1.133 |
| R&D supply | 1.845 | 0.367 | 0.258 | −0.492 | 0.076 | −0.230 | −0.457 | −0.908 | −0.459 |
| Diffusion | 0.906 | 1.276 | 0.365 | −0.072 | −0.674 | −0.297 | −0.328 | −0.555 | −0.622 |
| Demand | 0.492 | 0.465 | 0.563 | 0.606 | 0.224 | −0.464 | −0.480 | −0.455 | −0.952 |

*Note*: Data for Albania and for Bosnia and Herzegovina are insufficient for a calculation of aggregate values of the four dimensions and of the overall value of NIC.
*Source*: Calculation of NIC according to methodology in Radosevic (2004).

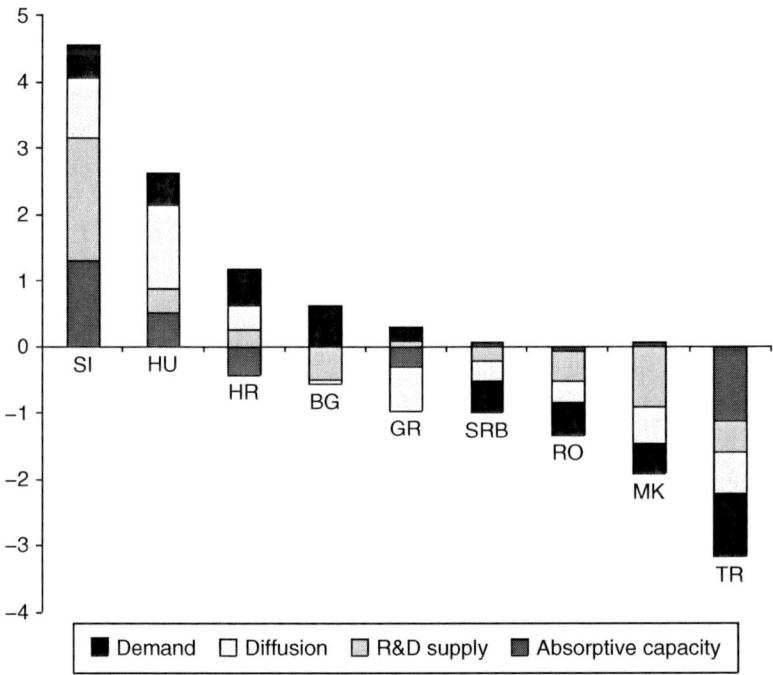

*Figure 9.2*  National innovation capacity of the SEE countries
*Source*: Calculation of NIC according to methodology in Radosevic (2004).

The aggregation of different dimensions of innovation capacity into the NIC index reveals considerable differences in innovation capacity between countries, which is to be expected given the analysis above. Slovenia emerges as the clear regional leader. It is the only SEE economy which ranks around the EU average in the majority of NIC indicators. In terms of innovation capacity in the region, Slovenia is followed by Hungary, Croatia, Bulgaria and Greece. These countries are above the SEE average. The national innovation capacities of Serbia, Romania, FYR of Macedonia and Turkey are least developed. If data were available for Bosnia and Herzegovina and for Albania, we suspect that these economies would belong to the lower segment of SEE countries. These results are in line with expectations when one looks at the individual components of NIC, but they are not identical to rankings by the European Innovation Scoreboard.

The European Innovation Scoreboard (EIS) is an alternative composite indicator, which has become an established measure for innovation in the European Union. EIS 2009 presents the current innovation performance in Bulgaria, Greece, Hungary, Romania, Slovenia, Croatia, Turkey and Serbia. Most of the innovation scoreboard data are still not available for other SEE countries. The Summary Innovation Index (SII) is a composite of 29 indicators representing innovation performance in the observed countries. According to SII and compared with the EU-27 average, different SEE countries are classified as being at different stages of innovation development (EIS, 2009) (see Table 9.7).

As was shown above, the ranking of countries differs when they are grouped on the basis of alternative composite indicators of NIC. Hence the question to be asked is: what does EIS actually measure? We would argue that EIS indicates the degree to which the growth of economies is based on the world frontier innovation, not necessarily on its own innovation capacity, which should include innovation activities typical

*Table 9.7* SEE economies based on the European Innovation Scoreboard index (SII)

| | |
|---|---|
| Innovation follower | Slovenia |
| Moderate innovator | Greece (SII = 0.370), Hungary (SII = 0.328) |
| Catching-up countries* | Bulgaria (SII = 0.231), Croatia (SII = 0.286), Romania (SII = 0.294), Serbia (SII = 0.227) |

*: No data for SII are available for Albania, for Macedonia and for Bosnia and Herzegovina, but these countries can confidently be grouped under the catching-up countries category.
*Source*: Based on European Innovation Scoreboard (2009).

for countries behind the technological frontier. The EIS was originally designed to measure the innovativeness of EU economies in relation to the technology leader, the USA. Hence this composite indicator has a built-in bias towards technology effort that takes place at the world's technological frontier. However, SEE countries are countries operating behind the technological frontier, with their growth largely based on imported technology and on its adaptation and improvements (Kutlača, 2006). Therefore our composite indicator seems to be a better approximation of the type of technology effort that takes place in SEE countries.

Inevitably, ranking countries on the basis of two different composite indicators will lead to different results. The biggest difference between NIC and EIS lies in the ranking of Greece. According to EIS, Greece ranks second among the SEE countries, while according to our NIC it only ranks fifth. Greece ranks much better when its innovativeness is measured by the extent to which the country relies on world frontier innovation activities than when it is measured by NIC. However, having a high score based on world frontier innovation activities does not necessarily mean that a country will grow faster, or that its GDP per capita will necessarily be higher. Countries should grow on the basis of the type of technology effort that is appropriate to their current and future level of development. For example, countries behind the technological frontier should grow at the highest rate if they improve their technology imitation and absorption activities. A high share of growth based on world frontier activities, which is combined with a low share of imitation and activities behind the world frontier, may indicate imbalances in the national innovation system rather than being an appropriate model of growth.

In addition, EIS contains 29 indicators while NIC contains 25, of which only 9 are identical. Among others, EIS contains more indicators that measure activities associated with world frontier technology activities like doctorate graduates, venture capital, technology balance of payment and export of knowledge-intensive services. On the other hand, NIC leans more towards measuring activities behind the technological frontier like resident patents and ISO 9000-certificates. In addition, differences also result from the general availability of indicators, which is much more restricted for some SEE countries.

On the basis of the analysis above, we now explain the relevance of our approach for understanding industrial upgrading in SEE countries. First, NIC indicates that the extent to which countries grow is based on innovation (albeit not necessarily on world frontier innovation activity). Current NIC, however, is not necessarily reflected in current growth. So NIC indicates *potential* for technological upgrading as well as the degree to which current levels of development are a reflection of innovation-based activities. For example, Greece has a much higher income per capita, but its innovation capacity is much lower than would be expected (see Figure 9.3). This simply points to the fact that the source of the Greek economic growth is in activities that are not based on technology, but in services that do not have much technological content. On the other hand, Slovenia has a higher NIC than its current income would predict, which suggests that this country has greater potential for growth based on technology catch-up. Alternatively, one could argue that its national innovation system (NIS) is not contributing to growth as would be expected. In the case of other countries these mismatches are visibly lower, which suggests that their future growth would require more investment in innovation activities. However, it is important to note that the sample of countries taken here is far too small for broad generalizations. Nevertheless, these seem to be intuitively very indicative conclusions. In addition, current levels of NIC may affect

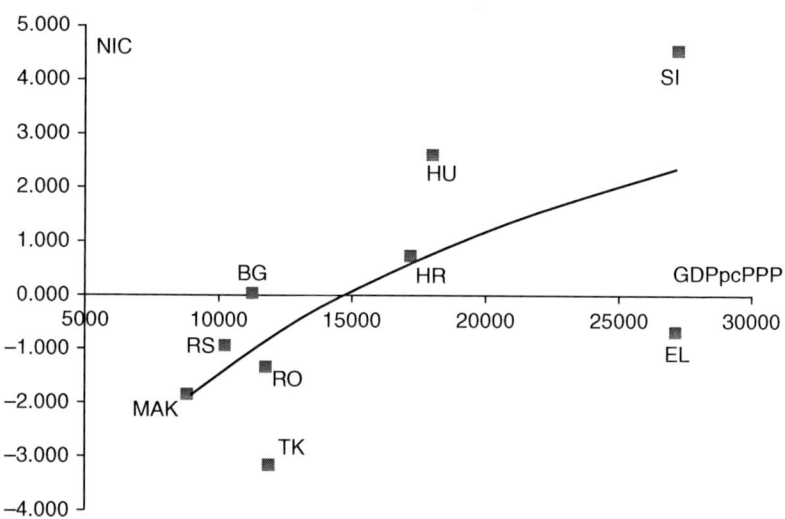

*Figure 9.3* Relationship between national innovation capacity index (NIC) and GDP per capita at PPP (GDPpc PPP) (2008)
*Source:* Authors for NIC; World Bank Development Indicators database for GDP per capita at purchasing power parity.

growth with sometimes significant delay – hence this relationship can be properly understood only from a longitudinal perspective.

SEE countries are operating behind the technological frontier in terms of knowledge generation and sources of growth, which are largely based on the acquisition and adoption of imported technologies. Thus their growth will be strongly dependent on how they are combining their internal process of technology accumulation with international technology import and export. We now turn to these issues, which are of equal importance for SEE.

## International technology integration in SEE

The current period provides a new and historic opportunity for the SEE region to integrate into the wider European economy. This should facilitate the catching up of this region with the EU core. From an industry upgrading perspective, countries can be integrated through production (industrial networks), but also through technology – or through knowledge-intensive networks. In this latter case we can speak of technology integration, by which we mean integration into the process of knowledge generation and diffusion across international borders. Obviously there is an overlap between production and technology integration, as production integration via foreign direct investment (FDI) and sub-contracting linkages may involve a significant degree of joint knowledge generation and exchange. Technology and knowledge integration are most visible in the field of R&D through the involvement in international R&D projects, through external funding of R&D or through the education of nationals abroad. This upstream integration at the level of R&D and human capital can be quite different from downstream integration at the level of trade and FDI. For example, Slovenia is highly integrated at the upstream or R&D level, but much less so at the level of FDI.

Subsequently we discuss first the integration at upstream or R&D level. We have recently seen an increasing integration of South East European R&D systems into EU R&D project networks. Table 9.8 shows that there are still very big differences in that respect between individual SEE countries, Greece and Slovenia clearly lying much ahead of the rest of the region. EU co-funding in these two countries is above the EU average, while per capita EU funding is several times lower than the average in other SEE countries. This is partly a reflection of much less developed R&D systems in these countries, as well as the effect of the 'early start' of these countries as regards the Seventh Framework Programme (FP7).

*Table 9.8*   SEE involvement in Seventh Framework Programme (FP7) projects: European Commission's contributions and requested contributions in FP7

| | Applicant-requested EC financial contribution in EUR (cumulative, not only of signed agreements) | Participant EC contribution in EUR (only in signed contracts of calls closed in reference year) | Share of signed contracts in requested contributions |
|---|---|---|---|
| | All FP7 PER 1MN POPULATION | All FP7 PER 1MN POPULATION | |
| Greece | 43.56 | 28.99 | 67% |
| Slovenia | 34.14 | 20.36 | 60% |
| Bulgaria | 7.69 | 4.35 | 57% |
| Croatia | 6.63 | 4.31 | 65% |
| Montenegro | 3.88 | 1.38 | 36% |
| Serbia | 3.73 | 2.24 | 60% |
| FYR of Macedonia | 3.68 | 2.65 | 72% |
| Romania | 3.64 | 2.08 | 57% |
| Turkey | 1.01 | 0.72 | 71% |
| Albania | 0.48 | 0.24 | 51% |
| Bosnia and Herzegovina | 0.37 | 0.32 | 86% |
| Average EU-27 countries | 32.49 | | |

*Source*: eCORDA, 8 June 2010, derived from Rivera León and Reid (2010).

We can expect that the SEE countries' R&D systems will become highly integrated into the European Research Area. This should have positive effects in terms of dynamism and excellence in R&D, as many countries' R&D groups will be 'plugged' into EU R&D networks. However, these effects by themselves will not ensure the relevance of these countries' R&D systems to their local economies (Radosevic, 2009). As the best, if R&D groups become integrated into EU networks, the gap between them and the local business sectors may widen. The situation of SEE may resemble the situation in Greece, where a competent R&D system has relatively limited links to the domestic business sector.

This orientation towards EU funding has made R&D systems of SEE already quite dependent on EU sources. Table 9.9 shows that the share of foreign funding of R&D is by far the highest in Greece, but also Bulgaria, Hungary and, surprisingly, Croatia have already recorded high shares.

*Table 9.9*  External funding of R&D: Total intramural R&D expenditure (GERD) by source of funds, % of GDP

|  | GERD by source of funds: All sectors | GERD by source of funds: Abroad | Share of GERD financed from abroad | Reference year |
|---|---|---|---|---|
| EU average (27 countries) | 1.9 | 0.17 | 8.9% | 2008 |
| Bulgaria | 0.48 | 0.04 | 8.3% | 2007 |
| Greece | 0.59 | 0.11 | 18.6% | 2005 |
| Hungary | 1 | 0.09 | 9.0% | 2008 |
| Romania | 0.58 | 0.02 | 3.4% | 2008 |
| Slovenia | 1.66 | 0.09 | 5.4% | 2008 |
| Croatia | 0.9 | 0.07 | 7.8% | 2008 |
| Turkey | 0.72 | 0 | 0.0% | 2007 |
| Serbia | 0.69 | 0.04 | 6.7% | 2007 |

*Source:* EUROSTAT database, September 2010; data for Serbia from Serbian Statistical Office.

If these early trends continue for new member states as well as for candidate states, it is to be expected that SEE countries will (just like Greece) be highly dependent on EU funding, which will have its own positive as well as negative effects. As was already pointed out, positive effects may include increasing international excellence, but not necessarily also increasing local relevance. It is significant that even countries like Serbia, which joined the Seventh Framework Programme quite recently, will soon reach EU average in the share of foreign R&D funding.

The Europeanization of R&D systems is accompanied by an increasing desire of students to study abroad, which can be classified either as 'brain drain' or as 'brain gain', or indeed as 'brain circulation'. It seems that this process is advancing at a somewhat slower rate than the increase in foreign funding of R&D. Table 9.10 shows that Albania is the major 'export' destination in this respect, while Greece and FYR of Macedonia are around the average level of the EU-27. Other SEE countries are lagging significantly behind. This can be explained by a variety of factors related to travel restrictions, size of countries as well as quality of life and living standards in individual countries.

While external conditions undoubtedly play an important role, internal conditions for retaining local talent are probably even more important. Data collected within the World Economic Forum (WEF) Global Competitiveness Report probed into this area by asking respondents about local conditions (Table 9.11). SEE countries vary greatly in terms

*Table 9.10* Foreign students in tertiary education (ISCED 5–6) by country of citizenship, % of total population

| Country of citizenship | Number of students from country in EU-27, year 2007 | % of total population |
|---|---|---|
| Albania | 18,965 | 0.603 |
| Greece | 34,878 | 0.324 |
| FYR of Macedonia | 6,205 | 0.304 |
| Bulgaria | 21,212 | 0.278 |
| Croatia | 9,126 | 0.216 |
| Bosnia and Herzegovina | 7,258 | 0.192 |
| Serbia and Montenegro | 9,617 | 0.121 |
| Slovenia | 2,309 | 0.114 |
| Romania | 20,074 | 0.093 |
| Hungary | 7,377 | 0.075 |
| Turkey | 37,588 | 0.054 |
| EU27 | 1,709,775 | 0.349 |

*Source*: EUROSTAT database, September 2010; data for Serbia from Serbian Statistical Office.

*Table 9.11* Evaluation of conditions for the prevention of 'brain drain' from country, World Economic Forum (WEF), 2010

| 'Does your country retain and attract talented people?' [1 = no, the best and brightest normally leave to pursue opportunities in other countries; 7 = yes, there are many opportunities for talented people within the country], 2009–10 weighted average | SCORE | RANK |
|---|---|---|
| Slovenia | 3.8 | 48 |
| Montenegro | 3.6 | 55 |
| Turkey | 3.0 | 90 |
| Hungary | 2.7 | 99 |
| Greece | 2.7 | 103 |
| Albania | 2.7 | 107 |
| Romania | 2.4 | 116 |
| Croatia | 2.3 | 122 |
| FYR of Macedonia | 2.2 | 126 |
| Bulgaria | 2.2 | 127 |
| Serbia | 2.0 | 136 |
| Bosnia and Herzegovina | 2.0 | 138 |

*Source*: Schwab (2010).

of the existence of conditions that would prevent the 'brain drain'. On the one hand, there are Slovenia and Montenegro, while Serbia and Bosnia and Herzegovina are at the other extreme and the majority of SEE countries are at the lower end of the spectrum. On the positive side, these divergences represent great opportunities for intra-SEE education and skills migrations.

To summarize, results from the analysis of selected data suggest that SEE has already become quite integrated into the EU R&D networks, with ambiguous effects on its R&D system. Also, EU integration has generated new opportunities in terms of migration of skilled people; however, these opportunities still vary widely between different countries.

This picture of upstream integration needs to be complemented by a picture of downstream integration (integration of SEE at the level of trade and production networks). Table 9.12 summarizes the situation by distinguishing between producer-driven and buyer-driven value chains. Producer-driven value chains are based on multinational companies' direct foreign investments, which are closely linked to intensifying

*Table 9.12* Network relationships of SEE countries by type of production networks

| Type of network relationship | Producer-driven value chains (largely equity relationships) | | Buyer-driven value chains (largely sub-contracting) | |
|---|---|---|---|---|
| | FDI stock in manufacturing per capita ($) (2003) | Networks' exports per capita (%) (2003) | Share of clothing export in manufactured export (%) (2003) | Average annual growth rate of clothing export in % (1996–2003) |
| Hungary | 1,694 | 1,847 | 4.1 | 3.8 |
| Slovenia | 824 | 1094 | 3.5 | −7.5 |
| Croatia | 694 | 69 | 15.5 | −0.9 |
| Bulgaria | 428 | 22 | 34,0 | 27,0 |
| Romania | 262 | 59 | 29.8 | 18.5 |
| Serbia and Montenegro | 217 | 15 | 14.5 | −4.4 |
| FYROM | 60 | 11 | 44.9 | 7.3 |
| Albania | | | 41.1 | 17.2 |
| Turkey | | | 26.3 | 7.3 |

*Source*: Based on Broadman (2005).

trade both in finished products and in semi-finished parts (network trade). Buyer-driven value chains are largely of the non-equity type – like sub-contracting, which is typical for instance for the clothing industry. Table 9.12 shows that FDI-driven networks and related network trade are characteristic of Hungary and Slovenia. Other SEE countries are largely excluded from producer-driven networks or network trade relationships. However, these countries (for example Albania, Bulgaria, Romania or Macedonia) are connected with the EU through sub-contracting linkages. This is largely cost-driven sub-contracting, which is unlike producer-driven networks, where local skills and technological knowledge play a more important role. Croatia and Serbia are not clearly integrated into either of these two forms of industrial networks.

From a developmental perspective, upstream and downstream types of integration should complement each other. This is more likely to happen in the case of countries that are integrated through producer-driven networks than in those integrated through buyer-driven networks. Producer-driven networks are more technologically driven, or at least they contain significantly higher potential for further industrial upgrading as well as links with R&D and innovation activities. For countries characterized by buyer-driven networks this is a much bigger challenge.

## Conclusion

This chapter has demonstrated major differences between SEE countries in terms of their innovation capacities. In the context of EU integration and international business this represents a specific set of constraints as well as opportunities. In several respects, South East Europe is the most complex region in contemporary Europe (Radosevic, 2009). From an international business perspective, it represents a complex institutional fabric of different degrees of integration into the EU economy, as well as a variety of different institutional arrangements in terms of intra-regional trade and cooperation. On the other hand, a diversity of 'production functions' in the region – in part due to differences in labour costs and in productivity levels – offers opportunities for intra-regional FDI and sub-contracting arrangements. Despite its close proximity to core EU economies, SEE remains only very partially integrated into the EU economy. Improvements in the national innovation systems of SEE countries have mainly occurred through vertical linkages on the upstream (through the integration of R&D into the European Research Area) and on the downstream (through positive direct effects of FDI and through sub-contracting linkages) sides. Whether these vertical linkages will be enhanced and whether they will mutually interact will also depend on the activities of local governments and of other stakeholders. The capacity to work with foreign investors in enhancing both local and external linkages remains to be developed.

## Notes

1. For the purpose of this chapter and from the perspective of European integration and of the European Research Area, the expression 'SEE' will cover the four Western Balkan countries (Albania, Bosnia and Herzegovina, Montenegro and Serbia), three EU candidate countries (Croatia, FYR of Macedonia and Turkey) and five EU Member states (Bulgaria, Greece, Hungary, Romania and Slovenia).
2. Data are not available for Bosnia and Herzegovina, FYR of Macedonia, Albania and Montenegro. However, given other available indicators for these economies, it is safe to conclude that these economies rank at the bottom of the EU scale in terms of their innovation capacity.
3. For a discussion of composite indicators, see OECD (2008), and for their critique, see Grupp and Mogee (2004).
4. The index of patent rights is constructed by Ginarte and Park (1997). The G–P index is constructed as a scoreboard of five features of patent protection: (1) extent of coverage; (2) membership in international patent agreements; (3) provisions for loss of protection; (4) enforcement mechanism; and (5) duration of protection. Each of these categories is broken down into several subcomponents and weighted in such a way that each category ranges in value from 0 to 1. These categories are summed up as unweighted components, so the index value ranges from 0 to 5. Higher values of the index indicate stronger levels of protection. Values used in this chapter are recalculations prepared by Park (2008).

## References

Broadman, H. G. (ed.) (2005) *From Disintegration to Reintegration: Eastern Europe and the Former Soviet Union in International Trade* (Washington DC: The International Bank for Reconstruction and Development/The World Bank).

EIS (2009) *European Innovation Scoreboard (EIS) 2009 – Comparative Analysis of Innovation Performance*, PRO INNO Europe paper no. 15 (Brussels: European Union).

EPO (2010) European Patents and Patent Applications – Statistics 2009, http://www.epo.org/about-us/office, date accessed 24 March 2011.

EUROSTAT (2010) http://epp.eurostat.ec.europa.eu/portal/page/portal/statistics/search_database, date accessed 24 March 2011.

Fagerberg, J. and Godhino, M. M. (2005) 'Innovation and Catching-Up', In Fagerberg, J., Mowery, D. and Nelson, R. R. (eds) *The Oxford Handbook of Innovation* (Oxford: Oxford University Press), 514–543.

Fagerberg, J. and Verspagen, B. (2003) 'Innovation, Growth and Economic Development: Why Some Countries Succeed and Others Don't'. Paper prepared for the First GLOBELICS Conference: Innovation Systems and Development Strategies for the Third Millennium, Rio de Janeiro, 2–6 November.

Freeman, C. and Soete, L. (1997) *The Economics of Industrial Innovation*, 3rd ed. (Cambridge, MA: MIT Press Books).

Ginarte, J. C. and Park, W. G. (1997) 'Determinants of Patent Rights: A Cross-National Study', *Research Policy*, 26, 283–301.

Grupp, H. and Mogee, M. E. (2004) 'Indicators for National Science and Technology Policy: How Robust Are Composite Indicators?', *Research Policy*, 33, 1373–1384.

ISO (2010) International Organization for Standardization Free Publications, http://www.iso.org/iso/publications_and_e-products/free_pubs.htm, date accessed 24 March 2011.

Kutlača, D. (2006) 'S&T System of Serbia: Between Survival and Restructuring', International Conference 'Why Invest in Science in South Eastern Europe', UNESCO Regional Bureau for Science and Culture in Europe (BRESCE), UNESCO Office in Venice, Proceedings of the International Conference and High Level Round Table, Ljubljana, 28–29 September, 131–138.

Lundvall, B. A. (ed.) (1992) *National Systems of Innovation: Towards a Theory of Innovation and Interactive Learning* (London: Pinter).

Mowery, D. C. (2005) 'The Role of Knowledge-Based "Public Goods" in Economic "Catch-Up": Lessons from History', Industrial Development Report 2005 Background Paper Series, May (Vienna: UNIDO).

Nelson, R. R. (2005) 'The Roles of Research in Universities and Public Labs in Economic Catch-Up', In Santangelo, G. D. (ed.) *Technological Change and Economic Catch-Up* (Cheltenham: Edward Elgar), 19–32.

OECD (2008) *Handbook on Constructing Composite Indicators: Methodology and User Guide* (Paris: OECD).

Park, W. G. (2008) 'International Patent Protection: 1960–2005', *Research Policy*, 37, 761–766.

Porter, M. E., Sachs, J. D., Cornelius, P. K., McArthur, J. W. and Schwab, K. (2002) *World Competitiveness Report 2001–2002* (New York: Oxford University Press).

Radosevic, S. (2004) 'A Two-Tier or Multi-Tier Europe? Assessing the Innovation Capacities of Central and East European Countries in the Enlarged EU', *Journal of Common Market Studies*, 42, 3, 641–666.

Radosevic, S. (2009) 'Research and Development and Competitiveness, and European Integration of South Eastern Europe', *Euro-Asia Studies*, 61, 621–650.

Rivera León, L. and Reid, A. (2010) *Participation of South – East European Countries in the Competitive Funding Programmes for Research in the European Commission*, Report to UNESCO-BRESCE, Technopolis group, July.

Salter, J. and Martin, B. R. (2001) 'The Economic Benefits of Publicly Funded Research: A Critical Review', *Research Policy*, 30 (3), 509–532.

Schwab, K. (ed.) (2010) *The Global Competitiveness Report 2010–2011* (Geneva: World Economic Forum).

USPTO (2010) U.S. Patent and Trademark Office General Patent Statistics Report, http://www.uspto.gov/web/offices/ac/ido/oeip/taf/reports.htm, date accessed 24 March 2011.

World Bank Development Indicators database (2010) World Development Indicators & Global Development Finance, World Bank, 19 April 2010, http://

databank.woldbank.org/ddp/home.do?Step=12&id=4&CNO=2, date accessed 24 March 2011.

WEF (2010) *The Lisbon Review 2010 – Towards a More Competitive Europe?* (Geneva: World Economic Forum).

Zinnes, C., Eilat, Y. and Sachs, J. (2001) 'Benchmarking Competitiveness in Transition Economies', *Economics of Transition*, 9 (2), 315–353.

Zysman, J. and Schwartz, A. (eds) (1998) *Enlarging Europe: The Industrial Foundations of a New Political Economy* (Berkeley: Institute for International Studies).

# 10
## Small Firms as a Development Factor in South East Europe

*Will Bartlett*

### Introduction

In recent decades, economic growth and development in the advanced economies has become increasingly dependent on the dynamism of entrepreneurial small firms. Analysts have noted the increasingly significant role of small firms in advanced economies in areas such as job creation, innovation and competitiveness (Acs and Audretsch, 1993; Storey, 1994). Since they tend to operate in more labour-intensive sectors of an economy than large firms do, the creation of a new small business sector may play an important role in the process of economic regeneration, and particularly in the process of job creation. In the context of high unemployment and of a declining role of large state firms, this aspect has been especially important in the transition economies of South East Europe (Bartlett and Hoggett, 1996). In creating jobs, there is an increasing understanding of the important role played by a minority of fast-growth small firms, which tend to create the greatest part of new jobs in most economies. Often based in more high-technology sectors, these 'gazelles' seem to thrive in economies in which institutional structures emphasize the importance of knowledge transfer and of freedom from government interference, which are more likely to characterize the business environment in developed market economies than in emerging and transition economies (Valliere and Peterson, 2009). This represents a challenge for policy makers in South East Europe (SEE), where knowledge transfer institutions are weak (Bartlett and Čučković, 2006) and where government has only recently become rather more supportive of the small-firm sector in some countries (OECD, 2009).

The shift away from a reliance on large firms to generate economic growth has been a global phenomenon over the last three decades. Thurik and Wennekers (2004) characterize it as a shift from a 'managed economy' of large firms in the immediate post–Second World War years to an 'entrepreneurial economy' of small and medium-sized firms in the 1980s and onwards. This entrepreneurial style of economy was initially developed in the USA and in the UK, where small firms were agents of innovation and flexible responses to rapidly changing consumer demand. They also played an important role in the Southern European countries such as Italy, where small firms organized in industrial districts were the main agents of the remarkable economic growth of the Emilia Romagna region in the 1980s and 1990s. The emphasis on the central role of small and medium-sized enterprises (SMEs) has more recently come to dominate policy thinking throughout the European Union (EU). In the transition countries of Eastern Europe, the entry of new entrepreneurial small firms was an essential element of the transition from state managed economies, based on gigantic enterprises, to more dynamic and competitive economies, based on the entry of myriad small firms in all sectors of their economies.

The countries of South East Europe have been rather different, especially in the post-communist transition countries, where the entry and growth of small firms has been held back by state policies that have been, at best, ambiguous about the support offered to new entrepreneurs. This has been mainly due to the close political connections between ruling elites and the large firm sector; the latter has created closed economies in which powerful monopoly interests have encouraged the persistence of significant barriers to the ability of entrepreneurs to establish new firms in many sectors of these economies (Bartlett, 2000). Monopolies and powerful coalitions have sought to stall reforms and to preserve the status quo in order to maintain the privileged positions gained during the chaos of the early stages in the transition. The non-transition countries of the region, Greece and Turkey, have also experienced difficulties in moving away from a managed economy, in which the state plays a large role in directing economic activity, towards a more entrepreneurial type of economy. Nevertheless, the environment for small firms has been more conducive in these two countries than in the transition countries of SEE. In Greece smaller firms generate proportionally more jobs than larger firms, primarily in the most dynamic sectors such as high technology, which have contributed the most to net job creation (Voulgaris et al., 2005).

## Small firms in South East Europe

Even before the breakdown of the communist system in 1989–91 in SEE, the regimes in some countries had introduced reforms that encouraged the development of private enterprise. In former Yugoslavia small private firms were prevalent in agriculture, construction, transport and tourism, although they were subject to a formal limit on employment, set at a maximum of five employees per business. Most of these firms were family concerns, established either as small farms or as craft businesses. In the 1980s the Yugoslav regime further liberalized the environment for private sector activity through the Enterprise Law of 1988, which abolished the employment limits on private businesses and permitted the creation of limited liability companies. In response, many thousands of new businesses were established at the end of the 1980s, well before the break-up of Yugoslavia. Many entered into sectors with low entry barriers, such as trade and consumer services. The Yugoslav successor states thus inherited relatively liberal laws on the formation and registration of private companies. In Bulgaria, economic reforms were introduced shortly before the communist system collapsed, which permitted the creation of private businesses. Decree 56, adopted in January 1989, permitted small private firms to hire up to ten permanent employees, while seasonal workers could be employed without limit. By February 1990, over 14,000 new private firms had been registered under this law, of which 11,285 were sole proprietorships, 2,556 were partnerships and 170 were cooperative firms (Jones and Meurs, 1991).

Between 1990 and 1995, SEE countries experienced a rapid burst of growth in the number of new small firms in the private sector, as pent-up demand for firm formation was released by the newly liberalized environment following the collapse of communism. By 1995–96 there were 125,000 registered private companies in Croatia,[1] 185,000 in Serbia[2] and 83,000 in Macedonia (Zarezankova-Potevska, 2000). In communist-ruled Albania, in contrast to former Yugoslavia, private enterprise of any form had been entirely forbidden, but following the collapse of the communist regime there was an equally explosive growth of new private companies. The Enterprise Law of 1992 liberalized the registration of new private firms, which led to a rapid increase in registered firms – from 20,000 in 1994 to 134,000 in 2004. Almost all, however, were very small micro-enterprises concentrated in trade, services and transport, and only 2 per cent employed more than 20 workers. The number of small firms also increased in Bulgaria, where, owing to the country's prior specialization in computer technology, there was a significant presence of high-tech fast growth small firms in the early 1990s (Bartlett and Rangelova, 1996, 1997).

Throughout SEE, most new job creation has been associated with the entry and growth of small enterprises, while employment in large and medium-sized enterprises has fallen. Yet, even though small private firms provided employment for many workers laid off from large enterprises in the state sector, the sector did not grown rapidly enough to prevent unemployment from increasing throughout the 1990s and the early 2000s in the region's transition countries.

The new entrepreneurs have faced many obstacles to developing their businesses, and entry rates in the transition economies slowed down in the late 1990s and early 2000s. One of the principal barriers to growth was the lack of finance from the underdeveloped banking system. The limited available bank finance was mainly channelled to the large enterprise sector, while loans to small enterprises were provided at high-interest rates, with heavy collateral requirements. Larger firms attempted to establish and maintain dominant or monopoly positions, making use of close connections between the economic and the political elites, which themselves rotated between positions of political and economic power. This convergence of political and economic power made it relatively easy for the large enterprise sector to establish and maintain monopoly positions and to influence economic policy in ways inimical to the development of the competitive small business sector. Additionally, there was relatively little policy impetus for the promotion of small firms in most of the SEE states throughout the 1990s.

Due to varying entry rates among countries, substantial differences emerged in the density of SMEs. By the early 2000s, the countries which had advanced least, with densities of small firms below 15 per thousand of population, were Albania, Bosnia and Herzegovina, Moldova, former Serbia–Montenegro and Turkey (IFC, 2007). An intermediate group of countries, including Bulgaria, Macedonia and Romania, had densities between 15 and 30 per thousand, while Greece and Slovenia had densities well above 40, while Greece, at 72.2 per thousand of population, was well above the EU average of 53. The data demonstrate the more conducive environment to small business in Greece compared to the transition economies of the region, and highlight the significant barriers that have existed to the creation of new businesses in those countries. In contrast, Turkey, with the lowest density of small firms, had more of the characteristics of the transition countries in this respect.

Research by the World Bank has investigated the relationship between entrepreneurship and economic growth. The results show a strong correlation between the density of registered firms as a percentage of the active population, the quality of the legal and regulatory environment and ease of access to finance (Klapper 2006). Across a sample of 95 countries, the study found a positive relationship

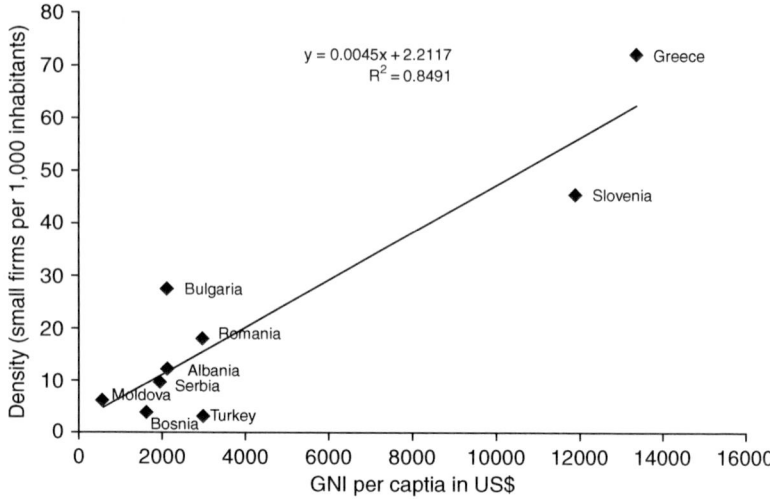

*Figure 10.1*   Firm density and level of economic development
Source: Author, on the basis of data from IFC (2007).

between economic development, business entry rates and business density. Figure 10.1 shows a similar relationship for the countries of SEE, the more developed countries, as measured by Gross National Income per capita, having a greater density of small firms than the less developed countries. The data show a strong positive relationship between the density of small firms and the level of economic development in the region. Although the chart does not imply causality, it does suggest that there is a strong link between the openness of a country to entrepreneurship and its level of economic development.

## The craft sector and self-employment

In addition to incorporated small and medium-sized companies, many new businesses are owned by sole proprietors, who are sometimes referred to as self-employed entrepreneurs. The tradition of the independent sole proprietor has played an important role in SEE countries in the form of the 'craft firm' (*obrt*) in Croatia or of the 'private shop' (*privatna radnja*) in Serbia. Due to the lower cost of entry and the greater flexibility of sole proprietorships compared to incorporated businesses, the sector has proved to be more dynamic in terms of employment growth. Even though these firms typically have just a few employees, they have a tradition of skilled work, they are important agents for the preservation and development of skills and they are a source of demand for skilled labour.

Sole proprietorships have increased in number in most of the Yugoslav successor states due to the relative simplicity and low cost of the procedure.[3] In Croatia, the number of sole proprietorships increased from 64,500 in 1991 to 100,500 by 2003, when they accounted for 62 per cent of all enterprises in the economy and for 24 per cent of employment.[4] In Serbia the number of sole proprietorships (*privatne radnje*) increased from 166,500 in 1993 (Popović, 1995) to 216,000[5] in 2008, providing employment for 571,000 owners and employees[6] at a time when employment elsewhere in the economy was falling. In Bosnia and Herzegovina the number of craft firms exceeds the number of incorporated firms by a significant margin (43,000 compared with 33,000) and is growing more rapidly, the fastest growth having occurred between 2004 and 2005 in agriculture, transport and financial services. In Macedonia in 2004 there were 49,000 active sole proprietors of various types, including craft firms, self-employed persons and 'small traders'.

There are two main factors driving this growth of self-employment. The first is poverty, which pushes unemployed or marginalized people into self-employment in easy-to-enter sectors such as retail trade or small retail kiosks with low prospects for growth. The second is the response to new opportunities, which pulls 'high-expectation' entrepreneurs into dynamic segments of the economy (Storey, 1994; Bartlett and Hoggett, 1996).[7] Research into self-employment in other transition contexts has suggested that self-employed persons with employees are more likely to be dynamic and upwardly mobile entrepreneurs, while self-employed individuals working on their own account are more likely to be struggling to make ends meet (Earle and Sakova, 2000; Hanley, 2000).

Both types of entrepreneurs can be observed in SEE. High unemployment and weak social security systems have pushed many people into self-employment as a means of ensuring a living, while there are also many cases of adventurous individuals who have been pulled into self-employment by the desire to take advantage of the new market opportunities opened up by economic liberalization. Data on self-employment rates taken from the Labour Force Surveys for Croatia, Greece and Serbia are presented in Table 10.1. These data suggest that Greece and Serbia have a greater overall propensity for self-employment than Croatia, although the smaller proportion of own-account self-employed without employees in Croatia suggests weaker 'push' factors than in Greece and Serbia. However, Greece has almost twice as many self-employed

*Table 10.1* Self-employed employers and own-account workers (% of all in work)

| | Self-employed employers with employees | Own-account self-employed without employees |
|---|---|---|
| Croatia (2010) | 4.9 | 14.6 |
| Serbia (2010) | 3.8 | 22.8 |
| Greece (2010) | 8.2 | 22.4 |

*Sources*: Labour Force in the Republic of Croatia First Quarter 2010, First Release 9.2.7/1, State Statistical Office of Croatia, July 2010; Labour Force Survey, Statistical Office of the Republic of Serbia, Communication No. 180, June 2010; Hellenic Statistical Authority, Press Release, Labour Force Survey 1st Quarter 2010, June.

employers as the other two countries, which suggests stronger 'pull' factors encouraging entrepreneurs to create jobs in Greece where the environment is more conducive to entrepreneurial activity. However, it should be noted that in all three countries many dynamic entrepreneurs are frustrated by high taxation and administrative burdens, avoid formal registration of all or part of their activities and operate in the informal economy that is widespread in the region.

## Barriers to entry and growth

In most transition countries in SEE, entry rates slowed down following an initial surge in the early stage of transition. Even in Croatia, one of the most advanced transition countries in the region, entry rates among small companies have been sluggish in recent years (Čučković and Bartlett, 2007).

Comparable cross-country data on entry rates taken from the World Bank Group Entrepreneurship Survey 2008 are presented in Table 10.2. These data show that Croatia has the lowest entry rate of small firms, being closely followed by Greece. However, these two examples reflect quite different contexts: Greece as a more mature market economy, with a high density of small firms, naturally shows a relatively low entry rate, while Croatia has a below optimal performance in relation to other transition economies of the region. Most countries of the region have entry rates below 10 per cent, well below the benchmark case of the UK which has practised a very liberal business regulatory policy for many years. The exceptions are Bulgaria, Romania, Serbia and Turkey, which have entry rates of 10 per cent and above – a fact suggesting that these economies have recently developed a more pro-enterprise business environment than other transition countries in the region.

*Table 10.2*   Entry rates of small firms in SEE and in the UK

| | |
|---|---|
| Croatia | 0.04 |
| Greece | 0.06 |
| BiH | 0.06 |
| Slovenia | 0.07 |
| Moldova | 0.08 |
| Albania | 0.09 |
| Romania | 0.10 |
| Turkey | 0.10 |
| Serbia | 0.12 |
| Bulgaria | 0.13 |
| UK | 0.16 |

*Note*: The entry rate is calculated as the number of newly registered corporations divided by the number of total registered corporations.
*Source*: World Bank Group Entrepreneurship Survey 2008.

The main causes of slow entry and growth in the transition countries in the region have been the financial and institutional barriers (Bartlett and Bukvič, 2002). The 'finance-first' view holds that financial constraints have been the most significant barrier to the entry and growth of small enterprises (Pissarides, 1999). In the absence of a well-developed capital market, firms that wish to expand are constrained by the amount of initial capital at the disposal of the owner and by the amount of profits available for reinvestment. The absence of external finance was especially important in the transition economies in which banks initially had little experience in lending to small firms and found it easier to lend to politically connected large enterprises. Absence of collateral to guarantee a bank loan was a further significant barrier to obtaining external finance.

In contrast, the 'institutional view' holds that no amount of finance will assist small firms if institutional constraints inhibit entry and growth. Especially problematic have been the political networks and ties that link banks to the state and to larger enterprises and divert investment finance from profitable small firms to large loss-making companies supported by political connections. In addition, a lack of effective property rights inhibits the entry of new firms and reduces investment in established ones. Consequently, the growth of new enterprises will be lower when institutional barriers are high and property rights are weak (McMillan and Woodruff, 2002). The scope of such institutional barriers is wide. The most significant barriers are inadequate property rights, but other issues are also relevant; these include administrative costs, costs of obtaining licences, delays in registering a company or, for example, the need to pay bribes to inspectors. Property rights are especially weak in the ex-Yugoslav countries, where inheritance laws have produced multiple ownership of land and properties among members of extended families; this phenomenon, combined with migration and poor cadastral records, often makes the identification of owners a difficult and cumbersome process. Aidis (2005) points to the interrelatedness of institutional barriers, which complicates attempts to overcome their adverse effects on economic development.

### Evidence on barriers to entry

According to a policy assessment of the environment facing small business in the region carried out in 2002 by the OECD (2003, p. 11), 'barriers to business entry [...] remain unnecessarily high [...] in addition, companies [...] face complex and often non-transparent procedures for obtaining and renewing permits and licenses, particularly building and land development permits.' Since the publication of the report, corrective policies have reduced many of the barriers to business entry and have created a more favourable investment climate. In Macedonia recent reforms have led to major improvements in the ease of doing business, which propelled the country to the top ten in a list of global reformers compiled by the World Bank in 2010. On the ease of doing business, the World Bank survey focused on a number of indicators that are relevant to the issue of business entry. The most recent survey, carried out in 2008–09, covers 183 countries, including those in SEE. Although it only covers limited liability companies based in the capital cities, the information provided is useful for gauging progress in reform and for benchmarking the ease of starting up a business in different countries.

Table 10.3 shows the results of the survey for the dimension of ease of business start-up. Only 5 out of the 13 SEE countries shown in the table appear in the top 50 of the global ranking, Macedonia being the outstanding country in this respect, after recent reforms to liberalize business start-up that have put the country in sixth place globally. A further 4 countries were ranked between 51st and 100th place, 3 countries being placed close to the bottom of the rankings – notably Bosnia and Herzegovina at 160th and Kosovo at 164th position. In comparison to the transition-country averages for the number of procedures required, the time taken and the cost of business start-up, Bosnia and Herzegovina, Croatia, Greece and Kosovo stand out as having the most difficult conditions for business start-up. In comparison with the

*Table 10.3* Ease of starting a business in SEE

| Country | Number of procedures needed to register a business (2009) | Number of days taken to register a business (2009) | Cost of registering a business in percent of income per capita (2009) | Minimum capital needed to register a business in percentage of income per capita (2009) | Rank overall ease of starting a business (2006) | Rank overall ease of starting a business (2009) |
|---|---|---|---|---|---|---|
| Macedonia | 4 | 4 | 2.5 | 0.0 | 76 | 6 |
| Slovenia | 3 | 6 | 0.0 | 43.3 | 98 | 26 |
| Romania | 6 | 10 | 2.9 | 0.9 | 7 | 42 |
| Albania | 5 | 5 | 17.0 | 0.0 | 120 | 46 |
| Bulgaria | 4 | 18 | 1.7 | 20.7 | 85 | 50 |
| Turkey | 6 | 6 | 14.2 | 9.5 | 53 | 56 |
| Serbia | 7 | 13 | 7.1 | 6.1 | 60 | 73 |
| Moldova | 8 | 10 | 7.0 | 11.4 | 84 | 77 |
| Montenegro | 12 | 13 | 2.6 | 0.0 | 83 | 85 |
| Croatia | 7 | 22 | 8.4 | 13.4 | 100 | 101 |
| Greece | 15 | 19 | 10.9 | 21.4 | 140 | 140 |
| Bosnia and Herzegovina | 12 | 60 | 15.8 | 29.8 | 141 | 160 |
| Kosovo | 9 | 52 | 43.3 | 169.5 | n/a | 164 |
| Eastern Europe and Central Asia | 6.7 | 17.4 | 8.3 | 21.5 | | |
| OECD | 5.7 | 13 | 4.7 | 15.5 | | |

*Source:* World Bank Ease of Doing Business Database 2010 and 2007.

OECD country average, Bulgaria, Moldova, Serbia and Turkey are also relatively unfriendly to business start-up. Several countries, including Albania, Bulgaria, Macedonia and Slovenia, have moved up in the overall rankings by more than ten places between 2006 and 2009, which indicates the rapid pace of reform in business start-up legislation and practice. Others had slipped back in relative rank, including Bosnia and Herzegovina, Romania and Serbia.

The number of procedures required to register a company in SEE has fallen sharply in recent years, and by 2009 was below the average of transition countries of Eastern Europe and Central Asia in six of the SEE countries, and below the OECD average in four of them. The time taken to register a company had fallen even further, eight countries being below the transition country average and six being below the OECD average. Similarly, seven countries had relative costs of registration below the transition country average, and five below the OECD average; while ten countries had minimum capital requirements below the transition country average, and eight below the OECD average.

Figure 10.2 shows the relationship between small firm entry and the ease of starting up a firm as measured by the World Bank surveys. It shows a positive relationship between the two variables, with a more

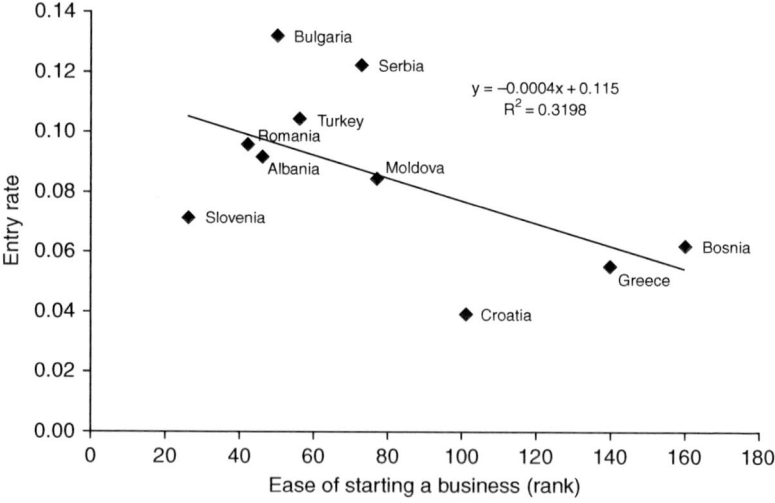

*Figure 10.2*  Relationship between business start-up regime and entry rate in SEE
*Source*: World Bank Ease of Doing Business Database 2010 and World Bank Group Entrepreneurship Survey 2008.

conducive business start-up regime (indicated by a lower value of the horizontal axis) being associated with a higher rate of small firm entry. The relationship is not exact and explains only 32 per cent of the variation in entry rates, indicating that other factors are involved – such as industry structure and other non-institutional barriers to entry. The relationship also points out that some countries are somewhat impervious to regulatory changes, and Croatia and Slovenia in particular seem to underperform in terms of entry rates, given the regulatory environment that their entrepreneurs face.

### Evidence on the barriers to the growth of small firms

When he took up his position as High Representative in Bosnia and Herzegovina in June 2002, Paddy Ashdown stated that job creation was one of his main priorities. In an inaugural speech, he observed that

> the challenge is to stimulate growth in the new private sector and especially among small businesses, which are already becoming the engine that will drive Bosnia's economy. We must sweep away the unnecessary red tape and bureaucracy that makes it so difficult to run an honest business and drives so many into the grey economy.[8]

This emphasis on barriers to the growth of small businesses has been one of the main themes of the research into the small business sector in the Balkans.

A survey of 800 small- and medium-sized enterprises in 3 SEE countries, carried out in 2000 by the present author and colleagues, demonstrated that SMEs in Bosnia and Herzegovina faced the most difficult business environment, reflecting delayed transition and the effects of war, while Slovenia faced the least difficult environment and Macedonia fell in between (Bartlett and Bukvič, 2002; Bartlett, 2003). The results of the survey revealed that the most significant barriers to the growth of small firms were high taxation and financial constraints. Taxation was the most serious barrier to growth at the time of the survey, mainly because business tax rates were still high in 2000. Businesses considered taxes to be a barrier to expansion and growth, but the main effect of taxes has been to provide an incentive for companies to operate in the informal economy. Even registered companies often declare an unrealistically low wage bill, in order to minimize payment of social contributions or just to avoid paying social contributions altogether. Recently tax rates have begun to fall, as several countries have introduced flat tax regimes. The most ardent tax reducing country has been Macedonia, which has cut the rate of profit tax to 10 per cent, followed closely by Serbia and several other countries.

The importance of financial constraints to growth can be explained by a number of factors. First, banks perceived small firms as high credit risks and typically required two or three times the value of a loan as collateral. Commercial banks often preferred to lend to larger firms, due to political connections as well as to limited capacity to evaluate credit risks presented by small firms. Bank credit was often provided on a short-term basis at a relatively high cost (Kraft, 2002), and owners of small firms therefore often self-financed their business investments. However, since the survey was carried out, this situation has changed dramatically, as most banks in the region were taken over by foreign banks. Credit to businesses expanded rapidly in many SEE countries, while the rate of interest fell, generating booming economies that powered along at 5 per cent growth rates through much of the 2000s. Recent analysis of surveys carried out in a large sample of transition economies have shown that the force of these financial barriers has diminished in many countries as transition has progressed, and that in the higher middle income countries the most significant barriers to business are now a lack of skilled labour and infrastructure gaps (Mitra et al., 2010). However, the global economic crisis, which hit the region at the end of 2008, has once again brought the financial constraints to the fore, as bank credit has dried up on a global scale. In SEE there is some evidence that small businesses are in increasing financial distress and that the proportion of non-performing loans in the business sector is on the increase.

The survey also revealed that institutional barriers – including social barriers (lack of trust, need to bribe officials) and administrative barriers (too much bureaucracy, too many licences required and so on) – were important impediments to growth. Social barriers were relatively high in Bosnia and Herzegovina and low in Slovenia. This reflects the finding from the survey that business relations between small firms in Slovenia were based more on arms-length trust relations, while in Bosnia and Herzegovina business relations were based more on interpersonal trust relations – which means that in Bosnia, unlike Slovenia, business owners were less willing to make business contracts with strangers. This lack of trust in anonymous business partners has increased the transaction cost of doing business in Bosnia in relation to Slovenia (Rus and Iglič, 2005).

The survey also showed that employment regulations were perceived to be the least important barrier to growth in each of the three countries. Employment legislation was a more serious barrier in Slovenia than in the other two countries, which suggests that some of the concerns about restrictive employment legislation voiced in the literature may have been overplayed (Bartlett, 2003). Lack of support services from the state was a medium-level barrier indicating an important role for the state in these countries in improving the provision of business support services – an issue that has subsequently been the subject of several projects organized by international donors and financial institutions.

Several studies of barriers to small firm growth have been carried out in Albania. These have also found that access to finance has been a major constraint to growth. A survey of fifty private enterprises in Albania employing fewer than 200 employees, carried out in early 1997, found that financial barriers were the most significant barriers to the growth of small firms (Hashi, 2001). A later survey carried out in 1999 found that the force of financial constraints had diminished and that the most important barrier was unfair competition from the informal economy (Muent et al., 2001). A more recent survey of 110 small firms in the manufacturing sector in Albania, carried out in 2004, also showed that finance was less of an issue and that growth was fastest among smaller, more recently established firms, in firms run by older, more experienced entrepreneurs, and in firms run by entrepreneurs with a recent business qualification and with business skills (Xheneti and Bartlett, 2006). The analysis also revealed that lack of information was a serious obstacle to growth, which reflects the weaknesses in the institutional support structure in Albania (Xheneti, 2005).

Numerous studies have emphasized the role of corruption in holding back business growth (Aidt, 2009). Corruption arises in a situation of social disruption and anomie and of breakdown of moral and legal norms, as has been the case in post-conflict situations in SEE. The survey by Muent et al. (2001) showed that small firms in Albania typically pay 3.3 per cent of their revenues in bribes, and 36 per cent of respondents reported paying bribes frequently. Corruption in the region has also been a concern for the EU, especially when it extends beyond the petty corruption of bureaucrats into the higher sections of society, such as politicians and high government officials, undermining the administrative efficiency necessary for adherence to Single Market regulations.

## Policies for small firms in SEE

The removal of barriers to entry and growth is an important point of focus in any policy designed to stimulate entrepreneurship in the transition economies of SEE. The situation is not much different in the non-transition economies. Turkey still has a long way to go in liberalizing its economy, and it is now included among the transition economies covered by the European Bank for Reconstruction 'Transition Report'. Greece, as an EU member, has a more developed market economy, but even there the state has played a dominant role in the economy and, as the recent economic crisis has revealed, has overstretched itself to the detriment of the private sector. In all SEE economies, therefore, the liberalization of the business environment is needed in order for these economies to stimulate the further development of the small firm sector.

However, from another point of view, the state has an important constructive and supportive role to play in promoting the development of the small firms sector. It has a major role to play in establishing the basic institutional framework in which entrepreneurship can flourish, new firms are encouraged to enter the market and established firms have appropriate incentives to undertake investment and generate employment opportunities (Tyson et al., 1994). In addition to macro-economic stability and secure property rights, governments need to establish an effective institutional support structure for the development of the SME sector (Kolodko, 2000). In particular, the establishment of formal institutions to monitor and enforce competition and to reduce the ability of large monopolistic firms to stitch up local markets is an important element of building the institutional framework supportive of a dynamic market economy and economic growth. Such structures have been established in most of the SEE states in recent years. Competition agencies have been established in most countries, and specific institutions to promote small firms have also been set up. The Croatian government began to develop an institutional support structure for SMEs in the 1990s, passing a Law on the Encouragement of Small Business Development in 2002. The Albanian government adopted a Medium Term Strategy for SME development in 2001 and an SME Law in 2002, and established an SME Development Agency in 2003. In Bosnia and Herzegovina, the Republika Srpska adopted a Law on the Development of Small- and Medium-Sized Enterprises in the same year. National strategies for SMEs were adopted in Macedonia in 2002 and in Serbia in 2003. Only the Federation of Bosnia and Herzegovina now lacks a formal agency for supporting the development of the SME sector.

Over the last decade the OECD and the European Commission have been active in monitoring and encouraging transition countries in SEE to adopt the European Charter for Small Enterprises, and the OECD produced a regular report, known as the SME Policy Index, which provides an assessment of progress in building a supportive institutional environment for small business development. Institutional and policy advances in fields such as ease and speed of business registration, business-friendly legislation and regulation, entrepreneurship education and training, reduced company taxation and access to finance are assessed across all the countries of the Western Balkans. In its latest report (OECD, 2009), the OECD classifies the countries into three groups. Croatia is assessed as the most advanced in terms of formal institutional structures designed to support the small business sector. The policy framework is assessed as good, and the country is considered to be moving ahead with implementation. A second group of countries, comprising Macedonia, Montenegro and Serbia, is assessed to be making good progress with policy formulation and institution-building, but as not yet having reached the stage of effective implementation. The third group of countries, consisting of Albania, Bosnia and Herzegovina and Kosovo, is assessed as being in the early stages of building a supportive institutional framework for small business development.

As the analysis presented earlier in this chapter suggests, however, progress with creating a formal institutional framework for the support for SMEs is not the whole of the story. This is clear from the relatively poor performance of the Croatian economy in generating a dynamic small firm sector, despite the formal progress in developing policies and institutions nominally supportive of small business development. The ingredients missing from that story are informal institutions that either promote or hinder the development of small businesses, and factors such as the extent of corruption, informal norms of business behaviour and the extent of the informal economy. In addition, the degree of interpersonal trust is an important factor. As Rus and Iglič (2005) showed in the case of Bosnia and Herzegovina, the legacy of conflict and ethnic tension can undermine this trust relationships and make it difficult for entrepreneurs to do business on the basis of arms-length anonymous contracting. Instead they are reduced to a smaller circle of business partners, whom they know personally and can trust to do business with them. Such trust is hard to rebuild once it has been damaged by civil conflict. A further dimension of informal institutions is the political connectedness between the large firm sector and the political elite. This connectedness supports the monopoly positions of local tycoons and provides both overt and hidden barriers to small business entry and growth. The economies of the region are relatively small and, in many sectors, easily monopolized. This drives up business costs and reduces the quality of goods and services, thus reinforcing the lack of international competitiveness of most of the economies of the region. Policy makers will need to address these issues in a serious way if the potential of the small firm sector to promote economic growth in an increasingly difficult global market environment is to be fully achieved.

## Notes

1. Statistički ljetopis 1995 [Statistical Yearbook 1995] (Zagreb: Državni zavod za statistiku), p. 54.
2. Statistički godišnjak Jugoslavije 1997 [Statistical Yearbook of Yugoslavia 1997] (Beograd: Savezni Zavod za Statistiku), p. 49. Of these, 127,000 were private enterprises without limited liability (sole proprietorships) and 58,000 were limited liability companies (društva sa ograničenom odgovornošću – d.o.o.).
3. In the Croatian case this amounted to DEM 5,000 according to the Company Law of 1993.
4. Croatian government response to the questionnaire of the European Commission, 2004, chapter 16, p. 1. The Crafts Law regulates the registration of craft firms, and requires that the owner should have a professional qualification or master craftsman's certificate.
5. Statistical Office of Serbia, Statistical Yearbook 2009, Table 3.14.
6. Ibid., Table 5.1.
7. These push-and-pull factors are frequently characterized as factors of 'necessity' and 'opportunity' entrepreneurship respectively.
8. 'Bosnia: Reform Will Bring Justice and Jobs', speech by Paddy Ashdown quoted in IWPR's *Balkan Crisis Report No. 341*, 7 June 2002.

## References

Acs, Z. and Audretsch, D. B. (eds) (1993) *Small Firms and Entrepreneurship: An East–West Perspective* (Cambridge: Cambridge University Press).

Aidis, R. (2005) 'Institutional Barriers to Small and Medium Sized Enterprise Operations in Transition Countries', *Small Business Economics*, 25, 305–318.

Aidt, T. (2009) 'Corruption, Institutions and Economic Development', *Oxford Review of Economic Policy*, 25, 271–291.

Bartlett, W. (2000) 'Economic Transformation and Democratization in the Balkans', in Pridham, G. and Gallagher, T. (eds), *Experimenting with Democracy: Regime Change in the Balkans* (London: Routledge), 132–151.

Bartlett, W. (2003) 'Barriers to SME Development in Bosnia and Herzegovina, Macedonia and Slovenia: A Comparative Analysis', in Franičević, V. and Kimura, H. (eds), *Globalization, Democratization and Development* (Zagreb: Masmedia), 363–376.

Bartlett, W. and Bukvič, V. (2002) 'What Are the Main Barriers to SME Growth and Development in South-East Europe?', in Bartlett, W., Bateman, M. and Vehovec, M. (eds), *Small Enterprise Development in South-East Europe: Policies for Sustainable Growth* (Dordrecht: Kluwer).

Bartlett, W. and Bukvič, V. (2006) 'Knowledge Transfer in Slovenia: Promoting Innovative SMEs through Spin-Offs, Technology Parks, Clusters and Networks', *Economic and Business Review for Central and Eastern Europe*, 8, 337–358.

Bartlett, W. and Čučković, N. (2006) 'Knowledge Transfer, Institutions, and Innovation in Croatia', *Društvena istraživanja [Social Research]*, 15, 371–400.

Bartlett, W. and Hoggett, P. (1996) 'Small firms in South East Europe: The Importance of Initial Conditions', in Brezinski, H. and Fritsch, M. (eds), *The Economic Impact of New firms in Post-Socialist Countries: Bottom-Up Transformation in Eastern Europe* (Cheltenham: Edward Elgar), 151–175.

Bartlett, W. and Rangelova, R. (1996) 'Small Firms and New Technologies: The Case of Bulgaria', in R. Oakey (ed.), *New Technology-Based Small Firms in the 1990s*, vol. 2 (London: Paul Chapman), 66–79.

Bartlett, W. and Rangelova, R. (1997) 'Small Firms and Economic Transformation in Bulgaria', *Small Business Economics*, 9, 319–333.

Čučković, N. and Bartlett, W. (2007) 'Entrepreneurship and Competitiveness: The Europeanization of Small and Medium-Sized Enterprise Policy in Croatia', *Southeast European and Black Sea Studies*, 7, 37–56.

Earle, J. S. and Sakova, Z. (2000) 'Business Start-Ups or Disguised Unemployment? Evidence on the Character of Self-Employment from Transition Economies', *Labour Economics*, 7, 575–601.

Hanley, E. (2000) 'Self-Employment in Post-Communist Eastern Europe: A Refuge From Poverty or a Road to Riches?', *Communist and Post-Communist Studies*, 33, 379–402.

Hashi, I. (2001) 'Financial and Institutional Barriers to SME Growth in Albania: Results of an Enterprise Survey', *MOCT-MOST: Economic Policy in Transition Economies*, 11, 221–238.

IFC (2007) *Micro, Small, and Medium Enterprises: A Collection of Published Data*, International Finance Corporation, http://rru.worldbank.org/Documents/other/MSMEdatabase/msme_database.htm, accessed 21 August 2010.

Jones, D. C. and Meurs, M. (1991) 'On entry in Socialist economies: Evidence from Bulgaria', *Soviet Studies*, 43 (2), 311–328.

Klapper, L. (2006) 'Entrepreneurship' World Bank Viewpoint No. 313.

Kolodko, G. W. (2000) 'Transition to a Market and Entrepreneurship: The Systemic Factors and Policy Options', *Communist and Post-Communist Studies*, 33, 271–293.

Kraft, E. (2002) 'Bank Lending to SMEs in Croatia: A Few Things We Know', in Bartlett, W., Bateman, M. and Vehovec, M. (eds), *Small Enterprise Development in South-East Europe: Policies for Sustainable Growth* (Dordrecht: Kluwer), 127–144.

McMillan, J. and Woodruff, C. (2002) 'The Central Role of Entrepreneurs in Transition Economies', *Journal of Economic Perspectives*, 16, 153–170.

Mitra, P., Selowsky, M. and Zalduendo, J. (2010) *Turmoil at Twenty: Recession, Recovery, and Reform in Central and Eastern Europe and the Former Soviet Union* (Washington: The World Bank).

Muent, H., Pissarides, F. and Sanfey, P. (2001) 'Taxes, Competition and Finance for Albanian Enterprises: Evidence From a Field Study', *MOCT-MOST: Economic Policy in Transition Economies*, 11, 239–251.

OECD (2003) *South East Europe Region: Enterprise Policy Performance– A Regional Assessment* (Paris: Organisation for Economic Co-operation and Development).

OECD (2009) *Progress in the Implementation of the European Charter for Small Enterprises in the Western Balkans* (Paris: Organisation for Economic Cooperation and Development).

Pissarides, F. (1999) 'Is Lack of Funds the Main Obstacle to Business Growth? EBRD's Experience with Small- and Medium-Sized Businesses in Central and Eastern Europe', *Journal of Business Venturing*, 14, 519–539.

Popović, P. (1995) *Preduzetnistvo: granice rasta* (Beograd: Ekonomski Institut).

Rus, A. and Iglić, H. (2005) 'Trust, Governance and Performance: The Role of Institutional and Interpersonal Trust in SME Development', *International Sociology*, 20, 371–91.

Storey, D. (1994) *Understanding the Small Business Sector* (London: Routledge).

Thurik, R. and Wennekers, S. (2004) 'Entrepreneurship, Small Business and Economic Growth', *Journal of Small Business and Enterprise Development*, 11, 140–149.

Tyson, L. d'Andrea, Petrin, T. and Rogers, H. (1994) 'Promoting Entrepreneurship in Eastern Europe', *Small Business Economics*, 6, 165–184.

Valliere, D. and Peterson, R. (2009) 'Entrepreneurship and Economic Growth: Evidence from Emerging and Developed Countries', *Entrepreneurship & Regional Development*, 21 (5/6), 459–480.

Voulgaris, F., Papadogonas, T. and Agiomirgianakis, G. (2005) 'Job Creation and Job Destruction in Greek Manufacturing', *Review of Development Economics*, 9, 289–301.

Xheneti, M. (2005) 'Exploring the Role of Business Support Infrastructure in Albania: The Need for a Rethink?', *Environment and Planning C: Government and Policy*, 23, 815–832.

Xheneti, M. and Bartlett, W. (2006) 'SME Development in Albania – An Analysis of the Determinants of Business Growth', *Proceedings of the ICES 2006 Conference 'From Transition to Sustainable Development: The Path to European Integration'* (Sarajevo: School of Economics and Business), 255–260 [abstract, full paper on CD ROM].

Zarezankova-Potevska, M. (2000) *Perspektivite na maloto stopanstvo* (Skopje: Neol-Risto-DOOEL).

# 11
# Direct Taxation of Business in South East European Countries

*Christian Bellak and Mario Liebensteiner*

## Introduction

This chapter sets out to assess changes in the direct taxation of business and tax policy in South East European Countries (SEECs), and its role in the location choice of foreign firms in particular. The role of direct business taxation for investment and location choice is twofold. First, direct taxation may be a limiting factor or a stimulating factor for investment and location choice. Second, direct taxation may interact with other location factors and thus either amplify or reduce their effects on investment and location choice. This explains why direct taxation is an important policy variable.

In recent years, the SEECs have revised and reformed their tax systems, which are generally characterized by an emphasis on indirect rather than direct taxes. Nevertheless, direct taxation of business is an important location factor for the investment of domestic, but also of foreign, firms, which raises important conceptual and empirical questions. The aim of the chapter is to assess some of the policy challenges that lie ahead for the tax policies of governments in the SEECs. The SEECs and their acronyms are Albania (AL), Bosnia and Herzegovina (BiH), Bulgaria (BG), Croatia (HR), Greece (GR), Macedonia (MK), Moldova (MD), Montenegro (MN), Romania (RO), Serbia (SRB), Slovenia (SLO) and Turkey (TR).

This chapter is structured as follows. In a first step a brief outline of the role of the direct taxation of business is sketched, taking the viewpoint of the governments (policy-makers) and of the firms, including multinational enterprises (MNEs). Next, recent developments in direct business taxation in SEECs are discussed, with a special emphasis on tax rates (tax burden) and tax system changes – the introduction of flat tax regimes in particular. Since Foreign Direct Investment (FDI) provides an important source of total investment in SEECs, a third step offers a description of the evolution of FDI in the SEECs over the last decade and discusses the likely impact of direct business taxation on FDI. Finally, we consider some policy aspects related to direct business taxation and tax competition.

While there are many relevant questions related to the conceptual and empirical aspects of direct business taxation in SEECs, literature and results of empirical analysis are scarce. Therefore the aim of this chapter is to emphasize relevant aspects and to provide some descriptive evidence, while more thorough analysis is left to future research.

## Conceptual aspects: The role of direct taxation of business

### Viewpoint of governments

The aims pursued by governments in direct business taxation are twofold: first, governments want to achieve tax revenues (macro-economic) and, second, they try to avoid economic distortions[1] and to ensure efficiency (Nicodeme, 2009). Concerning *tax revenues*, governments may view the direct taxation of business as a contribution to the financing of public goods, services and infrastructure, which are used by firms in particular. However, the fact that corporate income tax (CIT) alone will never be sufficient to finance all public goods and services consumed by enterprises must be emphasized. Turning to *efficiency*, the objective of governments is not to bias investment decisions, and hence to ensure *investment neutrality* (Homburg, 2007),[2] *financial and legal form neutrality*.

Governments are generally aware that the goal of revenue maximization may conflict with other economic policy goals, in particular the stimulation of investment for growth. Thus governments have a clear incentive to evaluate changes in their tax policy with regard to possible negative effects on investment. The room for tax reductions will depend, *inter alia*, on the quality of the provision of public goods (Baldwin and Krugman, 2004).

### Viewpoint of firms

The viewpoint of firms can be described as the mirror image of what has been said in the previous section. We distinguish between domestic and foreign firms, since the tax burden may differ between these two groups of firms.

## Taxes and investment of domestic firms

Business and its lobbying organizations (employers' federations and so on) frequently demand a reduction in tax rates and maintain that the CIT rates are too high in general. Direct business taxation is a direct production cost, as it reduces after-tax profits and/or the cost of capital. Therefore, *ceteris paribus*, for profit maximizing firms, higher direct business taxation in the form of CIT will lead to lower investment. Yet the other side of the coin is that profit maximization requires *inter alia* the provision of certain public goods conducive to investment in a world of heterogeneous locations.

The viewpoint of the firms implies that, while firms are lobbying against taxation, they take advantage of many location factors without direct contributions. It can be equally assumed that firms are more ready to pay taxes if they are compensated by the provision of favourable location factors, which implies that the tax elasticity of the investment is reduced.

## Taxes as a location factor for multinational enterprises

While what has been said about domestic firms applies in principle also to subsidiaries of foreign multinational enterprises (MNEs) cross-border investment (or FDI) may trigger tax burdens, which differ from those discussed in the section above. This rests on the fact that additional tax codes become relevant (for example at the supranational level, at the international level) and may result in higher or lower tax burdens than in the case of national income (due for example to double taxation or exemptions). Therefore taxes may be an important location factor in the decision for FDI. To be more precise, taxes may affect the scale of investment, as well as the choice of locations (Devereux and Griffith, 1999, 2003).

Taking these points into consideration, in practice it is likely that governments will rely on *some* direct business taxes together with *some* tax incentives, so as to solve the conflicting goals between raising revenue and ensuring efficiency, and at the same time firms will be compensated with some infrastructure for their tax payments. We now turn to the description of some elements of tax policies in SEECs. The distinction between national income and cross-border income will consequently be applied in our description of direct business taxation in SEECs in the forthcoming section.

## Recent developments and current trends of business taxation in SEECs

### Tax rates

*Tax rates on domestic corporate income in SEECs*

Substantial reductions of the nominal CIT rates characterize the development of direct business taxation in SEECs, from an average rate of 24 per cent in 2003 to 13 per cent in 2010. While this clear downward trend is not very different from trends in other areas (Central and East European Countries – CEECs; EU), the mean nominal CIT rate in SEECs is almost one half of that in the EU (see Figure 11.1).

Despite the uniform trend, there is still a large spread of tax rates across countries. Two facts stand out: first, tax rates in those countries where governments have substantially lowered the rates have been politically stable over the last years (for example AL, BU, MN, RO, SRB). Second, some countries are the frontrunners of tax lowering strategies, Moldova reducing the CIT rate to 0 per cent or Montenegro to 9 per cent. It seems that countries with a lower level of development rely more on tax lowering strategies. Among other factors, the infrastructure

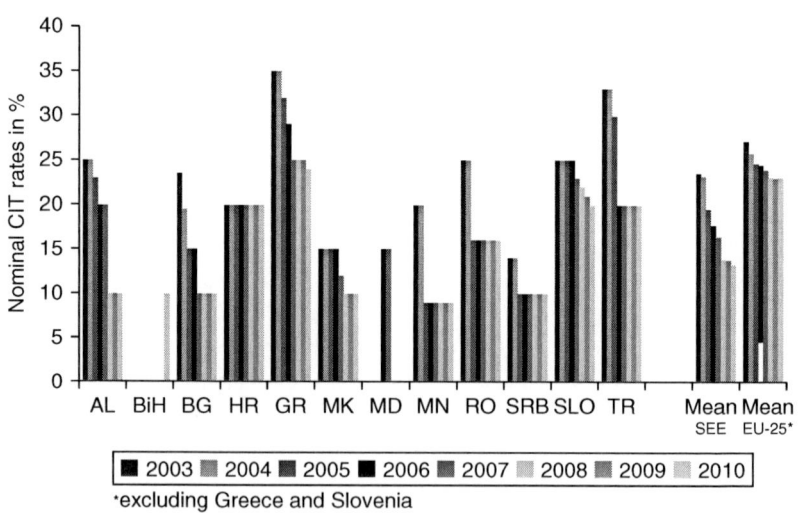

*Figure 11.1*  Nominal corporate income tax rates in %, by country

*Sources*: Devereux et al. (2008), European Commission: Taxes in Europe Database, and IBFD (various years).

endowment of these countries will be insufficient to reduce the tax rate sensitivity of FDI.

However, nominal tax rates do not tell the full story about the actual tax burden of firms, since they do not take into account other parameters of tax systems, such as tax exemptions or tax incentives. Put differently, the tax base is also relevant. MNEs often have to choose between different locations. Therefore we turn to effective average tax rates now, since for discrete choices like the location decision of MNEs the effective average tax rate is the relevant measure of tax burden (Devereux and Griffith, 1999). Effective average tax rates (EATRs) are defined as the net present value of a typical investment that is profitable. First we focus on domestic EATRs only, which unfortunately are only available for some of the SEECs and only from 2005 to 2007.

The across-countries averaged domestic EATRs in SEECs are below the across-countries averaged EATRs in EU countries (see Figure 11.2). At a first glance one might conclude form the impression that, for EU investors, SEECs may be preferred locations from a taxation point of view. Another indication of the appeal of a location from a taxation point of view may be gained from a comparison between the nominal and the effective tax burden: Figure 11.3 shows that the effective tax rates in SEECs are significantly below the nominal tax rates, while these

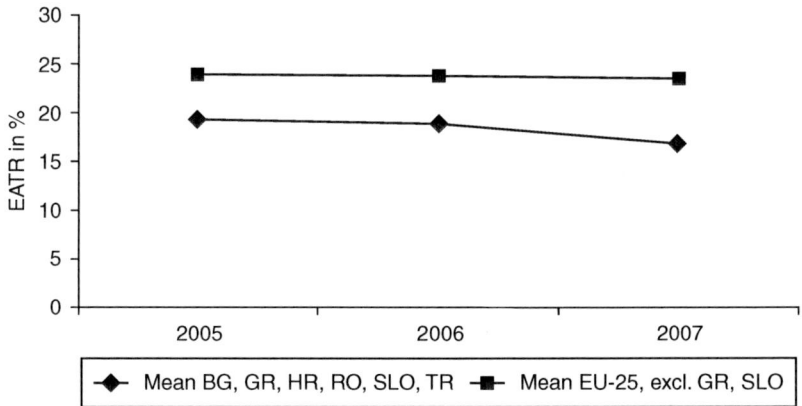

*Figure 11.2*  Domestic EATR, only corporation taxes in percentage
*Note*: EATRs are built on a number of assumptions. For assumptions underlying the calculation of the EATRs, see Devereux et al. (2008). This applies also to all the following EATRs below.
*Source*: Devereux et al. (2008).

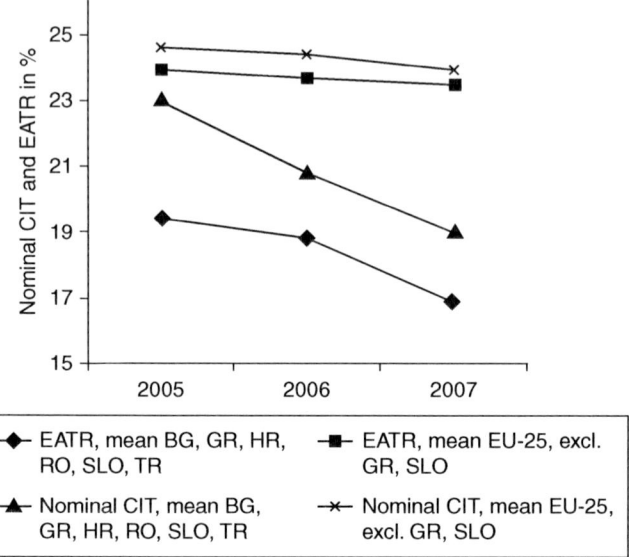

*Figure 11.3* Comparison of nominal CIT rate vs. domestic EATR in %
*Source*: Devereux et al. (2008).

tax rates are much more similar in the EU. This fact again points to the existence of various tax incentives in the CEECs.

In summary, domestic tax rates are decreasing and converging in the SEECs, and they are considerably different from domestic tax rates in the EU. Yet, for cross-border investments, additional tax parameters enter the location decision (see section below); therefore this assessment is only preliminary. Since EU companies are important investors in SEECs, we now turn to the tax burden of cross-border investment in SEECs.

*Effective tax rates on* cross-border *income*

As with the nominal tax rates at *domestic* level, described in the section above, the nominal tax rate does not reflect the actual tax burden in the case of *cross-border* inward investment, since regulations contained in double tax treaties, supranational and international tax law are not reflected in nominal tax rates. EATRs also need to include the tax burden on repatriated profits (for example dividend taxes). We emphasize here the tax burden arising for an *out*ward investment of EU countries directed to SEECs and for an *in*ward investment in the SEECs originating in the EU, as is the case for the bulk of inward FDI in SEECs.

An important additional tax code entering effective tax rates consists in double tax treaties. Double tax treaties may have a number of positive effects on FDI by reducing uncertainty and double taxation, but they may also impact negatively, as firms loose arbitrage possibilities (Blonigen and Davies, 2004). As can be seen from Table 11.1, SEECs have concluded double tax treaties with a large number of EU countries.

Turning to EATRs for cross-border investment, Figure 11.4 and Table 11.2 depict the main trends. Since EATRs are country-pair specific, as they differ between country pairs, many bilateral EATRs between EU countries and SEECs exist. In order not to complicate the picture, the figures on the *country level* presented here are averaged across home countries. For example, the EATR figure for Romania is the averaged EATR over all bilateral EU country inward investments with Romania. The figures on the *country-group level* (SEECs, EU), then, represent the averaged country-level EATRs, now averaged across those countries pertaining to a country group. For example, the EATR for the SEECs is calculated as the average of the averaged country-level EATRs of all SEECs. Beside the EU countries, several SEECs which are non-member states were included in the study – their figures are to be interpreted likewise. It must be kept in mind, however, that the variation of these bilateral tax rates is large, because home countries differ in their tax treatment of the proceeds of FDI. Therefore, the averaged figures presented here should be taken only as being indicative of a certain tax burden, while the actual tax burden of a home country/host country pair may differ considerably.

Comparing domestic and inward cross-border EATRs for the year 2007 (see Figure 11.4) in SEECs reveals that both tax rates go hand in hand: countries with nominal tax rates below the SEEC average also have below average inward cross-border EATRs. Comparing the SEEC figures to EU figures shows, additionally, the much lower level of inward cross-border EATRs in SEECs (with the exception of Turkey) than in the EU. Hence, for an EU company, investment in a SEEC rather than in another EU country pays off taxwise.

Table 11.2 shows the short-term development of these tax rates, which on average have fallen between 2005 and 2007. Keeping in mind that the nominal tax rate (see above) is an important determinant of the inward cross-border, EATR suggests that the downward trend continues at present.

Evidence on inward cross-border EATRs suggests therefore that SEECs are not an exception within Europe, as most countries show a decreasing effective tax burden for MNEs undertaking cross-border FDI within Europe.

*Table 11.1*  Double tax treaties as of 1 June 2010

| AL: | BiH: | BG: | | HR: | GR: | | MK: | MN: | SRB: | SLO: | TR: | |
|---|---|---|---|---|---|---|---|---|---|---|---|---|
| AT | AT | AL | RU | AL | AL | SY | AL | MT | AL | AL | AL | NL |
| BE | HR | DZ | SRB | AT | AR | TN | AM | | BY | AT | DZ | NO |
| BG | CZ | AM | SG | BY | AM | TR | AT | | BE | BE | AZ | PK |
| CN | FI | AT | SK | BE | AU | GB | AZ | | BiH | BG | BH | PL |
| HR | MY | BY | SLO | BiH | AT | US | BY | | BG | CA | BD | PT |
| CZ | MD | BE | ZA | BG | AZ | | BE | | CN | CN | BY | QA |
| GR | SRB | CA | ES | CA | BE | | BiH | | HR | HR | BE | RO |
| HU | ES | CN | SE | CL | BG | | BG | | CY | CZ | BiH | RU |
| KR | TR | HR | CH | CN | CA | | CA | | CZ | DK | BG | SA |
| LV | | CZ | SY | CZ | CN | | CN | | DK | EE | CN | SRB |
| MK | | DK | TH | DK | HR | | CY | | EGFI | FI | HR | SG |
| MY | | EG | TR | EG | CY | | CZ | | FR | GER | CZ | SK |
| ML | | EE | UA | EE | CZ | | EE | | GER | GR | DK | SLO |
| MD | | FI | GB | FI | DK | | FI | | GH | HU | EG | ZA |
| NL | | FR | US | FR | EE | | GER | | GR | IL | EE | ES |
| PL | | GE | ZU | GR | FI | | GR | | GN | KR | ET | SD |
| RO | | GER | VN | HK | FR | | HU | | HU | LV | FI | SE |
| SRB | | GR | ZW | HU | GE | | IL | | IN | LT | FR | SY |
| SLO | | HU | | ID | GER | | IT | | IR | LU | GER | TJ |
| SE | | IN | | IR | HU | | KZ | | IT | ML | GR | TH |
| CH | | ID | | IE | IN | | KG | | KP | MD | HU | TN |
| TR | | IE | | IL | IE | | LV | | KW | NL | IN | TM |
| | | IL | | IT | IL | | LT | | LV | PL | ID | UA |
| | | IT | | JO | IT | | LU | | LT | PT | IR | AE |
| | | JP | | KR | KR | | MK | | MK | SRB | IE | GB |
| | | KZ | | KW | KW | | NL | | MY | SK | IL | US |
| | | KP | | LV | LV | | OM | | MD | ES | IT | ZU |
| | | KR | | LT | LT | | PL | | NL | CH | JP | YE |
| | | KW | | MK | LU | | RO | | NO | TH | JO | |
| | | LV | | NL | MX | | RU | | PH | TR | KZ | |
| | | LB | | PL | MD | | SRB | | PL | GB | KR | |
| | | LT | | RO | MA | | SK | | RO | US | KW | |
| | | LU | | RU | NL | | SLO | | RU | | KG | |
| | | MK | | SM | NO | | ES | | SK | | LV | |
| | | ML | | RS | PL | | CH | | SLO | | LB | |
| | | MD | | SL | PT | | TJ | | LK | | LT | |
| | | MN | | SLO | RO | | TR | | SE | | LU | |
| | | ML | | ZA | SRB | | UA | | CH | | MK | |
| | | NL | | ES | SK | | GB | | TR | | MY | |
| | | NO | | CH | SLO | | ZU | | UA | | MD | |
| | | PL | | SY | ES | | | | GB | | MN | |
| | | PT | | TR | SE | | | | ZW | | MA | |
| | | RO | | UA | CH | | | | | | | |

*Source*: UNCTAD.org, International Arrangements Section.

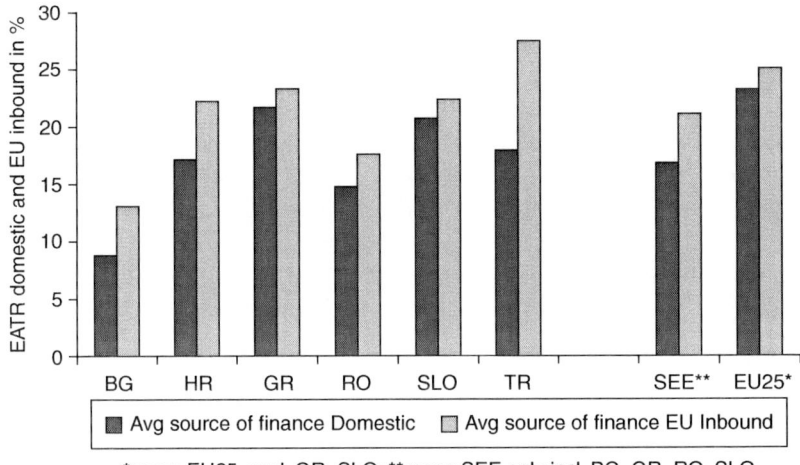

*mean EU25, excl. GR, SLO; **mean SEE only incl. BG, GR, RO, SLO

*Figure 11.4*   Comparison of domestic and inward cross-border effective tax rates, by country

*Note*: There are also effective tax rates available, which apply to the investment of small and medium-sized enterprises (SMEs).

*Source*: Devereux et al. (2008).

*Table 11.2*   Comparison between domestic and cross-border effective tax rates, averaged across country groups

|  | Nominal CIT | | EATR domestic | | EATR inbound EU27 | |
|---|---|---|---|---|---|---|
|  | mean EU25* | mean SEE** | mean EU25* | mean SEE** | mean EU25* | mean SEE** |
| 2005 | 22.0 | 24.6 | 24.0 | 19.5 | 25.8 | 23.4 |
| 2006 | 21.3 | 24.4 | 23.7 | 18.8 | 25.7 | 22.7 |
| 2007 | 18.5 | 23.9 | 23.5 | 16.9 | 25.1 | 19.1 |

\* mean EU25 excl. GR, SLO; ** mean SEE only includes BG, GR, RO, SLO.
*Sources*: Devereux et al. (2008), IBFD (various years).

## Tax systems in SEECs, flat tax systems in particular

The idea of a flat tax is not a novel one. In its purest form, private and corporate incomes are taxed at one rate, which is typically low. An idealized flat tax usually consists of the following elements: a single flat rate; elimination of special preferences; absence of double taxation; and the territorial tax system (Rabushka and Hall, 2007).

CEECs and SEECs comprise a group of countries where the flat tax idea has gained considerable importance in tax policy strategies. Estonia was the first to change its tax system to a flat rate of 26 per cent, combined with other neo-liberal incentives (for example zero-tariff trade). Within the following decade almost a dozen CEECs joined the 'flat tax revolution'. Even in the first year after Estonia's reform, the other two Baltic countries, Latvia and Lithuania, changed to a flat tax policy (see Table 11.3). One should keep in mind, however, that the changes in the tax systems do not reflect this idealized flat tax in these countries. Rather, these countries have introduced *flat rate* taxes in the area of personal income tax, corporate income tax or both.

While it was an absolute no-go in mature European economies to implement such radical tax reforms, the post-Soviet countries provided 'a fluid environment for policy change', while 'competition created

*Table 11.3*  Introduction of Flat Tax Reform

| Country | Year of reform |
| --- | --- |
| Jersey | 1940 |
| Hong Kong | 1947 |
| Estonia | 1994 |
| Latvia | 1995 |
| Lithuania | 1996 |
| Russia | 2001 |
| Serbia | 2003 |
| Slovakia | 2004 |
| Ukraine | 2004 |
| Georgia | 2005 |
| Romania | 2005 |
| Albania | 2007 |
| Iceland | 2007 |
| Kyrgyzstan | 2007 |
| Macedonia | 2007 |
| Mongolia | 2007 |
| Montenegro | 2007 |
| Bulgaria | 2008 |
| Czech Republic | 2008 |
| Bosnia and Herzegovina | 2009 |
| Mauritius | 2009 |
| Belarus | 2009 |
| Belize | 2009 |

*Sources*: Baturo and Gray (2009), Keen et al. (2008).

conditions that made adopting the flat tax persuasive' (Baturo and Gray, 2009, p. 131). Keen et al. (2008, p. 742) support this argument by saying that flat tax systems have usually been adopted 'by relatively new governments anxious to signal a fundamental regime shift, towards more market-oriented policies'. This creates the assumption that the flat tax reform processes are closely related to an ideological shift of the new government parties. Mitchell (2008) states that flat tax systems are designed to have low rates, so that investors are not penalized for risk-taking and entrepreneurship.

Liberal economists promote the idea of a flat tax system because it bears great potential for boosting the overall economic performance in relation to the following issues. Administration and compliance costs are reduced to a minimum, as are incentives for tax evasion. This leads to an increase in the government's tax revenue. 'The introduction of a flat tax system is widely seen as a reform which may boost efficiency, employment and growth through simplification and higher incentives', as Peichl (2009, p. 301) points out. In addition, a flat tax rate contributes to the principles of simplicity, reduced bureaucracy and territoriality and makes the tax system more easily comparable with other contemporaneous tax systems.

After a new coalition government came to power in Croatia in 2000, an encompassing tax reform was introduced that applied the reduction of corporate income tax from 35 to 20 per cent (Keen and King, 2002). The government parties justified the reform with the following arguments: the new tax system would promote domestic and foreign direct investment that, in turn, would enhance employment; the simplification of the tax system reduces costs and makes it easier to compare with other systems, and leads to a harmonization with the tax systems of the EU countries (Svaljek, 2005).

The main advantage of a low, flat tax rate comes with the attraction of foreign investors. Countries that do not adopt their neighbours' flat tax policies risk losing foreign direct investments: 'On average, "flat" countries receive 4.3 per cent of their GDP in FDI inflows after adoption, while non-flat countries receive 2.5 per cent. Also, on average, FDI inflows increase by 2.5 per cent after country adopts flat tax' (Baturo and Gray, 2009, p. 138). Thus flat countries would lure investors away from non-flat countries. Due to increased competition in implementing low flat tax systems in the post-Soviet countries over the last decade, some of the mature Western European economies started to examine the flat tax.

Russia's introduction of a rigorous 13 per cent personal income flat tax in 2001 and a cut of the corporate income tax from 35 to 24 per cent in 2002 yielded positive results. Tax evasion and avoidance became much less profitable (improved tax compliance); thus the government's tax revenue increased significantly. Moreover, the economy was given a boost due to the tax cut as well as to other free market reforms. Not only Russia, but also other countries experienced increased tax collections that exceeded expectations (Mitchell, 2008). Baturo and Gray (2009, p. 133) state in that case: 'One senior government tax official estimated that before the flat tax took effect at the beginning of 2001, Russians on average had declared as little as 25 per cent of their incomes.'

Despite all arguments in favour of the introduction of a flat tax system, there are some questionable points. The first relates to the distributional consequences of tax systems. A flat tax system seems to be infeasible in the welfare states of Western Europe because tax payers with low incomes do not want to be taxed at the same rate as people with high incomes, who should bear a greater share of the payment burden. Yet adverse distributional effects could be mitigated by generous tax exemptions for low-income groups. Furthermore, Western economies 'fear a race to the bottom, as countries compete for mobile international investment by offering lower tax levels and, thus, greater return to that investment' (Baturo and Gray, 2009, p. 132). The second point argues that a low flat tax could create marginal disincentives to work and invest. This is the case if a worker chooses to work less (due to the tax cut) to enjoy more leisure time while remaining on the same level of salary (Baturo and Gray, 2009). Thus inequality is likely to increase as a consequence of a flat tax reform. This in turn reduces the chances of the political parties in power gaining political support.

Summing up, simplification of the tax code and easier international comparability of the tax system, combined with reduced bureaucracy costs and higher tax compliance strongly support the idea of a flat tax. Amongst other economic reforms made during a reform process, the adoption of a flat tax system is likely to enhance FDI inflows and to boost the economy. The major drawback to be mentioned is a potential welfare loss due to a redistribution of resources that is considered to be unfair by Western European welfare states. The flat tax system treats all workers and companies equally, so the poor would not be financially supported by the rich. As a consequence, inequality is likely to be increased.

One immediate question concerning the introduction of flat tax regimes is their impact on tax revenues. However, as the OECD (2010,

p. 193) writes: 'No SEE economy has fully implemented a corporate income tax (CIT) microsimulation model for analysing the revenue impact of alternative tax regimes and allowing disaggregated analysis of the current tax regime.' Therefore, to date, it has been impossible to disentangle the revenue effects of the introduction of flat tax from other factors such as the business cycle effects on tax revenues.

## FDI in SEE

### Economic rationale of FDI attraction

The SEECs lack a necessary, but not alone sufficient, prerequisite for growth: capital. Therefore SEECs' governments have tried to attract FDI in order to ensure a certain growth of the investment volume. Beside these direct effects, host country governments also expect certain indirect effects, including technology transfer, spillover effects to domestic firms and so on. However, as empirical studies have shown, these effects need neither be positive in general (as there may exist important crowding-out forces), nor be substantial in macro-economic terms.

Therefore policy makers usually combine measures of FDI attraction with investment incentives at the national level. Moreover, there is less and less discrimination found between domestic and foreign firms, which is due to stricter competition policies in some countries. It is important, however, not to forget that there are exceptions as large foreign investment projects often being decided politically and receiving 'special treatment'.

### How much FDI has been attracted?

FDI may be measured as a *stock* value, reflecting the total amount of capital invested in a host country, including locally raised capital. Figure 11.5 shows the strong increase in FDI stocks over the last decade, as well as the negative effect of the economic crisis on FDI in the SEECs that even reduced FDI stocks, presumably mostly due to valuation adjustments of existing investment by foreign MNEs. The cross-country distribution of FDI stocks reflects partly the size of the host countries and partly their level of development.

Figure 11.6 includes the normalized inward FDI stocks (by population size). Ratios are not available for all the countries. HR (somewhat surprisingly, as it is not an EU member) and SLO are in the lead. RO and BU are catching up rapidly and strongly. AL is found towards the lower end of the figure. To some extent, this shows the strong variations in the capacity to attract FDI across SEECs.

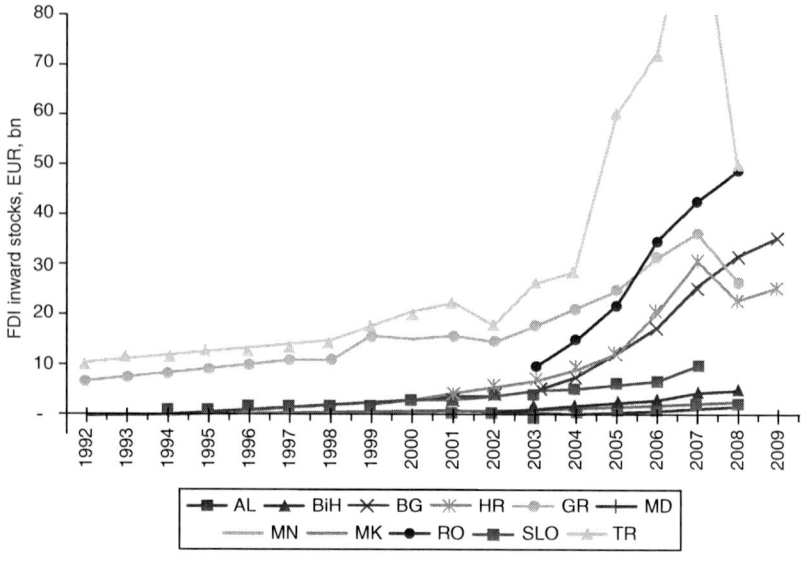

*Figure 11.5*    FDI stock total, euros, bn
*Sources*: WIIW database; Data on GR, MD, MN, TR: UNCTAD.

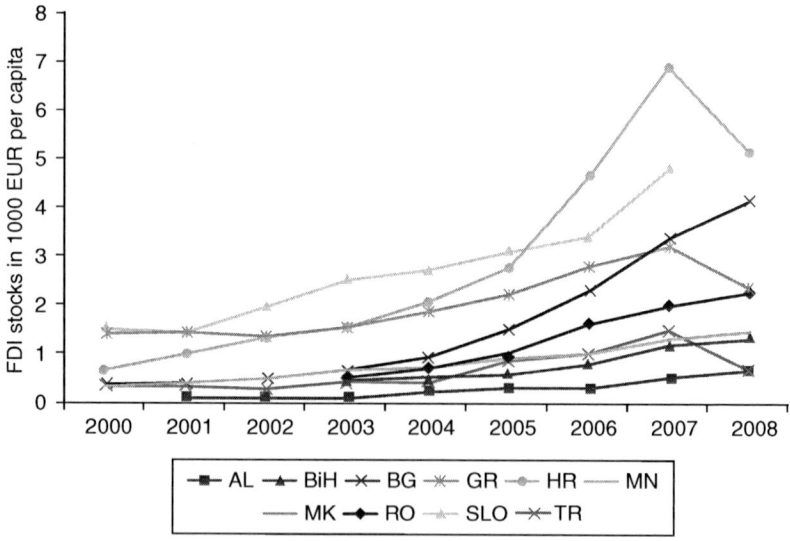

*Figure 11.6*    FDI stocks in 1000 euros per capita
*Sources*: FDI stocks: WIIW database, UNCTAD; Population data: WIIW Handbook of Statistics,
except for GR and TR: World Development Indicators online database.

However, FDI may also be measured as a *flow* value measuring the current (annual) contribution to existing FDI stock, as well as new investment. Ideally, beside equity, FDI flows also include reinvested earnings abroad and intra-company indebtedness. In practice not all countries stick to this definition, and thus comparability between countries is limited. Apart from the limited FDI inflows into Slovenia, Figure 11.7 shows a clear pre-membership effect for Romania and Bulgaria, as inward FDI flows surged, while all other SEECs' inflows remained below euro 1 bn annually. Also, a clear effect of the economic crisis is evident.

Figure 11.8 attemps to reflect the importance of inward FDI flows for domestic capital formation in the countries lacking capital mentioned in the section above. Despite some conceptual problems arising from comparisons between domestic and foreign investment flows, the picture gives a clear message: Figure 11.8 first shows that FDI makes an important contribution to the gross fixed capital formation, and thus to the growth of the capital stock in the host economies. Second, apart from two countries, where the share is larger than 100 per cent and the figures have therefore not been interpreted, the average share in the remaining SEECs is increasing and lies just below 40 per cent. The high share suggests that SEEC governments are inclined to introduce measures avoiding the loss of FDI, or even try to increase FDI to their country.

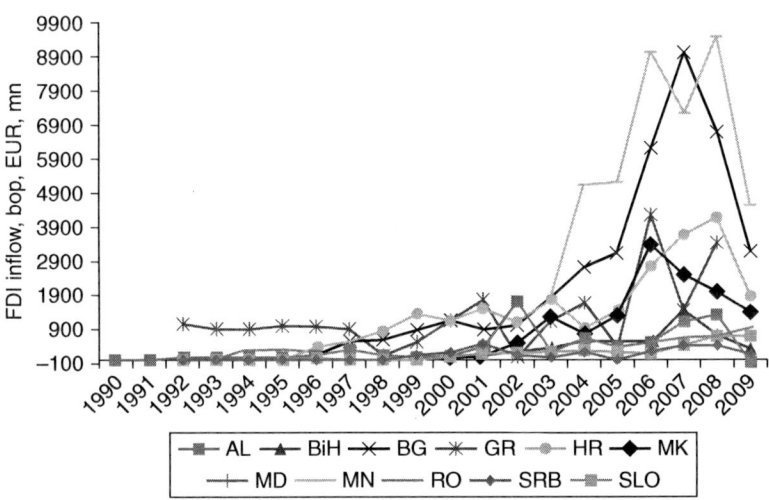

*Figure 11.7*   FDI inflows total, euros, mn, excluding TR
*Sources:* WIIW FDI database; Data on GR: UNCTAD.

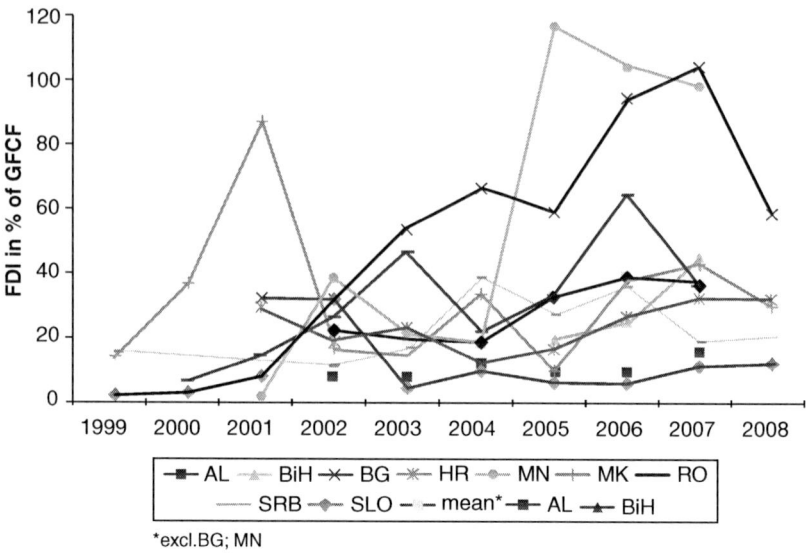

*Figure 11.8*   FDI in % of gross fixed capital formation
*Source*: WIIW Statistical Handbook database.

## Impact of taxes on FDI

Taxes, direct taxes such as the CIT in particular, are believed to exert a negative impact on inward FDI. The theoretical argument is as simple as it is convincing: an increase in the CIT, *ceteris paribus*, leads to an increase in the effective average tax rate, which determines the location of an inframarginal investment. Moreover, a rising CIT likely also increases the cost of capital, which is the required pre-tax return of the marginal investment project. Hence a rising CIT also reduces the scale of FDI. This so-called negative tax elasticity of FDI has been studied empirically in a number of analyses. Yet empirical information on tax elasticities in SEECs is scarce, as they are hardly covered in empirical studies which mainly focus on OECD countries. DeMooij and Ederveen (2008) provide a recent survey of the studies available. They reveal that the predicted semi-elasticity of the EATR is −5.9 when applied to financial FDI data.

With respect to a country group that is 'closer' to the SEECs, Bellak and Leibrecht (2009) study fifty-six bilateral country relationships by combining seven home countries from the EU and the US and eight Central and East European host countries (CEECs) of FDI from 1995 to 2003 and find a tax semi-elasticity of FDI of −4.3 on average. This implies that every reduction in the effective tax rate in the CEECs by one percentage point increases inward FDI by 4.3 per cent, which clearly is a non-negligible amount. In addition, this result is in line with the findings of DeMooij and Ederveen, quoted above. One should keep in mind that there are strong variations in the results depending on time frame, method applied, tax measure used, FDI indicator employed, the quality of data in general and so on, but negative and statistically significant results are derived in the majority of studies.[3]

Summarizing the previous considerations, SEEC governments have expressed clearly their aim to attract FDI via tax policy; substantial FDI has indeed flown into the SEECs; and empirically the probability that FDI directed into SEECs responds to changes in the structure and level of direct business taxes is high.

## Conclusions

This chapter has set out to discuss the role of direct taxation of business in SEECs for domestic investment in general, and the location choice of foreign firms in particular. Empirical evidence on various aspects of direct business taxation in SEECs is scarce.

As a starting point, we have discussed the positive and the negative impacts of taxation on domestic investment in general and the location choice of foreign firms in particular. We have taken both the viewpoint of firms and of governments. In conclusion, tax policy is a very dynamic field of policy making in SEECs. With respect to national corporate income tax rates, the main trend may be summarized as falling tax rates, which are converging across SEECs. The substantial difference between the (higher) *nominal* tax burden and the lower *effective* tax burden of firms (shown for domestic as well as for cross-border investments) suggests a high willingness of governments to stimulate investment in general.

Concerning policy strategies in direct business taxation, Bellak and Leibrecht (2008, p. 152) examine, for eight CEECs, four preconditions for tax competition[4] and conclude that 'all four preconditions for corporate income tax competition are fulfilled. [...] Tax competition for FDI is indeed a driver of the falling tax rates in these countries'. The information presented in this chapter, three facts in particular, suggests that not only CEECs', but also SEECs' governments are following a 'race-to-the-bottom' tax competition strategy, namely: (i) rapidly and strongly decreasing as well as converging nominal and effective CIT rates in the SEECs and introducing flat rate tax systems in particular, combined with much higher tax rates on wages (immobile factor labour) than on capital in the SEECs; (ii) the stated aim of tax reductions, namely the attraction of FDI, as published by many governmental investment promotion agencies in SEECs; and (iii) the technical feasibility of FDI, due to liberalization policies and to the fact that MNEs make use of this opportunity. Whether the fourth precondition, namely that 'corporate income taxes are a significant determinant of FDI', is fulfilled has not been examined analytically in this chapter. Yet the chapter has shown the strong increase of FDI in all SEECs up to 2008.[5] Moreover, direct business taxes have decreased substantially, a process that is sometimes paralleled by a change in the tax system. However, any causal link between these two parameters for SEECs would still have to be established empirically; but there are strong signs that tax competition for FDI between the governments in SEECs exists (Owens, 2004).

Following a strategy of tax competition may, however, be dangerous: As domestic investment and FDI respond to various location factors at the same time, no single location factor (in particular, certainly not the tax burden) will usually determine an investment, and thus location decision. The interrelationship of location factors may be neutral (as for example level of schooling and exchange rate), conflicting (for example infrastructure and taxes) or positive (for example infrastructure and level of schooling). The policy *challenge ahead*, for governments in SEECs trying to stimulate investment, is therefore to manage these complex relationships between the location factor 'taxes' and 'regulations' and the 'other business environment'. Finding the right balance is, however, difficult. This applies to the *design of a tax system*, enabling SEECs to finance those location factors conducive to investment (education, infrastructure etc.) and respective incentives on the one hand, but not leading to negative welfare consequences via large distortions (for example hampering FDI) or a loss of revenues (by low tax rates resulting from tax competition) on the other hand. The constraining factor concerning the development of such tax systems – beside national priorities – will be the evolving system of tax coordination in the EU – be it for members or non-members (applicants and future applicants) alike.

In this chapter, the tax environment has been characterized as being quite favourable to doing business in SEECs. MNEs may therefore relocate activities to the SEECs, which benefit from these conditions, comprising certain production and service activities, profit shifting and the like. Yet, for some activities, the efficiency losses from overregulations and a lack of infrastructure will prevent MNEs from engaging in further investment in the SEECs.

# Notes

1. See Nicodeme (2009) for a summary and discussion of possible distortions of the CIT at national and international level relating to the benefit principle, tax exporting, treasury effects and the erosion of personal income tax.
2. Apart from efficiency effects, there are important equity problems, for example whether companies contribute a 'fair share' to overall tax revenues. This – political – discussion is excluded from the present paper.
3. The magnitude of these variations may be found in DeMooij and Ederveen (2008).
4. These preconditions are (1) Governments reduce tax rates on corporate income which are relevant for FDI decisions of MNEs; (2) One explicit motivation of tax rate cuts is to attract FDI or to react to downward revisions of other countries' corporate income tax rates to avoid loosing investment; (3) FDI is technically possible and MNEs make use of this possibility; (4) Corporate income taxes are a significant determinant of FDI.
5. Except in GR and HR in 2008, which was the year of the economic crisis.

# References

Baldwin, R. E. and Krugman, P. (2004) 'Agglomeration, integration and tax harmonisation', *European Economic Review*, 48, 1–23.

Baturo, A. and Gray, J. (2009) 'Flatliners: Ideology and Rational Learning in Adoption of the Flat Tax', *European Journal of Political Research*, 48, 130–159.

Bellak, C. and Leibrecht, M. (2008) 'Corporate Income Taxation in Central- and Eastern European Countries and Tax Competition for Foreign Direct Investment', in Dunning, J. H. and Gugler, Ph. (eds), *Foreign Direct Investment, Location and Competitiveness, Progress In International Business Research*, vol. 2 (Oxford: Elsevier), 133–156.

Bellak, C. and Leibrecht, M. (2009) 'Do Low Corporate Income Tax Rates Attract FDI? – Evidence from Central- and East European countries', *Applied Economics*, 40, 2691–2703.

Blonigen, B. and Davies, R. B. (2004) 'The Effects of Bilateral Tax Treaties on U.S. FDI Activity', *International Tax and Public Finance*, 11, 601–622.

DeMooij, R. and Ederveen, S. (2008) 'Corporate Tax Elasticities: A Reader's Guide to Empirical Findings', *Oxford Review of Economic Policy*, 24, 680–697.

Devereux, M. P. and Griffith, R. (1999) 'The Taxation of Discrete Investment Choices', Working Paper 98/16 (Revision 2) (London: Institute for Fiscal Studies).

Devereux, M. P. and Griffith, R. (2003) 'Evaluating Tax Policy for Location Decisions', *International Tax and Public Finance*, 10, 107–126.

Devereux, M. P., Elschner, C., Endres, D., Heckemeyer, J. H., Overesch, M., Schreiber, U. and Spengel, C. (2008) 'Effective Levels of Company Taxation within an Enlarged EU', Project for the EU Commission TAXUD/2005/DE/3 10, Final Report, ZEW (Mannheim and Oxford: Zentrum für Europäische Wirtschaftsforschung).

Homburg, S. (2007) *Allgemeine Steuerlehre* (München: Vahlen).

IBFD (various years) *European Tax Handbook* (Amsterdam: IBFD).

Keen, M. and King, J. (2002) 'The Croatian Profit Tax: An ACE in Practice', *Fiscal Studies*, 23(3), 401–418.

Keen, M., Kim, V. and Varsano, R. (2008) 'The "Flat Tax(es)": Principles and Experience', *International Tax and Public Finance*, 15, 712–751.

Mitchell, D. J. (2008) 'The Global Flat Tax Revolution: Lessons for Policy Makers', *Prosperitas*, VIII(I), 1–12.

Nicodeme, G. (2009) 'Corporate Income Tax and Economic Distortions', *Taxation Papers* (Brussels: European Commission's Directorate-General for Taxation and Customs Union).

OECD (2010) *Investment Reform Index 2010* (Paris: Organisation for Economic Co-Operation and Development).

Owens, J. (2004) 'Competition for FDI and the Role of Taxation: The Experience of South Eastern European Countries', *Working Papers No 316* (Pavia: Università di Pavia).

Peichl, A. (2009) 'The Benefits and Problems of Linking Micro And Macro Models – Evidence from a Flat Tax Analysis', *Journal of Applied Economics*, 12(2), 301–329.

Rabushka, A. and Hall, R. (2007) *The Flat Tax* (Stanford: Hoover Institution).

Svaljek, S. (2005) 'The 2000 Tax Reform in Croatia: Causes and Consequences', *Economski Pregled*, 56(12), 1217–1236.

# 12
# Consumer Behaviour and Food Consumption Patterns in South East Europe

*Elka Vasileva and Daniela Ivanova*

## Introduction

In recent years the countries of South East Europe (SEE) have turned into market economies. This, quite naturally, has made the study of consumers in the region necessary. The aim of this chapter is to describe consumption patterns and consumer behaviour in SEE in general, emphasizing both national and regional characteristics and outlining the similarities with European and global consumers. An attempt is made to summarize and analyse the research studies published in scientific literature in this area.[1]

Communities with a shared history, specific cultural and religious traits, people with different lifestyles, which form certain patterns of behaviour, co-exist in SEE. This is a region with unique characteristics, which makes the description of consumer behaviour rather challenging. Despite the many differences, a number of similarities can nevertheless be found in local consumption patterns.

In the last decades these countries have gone through major economic and social changes. After the collapse of communism they embarked on the path of difficult adaptation from a controlled and centralized economy to a free market system. Some, like Bulgaria, Hungary, Romania and Slovenia, have already become members of the European Union (EU). The youngest countries can be found in the region of the Western Balkans, with the exception of Albania: Bosnia and Herzegovina, Croatia, the Former Yugoslav Republic of Macedonia, Kosovo, Montenegro and Serbia. Successor states of the former Republic of Yugoslavia, these countries are going through a difficult transition period, often connected with violence. Moldova, a former Soviet

271

republic, which represents the eastern neighbours of the region, is also included here. All are trying hard to find their way as regards the 'new' economy and their place in today's globalized world.

Since the fall of 'the iron curtain', most research studies have focused on the economic and social changes of the SEE reforming countries, on the institutional reforms, their economic consequences and the overall progress of the transition from planned to free market economy. Relatively little attention is paid to the consumer and to the changes which he or she experiences.

The entering of Western multinational corporations into these countries made the introduction of new marketing approaches possible and 'flooded' the newly emerged markets with a diverse range of products and international brands. This placed the consumer of the post-socialist era in a totally different situation, by allowing the consumer to get information on, and to evaluate, the products available and then to make a rational choice.

In the context of the new tendencies towards loss of confidence and pride in the local culture, alienation, frustration and increased stress, emerging consumers are seeking to catch up with Western levels of consumption patterns (Shama, 1992; Belk and Ger, 1994; Feick et al., 1995; Money and Colton, 2000; Coulter et al., 2003; Sredl, 2007).

The choice of the 'new consumer' in these transitional SEE economies is defined by a person's individuality, which is connected with needs, a perception of brands' characteristics, attitudes towards alternatives and also with demographic characteristics and lifestyle. On the other hand, the environment in which the consumer makes the choices has an especially strong influence; and this includes culture (the norms of society, regional or ethnic sub-culture), social class, as well as friends, family members and other reference groups. Consumer behaviour in the SEE countries is the result both of the communication between consumers as individuals and of environmental influences.

## Emerging consumer cultures in the transitional economies of South East Europe

The transition to a market economy in the SEE countries created unique conditions for revealing the nature of consumer transformation. Numerous studies put socio-cultural beliefs about consumption at the centre of post-socialist consumer culture. Some focus on consumer culture during state socialism and reveal the effects of this period, which have become manifested in modern-day consumer patterns and behaviour

(Belk and Ger, 1994; Sredl, 2007). It should be noted that consumers from Hungary and from the countries that made up former Yugoslavia, which are considered the most liberalized of the former command economies in Europe, have ample experience with products from other cultures and countries. Other researchers explore how new cultural beliefs about consumption, strongly influenced by Western media and by new products and brands, alter the role of consumption in everyday life (Money and Colton, 2000; Coulter et al., 2003, 2005).

Research into product involvement and brand commitment was carried out in two post-socialist countries from SEE: Hungary and Romania (Coulter et al., 2003). This work demonstrates that prominent political–cultural discourses, cultural intermediaries, social influences and life themes and projects collectively prompt product involvement. The research illustrates that consumers with little interest either in the product category or in the idea of branded products may be committed to particular brands.

Research carried out in Hungary during the period of transition to a market economy provides an ideal opportunity to examine the evolving relationships between consumer product knowledge and sources of information, including advertising, personal search, interpersonal sources and brand experience (Coulter et al., 2005). The results indicate that the market information variables explain more variance in consumer knowledge later rather than earlier in the transition period. Advertising is an important predictor of consumer knowledge for the later transition period, but not for the earlier transition period. Personal search is important both earlier and later in transition times, while interpersonal sources are not important in either time period. Brand experience is negatively related to knowledge earlier in the transition and positively related to it at later stages of that period.

Cross-national differences in consumer response to the framing of advertising messages are shown in a survey of consumers from Croatia, the Czech Republic, Hungary and Poland (Orth et al., 2007). The findings indicate different emotional, cognitive and attitudinal responses across countries. Another survey, carried out at the same time, confirms that consumers in the major urban areas of Bulgaria and Romania are more positive about advertising as an institution than the instruments used to promote advertising (Petrovici and Marinov, 2007). While acquisition of product information is the main personal use of advertising, which influences general attitudes to advertising in Bulgaria, the entertainment value of advertising was found to be the strongest personal use in Romania. No significant differences were found in the attitudes towards the institution and instruments of advertising in the two countries.

A cross-national study conducted in Bulgaria, Hungary and Romania examines the influence of Western brands and advertising in the field of fashion on consumer values. The study finds that former collectivist values are being gradually replaced by individualism (Manrai et al., 2001). The results show that fashion consciousness, a style that represents individualism, is highest for Westernized Hungarian consumers, while dress conformity, a style that captures collectivism, is highest for Bulgarian respondents. At the same time, younger individuals are more fashion conscious than older individuals, whereas dress conformity is higher for older than for younger individuals.

These empirical studies substantiate the conceptual model of Money and Colton (2000) for the 'new consumer' in transition economies exposed to Western-style advertising. According to this model, the factors affecting the consumer attitude and response to advertising are connected both with the degree of the country's transition to a market economy and with the demographic characteristics of age and income and with a number of individual difference variables specifically appropriate to post-socialist countries.

## Cultural and ethnic aspects of consumer behaviour in South East Europe

Culture as the collective memory of a society is the accumulation of shared meanings, rituals, norms and traditions by its members. It includes both abstract ideas, such as values and systems of ethics, and the material objects and services that are produced or valued by a group of people (Solomon et al., 2006). Traditional cultural patterns, together with the rapid infiltration of Western European and global cultures, have a strong impact on consumer behaviour in the SEE countries.

### Consumer behaviour induced by product nationality

Analysis of existing research findings shows that ethnocentrism has a definite impact on consumer behaviour in SEE countries. These studies, which will be explained in more detail within the subsequent paragraphs, make it possible to validate and generalize the existing models of consumer behaviour (for a survey of the existing economic models, see Rischkowsky and Döring, 2008) in a new cultural context, connected with socio-economic transformations, ethnic conflicts or even wars.

Consumer behaviour induced by product nationality is studied in two streams in literature – country of origin and consumer ideology (Dmitrovic and Vida, 2010). The two streams of research adopt different theoretical perspectives and are based on the different mechanisms of consumer preference formation. Most empirical research studies on the countries in the SEE region adopt the first approach to the influence of the national origin of products (country of origin) in consumer choice behaviour. There are also others, which take into account the influence of consumer ideology.

In an attempt to reveal the sources of consumer ethnocentricity in four Central European countries (the Czech Republic, Estonia, Hungary and Poland), Vida and Fairhust (1999) study cultural openness and demographic variables as antecedents to this phenomenon. The results show that brand awareness as an indicator of cultural openness, age and gender were all found to be significant determinants of the phenomenon of consumer ethnocentricity. An additional study, conducted in Kazakhstan and Slovenia, examines the effects of ethnocentrism and economic development on the formation of brand and advertisement attitudes depending on the degree of country's transition to market economy (Reardon et al., 2005). Considered representative of transitional economies, Kazakhstan and Slovenia were choosen: Kazakhstan represented the early stages of transition and Slovenia represented a highly advanced stage of transition. The results show that the effect of ethnocentrism on attitudes towards the advertisement of foreign products was stronger in the newly transitional economy. On the other hand, there was only limited support for the idea that the effect of ethnocentrism on brand attitudes was stronger in newly transitional economies.

A number of studies on the Western Balkans show that ethnic sentiment is becoming one of the strongest motivations in consumer purchasing behaviour in a multiethnic transitional economy. For instance Cicic et al. (2003), as well as Cutura (2006), found evidence that consumer ethnocentrism is positively related to willingness to buy domestic goods versus goods imported from the most important trade partners of Bosnia and Herzegovina (Croatia, Serbia and countries of the EU). The authors suggest that the appearance of ethnic affiliation as an important independent variable in influencing the level of ethnocentric tendencies is unique to Bosnia and Herzegovina. Similar conclusions about the effects of ethnic affiliation on ethnocentrism and on domestic purchase bias are made in another piece of research on Bosnia and Herzegovina (Vida et al., 2008). The findings confirm that both national identity and nationalism are significant predictors of consumer ethnocentrism and that ethnic affiliation has a direct effect both on consumer ethnocentrism and on domestic purchase bias. However, the antecedent nature of cultural openness in relation to consumer ethnocentrism was not confirmed.

The importance of information related to the national origin of products in consumer choice behaviour is investigated in another country from the region – Croatia (Dmitrović and Vida, 2007). The results of this empirical analysis show that the significance of country of origin information is a function of consumer ethnocentrism, and that the strength of this relationship is indeed mediated by a product/service type. Moreover, age and income were significant discriminators of consumers characterized by ethnocentric and polycentric purchase orientation.

In order to fill in the gaps in the examined behavioural manifestations of consumers' choice of domestic versus foreign products on a crossnational level, research has been carried out in four transitional post-war markets in the Western Balkans in recent years: Bosnia and Herzegovina, Croatia, Montenegro and Serbia (Dmitrovic et al., 2009). For all four countries it is evident that consumer ethnocentrism has affected domestic purchase behaviour both directly and indirectly, through domestic product appraisal. At the same time, consumer materialism is uniformly negatively related to ethnocentrism. The findings relating to the role of national identification as an antecedent to consumer ethnocentrism and domestic product appraisal were inconsistent across the countries.

The effect of ethnocentrism on consumer behaviour has been shown to be barely evident in Bulgaria, Romania and Hungary. Here the impact of the transition to market economy and accession to the EU can be seen in the dilemma 'domestic vs. foreign products'. Throughout Hungary's communist past, Western products were greatly desired and domestic brands belittled. Consumer ethnocentrism was only significantly correlated with age (Witkowski, 1998). In the years of transition in Bulgaria a new attitude emerged, the opposite of the popular consumer opinion that prevailed throughout the planned economy. In the Communist years foreign goods were equated with high quality, while 'Made in Bulgaria' was associated with inferior products. In contrast to that attitude, Bulgarian products are now perceived to be of good quality and in general to provide better value for money (Milanova, 1999).

Sredl (2007), Schuh and Holzmüller (2003), as well as Milanova (1999) pointed out that consumers in Central and Eastern Europe (Bulgaria, Croatia, the Czech Republic, Hungary, Poland, Romania and Serbia) were familiar with Western brands from trips to the West or from media coverage and were willing to pay a higher price for them, or at least as long as the price–quality ratio in relation to locally produced goods was considered fair. The incorporation of Western quality and modern image into reasonably priced products that meet certain demands is very appealing to consumers from this region.

A survey conducted in Bulgaria in 2005 showed that Bulgarians are divided in their opinion on whether, by buying a Bulgarian brand, they are supporting local industry (GfK – Bulgaria-Market Research Institute, 2005). They were more inclined to gain maximum advantage for themselves from the purchase. Their motivation in choosing between the foreign and the local brand remains rational. Mainly young people and those with higher incomes were of the attitude that the foreign product is a sure guarantee of good quality. Additonal research on Bulgarian consumers' perceptions of products made in Asia-Pacific countries (Japan, Hong Kong, Singapore, Indonesia and India) confirms the role of quality in the choice of foreign products. Products from Japan rank first and are deemed to be of high quality, being followed by the products from Hong Kong, Singapore, Indonesia and India (Leonidou et al., 1999).

A survey of the possible behaviour of Romanian consumers in the case of 'Buy Romanian' indicates a positive correlation with the general attitudes of the Romanian public towards Romanian products and with nationalist sentiment (Crăciun and Barbu, 2010). The orientation towards internationalism does not diminish the consumers' propensity to buy Romanian products.

Finally, a comparative research study focused on the market in East European countries such as Romania, Ukraine and Russia on the one hand and the US market on the other hand shows that consumers across all four countries expressed strong favouritism towards global brands and displayed relatively low levels of consumer ethnocentrism (Strizhakova et al., 2008). It was found that the belief in global citizenship had a significant positive effect on the importance of branded products in consumers' daily lives, and this effect was equally strong across all countries.

### The role of the family in consumer behaviour

The family and some reference groups have a significant influence on consumer patterns in SEE. Extended families often celebrate special occasions with large meals, which can cost the hosts a significant share of their income. In anthropological studies conducted in Bulgaria, emphasis is placed on the importance of the abundance of foods and drink at weddings and on the extravagance of the wedding gifts (Creed, 2002).

High levels of investment are also evident in the descriptions of weddings in Romania and Macedonia. These studies highlight the fact that the decline of rituals is not a universal phenomenon in post-socialist Bulgaria, but a pervasive one, which correlates closely with economic difficulty. An ethnographic description of Romania and other countries in Central and Eastern Europe supports this correlation (Creed, 2002). Similar patterns can be seen, though now to a lesser extent, in other South European countries such as Greece, Italy and Spain.

## Social class and luxury product consumption as a status symbol in South East Europe

Modern societies are not monolithic, and different social groups can have different consumption patterns. In the last century researchers typically divided social groups into classes based on economic status. Social class refers to a national status hierarchy by which groups and individuals are distinguished in terms of esteem and prestige. A consumer's standing in society, or social class, is determined by a complex set of variables, including income, family background and occupation (Solomon et al., 2006).

As ethnographic research conducted in Croatia suggests, consumption and class have a specifically local meaning, the roots of which lie in the dynamics of consumption in the socialist era (Sredl, 2007). This research emphasizes that class and consumer culture during the period of state socialism might seem to contradict notions of socialist equality and communist shortage. Consumption as a display of affiliation to a certain class (the communist elite, the middle class, youth culture or the working class) was embedded in everyday life (Sredl, 2007). The political dynamics of transformation mostly abolished the class structure, creating an awareness of consumption as a sign of social rank in the new state. This research looks also at how privatization has led to changes in local class relationships, in ways that influence socio-cultural beliefs about consumption. The conclusions reached in this research are relevant for the other former socialist countries in SEE, where consumer culture during the transition period is rooted in prior social tensions and political upheavals of transformation.

At the same time, research studies in the field of behavioural economics are analysing groups on the basis of their post-materialist needs and of their values. In these analyses the different groups influence their own patterns of consumption. For example, the consumption of luxury goods involves purchasing products and services that represent value both to the individual and to his or her reference group.

In SEE countries the widespread phenomenon of the '*nouveaux riche*' can be observed. This is a phrase sometimes used in a derogatory manner, to describe consumers who have achieved extreme wealth and have relatively recently become members of upper social classes. The '*nouveaux riche*' phenomenon is also widespread in those countries where the transition to capitalism has paved the way for a new class of wealthy consumers, who are spending lavishly on luxury items (Solomon et al., 2006).

Research from Sarajevo, Bosnia and Herzegovina (Husic and Cicic, 2009) on luxury consumption, its motives and the styles of the consumers defines two sub-categories of consumers, namely the 'old aristocracy' and the '*nouveaux riche*', which accords with the situation of a developing market and society. The results show that in the luxury market consumers perceive quality as a brand determinant. Furthermore, strong patron status suggests a 'snob effect' among consumers who buy exclusive items in an attempt to distinguish themselves from others.

From the perspective of prestige-seeking consumer behaviour, the luxury consumers in the Balkan region (Bosnia and Herzegovina, Croatia, Serbia and Slovenia) can be classified as 'perfectionists' or 'hedonists' (Husic and Ostapenko, 2010). The 'perfectionists' are quality-oriented older consumers with higher incomes. The most important features they expect from a product are perfection (quality) and performance. The group of the 'hedonists' consists of middle-aged and middle-income consumers who want to indulge themselves as a reward for the hard work they do.

As the above studies show, consumers of luxury goods from the Balkan region feel a strong sense of 'luxury shame' in overcoming the post-socialist mindset, which was based on collectivistic values and equality in consumption. As in the case of the demographic portrait of the average European consumer of luxury goods, important differences between the countries were also detected. The luxury consumers in the Balkan region come from different social classes, have different incomes and education and are of different ages. Consumers who expressed more positive attitudes towards cultural change were also more likely to consume luxury goods, independently of their demographics and social class (Dubois and Duquesne, 1993). Research proves that people from the Balkan region purchase luxury goods for what they symbolize – that is, for status and recognition purposes, irrespective of the economic or social surroundings (Milanova, 1999; Husic and Cicic, 2009; Husic and Ostapenko, 2010).

## Food consumption in South East Europe

### The 'culture' of food consumption

Nowadays food consumption can be treated as a 'culture' constituted of specific social elements and endowed with certain characteristics, such as general food behaviour and attitudes ('consumption trends'), product-related food behaviour ('drinking habits') and health-related food behaviour and attitudes ('diet willingness').

Food consumption in the SEE countries should be viewed, above all, within the context of the transition from a centrally planned economic system, controlling the distribution and consumption of goods and services, to a system based on markets as an allocative mechanism. The period of transition in these countries involved substantial changes in the patterns of food consumption and significant year-to-year variation (Petrovici and Ritson, 2000). Liberalization of the economy led to lifestyle changes, uncertainties and employment insecurity, concerns about adequate nutrition or changes in consumption resulting from varying incomes. Individual responses to changes vary. The nature of the experienced change affects the system of values and preferences, and emerging preferences are reflected in consumption choices.

### General food behaviour and attitudes

During the 1990s, as a result of the ongoing economic and political changes in SEE countries, household incomes decreased rapidly. Food and clothes expenses in the period of recovery formed the most significant element in household expenditure. In recent years the proportionate spending on food in households has decreased, and considerable changes in the consumed foods have been noticed. The food diet of the populations in SEE countries includes cereals, milk, eggs, fish and vegetables in large quantities. An increase in the consumption of fish and milk has been observed in recent years. An exception from the general trend is Moldova, whose consumption of vegetables is lower than in the other countries in the region (FAOSTAT, 2009). The low consumption of fresh fruit is noted as a general trait in the consumption of fruits and fruit products in the countries of the Western Balkans (Serbia, Slovenia, Croatia, Macedonia, Bosnia and Herzegovina and Montenegro) – a trait related to the absence of habit (FOCUS-BALKANS, 2010). A trend of increased fruit consumption of both fresh and processed fruit, mainly as a result of raised awareness of healthy diet, is observed in all countries in this region.

The transition to a market economy led to a rapid increase in the variety of food items available, including beverages. Consumption of prepared and processed food as well as food imports have been increasing steadily since the end of the recession. This may be linked to growing customer preference for buying food in supermarkets instead of local shops and markets.

Along with economic factors, lifestyle and tradition play a significant role in food consumption. Another phenomenon explicitly manifested in this region is access to land where householders can grow their own food. In Bulgaria, the cultivation of a private plot of land is emerging as a main coping strategy designed to meet the basic food needs of a significant part of the population during the period of transition. The tradition of home food production and the making of fruit and vegetable preserves has its origins in the socialist era, but it has become so much a part of culture that it may continue long after the economic necessity for it has disappeared (Milanova, 1999; EEA, 2007). A current report on the European project 'FOCUS-BALKANS: Food Consumer Sciences in the Balkans' confirms that the tradition of growing fruit on private properties and of making sweet preserves is common to the countries of the Western Balkans (FOCUS-BALKANS, 2010).

The purchase of food in SEE countries is done mainly in small shops, open-air markets and the rapidly spreading supermarkets, which create new consumption patterns. The ratio between these three types of food retailers is different in the different countries of the region and is marked by being highly dynamic. The countries of the Western Balkans have seen a rapid growth in Western-style fast-food restaurants in large cities. These new retail outlets have brought with them Western brands and convenience foods, such as pre-prepared meals, many sold at low prices and supported by advertising. Big retail centres (the so-called 'malls') facilitate the transition to modern patterns of food consumption, typical of urban regions (Sik and Wallace, 2002; Millan and Howard, 2007; EEA, 2010).

*Product-related food behaviour*

The pattern of beverage consumption captures phenomena associated both with the traditions of the peoples of this region and with the dramatic socio-economic change induced by transformation of the countries' political and economic system. Drinking patterns are full of symbolic dimensions linked to gender, class, lifestyle, situations and rituals (Florkowski et al., 2006; Solomon et al., 2006).

In the SEE countries product traditions, drinking habits and social reactions to alcohol define the so-called Mediterranean pattern of drinking. Bulgaria, Hungary, Romania, Slovenia as well as other countries that were formerly part of Yugoslavia have traditionally been wine and fruit brandy countries; they are strongly influenced by the Mediterranean, especially the Greek and Italian, way of drinking. The Mediterranean style of drinking is characterized by the almost daily drinking of alcohol, by the frequent consumption of wine with meals and by lack of acceptance of public drunkenness (Popova et al., 2007). Information on the consumption of alcoholic beverages was expected to reflect an increased level of stress associated with the transition to the new socio-economic system in general, and uncertainties associated with employment in particular.

An overview of the volume of alcohol consumption, beverage preferences and patterns of drinking among adults (people 15 years of age and older) in Eastern European countries – among which Bulgaria, Hungary, Romania and Slovenia are included – allows a comparative analysis from a European perspective. The analysis is based on data for preferred beverage type for the year 2002 from the WHO Global Status Report on Alcohol and the WHO Global Alcohol Database (Popova et al., 2007). The highest overall per capita alcohol consumption, recorded and unrecorded (14–25 l of pure alcohol per year), for the year 2002 was found predominantly in Eastern European countries. The highest level of consumption was attained in Moldova, which was followed by Lithuania, Latvia, Slovakia, Hungary, Russia, Ukraine and Romania. Recorded consumption was noticeably lower in Bulgaria, where the beverages of choice were wine and spirits. It was revealed that the countries of Eastern Europe (that is, Croatia, Hungary, Moldova, Romania, Slovenia and Ukraine) have experienced a steep rise in mortality from alcoholic liver diseases and from cirrhosis (DHS, 2005; Popova et al., 2007).[2]

Finally, the changes in beverage consumption patterns in a new market economy were studied in Bulgaria for eight beverage categories: milk, coffee, tea, soft drinks, lemonade, beer, wine and spirits (Florkowski et al., 2006). The model developed includes factors (demographic, economic and geographic) influencing beverage choice using consumption frequency data. It was found that age, employment, education and income are the core characteristics of each beverage-consuming group, while gender and household characteristics, together with religion and geographical location, helped to outline the profile of Bulgarian beverage consumers.

*Health-related food behaviour and attitudes*

Food diets are directly related to personal well-being. Across the region of SEE malnourishment has declined since the 1990s, and currently malnourished people make under 5 per cent of the total population of all the countries in the region, according to FAO data for 2005 (FAOSTAT, 2009). This is the result of the end of conflicts in the Western Balkans and of a return to extensive economic growth.

Another health problem, connected with food patterns, has become very prominent – the increase in the number of overweight and obese adults in the region. In all countries in SEE more than 40 per cent of adults are either overweight or obese – as is the case in many other European countries (WHO, 2008).

Low incomes and inadequate resources for medical care in some of the countries of the region, food diet and lifestyle appear to be the main reasons for high mortality rates related to cardio-vascular diseases among the population. Almost all countries in SEE except Slovenia have a higher than average mortality rate by comparison with the rest of Europe (DHS, 2005; WHO, 2008).

Under the influence of the above-mentioned phenomena, the tendency for change in attitudes to diet, health and nutrition is gaining significance in the SEE countries. The future of food consumption patterns in the region and any related environmental and health problems will be connected with the evolution of cultural patterns, such as preferences for locally grown food and for traditional and organic products. The continuing preference of many householders for locally and nationally produced foods, which is due to perceptions of better quality, national sympathies and healthy effects, supports this prediction. At the same time, food consumption patterns connected with shopping from big retail centres, which incorporate supermarkets, restaurants, fast food shops and other retail outlets (i.e. cafés, sushi bars etc.) will continue to develop rapidly in the urban regions.

## The consumer of foods as an individual

Understanding consumption patterns also means understanding how individuals make choices. Food choice is intensely personal, based on individual tastes and household experiences of domesticity, and is an important aspect of citizenship nationally and indeed globally. There is a number of empirical research studies from recent years that deal with the specific attitudes and perceptions of consumers from SEE countries in relation to various groups of foods. The geographical focus of most of these studies restricts their generalizability. Many locally specific studies can be criticized for their lack of representativeness, since the sample of respondents is limited by the place where the studies were conducted or by the type of foods they deal with. Other studies are more general in nature but are unfortunately not cross-national. The examples presented here offer a general overview of the variety of these research studies.

In a comparative study on the perceptions of poultry meat in Bosnia and Herzegovina, Serbia and Slovenia, no considerable differences were found. Consumers were found to perceive the following features as important factors in buying: the taste, the fact that poultry meat is considered healthy and the origin of the food (Vukasovic, 2010). The results obtained among Croatian consumers of milk are similar: the sensory quality is the most important motivational factor in buying (Krešić et al., 2010). Product attributes such as quality, safety, taste and price were the main features motivating consumers from Kosovo to purchase dairy products (Bytyqi et al., 2008). A survey in Romania identifies four main dimensions of motivaton in relation to the purchasing of honey: the medical benefits of its consumption, its dietary quality, the ethical character associated with it and its compatibility with food consumption lifestyle (Krystallis et al., 2007).

Among consumers in SEE, interest in organic foods has been growing, because these foods are perceived, above all, as healthy. Positive attitudes towards organic food are confirmed in a cross-national survey carried out in Bosnia and Herzegovina, Croatia and Slovenia. The most important motives for buying organic food products in Croatia and Slovenia are the health value of organic food and care for the environment, and in Bosnia and Herzegovina the idea of return to nature, health value and safety of organic food products (Radman, 2005; Cerjak et al., 2010). In a comparative study conducted among Bulgarian and Romanian consumers, respondents from both countries appear to perceive organic agricultural products as 'clean' foods, which do not contain chemical ingredients harmful to health and are produced 'by a natural method or as naturally grown foods' (Vassileva et al., 2008, p. 370). In addition, consumer motivations in the purchase of organic Bulgarian yoghurt were studied using the means–end approach. This research showed that the most significant factors for consumers are the experience of pleasure in consuming this food and the need for a guarantee that the products are organic. Bulgarian consumers of organic yoghurt represent the person 'experiencing pleasure' (gourmet) and the person looking for a healthy food diet (OrganicBG, 2009).

Studies on the effect of consumer risk perceptions on the propensity to purchase genetically modified foods in Romania reveal the scepticism of consumers regarding the consumption of these foods (Curtis and Moeltner, 2007). In addition, the knowledge, attitude and expectations of Hungarian consumers in relation to genetically modified foods were also studied. Hungarian consumers unequivocally perceive these foods as harmful to health (Bánáti and Szabó, 2008). Croatian citizens are becoming deeply sceptical about the benefits of genetically modified foods, and also more generally about the foods they eat (Renko et al., 2003).

The traditionally strong connection, among consumers from the countries of the Western Balkans, with agrarian regions and family farms is confirmed by research on products made in households in Serbia. Most consumers have positive attitudes towards such products and believe that these products are of a high quality and are made without polluting the environment (Zaric et al., 2009). Family farm food products enjoy a very good image in Croatia as well. For Croatian consumers such products are very healthy, of high quality and very tasty (Radman et al., 2006).

Finally, Petrovici et al. (2004) used a modified version of the theory of reasoned action to find the determinants of food choice in Romania. The model included attitude towards intention, habit and food preference as independent variables. The authors suggest that the influence of non-economic variables may be growing in importance in explaining food choice and consumer behaviour in the emerging economies. The results point towards the fact that the influence of these variables may still be limited by comparison with that of economic factors.

### Towards a convergence with European 'food culture'?

The cultural borders dividing Europe into regions with individual cultural backgrounds also define the variety of food consumption patterns in Europe. On the one hand, the results of an analysis of data from the 1989 pan-European lifestyle survey, which was carried out in 15 European countries divided into 79 regions,[3] showed that national or linguistic borders still have a strong impact on European food cultures (Askegaard and Madsen, 1995). In addition, the macro-environment in Eastern Europe (low income, food budget share and the like) was (and still is) very often expected to be associated with consumption patterns that are distinct from those of Western Europe. In accordance with this proposition, research carried out by Elsner and Hartmann

(1998) on convergence in the consumption levels as well as on the structure of food consumption in Western and Eastern Europe (including in Bulgaria, Hungary, Romania and Slovenia) shows that the features of this process of convergence are strongly dependent on the country and on the food products.

On the other hand, Petrovici et al. (2005) investigated the heterogeneity of food consumption patterns in Europe through a set of indicators, namely the structure of calorie, protein and fat consumption, as well as the consumption of main food products. The authors found that, in some post-socialist countries from Central and Eastern Europe (including Bulgaria, Hungary, Romania and Slovenia), some dietary patterns such as those of energy and nutrient intake have become more similar to the patterns of Western Europe. Along with similarity in marketing environments, several demographic and cultural trends found in Western Europe have become more visible in Eastern Europe too, for instance the ageing population and health concerns in dietary choice (Petrovici et al., 2004).

Irrespective of common cultural, religious, social, linguistic and overall historical heritage, the SEE region is one of the most heterogeneous areas of the European continent. In the countries of the Western Balkans cultural and religious differences still divide the populations living across the newly drawn borderlines. These national and regional differences can exert a major impact on food consumption patterns. At the same time, the economic development of these countries opens up an opportunity for change.

The lack of detailed information about the specifics of food consumption patterns in different countries of the Western Balkans, together with information gaps in cross-country comparative studies, does not allow an analysis of the tendency towards convergence with Western European food cultures. The need to gather new, specific, empirical evidence about food-related behaviour and attitudes in the SEE countries, and in the Western Balkans in particular, in order to provide explanations and interpretations of the observed differences and similarities within the context of European food cultures is evident.

## Sustainable consumption in South East Europe – changing patterns

Sustainable consumption makes possible the use of products and services that meet consumer needs in an effective and efficient manner by minimizing the negative impact of a globally growing consumption of products and services on society, on the economy and on the environment. The ultimate aim of sustainable consumption is to improve the quality of living for all consumers of present-day and future generations by reducing the harmful influences on the environment. Sustainable consumption is based on the idea that meeting present-day consumer wants will not limit the needs and opportunities of future generations (UNEP, 2001; UNEP and Consumers International, 2002; United Nations, 2003).

At the same time, about two-thirds of all environmental pressures in Europe, and in the SEE, result from consumption in three areas. These are food and drink; housing and infrastructure, including residential heating; and the transport of persons and goods. A change of consumer behaviour, at individual and household level, in these three areas would allow for sustainable consumption in SEE countries (EEA, 2005, 2007). In this context, some of the existing (traditional) behaviour patterns could serve as role model for sustainable consumption in the SEE region. One illustration of this principle is the supply of food products from rural areas and family farms to households, which is especially evident in the countries of the Western Balkans. The organic production of foods is another example of sustainable agricultural practice. This has good prospects for development, due to the reduced use of artificial fertilizers and pesticides in agriculture over recent years (EEA, 2010). On the other hand, in many countries of the region residential buildings are very big consumers of energy for heating, and households still continue to use inefficient heaters (fuelled with wood and coal). This adds to local air pollution. In recent years a boom in construction has been observed in this region, which provides an excellent opportunity for improving the heating and energy efficiency of new buildings.

As a result of economic growth, the amount of passenger and freight transport in the region has increased; but many of the private motor vehicles are old. All this causes air pollution in urban areas and leads to an increase of greenhouse gas emissions. Moreover, the increase in the size of the population in big cities has a negative impact on the environment. However, ongoing economic and social restructuring in the SEE region provides a unique opportunity for establishing more resource-efficient, safe and sustainable production patterns and at the same time for improving the quality of life and of consumption patterns. This is one way for SEE countries to 'leapfrog' Western European countries and to avoid many of the production- and consumption-related problems common to Western Europe.

Studies on the perception of, and attitudes to, sustainable consumption in the SEE countries (Jackson, 2005; SCORE, 2006; Vadovic and Gulyás, 2008) show the following results:

- The provision of systematic, accessible and relevant information in order to facilitate consumer choice is a key element of the policy of sustainable consumption.
- The change of consumer behaviour is a complex and difficult process. The prerequisites for the success of initiatives for change lie in influencing consumers 'locked' into their specific behavioural model through institutional factors, which as a rule are out of their control; 'unfreezing' old habits; and negotiating new social conditions and expectations to govern consumer behaviour.
- There is a need for engagement by setting examples for the desired changes through governmental policies and practices.

For the successful development of sustainable consumption patterns it is necessary to change the attitudes and the behaviour of all stakeholders engaged in the process. Only when the need for information has been recognized by all stakeholders can sustainable behaviour patterns be adopted in SEE countries.

## Conclusion

The democratization of SEE countries and their impending accession to the EU brought about profound changes in people's lives and a transformation of consumption patterns and consumer behaviour. The transition to market economy has turned the region into a kind of laboratory for research on the nature of consumer transformation.

'New consumers' are influenced both by different economic and political circumstances and by regional or ethnic factors. Faced with the dilemma of choice between 'Western quality and modern image' and 'national product', or 'consumerism and catching up with the West' and 'traditional and green values', consumers in the transitional economies of SEE are creating specific consumer cultures. The current change in the consumer patterns of individuals and households is opening up unique opportunities for the implementation of sustainable consumption in these countries.

## Notes

1. In the course of our work we faced a number of limitations in current research, mainly stemming from the lack of sufficient information about consumption patterns in some countries and from the lack of comparative cross-national studies, which would allow an in-depth analysis of consumer behaviour. Additional difficulties result from the fact that the larger part of the information on consumer behaviour is published in local publications and in local languages.
2. In addition, a current research identifies wine customer profile in Kosovo with its characteristic demographic and socio-economic features (Gjonbalaj et al., 2009). The data show that wine is not very popular in the country.
3. The survey was organized by the CCA (Centre de Communication Avancé), a marketing research agency in Paris, in cooperation with the Euro-panel network of opinion-research institutes in 15 countries, namely the 12 EC countries at that time and the 4 EFTA countries Norway, Sweden, Austria and Switzerland (Luxembourg was considered a region in Belgium), and comprises the questioning of around 20,000 people in these countries.

## References

Askegaard, S. and Madsen, T. (1995) 'European Food Cultures: An Explanatory Analysis of Food Related Preferences and Behaviour in European Regions', *MAPP Working Paper 26* (Aarhus: The Aarhus School of Business).

Bánáti, D. and Szabó, E. (2008) 'A Study of Consumer Behaviour in Hungary', *Food Science and Technology*, 22, 24–25.

Belk, R. and Ger, G. (1994) 'Problems of Marketization in Romania and Turkey', in Shultz II, C., Belk, R. and Ger, G. (eds), *Special Volume of Research in Consumer Behavior on Consumption in Marketizing Economies* (Greenwich, Connecticut: JAI Press Inc.), 123–155.

Bytyqi, H., Vegara, M., Gjonbalaj, M., Mehmeti, H., Gjergjizi, H., Miftari, I. and Bytyqi, N. (2008) 'Analysis of Consumer Behavior in regard to Dairy Products in Kosovo', *Journal of Agricultural Researches*, 46, 311–320.

Cerjak, M., Mesić, Z., Kopić, M., Kovaćić, D. and Markovina, J. (2010) 'What Motivates Consumers to Buy Organic Food: Comparison of Croatia, Bosnia Herzegovina, and Slovenia', *Journal of Food Products Marketing*, 16, 278–292.

Cicic, M., Brkic, N. and Praso-Krupalija, M. (2003) 'Consumer Animosity and Ethnocentrism in Bosnia and Herzegovina: The Case of a Developing Country in a Post-War Time', *Akademija MM – Slovenian Marketing Research Journal*, 6, 59–73.

Coulter, R., Price, L. and Feick, L. (2003) 'Rethinking the Origins of Involvement and Brand Commitment: Insights from Postsocialist Central Europe', *Journal of Consumer Research*, 30, 151–169.

Coulter, R., Price, L., Feick, L. and Micu, C. (2005) 'The Evolution of Consumer Knowledge and Sources of Information: Hungary in Transition', *Journal of the Academy of Marketing Science*, 33, 604–619.

Crăciun, L. and Barbu, M. (2010) 'How Would Romanian Consumers Act to a "Buy Romanian" Call?', *Globalization and Higher Education in Economics and*

*Business Administration – GABA 2010*, 21–23 October 2010, Iasi, Romania, http://www.feaa.uaic.ro/geba/abstracts/7-10-176.doc, accessed 16 August 2010.

Creed, G. (2002) 'Economic Crisis and Ritual Decline in Eastern Europe', in Hann, C. (ed.), *Postsocialism: Ideals, Ideologies, and Practices in Eurasia* (London: Routledge), 57–73.

Curtis, K. and Moeltner, K. (2007) 'The Effect of Consumer Risk Perceptions on the Propensity to Purchase Genetically Modified Foods in Romania', *Agribusiness*, 23, 263–278.

Cutura, M. (2006) 'The Impacts of Ethnocentrism on Consumers' Evaluation Processes and Willingness to Buy Domestic vs. Imported Goods in the Case of Bosnia and Herzegovina', *South East European Journal of Economics and Business*, 1, 54–63.

DHS (2005) *Moldova Demographic and Health Survey 2005*, http://www.measuredhs.com, accessed 16 August 2010.

Dmitrović, T. and Vida, I. (2007) 'Saliency of Product Origin Information in Consumer Choices', *Management*, 12, 1–23.

Dmitrovic, T. and Vida, I. (2010) 'Consumer Behavior by Product Nationality: The Evolution of the Field and Its Theoretical Antecedents', *Transformation in Business and Economics*, 9, 145–165.

Dmitrovic, T., Vida, I. and Reardon, J. (2009) 'Purchase Behavior in Favor of Domestic Products in the West Balkans', *Journal of International Marketing*, 18, 523–535.

Dubois, B. and Duquesne, P. (1993) 'The Market for Luxury Goods: Income versus Culture', *European Journal of Marketing*, 27, 35–44.

Elsner, K. and Hartmann, M. (1998) 'Convergence of Food Consumption Patterns between Eastern and Western Europe', *Discussion Paper 13* (Halle: Institute of Agricultural Development in Central and Eastern Europe).

EEA – European Environment Agency (2005) *Household Consumption and the Environment, EEA Report No 11/2005* (Copenhagen: European Environment Agency).

EEA – European Environment Agency (2007) *Sustainable Consumption and Production in South East Europe and Eastern Europe, Caucasus and Central Asia, EEA Report No 3/2007* (Copenhagen: European Environment Agency).

EEA – European Environment Agency (2010) *Environmental Trends and Perspectives in the Western Balkans: Future Production and Consumption Patterns, EEA Report No 1/2010* (Copenhagen: European Environment Agency).

FAOSTAT (2009) *Statistical Yearbook 2009*, http://faostat.fao.org/, accessed 16 August 2010.

Feick, L., Coulte, R. and Price, L. (1995) 'Consumers in the Transition to a Market Economy: Hungary, 1989–1992', *International Marketing Review*, 12, 18–34.

Florkowski, W., Bilgic, A., Paraskova, P., Beuchat, L., Chinnan, M., Resurreccion, A. and Jordanov, J. (2006) 'Beverage Consumption Patterns in a New Market Economy', *Economic Revue, Poznan University*, 6, 25–53.

FOCUS-BALKANS: *Food Consumer Sciences in the Balkans: Frameworks, Protocols and Networks for a Better Knowledge of Food Behaviours*, FP7 Cooperation Work Programme, Report on the production and consumption of fruits and fruits products in the Balkans, Finalised Draft, 25 February 2010, http://www.focus-balkans.org, accessed 16 August 2010.

GfK – Bulgaria-Market Research Institute (2005) 'Do we choose "Made in Bulgaria"?', *Kapital*, 23 July 2005 (29), K 2.

Gjonbalaj, M., Miftari, I., Pllana, M., Fetahu, S., Bytyqi, H., Gjergjizi, H. and Dragusha, B. (2009) 'Analyses of Consumer Behavior and Wine Market in Kosovo', *Agriculturae Conspectus Scientificus*, 74, 333–338.

Husic, M. and Cicic, M. (2009) 'Luxury Consumption Factors', *Journal of Fashion Marketing and Management*, 13, 231–245.

Husic, M. and Ostapenko, N. (2010) 'Celebrating Recession in Style: The Mainstreaming of Attitudes toward Luxury Consumption in the Balkans and European Russia', Paper presented at the 2010 Oxford Business and Economics Conference, 28–29 June 2010 (Oxford: Oxford University).

Jackson, T. (2005) *Motivating Sustainable Consumption, a Review of Evidence on Consumer Behaviour and Behavioural Change, Report to the Sustainable Development Research Network* (Surrey, UK: University of Surrey).

Krešić, G., Herceg, Z., Lelas, V. and Jambrak, A. (2010) 'Consumers' Behaviour and Motives for Selection of Dairy Beverages in Kvarner Region: A Pilot Study', *Mljekarstvo*, 60, 50–58.

Krystallis, A., Petrovici, D. and Arvanitoyannis, I. (2007) 'From Commodities to the Consumption of Quality Foods in Eastern European Context. An Empirical Examination of the Determinants of Consumer Behavior towards Honey', *Journal of East–West Business*, 12, 5–37.

Leonidou, L., Hadjimarcou, J., Kaleka, A. and Stamenova, G. (1999) 'Bulgarian Consumers' Perceptions of Products Made in Asia Pacific', *International Marketing Review*, 16, 126–142.

Manrai, L., Lascu, D., Manrai, A. and Babb, H. (2001) 'A Cross-Cultural Comparison of Style in Eastern European Emerging Markets', *International Marketing Review*, 18, 270–285.

Milanova, E. (1999) 'Consumer Behavior in an Economy of Distress', *Advances in Consumer Research*, 26, 424–430.

Millan, E. and Howard, E. (2007) 'Shopping for Pleasure? Shopping Experiences of Hungarian Consumers', *International Journal of Retail and Distribution Management*, 35, 474–487.

Money, R. and Colton, D. (2000) 'The Response of the "New Consumer" to Promotion in the Transition Economies of the Former Soviet Bloc', *Journal of World Business*, 35, 189–205.

OrganicBG (2009) *Sustainable Attitude and Behaviour over the Delivery Chain for Organic Products in Bulgaria, National Science Fund, Research Report No 3, September 2009* (Sofia: National Science Fund).

Orth, U., Koenig, H. and Firbasova, Z. (2007) 'Cross-National Differences in Consumer Response to the Framing of Advertising Messages: An Exploratory Comparison from Central Europe', *European Journal of Marketing*, 41, 327–348.

Petrovici, D. and Ritson, C. (2000) 'Food Consumption Patterns in Romania', *British Food Journal*, 102, 290–308.

Petrovici, D. and Marinov, M. (2007) 'Determinants and Antecedents of General Attitudes towards Advertising: A Study of Two EU Accession Countries', *European Journal of Marketing*, 41, 307–326.

Petrovici, D., Ritson, C. and Ness, M. (2004) 'The Theory of Reasoned Action and Food Choice: Insights from a Transitional Economy', *Journal of International Food and Agribusiness Marketing*, 16, 59–87.

Petrovici, D., Ritson, C. and Ness, M. (2005) 'Exploring Disparities and Similarities in European Food Consumption Patterns', *Cahiers d'économie et sociologie rurales*, 75, 24–49.

Popova, S., Rehm, J., Patra, J. and Zatonski, W. (2007) 'Comparing Alcohol Consumption in Central and Eastern Europe to other European Countries', *Alcohol and Alcoholism*, 42, 465–473.

Radman, M. (2005) 'Consumer Consumption and Perception of Organic Products in Croatia', *British Food Journal*, 107, 263–273.

Radman, M., Kovaćić, D. and Markovina, J. (2006) 'Croatian Consumers' Attitudes towards Family Farm Food Products', *Journal of Food Products Marketing*, 12, 79–88.

Reardon, J. Miller, C., Vida, I. and Kim, I. (2005) 'The Effects of Ethnocentrism and Economic Development on the Formation of Brand and Ad Attitudes in Transitional Economies', *European Journal of Marketing*, 39, 737–754.

Renko, N., Brcić-Stipcević, V. and Renko, S. (2003) 'Attitudes of the Croatian Population toward Genetically Modified Food', *British Food Journal*, 105, 148–161.

Rischkowsky, F. and Döring, T. (2008) 'Consumer Policy in a Market Economy: Considerations from the Perspectives of the Economics of Information, the New Institutional Economics as well as Behavioural Economics', *Journal of Consumer Policy*, 31, 285–313.

Schuh, A. and Holzmüller, H. (2003) 'Marketing Strategies of Western Consumer Goods Firms in Central and Eastern Europe', in Stüting, H., Dorow, W., Claasen, F. and Blazejewski, S. (eds), *Change Management in Transition Economies – Integrating Corporate Strategy, Structure and Culture* (New York: Palgrave Macmillan), 176–188.

SCORE – Sustainable Consumption Research Network (2006) 'Sustainable Consumption and Production: Opportunities and Challenges', Proceedings Referreed Session III, Launch Conference of the Sustainable Consumption Research Exchange, 23–25 November 2006 (Wuppertal: Score-network).

Shama, A. (1992) 'Transforming the Consumer in Russia and Eastern Europe', *International Marketing Review*, 9, 43–59.

Sik, E. and Wallace, C. (2002) 'The Development of Open-Air Markets in East-Central Europe', *International Journal of Urban and Regional Research*, 23, 697–714.

Solomon, N., Bamossy, G., Askegaard, S. and Hogg, M. (2006) *Consumer Behavior: A European Perspective*, 3rd edn (Harlow: Pearson Education).

Sredl, K. (2007) 'Consumption and Class during and after State Socialism', in Belk, R. and Sherry, J. F. (eds), *Consumer Culture Theory, Research in Consumer Behavior*, 11 (Oxford: Elsevier), 187–205.

Strizhakova, Y., Coulter, R. and Price, L. (2008) 'Branded Products as a Passport to Global Citizenship: Perspectives from Developed and Developing Countries', *Journal of International Marketing*, 16, 57–85.

UNEP (2001) *Consumption Opportunities: Strategy for Changes* (Geneva: United Nations Environment Programme).

UNEP and Consumers International (2002) *Tracking Progress: Implementing Sustainable Consumption Policies*, 2nd edn (London and Paris: Consumer International and United Nations Environment Programme).

United Nations (2003) *United Nations Guidelines for Consumer Protection* (New York: United Nations).

Vadovic, E., and Gulyás, E. (2008) (eds), *Sustainable Consumption 2008 – Academic Conference Proceedings* (Budapest: Corvinus University of Budapest).

Vassileva, E., Ivanova, D., Botezat, E. and Tomescu, A. (2008) 'Comparative Study of Consumers' Perceptions and Attitudes to Organic Agricultural Products in Bulgaria and Romania', in Lee, Y.-H. and Shin, H. (eds), *Achieving Commodity and Service Excellence in the Age of Digital Convergence*, Proceedings of the 16th Symposium of IGWT 2 (Korea: Suwon), 370–3.

Vida, I. and Fairhurst, A. (1999) 'Factors Underlying the Phenomenon of Consumer Ethnocentricity: Evidence from Four Central European Countries', *The International Review of Retail, Distribution and Consumer Research*, 9, 321–337.

Vida, I., Dmitrovic, T. and Obadia, C. (2008) 'The Role of Ethnic Affiliation in Consumer Ethnocentrism', *European Journal of Marketing*, 42, 327–343.

Vukasovic, T. (2010) 'Buying Decision-Making Process for Poultry Meat', *British Food Journal*, 112, 125–139.

WHO – World Health Organization (2008) *World Health Statistics 2008* (Geneva: WHO Press).

Witkowski, T. (1998) 'Consumer Ethnocentrism in Two Emerging Markets: Determinants and Predictive Validity', *Advances in Consumer Research*, 25, 258–263.

Zaric, V., Petkovic, D. and Radosevic, M. (2009) 'Consumer Perception towards Traditional Serbian Agriculturaland and Food Products', *European Association of Agricultural Economists*, 113th Seminar, 9–11 December 2009, Seminar Volume (Belgrade: EAAE), 313–321.

# 13
# The Transport and IT Infrastructure in South East European Countries

*Markus Leibrecht and Mario Liebensteiner*

## Introduction

A well-established infrastructure endowment is frequently seen to be an important prerequisite for the catching up of emerging and transition economies. Broadly speaking, infrastructure can be defined as the 'social overhead capital' of an economy (Hirschman, 1958), which is necessary for economic agents, for example firms, to start and conduct their activities (Frey, 1988). With a focus on the catching up of emerging and transition economies, and thus on the growth performance of such countries, it is especially important that infrastructure can be seen as 'the economic growth framework of the market economy' (Buhr, 2009, p. 1). Thus, *inter alia*, the growth potential of an economy crucially hinges upon its infrastructure endowment. From an (international) business viewpoint, infrastructure matters insofar as it impacts on production costs and, hence, on the profitability of an investment. Moreover, as infrastructure may induce higher economic growth rates, increases in the infrastructure endowment lead, *ceteris paribus*, to the larger market size of an economy. The market size of an economy is among the most important determinants in the investments of foreign firms (Bellak and Leibrecht, 2009).

Against this background, the aim of this chapter is to provide an overview of the transport and information and communication (IT) infrastructure endowment in several South East European countries (SEECs). As shown by empirical studies, these two types of infrastructure are especially important for (international) business activities. The country focus here is on Albania, Bosnia and Herzegovina, Bulgaria, Croatia, Macedonia, Moldova, Romania and Serbia.

To achieve this goal, we proceed as follows. In a first step we define what is understood by 'infrastructure', also exploring the role of the government in its provision. The second step offers insights into the role of infrastructure in determining foreign direct investment (FDI) and a country's economic growth potential. FDI is frequently considered to be an 'engine for economic growth' in emerging and transition countries, which are usually confronted with a lack of domestic capital for financing investments.[1] Moreover, touching on the interrelationship between infrastructure and FDI directly indicates the importance of a well-functioning infrastructure as a location factor from the viewpoint of foreign investors (international business view). With the third step, descriptive evidence concerning the quantity and the quality of the transport and IT infrastructure in SEECs is provided. This step also gives selective information on proposed major projects in the transport infrastructure sector in several SEECs. In addition, the degree of private sector participation in infrastructure provision is specifically explored in this section. This includes the presentation of several indicator variables that capture important quantitative aspects of the transport and IT infrastructure.[2] The chapter ends with a summary of the findings and a conclusive discussion.

## The definition of infrastructure and the role of the government

The definition of infrastructure as 'social overhead capital' is too general to be of use in exploring the extent of the infrastructure endowment of an economy or in analysing the impact that changes in the infrastructure endowment have on a country's economic growth and on its FDI inflows. Unfortunately, a precise and generally accepted definition of infrastructure is still lacking (Buhr, 2003).[3] In empirical work one has to work, basically, with definitions of infrastructure that list activities and types of capital that comprise a country's infrastructure endowment.

One useful definition was introduced by Jochimsen (1966) and incorporates the various categories of infrastructure. According to this author, infrastructure can be separated into material, institutional and personal types. Material infrastructure includes 'capital goods in the form of transportation, education, and health facilities, equipment of energy and water provision, facilities for sewage, garbage disposal, and air purification, building and housing stock, facilities for administrative purposes and for the conservation of natural resources' (Jochimsen, 1966, as cited in Buhr, 2003, p. 8). A more recent definition would also include telephone mainlines and other types of material IT infrastructure. Institutional infrastructure 'comprises all customary and established rules of the community' (Buhr, 2003, p. 4), which determine the behaviour of economic agents. It also incorporates 'the facilities and procedures for guaranteeing and implementing these rules by the state' (ibid.). The personal infrastructure of an economy basically consists of the quantity (for example, number of persons of working age) and the quality (human capital) of an economy's working population (ibid.).

The focus of this chapter is on the sub-categories of material infrastructure. Material infrastructures can be divided into those that are production-related and those that are consumer-related. Production-related material infrastructure – if it is complementary to private capital – reduces production and transport costs, increases total factor productivity and has a positive impact on firms' profits. This, *ceteris paribus*, encourages investments from domestic and foreign firms and leads to economic growth. Moreover, as argued by Agion and Schankerman (1999), production-related infrastructure lowers communication, information and transportation costs, which reduce the barriers for low-cost firms to enter the market. This, in turn, intensifies market competition and enhances the speed of structural change in the economy. Thus, beside an investment expansion effect, infrastructure may also have a selection (structural) effect (Holzner et al., 2006). In contrast, consumer-related material infrastructure provides basic services to households. This type of infrastructure directly enters 'into household utility, rather than firms' production functions' (Barro, 1991, p. 282).[4]

According to Gramlich (1994) and to the OECD (2003), economically relevant production-related material infrastructure includes transport, communication and electricity production facilities. Transmission facilities for electricity, gas and water are relevant too (Regan, 2004). Given this definition, production-related material infrastructure excludes assets like schools, universities or hospitals of an economy. Although this latter classification is not indisputable – for instance, the transport network is also used by consumers – it does help to target empirical work with a business focus towards the most important infrastructure categories.

From an economic policy perspective it is relevant to isolate the role of the state in the provision of the different infrastructure types. Whereas it is clear that (formal) institutional infrastructure is provided by the government,[5] public involvement in the provision of personal and material infrastructure needs to be justified specifically. Public economics literature thereby uses the concept of 'market failure' to justify state intervention in a market economy (Stiglitz, 2000). The most important causes of market failure include the presence of positive technological externalities, sub-additivity of cost functions, public and merit goods characteristics and information asymmetries (Frey, 1988; Fritsch et al., 2007). Apart from market failure arguments, state intervention in infrastructure sectors may be justified on the grounds of distributional concerns.

It is not difficult to realize that market failure and/or distributional aspects may be of concern in the provision of material infrastructure. For instance, public involvement in transport infrastructure may be justified on the grounds of the sub-additivity of cost functions (railway network) or from the perspective of public good characteristics (non-rivalry in consumption up to some extent and non-excludability). Similarly, state intervention in IT infrastructure can be justified through the presence of technological externalities (in the form of network externalities) and the sub-additivity of cost functions (Fritsch et al., 2007).

Once we have highlighted the vital role of the state in the provision of production-related material infrastructure, transport and IT infrastructure in particular, it should be stressed that state intervention in infrastructure can take various forms. A substantial part of production-related material infrastructure is owned and maintained by the public sector. Yet, recently, infrastructure has also been provided, to an increasing extent, by the 'private sector' paired with public regulation, especially in the field of telecommunication and electricity.

## Production-related material infrastructure, FDI and economic growth

From a theoretical perspective, production-related infrastructure matters for firms' investments, as it impacts on production costs and hence on the profitability of an investment. Moreover, infrastructure may induce higher economic growth rates that, *ceteris paribus*, lead to a larger market size of an economy. As noted above, production-related material infrastructure may impact on economic growth via an expansion effect, a selection effect and an income effect. Yet empirical studies dealing with the FDI or the growth impact of infrastructure are confronted with severe data problems: indicator variables for a country's endowment with infrastructure are hardly available on an internationally comparable basis and for a longer time span. Variables capturing the quality of the infrastructure endowment are particularly scarce.

Empirical analyses, thus, have to rely on rather crude measures of the infrastructure stock.

For instance, some studies use public investment as a share of GDP to capture a country's infrastructure endowment. However, this approach is questionable, not least because of the increasing importance of private enterprises in infrastructure projects. This latter aspect is especially relevant for transition countries, where the privatization of public enterprises is an important aspect along the transition path. A better approach is to use variables that directly capture the extent of a certain infrastructure category in a country. For example, the length of the railway and road networks as a percent age of the total land mass in the given area are useful calculations for transport infrastructure endowment. Similarly, the number of telephone mainlines and mobile phone subscribers are a suitable basis for the analysis of the IT infrastructure endowment.

Concerning FDI, empirical evidence points towards a positive relationship with infrastructure. On the basis of a panel-gravity model approach, Bellak et al. (2009) show that FDI in Central and Eastern European Countries (CEECs) is attracted by increases in the IT as well as by the transport infrastructure. They use infrastructure indices derived from principal component analysis. These findings are in line with Wheeler and Mody (1992), who study the importance of infrastructure for the location decision of US Multinational Enterprises (MNEs). They find that a comprehensive index capturing various dimensions of infrastructure is positively correlated with FDI. Furthermore, infrastructure seems to be especially relevant as a location factor for less developed countries. Empirical evidence also suggests that a favourable transport infrastructure is a relevant determinant of FDI in Chinese regions (Cheng and Kwan, 2000).

Goodspeed et al. (2006) analyse FDI determinants on the basis of variables from a broad range of countries. They include in their empirical model the consumption of electric power, the number of mainline telephone connections and a composite infrastructure index. For the latter two variables they find a significant positive correlation with FDI. In a related paper, Goodspeed et al. (2009) find that the infrastructure endowment is an important location factor in developed as well as in less developed countries. However, the importance is greater for the less developed country group. Goodspeed et al. (2009) use a composite infrastructure index comprising transport, IT, energy and environmental infrastructures. Mollick et al. (2006), too, find a positive impact of infrastructure on FDI. These authors analyse the role of IT and transport infrastructure for FDI into Mexico. Bénassy-Quéré et al. (2007) use data on the net stock of public capital and analyse FDI from the US to several EU countries. They find a significant positive impact of the net stock of public capital on FDI.

Thus the empirical evidence available suggests that production-related material infrastructure is an economically and statistically significant determinant of FDI, especially in developing and transitional economies. From an economic policy viewpoint, this implies that improvements in the infrastructure endowment can be used by SEEC governments to attract FDI.

The empirical studies surveyed usually control for a country's market size in their econometric analyses. Thus they isolate a positive relationship between infrastructure and FDI, which is most likely due to a favourable effect of infrastructure on production costs. However, a better infrastructure endowment may also lead to more FDI if it induces higher economic growth rates and if it increases an economy's market size. Several empirical studies have focused on the relationship between infrastructure and economic growth performance. Economic growth performance is usually measured either by productivity growth or by GDP (per capita) growth (Aschauer, 1989; Norton, 1992; Nadiri and Mamuneas, 1996; Roeller and Waverman, 1998; Calderón and Servén, 2004; Égert et al., 2009; De la Fuente, 2010). Extensive literature reviews already exist, which offer a basis for the forthcoming considerations (Holzner et al., 2006; Égert et al., 2009; De la Fuente, 2010). This contribution focuses on papers that provide especially interesting insights from an economic policy viewpoint.

Among the seminal papers exploring the infrastructure–growth nexus are Barro (1991) and Easterly and Rebelo (1993). Barro (1991) concentrates on the long-term determinants of per capita growth (amongst other variables), in a study based on data for 72 countries over the period 1960–85. The potential determinants in his regressions include public expenditures that are split up into government consumption and government investment. The latter variable aims to capture infrastructure. Barro finds a statistically significant positive impact of infrastructure on economic growth. These results are corroborated by the study of Easterly and Rebelo. They find that '[t]ransport and communication investment seem to be consistently positively correlated with growth with high coefficient (between 0.59 and 0.66)' (Easterly and Rebelo, 1993, p. 431). The message from these two seminal studies is that policy makers should be aware that infrastructure is a relevant economic policy instrument to spur on economic growth.

In a widely cited study, Fernald (1999) shows that diminishing returns to infrastructure investment may exist. Specifically, Fernald finds that the construction of the US interstate highway system substantially boosted productivity during the 1950s and 1960s. In 1973, when the highway system was broadly finished, productivity growth dropped around the same time. Using data on inputs and outputs for 29 sectors of the US economy for the years from 1953 to 1989, Fernald finds that the growth in roads (the construction of the interstate highway system) is significantly positively related to productivity growth before 1973. But the relationship turns out to be insignificant in the post-1973 years. This leads to the simple conclusion that 'building a network may have a very high rate of return; but building a second network may have a very low marginal return' (Fernald, 1999, p. 630). Thus, returning to public investment rates similar to those of the 1950s and 1960s would not have contributed to a productivity growth, as happened during this time span. The construction of the interstate highway system 'offered a one-time increase in the level of productivity, rather than a continuing path to prosperity' (Fernald, 1999, p. 633). Thus policy makers must be aware not to over-invest in (certain types of) infrastructure.

These findings are consistent with Canning and Bennathan (2000). On the basis of a panel regression analysis (which includes a broad range of countries over the period from 1960 to 1990), they also show that diminishing returns to infrastructure investment exist. Specifically, in their trans-log production function model, which includes proxy variables for the infrastructure endowment as well as their squared terms, the squared terms enter significantly with a negative coefficient.

Hulten (1996) was among the first who analysed in depth the *quality aspect* of infrastructure and its impact on economic growth. His analysis is based on 46 low and middle income countries between 1970 and 1990. Hulten develops an infrastructure effectiveness indicator,[6] which is based on the number of reported telephone call faults, electricity generation losses, the condition of paved roads and of diesel locomotives. He finds that controlling for infrastructure quality leads to an insignificant impact of the infrastructure quantity variable (in Hulten's case, public investment), but to a significant positive impact of the effectiveness indicator. Hulten points out that 'a one percent increase in the infrastructure effectiveness parameter is found to have an impact on growth that is more than seven times higher than the impact of the same percentage increase in the rate of public investment' (Hulten, 1996, p. 2).

Several studies analyse the infrastructure–growth nexus by splitting the sample into high and low-income countries. These studies frequently detect a non-linearity in the relation between infrastructure endowment and economic growth (De la Fuente, 2010). Infrastructure seems to matter for economic growth particularly in countries with initially low provision of infrastructure facilities. This latter finding is consistent with the findings of Fernald (1999), and it is of importance for the SEECs with low levels of infrastructure endowment.

Thus, summarizing the empirical evidence concerning the impact of infrastructure on economic growth, we conclude with De la Fuente (2010, p. 55) that 'there are sufficient indications that public infrastructure investment contributes significantly to productivity growth, at least for countries where a saturation point has not been reached'. A solid endowment with production-related material infrastructure is vital for the growth performance of emerging and transition countries.

However, policy makers should be aware not to over-invest in certain types of infrastructure, as diminishing returns to infrastructure investments exist. Moreover, policy makers should consider that the quality of the infrastructure services provided matters for the growth performance. Specifically, putting the results of Fernald (1999) and Hulten (1996) together implies that countries with a low endowment in certain infrastructures should first establish a sufficiently large infrastructure network in quantity (and quality) terms. Once such a network exists, policy makers should keep an eye on the maintenance of the infrastructure network in quality terms.[7]

## Transport and IT infrastructure in SEE countries

The following section sketches the degree of private sector involvement ('commercialization') in the provision of infrastructure services. It intends to give a first impression concerning the quality of infrastructure services provided in SEECs. On the basis of summary measures, the next section gives a descriptive overview of the quantitative dimension of the transport and IT infrastructure in SEE countries. The final section gives a brief outline of proposed major transport infrastructure projects in the SEE region covered.

### Private sector involvement (commercialization) in the provision of infrastructure

As noted above, due to different types of market failure and/or distributional concerns the vital role of the public sector in the provision of transport and IT infrastructure is economically justified. The forms of public sector participation range from public production and provision and from financing via taxes to private production and provision and to financing via user fees with public regulation of prices and/or quality of the infrastructure service (Frey, 1988).

In the SEE countries, as former communist nations, the provision and maintenance of infrastructure was under full state control. Since the fall of the iron curtain private sector involvement has increased in all of the SEE countries. However, the pace of privatization and commercialization differs across countries and infrastructure sectors (railway, road, IT, electricity and so on).

Private sector involvement in the provision of infrastructure is frequently seen as a device to increase allocative efficiency and the quality of infrastructure services (see European Bank for Reconstruction and Development (EBRD) 2004, chapter 3 for details). For instance, in a recent survey Kessides (2005, p. 91)[8] argues that '[p]rivatization and deregulation have significantly improved physical performance, [infrastructure] service quality, and other aspects of efficiency in many developing and transition economies'.

The EBRD calculates and publishes transition indicators which include, *inter alia*, information concerning the degree of private sector involvement in the provision of infrastructure services. The indicators range between 1 and 4+. An entry of 1 implies full state control, and a value of 4+ implies widespread private sector participation, with public regulation of prices and quality (see for details EBRD, 2010).[9]

Table 13.1 provides information on the degree of private sector involvement for each of the considered SEE countries, for two years (2000 and 2009) and across three infrastructure sectors (railway, roads and telecommunication). In addition, the overall infrastructure reform index is shown. This index is an average over five infrastructure sectors (including electric power and water and waste water in addition). For the purpose of comparison, the average values for the eight CEECs which joined the EU in 2004 (CEEC-8) are also provided.

Table 13.1 implies that private sector involvement is increasing over time, although it is relatively low. These developments are consistent with an increase in the allocative efficiency in the provision of infrastructure services and in their quality in recent years (Kessides, 2005). In 2000 the mean values of the SEECs are between 2.2 (roads) and 2.6 (IT). These values indicate minimal private sector involvement in railways and roads and some commercialization in the IT sector. Over time the private sector involvement increases in each sector. Moreover, in the year 2009 the difference between the mean values for the SEECs and those for the CEECs is smaller in the IT and in the road sector by comparison to the situation in the year 2000.

*Table 13.1* Private sector involvement in infrastructure (EBRD infrastructure reform index)

|  | Overall | | IT | | Rail | | Road | |
|---|---|---|---|---|---|---|---|---|
|  | 2000 | 2009 | 2000 | 2009 | 2000 | 2009 | 2000 | 2009 |
| Albania | 2.0 | 2.3 | 3.0 | 3.3 | 2.0 | 2.0 | 2.0 | 2.3 |
| Bosnia and Herzegovina | 2.0 | 2.3 | 2.3 | 2.3 | 2.0 | 3.0 | 2.0 | 2.7 |
| Bulgaria | 2.7 | 3.0 | 3.0 | 3.7 | 3.0 | 3.3 | 2.3 | 2.7 |
| Croatia | 2.3 | 3.0 | 3.0 | 4.0 | 2.3 | 2.7 | 2.3 | 3.0 |
| Macedonia | 2.0 | 2.7 | 2.0 | 3.7 | 2.0 | 2.0 | 2.3 | 2.3 |
| Moldova | 2.3 | 2.3 | 2.3 | 3.0 | 2.0 | 2.0 | 2.0 | 2.0 |
| Romania | 3.0 | 3.3 | 3.0 | 3.3 | 4.0 | 4.0 | 3.0 | 3.0 |
| Serbia | 2.0 | 2.3 | 2.0 | 2.7 | 2.0 | 2.3 | 2.0 | 2.7 |
| Mean SEECs | 2.3 | 2.7 | 2.6 | 3.3 | 2.5 | 2.7 | 2.2 | 2.6 |
| Mean CEEC-8 | 2.9 | 3.2 | 3.4 | 3.7 | 3.1 | 3.4 | 2.7 | 2.8 |

*Note*: For Serbia the value for 'Rail' is that prevailing in the year 2001.
*Source*: EBRD Transition indicators database.

The current situation (as of 2009) in the IT sector can be characterized as considerably liberalized in the mobile phone segment and in value-added services, especially in Croatia ('complete commercialization'), Bulgaria and Macedonia. In the two remaining sectors the involvement of the private sector is lower. Yet substantial country heterogeneity is given. For instance, in Romania the private sector is heavily involved in the rail sector. Furthermore, in Bulgaria some private sector participation is present. Some private participation in the road infrastructure sector is given in Romania and Croatia. In the least developed SEECs (Albania, Bosnia and Herzegovina, Macedonia, Moldova and Serbia) private sector participation is low in the rail and road infrastructure sectors.[10]

## Current state of the transport and IT infrastructure endowment[11]

This section sketches the current state of the transport and IT infrastructure in the SEECs, focusing on quantitative aspects.[12] Due to a lack of data, the most recent year examined is 2007. However, in the case of road infrastructure, the most recent year available is often even prior to 2007 (see Appendix A.1). Following related literature (Holzner et al., 2006), we use different variables (for example road and rail density, telephone mainlines per capita) to capture a country's infrastructure endowment in quantity terms. For the sake of comparison we also present mean values for the EU-15 countries, as well as for the CEEC-8.

Data are mainly taken from the World Bank's World Development Indicators (WDI) 2009 database.

Figure 13.1 includes summary information on various aspects of the transport and IT infrastructure endowment, for the SEECs, for the CEEC-8 and for the EU-15 for the year 2007.[13] Specifically, the total road density, the rail density, the penetration rate with telephones and mobile phones as well as the penetration rate with broadband internet connections and internet users are shown. The rail density is calculated as km of railways divided by $1000\,km^2$ of surface area. The road density is calculated as km of roads divided by $100\,km^2$ of surface.[14] The penetration rates are measured in units of 100 inhabitants. The figure signals the underdevelopment both of the transport and of the IT infrastructure (in quantity terms) in the SEE economies compared with the CEEC-8 and the EU-15. Note that the mean railway density of the CEEC-8 exceeds that of the EU-15 in 2007.

It is interesting to compare the values given in Figure 13.1 with the corresponding values in the year 2000 (cf. Figure 13.2). This

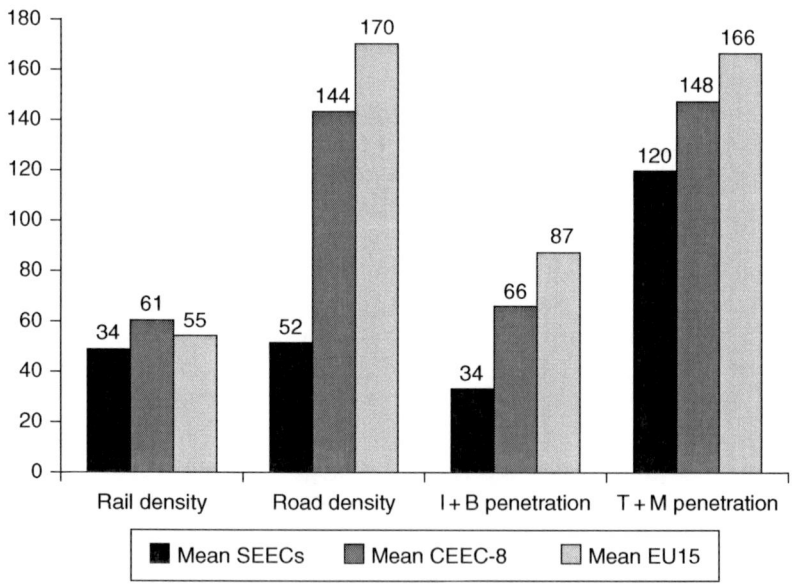

*Figure 13.1*   Summary of the infrastructure endowment in 2007
*Notes:* I + B = internet and broadband; T + M = telephone and mobile phone; for some countries road network values are taken from years prior to 2007.
*Source*: WDI database.

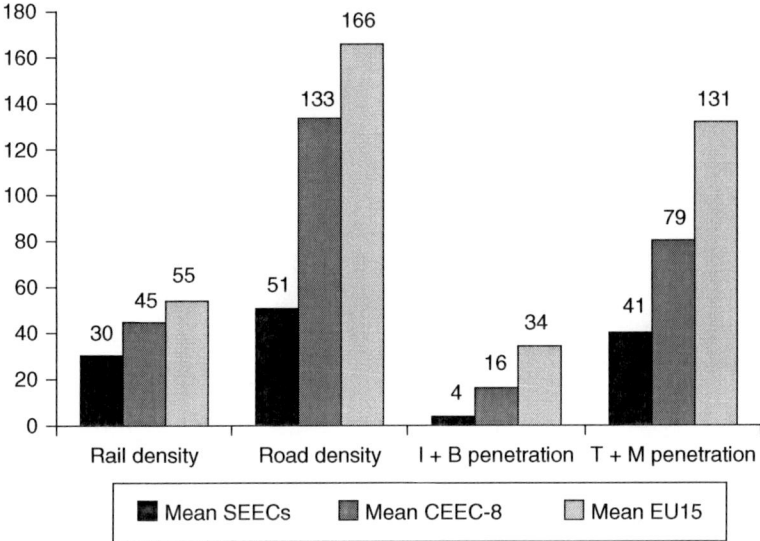

*Figure 13.2* Summary of infrastructure endowment measures in 2000
*Notes*: I + B = internet and broadband; T + M = telephone and mobile phone; for some countries (Latvia, Sweden, Macedonia, Bosnia and Herzegovina) road network values are taken from years prior to or later than 2000; the value on railway length for Moldova is for 2005.
*Source*: WDI database.

provides information on the developments in infrastructure endowment over time.

Comparing the figures shows that, on average, the SEECs could not manage to increase substantially their transport infrastructure in the 2000–2007 period. This is in marked contrast to the CEECs, which increased their rail as well as road density. However, the figures also imply that the SEECs have substantially improved their IT infrastructures, as illustrated by the penetration rates.

Although these two figures provide an initial picture of the infrastructure position of the SEECs, they hide substantial country heterogeneity. Therefore Tables 13.1 to 13.6 provide more detailed information, on a country-by-country basis. Table 13.2 includes data on the railway system in each of the SEECs in 2000 and 2007. It also contains the mean values over the SEECs, the CEEC-8 and the EU-15. According to the density measure, each of the SEECs was, and still is, less endowed with railway infrastructure when compared with the CEEC-8 and the EU-15. This result underlines what has been stated above.

*Table 13.2*   Railway network (per country; 2000 and 2007)

|  | Length of lines (km; 2000) | Density of lines (km/1000 km²; 2000) | Length of lines (km; 2007) | Density of lines (km/1000 km²; 2007) |
|---|---|---|---|---|
| Albania | 440 | 16 | 423 | 15 |
| Bosnia and Herzegovina | 1,032 | 20 | 1,103 | 22 |
| Bulgaria | 4,320 | 39 | 4,027 | 36 |
| Croatia | 2,727 | 48 | 2,722 | 48 |
| Macedonia | 699 | 27 | 699 | 27 |
| Moldova | 1,075 | 32 | 1,154 | 34 |
| Romania | 11,364 | 48 | 10,646 | 45 |
| Serbia | 4,058 | 46 | 4,057 | 46 |
| Mean SEECs | 3,210 | 30 | 3,104 | 34 |
| Mean CEEC-8 | 5,927 | 45 | 5,841 | 61 |
| Mean EU-15 | 9,933 | 55 | 9,900 | 55 |

*Note*: The value for Moldova is for 2005.
*Source*: WDI database.

Out of the eight SEECs, Croatia had the highest rail density in 2007, whereas Albania lagged far behind. Comparing the values for 2000 and 2007 reveals that only two countries have (slightly) improved their railway density scores: Bosnia and Herzegovina, and Moldova. In three countries the score did not change over the 2000–2007 period: Croatia, Macedonia and Serbia. In the remaining three countries – Romania, Bulgaria and Albania – the density value even decreased. The decrease might be an indication that countries have closed some lines that were in poor condition but of minor importance.

Table 13.3 contains information on the 'efficiency' of the rail network, whereby efficiency is measured as the ratio of passenger kilometres (Pkm) or freight tonne kilometres (Tkm) and the length of the railway lines (Holzner et al., 2006). It is important to stress, however, that these ratios are only a rough approximation of the efficiency of the infrastructure endowment. For instance, the numerator of the ratios depends on the macro-economic situation (boom or recession). Thus comparing the ratios of different years can only be done under substantial uncertainty (business cycle vs. structural efficiency effect).

In terms of 1,000 passenger kilometres per kilometre of railway, not only the SEECs but also the CEECs lag behind the EU-15 countries in 2007. The SEECs are only about 17 per cent as 'efficient' as the EU-15 when it comes to passenger transport (353 divided by 2,044). In terms

*Table 13.3* Rail efficiency (per country; 2001 and 2007)

| | Length of lines (km; 2001/2007) | Passenger km (million; 2001/2007) | Freight tonnes km (million; 2001/2007) | 1000 Pkm per km of lines (2001/2007) | 1000 freight Tkm per km of lines (2001/2007) |
|---|---|---|---|---|---|
| Albania | 447/423 | 138/51 | 19/53 | 309/121 | 43/125 |
| Bosnia and Herzegovina | 1,101/1,103 | 53/68 | 264/1,148 | 48/62 | 240/1,041 |
| Bulgaria | 4,320/4,027 | 2,990/2,424v | 4,905/5,242 | 692/602 | 1,135/1,302 |
| Croatia | 2,727/2,722 | 1,241/1,611 | 2,047/3,574 | 455/592 | 751/1,313 |
| Macedonia | 699/699 | 133/109v | 462/778 | 190/156 | 661/1,113 |
| Moldova | –/1,154 | –/468 | –/3,092 | –/406 | –/2,679 |
| Romania | 11,364/10,646 | 10,965/7,417 | 17,754/13,471 | 965/697 | 1,563/1,265 |
| Serbia | 3,900/4,057 | 1,170/762 | 1,989/4,417 | 300/188 | 510/1,089 |
| Mean SEECs | 3,508/3,104 | 2,384/1,777 | 3,920/4,098 | 423/353 | 700/1,237 |
| Mean CEEC-8 | 5,927/5,841 | 5,040/4,351 | 14,693/15,130 | 656/574 | 3,911/4,321 |
| Mean EU-15 | 9,933/9,900 | 21,673/22,293 | 17,088/17,120 | 1,916/2,044 | 1,395/1,696 |

*Note:* The 2001 values are used, since in 2000 many values on passengers and freight rail transport kilometres are missing; the 2001 mean values exclude Moldova and Luxemburg.
*Source:* WDI database.

of freight tonnes per kilometre of railway, the SEECs reach about 72 per cent of the efficiency of the EU-15 (1,237 divided by 1,696). In contrast, the CEECs outperform the EU-15 by more than 250 per cent (4,321 divided by 1,696). This indicates that the CEECs were strongly integrated in the Soviet Union's heavy industry production (Holzner et al., 2006).

Among the SEECs, Bosnia and Herzegovina and Albania have (by far) the lowest rail efficiency scores. Bulgaria, Croatia and Romania are among the SEE countries with the largest rail efficiency scores. However, according to the WDI data, Moldavia outperforms the other SEECs in terms of freight tonnes per kilometre railway in 2007.

Table 13.3 also indicates that the SEECs may have increased their rail efficiency in terms of freight tonnes per kilometer of railway (700–1,237). In the case of passengers per kilometre of railway, the SEECs lost ground (423–353). The SEECs share this development with the CEEC-8. In contrast, the EU-15 managed to increase their average rail efficiency in both categories (freight and passengers). Among the SEECs, Bosnia and Herzegovina substantially raised its score in rail freight (240–1,041), whereas Romania lost somewhat (1,563–1,265). In the case of passengers per kilometre of railway, all SEECs except Croatia and Bosnia and Herzegovina may have lost rail efficiency.

Tables 13.4 and 13.5 provide information on the quantity and 'efficiency' of the road network. Note that many values are missing in the WDI dataset for the road network. For some countries (for example, Bulgaria and Albania) only one value is available at all. In these cases no comparison across years is possible. This is unfortunate, as the road infrastructure is likely of greater importance for firms than the rail infrastructure. Appendix A shows, on a country-by-country basis, which years are used as 'first' and 'last' year.

Table 13.4 provides information about the length of the road network, the percentage of paved roads of total roads and the road density. The last value is calculated as the length of roads in relation to 100 km² of surface area.

The SEE economies are poorly endowed with road infrastructure when compared to the EU-15 and CEE countries. On average, the SEECs have only about 37 (30) per cent of the road density of the CEEC-8 (EU-15). In contrast, the CEECs are well endowed with roads: their average road density in relation to that of the EU-15 is about 80 per cent ('last year'; 141 divided by 175).

Among the SEECs, Romania has by far the highest road density. Interestingly, Bulgaria is the SEEC with the lowest density (Holzner et al., 2006). The percentage of paved roads may be used to indicate the quality

*Table 13.4* Road density (per country, first and last year)

| | Length of roads (km; 1st year/last year) | Paved roads in per cent of total roads (first year/last year) | Density of roads (km/100 km$^2$; first year/last year) |
|---|---|---|---|
| Albania | −/18,000 | −/39 | −/63 |
| Bosnia and Herzegovina | 21,846/21,846 | 52/52 | 43/43 |
| Bulgaria | −/40,231 | −/98 | −/36 |
| Croatia | 28,123/28,788 | 85/89 | 50/51 |
| Macedonia | 13,182/13,840 | 64/70 | 51/54 |
| Moldova | 12,705/12,731 | 86/86 | 38/38 |
| Romania | 198,603/198,817 | 50/50 | 83/83 |
| Serbia | 39,937/38,507 | 63/63 | 45/44 |
| Mean SEECs | 52,399/46,522 | 67/68 | 52/51 |
| Mean CEEC-8 | 117,639/122,180 | 74/71 | 134/141 |
| Mean EU-15 | 279,074/296,071 | 88/92 | 173/175 |

*Notes*: − implies that only one value is available in the WDI database which is used as 'last year' value. Mean values given in this table do not exactly correspond to the values shown in Figures 13.1 and 13.2, as the first and last year used for Table 13.4 differ slightly from the years the two figures are based upon; the reason is that the first and last year used in Table 13.4 are those years for which total road network as well as data for freight and passenger transport are available; the data used for Figures 13.1 and 13.2 abstract form the availability of freight and passenger transport data (also see Appendix A.1).
*Source*: WDI database; value for per cent of paved roads in Romania in 2007 is taken from http://www.romania-belgium-bc.com/romania, accessed 5 August 2010.

of the road network. Table 13.4 implies that the SEE and CEE countries have broadly similar shares. In contrast, the EU-15 economies have a substantially larger mean share, of about 90 per cent.[15] Of interest is that Albania, despite having a low percentage of paved roads, scores relatively well with respect to road density (value of 626). Thus Albania seems to have a relatively large road network, which, however, is of low quality.

Comparison between first year and last year values, where both scores are available, suggests that the road density has neither changed substantially in any of the SEECs nor increased or decreased dramatically in the CEEC-8 or in the EU-15. The same is true for the percentage of paved roads in total roads.

The same approach that was used for rail efficiency is now adopted to obtain values for the road efficiency (cf. Table 13.5). Concerning the comparison of values across years, the same caveat (business cycle effect) applies that was mentioned above in case of the rail efficiency. It turns out that the EU-15 countries do far better than the CEECs and the SEECs in terms of road passenger and road freight efficiency. The SEECs only reach 15 per cent of the EU-15 in passenger transport efficiency and

Table 13.5 Road efficiency (per country, first and last year)

| | Length of roads (km; first year/last year) | Passenger km (million; first year/last year) | Freight tonnes km (million; 1st year/last year) | 1,000 Pkm per km of roads (first year/last year) | 1,000 freight Tkm per km of roads (first year/last year) |
|---|---|---|---|---|---|
| Albania | –/18,000 | –/197 | –/2,200 | –/11 | –/122 |
| Bosnia and Herzegovina | 21,846/21,846 | –/– | 300/300 | –/– | 14/14 |
| Bulgaria | –/40,231 | –/13,688 | –/11,843 | –/340 | –/294 |
| Croatia | 28,123/28,788 | 3,331/3,094 | 6,783/10,175 | 118/107 | 241/353 |
| Macedonia | 13,182/13,840 | 842/1,027 | 2,693/8,389 | 64/74 | 204/606 |
| Moldova | 12,705/12,731 | 1,169/1,640 | 964/1,577 | 92/129 | 76/124 |
| Romania | 198,603/198,817 | 7,700/8,638 | 14,288/37,220 | 39/43 | 72/187 |
| Serbia | 39,937/38,507 | –/3,865 | 582/1,161 | –/100 | 15/30 |
| Mean SEECs | 52,399/46,522 | 3,261/4,593 | 4,268/9,108 | 78/115 | 104/216 |
| Mean CEEC-8 | 117,639/122,180 | 21,120/23,474 | 15,467/34,352 | 227/209 | 124/258 |
| Mean EU-15 | 279,074/296,071 | 303,593/310,719 | 66,977/104,161 | 884/768 | 363/414 |

Source: WDI database and International Transport Forum database (for Serbia), http://www.internationaltransportforum.org/statistics/trends/index.html, accessed 5 August 2010.

52 per cent in freight transport efficiency ('last year'). The CEECs perform somewhat better, having 27 per cent passenger transport efficiency and 52 per cent freight transport efficiency. However, in contrast to the CEEC-8 and the EU-15, the SEECs could – on average – improve their efficiency score in both dimensions (passengers and freight transport).

Among the SEECs, Albania, Bosnia and Herzegovina and Serbia have particularly low levels of passenger transport and/or freight transport efficiency. In the case of passengers, Croatia's efficiency score declined somewhat (from 118 to 107).

Turning to the IT infrastructure, Table 13.6 contains information on the penetration of information and communication technology in the SEECs. This information is separated into two categories: (a) internet and broadband subscribers; and (b) telephone and mobile phone subscribers. Again, the SEECs' scores on these indicators fall behind those of the CEEC-8 and the EU-15 in 2007. However, the development over time suggests that the SEECs substantially reduced the gap between themselves on the one hand, the CEEC-8 and the EU-15 on the other. This is especially the case for the telephone and mobile phone penetration rate. Here three countries (Serbia, Croatia and Bulgaria) come close to the EU-15 average in 2007. Croatia also scores relatively well in terms of internet and broadband penetration.

*Table 13.6* Information and communication technology penetration (per country; 2000 and 2007)

| | Internet and broadband subscribers (per 100 inhabitants; 2000) | Internet and broadband subscribers (per 100 inhabitants; 2007) | Telephone and mobile phone subscribers (per 100 inhabitants; 2000) | Telephone and mobile phone subscribers (per 100 inhabitants; 2007) |
|---|---|---|---|---|
| Albania | 0 | 15 | 19 | 84 |
| Bosnia and Herzegovina | 1 | 30 | 34 | 93 |
| Bulgaria | 8 | 39 | 56 | 159 |
| Croatia | 12 | 53 | 80 | 155 |
| Macedonia | 3 | 32 | 38 | 118 |
| Moldova | 1 | 22 | 21 | 81 |
| Romania | 5 | 33 | 36 | 115 |
| Serbia | 0 | 44 | 42 | 155 |
| Mean SEECs | 4 | 34 | 41 | 120 |
| Mean CEEC-8 | 16 | 66 | 79 | 148 |
| Mean EU-15 | 34 | 87 | 131 | 166 |

*Source: WDI database.*

Sections 4.1 and 4.2 imply that especially the transport infrastructure in SEECs is inferior in quantity and quality, when compared to the CEEC-8 and the EU-15. This conclusion was already drawn by Holzner et al. (2006), who based their analysis on data from 2001 (or prior years).[16] Thus, although some progress has been achieved by comparison to CEECs and the EU-15, the transport infrastructure in SEECs is still rather weak. The SEECs with the weakest transport infrastructure are Albania and Bosnia and Herzegovina. Overall, Croatia performs best among the SEECs in terms of transport infrastructure. The EU and other Western institutions provide substantial financial support for the improvement of transport infrastructure networks in SEECs. Basic features of some major projects are sketched in the next section, where the focus is on the SEECs that are not member countries of the EU (Albania, Bosnia and Herzegovina, Croatia, Serbia, Macedonia and Moldova), and as such are not covered by the Trans-European Transport Network (TEN-T) in the enlarged EU (European Commission, 2010).[17]

In contrast, the gap in endowment with IT infrastructure between the SEECs and the CEEC-8, and even the EU-15, is smaller. SEECs have improved their IT infrastructure substantially in the last years. Again, Croatia performs best among the SEECs.

### Some major current transport infrastructure projects in SEE countries

In December 2009 the Western Balkans Investment Framework (WBIF) was launched by the European Commission, the European Investment Bank (EIB), the EBRD and the Council of Europe Development Bank. The objective of the WBIF is to finance priority projects in the Western Balkans (Santarelli, 2009). Part of the WBIF is the Infrastructure Projects Facility in the Western Balkans (IPF), which aims, *inter alia*, to help to develop new and modern transport infrastructure in Albania, Bosnia and Herzegovina, Croatia, Macedonia, Kosovo, Montenegro and Serbia.[18] The IPF sub-framework was initiated because the transport infrastructure throughout South East Europe is considered to be of poor quality – not least as it has suffered from war and from a lack of maintenance and investment (IPF, 2010). Several major projects in the transport infrastructure sector financed by the EBRD and/or by the EIB are scheduled for the 2009–12 period (IPF, 2010):

– Albania: Albanian Railway Network: Infrastructure and Signaling Improvement Project; Lead International Finance Institution: EBRD;

Estimated investment sum: 225 mn euros. The aim of the project is to improve the operational capability of the Albanian railway system. In the end the system should fully comply with the European requirements for well established railway networks.[19]
- Bosnia and Herzegovina: Construction of the main Foca-Hum Road; Lead International Finance Institution: EBRD; Estimated investment sum: 80 mn euro. This project seeks to upgrade the road between Foca in the Republica Srpska and the Montenegrin border. This road is part of the link that forms the shortest connection between the two capital cities, Sarajevo and Podgorica.
- Bosnia and Herzegovina: Bosnia and Herzegovina motorway in the Pan European Corridor Vc; Lead International Finance Institution: EIB; Estimated investment sum: 180 mn euro. This project is part of the Trans-European Network (TEN) of inland corridors. Corridor Vc connects the Port of Ploce, the main sea gate of the Bosnian economy, with Bosnia and Herzegovina's capital city, Sarajevo, Osijek and Zagreb in the Republic of Croatia, Belgrade in Serbia and Budapest in Hungary.
- Bosnia and Herzegovina: Railway Sarajevo-Podlugovi; Lead International Finance Institution: EIB; Estimated investment sum: not provided. The section Podlugovi-Sarajevo is on the railway line from Ploce to Budapest, which is part of Pan European Corridor Vc. The project aims to finance expenditures for new tracks and new switches in stations or for the repair of bridges and for the installation of signaling at stations.
- Bosnia and Herzegovina: In May 2009 the government signed a contract with the Austrian construction company Strabag to establish a joint venture company with the aim to construct highways. Strabag builds, operates and maintains major roads in the region. The first project will be a highway from Banja Luka to Doboj (EBRD, 2009)
- Serbia: Railway reconstruction Nis-Presevo; Lead International Finance Institution: not provided; Estimated investment sum: not provided. The financed rail line is part of Corridor 10, a key European defined transport corridor. Corridor 10 connects Macedonia and Greece with Central Europe. As the line is in bad condition, far-reaching reconstruction efforts are intended.
- Moldova: The EIB started to finance improvements of Moldova's transport network in 2009 (Tarnosauskas, 2010). Specifically, two main roads that connect Chisinau with Romania will be improved (the Chisinau–Hincesti road and the Chisinau–Calarasi road). Financial support for the renovation and upgrading of

Moldova's main airport (Chisinau airport) is provided by the EIB (Tarnosauskas, 2010).

– Macedonia: In March 2010 the EBRD launched a new strategy to improve the transport infrastructure network in Macedonia. There the EBRD focuses on promoting road and railway transport networks and their regional interconnection, on supporting Macedonian Airports and on the restructuring of the road maintenance sector. Moreover, the EBRD will promote private sector involvement in the transport infrastructure sector (Coretchi, 2010), which is among the lowest within the SEECs (see Table 13.1).

## Summary and conclusions

This chapter provides an overview of the current state of the infrastructure endowment in eight SEE countries. The focus is on two types of production-related material infrastructure: the transport and IT infrastructure. The main findings presented in the chapter can be summarized as follows: (i) production-related material infrastructure is a relevant determinant of FDI in emerging and transitional economies and it is positively correlated with economic growth in such countries; (ii) private sector involvement (commercialization) in the provision of infrastructure is comparably low in SEECs, even if it has gained importance over the last years. Moreover, substantial country heterogeneity is given. Private sector participation is highest in Bulgaria, Croatia and Romania; (iii) the current state of production-related material infrastructure (quality and quantity) in the analysed SEECs is poorer than that of the CEEC-8 and of the EU-15 – and this is especially the case in the transport sector; overall, Albania and Bosnia and Herzegovina have the worst and Croatia the best transport infrastructure endowment among the SEECs; (iv) European institutions recently agreed to (co-)finance the improvements of major transport networks, which aim to connect the SEECs with the 'heart' of EU-Europe.

From an international business viewpoint the low level of private sector participation (commercialization) suggests that the potential to undertake FDI in infrastructure sectors (Unctad, 2008) in these countries is considerable. However, international firms need to be aware that labour and/or total factor productivity in their SEE subsidiaries is unlike to reach the level of their Western subsidiaries or of the parent company due to the lack of adequate transport infrastructure (Bellak et al., 2000). Yet the selective overview of major infrastructure projects contained in section 4.3 suggests that main roads and railway lines that connect the

SEECs with EU countries will improve in quality (and quantity) in the near future. This development is especially important for EU investors who plan to finance vertically motivated FDI in the SEECs, for instance with the aim of exploiting the low labour costs in this region. As this type of FDI is export-generating in nature (Barba Navaretti and Venables, 2004) a well-functioning transport infrastructure to connect the SEECs with the EU is particularly important. In contrast, in most SEECs, the IT infrastructure endowment should not be an impediment to start a business.

From a national economic policy viewpoint, the inferior endowment with production-related material infrastructure implies that SEEC governments have an effective economic policy device at hand to spur economic growth and to attract FDI inflows. However, improvements in the quality and quantity of infrastructure are a medium-run task. Thus SEE governments need to use other economic policy tools, *in addition* to investments in infrastructure, to spur economic growth in the short run. Viable options in this respect are cuts in corporate taxes and a cut in administrative burdens for firms wanting to start a business in the region (The World Bank, 2009). Therefore host country governments should keep in mind that cutting taxes results in a loss of tax revenues. This in turn may hinder the improvement of the infrastructure endowment if other financial means are not raised or set free at the same time. Increases in tax morality, financing via debt (in the case of low debt levels) as well as administrative reforms in the public sector could result in this required 'room for maneuver'.

From an EU, or even from a global, perspective the gap in the infrastructure endowment in most SEECs points to the need to help these countries to extend their infrastructure endowment. The latter can be considered as a crucial factor in the theory of the 'Big Push' by Rosenstein-Rodan (1943). Specifically, increasing the infrastructure endowment can lead to a speeding up of the industrialization of depressed areas, which 'is in the general interest not only of those countries, but of the world as a whole' (Rosenstein-Rodan, 1943, p. 202).

Policy makers at the national and at the EU level are well aware of this role of production-related material infrastructure in the catching-up process of the SEECs. Thus these countries will experience a substantial improvement in their infrastructure endowments and, in consequence, in their economic growth rates and market sizes in the near future. It is also likely that the degree of private sector participation in the provision of infrastructure services will increase over time. Both these developments will be 'good news' for international firms that are considering investing in the SEECs.

## Appendix A.1: Road data availability

| Country | first year | last year |
|---|---|---|
| Albania | – | 2001 |
| Austria | 2000 | 2003 |
| Belgium | 2000* | 2006 |
| Bosnia and Herzegovina | 2000* | 2003* |
| Bulgaria | – | 2005 |
| Croatia | 2000 | 2006 |
| Czech Republic | 1999 | 2002 |
| Denmark | 2000 | 2005 |
| Estonia | 2001 | 2005 |
| Finland | 2000 | 2006 |
| France | 2003 | 2006 |
| Germany | – | 2006 |
| Greece | – | 1999 |
| Hungary | 2001 | 2006 |
| Ireland | 1999* | 2003* |
| Italy | 1999 | 2002 |
| Latvia | 2002 | 2006 |
| Lithuania | 2002 | 2006 |
| Luxembourg | 2001* | 2003* |
| Macedonia | 2002 | 2007 |
| Moldova | 2001 | 2003 |
| Netherlands | 2001 | 2003* |
| Poland | 2002 | 2006 |
| Portugal | 1999* | 2002* |
| Romania | 2000 | 2004 |
| Serbia | 2000 | 2007 |
| Slovak Republic | 2000 | 2006 |
| Slovenia | 2000 | 2006 |
| Spain | 1999 | 2003 |
| Sweden | 2003 | 2006 |
| UK | 2003 | 2005 |

*Notes*: * = no passenger km data available; – = only one value is contained in WDI database, which is used as 'last year' value; especially data on passengers and freight carried are missing; data on the total road network are more fully available (the most recent years are usually 2005, 2006 or 2007).

# Notes

1. FDI impacts on economic growth due to its direct capital stock effect and due to various spillover effects on the domestic economy (for example, knowledge spillover effects, competition effects, technology transfer to domestic firms and so on (see for example Barba Navaretti and Venables, 2004).

2. Directly capturing the quality of a country's infrastructure endowment is made difficult by the lack of meaningful indicator variables.

3. Beside the definition of infrastructure as social overhead capital, several other definitions were given in the literature (see Frey, 1988; Buhr 2003). For instance, Nijkamp (2000) defines infrastructure as material public capital like roads, railways, airports, ports, pipelines and so on. He distinguishes infrastructure from *suprastructure*, which comprises immaterial public capital like knowledge networks, communication, education, culture and so on (see Buhr, 2003).

4. We want to stress that improvements of the production- and consumer-related infrastructure endowment also exert an income effect: rising incomes imply a rising purchasing power in the country, which probably leads to increases in investments.

5. Of course informal institutional infrastructure is also provided by non-governmental entities like the church.

6. For a detailed description of the construction of the effectiveness indicator see Hulten (1996).

7. Improvements of the infrastructure endowment may not only lead to higher economic growth. Empirical evidence also points towards a reduction in income inequality in developing countries: job opportunities and human capital enhancement arise from higher infrastructure endowment (Calderón and Chong, 2004; Calderón and Servén, 2004). There are even spill-overs to other development-related aspects: better transportation infrastructure leads to an enhanced aggregate health level of the economy, because sanitary facilities and hospitals can be reached more easily. Thus child mortality decreases and school attainment rises (Leipziger et al., 2003).

8. Of course, distributional effects of infrastructure reforms (in the sense of increasing private sector participation) must also be considered. Kessides (2005) points out that infrastructure reforms may especially hurt higher-income groups, for instance via higher user fees, which have access to infrastructure before the reform. The poorest income group often has no access to infrastructure before the reform. However, in the transition countries, many poor persons have access to infrastructure services before the reform (Kessides, 2005). The solution for these countries 'is not to halt the needed reforms but to put in place safety nets and tariff rebalancing schemes that do not involve radical, across-the-board price increases' (Kessides, 2005, p. 94).

9. It should be noted that public regulation of private provision plays a crucial role for ownership changes having a positive impact on service quality. For instance, simply changing ownership structures from a public monopolist to a private monopolist will probably not lead to increases in service quality (see EBRD, 2004).

10. According to EBRD (2004), the bulk of private sector participation is through FDI from Western European utilities. However, recently, private investors from other transition countries and local investors are also becoming increasingly important.

11. This section updates and complements the analysis given by Holzner et al. (2006) and by Agion and Schankerman (1999).

12. In this section transport sector infrastructure is confined to the rail and road infrastructure. Waterways, sea-ports and airports, which clearly are other

types of transport infrastructure, are not considered here, because mean-ingful data, which are comparable over time and across countries, are not available.

13. For some countries, values for the road density are taken from prior years (usually 2005 and 2006) due to lack of more recent data (also see Appendix A.1).

14. Thus one should not compare densities in the rail and road sectors.

15. According to the WDI database, the percentage of paved roads substantially declined over time in Romania (50 to 30 per cent). In contrast, Bulgaria has 98 per cent of its roads paved (even Moldova has 86 per cent of its roads paved). This result for Romania is surprising. The drop in the value to 30 per cent may be seen as an indication of the weak quality of the WDI data for many developing and transitional countries. Indeed, inter-net search revealed that currently the percentage of paved roads still is 50 per cent (see the notes to Table 13.4).

16. Holzner et al. (2006, p. 42) state that 'these countries are poor countries with poor infrastructure'.

17. Romania and Bulgaria are covered by TEN-T. Several TEN-T priority projects include these two countries. For instance, TEN-T Priority Project 22 (rail-way axis Athens–Sofia–Budapest–Vienna–Prague–Nuremberg/Dresden) aims to connect Romania and Bulgaria (and Greece) with Central Europe. TEN-T Priority Project 18 (waterway axis Rhine/Meuse-Main-Danube) aims to con-nect the North Sea at Rotterdam and the Black Sea in Romania (see European Commission, 2010 for more details).

18. See http://www.westernbalkans-ipf.eu/?page_id=330&sector=transport, acc-essed 5 August 2010.

19. According to the EBRD (2009), Albania has substantially enhanced its trans-port infrastructure since 2007 (last year in our sample). For instance, major improvements have been achieved to connect Tirana International Airport with the city of Tirana. Moreover, the north- and south-bound highways have improved substantially.

## References

Agion, P. and Schankerman, M. (1999) 'Competition, Entry and the Social Returns to Infrastructure in Transition Economies', *Economics of Transition*, 7, 79–101.

Aschauer, D. (1989) 'Is Public Expenditure Productive?', *Journal of Money, Credit and Banking*, 23, 177–200.

Barba Navaretti, G. and Venables, A. J. (2004) *Multinational Firms in the World Economy* (Princeton: Princeton University Press).

Barro, R. J. (1991) 'A Cross-Country Study of Growth, Saving, and Government: NBER Chapters', in Bernheim, B. D. and Shoven, J. B. (eds), *National Saving and Economic Performance*, National Bureau of Economic Research (Chicago: The University of Chicago Press), 271–304.

Bellak, C. and Leibrecht, M. (2009) 'Do Low Corporate Income Tax Rates Attract FDI? – Evidence from Central- and East European Countries', *Applied Economics*, 41, 2691–2703.

Bellak, C., Leibrecht, M. and Damijan, J. P. (2009) 'Infrastructure Endowment and Corporate Income Taxes as Determinants of Foreign Direct Investment in Central and Eastern European Countries', *World Economy*, 32, 267–290.

Bellak, C., Beer, E. and Altzinger, W. (2000) 'Fallstudien zu den Auswirkungen der Ostöffnung auf Beschäftigung und Zahlungsbilanz Österreichs', *Research Report of a Project of Jubiläumsfonds of the Austrian Nationalbank*, No. 6700.

Bénassy-Quéré, A., Gobalraja, N. and Trannoy, A. (2007) 'Tax and Public Input Competition', *Economic Policy*, 15, 387–430.

Buhr, W. (2003) 'What Is Infrastructure?', *Volkswirtschaftliche Diskussionsbeiträge 107–103* (Siegen: Universität Siegen).

Buhr, W. (2009) 'Infrastructure of the Market Economy', *Volkswirtschaftliche Diskussionsbeiträge 132–109* (Siegen: Universität Siegen).

Canning, D. and Bennathan, E. (2000) 'The Social Rate of Return on Infrastructure Investments', *World Bank Policy Research Working Paper No 2390* (Washington, DC: World Bank).

Calderón, C. A. and Chong, A. (2004) 'Volume and Quality of Infrastructure and the Distribution of Income: An Empirical Investigation', *Review of Income and Wealth*, 50, 87–106.

Calderón, C. A. and Servén, L. (2004) 'The Effects of Infrastructure Development on Growth and Income Distribution', *World Bank Policy Research Working Paper No. 3400* (Washington, DC: The World Bank).

Cheng, L. K. and Kwan, Y. K. (2000) 'What are the Determinants of the Location of Foreign Direct Investment? The Chinese Experience', *Journal of International Economics*, 51, 379–400.

Coretchi, I. (2010) 'EBRD Launches New Strategy for FYR Macedonia', *EBRD Newsletter*, 31 March 2010, http://www.ebrd.com/pages/news/press/2010/100331b.shtml, accessed 5 August 2010.

De la Fuente, A. (2010) 'Infrastructures and Productivity: An Updated Survey', *Working Paper 10/18, Instituto de Análisis Económico* (Barcelona: CSIC).

Easterly, W. and Rebelo, S. (1993) 'Fiscal Policy and Economic Growth: An Empirical Investigation', *Journal of Monetary Economics*, 3, 417–458.

EBRD (2004) *Transition Report 2004* (London: European Bank of Reconstruction and Development).

EBRD (2009) *Transition report 2009* (London: European Bank of Reconstruction and Development).

EBRD (2010) *Transition Indicators Methodology*, http://www.ebrd.com/russian/pages/research/analysis/surveys/ti_methodology.shtml, accessed 5 August 2010.

Égert, B., Kozluk, T. and Sutherland, D. (2009) 'Infrastructure and Growth: Empirical Evidence', *OECD Economics Department Working Papers*, No. 685 (Paris: Organisation for Economic Co-Operation and Development).

European Commission (2010), *TEN-T Projects by Country*, http://tentea.ec.europa.eu/en/ten-t_projects/ten-t_projects_by_country/, accessed 5 August 2010.

Fernald, J. (1999) 'Roads to Prosperity? Assessing the Link Between Public Capital and Productivity', *American Economic Review*, 89, 619–638.

Frey, R. L. (1988) 'Infrastruktur', in W. Albers et al. (eds), *Handwörterbuch der Wirtschaftswissenschaft* (Göttingen: Vandenhoeck and Ruprecht), 200–215.

Fritsch, M., Wein, T. and Ewers, H.-J. (2007) *Marktversagen und Wirtschaftspolitik*, 7th edn (München: Verlag Vahlen).

Goodspeed, T., Martinez-Vazquez, J. and Zhang, L. (2006) 'Attracting FDI: Further Evidence on Infrastructure, Corruption, and Taxes from Panel Data', *ISP Working Paper Series* (Boston: Boston University).

Goodspeed, T., Martinez-Vazquez, J. and Zhang, L. (2009) 'Public Policies and FDI Location: Differences between Developing and Developed Countries', *Andrew Young School of Policy Studies, International Studies Program Working Paper*, 09–10 (Atlanta: George State University).

Gramlich, E. M. (1994) 'Infrastructure Investment: A Review Essay', *Journal of Economic Literature*, 32, 1176–1196.

Hirschman, A. O. (1958) *The Strategy of Economic Development* (New Haven: Yale University Press).

Holzner, M., Christie, E. and Gligorov, V. (2006) 'Infrastructural Needs and Economic Development in South-Eastern Europe: The Case of Rail and Road Transport Infrastructure', *South East Europe Review*, 01, 15–50.

Hulten, C. R. (1996) 'Infrastructure Capital and Economic Growth: How Well You Use It May Be More Important Than How Much You Have', *NBER Working Paper No. 5847* (Massachusetts: National Bureau of Economic Research).

International Bank for Reconstruction and Development/The World Bank (2009) *Doing Business 2010* (Washington DC and New York: The World Bank, International Finance Corporation and Palgrave Macmillan).

IPF (2010) *Infrastructure Projects Facility in the Western Balkans: Transport*, http://www.westernbalkans-ipf.eu/index.php?page_id= 330&sector= transport, accessed 5 August 2010.

Jochimsen, R. (1966) *Theorie der Infrastruktur: Grundlagen der marktwirtschaftlichen Entwicklung* (Tübingen: J. C. B. Mohr, Paul Siebeck).

Kessides, I. N. (2005) 'Infrastructure Privatization and Regulation: Promises and Perils', *World Bank Research Observer*, 20, 81–108.

Leipziger, D., Fay, M. and Yepes, T. (2003) 'The Importance of Infrastructure in Meeting MDGs', *mimeo* (Washington DC: The World Bank).

Mankiw, G. N., Romer, D. and Weil, D. N. (1992) 'A Contribution to the Empirics of Economic Growth', *The Quarterly Journal of Economics*, 107, 407–437.

Mollick, A. V., Ramos Duran, R. and Silva Ochoa, E. (2006) 'Infrastructure and FDI into Mexico: A Panel Data Approach', *Global Economy Journal*, 6, 1–25.

Nadiri, M. I. and Mamuneas, T. (1996) 'Contribution of Highway Capital to Industry and National Productivity Growth', *New York University Working Paper* (New York: New York University).

Nijkamp, P. (2000) 'Infrastructure and Suprastructure in Regional Competition: A Deus Ex Machina?', in Batey, P. W. J. and Friedrich, P. (eds), *Regional Competition* (Berlin, Heidelberg and New York: Springer-Verlag), 87–107.

OECD (2003) 'Policies and International Integration: Influences on Trade and Foreign Direct Investment', *Economics Department Working Paper*, 359 (Paris: Organisation for Economic Co-operation and Development).

Regan, M. (2004) 'Measuring Up: Dimensions of the Australian Infrastructure Sector', *Public Infrastructure Bulletin*, March, 16–19.

Roeller, L. and Waverman, L. (1998) 'Telecommunications Infrastructure and Economic Development: A Simultaneous Approach', *Working Paper* (London: London Business School).

Rosenstein-Rodan, P. N. (1943) 'Problems of Industrialisation of Eastern and South-Eastern Europe', *The Economic Journal*, 53, 202–211.

Santarelli, M. (2009) 'Western Balkans Investment Framework Launched', *European Investment Bank Newsletter*, 2009-246-EN, http://europa.eu/rapid/pressReleasesAction.do?reference= BEI/09/246&type= HTML, accessed 5 August 2010.

Stiglitz, J. (2000) *Economics of the Public Sector*, 3rd edn (New York: W. W. Norton & Co).

Tarnosauskas, T. (2010) 'Moldova Transport Infrastructure Project Take Off', *The EIB – The EU Bank INFO*, Special edition, May, 28–29.

Unctad (2008), *World Investment Report* (Geneva: United Nations Conference on Trade and Development).

Wheeler, D. and Mody, A. (1992) 'International Investment Location Decisions: The Case of US Firms', *Journal of International Economics*, 33, 57–76.

# Part III

# Social and Cultural Perspectives on South East Europe

# 14
## 'Social Capital' in Central, Eastern and South East Europe: Methodological, Theoretical and Epistemological Debates

*Dimitrina Spencer*

### Introduction

The concept of 'social capital' has recently become widely adopted in both research and development practice. Until the 1990s very few scholars had referred to it, drawing either on Bourdieu (1980, 1984, 1986, 1993, 1996; among others)[1] or on the rational choice theorist James S. Coleman (1988a, 1988b; among others).[2] The popularity of 'social capital' since the 1990s is due mainly to the political scientist Robert Putnam. His book on Italian civic culture (Putnam et al., 1993, see also Putnam 1995, 2000) referred to 'social capital' mostly as 'membership in groups' – assuming this to be a precondition for good governance and growing economic development. Putnam et al. (1993) conceptualized 'social capital' more specifically as 'features of social organization, such as trust, norms and networks, that can improve the efficiency of society by facilitating coordinated actions' (p. 167). As his numerous critics (for instance Fine, 2010, p. 166; see also Navarro, 2002; Mohan and Nohan, 2002; White, 2002; Shortall, 2004; Cheshire and Lawrence, 2005) have pointed out, Putnam's understanding may have neglected the language of power, class, race, gender or conflicting interests while employing 'social capital' as a romantic, essentialist and universalist notion of the structural contexts that influence political participation and economic life. Some of the limitations of his approach (see for instance Spies-Butcher, 2002) have been related to the rational choice theory underpinning Coleman's work. At the same time, this theory has been valued by the neoclassical economists, who form the majority of staff in one of the most powerful social science research organizations – the World Bank (Harriss, 2002). Indeed, the World Bank (since Grootaert, 1998) has adopted this particular notion of 'social capital', promoting the idea that it is 'membership in groups' that forms the 'the missing link in development'. However, the ensuing developmental agendas and policy making have been criticized extensively for failing to address the role of power and interests as well as the role of the state and its shortcomings in dealing with social disadvantage and inequalities (see Harriss, 2002; also Chiveralls, 2006; Edwards et al., 2006). For example, Chiveralls (2006) argues that 'social capital subsumes the social and the political in the economic and allows policy makers not to address any' (p. 142).

Despite such critique, 'social capital' has remained an important tool in development practice and in policy making and has entered and is informing various research strands. As Ben Fine (2001) argues, studying the economic consequences of 'membership in groups' or 'local associations' through the lens of 'social capital' has become almost a 'cottage industry'. This chapter explores some of the ways in which 'social capital' has been employed in research and practice in Central and Eastern Europe (CEE) as well as in South East Europe (SEE) and calls for caution in relying on it as a useful concept or research framework, if not entirely dismissing it in the first place. The first part of the chapter introduces some of the limitations of the 'social capital industry', drawing mainly on the work of Ben Fine (2001, 2010) and, briefly, of John Harriss (2002). The second part describes some of the channels through which 'social capital' has entered CEE/SEE as a hegemonic discourse limiting local agency in the conceptualization of social, economic and political processes – it is notable that local actors self-subject themselves to the uncritical discourses of 'social capital' through affective mechanisms such as cynicism, enthusiasm, desire, optimism and hope. The third part begins with some of the main ways in which 'social capital' has been defined by researchers and practitioners in CEE/SEE, and then addresses critically the use of social capital in terms of 'informal networks' and 'trust'. This will be done by juxtaposing examples from work relying on 'social capital' in CEE/SEE with work that does not use the concept but sets itself similar tasks – for instance, to understand the role of social networks, socio-cultural transformation and political change (such as in the volume of Bougarel et al., 2007) or 'trust' in economic development (for instance Harriss, 2002).

## Critical evaluations of 'social capital'

In a recent book, the economist Ben Fine (2010) critically surveys the enormous literature on social capital worldwide and describes its spread in academia as a 'McDonaldization' of social science and as 'hack academia' or 'hackademia'. Some of the critical points he makes will be summarized here below, although the reader would benefit from consulting his volume directly for a fuller picture.

### 'Social capital' as 'McDonaldization'[3]

Perhaps the main problem with the way economics employs 'social capital' is that this concept has confirmed rather than challenged the presumption that 'the social' and 'the economic' are separate. This separation pertains to the process through which economics has developed as a discipline and has interacted with other social sciences. Ben Fine (2010) noted that the discipline of economics has made a number of intellectual compromises since its independent formation after the Second World War. While it was separating itself from the other social sciences, it became devoted to the study of 'economy rationality', and its scope of analysis was confined to 'individual optimisation directed towards or even within the market' (Fine, 2010, p. 45). Economics was then established as 'a science of economic behaviour through attention to the technical details of utility optimisation', 'assumptions being made in order to attain this goal irrespective of their realism and conceptual validity from other perspectives or aims' (p. 45).

Fine further describes how this was strengthened by 'the rise of econometrics so as to incorporate variables at will into a regression to explain economic performance such as growth or poverty alleviation' (p. 44). 'Social capital' seems to have appeared within economics at a time when economists have considered the need to include 'the social' into the economic. Unfortunately, although such an aim is commendable (as in fact 'the social' and 'the economic' do not exist as separate realms in reality), the way it was done on this occasion is highly problematic academically. Since economics is one of the more powerful disciplines (better funded and informing decision-makers), the way it adopted 'social capital' has led to the colonization of the social sciences without an adequate inclusion either of the economic or the social (p. 18). Fine (pp. 17–21) describes this process as 'the imperialism of economics': economic approaches reduced the social the same way as they have reduced the economic to thinking through 'optimising individuals' interacting in a market where "the social" is a response to market imperfections' (pp. 17–18). Because such a reduction of the social to rational decision-making is methodologically questionable yet seems to have spread globally, Fine argues that 'social capital is to social science as McDonald is to gourmet food' (pp. 17–18).

Fine (p. 23) also explains that most of the research consists of badly conducted middle-range theoretization, which, instead of posing questions, claims outcomes by translating the middle-range concepts directly onto observable and measurable categories. It then claims the strength of empirical evidence but puts aside a deeper understanding of all phenomena under study and ignores both wider considerations and deeper determinants, which may be key to understanding the phenomenon under study. Such approaches claim that social capital is a determinant, while it may only be a proxy or a conduit of a more important determinant, depending on what it stands for. More importantly, 'it omits standard variables of socio-economic analysis such as power, class, conflict and hierarchy, as emphasis is placed upon the possibility and virtues of cooperation and collectivity' (p. 33).

Further, Fine (pp. 32–3) describes how researchers often seem to reinterpret social theory through the prism of 'social capital', adding another element X (for instance health, or education, or others). He refers to such methodological approaches as 'hackademia'. 'Hackademic' logic becomes possible through ignoring existing research and through prioritizing the need for the researcher's career advancement rather than the research task at hand:

> Whatever I, or even somebody else, published before, I can publish again as if a new contribution [...] Of course, this may be disguised by [a] new case study or empirical analysis, but these could equally have been done, and often have been, before social capital had ever been heard of. In addition, social capital opens access to research grants and other marks and perks of academic life.
>
> (pp. 32–3)

In the conclusion to his volume (the subtitle of which is 'Researchers Behaving Badly'), Fine argues that 'the problem with social capital is not that it is hard to define and measure', but that 'why and how this is so is a reflection of the legion of analytical deficiencies that it displays in practice, not least that it intends to preclude the presence of power, oppression and violence other than an afterthought' (p. 205). The functionalist, a-historical and a-cultural basis of 'social capital', as well as its misinterpretation of 'the social' while claiming for itself the status of a 'cure-all' social theory, invalidate it academically to the extent that, Fine suggests, it must not be used at all as a concept.

Like Fine, the social anthropologist John Harriss, in his volume *Depoliticizing Development: The World Bank and Social Capital* (2002), provides a penetrating, thorough and robust critique of 'social capital'. Harriss focuses on development practice that relies on the World Bank discourse of 'social capital'. He argues that the underlying message in such development discourse often refers to an expectation for 'the most disadvantaged people to pull themselves up by their own straps, in a way which is remarkably convenient for those who wish to implement large-scale public expenditure cuts' (Harriss, 2002, p. 7; see also Fine, 2001, 2010). In this way, the result is one of depoliticizing development and ignoring political process, power, interests, conflict and class. As Harriss notes, Putnam (whose approach the World Bank adopted) has recognized the importance of government and that it should not be replaced by civil society. Yet his argument has served well those who are keeping the state out, both in US government and in international development.

At the same time, Harriss (2002) undisputedly points out the major limitations in thevolume *Making Democracy Work* by Putnam et al. (1993) Some of the flaws are methodological (for instance regarding the construction of measures, the selection of data and so on); others include problems of logic (for instance the equation of interpersonal trust generated in face-to-face relationship with generalized trust); and yet others pertain to questions of historical significance. In contrast to the Putnamian approach employed by the World Bank, Harriss reminds us that social ties and local social networks depend on their socio-political contexts (they need to be contextualized), and that the collaboration between state agencies and communities of groups of people involves a political process, which is influenced by the nature of underlying social conflicts and by the nature and extent of inequality.

Treating social capital only as referring to horizontal voluntary organizations would obscure the role that state-backed institutions may have in creating the very conditions for civic engagement. As Harriss argues, it is such disregard for the state and for politics that leads to a reductionist view of 'civil society'. Instead, he proposes that we need to consider how local or grassroots organizations are situated within the overall structure of social relations, including power relations.

These power relations contain, among others, internal and external institutional practices promoting the discourse of social capital.

For example, with regard to the World Bank's external relations, Fine (2010) asks:

> Is it a coincidence that "social capital" came to the fore just as the World Bank proposed the reallocation of billions of dollars for infrastructural funding from International Development Assistance (IDA), which makes concessional loans to governments, to the International Financial Corporation (IFC), which lends exclusively to the private sector?
>
> (p. 218)

The external interests of the World Bank seem to be aligned with the institutional logic of promoting 'social capital' within the Bank. As Fine (2010) describes it, some of the internal politics of the Bank (for instance, compromises with economists) played a role in the making of 'social capital'. This goes in concert with employees' concerns about hiring and promotion (for the sake of which some got involved in paradigm promotion); with the marginalization of those who do not comply; with the manipulation of data to falsehood; or with the external projection of those who do conform to paradigm maintenance. In this context, in order to deconstruct 'social capital' as a 'buzz word' in development discourse, Fine asserts that we have to examine it as: constructed; contextual; chaotic (full of contradictions); construed (reinterpreted by those who construct it); contradictory (how could economists address the social through 'social capital' while ignoring so much that social science has to offer beyond 'social capital'?); contested, collective (social capital has created a community of its own, which is absorbing criticism); and closed (allowing the presence of some ideas only, and imposing the closure of others).

Having reviewed some of the key developments in the field through a critical prism, we can now turn to the way in which 'social capital' has entered the context of Central, Eastern and South East Europe.

## The arrival of 'Social Capital' in Central, Eastern and South East Europe

Social capital is, relatively, a newcomer to research and practice in CEE/SEE. Interest in the topic has been stirred largely by the activities of development agencies such as the World Bank and the United Nations Development Programme (UNDP). Indeed, much of the social capital research published in English is somehow related to the practical development initiatives taken, particularly after 1996, when the World Bank proclaimed that social capital is the 'missing link in development'. Usually, in CEE/SEE, the academics and practitioners working on 'social capital' tackle central debates related to the 'transition' from post-socialism, namely relationships between markets, states and formal or informal institutions, and the significance of culture in institutional building and economic development. To a greater or lesser extent, all of these works address two basic questions: how to improve economic growth and how to achieve successful institutional change (Mihaylova, 2004).

These studies are often trapped in a modernization paradigm, according to which the countries in CEE/SEE have been described as lacking in many areas of development. In many cases such a description may not have been critically scrutinized. To a certain extent, it has fitted the public self-perception of CEE/SEE countries as 'underdeveloped' (some of this may have been an instrumental approach when applying for funding). As pointed in Mihaylova (2004), some Western authors often assume a 'missing', or 'negative' 'social capital' in these countries which they sometimes see as 'pre-modern', or even 'primitive' (for instance Rose, 1999; Paldam and Svendsen, 2000). The 'absence' of social capital or the abundance of some presumed 'negative' type of social capital have been pointed out as the main causes for difficulties in transition societies. Such thinking may be interpreted as a way of idealizing the Western market or democracy, or of justifying colonizing discourses; and it establishes a patronizing dichotomy between 'us' ('developed' and 'civilized') and 'them' ('underdeveloped' and 'uncivilized').

The development agencies' initiatives and daily practices in the region have undoubtedly provided an important stimulus to the growing interest in the topic of social capital. The World Bank has organized various workshops on it in most CEE and SEE countries, which gave rise to a lot of enthusiasm around this buzz tool for development. Leading scholars and practitioners from the West have taken part in these workshops in order to 'help' train and enthuse local experts in using the concept and in carrying out research on this topic. The approach of this research has been mostly sympathetic to 'social capital' and has tended to have only intermittent (if any) engagement with polemics in the 'social capital' field worldwide. It can be argued that this predominant lack of criticism in CEE/SEE research (for exceptions, see for instance Tardos, 1996; Angelusz and Tardos, 2001; Adam and Roncevic, 2003) possibly reflects the relatively recent entrance of 'social capital' in the field of development studies, as well as its undeserved reputation as a 'cure-all option'.

However, another reason for it may be the power of this hegemonic discourse on 'social capital' and its agents as well as the power of enthusiasm employed in its dissemination which has diminished local agency or interest to question it locally.

The hegemonic presence of development and political discourses has imposed the notion of 'social capital' locally as a solution to a multitude of problems encountered in the transition from Socialism, in economic crises and in the search for political models for the young democracies. The interesting question here is how exactly such a flawed concept as 'social capital' is being embraced by local people in various countries as a way of making sense and conceptualizing reality, theoretically and practically. What motivates its local use? Some of the encounters with practitioners in the region provide clues about some possible mechanisms that are at work through individual agency and are situated within day-to-day development practice, including the 'projectification of research' funded by Western agencies in CEE/SEE.

At a workshop on 'social capital' in one of the CEE/SEE countries funded by the World Bank, I met a middle-aged female local government counsellor. Although her story is an individual experience and serves mainly as illustration rather than proper ethnographic evidence here, it may not be uncommon in the region and needs to be examined further. She described how she had never heard about 'social capital' prior to a conversation with a World Bank consultant two years before the conference at which I met her (in the early 2000s). The World Bank consultant had been very enthusiastic about the concept and the counsellor said (in a bit too self-critical and self-discounting a manner) that following that meeting she thought to herself:

> What an inspiring new way to look at our situation! How could it not occur to me that the problem we have is related to 'social capital'! Well, I am not educated well – I went to university during socialism and then no one taught us such things. That consultant came from a democratic country. He had many years of experience supporting democratization around the world. What do I know about democracy!? I took his thinking on board and then I realized that there is a lot of literature on it. I received materials from the World Bank. It was clear to the consultant and it became clear to me that we need to build social capital. Indeed – look at our country – it is a complete mess! If they [consultants] say we need to build social capital, we need to. Of course, I never questioned it. Plus, they funded the project and wanted us to write it within this framework. Now, at this

conference, I hear that there are problems with the concept and the methodology, and so on. But our project and our salaries are all tied to it now. Why should I protest against it – there is nothing harmful about it and it brings us funding. Plus, I think it is a good idea and it now makes sense to me. And, you do not kick against the hand that is feeding you.

(50-year-old woman, informal discussion)

This account of personal experience suggests that some of the mechanisms leading to a rather uncontested adoption of 'social capital' may be entwined with an enactment of a relative lack of self-confidence (which may or may not be justified), an inferior self-belief, as well as a slightly idealized view about the international consultants and the Western democracy; dependency on project money funding; and, possibly, fear to question a more powerful actor. Importantly, the motivation to find a better way of doing one's job and the enthusiasm stirred by the arrival of a 'cure-all' concept in a country that is 'in a mess' have also played a role in the counsellor's self-subjection to this powerful Western discourse. In similar ways, cynicism, despair, fantasies of the West and its supposed experience with democracy, feeling powerless or not powerful enough and the lack of confidence may have also opened the doors for the establishment of an uncritical adoption of 'social capital' theories and practices locally. Some level of reinterpretation, questioning and adaptation of 'social capital' to local practices was visible in other conversations and in the course of the workshop – as they may be across the region – but official reports published by the development organizations seem mostly to adhere to the official universalizing discourses on 'social capital' empowered by Western institutions (for a recent example, see UNDP, 2009), even when they attempt to be context-specific.

Another way in which social capital has penetrated local context has been through individual or collective scholarly enthusiasm and a desire to succeed professionally. Rather than by brute force, 'social capital' discourses discipline through optimism, desire and hope, or more precisely, local academics and practitioners self-subject to the uncritical discourses of 'social capital' through such affective mechanisms underlying daily practices. For example, a colleague in another country has become active in writing about social capital because she was initially included in some development projects funded from a Western agency. She was really happy with this opportunity for personal and professional fulfilment, and she also realized that she could keep herself employed, network professionally, get invited to conferences and try to publish within the new field of social capital, thus also obtaining more project funding. It should be stressed that in addition to cynicism, insecurity or desperation, often local actors have embraced uncritically Western discourses because those may allow some space for real or imaginary personal and professional growth. Kovác and Kučerová (2006) have also described the development of a 'project class' in Hungary and the Czech republic that exists on the benefits from 'social capital' project work in local NGOs (see also Krastev, 2000; Cellarius and Staddon, 2003; Cellarius, 2004; Jeffrey, 2007). It is the enthusiasm of this 'project class' as well as its networks, ambitions and power, that may allow problematic buzz words and development tools such as 'social capital' to enter local practice without due criticism and accountability of its Western promoters.

Local practices driven by all sorts of affect, hope, survival strategies or idealism may have limited the creation of alternative discourses of development and political change. This may not be very different from what some of the leading social scientists in CEE/SEE have argued about other important ideas arriving to CEE/SEE from the West after the end of the Cold War (see for instance Krastev, 2010, p. 118 on the 'ideology of normality' surrounding Western models of democracy and their imitation). A number of ideas, not just 'social capital', have been imitated without sufficient questioning in the region. This may have diminished the 'creative tensions' of their development locally, which could have led to more adequate and sustainable political and economic change.

## Main themes in the study of social capital in CEE/SEE

As is the case anywhere else, the definitions of social capital used in CEE/SEE differ tremendously, not only from discipline to discipline but also from author to author. Some adopt the definition given by Putnam, others subscribe more directly to rational choice theories, drawing on Coleman, while only a limited number rely on Bourdieu and some claim to use a mixture of approaches. Most work could be grouped into several wider thematic areas (Mihaylova, 2004):

1. Social capital in the sense of networks and/or resources acquired through them.
2. Social capital as a form of culture.
3. Social capital as a socialist legacy.
4. Social capital as trust.

At the same time, as in other parts of the world, all theoretical and empirical debates addressed by social capital research in CEE/SEE already exist in numerous other publications, drawing on earlier traditions in academia and practice. Thus research on civil society, economy (and particularly the informal economy), informal networks, post-socialism or culture does not always incorporate the 'social capital' concept or research framework (see further below). A lot of research that addresses similar topics and questions to those in the social capital field still thrives without having to rely on the 'social capital' concept, and must not be ignored. Indeed, some research may not overtly use the notion of 'social capital' while addressing key social capital themes such as informal networks, trust or civic engagement. When social capital enters an existing academic field, it redresses older academic discourses such as in the case of health, where it repackages 'community capacity', 'empowerment' and 'social support' (Pearce, 2003 in Mihaylova, 2004).

In the following sections, examples will be used from the application of social capital in two main thematic areas: informal networks and trust. Furthermore, research that does not rely on the concept, as well as some examples from the 'social capital' genre that either conflict or support some of the findings, but in either case pose more questions than they offer solutions, will be introduced.

## Studies of informal networks

In the existing research in CEE/SEE, 'social capital' may refer to anything from individual to institutional networks (Mihaylova, 2004). Work on the informal economy, subsistence economy, institutional change, elites, social support, social cohesion and participation fall within this category. Many authors seem to have provided extremely insightful work without ever referring to the concept of 'social capital' – examples include 'network capital' in Sik and Wellman (1999), 'blat' in Ledeneva (1998), 'weak and strong ties' in Sik and Wallace (1999), 'social networks' in Torsello and Pappova (2003) or 'social-network resources' in Angelusz and Tardos (2001).

The main problem with the arrival of social capital in this field is that authors write as if the world-wide literature studying social networks did not exist. For example, hardly anyone seems aware that, in addition to the sociological work of Granovetter (1973) and his followers in sociology (for a review, see Portes, 1998), there has been some important anthropological experience on this topic accumulating since the mid-1950s, when Barnes (1954) introduced the concept (about some of the early achievements and struggles with methodology and analysis, see also Boissevain and Mitchell, 1973, Mitchell 1975). More recently, research has pointed strongly to the importance of the historical, national and political – as well as individual – contexts of social networks. Anthropologists (as well as sociologists) have made numerous contributions to the field, particularly by highlighting the links between macro socio-economic and political processes in the formation and dynamics of social networks. Thus, for example, work on various aspects of culture, on the 'moral economy' (since Scott, 1976; for SEE – see Mandel and Humphrey 2002), on identity economics (for instance Meagher, 2010) or on sentiment (Svašek, 2006) and also on the relationships between people and state in daily life (for instance, Fuller and Bénéï, 2001; Sharma and Gupta, 2006) has provided important insights. For the context of CEE/SEE, see for instance, among others, Herzfeld, 1985, 1987, 1991, 1992, 2004, 2005; Sorabji, 1989, 1995; Kideckel, 1993; Bringa, 1995; Creed, 1995, 1999, 2002, 2004; Verdery, 1995, 1998, 1999; Hann and Dunn, 1996; Burawoy and Verdery, 1998; Bridger and Pine 1998, Kaneff, 1998a, 1998b, 2002a, 2002b, 2002c, 2004a, 2004b; Berdahl et al., 2000; Hann, 2002; Navaro-Yashin, 2002; Iliev, 2004; Bougarel et al., 2007).

More recently, the field of migration studies has made significant theoretical and methodological contributions to understanding 'social networks' in the context of mobility and globalization, which also play an important role in CEE/SEE today. Such literature pays attention to issues of power, interests and hierarchy along social networks, both horizontally and vertically (Kearney, 1986; Portes, 1995, 1998; Vertovec and Cohen, 1999).[4] Some of the state-of-the-art methodological and theoretical approaches to understanding social networks can be found in the interdisciplinary journal *Global Networks: A Journal of Transnational Affairs*. In the context of this rich research experience, some of the work on social capital that ignores such earlier research experience or other disciplinary or regional expertise and follows strictly only the work of Putnam or Coleman may lack significantly in either methodology or theory, if not in both (see for instance Rose, 1999; Paldam and Svendsen, 2002).

Most authors working on 'social capital' as social networks in CEE/SEE are concerned with the way in which informal networks and formal institutions interact, as well as with the ways in which formal networks could become conducive to market development and democratization. While some suggest that socialism demolished social networks and created a sterile social environment, others, particularly anthropologists, have demonstrated more convincingly the continuing, although changing, role of social networks as a political transformation – that is, in relation to the state (Creed, 1995, 2002, 2004; Ledeneva, 1998; Kaneff, 2002b – among others). Anthropologists have also argued against the simplified models of transition that ignore the continuity, dynamics and complexity of social relationships, including the strict separation of institutions into 'formal' and 'informal' (Hann, 1990; Hann and Dunn, 1996; Lampland, 2002). Lampland (2002 as cited in Mihaylova, 2004), for example, invites us to think critically by asking: 'Is this division between formal structures and informal networks, routines and practices a helpful one in analyzing the historical impact of socialism?' (pp. 36–37). Her answer is that such divisions may 'tell us how people wished to live their lives but not in actuality how their lives were lived' (pp. 36–37). This points to the methodological problems arising in cases where there is no distinction between what people say they do and their actual practices, which seems to mark a lot of the research on social capital.

Some authors may be sceptical about the use of 'social capital', but nevertheless adopt it themselves. Bougarel et al. (2002) have accepted the task of preparing a report for the World Bank on social capital. However, they prefer the phrase 'social relations' instead of networks and attempt to identify the quality of interpersonal relations, trust, forms of cooperation and conflict management both among individuals and among groups (Mihaylova, 2004). Although the authors feels obliged to stick to the official paradigms, they still attempt to bring some 'reality' to the approach. They introduce a nuanced analysis between different categories such as rural/urban, rich/poor or various ethnic and religious backgrounds, and they draw attention to the role of institutions and poverty in shaping local relations.

Other authors (as described in Mihaylova, 2004) have paid attention to the shrinking of social networks in transition which is seen as closing off access to various services. For example, Angelusz and Tardos (2001 discussed in Mihaylova, 2004) discuss 'social network resources' and argue that, with the growing differences in wealth and political involvement, network resources are becoming more polarized and closing in, thus becoming a source of inequality. Ganev (2001 also as discussed in Mihaylova, 2004) contributes to a better understanding of mutual effects between a particular type of closed elite networks and 'state weaknesses'. He explores the nature of redistributive conflicts within a historical perspective, arguing that 'winners' networks' perpetuate deficits in good governance. One possible way to improve the socio-economic situation could be through investment in social activities that renew the social networks, for example activities that are supportive of individuals in their finding a job (see also Creed, 2002).

In the case of economic change, Lampland's (2002) ethnographic study of managers of cooperative farms during and after socialism demonstrates how social networks were very important resources in maintaining economic and political power in the transition from the socialist to the post-socialist context (Mihaylova, 2004). She shows how 'successful entrepreneurship depends in the first instance on a variety of social relations, often including relations by kin' (p. 47). The most important form of social capital for these managers includes contacts, ranging from simple friendships to complex bureaucratic and commercial connections (p. 48). The reliance on these contacts is diffusing some of the uncertainties produced by the new market economy and offers an advantage for entrepreneurs. Despite this, Lampland shows that the negotiation of a good contract or a fair price for one's goods cannot and should not be attributed to personal contacts alone – knowing how to run the business effectively emerges as the most important factor of success. Examining the current ideologies of success and failure, the author also warns against exaggerating the influence of the personal or family history of a manager on success or a lack thereof. One could often simultaneously hear self-aggrandizing accounts of managers alongside villagers' charges of corruption, and these may be disguising the crucial management practices in action: expert knowledge and extensive experience (pp. 44–47). This is a useful reminder not to take at face value some answers to surveys that are not embedded in knowledge of the local context. In this way the advantage of qualitative studies becomes apparent, especially when the goal is to understand thoroughly the very mechanisms and processes surrounding different forms and transformations of 'social networks'.

Analysing the transformation of social networks in Bulgaria, Ivan Krastev (2003) discusses the absence of policies directly, addressing social inequalities produced in the time of transition, and suggests that these may be the main reason for preventing societies to start trusting their institutions. His work draws on historical, sociological and anthropological thinking, tracing the nature of informal networks and forms of, or attitudes towards, corruption during socialism and after. The author demonstrates that the moral economy of favours during socialism was an acceptable social form because it was based on favours, not on money. Today, however, bribes involve money, and this monetarization of favours begins to reveal the new inequalities. The discourse on corruption is therefore not so much about fairness as about social equality – it is a mechanism for regulating inequality in society. Such research argues for an examination of the moral economy – the interplay between culture and economy and, in particular, the local meanings and role of 'trust' along social networks.

I will now turn towards a volume edited by Bougarel et al. (2007), which does not study social capital per se but discusses different topics often subsumed by the 'social capital' concept. The volume is devoted exclusively to one country, Bosnia and Herzegovina. However, some insights (particularly the methodological ones) may also be comparable with research in other CEE/SEE countries, even in those countries that have not been at war. In the introduction, the authors share their discontent with the ongoing disconnection between 'top-down' political analyses and research 'on the ground' and critically discuss various approaches to understanding the role of social networks in post-socialist and post-war societies. They note, for example, that one of the major obstacles to understanding Bosnian society is the dominant top-down approach and an over-reliance on official reports and websites or interviews with representatives of international organizations, local 'experts' or NGO leaders (Bougarel et al., 2007, p. 13). Another reductionist approach discussed by these authors is the overemphasis on 'ethnic' issues in the interaction between local and international actors or in the (non)regeneration of social and political bonds (ibid., p. 14). In contrast to such a reductionist approach, the ethnographic studies in the volume show the important dynamics of local contexts, the role of historical continuity and discontinuity as well as the concerns and agency of ordinary people in a more nuanced and holistic way (cf. Hann, 1994; Nordstrom, 1995; Burawoy and Verdery, 1998; Das and Kleinman, 2000, 2001). The authors invoke earlier work by Lockwood (1975), Sorabji (1989) and Bringa (1995), describing eloquently the fluid and contextual nature of ethnic identifications and the importance of status, origin (rural or urban) and access to resources. Although after the war ethnic and religious differences have become more pervasive and rigid (Sorabji, 1995; Halpern and Kideckel, 2000), they continue to be relative, changing and contested (Jansen, 1998), some interethnic cooperation having survived the war (Macek, 2000; Pickering, 2003).

New important social categories have emerged such as those of war veterans, families of missing people or displaced people, most of which are defined through memories about the war and are articulated through moral categories such as victimhood, crime, poverty, treason, organized crime, illegitimate enrichment or heroism, in addition to older categories such as cultured (for instance 'of the city') versus uncultured (for instance 'peasant') (Bougarel et al., 2007, p. 20). These categories form the basis of moral claims and struggles for legitimacy in the conflicts of interests and in the competition for scarce resources – housing, jobs, collapsing public services and so on. For example, while displaced persons stressed their material needs and rights to settle in their new locations, the returnees claimed their pre-war property rights and compensation for wartime injustice. According to the authors, this points to the ongoing significance of war-related groups and conflicts where the brutality of war and ethnic cleansing have had a lasting impact. The latter is fuelled continuously by political actors and international involvement, in addition to social and material insecurity and the lack of economic opportunities for survival resulting from competition over scarce resources (pp. 20–21). All these deepen the social, ethnic and political divides while at the same time creating new ones within each group (p. 22).

In addition to offering such in-depth understanding of how 'social networks' form and change in one CEE/SEE country, this volume calls for more attention to the anthropological studies of state-building, 'transition' and violence and recovery in other parts of the world. Introducing such research experience immediately questions the 'novelty' of 'civil society' in Bosnia as well as some current political visions (p. 32). Rather than relying on ready-made concepts such as social capital, it may be more productive, as this volume suggests, to explore 'the everyday practices of state bureaucracies' simultaneously with the discursive construction of the state in public culture (Gupta, 1995, p. 375; see also Mitchell, 1999; Trouillot, 2001; Ferguson and Gupta, 2002; Kalb, 2002 cited in Bougarel et al., 2007, p. 32). Thus the new forms of governmentality and the 'state as an effect' (Mitchell, 1991) have to be studied by observing the local level and how 'the local' and 'the national' form part of wider international influences and globalization. These are expressed through moral categories and claims, within normative frameworks that are difficult to establish as 'common'. Bougarel and colleagues (2007) ask whether moral 'categories and claims contribute to the restoration of common normative frameworks or, by turning social conflicts into unyielding moral hierarchies, prevent Bosnian society from successfully managing its inner contradictions' (p. 34).

Drawing on an anthropology of violence and recovery, some authors suggest that 'community healing' should be addressed as 'a form of repair but also of transformation into a different moral state where the fresh attempt to build communities or neighbourhoods is never purely a local affair [...] [it is] simultaneously an attempt to redefine and re-create the political society' (Das and Kleinman, 2000, p. 4, cited in Bougarel et al., 2007, p. 35). It seems that 'politics' of the nationalist parties, but also of the 'internationals' and NGOs, are seen as 'corrupt' by many Bosnians and that this, being fed by the existing practices and by discourses of international practices and discourses, may be preventing the formation of a shared political space (Bougarel et al., 2007, p. 35).

In the light of this high-quality research, which is dissecting all levels and complex dynamics of a transforming post-socialist and post-war society and articulating the underlying mechanism and challenges of social, economic and political life (rather than just describing what goes on), one wonders what may be the benefit of producing social capital research from a rather universalist, modernist or culturally essentialist standpoint devoid of an understanding of the lasting impact of the war, particularly on morality and on the social division into competing or conflicting groups – such as the recent UNDP report on social capital in Bosnia and Herzegovina (UNDP, 2009). With the study of Bougarel et al. (2007) in hand, it is unsatisfactory only to suggest (as the UNDP, 2009 does) that the social divides in Bosnia today result mainly from the persistence of 'family networks' and their potential to produce inequality. Although this report introduces some key social categories, it does not analyse them and it does not address the underlying issues – it simply states what people have said in a very descriptive fashion. The lack of articulation of the real problems in a post-war society may risk being identified as an intellectual collusion 'ignoring the elephant in the room' and perpetuating trauma and stagnation through staying with descriptions and illustrations suggesting (and re-creating) disconnection between people and state rather than offering analysis and interpretation which show how people and state mutually constitute each other.

In contrast to the UNDP report (2009), Bougarel et al. (2002; cf. Bougarel et al., 2007) have argued that simply mobilizing the poor 'to participate' will not resolve their situation or reduce poverty. Such initiatives may undermine the responsibility of the state institutions and policies in poverty reduction. Indeed, Bateman (2003) has also made similar arguments, criticizing the 'social capital industry' as a tool of neo-liberalism further enhancing the disconnection between people and state, when in actuality the state may still have a role to play and may still have some duties.

### Social capital as trust

Since the publication of *Trust: The Making and Breaking of Cooperative Relations*, by Diego Gambetta (1988), and more recently of *Trust: The Social Values and the Creation of Prosperity*, by Francis Fukuyama (1995), social scientists have become somewhat preoccupied with the study of trust. Fukuyama's work has been extremely influential over the way in which trust has been conceptualized as an aspect of culture shaped by specific features of family and kin organization, such as expectations arising 'within a community of regular, honest and cooperative behaviour, based on commonly shared norms, on the part of other members of that community' (p. 26). Fukuyama's conservative ideological agenda (according to Harriss, 2003, pp. 1–2) is visible in his idea that societies differ between those possessing a more generalized trust (where sociality outside the family is greater – as for instance in the US, Germany and Japan) and those dominated by 'familism' (where trust is present predominantly within the family and kin groups). The author asserts that, in the latter case, the private sector cannot produce large, strong and dynamic enterprises (Fukuyama, 1995, p. 114 cited in Harriss, 2003, p. 2).

In his article, Harriss (2003) critically addresses Fukuyama's culturally essentialist argument. Harriss presents detailed ethnographic evidence on the development of entrepreneurship in India. He compares several small and large companies from two cities in India and unpacks the ideological views underpinning Fukuyama's promotion of a 'soft' view of capitalism, which obscures power relations. He then poses very important questions: whether the absence of a generalized morality is a matter of culture or is instead connected with the weaknesses of the formal institutional framework; whether there is a problem with trust in business, and how it is dealt with if there is a greater need than ever for reliance on trust (p. 7). The findings from his anthropological research are similar to those of Whitley (1999) – who concludes that, where impersonal institutionalized procedures are 'weak or judged unreliable, personal and particularistic connections become especially important in organising exchange relationships' (p. 52, cited in Harriss, 2003, p. 9). Exploring the interactions between smaller and larger companies in the software industry, Harriss finds that the larger firms have confidence in the institutionalized sanctions backed by law and by the dependence of smaller companies on them. This is not about trust but about

> confidence in the institutionalised sanctions to which their trading partners are subject, or in some cases in the incentives which inhere in their interdependence. Though transaction may still be embedded in a personalised relationship [...] the transactions between larger and smaller firms reflect power differences rather than trust, if this is understood to imply egalitarian mutuality.
>
> (Harriss, 2003, p. 12)

Further, Harriss shows that 'obligational contractual relationships' are 'contractual relationships which establish strong obligations on the part of both parties, and may therefore build "trust". These do not come about as a result of the prior existence of trust' (p. 13). The author then concludes that the role of trust is over-exaggerated in the literature at the expense of understanding the hierarchy and the power involved, for instance, in inter-company relationships. Such over-exaggeration is based on the assumption that trust is essentially egalitarian and involves shared norms and reciprocity. Harriss' view is supported by Sayer (2001), who argues that 'the social and cultural embedding of relations between firms usually depends not so much on trust per se but on overlaps in their self-interest' (p. 699, cited in Harriss, 2003, p. 13). Further, in the Indian context, where property rights and confidence in institutionalized sanctions are weak, companies depend on 'specific character assessment' and on the experience of collaboration (which can be referred to as 'process trust'). This means that the types of institutions determine whether a system of exchange is a 'high' or a 'low' trust system, and 'the influence of cultural factors on economic organisation is mediated through institutions' (Harriss, 2003, p. 14).

While the caste differentiation (sometimes verging on antagonism) does indeed create distrust, hindering collaboration, it is a factor of much less importance in big companies than it is among small companies at the bottom end of the market. The reliance on 'selective trust' or 'specific trust' may, to a certain extent, support Fukuyama's argument at first sight. However, while Fukuyama defines trust as a moral disposition of a community, in a culturally essentialist way, Harriss (2003) suggests that trust is more of an 'interplay of habits of thought and practice with formal institutions [rules, norms and conventions regulating economic activity]' (p. 19). Similarly, for China, Kipnis (1997, cited in Harriss, 2003) argues that *guanxi* (social networks) are not a cultural essence or form of adaptation to Communist socio-economic structures, but a form of practice, that is, a response to changing contexts where different actors have different meanings.

Thus, contra Fukuyama, Harriss (2003) convincingly suggests that, historically, culture is important, but the establishment of formal institutional frameworks can bring about changes in 'habits of thought and practice' (p. 20). According to Harriss, the current stress on the importance of trust in the organization of economic activity is an ideological instrument arguing against state intervention and regulation, or promoting a 'soft view of capitalism', where class divisions are swept under the carpet. Such analysis and conclusions were possible only as a result of a careful development of the methodology of the study. To start with, Harriss has carefully examined the definition of trust. The ethnographic approach, distinguishing between what people say and what they do and between simple description and holistic articulation of social processes, allows for a more refined understanding of the variety of concepts covered by the notion of 'trust'. For example, what is being labeled as 'trust' in the popular understanding (and then reproduced by scholars in survey designs) could be a moral discourse masking issues of common or contradicting interests, hierarchies and power relations. The distinction between 'character assessment' and 'incentive assessment' is an insightful way to define the variety of social bases of trust. Following Moore (1999), Harriss suggests that we should tease out the different phenomena usually referred to collectively as 'trust' if we want to avoid lumping very different types of social relations under one and the same label – particularly when the difference may lead to rather different conclusions. Thus, instead of talking about 'trust', or even 'generalized trust', according to Harriss (2003, pp. 6–9, building on Moore, 1999 and in part on Zucker, 1986: see also footnote 5 in Harriss, 2003, p. 24), we need to distinguish between:

1. *character assessment*, which denotes how A trusts B because of who s/he is. Character assessment may be:

    1.1. *specific*:

    – relying on experience of the other;
    – relying on a third-party assessment of him/her; *or*

    1.2. *generic*:

    – relying on the general reputation of those with such characteristics;
    – relying on characteristics shared by A and B, e.g. ethnicity.

2. *incentive assessment*, which shows how A trusts B because of her/his assessment of the incentives/sanctions acting upon the other. Incentive assessment refers to:

    2.1. institutionalized sanctions acting upon B;
    2.2. reputational jeopardy, to which B may be subject in the event of failing to behave appropriately;
    2.3. the possibility and effectiveness of direct retaliation against B;
    2.4. the effectiveness of future non-cooperation with B;
    2.5. interdependence of A and B.

The results of Harriss' study (discussed above) seriously question the validity and usefulness of Putnam's approach to trust in the realm of social capital studies (see also Harriss, 2002). Furthermore, drawing on Harriss' insights, our ethnographic approach, employed in a study of advertising agencies that we conducted in Bulgaria in 2004, confirmed that the role of interests, power and the institutional framework were the key determinants of social and cultural practices shaping the interactions between advertising agencies and between the agencies and their clients or sub-contractors (we reported the preliminary findings of this study in a conference paper; see Harriss and Mihaylova, 2003). This shows that researchers should not shy away from comparative ethnographic and interdisciplinary analysis or from finding out about research on similar topics conducted by anthropologists in other parts of the world when conducting research in CEE/SEE.

Most studies examining trust in the social capital literature in CEE/SEE do not make such distinctions. They usually conflate the social practices, ideas and concepts described above (for instance 'motives', 'dispositions', 'circumstances', 'interests' and 'power'). This lowers the quality of understanding as to whether what they mean by 'trust' impacts on economic development, although some of the conclusions may be similar. However, some of the work that I discuss in Mihaylova (2004) supports various aspects of Harriss' findings and I summarize these in the reminder of this section here below.

Raiser (1999) offers a strong argument that interpersonal trust is important for the emergence of entrepreneurship and forms a key ingredient for the market economy. The production of generalized trust (defined as social capital) is related to the quality of institutions. Extended trust can be a result of expanding networks or moral innovations (creation and establishment of new moral norms), of the homogeneity of a society and of a low risk of being cheated, but primarily it is the result of the enforcement of contracts by the state (Raiser, 1999, p. 6). That is, a 'kick start' of generalized trust may be produced by the state. However, the more extended the trust is, the greater the reliance that may be placed on state enforcement only. This in turn can create problems such as the stretching of administrative resources.

In contrast, Sandu (1999) argues that interpersonal (rather than generalized) trust is a root for trust in institutions. The author shows how poor government performance in Romania consistently diminishes trust, while good performance always increases trust. He also suggests that there is a tendency towards lowering trust, despite the incidence of good performance. The different case studies show the importance

of distinguishing between different contexts (rural/urban) and different segments of the population (for instance educated, religious, female,
aged, well-connected and other categories) before making assumptions
about generalized trust. Bjornskov (2002), in a study on Estonia and
Slovenia, suggests that social capital in CEE/SEE could be strengthened
through increasing the quality and credibility of national institutions,
which should increase trust. Petro (2001) shows how the local government in Novgorod managed to implement reforms successfully, secure
foreign investment, jobs and the support of the regional administration and stimulate the growth of civic organizations. It is suggested
that local government has thus created most of the social capital. Uhlir
(1998) emphasizes the key role of foreign investment in the production
of social capital in the Czech Republic. In a different country context –
for Bosnia and Herzegovina – Bougarel et al. (2002) suggested, however,
that top-down approaches to institutional reorganization may be of limited effect and that some efforts of cooperation may even be destroyed
by top-down approaches that neglect the local forms of social capital or
support clientelistic practices (especially through donor agencies).

One very useful work on trust is that by Giordano and Kostova (2002).
The authors examine the social production of mistrust in Bulgaria,
describing how the privatization process differed from what was
expected. Instead of producing family-run enterprises based on private
small holdings, it has created a host of new social agents, including individual and collective ones: *arendatori* (leaseholders), cooperatives and
commercial intermediaries and foreign actors. These agents represent
different interest and economic strategies in a context where there is a
gap between social practice and legal framework, that is, between legitimacy and legality. Public institutions are seen as foreign bodies and as
obstacles to be avoided, and the relationships between state and people
are characterized by misinterpretation, tensions and conflicts. Citizens
defend their adaptive strategies as 'weapons of the weak' or as legitimate,
even if they are not legal. Such relations of mutual suspicion between
state and society date back to the Ottoman Empire. However, the gap
has been widened during the socialist and post-socialist periods, where
the clientelistic strategies of elites and theoretical or physical separation
have increased the gulf between legality and legitimacy. The authors
conclude that 'the pernicious effects of the new public institutions' are
responsible for the production of mistrust – 'based on specific practices
that necessarily stem from the past negative experiences, which are reac-
tivated in the present through the group's collective memory' (Giordano
and Kostova, 2002, p. 75) and current practices.

## Conclusion

The studies of social capital and related themes have remained theoretically and methodologically disciplinary in nature: anthropologists, sociologists, economists, socio-legal scholars and political scientists have worked in isolation from each other on what might essentially demand an interdisciplinary approach. Instrumental and rational choice theories, uncritical adherence to the modernization paradigm, the insistence on rigid dichotomies between East and West and reliance on large-scale, badly operationalized surveys have characterized many of the studies on social capital in CEE/SEE, but have not led to 'bringing in the social'. These instruments have not received sufficient critique, even though they often muddle different ideas into one concept. For example patronage, protection, motivation, incentive and confidence have all been subsumed under the heading of 'trust', thereby disregarding the local meanings or relevance of such concepts. It is arguable that these shortcomings undermine the credibility of the resulting policy recommendations. In contrast, the qualitative studies – or at least those that incorporate qualitative approaches in the quantitative work – have been able to describe better the processes and mechanisms within which social relations operate. They allow for an investigation of specific contexts and situations in the interplay of social networks and the state. Thus research in related fields needs to be consulted before one chooses to close oneself off in the existing and rather narrow field of 'social capital'.

The explanatory potential of social capital is extremely limited due to its analytical weakness and history of misuse. The use of the phrase may be pseudo-scientific or may lead to poor-quality research, as well as depoliticize significant social processes and prevent us from fully understanding how power and inequality operate within society. On such grounds, it may be relevant to consider the existing critique and research closely (for instance Aberg, 2000; Bjornskov, 2002; Adam and Roncevic, 2003; and mainly Harriss, 2002, 2003 and Fine, 2001, 2010) and give up the notion of 'social capital' in the name of professionalism and research morality. Taking critically into account serious academic research from other fields of social science and considering the social, economic and political consequences of one's publications, as well as questioning the enthusiasm surrounding buzz words and 'tools' for local development and forming confidence in and loyalty to the locally existing needs, creativity and insight may lead to a better understanding of social, political and economic phenomena in the CEE/SEE region.

## Notes

1. In terms of an instrument of power converting social relationships into economic capital.
2. In terms of individuals seeking to maximize the realization of their interests – here the notion of 'interest' seems to have too much of a general meaning, disengaged from specific cultural, historical and socio-economic or political contexts.
3. Here Ben Fine makes an allusion to the McDonaldization thesis of George Ritzer, who was his co-plenary presenter at the CMS Conference and who argued that the hamburger could be taken as a model to understand modern capitalism as well as consumption.
4. For a review of the literature, see also Hilly et al. (2004) and Penninx et al. (2008).

## References

Aberg, M. (2000) 'Putnam's Social Capital Theory Goes East: A Case Study of Western Ukraine and L'viv', *Europe-Asia Studies*, 52, 295–317.

Adam, F. and Roncevic, B. (2003) 'Social Capital: Recent Debates and Research Trends, *Social Science Information*, 42(2), 155–183.

Angelusz, R. and Tardos, R. (2001) 'Change and Stability in Social Network Resources: The Case of Hungary under Transformation', in Lin, N., Cook, K. and Burt, R. S. (eds), *Social Capital: Theory and Research* (New York: Aldine de Gruyter), 297–323.

Barnes, J. A. (1954) 'Class and Committees in a Norwegian Island Parish', *Human Relations*, 7, 39–58.

Bateman, M. (2003) 'Imposing Ideology as "Best Practice": The Problems of the International Financial Institutions in the Reconstruction and Development of Eastern Europe', Conference paper, Dubrovnik Workshop of the PfP Consortium Study Group Regional Stability in South East Europe, *Through Economy to Democracy and Security? An Integrated Approach to Stability in South East Europe*, 23–25 October 2003, Dubrovnik, Croatia.

Berdahl, D., Bunzl, M. and Lampland, M. (2000) *Altering States* (Ann Arbor: University of Michigan Press).

Bjornskov, C. (2002) *Policy Implications of Social Capital in Post-Communist Europe: Is Slovenia Different From the Rest?*, http://www.sigov.si/zmar/conference2002/pdf/bjornskov.pdf, accessed 15 October 2010.

Bougarel, X. et al. (2002) *Local Level Institutions and Social Capital Study: Findings and Recommendations*, World Bank Report, vol. 2, June 2002.

Bougarel, Xavier, Helms, E. and Duijzings, G. (2007) *The New Bosnian Mosaic: Identities, Memories and Moral Claims in a Post-War Society* (Aldershot: Ashgate).

Boissevain, J. and Mitchell J. C. (1973) *Network Analysis: Studies in Human Interaction* (The Hague and Paris: Mouton).

Bourdieu, P. (1980) 'Le capitale social: Notes provisoires', *Actes de la Recherces en sciences socials*, 31, 2–3. [Social Capital: provisional notes, in French].

Bourdieu, P. (1984) *Distinction: A Social Critique of the Judgement of Taste* (London: Routlege).

Bourdieu, P. (1986) 'The Forms of Capital', in J.G. Richardson (ed.) *Handbook of Theory and Research for the Sociology of Education* (New York: Greenwood), pp. 241–258.

Bourdieu, P. (1993) *Sociology in Question* (Landon: Sage).

Bourdieu, P. (1996) *The State Nobility: Elite Schools in the Field of Power* (Cambridge: Polity Press), first published in French, 1992.

Bridger, S. and Pine, F. (1998) *Surviving Post Socialism: Local Strategies and Regional Responses in Eastern Europe and the Former Soviet Union* (London: Routledge).

Bringa, T. (1995) *Being Muslim the Bosnian Way: Identity and Community in a Central Bosnian Village* (Princeton, NJ: Princeton University Press).

Burawoy, M. and Verdery, K. (1998) *Uncertain Transition: Ethnographies of Change in the Post-Socialist World* (Lanham: Rowman and Littlefield).

Cellarius, B. (2004) *In the Land of Orpehus: Natural Livelyhoods and Nature Conservation in Postsocialist Bulgaria* (Madison, WI: University of Wisconsin Press).

Cellarius, B. A. and Staddon, C. (2002) 'Environmental Nongovernmental Organisations, Civil Society and Democratisation in Bulgaria', *East European Politics and Societies*, 16, 182–222.

Cheshire, L. G. and Lawrence, G. (2005) 'Neoliberalism, Individualism and Community: Regional Restructuring in Australia', *Social Identities*, 11, 435–455.

Chiveralls, K. R. (2006) 'The Weakest Link: Social Capital in Australian Regional Development', in Edwards, R., Franklin, J. and Holland, J. (eds), *Assessing Social Capital: Concept, Policy and Practice* (Cambridge: Scholars Press), 129–145.

Coleman, J. S. (1988a) 'Social Capital in the Creation of Human Capital', *American Journal of Sociology*, 94 (Supplement), S95–S120.

Coleman, J. S. (1988b) 'The Creation and Destruction of Social Capital: Implications for the Law', *Notre Dame Journal of Law, Ethics and Public Policy*, 3, 375–404.

Corrin, C. (ed.) (1999) *Gender and Identity in Central and Eastern Europe* (London: Frank Cass).

Corrin, C. (2000) *Gender Audit of Reconstruction Programmes in South Eastern Europe* (New York: Women's Commission for Refugee Women and Children and Urgent Action).

Corrin, C. (2001) 'Post-Conflict Reconstruction and Gender Analysis in Kosova', *International Feminist Journal of Politics*, 3, 77–103.

Creed, G. W. (1995) 'The Politics of Agriculture: Identity and Socialist Sentiment in Bulgaria', *Slavic Review*, 54, 843–868.

Creed, G. W. (1998) *Domesticating Revolution: From Socialist Reform to Ambivalent Transition in a Bulgarian Village* (University Park, PA: Penn State Press).

Creed, G. W. (1999) 'Deconstructing Socialism in Bulgaria', in Burawoy, M. and Verdery, K. (eds), *Uncertain Transition: Ethnographies of Change in the Socialist World* (Lanham: Rowman and Littlefield), 223–244.

Creed, G. W. (2002) 'Economic Crisis and Ritual Decline in Eastern Europe', in Hann, C. M. (ed.), *Postsocialism: Ideals, Ideologies and Practices in Eurasia* (New York: Routledge), 57–73.

Creed, G. W. (2004) 'Constituted through Conflict: Images of Community (and Nation) in Bulgarian Rural Ritual', *American Anthropologist*, 106, 56–70.

Das, V. and Kleinman, A. (2000) 'Introduction', in Das, V., Kleinman, A., Ramphele, M. and Reynolds, P. (eds), *Violence and Subjectivity* (Berkeley, CA: University of California Press), 1–18.

Das, V. and Kleinman, A. (2001) 'Introduction', in Das, V., Kleinman, A., Lock, M., Ramphele, M. and Reynolds, P. (eds), *Remaking a World: Violence, Social Suffering and Recovery* (Berkeley, CA: University of California Press), 1–30.

Dowley, K. M. and Silver, B. D. (2002) 'Social Capital, Ethnicity and Support for Democracy in the Post-communist States', *Europe-Asia Studies*, 54, 505–527.

Edwards, R., Franklin, J. and Holland, J. (eds) (2006) *Assessing Social Capital: Concept, Policy and Practice* (Cambridge: Scholars Press).

Ferguson, J. and Gupta, A. (2002) 'Spatializing States: Toward an Ethnography of Neoliberal Governmentality', *American Ethnologist*, 29, 981–1002.

Fine, B. (2001) *Social Capital versus Social Theory: Political Economy and Social Science at the Turn of the Millennium* (London: Routledge).

Fine, B. (2010) *Theories of Social Capital: Researchers Behaving Badly* (London: Pluto).

Frane, A., Tomsic, M. and Roncevic, B. (2000) 'Social, Cultural and Political Aspects and Indicators of Socio-Economic Development', in Sicherl, P. and Vahcic, A. (eds), *The Indicator Model for Design of Development Policy and for Monitoring the Implementation of the Strategy of Economic Development of the Republic of Slovenia* (Ljubljana: SICENTER).

Fukuyama, F. (1995) *Trust: The Social Virtues and the Creation of Prosperity* (London: Hamish Hamilton).

Fuller, C. J. and Bénéï, V. (2001) *The Modern State and Society in India* (London: Hurst).

Gal, S. and Kligman, G. (eds) (2000) *Reproducing Gender: Politics, Publics and Everyday Life after Socialism* (Princeton: Princeton University Press).

Gambetta, D. (ed.) (1988) *Trust: Making and Breaking Cooperative Relations* (Oxford: Blackwell).

Ganev, V. (2001) 'The Dorian Gray Effect: Winners as State Breakers in Post Communism', *Communist and Post-Communist Studies*, 34, 1–25.

Giordano, C. and Kostova, D. (2002) 'The Social Production of Mistrust', in Hann, C. (ed.), *Postsocialism: Ideals, Ideologies and Practices in Eurasia* (London: Routledge), 74–91.

Granovetter, M. (1973) 'The Strength of Weak Ties', *American Journal of Sociology*, 78, 1360–1380.

Grootaert, C. (1998) 'Social Capital: The Missing Link', *Social Capital Initiative Working Paper 3*, http://siteresources.worldbank.org/INTSOCIALCAPITAL/Resoources/Social-Capital-Initiative-Working-Paper-Series/SCI-WPS-03.pdf, accessed 15 November 2010.

Gupta, A. (1995) 'Blurred Boundaries: The Discourse of Corruption, the Culture of Politics and the Imagined State', *American Ethnologist*, 22, 375–402.

Halpern, J. M. and Kideckel, D. (eds) (2000) *Neighbours at War: Anthropological Perspectives on Yugoslav Ethnicity, Culture and History* (University Park, PA: Pennsylvania State University Press).

Hann, C. (ed.) (1990) *Market Economy and Civil Society in Hungary* (London: Frank Cass).

Hann, C. (ed.) (1994) *When History Accelerates: Essays on Rapid Social Change, Complexity and Creativity* (London: Athlone).

Hann, C. (ed.) (2002) *Postsocialism: Ideals, Ideologies and Practices in Eurasia* (London: Routledge).

Hann, C. and Dunn, E. (eds) (1996) *Civil Society. Challenging Western Models* (London: Routledge).

Harriss, J. (2002) *Depoliticizing Development: The World Bank and Social Capital* (London: Anthem).

Harriss, J. (2003) 'Widening the Radius of Trust: Ethnographic Explorations of Trust and Indian Business', *The Journal of the Royal Anthropological Institute*, 9, 755–773.

Harriss, J. and Mihaylova, D. (2003) 'Breaking Out of the Vicious Circle, Trust and Economic Development in the Balkans', Conference paper, *From Transition to Development: Globalisation and the Political Economy of Development in Transition Economies*, The Faculty of Economics, Sarajevo, 9–11 September 2003.

Herzfeld, M. (1985) *The Poetics of Manhood: Contest and Identity in a Cretan Mountain Village* (Princeton: Princeton University Press).

Herzfeld, M. (1987) *Anthropology through the Looking-Glass: Critical Ethnography in the Margins of Europe* (Cambridge: Cambridge University Press).

Herzfeld, M. (1991) *A Place in History: Monumental and Social Time in a Cretan Town.* (Princeton: Princeton University Press).

Herzfeld, M. (1992) *The Social Production of Indifference: Exploring the Symbolic Roots of Western Bureaucracy* (Oxford: Berg).

Herzfeld, M. (2004) *The Body Impolitic: Artisans and Artifice in the Global Hierarchy of Value* (Chicago: University of Chicago Press).

Herzfeld, M. (2005) *Cultural Intimacy: Social Poetics in the Nation–State*, 2nd rev. edn (New York: Routledge).

Hilly, M.-A., Berthomiere, W. and Mihaylova, D. (2004) 'La Notion de "reseaux sociaux" en migration', *Hommes et Migrations*, No. 1249.

Iliev, I. (2004) 'Small Farms in Bulgaria: Four Decade Anomaly', in Kabakchieva, P. and Abramov (eds), *'East'–'West' Cultural Encounters* (Sofia: Iztok Zapad), 181–201.

Jansen, S. (1998) 'Homeless at Home: Narrations of Post-Yugoslav Identities', in Rapport, N. and Dawson, A. (eds), *Migrants of Identity: Perceptions of 'Home' in a World of Movement* (Oxford: Berg), 85–109.

Jeffrey, A. (2007) 'The Geopolitical Framing of Localised Struggles: NGOs in Bosnia and Herzegovina', *Development and Change*, 38, 381–396.

Kalb, D. (2002) 'Afterward: Globalism and Postsocialist Prospects', in Hann, C. M. (ed.), *Postsocialism: Ideal, Ideologies and Practices in Eurasia* (London: Routledge), 317–334.

Kaneff, D. (1998a) 'When "Land" Becomes "Territory": Land Privatisation and Ethnicity in Rural Bulgaria', in Bridger, S. and Pine, F. (eds), *Surviving Post-Socialism: Gender, Ethnicity and Underclass in Eastern Europe and the Former USSR* (London: Routledge).

Kaneff, D. (1998b) 'State Building and Local Level Resistance', in Schopflin, G. and Bianchini, S. (eds), *State Building in the Balkans: Dilemmas on the Eve of the 21st Century* (Ravenna: Longo Editore).

Kaneff, D. and Leonard, P. (eds) (2002a) *Post-Socialist Peasant? Rural and Urban Constructions of Identity in Eastern Europe, East Asia and the Former Soviet Union*, (Basingstoke and New York: Palgrave Macmillan).

Kaneff, D. (2002b) 'Why People Don't Die "Naturally" Anymore: Changing Relations between "the Individual" and "the State" in Post-Socialist Bulgaria', *Journal of the Royal Anthropological Institute*, 8, 89–105.

Kaneff, D. (2002c) 'Global Policies, Local Solutions: The Value of Local Studies', in Krasteva, A. and Privitera, F. (eds), *Ten Years of Post-Communist Transition in Central European Initiative Countries: The Inner Dynamics Compared* (Ravenna: Longo Editore).

Kaneff, D. (2004a) *Who Owns the Past? The Politics of Time in a 'Model' Bulgarian Village* (Oxford: Berghahn).

Kaneff, D., Pine, F. and Haukanes, H. (eds) (2004b) *Politics, Religion and Memory: The Present Meets the Past in Europe*, Halle studies in the Anthropology of Eurasia No. 4 (Münster: Lit Verlag).

Kearney, M. (1986) 'From the Invisible Hand to Visible Feet: Anthropological Studies of Migration and Development', *Annual Review of Anthropology*, 15, 331–361.

Kideckel, D. A. (1993) *The Solitude of Collectivism: Romanian Villagers to the Revolution and Beyond* (Ithaca: Cornell University Press).

Kipnis, A. (1997) *Producing Guanxi Sentiment, Self and Sub-Culture in a North China Village* (Durham, NC: Duke University Press).

Kovác, I. and Kučerová, E. (2006) 'The Project Class in Central Europe: The Czech and Hungarian Cases', *European Journal for Rural Sociology*, 46, 3–21.

Krastev, I. (2000) 'Post Communist Think Tanks: Making and Faking Influence', in Stone, D. (ed.), *Banking on Knowledge: The Genesis of the Global Development Network* (London: Routledge), 142–161.

Krastev, I. (2003) 'A Moral Economy of Anti-Corruption Sentiments in Transition', Unpublished paper, Centre for Liberal Strategies, Sofia, http://www.wiiw.ac.at/balkan/files/Krastev.pdf, accessed 15 December 2010.

Krastev, I. (2010) 'Twenty Years of Postcommunism: Deepening Dissatisfaction', *Journal of Democracy*, 21, 113–119.

Lampland, M. (2002) 'The Advantages of Being Collectivized: Cooperative Farm Managers in the Postsocialist Economy', in Hann, C. (ed.), *Postsocialism: Ideals, Ideologies and Practices in Eurasia* (London: Routledge).

Ledeneva, A. V. (1998) *Russia's Economy of Favors: Blat, Networking and Informal Exchange* (Cambridge: Cambridge University Press).

Macek, I. (2000) *War Within: Everyday Life in Sarajevo under Siege*, Uppsala Studies in Cultural Anthropology, 28 (Uppsala: Acta Universitatis Upsaliensis).

Mandel, R. and Humphrey, C. (2002) *Markets and Moralities: Ethnographies of Postsocialism* (Oxford: Berg).

Meagher, K. (2010) *Identity Economics: Social Networks and the Informal Economy in Africa* (Woodbridge: James Currey).

Mihaylova, D. (2004) *Social Capital in Central and Eastern Europe: A Critical Assessment and Literature Review*, Policy Studies Series (Budapest: Centre for Policy Studies, Central European University).

Mitchell, J. Clyde (1975/1969) 'The Concept and Use of Social Networks', in Mitchell, J. Clyde (ed.), *Network Analysis: Studies in Human Interaction* (Paris: Mouton), pp. 1–50.

Mitchell, T. (1991) 'The Limits of the State: Beyond Statist Approaches and Their Critics', *American Political Science Review*, 85, 77–96.

Mitchell, T. (1999) 'Society, Economy and the State Effect', in Steinmetz, G. (ed.), *State/Culture: State Formation after the Cultural Turn* (Ithaca: Cornell University Press), 76–97.

Mohan, G. and Mohan, J. (2002) 'Placing Social Capital', *Progress in Human Geography*, 25, 67–82.

Moore, M. (1999) 'Truth, Trust and Market Transaction: What Do We Know?', *Journal of Development Studies*, 36, 74–88.

Navarro, V. (2002) 'A Critique of Social Capital', *International Journal of Health Services*, 81 423–432.

Navaro-Yashin, Y. (2002) *Faces of the State: Secularism and Public Life in Turkey* (Princeton: Princeton University Press).

Nordstrom, C. (1995) 'Creativity and Chaos: War on the Frontlines', in Nordstorm, C. and Robben, A. (eds), *Fieldwork under Fire: Contemporary Studies of Violence and Survival* (Berkeley, CA: University of California Press), 129–153.

Paldam, M. and Svendsen, G. T. (2002) 'Missing Social Capital and the Transition in Eastern Europe', *Journal of Institutional Innovation, Development and Transition*, 5, 21–34.

Pearce, Neil (2003) Is Social Capital the Key to Inequalities in Health? *American Journal of Public Health*, 93(1), 122–129.

Penninx, R., Spencer, D and N. Van Hear (2008) 'Migration and Integration in Europe: The State of Research' Report, COMPAS, University of Oxford, available online: http://www.norface.org/files/migration-COMPAS-report.pdf.

Petro, N. N. (2001) 'Creating Social Capital in Russia: The Novgorod Model', *World Development*, 29, 229–244.

Pickering, P. M. (2003) 'The Choice the Minorities Make: Strategies Negotiation with Majority in Postwar Bosnia–Herzegovina', in Kerid, D., Eias-Bursac, E. and Yatromalonakis, N. (eds), *New Approaches to Balkan Studies* (Dulles, VA: Brassey's), 255–309.

Portes, A. (1995) 'Economic Sociology and the Sociology of Immigration: A Conceptual Overview', in Portes, A. (ed.), The *Economic Sociology of Immigration* (New York: Russell Sage Foundation), 1–41.

Portes, A. (1998) 'Social Capital: Its Origins and Applications in Modern Sociology', *Annual Review of Sociology*, 24, 1–24.

Putnam, R. D., Leonardi, R. and Nanetti, Raffaella Y. (1993) *Making Democracy Work: Civic Traditions in Modern Italy* (Princeton: Princeton University Press).

Putnam, R. D. (1995) 'Bowling Alone: America's Declining Social Capital', *Journal of Democracy*, 6, 65–78.

Putnam, R. D. (2000) *Bowling Alone: The Collapse and Revival of American Community* (New York: Simon and Schuster).

Raiser, M. (1999) 'Trust in Transition', European Bank for Reconstruction and Development Working paper 39, http://www.colbud.hu/honesty-trust/raiser/pub02.PDF, accessed 22 December 2010.

Rose, R. (1999) 'Modern, Pre-Modern and Anti-Modern Social Capital in Russia', Studies in Public Policy Working paper No. 324, Centre for the Study of Public Policy, University of Strathclyde, Glasgow.

Sandu, D. (1999) *Structure of Social Capital in Europe* (Bucharest: Universitatea Bucuresti).

Sayer, A. (2001) 'For a Critical Cultural Political Economy', *Antipode*, 33, 687–708.

Scott, J. (1976) *The Moral Economy of the Peasant* (New Haven: Yale University Press).

Sharma, A. and Gupta, A. (2006) *Anthropology of the State: A Reader* (Malden, MA: Blackwell).

Shortall, S. (2004) 'Social or Economic Goals, Civic Inclusion or Exclusion? An Analysis of Rural Development Theory and Practice', *European Society for Rural Sociology*, 44, 109–123.

Sik, E. and Wellman, B. (1999) 'Network Capital in Capitalist, Communist and Postcommunist Countries', in Wellman, B. (ed.), *Networks in the Global Village: Life in Contemporary Communities* (Boulder: Westview), 225–253.

Sik, E. and Wallace, C. (1999) 'The Development of Open-Air Markets in East-Central Europe', *International Journal of Urban and Regional Studies*, 23, 697–714.

Sorabji, C. (1989) *Muslim Identity and Islamic Faith in Sarajevo*, PhD Dissertation, University of Cambridge.

Sorabji, C. (1995) 'A Very Modern War: Terror and Territory in Bosnia–Herzegovina. In War: A Cruel Necessity?', in Hinde, R. A. and Watson, H. (eds), *The Bases of Institutionalized Violence* (London: Tauris), 80–95.

Spies-Butcher, B. (2002) 'Tracing the Rational Choice Origins of Social Capital: Is Social Capital a Neo-Liberal "Trojan Horse"?', *Australian Journal of Social Issues*, 37, 173–192.

Svašek, M (2006) *Postsocialism: Politics and Emotions in Central and Eastern Europe* (Oxford: Berghan).

Tardos, R. (1996) 'Some Remarks on the Interpretation and Possible Uses of the Social Capital Concept with Special Regard to the Hungarian Case', *Bulletin de Méthodologie Sociologique*, 53, 52–62.

Torsello, D. and Pappova, M. (2003) *Social Networks in Movement: Time, Interaction and Interethnic Spaces* (Dunajska Streda, Slovakia: Lilium Aurum).

Trouillot, M.-R. (2001) 'The Anthropology of the State: Close Encounters of a Deceptive Kind. Forum on Theory in Anthropology', *Current Anthropology*, 42, 125–138.

Uhlir, D. (1998) 'Internationalisation and Institutional and Regional Change: Restructuring Postcommunist Networks in the Region of Lanskroun, Czech Republic', *Regional Studies*, 32, 673–685.

UNDP (2009) *Ties that Bind Social Capital in Bosnia and Herzegovina*, Human Development Report, http://europeandcis.undp.org/home/show/56BA37D8-F203-1EE9-BDBA5775318AC81E, accessed 12 December 2010.

Verdery, K. (1995) ' "Caritas": And the Re-Conceptualisation of Money in Romania', *Anthropology Today*, 11(1), pp. 3–7.

Verdery, K. (1998) 'Property and Power in Transylvania's Decollectivisation', in Hann, C. (ed.), *Property Relations: Renewing the Anthropological Tradition* (Cambridge: Cambridge University Press), 160–180.

Verdery, K. (1999) 'Fuzzy Property: Rights, Power and Identity in Transylvania's Decollectivisation', in Burawoy, M. and Verdery, K. (eds), *Uncertain Transition: Ethnographies of Change in the Post-Socialist World* (Lanham: Rowman and Littlefield), 53–82.

Vertovec, S. and Cohen, A. (1999) 'Introduction in Migration and Transnationalism', in Vertovec, S. and Cohen, R. (eds), *Migration, Diasporas and Transnationalism* (Aldershot: Edward Elgar), xiii–xxviii.

White, L. (1992) 'Connection Matters: Exploring the Implications of Social Capital and Social Networks for Social Policy', *Systems Research and Behavioural Science*, 19, 255–269.

Whitley, R. (1999) *Divergent Capitalisms: The Social Structuring and Changes of Business Systems* (New York: Clarendon Press).

Zucker, L. (1986) 'Production of Trust: Institutional Sources of Economic Structure, 1840–1920', *Research in Organizational Behaviour*, 8, 53–111.

# 15
# Trends in the Western Balkan Labour Markets

*Hermine Vidovic*

## Introduction

Labour markets in the Western Balkan countries (WBC)[1] differ substantially from those in the new EU member states (NMS) due to the delayed start of transition, the scale and character of labour migration (including brain drain) and the already high level of unemployment at the outset of transition, particularly in some of the successor states of the former SFR Yugoslavia. Taking these 'starting conditions' into account, output recovery has been much slower in the Western Balkans than in the Central European countries. Thus labour markets in the WBC began to improve with some delay as compared to labour markets in the NMS. Following the high GDP growth that started in most countries of the region by the end of 1999, employment increased everywhere, but with a considerable lag. In Serbia and in Montenegro employment growth resumed only in 2007 (Figure 15.1).

This implies that increased productivity rather than the creation of new jobs has been the driving force behind growth ('jobless growth') throughout the first years of recovery, a situation resembling the labour market developments in the Central and East European countries during the initial years of transition. The employment structure shows a picture that diverges from that of the NMS and of the EU-15, with continued heavy dependence on agricultural employment in some countries, which absorbs workers laid off in other sectors or serves as subsistence activity due to the low job creation in the formal and informal sectors. A common feature of all countries in the region is the sharp contraction of industrial employment, which reflects the slow recovery of the industry. The services sector is underdeveloped by comparison with that of the NMS and EU-15. But, taking into account the large

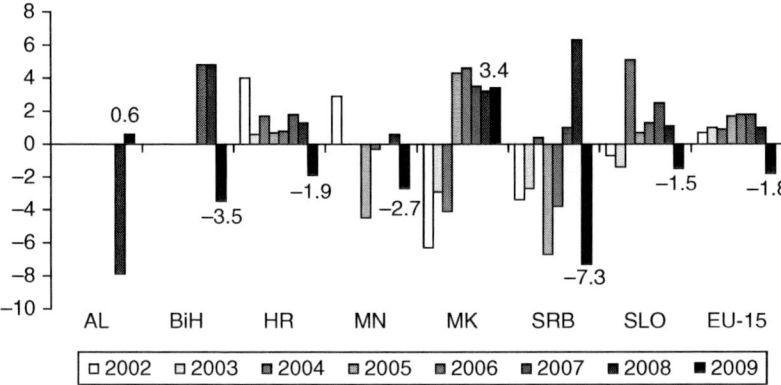

*Figure 15.1* Employment evolution in the Western Balkan countries, Slovenia and EU-15 (annual change in %)
*Source*: EUROSTAT; National Labour Force Survey.

informal sector that concentrates traditionally on services sector activities (together with agriculture and construction), it would seem that the information obtained from official figures underestimates the actual size of that sector.

As in the case of the Southern EU member states, self-employment accounts for a notable share in total employment in the Western Balkan countries, reflecting the still high share of self-employment in agriculture and probably also in trade (tourism). Apart from this, the employment structure by ownership has changed significantly, from the state (socially-) owned sector towards the private sector. Today private sector employment varies between 60 per cent in Serbia and in Montenegro and close to 70 per cent in Croatia and Macedonia. Large informal sector activities are another important feature of these economies. Irrespective of the method used, estimates on the size of this sector indicate a considerably larger share of the unofficial economy in the Western Balkan countries than in the new EU member states.

Almost the entire region is facing a demographic contraction and the population is ageing. Only Kosovo and Albania have a high share of population in the pre-productive age. Negative trends are projected to persist in the medium term (World Bank, 2009). International migration played an important role in alleviating unemployment in Yugoslavia already before 1989 and has continued to be of great importance in most of the successor states, as well as in the other countries of the region (e.g. Albania, Bulgaria and Romania). For all these countries, worker remittances secure substantial parts of income for many households, providing insurance against income losses due to labour market shocks.

Data limitations may impede the analyses of the Western Balkan countries' labour markets and the outcome might be controversial in some cases, depending on the data source used. In the following analysis we employ primarily data obtained from the Labour Force Surveys (LFS) of individual countries and, where possible, compare them with three selected new EU member states (Bulgaria, Romania and Slovenia) as well as with EU-15.

## Structural features of Western Balkan labour markets

The entire region is characterized by extremely low employment rates and exceptionally high unemployment rates. With the exception of Croatia, where some recovery started from 2002 onwards, activity and employment rates only began to rise in most Western Balkan countries from 2004/2005. Activity rates range between 51–53 per cent in Montenegro and in Bosnia and Herzegovina and slightly over 60 per cent elsewhere. These values are somewhat lower relative to Romania and Bulgaria, but are far from the results obtained for Slovenia (70 per cent). Similarly, employment rates are very low, varying between 22 per cent in Kosovo and 57 per cent in Croatia (Table 15.1). In Bosnia and Herzegovina and in Macedonia only 40 per cent of the working-age population is in employment. In all other countries the employment rate hovers around 50 per cent.

In almost all countries of the region low female participation is one of the main factors that impinge markedly on overall employment rates. However, male employment and activity rates also deviate significantly from the values obtained for the European Union (Figure 15.2). As for Croatia, the World Bank (2009) argues that the low male labour market participation might be partly caused by the 'war veteran' benefits and partly by the low effective retirement age. Croatia exhibits the highest female employment rate in the region, but still ranges at the lower end of the scale when compared to the EU countries – resembling the pattern of Southern European countries such as Spain and Italy. Kosovo is an extreme case in that respect, with a value of only 9 per cent. Declines in the employment rates during the transition period were somewhat more severe for women than for men in Montenegro and Albania, while men were hit harder than women in Macedonia. In 2009 only in Croatia did the gender gap remain below the EU-15 average (12 percentage points), while in the other countries it varied between 17 percentage points in

*Table 15.1* Employment rates in the Western Balkan countries and selected new EU member states (employed in % of working-age population 15–64)

|  | 2000 | 2001 | 2002 | 2003 | 2004 | 2005 | 2006 | 2007 | 2008 | 2009 |
|---|---|---|---|---|---|---|---|---|---|---|
| Albania[1] | 55.1 | 52.1 | 52.1 | 50.1 | 49.4 | 45.6 | 48.7 | 56.4 | 53.8 | n.a. |
| Bosnia & Herzegovina | n.a. | 44.3 | 45.4 | n.a. | 45.4 | n.a. | 35.0 | 36.8 | 40.7 | 40.1 |
| Croatia | 53.2 | 51.6 | 52.9 | 53.4 | 54.9 | 55.0 | 55.6 | 57.1 | 57.8 | 56.6 |
| Macedonia | 40.8 | 42.6 | 40.4 | 38.5 | 36.8 | 37.9 | 39.6 | 40.7 | 41.9 | 43.3 |
| Montenegro[2] | 54.9 | 48.6 | 50.9 | 49.8 | 43.4 | n.a. | 41.0 | 49.2 | 50.8 | 48.8 |
| Serbia[2] | 50.1 | 50.3 | 48.6 | 47.6 | 45.2 | n.a. | 49.8 | 51.5 | 53.3 | 50.8 |
| Kosovo | n.a. | n.a. | 23.8 | 25.3 | 27.7 | 25.7 | 25.8 | 23.7 | 21.8 | n.a. |
| Bulgaria | 51.5 | 50.7 | 51.1 | 53.1 | 55.1 | 55.8 | 58.6 | 61.7 | 64.0 | 62.6 |
| Romania | 64.2 | 63.3 | 58.6 | 58.7 | 58.7 | 57.6 | 58.8 | 58.8 | 59.0 | 58.6 |
| Slovenia | 62.7 | 63.6 | 64.3 | 62.5 | 65.6 | 66.0 | 66.6 | 67.8 | 68.6 | 67.5 |
| EU-15 | 63.2 | 63.9 | 64.2 | 64.4 | 64.6 | 65.4 | 66.2 | 66.9 | 67.3 | 65.9 |

*Notes*: 1 Registration data; Working-age population: male = 15–59, female = 15–54. From 2007 LFS. – 2 1999–2003: working-age population: male = 15–59, female = 15–54.
*Source*: EUROSTAT; wiiw incorporating national statistics.

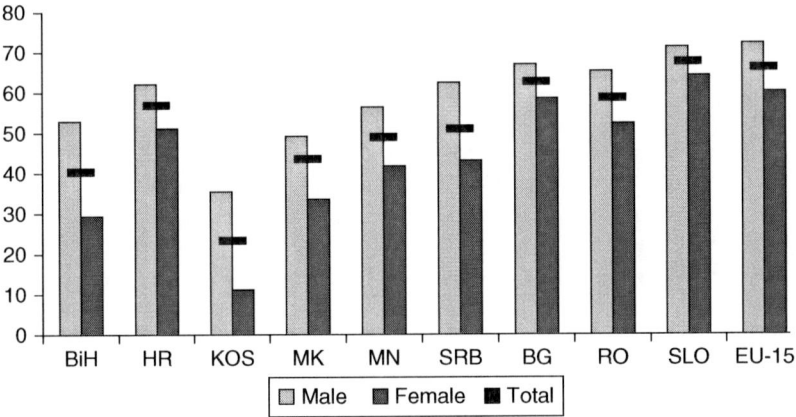

*Figure 15.2* Employment rates by gender, 2009 (employed in % of working-age population 15–64)
*Source*: EUROSTAT; National Labour Force Survey.

Macedonia and 22–25 percentage points in Bosnia and Herzegovina and in Kosovo.

Notable differences between the Western Balkan countries and the EU-15 exist also with regard to youth employment rates. Despite some improvements of the labour markets in the years prior to the crisis,

*Table 15.2*  Youth employment rates in the Western Balkan countries and selected new EU member states (employed in % of working-age population 15–24)

|  | 2000 | 2001 | 2002 | 2003 | 2004 | 2005 | 2006 | 2007 | 2008 | 2009 |
|---|---|---|---|---|---|---|---|---|---|---|
| Albania | n.a. | n.a. | n.a. | n.a. | n.a. | n.a. | n.a. | n.a. | n.a. | n.a. |
| Bosnia and Herzegovina | n.a. | n.a. | n.a. | n.a. | n.a. | n.a. | 12.6 | 13.9 | 17.4 | 16.7 |
| Croatia | n.a. | n.a. | 25.7 | 24.7 | 26.9 | 25.8 | 25.5 | 56.5 | 27.1 | 25.7 |
| Macedonia | 17.5 | 14.8 | 12.1 | 11.5 | 12.3 | 14.4 | 15.2 | 15.7 | 15.7 | n.a. |
| Montenegro | n.a. | n.a. | n.a. | n.a. | n.a. | 14.2 | 20.1 | 23.4 | 18.6 | n.a. |
| Serbia | n.a. | n.a. | n.a. | n.a. | n.a. | n.a. | 19.5 | 18.7 | 21.2 | 16.8 |
| Kosovo | n.a. | n.a. | n.a. | n.a. | 10.5 | 11.5 | 9.4 | 8.1 | n.a. | n.a. |
| Bulgaria | 19.7 | 19.8 | 19.4 | 20.7 | 21.5 | 21.6 | 23.2 | 24.5 | 26.3 | 25.8 |
| Romania | 33.1 | 32.6 | 28.7 | 26.4 | 27.9 | 24.9 | 24.0 | 24.4 | 24.8 | 24.5 |
| Slovenia | 32.8 | 30.5 | 30.6 | 29.1 | 33.8 | 34.1 | 35.0 | 37.6 | 38.4 | 35.3 |
| EU-15 | 39.9 | 40.5 | 40.4 | 39.9 | 39.6 | 40.0 | 40.4 | 41.0 | 41.0 | 38.2 |

*Source*: National Labour Force Survey.

the situation among the young (15–24 years) remains a matter of concern (Table 15.2). Employment rates of the young have changed only marginally over recent years. Croatia has the highest youth employment rate, which is comparable to those in Bulgaria and Romania (at 26 per cent), but is still very low relative to Slovenia or the EU-15 (35–38 per cent). At the other end of the spectrum, apart from the extreme of Kosovo, where only 8 per cent of young people are in employment, all other countries report an employment rate below 20 per cent. In general, employment rates are higher for young men than for women, the gap being in all countries (but Montenegro) much higher than in the EU-15; Kosovo was close to Romania and Slovenia in this regard.

## Supply of and demand for skills

Although the labour force of former Yugoslavia is considered well educated, adverse political and consequently economic developments during the 1990s have impeded human resource development according to the requirements of the newly created market economies. In the following pages the developments on the supply and demand side regarding the skill structure of the working-age population (15 years and over) in the Western Balkan countries will be examined. We also set these developments in relation to those in Bulgaria, Romania, Slovenia and the EU-15. As illustrated in Figure 15.3 and in Table 15.3, there are significant differences between the Western Balkans and EU countries respect

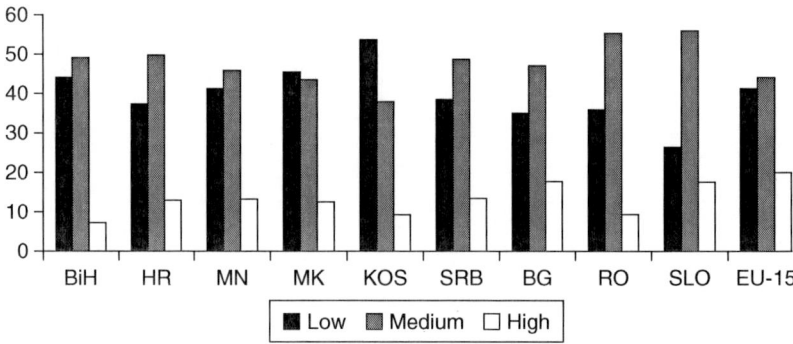

*Figure 15.3* Educational structure of the working-age population 15+, 2007–09
Source: CPESSEC, EUROSTAT and own calculations based on the national Labour Force Survey.

to both supply- and demand-side features, reflecting different inherited structures of education and different stages of structural adjustment processes relative to these economies.

As regards the educational attainment levels of the working-age population, all Western Balkan countries except Croatia have a significantly higher share of low-educated population than either the EU-15 or the three new EU member states. Close to 40 per cent of the entire working population belong to this group, in Bosnia and Herzegovina and in Macedonia almost half of the working-age population, as compared to around 35 per cent in the EU-15 and in Slovenia, Bulgaria and Romania. On the other hand, the proportions of the highly educated are in some cases (Bosnia and Herzegovina; Macedonia) much lower than either in the EU-15 or in Bulgaria and Slovenia. Romania and Macedonia have similar shares of highly educated working-age population. The Western Balkan countries have a lower representation of the medium-educated compared to Bulgaria, Romania and Slovenia (only Croatia is similar), but a much higher share compared to the EU-15.

Experience from other transition countries shows that particularly the low-skilled were heavily affected by employment losses during transition, while the high-skilled reported employment gains from the very beginning. Available data for the Western Balkans are patchy, thus comparable time series are not existent for the whole region. However, on the basis of the information available, one may conclude that these countries follow a similar pattern to that of the new EU member states.

There is a clear link between educational attainment and employment rate. Table 15.3 shows employment rates referring to low-, medium- and

*Table 15.3*  Employment and unemployment rates by educational attainment 2009

|  |  | Employment rate | Unemployment rate |
|---|---|---|---|
| Albania |  |  |  |
|  | Low | 49.4 | n.a. |
|  | Medium | 55.6 | n.a. |
|  | High | 75.1 | n.a. |
| Bosnia and Herzegovina |  |  |  |
|  | Low | n.a. | 34.3 |
|  | Medium | n.a. | 34.3 |
|  | High | n.a. | 12.5 |
| Croatia |  |  |  |
|  | Low | 34.2 | 10.6 |
|  | Medium | 60.3 | 10.3 |
|  | High | 81.1 | 5.3 |
| Macedonia |  |  |  |
|  | Low | 27.2 | 39.2 |
|  | Medium | 49.9 | 32.3 |
|  | High | 70.6 | 21.3 |
| Kosovo |  |  |  |
|  | Low | 9.3 | 64.0 |
|  | Medium | 34.9 | 46.3 |
|  | High | 76.9 | 14.9 |
| Serbia |  |  |  |
|  | Low | 38.7 | n.a. |
|  | Medium | 56.3 | 20.0 |
|  | High | 74.1 | 9.2 |
| Slovenia |  |  |  |
|  | Low | 41.1 | 9.5 |
|  | Medium | 70.0 | 6.4 |
|  | High | 88.1 | 3.2 |
| EU-15 |  |  |  |
|  | Low | 50.8 | 14.7 |
|  | Medium | 70.9 | 8.3 |
|  | High | 82.8 | 5.1 |

*Note*: Albania 2008.
*Source*: National Labour Force Survey.

high-skilled workers in the Western Balkan countries. Employment rates in Croatia are very similar to those in the EU-15 regarding the highly educated (above 80 per cent are employed in that group of educational attainment), but they are much lower than in Slovenia.

In most other countries the rate of employment of the high-skilled is hovering around 75 per cent, in Macedonia only at 71 per cent.

Employment rates of the medium-educated in Croatia, Macedonia, Kosovo and Serbia are lower than in Slovenia and the EU-15, while there is a big difference with respect to the low-educated, who show apart from the extreme of Kosovo (9 per cent), also a low level for Macedonia (27 per cent) – particularly if compared to Slovenia (around 40 per cent). Albania[2] is an exception; here the employment rate for the low educated (49 per cent) is much higher than in any other country of the region, but compares well with EU-15.

As shown in Table 15.3, unemployment rates decline significantly with higher levels of educational attainment. The highly unfavourable labour market position of the low-educated in the Western Balkans is also borne out by very high unemployment rates (64 per cent in Kosovo, close to 40 per cent in Macedonia, over 30 per cent in Bosnia and Herzegovina, while the unemployment rate in Slovenia is below 10 per cent). For the other two groups, the high and medium-educated, the unemployment rates are again very high for Kosovo, Bosnia and Herzegovina and for Macedonia as compared to Slovenia and the EU-15, indicating a rather tight labour market for these educational categories of the labour force. The unemployment rate for the highly educated in Croatia is higher than in Slovenia, but below the level of all other countries of the region.

## Unemployment

Unemployment has been traditionally high in all Western Balkan countries, which is partly due to already high levels of unemployment inherited from the past. Apart from the extremes of Kosovo and Macedonia, where the Labour Force Survey (LFS) unemployment rate stands at 45 and 33 per cent respectively, the incidence of unemployment is highest in Bosnia and Herzegovina (29 per cent).[3] Both in Serbia and in Montenegro large-scale lay-offs and consequently the rise of unemployment started only after the implementation of economic reforms at the beginning of the new millennium, with some signs of improvement in the two years prior to 2009. In Croatia unemployment fell steadily from 2001 onwards and stood at 9.6 per cent in 2007, but it started to rise again in the course of the economic crisis. In 2009 it was similar to the EU-15 average and (much) lower than in a number of new EU member countries, for example, the Baltic States or Slovakia. Table 15.4 shows total unemployment rates in the Western Balkan countries compared with the rates in three selected new EU member states.

With the exception of Albania and Montenegro, unemployment measured by registration is (much) higher almost everywhere than in the

*Table 15.4*   Unemployment rate in the Western Balkans and selected new EU member states (%)

|  | 2000 | 2001 | 2002 | 2003 | 2004 | 2005 | 2006 | 2007 | 2008 | 2009 |
|---|---|---|---|---|---|---|---|---|---|---|
| Albania | 16.8 | 16.4 | 15.8 | 15.0 | 14.4 | 14.1 | 13.8 | 13.5 | 13.0 | n.a. |
| Bosnia and Herzegovina | 39.7 | 40.0 | 41.1 | 41.6 | 41.8 | 43.9 | 31.1 | 29.0 | 23.4 | 24.1 |
| Croatia | 17.0 | 16.3 | 14.7 | 14.1 | 13.6 | 12.6 | 11.1 | 9.6 | 8.4 | 9.1 |
| Macedonia | 32.2 | 30.5 | 31.9 | 36.7 | 37.2 | 37.3 | 36.0 | 35.0 | 33.8 | 32.2 |
| Montenegro | 19.3 | 21.2 | 20.7 | 22.7 | 27.7 | 30.3 | 29.6 | 19.3 | 16.8 | 19.1 |
| Serbia | 13.3 | 13.3 | 14.5 | 16.0 | 18.7 | 21.1 | 21.0 | 18.3 | 13.6 | 16.1 |
| Kosovo | n.a. | 57.1 | 55.0 | 49.7 | 39.7 | 41.4 | 44.9 | 43.6 | 47.5 | 45.4 |
| Bulgaria | 16.4 | 19.5 | 18.2 | 13.7 | 12.1 | 10.1 | 9.0 | 6.9 | 5.6 | 6.8 |
| Romania | 7.3 | 6.8 | 8.6 | 7.0 | 8.1 | 7.2 | 7.3 | 6.4 | 5.8 | 6.9 |
| Slovenia | 6.7 | 6.2 | 6.3 | 6.7 | 6.3 | 6.5 | 6.0 | 4.9 | 4.4 | 5.9 |
| EU-15 | 7.7 | 7.3 | 7.6 | 8.0 | 8.1 | 8.1 | 7.7 | 7.0 | 7.1 | 9.0 |

*Source*: EUROSTAT; National Labour Force Survey.

data obtained from the LFS. In 2009 the widest gaps occurred in Bosnia and Herzegovina and in Serbia, where registered unemployment was 14 percentage points and 9 percentage points higher than the LFS rate. In Croatia the difference has constantly been about 5–6 percentage points (but the gap widened in the course of the crisis), while in Serbia the gap has been narrowing steadily over the past years.

These discrepancies in unemployment rates may be explained by the fact that a large number of registered unemployed are *de facto* self-employed in agriculture or work in the informal economy. Many are often not actively seeking a job but do register because of health insurance (Macedonia)[4] or in order to get access to some other social benefits (such as in Bosnia and Herzegovina and in Croatia). Over the past few years attempts were made in most countries to de-couple registration from health insurance. Hence the reduction in the number of registered unemployed in Serbia is mainly a consequence of changes in the health insurance system in 2007; since then, an unemployed person is offered health insurance only if it is confirmed that he or she is 'really' unemployed and has a terminated labour contract. In Albania registered unemployment fell from about 23 per cent in 2003 to some 13 per cent in 2007, but it was not accompanied by new job creation.

*Long-term unemployment*

High and persistent long-term unemployment has become a salient feature of the labour markets of the region; those affected are running the risk of permanent exclusion and of finally exiting the official labour market. The problem of long-term unemployment is much more severe in the Western Balkans than in the other transition countries, and the proportion of those affected is by far higher there. The most outstanding share of long-term unemployed is reported for Albania, where more than 90 per cent of the registered unemployed have been out of work for more than one year. In Macedonia, Bosnia and Herzegovina, Montenegro and Kosovo around 80 per cent of the total unemployment is long term, while these figures are 'lowest' in Croatia, with still almost 50 per cent long-term unemployed.[5] Serbia witnessed the strongest decline of long-term unemployed (by 15 percentage points), which is very likely the consequence of the clearing up of the unemployment registers starting from 2007. In general, it can be assumed that these high shares of long-term unemployment do not reveal the actual situation in the respective countries because of the large flows between the informal sector, employment and unemployment. Long-term unemployment is high among laid-off workers and young first-time job seekers; in addition, vulnerable groups such as refugees, displaced persons, war veterans and members of ethnic minorities are heavily affected. In most cases women are more affected by long-term unemployment than men.

Unemployment hits young people disproportionately. In most countries of the region the unemployment rate among people younger than 25 years is twice as high as the total unemployment rate. Croatia, however, had made substantial progress in reducing youth unemployment up to the beginning of the economic crisis. The high rates of 73 and 56 per cent in Kosovo and Macedonia, but also in the other countries, indicate the quite critical situation of young people on the Western Balkan countries' labour markets. In many cases young people lack the skills and professional experience for employment, their options being either to emigrate or to enter the informal economy (poor working terms).

*Regional disparities widening*

Most transition countries have been suffering from high and growing disparities in regional unemployment. The development of these widening disparities is closely linked to the process of transition; in the socialist past regional differences tended to be small (Huber, 2005). As in the new EU member states, there is a sizeable and persistent regional mismatch of unemployment in most Western Balkan countries, which suggests that there are strong barriers to regional labour mobility. Differences between the regions with the highest and lowest unemployment rates are particularly high in Macedonia and in Serbia and are still significant in most other countries of the region. However, the results of a comparison between these differences should be taken with caution, since the number of districts varies across countries. Internal migration in Albania, which is still underway, is mostly from the northern districts of the country towards the urban centres in the central and coastal regions; Tirana and Durres are the most important destinations. More than half of the recent internal movements have been towards the capital city of Tirana. As a consequence, unemployment has been declining in the disadvantaged areas and growing in other, more developed and urbanized regions over the years, which led partly to a narrowing of the unemployment gap between regions (UNDP, 2010).

LFS data for Croatia show that more than 60 per cent of the employed work in the area in which they live, and additionally 28 per cent work within the same county. When analysing the effect of the lack of regional mobility on the persistence of differences in the regional unemployment rate, Botric (2007) found that low mobility in a county is associated with increased unemployment. An attempt made by the Croatian Employment Service to increase mobility within the country by making the entitlement to unemployment benefit conditional on the readiness of an unemployed person to accept a job offer within a 50-kilometre distance from the place of residence did not succeed.

Despite the country's small size, unemployment has also a strong regional dimension in Macedonia. It is particularly high in rural areas and in regions affected by restructuring. But, even within urban and rural areas, there are large differences in the incidence of unemployment, rates ranging between 27 and 59 per cent in urban areas and between 24 and 67 per cent in rural areas (ILO and Council of Europe, 2006 and 2007). This seems also to reflect the ethnic diversity of the country. Among ethnic groups, the Roma population is the most affected by unemployment in Macedonia.

In Serbia regional unemployment rates by districts vary within a ratio of more than 1:3. The highest unemployment rates are recorded for Central Serbia (excluding Belgrade) and Vojvodina (close to 21 per cent each in April 2010), while working conditions are better in the capital city of Belgrade (but there is still an unemployment rate of 14 per cent). Central Serbia is also the region with the highest incidence of long-term unemployment. As in the new EU member states, limiting factors for the geographical mobility of the population are the high cost of living outside the place of permanent residence and the inefficient housing market – but also cultural factors (Arandarenko and Jovicic, 2007).

*Informal labour markets*

In the Western Balkan countries large informal sectors and activities with important ties with the states have developed due to the weakness of state structures as well as to the functioning of the formal sector. Among the employed, a significant number of people partly or in full work in the informal markets. Informal employment has characteristics of involuntary employment, because it comes with much higher risks and lower rights than in the formal labour market. In that respect, these countries have characteristics that can also be found in the developing world. As Arandarenko and Vukojevic (2008, p. 11) state, 'formality and informality in the region do not appear as binary choice, but rather along a spectrum of statuses, from full informality through semi-formality (agriculture, self-employment, double payrolls in many small private firms), to full formality most typically in the public sector'.

The estimates of informality vary according to the methodology used. Still, most estimates point to about one-third of the GDP being produced informally; and in some cases – such as in Kosovo, Albania and Macedonia – that share is even higher. In terms of employment, the informal sectors' share varies between 30 and 60 per cent of the total employment. According to the 2007 Household Budget Survey (HBS) data, about 30 percent of the labour force in Bosnia and Herzegovina classified themselves as informally employed. Most of the informal sector employment (about 60 per cent) is concentrated in rural areas, in a situation where formal sector employment is equally split between urban and rural areas (World Bank, 2009). More than two-thirds of those informally employed are men, while for the formal economy that ratio is somewhat lower, at 63 per cent. In addition, the HBS data indicate that educational attainment is higher for the people in the formal sector, especially for those with post-secondary and tertiary education.

In most countries of the region the incidence of informality has been growing throughout transition, being driven by incentives to evade taxes and labour regulations as well as by the failure of the formal sector to provide jobs (Micevska, 2007). Croatia is probably the only country in the region where informal sector activities have been on the decline over the past years (Šošić, 2004; Nastav and Bojnec, 2007).

A more recent study, by Sanfey and Krstic (2009), on the informal sector in Serbia – based on data obtained from the Living Standards Measurement Surveys (LSMS) from 2002 and 2007 – found that the informal sector employs a significant share of the Serbian workforce. The share of informal sector employment increased significantly during the period under consideration, from 28 per cent to 35 per cent, or even 37 per cent, if one includes workers with a verbal contract with the employer, or with none. If one considers only employees, excluding self-employed people, farmers and unpaid family workers, the portion of those working in the informal economy has doubled from 10 per cent in 2002 to 20 per cent in 2007. This increase is particularly striking, as the economic environment has improved remarkably over this period.

A large part of the workforce in the informal sector consists in young workers and males with low educational attainment levels (Ognjenovic, 2008). Sanfey and Krstic (2009) found that the share of older workers, better educated persons with secondary education or more, self-employed and unpaid family workers had increased between 2002 and 2007, while the share of workers in the services sector declined. In addition, it turned out that wages in the informal sector were lower than in the formal sector in both years, with the gap between the two even increasing. Similar results were obtained from a World Bank study published in 2006.

In almost all countries of the region a significant number of registered unemployed are working informally and register to receive free health insurance (see above). Low-skilled workers, most affected by the disintegration of the formal job market, have higher incentives to rely on employment in the informal sector than others. Heavy labour taxes are identified as being the ones most conducive to informality. As for Bosnia and Herzegovina, Bojicic-Dželilovic et al. (2004) found that tax evasion and non-payment of social insurance contributions were, apart from the non-registration of workers, particularly evident in the small firm sector.

*Employment protection legislation*

As in other transition countries, labour market flexibility became an important issue in the Western Balkans. Starting from rather strict labour legislation, most countries have introduced more flexible legislation over the past ten years or so. A comparative analysis of the overall Employment Protection Legislation (EPL) index on the basis of the Organisation for Economic Co-Operation and Development (OECD) methodology (Micevska, 2007)[6] reveals substantial disparities: the index values vary between 2.5 in Kosovo and 3.6 in Montenegro – figures that are above the CEE and EU averages.[7] A comparison between the Western Balkan countries on the one hand and the CEE and OECD countries on the other shows that the Western Balkans tend to be relatively restrictive. However, this rigidity stems mainly from their legislation on temporary employment and collective dismissals, while the legislation on regular employment in the Western Balkan countries is quite flexible. These cross-regional comparisons suggest that, in adopting and amending their labour legislation during the transition period, the countries in the Western Balkans have focused mainly on relaxing the regular employment restrictions, while insufficient attention has been paid to the benefits of adopting more flexible legislation on temporary employment and, in some countries, more flexible legislation on collective dismissals.

## Labour market policies

Labour market policies in the Western Balkan countries are mainly concentrated on passive measures in the form of unemployment benefits. By contrast, expenses for active labour market policies are still rather low compared with the EU-15, but similar to, or even higher than, expenses in some new EU member states. Action is constrained by fiscal problems and by the difficulty of expanding the finance available for such policies, especially in the context of very high unemployment and where, accordingly, substantial funding is earmarked for passive measures of income support.

### Unemployment benefit systems

Unemployment insurance systems in the Western Balkan countries are characterized by low replacement rates and a relatively short duration of unemployment benefit, contrasting with long unemployment durations and the limited coverage – in particular if these features are compared with the situation in old and new EU member states. Only in Montenegro and Croatia is the proportion of unemployment benefit recipients comparable to that of some new EU member states, or even higher. Though there are a unemployment benefit recipients in growing numbers in Bosnia and Herzegovina, the coverage is extremely low (1.6 per cent of those registered unemployed). Also in Albania the proportion has dramatically decreased over time, from 35 per cent in 1993 to about 7 per cent during the 2000 to 2007 period (of the total of those unemployed). The reasons behind the low share of beneficiaries are the high proportion of first-time job seekers and the large number of the long-term unemployed, who are either not eligible for unemployment benefits or have already exhausted their benefit rights.

Low levels of benefit rates are another salient feature of the unemployment benefit system in the Western Balkan countries – one that is 'questioning their effectiveness as a poverty alleviation tool' (European Commission, 2009, p. 43). In general, unemployment benefit is calculated at about 40–60 per cent of the wages earned three to six months prior to unemployment. In Croatia and Montenegro, benefits are linked to minimum wages.

In the majority of the Western Balkan countries the benefit entitlement is limited to 12 months; Serbia, and Bosnia and Herzegovina (the Federation BiH in particular) are exceptions in envisaging a maximum of 24 months of the (official) unemployment benefit duration. However, the average duration is very likely much longer, since the bulk of unemployment benefit recipients accounts for older persons, who enjoy more generous regulations than those with a shorter working period before unemployment. Kosovo does not provide unemployment benefits to the registered unemployed; there is only a social assistance programme, which was introduced in 2000 and targets poor households (Hoti, 2007). Apart from persons close to retirement age, there are also some other target groups – for instance demobilized soldiers and redundant workers – who benefit from more generous arrangements. In Bosnia and Herzegovina the Law on the Rights of Demobilized Soldiers, enacted in October 2006 and expiring in April 2010, envisaged the entitlement to more generous provisions for registered unemployed soldiers, war veterans and families of war victims. Altogether, expenditures on passive labour market policy measures in the Western Balkan countries range between 0.08 per cent of the GDP in Albania and about 1 per cent in Serbia – the latter being close to the EU average.

### Active labour market policies

Active labour market policies (ALMPs) aimed at counteracting imbalances on the labour market still play a less important role in the Western Balkan countries. Spending on active labour market policies differs by country: in Bosnia and Herzegovina and in Croatia active measures concentrate on employment incentives (wage subsidies to employers in order to maintain or create new jobs), while Macedonia focuses on start-up schemes. Serbia and Montenegro rely on a mix of measures, including training, employment incentives, direct job creation and start-up schemes. By contrast, in most of the old and new EU countries expenditures on ALMPs are primarily earmarked for training programmes, job search assistance and public work. Expenditures on active labour market policies vary from 0.02 per cent of the GDP in Albania to 0.43 per cent in Montenegro.[8] As a response to the economic and financial crisis, Macedonia increased its spending on active measures from 0.06 per cent of the GDP in 2008 to 0.17 per cent in 2009.

## The impact of the economic crisis on labour markets in the Western Balkan countries

The impact of the economic crisis on the labour market varies significantly across the region. Both in Albania, reporting a GDP growth in 2009, and in Macedonia, where the GDP dropped only moderately, employment has even increased, while Bosnia and Herzegovina, Montenegro, Croatia and Serbia in particular suffered from substantial employment reductions. The declining trend in the respective countries has been continuing during the first half of 2010. In Serbia and Croatia additional job losses can be expected with the reduction of employees in the public sector, as announced by the governments. The figures depend on the sources used: in 2009 between 160,000 (registration) and 240,000 (LFS) jobs were lost in the Western Balkan countries. Irrespective of the measure applied, the brunt of the cutback was borne by Serbia and, to a lesser extent, by Croatia and by Bosnia and Herzegovina. Employment drops were most pronounced in construction, manufacturing, retail trade and tourism (Croatia, Montenegro), and in Serbia also in agriculture, which could not have been offset by new job creation in public administration and in the health and education sectors. In Serbia the strong employment losses in agriculture may be attributed to shrinking job opportunities in the informal sector, but also to the ageing of the population and to the increasing concentration of agricultural land (Matkovic et al., 2010). In Croatia, since the beginning of the crisis, almost 70,000 jobs in manufacturing have been lost.

In 2009 only in Montenegro and in Serbia were the strong employment declines (at least) partly translated into rising LFS unemployment (by 2–2.5 percentage points). In Croatia and in Bosnia and Herzegovina the rise in unemployment was negligible (around 0.7 percentage points each), which is probably due to the discouraged worker effect, as people decided to leave the labour market altogether. The picture differs quite substantially if one takes registration data. According to this measure (i.e. registration data), the unemployment rates were higher by 3 percentage points in Croatia and by almost 2 percentage points in Bosnia and Herzegovina, while both in Serbia and in Montenegro the rise in unemployment is lower when one is using this measure. In Macedonia increasing employment was reflected in declining unemployment – from very high levels – while in Albania unemployment remained stagnant despite rising GDP and employment.

Young people are disproportionately affected by the economic crisis: between 2008 and 2009 the youth employment rate in Montenegro dropped by 4.8 percentage points, in Serbia by 4 percentage points and in Croatia by 1.8 percentage points. The deterioration of employment rates for young people was accompanied by an acceleration of unemployment in this age group, which went up by 6.4 percentage points in Serbia, by 5.1 percentage points in Montenegro and by 3.1 percentage points in Croatia. However, in all three countries youth unemployment rates were still lower during these years than throughout most of the 2000s.

In most countries (an exception being Serbia) men have been more affected by rising unemployment than women, the reason behind this being the huge job losses in male-dominated sectors such as manufacturing and construction (which was booming in the pre-crisis period). Despite these developments, in the entire region female unemployment rates remained higher than those of men.

As in the new EU member states, the incidence of job reduction was felt strongly by the low-skilled, a trend that was already evident in the past and accelerated during the crisis; but recently also the medium-skilled (manufacturing) workers have become more affected by employment reductions. In contrast, the employment of the high-skilled has continued to grow.

As in the case of Croatia, the World Bank and UNDP (2010) concluded that regions dominated by those industries that were most affected by the crisis (manufacturing, trade, tourism and construction) were naturally hit hardest. Regions where unemployment was initially low were therefore affected more than those where unemployment was high; in other words, labour market conditions worsened in industrialized regions rather than in agricultural regions. Thus regional disparities have been narrowing as a result of the crisis.

In most countries, the position of vulnerable groups (Roma, internally displaced persons (IDPs), social assistance beneficiaries) has further deteriorated during the crisis due to the decreasing availability of jobs in the informal sector, which these groups rely heavily on, but also due to the loss of formal employment, low chances of finding a new job and decreased wages both in the formal and in the informal economy.

In response to the crisis, apart from passive measures (unemployment benefits in particular), Croatia implemented training and public works programmes. Only these two programmes were expanded in 2009, while all remaining programmes were reduced in size (total enrolment in ALMPs fell by 26 per cent in 2009 by comparison with 2007).

## Conclusions

Labour markets in the Western Balkans differ significantly from those in the new EU member states. Employment rates are very low compared with those of the European Union and unemployment has been much higher. The upgrading of skills will be one of the major tasks designed to overcome the problem of the skill mismatch. A particular focus should be placed on the change of the educational system, in particular in relation to vocational training. The huge proportion of long-term unemployed may lead to the further erosion of skills, and many of these might be expected to exit the labour market altogether, which points to a further decline in activity rates. As for future economic development, the economies of the Western Balkan countries will recover only slowly; a slight improvement can be expected in 2011. Given that the employment threshold (growth rate necessary to keep employment constant) is still much higher in the Western Balkan region than in the EU-15, one may conclude that the coming years will still be characterized by 'jobless growth' or by very low job creation. Taking into account the fact that restructuring in state-owned companies has not yet been completed, the labour market situation will remain strained.

## Notes

1. Western Balkan countries comprise Albania (AL), Bosnia and Herzegovina (BiH), Croatia (HR), the former Yugoslav Republic of Macedonia (MK), Montenegro (MN), Kosovo under UNSCR 1244/99 (KOS) and Serbia (SRB).
2. Albania introduced the LFS only in 2007.
3. All of these countries had entered the transition period already with a considerable level of unemployment in 1990: Kosovo: 40.8 per cent, Macedonia: 23 per cent, Montenegro: 22.9 per cent, Bosnia and Herzegovina: 21.2 per cent; Serbia (including Vojvodina): 16.7 per cent.
4. In December 2008 two-thirds of the total number of the registered unemployed benefited from free health insurance via the Public Employment Service (euro – Balkan Institute, 2009).
5. The share of long-term unemployment has been decreasing since the beginning of the crisis due to statistical reasons, as a high number of newly unemployed entered the unemployment pool. This does not save them from becoming long-term unemployed in the next years.
6. The EPL index takes values from 1 to 6. The higher the EPL index, the stricter the employment protection legislation is.

7. In this comparison the CEE countries include the Czech Republic, Hungary, Poland, the Slovak Republic and Slovenia.
8. As for the remaining countries, expenditures on active labour market policies as a percentage of the GDP are the following: Bosnia and Herzegovina 0.08 percent, Croatia 0.14 per cent, Kosovo 0.07 per cent, Macedonia 0.17 per cent and Serbia 0.11 per cent.

# References

Arandarenko, M. and Vukojevic, V. (2008) *Labor Costs and Labor Taxes in the Western Balkans* (Washington DC: The World Bank).

Bojicic-Dželilovic, V., Causevic, F. and Tomaš, R. (2004) 'Bosnia and Herzegovina: Problems, Obstacles and Outcomes of the Reforms', *European Balkan Observer*, 2 (4), 2–9.

Botric, V. (2007) 'Croatia', Background Paper for the Study on the Adjustment Capacity to External Shocks of EU Candidate and Potential Candidate Countries of the Western Balkans, with a Focus on the Labour Markets (Zagreb: Institute of Economics).

Euro – Balkan Institute (2009) *Labour Market in the Former Yugoslav Republic of Macedonia* (Skopje: Euro-Balkan Institute).

European Commission (2009) *Social Protection and Social Inclusion in the Western Balkans – Summary of the Synthesis Report* (Brussels: European Commission).

Hoti, A. (2007) 'Kosova', Background Paper for the Study on the Adjustment Capacity to External Shocks of EU Candidate and Potential Candidate Countries of the Western Balkans, with a Focus on the Labour Markets (Prishtina: University of Prishtina).

Huber, P. (2005) 'Inter-Regional Mobility in the Accession Countries: A Comparison to EU-15 member States', *WIFO Working Papers*, No. 149/2005 (Vienna: The Austrian Institute for Economic Research).

ILO and Council of Europe (2006 and 2007) *Employment Policy Review: The former Yugoslav Republic of Macedonia* (Geneva and Strasbourg: International Labour Organisation and Council of Europe).

Matkovic, G., Mijatovic, B. and Petrovic, M. (2010) *Impact of the Financial Crisis on the Labor Market and Living Conditions Outcomes* (Belgrade: Center for Liberal-Democratic Studies).

Micevska, M. (2007) 'Employment Protection Legislation in Southeast Europe', Background paper for the Study on the Adjustment Capacity to External Shocks of EU Candidate and Potential Candidate Countries in the Western Balkans, with a Focus on Labour Markets (Klagenfurt: University of Klagenfurt).

Nastav, B. and Bojec, S. (2007) 'The Shadow Economy in Bosnia and Herzegovina, Croatia and Slovenia: Labour Approach', *Eastern European Economics*, 45, 29–58.

Ognjenovic, K. (2008) 'Serbia', in European Commission (ed.), *Adjustment Capacity of Labour Market of the Western Balkans Countries: Countries Studies II* (Brussels: European Commission), 199–229.

Sanfey P. and Krstić, G. (2010) 'Earnings Inequality and the Informal Economy: Evidence from Serbia', *EBRD Working Paper 114* (London: European Bank of Reconstruction and Development).

Šošić, V. (2004) *Regulation and Flexibility of the Croatian Labour Market*, (Vienna: The Vienna Institute for International Economic Studies).

UNDP (2010) *Overview of Regional Disparities in Albania (Preliminary), 10 March 2010* (Tirana: The United Nations Development Programme (UNDP) in Albania).

World Bank (2006) *Serbia – Labour Market Assessment*, Report No. 36576-YU, September 2006 (Washington DC: The World Bank).

World Bank (2009) *Croatia's EU Convergence Report: Reaching and Sustaining Higher Rates of Economic Growth*, vol. 2: Full Report, Report No. 48879- HR, June 2009 (Washington DC: The World Bank).

World Bank and UNDP (2010) *Croatia: Social Impact of the Crisis and Building Resilience, Main Report* (Washington DC and New York: The World Bank and United Nations Development Programme).

# 16
# Higher Education in Former Yugoslav Countries: Impact of the Bologna Process

*David Crosier and Elizabeth Heath*

## Introduction

The past ten years have seen unprecedented developments in higher education in all European countries. Student numbers have increased by an average of 25 per cent (Eurydice, 2009), while the range of societal demands has also broadened considerably. Higher education is now expected to meet a wide range of needs of evolving knowledge society and economies: educating ever larger numbers of the population, creating new opportunities for non-traditional students, developing research excellence and acting to improve quality and efficiency in all aspects of the higher education mission. While these trends certainly began before the turn of the twenty-first century – indeed they can be traced in a perspective of post–Second World War evolution – the speed of change has accelerated in recent years. This reality of a fast-moving landscape for higher education with ever-increasing demands is now coupled with the impact of the global financial and economic downturn. The result is a higher education landscape of considerable turbulence, with major challenges emerging for the future.

## Additional challenges in former Yugoslav countries

As well as facing these common challenges of our age, the countries of former Yugoslavia are also attempting to cope with new geo-political, social and demographic realities, and with the individual and societal trauma related to the conflicts of separation. These realities cannot be overlooked. Higher education students of today's generation were born as the first steps in the break-up of Yugoslavia were taking place, and their childhood was lived through a period of tumultuous conflict.

Many of today's students will have experienced direct losses of close family members in their early childhood, and will also have been taught by school teachers who have lost relatives. Conflict and its associated trauma have been the formative experience of many lives. Indeed, the current generation of higher education students in several former Yugoslav countries has been affected by conflict in a way that is unlike anything that their counterparts around Europe will have experienced.

Staff working in higher education institutions has been similarly affected, and many of its members are also struggling to come to terms with their troubled past. Like their students, they too live with the trauma of loss. At a professional level, they are also keenly aware that many former colleagues have left to establish new lives abroad, from where it is perhaps easier to leave the troubled past behind. For those who did not leave, the present reality makes the past impossible to put behind. They work in a degraded academic environment, with poor salaries, poor facilities, lack of incentives and, in the worst cases, in an endemic culture of corruption and nepotism.

It is important to recognize that the citizens and countries of former Yugoslavia are part of the wider European context. However, the impact of these specific aspects of their reality should not be ignored.

## Main objectives of the Bologna Process

Part of today's challenge is dealing with a fast-changing global transformation, from industrialized to post-industrial knowledge society. As far as higher education is concerned, a concerted pan-European response to pressures of globalization and the rise of knowledge societies has been crystallized over the last decade through what is known as the Bologna Process. Essentially the Bologna Process is an informal and voluntary agreement, first signed by 29 European governments in 1999. The ministers pledged to reform their higher education systems in similar ways, with the same major objective in mind – the creation of a European Higher Education Area by 2010. Thus higher education systems in European countries should be organized in such a way that it would be easy to move from one country to the other for the purpose of study or employment; the attractiveness of European higher education to other world regions would be increased; and Europe would have a broad high-quality knowledge base.[1]

The Bologna Process has a number of different action lines, ranging from the reform of degree structures to addressing issues of student support and study conditions. However, there is nothing legally binding about the commitments made. Instead there is a process of self-reporting of countries in relation to these commitments, and hence a kind of peer pressure to reform.

The number of countries involved in the process has now expanded to 47, and so it can therefore be claimed as genuinely pan-European. All of the countries of former Yugoslavia, with the exception of Kosovo, are official members of the Bologna Process (to date, Kosovo has been considered ineligible for official recognition as a member). Moreover, tackling Bologna reforms is the substance of much international donor support. The Bologna Process is therefore a significant aspect of higher education reality for all countries, and the way in which it has been addressed merits deeper consideration.

## Impact of the Bologna Process in Europe

There is little doubt that the Bologna Process has triggered major advances in higher education reform across the continent. Degree systems are becoming increasingly harmonized (a word that was politically taboo ten years ago, but is now increasingly commonplace as a description of European higher education system developments), quality assurance systems are developing through close consultation between countries and the tendency to adapt higher education systems to the needs of a wider group of learners can be seen everywhere. The Bologna Process has given a sense of direction and common purpose to higher education development, and has also helped countries to adapt to societal demands for mass higher education systems.

Yet Bologna has also become the focus of scepticism and criticism – much of which is, arguably, misplaced. Instead of recognizing the underlying phenomena of societal change that should really be at the heart of discussion, many commentators and stakeholders have found it easier to attack Bologna. Thus the Bologna Process is often portrayed – by some students and academics alike – as a front for economic liberalization and for the release of market forces in higher education. In reality, these trends were already in motion independently of Bologna. Indeed, if anything, the Bologna Process, through its rhetorical emphasis on public responsibility, has provided some means of resistance to such trends.

There is still much more to be done if a European higher education area is to become a meaningful reality. Bologna implies a profound shift in education philosophy and practice – and it is here that attention needs to focus in the future. Indeed, the most significant purpose of Bologna is to respond to societal needs by moving from a system of teacher-driven provision towards a student-centred concept. No longer can higher education be essentially a matter of transmitting knowledge. Instead the reforms are laying the foundations for a system that responds to a growing variety of student needs within a framework of lifelong education. The impact of the economic crisis is also likely to focus attention on to this agenda of lifelong learning in a far more meaningful way than before – but with the risk that the needs of the labour market for skilled workers are prioritized over the needs of individuals to fulfil their potential.

## Legacy of the Yugoslav higher education system

In order to assess the impact of the Bologna Process in the countries of former Yugoslavia, it is important to consider the historical evolution of higher education prior to the break-up of Yugoslavia, as this has done much to shape the way in which the higher education sector is conceived. Unlike in other European regions, many would characterize higher education in former Yugoslav countries today by a general feeling of inertia and resistance to change. There are many reasons for this perception, but one that is often overlooked is the cultural impact of the higher education model in former Yugoslavia.[2]

This model for higher education developed greatly in the post–Second World War period. It also proved to be very successful and brought enormous benefit to citizens in Yugoslavia. Indeed, progress in both qualitative and quantitative terms was spectacular. While in 1945 0.5 per cent of the population had been university-educated, by the mid-1980s Yugoslavia could count 7.5 per cent university graduates among its population, and access to the university system was available to all who completed secondary education. Other statistics illustrate the same positive and expansionist trend. The number of universities rose from 5 in 1945 to 19 at the beginning of the 1980s, and faculties extended from 17 to 75 in the same period. Meanwhile the number of students expanded from 17,000 to about 350,000. By the 1980s Yugoslavia had, by the standards of its day, an extremely well-educated population, and the development of the university system underpinned this knowledge base.

As well as expansion in higher education, the post-war period also saw the development of the concept of self-management in all aspects of society, including higher education. Under this governance system, faculties became self-governing, with many elections among peers, and the university was conceived of as a system of associated, autonomous faculties. This cultural system, very strongly embedded in Yugoslav society, has also been highly influential in all the post-Yugoslav successor nations.

While higher education in Yugoslavia certainly had very strong and positive features, by the end of the 1980s it also faced serious problems. University drop-out rates were high, and students took an average of seven years to complete a four-year degree, and five years to finish a two-year programme. At a time of economic difficulty, high tuition and living expenses made it difficult for many students to participate, and university education was therefore inaccessible for many Yugoslav families. However, the break-up of Yugoslavia meant that these and other issues were never to be addressed – or at least were only to be tackled in a vastly altered context. Inevitably, along with all normal features of society, higher education was to break down in many parts of former Yugoslavia during the conflicts of separation, and universities became places where political interference was widespread. These realities have proved to be extremely difficult to address in the new era of post-conflict independent states.

## Regenerating higher education in South East Europe

In June 1999, at the same time as Ministers of Education were busy signing the Bologna Declaration, the Stability Pact for South Eastern Europe was launched as the first comprehensive conflict prevention strategy for the region. It aimed at strengthening the efforts of the countries of South Eastern Europe to foster peace, democracy, respect for human rights and economic prosperity, and at providing a framework to stimulate regional cooperation and to facilitate integration into European and Euro-Atlantic structures.

Education and higher education were almost completely neglected in the original documents announcing the establishment of the Stability Pact. Although this was soon rectified (thanks to strong lobbying by individuals and organizations with a concern for educational development), the initial omission reveals much about prevailing attitudes in the international community towards societal reconstruction and regeneration. Indeed more attention was focused on concrete (and sometimes literally so) projects than upon the need to empower citizens and to develop a genuine sense of belonging in Europe. Education and culture were considered to be 'soft sector' activities, to be tackled after more urgent priorities had been addressed (Daxner, 2006).

Thus it was assumed that major problems such as poverty, unemployment, brain drain and stagnant economies should be addressed before other issues were broached. The importance of education and higher education in providing societal conditions for long-term sustainable development was largely ignored. This failure to see education and higher education as a major priority was symptomatic of international action to 'help' the countries of South East Europe, and it contributed to a failure to develop any real concept of strategic development. This contributed to condemning the countries of South Eastern Europe to a long, ongoing struggle to come to terms with the challenges of the twenty-first century.

## Reform efforts in South East Europe higher education

Higher education reform efforts have nonetheless intensified in recent years. As the infrastructure and 'hard sector' have improved in the immediate post-war years, international donor focus has become increasingly directed towards higher education reform. National governments in South Eastern Europe have also been quick to sign up to the Bologna Process – often perceiving this action as a required step towards becoming an EU member state. With EU integration the key to economic and development strategy, reforming a higher education system and adopting Bologna action lines appear to be two of the more straightforward boxes to tick for governments trying to achieve EU membership.

However, there are four key problems regarding the approach taken to higher education reform:

(1) There is a lack of guiding vision for this reform. Where is the region and its constituent countries going? Why move in this direction rather than another? What will be the impact of the policy choices made? How will success and failure be measured and understood? These and other key questions are left unanswered – and often unasked.

(2) The legacy of the former Yugoslav system and the practice of equating new legislation with change hinders reform efforts. Thus, when legislation or regulations change, the reality on the ground often stays the same, as there is no strategy or mechanism for implementation.

Conversely, for issues that have not been addressed through legislative reform, the lack of legislation is routinely used as an excuse for not changing academic practice. Rather than seeing legislation as setting the framework and boundaries of acceptable practice, it is as if no innovation and change in academic behaviour were possible *unless* required by legislation.

(3) Information to help understand and tackle key problems is often unreliable and/or unavailable. This can range from basic data regarding student enrolment, graduation and employment rates to information on the funding of different aspects of the higher education mission (for instance research funding) or information on the impact of reforms.

The main problem is that the kind of statistical and management information infrastructure that is used as a matter of routine in most European countries and higher education institutions has not been developed coherently in former Yugoslav countries. This is linked to the culture of decentralized higher education management, whereby each faculty is responsible for its own actions and initiatives, and as a result there is no harmonization in the methods for collecting information. Thus statistics are collected in different ways, for different purposes and, when amalgamated at institutional and/or national level, they are often not comparable and therefore they are less than completely reliable.

(4) Finally, universities remain teacher- rather than student-centred and maintain an elite approach to higher education. This leads to many aspects of the recognized Bologna 'tools' – Diploma Supplement (European Commission, 2010a), ECTS (European Commission, 2010b), National Qualifications Frameworks (Bologna Secretariat, 2010) – being not understood and not used for their intended purpose. This purpose can be simply described as creating a high-quality student-centred learning environment, with opportunities for mobility and flexible learning. Unfortunately this is not a vision that is a common aspiration of higher education institutions in the former Yugoslav countries.

## Misunderstanding the Bologna Process

Many governments and universities appear to have thought that the Bologna Process would provide a blueprint for higher education reform. This led to confusion when they discovered that the process provided aims and objectives with guidelines to move forward rather than a set of prescriptive rules and 'how to' manuals. This misunderstanding of the Bologna Process has also contributed to the higher education sector failing to address specific problems of national systems. As long as these issues are left untouched, coherent efforts to implement Bologna reforms are simply not possible.

Bologna is often perceived as a top-down initiative, and this causes its own inherent problems throughout Europe. Governments sign up, thus putting public universities and other higher education institutions under pressure to reform. At some point, however, if pressure is the main method for inducing change, there may come a backlash and a lack of engagement from the academic staff. This attitude could be described as 'indignant inertia'.

In universities of former Yugoslav countries, problems are further compounded by contradictions between higher education legislation and academic practice. For example, it is typical for the recognition of qualifications or learning periods to be granted by groups of experts who compare the content of a written curriculum in a foreign institution with the local curriculum. If contents are not identical, recognition is not granted. This prescription of input is in total conflict with the conceptual move in higher education towards a focus on learning outcomes, whereby it is what a graduate knows and is able to do that matters, rather than the particular content that she or he has studied. Such practice also leaves very little space for mobility, and thus undermines another of the Bologna goals for European higher education.

In some ways, pressure for higher education reform is less noticeable in former Yugoslav countries than in other parts of the continent. This is partly because most of the student mobility flows are within the former Yugoslav region. As students and staff come from similar institutions, it is difficult to create the peer pressure and student demand for reform that exists in parts of Europe where mobility is a more common phenomenon. While universities in other European countries also struggle with implementing the Bologna Process, there are a number of incentives for them to engage in it. For example, in addition to the benefits of establishing wider teaching and research contacts and improving quality, universities may be motivated towards developing internationalization strategies by the prospect of enrolling fee-paying students, who can be an important source of additional income. This may seem particularly enticing at a time of economic hardship.

Interest in internationalization and mobility was not a significant aspect of higher education before the Bologna reforms, except in a few leading European institutions and in countries with strong post-colonial connections. In these countries, the mobility flows also tended to be one way – towards the elite institutions and former colonial powers. Now, however, a well-functioning Bologna-reformed university can offer an easy to understand and accessible environment for overseas students. This is one of the key drivers to create a European Higher Education

Area that attracts overseas students to the continent as a whole, rather than to a small number of internationally reputed institutions.

In contrast, in the former Yugoslav countries many universities are not even regionally focused, let alone European or internationally focused, and they continue to ignore the opportunities of developing programmes in widely spoken international languages – particularly English – that would be attractive to students from outside the region. In addition, they maintain the most off-putting recognition practices possible, further discouraging any potential international students. Despite the theoretical commitment to the Bologna goals of establishing an open and inclusive higher education area, few attempts are being made in this direction at the moment.

Bologna reform continues to be a difficult process in most parts of Europe. However, the combination of non-enabling higher education laws, unfavourable economic climate and inherited former Yugoslav systems creates a particularly challenging environment in the Western Balkans. As there is so little exposure to higher education systems in other parts of Europe, it is difficult for higher education staff and students to gain any picture of more positive reform trends and to understand what the potential benefits could be in the region. The mixed top-down messages – Bologna reform within a non-enabling higher education legislative framework – combined with internal resistance to change, from staff and sometimes also from students, mean that universities are likely to conform to higher education legislation, but to make little effort at an effective implementation of Bologna goals.

## Obstacles to reform

In addition to the overarching tension between Bologna reforms and non-accommodating higher education laws, there are also a number of technical and university infrastructure-related obstacles.

### European Credit Transfer and Accumulation System

European Credit Transfer and Accumulation System (ECTS) is a student-centred credit system based on the student workload required to achieve specified learning outcomes. It was originally set up in 1989 in order to facilitate the recognition of periods of study abroad within the European Union's Erasmus programme. More recently, it has been developing into an accumulation system, to be implemented in all programmes at institutional, regional, national and European levels.

ECTS would typically consider the hours of contact time, pages of required reading or laboratory work, hours of self-study and also the assessment of learning. It is a convention of the system that each academic year should typically comprise 60 credits, which results in the accrual of 180 ECTS credits for a three-year Bachelor degree, and between 60 and 120 ECTS for a Masters degree. Since the launch of the Bologna process, ECTS has increased in importance as a tool, also to assist the development of reformed curricula in the three-cycle structure and to develop more harmonized systems across the European Higher Education Area (EHEA). First and second cycle (Bachelor and Master) degrees from any country within the EHEA would have similar workload and learning outcomes, while the course content would differ between universities and countries.

The introduction of ECTS also facilitates the design of degree programmes made up of 'building blocks' or modules (some compulsory, others optional) that all fit together to create a harmonized degree programme. By unpacking, re-evaluating and re-designing courses so that a 20 credit module, for example, would feel similar across the EHEA, the system aims to create an environment that facilitates flexible learning routes and mobility. The degree might be developed within the same university with a student who takes a module from a different department of faculty; alternatively, a student may choose to study abroad for one or more semesters.

Many, if not all, universities across the former Yugoslav region claim to have implemented ECTS. However, there are countless cases of ECTS being implemented in name rather than in practice. This might mean that a five-year degree course has been squeezed into a three-year programme to fit the Bologna cycle. This results in students often being overloaded by content-driven programmes and examinations, as what was once achieved in four or five years of study has now be done in three years. Moreover, there are no benefits in terms of flexible learning to compensate for these problems. Although ECTS may be used in theory in all the faculties of a university, it will remain impossible for a student to take courses from another faculty.

## Learning outcomes and assessment methods

The development of 'learning outcomes' is an extremely important element of creating a flexible learning environment. Learning outcomes are part of the conceptual model of student-centred higher education. Statements of intended learning outcomes are used to express what students are expected to be able to do at the end of the learning period. Learning outcomes can be generic or subject specific, encompassing skills as well as content and normally addressing the cognitive development for which a certain module would strive. Learning outcomes are important for two main reasons: first, they help to ensure that students come away from a study programme with a range of skills and knowledge to use in future study or in the labour market; secondly, they make it possible for modules to be recognized without content being analysed to see if the modules are identical. The key question for graduates shifts from 'What did you study?' to 'What can you do as a result of your study?'

A range of learning outcomes also calls for a range of teaching and assessment methods. These could encompass such activities as group work, individual research, student presentation of project outcomes as well as more traditional final exams. All too frequently in former Yugoslav universities, a range of assessment methods may be introduced, but they will be added to the original assessment that the course required rather than replacing it. For example, a student may have to give an assessed presentation of a group project, but the final grade will still be determined by a final examination.

### Decentralized higher education institutions

The former Yugoslav university model, with decentralized and autonomous faculties, often remains intact today. Faculties are financially and administratively autonomous and often view any 'interference' from central management – for example, attempts to coordinate the introduction of Bologna reforms – as an unwelcome intrusion on their autonomy. This means that reform is often viewed as being imposed from outside and may be understood as a negative judgement on the quality of learning provision the faculty offers. Hence an atmosphere of distrust and dissatisfaction is often linked to reform efforts.

Some universities are moving towards more centralized systems and are implementing more streamlined approaches. However, these attempts at governance reform are also generally met with resistance from faculty deans anxious to safeguard their power and interests. Over the past decade this has led to university reformers using the term 'integration' rather than 'centralization' as the objective of reforms.

### Outdated pedagogy and assessment

Much old-fashioned pedagogy is still practised in former Yugoslav universities, and there is insufficient focus on developing critical thinkers. All too frequently the dominant educational model is 'one book, one professor, one examination'. Anonymous or blind marking is little practised in universities, with the inevitable consequence that the system is open to malpractice and corruption. Students are often reluctant to speak out or question the system for fear of individual reprisals from 'untouchable' professors. Teacher review by students is also an unusual and often unwelcome practice for many academics.

## Barriers to student mobility

The cosmetic introduction of ECTS, the lack of application in introducing learning outcomes, the lack of transparency in assessment and the tradition of strong, autonomous faculties all create major barriers to student mobility and flexible learning. Notwithstanding the non-enabling higher education laws for mobility, these additional factors mean that it is difficult for students to have a flexible learning route through their own university, or to study abroad.

Internal flexible learning routes are further hampered by decentralized faculties and budgets. Faculties are often not inclined to accept students or staff from other faculties, as demands could be made for compensation in budget or in teaching hours. Meanwhile, the reality that learning undertaken abroad may not be recognized by one's home institution – whether or not the correct formal arrangements for assuring recognition have been made – is a major obstacle to student mobility. Furthermore, because learning outcomes are neither understood nor used, faculties or departments will only accept module credits from abroad if the content is almost a perfect match. This can result in students studying abroad, being assessed abroad and then returning home and then learning new content and being assessed again to gain the same credits.

## Nature and outcomes of international support

The newly independent former Yugoslav nations have been receiving donor aid for education and for higher education, in a number of different forms and from a range of donors over the past 15 years. Although aid in higher education has been intended to support reform efforts, it has not always had the desired outcomes and has sometimes created unwelcome side effects.

In many cases, money intended for reform has been administered by those in the system who are most opposed to change. This has led to reforms being half-heartedly implemented and to most of the aid money being diverted and used for other purposes. Alternatively, positive reform efforts have been initiated through international projects; but, as soon as the international funding is no longer available, the effort also dries up. Sustainability has thus rarely been achieved.

Donor organizations have also arrived with their own 'pet problems' to solve, and this has distorted the nature of reform efforts. In particular, many organizations appear to have believed that what is most urgently needed in the region is the teaching of human rights and of democracy, and a focus on social sciences. While it is evident that the warfare experienced in the region has brought about a crisis in values and culture, it is perhaps misguided to believe that a focus on particular disciplines will be able to address such a complex issue adequately.

Even more problematic than these particular issues has been the rise of a dependency culture in the region. Rather than reform being initiated and developed by the main stakeholders of higher education, too often it is external organizations that have argued the case for reform. As these organizations are evaluated by their success in undertaking and carrying through projects supporting such reform agendas, there has been a tendency for local actors to sit back and leave the work to international players. However, this dynamic is inevitably changing now, as the focus of international organizations moves to other world regions. Having become dependent on external support, how will the region now support itself?

However, the picture is not all black. International support has also, at times, created pressure within the system to deal with many of the obstacles described above. For example, a number of initiatives have been introduced to support student mobility in the region – albeit with mixed results so far. Basileus,[3] CEEPUS[4] and Erasmus Mundus[5] are all organized for students in South East Europe to have study abroad periods, often in the EU states. Students who do go abroad for a semester are frequently exposed to different styles of teaching, learning and assessment methods that focus on a range of learning outcomes. Students are also exposed to the variety of degree programmes, structures and flexible learning paths now common in other parts of Europe.

As described previously, there are often issues with the recognition of study abroad periods even when students depart with a learning agreement signed by their university and the host university. Thanks to internationally funded projects, students are travelling abroad to study in increasing numbers, and this is creating a reality that universities have to deal with when their students return. Thus there is an inside-out movement for reform as students are now going abroad, participating in a different kind of university experience and then returning home. In some cases, these students are demanding that they have fair recognition and the kind of opportunities for flexible learning that other students increasingly take for granted in Europe.

International support has also helped to ease relations between universities or groups that are still operating within difficult political environments. For example, the University of Mitrovica (North Kosovo) considers itself to be part of the Serbian higher education system. However, it is only eligible to receive EU funds under the umbrella of Kosovo (1244).[6] The ministries of education of both Serbia and Kosovo are committed to Bologna reform. Therefore the University of Mitrovica is able to work on its Bologna reform agenda in line with the Serbian ministry's ambitions, while international organizations are able to work with the university on Bologna reform projects with funding earmarked for Kosovo (1244).

Similarly, a number of universities from the region, including the University of Novi Sad (Serbia) and the University of Pristina (Kosovo), have started a joint Masters programme. The Serbian ministry of education does not recognize the University of Pristina or any qualifications that it issues. However, students are enrolled on the course, and this pressure means that the Universities of Novi Sad and Pristina now have to work out a practical solution to this particular issue of recognition.

## The future for higher education in former Yugoslav countries

The biggest problem in thinking about higher education in the future is that no one actually knows what the future has in store. Thus there are two main dangers in future planning. The first is to underestimate how different tomorrow's world may become, and thus to fail to make significant change through lack of vision and ambition. The second is to recognize that change is inevitable, but to make the wrong judgement on the particular reforms needed. As the Danish Nobel-Prize winning physicist Niels Bohr wisely observed: 'prediction is very difficult; especially if it's about the future'.

Nevertheless, at European level, planning for the decade ahead is almost a routine matter – whatever reality subsequently emerges. Thus the European Commission has ambitiously announced a Europe 2020 strategy with sustainable education and growth at its heart. This is a clear continuation of the equally ambitious Lisbon strategy during the first decade of the twenty-first century. Whatever the merits and shortcomings of this new strategy may turn out to be, the former Yugoslav countries would be well advised to become involved in the processes that aim to realize these goals for European development.

There are, of course, many problems to consider. First, the Lisbon strategy that preceded the Europe 2020 strategy was not itself a great success – at least if success is to be judged in terms of achieving the declared goals of Europe becoming 'the most dynamic and competitive knowledge-based economy in the world capable of sustainable economic growth with more and better jobs and greater social cohesion, and respect for the environment by 2010' (European Parliament, 2000). There can be no guarantees that the Europe 2020 strategy will be more successful.

One of the changes that has taken place in the decade between the launch of the Lisbon and Europe 2020 strategies is a greater reliance on benchmarking and target-setting. Thus there are now more moves to measure progress towards benchmarks and targets in education and higher education, and there is no doubt that this is having a considerable impact on policy choices in the EU member states. It is important for the former Yugoslav countries to pay attention to these developments and to develop policy and practice to improve performance in these priority concerns across the continent.

Not only are EU countries setting common targets, they are also beginning to work together in addressing them. This can be seen in peer learning activities at many levels, for instance ministerial or institutional, and through the number of European level professional networks that have been established in recent years. Indeed this developing habit of working together across borders in higher education is a very positive sign of the times in which we live – and the last ten years have seen considerable change in this respect. As the world becomes more globally connected, it is clearly an advantage for Europe to have acquired a decade of experience in working together more closely.

There is still much more to be done if a European Higher Education Area is to become a meaningful reality; but, while acknowledging that creating and developing the European Higher Education Area is the Plan A for the member countries of the Bologna Process, it is important to face up to the reality that there is no Plan B. Indeed if countries fail to make a success of European higher education, it is very likely that, as a consequence, Europe will fall into decline by comparison to other world regions. This is also a reason why the countries of former Yugoslavia should continue to nail their banner to the European mast. They are part of Europe's future, just as Europe is part of theirs.

## Conclusion

The picture that this commentary has painted of the developments in higher education in former Yugoslav countries in the last ten years suggests that there are major steps to be taken and radical reforms to be made if the region is to face up to fast-changing societal realities. This conclusion is not intended to be alarmist, but it should give cause for concern. Many individuals and organizations have expended enormous efforts on trying to reform and modernize higher education in the region. Yet equally there have been many forces in place that have worked as obstacles to positive change. It is important to recognize the progress that has taken place, as well as the mistakes made and failures registered along the way.

The key question today, however, is: what path should be taken for the future? This question could be sub-divided for different organizations and actors. What should the EU and other international organizations be doing? What should national governments be doing? What should the role of higher education institutions be? And what about other societal stakeholders – students, parents, employers, trade unions and so on? While it is neither advisable nor possible for the authors of this article to answer all these questions, we would suggest certain elements for consideration.

First, it is important to work on re-establishing the role of higher education in society. This is a simple statement to write, but one that has enormous implications. Developing the role of higher education means addressing the question of the kind of society in which people would like to live. And that question, difficult anywhere and any time, is particularly difficult in a region where lives have been so much affected by recent history.

It is interesting to note that, during a period of post-conflict reconstruction, this question of the nature of society has often been ignored. This fact is no doubt related to the issue pointed out earlier: that, at first, education itself was also largely ignored in post-conflict nation-building efforts. However, societal development will only succeed if questions of education and higher education systems are given sustained attention.

It is important to look critically at the current reality, and to look forward. At the moment, the higher education systems in former Yugoslav countries are failing many people, and also failing the wider society at large. Overall enrolment rates are low compared to those in most European countries – and many citizens are not being offered the kind of higher education that can help them to develop as individuals and to contribute to societal development in the future. However, even when enrolled in higher education, many students are failing ever to graduate. Given the particular demographic problems of the region, with wildly unbalanced 'brain circulation', this situation of low enrolment and even lower graduation rates can be considered a tragic reality for individuals and for the wider community.

The idea that there is a simple recipe for redressing the weaknesses of higher education should, however, be discounted from the outset. While it is important to identify and discuss weaknesses and problems, it is also important to recognize that higher education development is a dynamic process. It might be theoretically desirable to stop time and undertake a full analysis of all the different issues, but this cannot be done in reality. Hence higher education must be considered as being under permanent construction, hopefully building on the stronger foundations and trying to dislodge the weaker elements of the system that are causing problems. Some fundamental changes are also necessary to the old systems, if the new structures and processes required by the Bologna reforms are to make sense.

For the countries of former Yugoslavia, integration within the EU should be regarded as a major incentive, and indeed the greatest opportunity for building a successful future. The closer the countries of the region coordinate their national policies with the long-term strategies in the EU, and the closer they cooperate with their respective neighbours, the more likely is it that the whole of Europe will become a well-educated and well-trained continent.

Improving quality implies the development of standards and of transparent and efficient models of quality assurance. At the moment, efforts in the region to develop effective quality assurance in higher education have been hampered, because the motivation for such developments is far from being shared. Universities undoubtedly feel threatened and challenged by national projects to establish quality assurance systems, especially as these projects appear often to be pushed and driven by international organizations or other 'external' forces. Yet in the long term it is the universities that stand to gain if they are able to demonstrate high-quality provision and the good use of public and private investment.

We should not, however, give the impression that there are few positive developments to report, or few significant foundations to build upon. On the contrary, the region is rich in human potential, and education holds the key to unlocking this potential and to overcoming the painful legacy of the past. The transition, in these countries, is not only away from a conflict-ridden past to a hopefully peaceful future, but also from a socialist to a market-oriented economy.

For such a transition to be positive, a changed mindset among citizens will be required. Rather than being dependent on the state or on another authority for their educational provision, citizens need to develop a new sense of ownership and responsibility. Often problems of educational institutions are treated as if they could not be changed, and as if the individual were powerless. This attitude needs to change. Each citizen should demand participation and ownership of the educational processes, which are so desperately required by individuals and societies. If such a new attitude to education can evolve, placing creativity and innovation at the heart of educational aspiration, there will again be hope within the region.

The European Higher Education Area is not only – and perhaps not primarily – a physical reality. It is also a symbolic reality for building cohesion, solidarity and quality. The path forward should therefore be, unequivocally, towards European integration, in order for the region to be part of an 'area of hope' for the further development of all levels of education. Both the educational systems and the development of society will be served by a close coordination between the region and the rest of Europe. This should not entail a new form of dependence – following standards and procedures developed elsewhere – but should rather be seen as an active engagement and as a strong commitment of all regional stakeholders to a sustainable and integrated European future.

Finally, in this quest for a renewed understanding of the role of education and higher education, lifelong learning requires particular attention. Higher education institutions cannot ignore their role in lifelong learning if a knowledge-based society is to emerge and thrive. There are many questions about how lifelong learning should be conceived, funded and delivered. These considerations need to be debated and discussed in institutions and in the wider society. However, for the future of the region, the provision of lifelong learning opportunities for all should be considered as a necessity and not as a fantasy.

## Notes

1. For further information on the Bologna Process, see the official website of the Bologna Secretariat www.ehea.info.
2. Information on the development of Yugoslav higher education is drawn from Šoljan (1989).
3. See http://www.basileus.ugent.be/, accessed 15 November 2010.
4. See http://www.ceepus.info/, accessed 15 November 2010.
5. See http://ec.europa.eu/education/external-relation-programmes/doc72_en.htm, accessed 15 November 2010.

6. Kosovo (1244) refers to the United Nations Security Council Resolution 1244, adopted on 10 June 1999, in which international civil and military presence was authorized and the call in previous resolutions for substantial autonomy and meaningful self-administration for Kosovo was reaffirmed.

## References

Bologna Secretariat (2010) 'National Qualifications Frameworks', http://www.ond.vlaanderen.be/hogeronderwijs/bologna/qf/national.asp, accessed 30 November 2010.

Daxner, M. (2006) 'The Balkans on the Way to Europe and to Themselves: An Agenda for Higher Education', Keynote presentation, *European University Association Conference*, Brno.

European Commission (2010a) 'The Diploma Supplement', http://ec.europa.eu/education/lifelong-learning-policy/doc1239_en.htm, accessed 30 November 2010.

European Commission (2010b) 'European Credit Transfer and Accumulation System (ECTS)', http://ec.europa.eu/education/lifelong-learning-policy/doc48_en.htm, accessed 30 November 2010.

European Parliament (2000) *Lisbon European Council 23 and 24 March 2000 Presidency Conclusions*, http://www.europarl.europa.eu/summits/lis1_en.htm, accessed 30 November 2010.

Eurydice (2009) *Key Data on Education in Europe 2009* (Brussels: Eurydice network/Eurostat).

Šoljan, N. N. (ed.) (1989) *Higher Education in Yugoslavia* (Zagreb: Androgoski Centar).

# 17
## Cultural Diversity in South East Europe
*Albert Simkus*

### Introduction

Discussions of cultural differences within South East Europe could cover many dimensions of culture, but this chapter will focus on three topics: first, the main divisions with regard to ethnic identities and their bases; second, some of the most important causes of cultural differences both between and within ethnic groups, on the basis of previously published research; and, third, evidence from social surveys about differences in attitudes and values across countries and ethnic groups in the South East Europe (SEE) region within their European contexts, paying particular attention to the complicated situation in the Western Balkans. The differences in attitudes and values concentrate on religiosity, moral values, gender role attitudes and attitudes towards ethnic relations.

South East Europe, as it is defined in this book, includes Albania, Bosnia and Herzegovina, Bulgaria, Croatia, Kosovo, Hungary, Macedonia, Moldova, Montenegro, Romania, Serbia and Slovenia. It should be noted that, while there is a general acceptance of this phrase and definition of the region, there are various national sensitivities and varying degrees of acceptance of the label (Ballinger, 1999; Bracewell and Drace-Frances, 1999; Schöpflin, 1999). Obviously, this definition does not perfectly follow geographical lines, either in terms of physical geography or in terms of historical contexts. Certainly most Hungarians now describe Hungary as belonging to Central Europe, much like Austria, which is not much more northern than Hungary. Slovenia and perhaps Croatia might also be considered more Central European than either East European or Southern European. Both share degrees of latitude with northern Italy and southern France, and degrees of longitude with Austria. Geographically, the exclusion of Greece might seem odd. In terms of political and economic integration within Europe, Slovenia, Hungary and gradually also Croatia are more tied to Central Europe than to the Balkans. For that matter, the precise definition of the 'Balkans' and characterizations of the 'Western' and 'Eastern' Balkans are also matters of disagreement and controversy, particularly in Croatia and Romania.

The definition of South East Europe is partly based on two additional aspects of these countries. First, all these states were previously dominated by state socialist political and economic systems. This had the consequence that they were, to varying degrees, isolated from political, economic and cultural integration with Western Europe during 1945–90. However, these countries had also been differentiated from the more 'Western' Europe prior to the establishment of socialist regimes following the Second World War.[1] Second, the regional distinction of South East Europe is also clearly related to divisions among major ethnic and language groups. The region involves countries in which the dominant languages are Albanian, Hungarian, Romanian and Southern Slavic, without counterparts in the more Western and northern European countries. There are also differences related to predominant religious denominations, although these differences are more mixed and ambiguous.

Thus the definition of South East Europe is cultural as well as geographic; at the same time, this region is deeply divided within itself culturally, partly on the basis of differences among countries and partly on the basis of ethnic divisions within these countries. The situation is complex, because cultural differences in this region are partly country-based, partly based on ethnic affiliation and partly caused by the interaction between the two – differences in ethnic groups within different state contexts and histories.

## The main bases of cultural differentiation in South East Europe

### Major ethnic groups

The predominant basis of cultural differentiation is determined and manifested by differences between ethnic groups, the distinctions between these ethnic groups being based on language, religion and history. Most of the SEE countries are now characterized by having a large single dominant ethnic majority constituting about 65–95 per cent of the population. The exception to this generalization is Bosnia and Herzegovina, where the largest group, Bosniaks, comprises approximately 47 per cent of the population, Serbs represent a large, second major minority of about 37 per cent and Croats are a third substantial minority of about 13 per cent. These percentages are approximate and controversial, given the absence of a recent census for Bosnia and Herzegovina as well as a substantial amount of cross-border fluidity in residence, particularly of Croats, and to a lesser extent also of Serbs.

At this point it makes sense to stress the meaning of the terms 'nation', 'nationality' and 'national' in this regional context, in contrast to conventions in more multiethnic states such as the US. Internationally, it is common to equate 'nation' with either 'nation–state' or 'country'. In this region, 'nationality' is generally equated with 'ethnic group' rather than with 'country', although this varies somewhat with the degree to which a country is ethnically homogeneous and is the only country in which that 'nationally' is numerically and politically dominant. There is also sometimes a distinction between 'national minorities' versus other smaller minorities, an important issue in arguments about constitutions in some of these countries.

Within the larger set of South East European states with majority nationalities, a distinction can be made between three groups of countries: (1) those without any *individual* ethnic minority reaching more than about 6 per cent of the population – Albania, Croatia, Kosovo, Hungary, Montenegro, Serbia and Slovenia; (2) those with ethnic minorities which are relatively small, 6 to 10 per cent, but large enough to be politically important, particularly with regard to relations with their ethnic kin in neighbouring countries – in Bulgaria, Moldova and Romania; and (3) Macedonia, with an Albanian minority of approximately 24 per cent, sizeable enough to be essential in maintaining social cooperation and even peace. Of course, in some countries, such as Croatia and Kosovo, this 6 per cent distinction is partly the result of coerced migrations of ethnic Serbs during the last two decades. Furthermore, the precise percentages of various ethnic groups are a matter of some debate and imprecision within a few percentage points. The distinction between these three main groups of countries in terms of ethnic diversity is simply intended to provide a way of simplifying differences in the situations of these 12 diverse countries.

In this discussion, the situation of Montenegrins is relatively special, in that large proportions of the Orthodox Serbian-speaking citizens of Montenegro have identified themselves either as ethnic 'Serbs' or as 'Montenegrins'. The percentage identifying themselves as one or the other has varied over the years, and the importance of the ethnic distinction has long been a subject of debate. These two groups are not distinguished mainly by differences in religious denomination, nor by a major language division (though linguistic differences exist and are given increasing political significance), but on historically based differences in self-identification.

The map in Figure 17.1 displays the geographic distribution of the major ethnic groups in the countries where ethnic composition is most complicated. This map does not indicate regions of ethnic groups for Hungary, Moldova and Slovenia; these three countries are relatively homogeneous ethnically, characterized by overwhelming majorities of Hungarians, Romanians/Moldovans and Slovenes, respectively. Nevertheless, there are significant concentrations of minorities in small regions of these countries, particularly in Moldova. Working in regions of particular countries, it is easy to find more detailed information on the distributions of the smaller local minorities, best from census data, which are often available through the Internet.

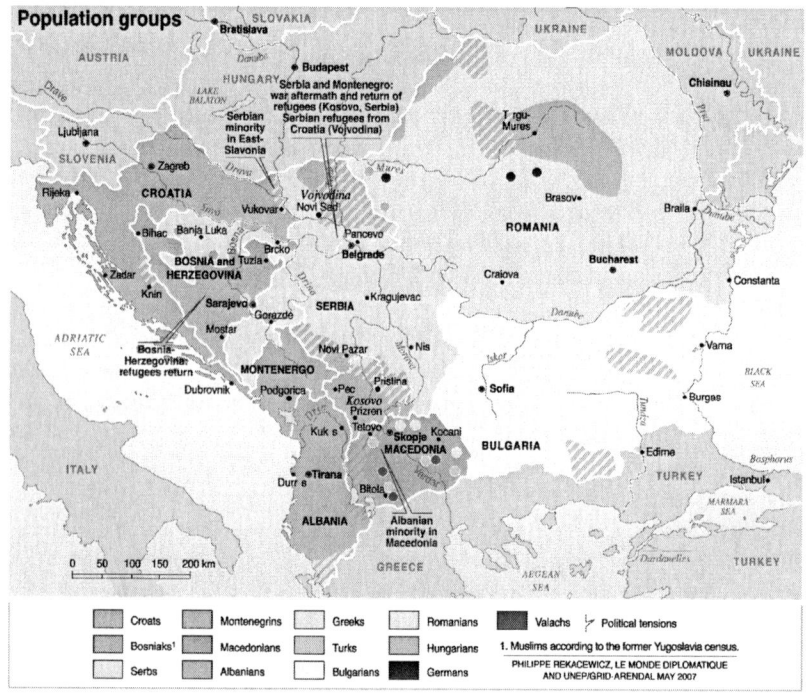

*Figure 17.1* The distribution of ethnic group concentrations in South East Europe (excluding Slovenia, Hungary and Moldova)
*Source*: UNEP/GRID-Arendal (GRIDA, 2007).

There are ten major ethnic groups in the region: Albanians, Bosniaks, Bulgarians, Croats, Hungarians, Macedonians, Montenegrins, Romanians, Serbs and Slovenes. These groups are clearly differentiated on the basis of language, particularly the distinctly different languages of Albanian, Hungarian, Romanian as well as the Southern Slavic languages of Bulgarian, Bosnian, Croatian, Macedonian, Serbian and Slovenian. There is no mutual intelligibility among the four main language groups of Albanian, Hungarian, Romanian and Southern Slavic languages, although they share many words.

Mutual intelligibility among the Southern Slavic languages varies. It is an issue of debate and has changed with the political and ethnic subdivision of the former Republic of Yugoslavia. Many passionate debates about differences among the Bosnian, Croatian and Serbian languages have raged without the necessity of translators. Mutual intelligibility between Slovenian and Croatian, as well as between Macedonian and both Serbian and Bulgarian, is lower and commonly reported to be asymmetric, Slovenes reporting that they understand Croats better than the other way around, and similarly with Macedonians understanding Serbian better than Serbs understand Macedonian.[2]

The dialects of Eastern Macedonian are similar to Bulgarian. While distinctions are made between the dominant Romanian language dialects of Romania and Moldova, they are generally considered to belong to a common Romanian language. There are significant differences in dialects within the major languages, but they are generally not associated with great cultural–political divisions, except to the degree that they are associated with divisions based on region, clan or state sovereignty, such as in the case of ethnic Albanians.

Religious denomination is a second basis for differentiation between the major ethnic groups, the four major religions of the region being Orthodox Christian, Muslim, Protestant and Roman Catholic. While the major ethnic groups are homogeneous with regard to language, some are heterogeneous with regard to religion. Slovenes and Croats are overwhelmingly Roman Catholic, while Hungarians, though predominantly Catholic, also include a substantial minority of Protestants, who are in turn subdivided into a majority of Calvinists and a minority of Lutherans. While there are significant differences among Catholics and Protestants in Hungary, this division is not a source of major cultural divisions among Hungarians to the extent of producing serious conflict.

Bulgarians, Macedonians, Moldovans, Montenegrins, Romanians and Serbs are overwhelmingly Orthodox, while Bosniaks are overwhelmingly Muslim, although the importance and meaning of this subjective identification as Muslim, to persons themselves as well as to others, varies immensely. While ethnic Albanians are predominantly Muslim, they also include important minorities of Albanian Orthodox, Roman Catholics and non-believers, particularly within Albania.

Beyond this general description, two further points should be made about the role of religion regarding cultural differences in the region. First, within these major religious denominations there are significant divisions related to national identity. The Orthodox Church is administratively and politically divided on the basis of nationality, and in both Macedonia and Montenegro there is conflict and competition between the Serbian Orthodox Church and the Macedonian and the Montenegrin Orthodox churches. Among Albanian Muslims, the majority are Sunni, but there is an important Bektashi minority, particularly in Albania. These divisions are of some significance for political views and values, but not a general threat to cooperation and peace. Second, as will be shown and discussed later in this chapter, different ethnic groups sharing the same religious identity show substantial differences in the intensity and orthodoxy of their religiosity. Roman Catholics show significant differences in doctrinal orthodoxy and intensity of belief among those living in Hungary, Slovenia, Croatia and Herzegovina. South-East European Social Survey Project (SEESSP) data (Simkus, 2007a, 2007b) show Croatian Catholics in Bosnia and Herzegovina to be most devout, Catholic Croats in Croatia less so and Slovenes and Hungarians even less so, while Montenegrins are apparently less religious than self-identifying Serbs in Montenegro, Kosovo and the Republika Srpska. In Bosnia and the Sandžak region of Montenegro and Serbia there are significant frictions between very secular and very orthodox Sunni Muslims. Thus the significance of religious differences for cultural differentiation in this region involves the importance of religiosity as well as differences among denominations and divisions within denominations.

A third basis for cultural differentiation grounded in ethnicity and country is historical context. Here the most important causal factors are related to the history of earlier inclusions of areas and populations in large empires and to the recent contexts of ethnic groups within different states. Among the most important older historical divisions are those related to the regions and periods, in this region, of control and independence from the Austrian/Austro-Hungarian, Ottoman and Russian empires, from the sixteenth up to early twentieth centuries. The Austrian and Austro-Hungarian territories of Slovenia, Hungary, Croatia and parts of present-day Romania (Transylvania) and Serbia (Vojvodina) were associated with the influence of the Roman Catholic Church and to a lesser extent of Protestantism, as well as with a more Western cultural orientation.

The Ottoman Empire had, together with the Orthodox Church, great influence on the Southern Balkan territories of Serbia, Bosnia, Macedonia, Bulgaria and parts of Romania. Some areas, such as Montenegro and parts of Dalmatia on the Croatian coast, enjoyed long periods of independence or of Venetian influence. The Russian Empire often controlled the territory of present-day Moldova. Various territories within these empires experienced quite different forms of rule, as well as 'parcelized sovereignty'. The details of the historical situation in the various regions are simply far too complex to be discussed here, since borders often changed, as did the various meanings of 'autonomy' and 'domination' for the resident populations.

The gradual dissolution of the Ottoman and Austro-Hungarian empires from the nineteenth century up until the end of the First World War gradually established Albanian, Bulgarian, Romanian and Serbian independence, the formation of the problematic new independent and combined state of the Southern Slavs – Yugoslavia – and the transfer of Transylvania, with its considerable Hungarian population, to Romanian control. The vicious large-scale interethnic conflict during the Second World War exacerbated already formidable animosity among nationalities within Yugoslavia.

The more recent historical circumstances of the period from the end of the Second World War up until 1990 involved significant, not to be forgotten differences among the socialist states of the period. Albania was very isolated from all other socialist regimes of this region (though variously associated with the Soviet Union and China), as it was isolated from the rest of the world and also from the Albanian communities in Kosovo and Macedonia. Under Enver Hoxha, the Albanian state experienced exceptionally severe religious repression and various measures of Stalinist and Maoist policies.[3] It should not be forgotten that there were very significant differences among 'communist' regimes in South East Europe, across both countries and historical periods.

The Republic of Yugoslavia was, within this group of countries, relatively more tolerant concerning religion, less politically repressive and had stronger relations with Western Europe. At a relatively early stage, and more so during subsequent historical periods, the post–Second World War Yugoslav state promoted ethnic tolerance, decentralization and cooperation within its territory. These positive aspects are criticized by those who emphasize that this state repressed democracy, 'national' identities, independence and the economic growth of its richer republics. This is quite true, while it is also true that Yugoslav policies were less repressive than those of other socialist states. This has continuing consequences. There is a degree of 'Tito nostalgia' through-out much of the territory of the former Republic of Yugoslavia, which has no full equivalent in terms of retained or revived warm feelings about other former socialist leaders in other countries of South East Europe.

The countries of Hungary, Romania and Bulgaria conformed to a more orthodox Soviet form of Socialism by comparison to Yugoslavia, but each featured varying degrees of cooperation with the West, internal repression and socialist economic orthodoxy. By the 1980s, Hungary had the most reformed economy and connections to the West, while Romania combined some international political independence with a Stalinist economic system, severe internal repression and strong policies to force the integration of the Hungarian minority into the ethnic Romanian majority. Bulgaria was a more typical Soviet Bloc state, while Moldova belonged to the Soviet Union and existed under direct Russian/Soviet control. The political division between Romania and the Soviet Union reinforced differences between Romanians and Moldovans, even though they are generally understood to belong to the same ethnic group.

The history of the most recent period, particularly 1990–2002, has been of great importance, especially for the successor states of the former Republic of Yugoslavia. The multiethnic state divided into seven states, which resulted in the formation of independent states of largely homo-geneous nationalities, accompanied by open warfare, especially between Croats and Serbs in Croatia, Bosniaks, Croats and Serbs in Bosnia and Herzegovina and Albanians and Serbs in Kosovo. Slovenia experienced a relatively brief and moderate military struggle for independence, while Macedonia was exposed to a relatively limited period of internal civil conflict between ethnic Macedonians and ethnic Albanians. Serbia suf-fered bombing by Western military forces, and Montenegrin and Serb soldiers were involved in fighting in Bosnia and Herzegovina and in Croatia.

The impact of these conflicts on current ethnic and cross-country relations may be interpreted as being a result of the recent character of the specific conflicts, of the intensity of conflicts and of the degree to which the political issues upon which the conflicts were based have been resolved. The most serious divisions within these countries now are those in Bosnia and Herzegovina between the Bosniak-Croat Fed-eration and the Republika Srpska. In Kosovo, the divisions between Albanians and Serbs lack political settlement. The two societies are nearly completely segregated, but there is an evidently inevitable *de facto* peaceful segregated co-existence in the absence of other alternatives acceptable for both sides. In Macedonia, the ethnic Macedonian and ethnic Albanian communities remain significantly socially separated; but, despite concerns about possible conflict, peace and a degree of economic and political integration seem secure.

In addition to the animosity caused or reinforced by these conflicts, these events are important in two other ways. They were accompanied by substantial migrations, which – while followed by significant return migration – still involve substantial numbers of persons forced from their former homes and territories and facing considerable insecurity, antagonism and difficulty in returning to their former homes. This concerns especially Serbs forced from Croatia and Kosovo and Bosniaks forced from the Republika Srpska.

Finally, there are several countries in which large ethnic minorities significantly differ culturally from the members of the same ethnic groups living in those countries where they are the dominant ethnic majority. Examples of such groups are ethnic Croats living in Bosnia and Herzegovina compared to Croats living in Croatia; Serbs living in Republika Srpska, Kosovo and Montenegro compared with those living in Serbia; Bosniaks living in the Sandžak region of Serbia and Montenegro compared to Bosniaks in Bosnia and Herzegovina; and Albanians living in Macedonia and Kosovo compared to each other, as well as compared to Albanians in Albania. These significant local minorities share the same language and often the same religious denomination as members of the same ethnic group living in the countries in which they are the dominant ethnic group. However, at the same time, compared to those living in the countries in which they are dominant, they show higher levels of ethnic intolerance and social distance related to other ethnic groups and they tend to be more conservative in their social values and more religious.

It is undoubtedly true that these differences are partly due to the fact that these large local minorities occupy regions that are peripheral to the main political and economic centres and are relatively rural. However, in multivariate social survey analyses, these differences are still substantial, even after controlling for rural residence and levels of education. This lends credence to the interpretation that these differences are also related to the fact that these groups are relatively isolated, feel threatened by being minorities within their states, yet are large enough and sufficiently concentrated within relatively small geographic regions to develop strong feelings of solidarity and social cohesion as regional communities.

The role of geographical and political boundaries has been important in some aspects of cultural differentiation in the region. The immense degree of political and social isolation of Albania from the rest of Europe, even from Yugoslavia, contributed to cultural differences between Albanians in Albania versus Albanians in former Yugoslavia, whose consequences are palpable even today. Geographical obstacles, particularly in the form of formidable mountain barriers, contributed to differences among Albanians in Kosovo, Macedonia and Albania. Mountainous terrain also contributed to Montenegrin independence and identity. Also, the Carpathian mountains in Romania were important in maintaining the social identity of the Hungarian population in Transylvania and the cohesion of the small Hungarian sub-group of the Székely.

## Smaller ethnic minorities within these countries

Thus far, distinctions among the largest national ethnic groups have been discussed. Before we end this discussion of cultural diversity based on ethnic groups, the significance of relatively small ethnic minorities in South East Europe, which add to the cultural diversity in the region, ought to be mentioned. These groups may be more important than their numbers might suggest and are linked to serious issues of discrimination and violence (this is most true of the Roma). They may also play a role as minority supporters of political coalitions in cases when national political groups are divided and deadlocked. These groups may band together for various political aims, and they can be internationally important with regard to political and economic relations with various countries. These groups generally constitute 1 to 6 per cent of the national populations in their respective countries.

These smaller ethnic minority groups include the Roma ('Gypsy' or 'Cigany') populations, forming about 1 to 4 per cent of the population mainly in Bulgaria, Macedonia, Hungary, Romania and Serbia. They speak various dialects of Romani and local languages, many live residentially segregated and they experience a high degree of discrimination, or even violent attacks. Jews are a very small minority in the region, and most of them live in Hungary, in the vicinity of Budapest. Slovenia has small populations of Croats, Bosniaks, Serbs, Hungarians and Italians. Croatia has a reduced Serbian minority of about 6 per cent. Montenegro has significant populations of Bosniaks (about 8 per cent) and Albanians (about 5 per cent). Serbia has a significant minority of Bosniaks, mainly in the Sandžak region in the south-west of the country, and significant Hungarian, Slovak and Croat communities in Vojvodina in the north.

Macedonia, in addition to its much larger Albanian minority, has significant communities of Turks, Serbs and Muslim Slavs. It is important to recognize that there are several groups of non-Albanian, Slavic-speaking Muslim Slavs in the Southern Balkans, mainly in Bulgaria, Macedonia and Kosovo, in addition to the Bosniaks. These include Pomaks, Torbeši and Gorani. Other small ethnic groups in the region include Vlachs and Ruthenians. Albania has a very small Greek population, mostly concentrated in the South. Romania has a relatively large Hungarian minority population of about 8 per cent, mostly concentrated in Transylvania. Moldova has significantly large minorities of Ukrainians, Russians, Gagauz (a Turkic group) and Bulgarians, concentrated by region.

Living and working in small geographical areas where such groups are prevalent, or working with colleagues from these ethnic groups, it would be wise to develop knowledge and appreciation of these groups. Such appreciation will undoubtedly be appreciated in return by colleagues and local residents. One on one, few people expressing aforementioned identities will be reluctant to educate outsiders about their group. Additionally, while such an education can be biased or inaccurate, there is not a great wealth of published expertise on these matters, especially in English. So efforts to understand, braced with a little scepticism and openness to listen to various views, will be very rewarding.

Unfortunately, while these groups are interesting and important, their small sizes make it impossible to compare them using large-scale public opinion surveys; they are more amenable to small-scale qualitative ethnographic studies, which are too numerous and detailed for this chapter. In large-scale surveys, analyses of differences across ethnic groups tend to find respondents in the smallest groups to be more ethnically tolerant than members of major minorities. It is not possible to tell whether this is because small, dispersed minorities wish and need to assimilate, whether members of such groups are more comfortable belonging to very small and politically unimportant minorities or whether such respondents are rarely interviewed in large national surveys by an interviewer of their group and are therefore more reluctant to express strong minority views.

## Diversity based on levels of economic and social development

Cultural diversity in this region is not only based on military history, language and religion, but also on levels and forms of economic and social development. Very important factors in the cultural differentiation of these countries and of major ethnic groups within these countries are the differences in the levels of industrialization, wealth, education, urbanization, per capita GDP, cosmopolitanism and modernization. Theories of modernization have a relatively long and complex history, but the contributions of Ronald Ingelhart and his colleagues are among the more recent, complex and influential, and they are well verified by empirical cross-national, cross-cohort and time-series comparisons across a wide group of countries (Inglehart and Baker, 2000; Inglehart and Norris, 2003; Welzel et al., 2003; Norris and Inglehart, 2004, 2009).

Inglehart and his colleagues have presented a cultural map of the world in which countries are located in two dimensions: (1) the prevalence of values of survival versus self-expression and (2) traditional versus rational–secular values (Inglehart and Norris, 2003). The central factor in survival values versus self-expression values reflects materialist versus post-materialist values. Post-materialist values have increased as survival values have decreased, in relation to increasing levels of economic and material conditions and decreasing levels of concern about personal and economic survival security. The increases in economic and material security are based partly on improvements in national wealth and income, but also on improvements in social welfare protections, medical care and lessened dangers of suffering from natural disasters and war.

The dimension of traditional versus secular–rational reflects contrasting value systems found in religious versus secular societies. As Ingelhart and Norris state:

> Traditional societies emphasize the importance of parent–child ties in traditional families and deference to authority, along with absolute moral standards, and they reject divorce, abortion, euthanasia, and suicide. Traditional societies are highly patriotic and nationalistic. Societies with secular – rational values display the opposite preferences on all these topics.
>
> (Inglehart and Norris, 2003, pp. 153–4)

Increases in rational–secular versus traditional values are seen as being closely related to the shift from agricultural to industrial societies, while increases in self-expression versus survival values are seen as being associated with the shift from industrial to post-industrial information societies. Both dimensions are related to general levels of socio-economic development. In cross-sectional, cross-national comparisons, countries with higher levels of economic and social development – measured by indices such as the Human Development Index, GDP, life expectancy, the dependency ratio, divorce rates, percentage urban population or the percentage of GDP from services – are strongly positively correlated with higher values on both scales of values: rational–secular versus traditional, and self-expression versus survival. Time-series analyses lead to the same conclusions. This empirical research is based on the extensive cross-national survey data of the European and World Values surveys,[4] covering a large number of countries from around the world.

In the cultural map of the world presented in this body of research, the formerly communist countries fall into the upper left quadrant, scoring high on secular–rational values but low on self-expression values. On this cultural map, high on the vertical, secular–rational dimension lie Japan, Sweden, Norway, East Germany, the Czech Republic, Denmark, Germany, China, South Korea, Estonia, Bulgaria, Russia, Ukraine and Belarus; slightly lower on this dimension are the South East European countries of Slovenia, Montenegro, Serbia, Albania, Moldova, Hungary, Macedonia, Croatia, Bosnia and Herzegovina and Romania (ranking from highest to lowest on secular–rational values in the order listed).

On the horizontal dimension representing survival versus self-expression values, the countries of South East Europe are relatively low on self-expression values in general. Among the SEE countries, Slovenia, Croatia, Bosnia and Herzegovina, Serbia, Montenegro, Macedonia, Hungary, Albania, Bulgaria, Romania and Moldova rank in order of decreasing self-expressive and increasing survival values. South East European countries exhibit lower self-expression values than the clusters of countries formed by English-speaking countries, Protestant Europe, Catholic Europe and 'Confucian' countries.

Inglehart and Norris (2003, 2004) stress that the clustering of countries on their cultural map of values seems to reflect the importance of factors in addition to economic development. In particular, they point out groupings based on religious denominations, such as predominantly Protestant and predominantly Catholic countries in Europe, suggesting that religious traditions may determine different 'path-dependent' trajectories of change. They also point out histories of socialist rule as another mitigating influence in the overall pattern of change along these value dimensions.

Some methodological caveats should be added before drawing too many conclusions out of small country differences on this 'cultural map'. First, it is possible that there are significant problems with data quality and comparability, particularly in the poorest and most socially disrupted countries in the Balkans; second, the precise confidence intervals for these estimates are not specified in graphic displays of the range of differences among countries; third, in the past, Kosovo has not been included independently but in conjunction with Serbia; and, fourth, these are all estimates for countries as wholes, thereby obscuring some very significant differences within the countries. Recent research has pointed out substantial variation between major ethnic groups in Bosnia and Herzegovina as well as in Macedonia, where minority groups are large and quite different from each other. In general, the World/European Values Survey data have not involved large enough samples to provide reliable estimates for the larger ethnic groups in these two countries. In this chapter we take advantage of the larger sample sizes for groups within the Western Balkans available in the South East European Social Survey Project data[5] to illustrate the differences among ethnic groups also within countries in the Western Balkans.

A number of recent studies have compared various civic and cultural values in the Western Balkan countries to those in other European countries, combining data from the SEESSP with data from the International Social Survey Programme (ISSP) and from the European Social Survey (ESS) (Listhaug et al., 2010; Ringdal et al., under review). These comparative studies have shown clear differences in values associated with national differences in Human Development Index (HDI) scores.

Thus far, the discussion of cultural differences in South East Europe has focused on differences across countries and ethnic groups as whole populations, differences based largely on language, religion, group history and economic development. Nevertheless, attention must also be given to the possibilities of cultural divisions *within* countries, between ethnic groups and between ethnic groups within countries. Specifically, there may be important divisions within the countries – constituting to some degree 'sub-cultures' – differences based on age groups associated with birth cohorts, which are sometimes imprecisely referred to as 'generations'. As can be shown for values such as nationalism, authoritarianism, traditionalism in sexual mores, traditionalism in gender role attitudes or in attitudes towards state egalitarian policies, there are important divisions based on levels of education, age and urban versus rural residence (Simkus, 2007b; Brajdić-Vuković and Stulhofer (under review); Pesić (under review); Simkus (under review a, under review b).

These three variables – age, education and size of place of residence – involve individual demographic divisions within SEE countries associated with differences in cultural attitudes and values within countries and between ethnic groups. Certainly within the Western Balkans, these individual demographic characteristics have different degrees of importance, depending on the specific kind of attitude or value being considered. Education is most important in terms of attitudes towards gender roles, while ethnicity is most important in terms of attitudes towards ethnic relations. In general, in multivariate analyses of value differences in the Western Balkans, education is most important, followed by age and residence, and all three have significant independent effects. As might be expected, higher education, younger age and urban residence are associated with lower than average measures of nationalism, authoritarianism, gender role traditionalism and sex-related moral values (Simkus, under review b). The relationship of these demographic variables to ethnic exclusionism and religiosity is less strong but varies across groups, and deserves more attention to detail than is possible here.

## Cultural diversity described in previous survey analyses

Descriptions of cultural diversity are enhanced by including comparative contextual perspectives. Three contexts are important here: first, the distribution of South East European country populations relative to other European state-defined populations; second, the range of differences among countries in South East Europe; third, differences between major ethnic groups within these countries, which may be as large as, or even larger than, cross-country differences. Four databases are available for such comparisons, each with possibilities for wider comparisons and each with possibilities for studying smaller groupings within these countries, especially within the Western Balkans.

Unfortunately, different international social survey projects are differently suited for measuring these different dimensions. In some cases the survey questions and scales for dimensions differ to varying degrees; in other cases the questionnaire items are quite different across survey projects and across the different topics included in specific survey waves. The comparisons presented here are based on cross-national and cross-group differences from a few individual questions that allow comparisons among European countries in the survey of the European Social Survey Project (ESS),[6] wave 4, conducted in 2008, the European surveys of the International Social Survey Project (ISSP),[7] wave of 2002 (family and gender roles) and the South East European Social Survey Project (SEESSP), conducted in 2003–04.[8]

These comparisons involve merging data for individual countries that were available for a broad range of European countries in the ESS and ISSP projects with data for Croatia, Bosnia and Herzegovina, Montenegro, Serbia, Kosovo, Macedonia and Albania only available in the SEESSP. And, as indicated earlier, while cross-national comparative data were available from the European Values Surveys, they were judged as less reliable for measuring values among ethnic minorities within the Western Balkans.[9] Differences among ethnic groups within countries will be shown for the Western Balkans (mainly an issue in Bosnia and Herzegovina, Macedonia and Kosovo) on the basis of the SEESSP data. Moldova is the only country thus far not included in the ESS, ISSP or SEESSP, although it is included in the World Values Survey (WVS). The WVS-based comparisons of Inglehart and Norris (2003) can be used to locate the general position of Moldova relative to the other South East European countries on the values of religiosity and gender role traditionalism.

As Inglehart and colleagues have stressed religiosity, sexual mores, gender role attitudes and attitudes towards marriage as basic measures of traditionalism, we will concentrate on such values. In addition, for the Western Balkan countries, we examine questions related to ethnic relations. The following discussion is divided into two sections. First we describe differences reported in previous social survey analyses. Second we present figures showing comparative differences for some specific variables for these countries.

### Generalizations based on earlier research, primarily for the Western Balkans

*Religiosity*

The wide set of comparisons has the advantage of placing nearly all the South East European countries within the comparative context of cross-national differences regarding religious fervour within Europe. This is possible by using published comparisons from the World Values Surveys as well as individual-level data merged between the surveys of the European Social Surveys of the mid-2000s and the SEESSP surveys.

On the basis of a scale of average strength of religiosity, for countries included in the World Values Surveys, Inglehart and Norris (2003) presented cross-national differences among 75 countries during 1981–2001.

In a broad global perspective, the countries of South East Europe roughly fall in the middle of the distribution of all countries under investigation, generally being more religious than countries in North West Europe and China, yet less religious than most of the non-European and less developed countries. However, there are very significant differences among the South East European countries also: Romania is most religious by far. In order of decreasing religiosity, Bosnia and Herzegovina, Croatia, Moldova, Albania, Macedonia, Serbia, Slovenia, Montenegro and Hungary follow, Bulgaria being the least religious country in the region.

As it was measured in the SEESSP surveys, the intensity of religiosity varies much between ethnic groups by country within the Western Balkans, ethnic Albanians in Macedonia being more religious than their ethnic kin in Kosovo and more likely to go to the mosque regularly (Simkus, 2007b). Ethnic Albanians in Albania are the least religious Albanians in the Western Balkans, measured by both belief and religious observance. This fact should not be oversimplified as a result of the extremely religiously repressive policies of the former Hoxha regime. The anti-religious repression of the Hoxha regime and the relatively weak embrace of conservative movements within Islam after the end of that regime are at least partly explained by the division of Albanians among Sunni, Bektashi, Orthodox, Roman Catholics and sceptics, and by an overwhelming devotion to Albanianism beyond sectarianism. Orthodox Southern Slavs tend to go to church less often than Catholics in Croatia and Herzegovina, and less often than men go to mosque in Macedonia. Roman Catholic Croats in Bosnia and Herzegovina attend church more often than any other group attends church or mosque apart from Albanians in Macedonia, and significantly more often than Croats in Croatia.

### Attitudes towards gender roles

Using data from the World Values Surveys, Inglehart and Norris (2003) reported cross-national differences on a scale of attitudes towards gender equality for 61 nations during 1995–2001. On average, the countries of South East Europe fall into the middle of the distribution of all countries internationally. Among European countries, they are relatively traditional. However, there are significant differences between the countries of South East Europe: Slovenia, followed by Croatia and Macedonia, are least traditional, while Moldova is by far the most traditional, followed by Romania. The other countries of South East Europe lie between these two extremes: listed in order of increasing traditionalism are Serbia, Bulgaria, Hungary, Albania and Montenegro.

Pesić (under review) reports differences among Western Balkan countries on two scales of attitudes towards gender roles and women's employment on the basis of the SEESSP data of 2003–04. In multivariate regression analyses controlling for individual differences based on education, age, urban versus rural residence and religiosity, she finds attitudes to be most traditional in Albania and Kosovo and most liberal in Croatia. Using somewhat different scales for gender role attitudes, multivariate analyses controlling for age, education and urban versus rural residence and the SEESSP data, Simkus (2007b, under review b) reports substantial differences within countries that are based on ethnic groups within the Western Balkan countries. Albanians in Macedonia, Kosovo and Albania are all among the most traditional, while Croats in Croatia are the least traditional. Within Bosnia and Herzegovina, ethnic Croats are the most traditional, ethnic Serbs least so, while Bosniaks rank between the other two groups.

*Attitudes towards sexual behaviour and marriage*

Attitudes towards sexual behaviour and marital mores are closely associated with religiosity. The evolution of these mores across age cohorts and ethnic groups by country is rather complicated and would demand a careful book rather than a chapter. Initial analyses of the SEESSP data seemed to indicate rather different patterns among different ethnic groups, which could not be described adequately in this chapter. There seems to be some evidence that religious mores have consolidated somewhat in the Croatian populations of Bosnia and Herzegovina, younger Croats being slightly more religiously traditional and morally conservative than younger Serbs in Republik Srbska and Muslims in Bosnia and Herzegovina lying in between (Simkus, under review a).

In the Western Balkans, the most conservative sex-related mores were observed for Albanians in Kosovo, Macedonia and Albania, in that order. The least conservative sexual mores were observed among Croats in Croatia, Serbs in Bosnia and Herzegovina, Montenegrins in Montenegro and Serbs in Serbia, which were not significantly different among themselves (Simkus, 2007b). Using a slightly different scale and a much larger portion of the SEESSP sample, slightly different conclusions were reached, with Kosovar and Macedonian Albanians still most conservative, but with Croats in Croatia being significantly more liberal than Serbs and Montenegrins (Simkus, under review b). Serbs in Kosovo,

Bosniaks in Serbia and Montenegro and Albanians in Montenegro were found to be strikingly conservative.

Attitudes towards homosexuality are a strong indicator of traditionalism in attitudes towards sexual mores. Brajdić-Vuković and Stulhofer (under review) present analyses comparing differences among Western Balkan countries in the SEESSP project, together with comparisons of these countries with Hungary and Slovenia in South East Europe, along with Portugal, Slovakia, Great Britain, France, Austria, the Czech Republic and the Netherlands. These comparisons are based on combining data from SEESSP (2003–04), the ESS (2002–03) and the ISSP (1998–99). They find the seven Western Balkan countries to show the highest homonegativity of all sixteen countries observed. Slovenia and Hungary show lower levels of homonegativity than the Western Balkan countries, but higher than the more Western European countries. Among the Western Balkan countries, Croatia showed the lowest level of homonegativity and Kosovo the highest.

*Ethnic tolerance and exclusionism*

A quite long tradition of survey research has tracked attitudes towards ethnic exclusionism, which is sometimes labeled 'ethnic intolerance', among groups in the Western Balkans since the late 1980s (Hodson et al., 1994; Sekulić et al., 2006; Simkus, 2007b; Strabac and Ringdal, 2008; Ellingsen et al., under review; Simkus, under review b). The questionnaire items for these attitudes reflect scepticism about interethnic marriage, security in mixed communities and the desire for national states rather more than for 'ethnic cleansing', although there is obviously some relation between feelings towards the three. There have been rather many analyses of such attitudes in the Western Balkans from the late 1990s up until at least 2004. The most detailed series of cross-sectional surveys has been conducted in Croatia, and to a lesser extent in Serbia during the last 15 to 20 years. For the other countries in the region, analyses of changes over time are restricted to comparisons of only two time points – the late 1980s, just prior to the break-up of Yugoslavia, and the period of the SEESSP surveys in 2003–04. Unfortunately, similar questions about ethnic tolerance and exclusionism have not been asked in the Eastern Balkan countries or among the participants in the ISSP and ESS surveys in Central Europe, which have been more concerned with immigrant populations.

Analyses of 'ethnic intolerance' or 'ethnic exclusionism' have produced consistent conclusions. Among ethnic groups, Croats in Croatia,

Serbs in Serbia and, even more so, Montenegrins in Montenegro have given responses which indicate that they are relatively tolerant ethnically. Albanians, especially in Kosovo and Macedonia, gave the least ethnically tolerant responses about ethnic intermarriage and the possibilities of living and working together with ethnic Croats and Serbs. Working together is easier than living together, as nearly all totally reject intermarriage. Ethnic Bosniaks are relatively open, despite their victimization in the war and perhaps because of their numerical superiority in the new state. While they prefer relations among their own, they are more open to cross-ethnic relations than either Croats or Serbs in Bosnia and Herzegovina are.

To the surprise of those analysing the post-war data on individual attitudes, individual personal reports of having experienced war events and tragedies seem to have had very little effect on individual attitudes about ethnic tolerance in the war zones of Croatia, Bosnia and Herzegovina and Kosovo (Strabac and Ringdal, 2008). On the basis of evidence from the SEESSP, there are considerable and understandable *average* differences in attitudes towards ethnic tolerance across countries and ethnic groups according to the severity of warfare at the national level. However, while correlated with the severity of warfare at the national level during 1990–2001, the relative differences across ethnic groups in 2003–04 are similar to those reported for the late 1980s. There are significant relationships between individually reported war experiences and individual post-war reports of war-trauma-related psychological symptoms, but very weak relationships between such experiences and attitudes towards ethnic tolerance.

## Survey-based comparisons: South East European countries in a European context and major ethnic groups by country in the Western Balkans

This section presents cross-national and cross-ethnic group comparisons for specific variables in the ESS, ISSP and SEESSP data not previously available in other publications. With the exception of interethnic attitudes in the Western Balkans, the figures are composed to provide matched pairs of comparisons, first showing cross-country differences for the countries of South East Europe in a European context, then showing comparable comparisons among groups in the Western Balkans. For each pair of figures, the variables on the vertical and on the horizontal axes are closely related to each other, there being identical ranges and scales on both axes.

### Differences in self-reported religious behaviour

The first pair of figures, Figures 17.2 and 17.3, display measures of how often people report attending services at a church or mosque per year and of how often they report praying per year, calculated as an average for each country or group. Since, especially for prayer, the differences can be very large, the measure is the natural logarithm of the number of attendance times per year. While this measure might seem arbitrarily abstract, it is based on considerable earlier analysis.[10]

Figure 17.2 displays cross-national differences in religiosity, which are based on these two measures of religious behaviour for countries in Europe and a few of its peripheral states. Average church/mosque attendance and prayer averages are obviously fairly consistent for country averages. In the European context, national averages do not make

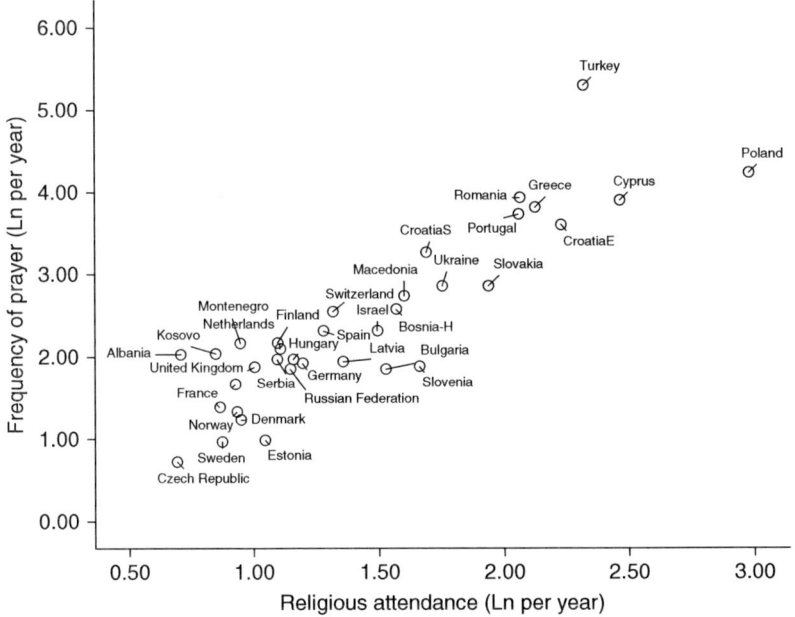

*Figure 17.2* Religious attendance by frequency of prayer for European and neighbouring countries

*Source*: Author, on the basis of merged aggregate measures for countries from the 2008 European Social Survey (ESS) and from the 2003–04 South East European Social Survey Project (SEESSP). The measures are based on the averages of the natural logarithms of the reported number of times per year (see note 10 for details). CroatiaE refers to ESS data; CroatiaS to SEESSP data.

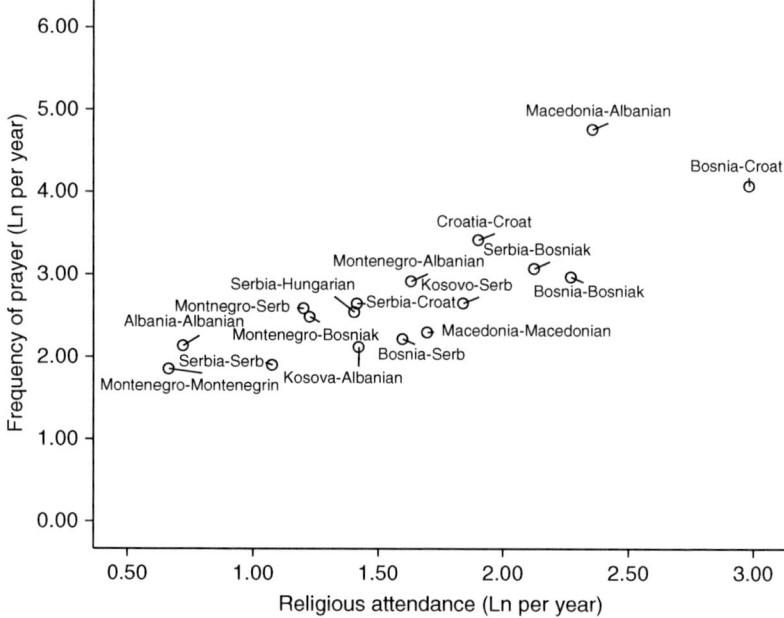

*Figure 17.3*    Religious attendance by frequency of prayer for major ethnic groups by countries in the Western Balkans

*Source*: Author, on the basis of aggregate measures for the major ethnic groups in seven countries of the Western Balkans from the 2003–04 SEESSP surveys. The first name in each label indicates the country, while the second name indicates ethnicity. The measures are the averages of the natural logarithms of the reported number of times per year (see note 10 for details).

South East European averages very exceptional, except for a few cases. Nationally, Romania and in some estimates Croatia are rather religious, being exceeded only by Poland, Turkey and perhaps Greece. Otherwise, within a European context, the countries of South East Europe are not very different from other European countries.

Figure 17.3 displays the same statistics on the same scale for subgroups within the Western Balkans. Here we can see that the differences within the country between ethnic groups in the Western Balkans are relatively large. In the European context, Croats in Bosnia and Herzegovina and Albanians in Macedonia are exceptionally religious. On the other hand, Albanians within Albania, self-identifying Montenegrins in Montenegro and Serbs in Serbia are not more religious than those West Europeans who are not very religious.

## Differences in self-reported religiosity and anti-homosexual attitudes

There is a strong relationship between religiosity and traditional mores concerning sexual behaviour. There are many dimensions of mores concerning sexual behaviour, but some display more cross-cultural variation than others. While mores against pre-marital sexual activity certainly exist and vary across countries, within Europe pre-marital sexuality is relatively acceptable, although not in the minds of many Balkan grandmothers. Similarly, extra-marital sex is largely condemned in survey research in Europe. However, opinions about acceptance of persons having sex with persons of their own gender vary widely among individuals, and certainly across countries.

Within countries, condemnation of gay and lesbian relationships is generally most highly correlated with traditional religiosity. Figures 17.4 and 17.5 present cross-national differences in attitudes towards homosexuality by self-reported religiosity, again between countries (Figure 17.4) and between ethnic groups by country for the Western Balkans (Figure 17.5). Figure 17.5 shows that, in the European context, tolerance of gays and lesbians is very low, especially among ethnic Albanians and ethnic Serbs. Nowhere in this region is tolerance as high as in North West Europe.

## Gender role attitudes

Figures 17.6 and 17.7 display differences in average answers regarding two questions related to gender role values. There are many different gender role questions among the ISSP, WVS and SEESSP surveys, but only a few allow broad cross-national comparisons including the Western Balkans. Here we have chosen a couple of questions that might seem simple but that reveal cross-national differences very clearly and consistently. These are based on two matching questions in the ISSP surveys of 2003 and the SEESSP surveys of 2003–04. Respondents were given five levels of agreement or disagreement with two questions: 'A job is alright but what women really want is a home with children'; and 'A man's job is to earn money; a woman's job is to look after the home.' Both questions are coded in such a way that a higher score reflects *disagreement* with these statements. In both figures, higher values express less traditional and more modern attitudes regarding gender roles.

Within the broader European context displayed in Figure 17.6, there is an impressively great difference between the countries of South East

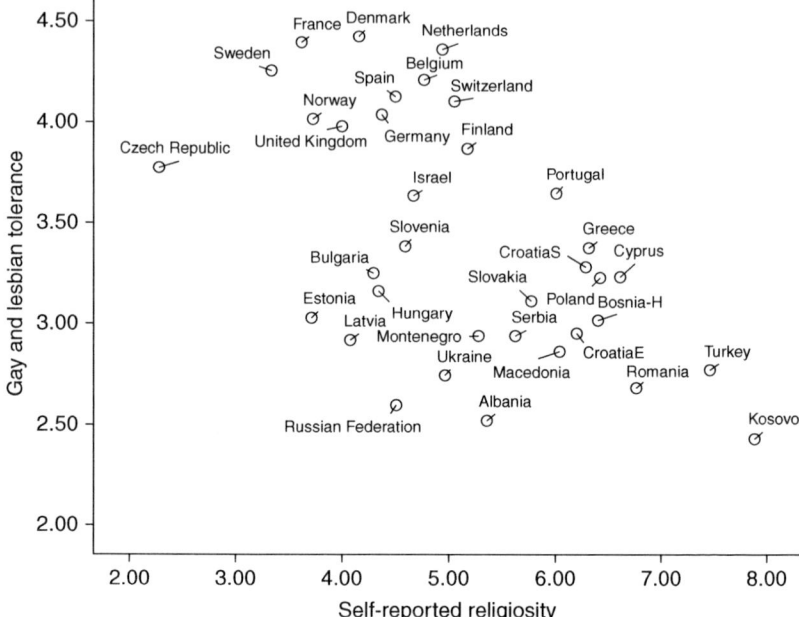

*Figure 17.4*  Self-reported subjective religiosity by gay and lesbian tolerance for European and neighbouring countries

Source: Author, on the basis of merged data for countries from the 2008 ESS and the 2003–04 SEESSP. The measures are the average values for each country on two survey items: self-reported religiosity is based on asking respondents to say how religious they are on a scale of 0 to 10, where 0 indicates 'not religious at all' and 10 indicates 'very religious'. Gay and lesbian tolerance is based on responses to the statement: 'Gay men and lesbians should be free to live their own life as they wish.' Possible responses to this item involved five categories, from 'strongly agree' to 'strongly disagree', given codes ranging from 1 to 5. The values here have been recoded such that high values reflect agreement. CroatiaE refers to ESS data; CroatiaS to SEESSP data.

Europe and the rest of Europe. The lower-left quadrant of the figure is almost completely dominated by the countries of South East Europe. The only other countries with similar gender attitudes are the formerly socialist states of the Czech Republic, Slovakia and Latvia, as well as the non-formerly socialist state of Portugal. Cross-national comparisons of gender role attitudes have generally shown that formerly socialist countries tend to have relatively traditional attitudes (Crompton and Harris, 1997). This may be partly due to generally lower levels of economic development in these countries. However, there is also another argument that very strong socialist policies of moving women into the labour force, combined with poor quality levels in public child care and

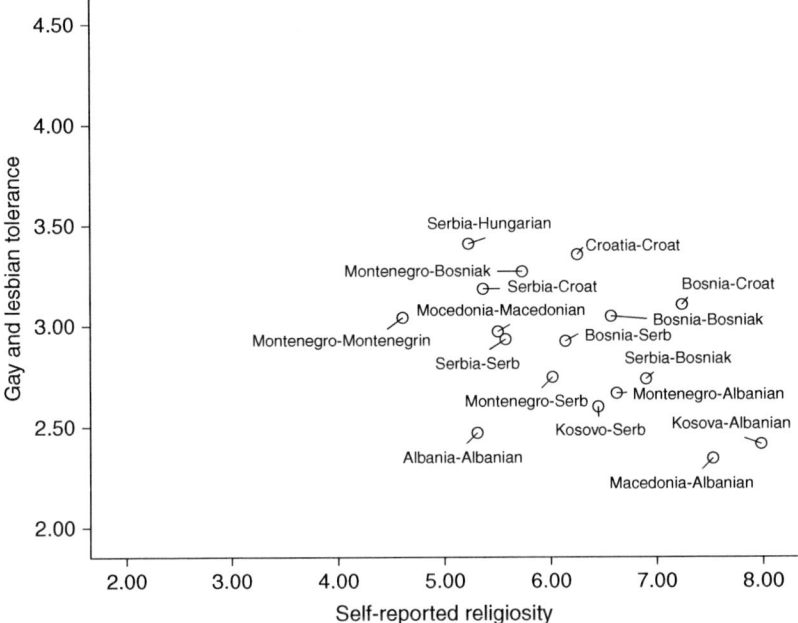

*Figure 17.5* Self-reported subjective religiosity by gay and lesbian tolerance for major ethnic groups, by country, for the Western Balkans
Source: Author, on the basis of the 2003–04 SEESSP. The questionnaire items, coding and scaling in the figure are the same as in Figure 5.4.

strong gender traditionalism persisting within family homes (even the hardest states could not make men change diapers or cook Sunday dinner), resulted in a kind of 'backlash' in which women wanted to claim pride for the 'jobs' they actually did.

Figure 17.7 displays the differences among different ethnic groups and countries within South East Europe. Clearly there are significant differences within as well as between countries. At the same time, these countries and groups are generally rather traditional. The most traditional groups are Albanians in Macedonia and Kosovo, ethnic Macedonians in Macedonia and Serbs in Kosovo and Montenegro. Out of this very traditional set of countries and groups, the most liberal are Croats in Croatia, Montenegrins and, in some ways, Albanians in Albania. Obviously there are some inconsistencies in the relative rankings of ethnic groups and countries depending on the two specific questions asked about gender roles for the horizontal and vertical dimensions of Figure 17.7. Based on the SEESSP surveys for the Western Balkans there is a much wider range

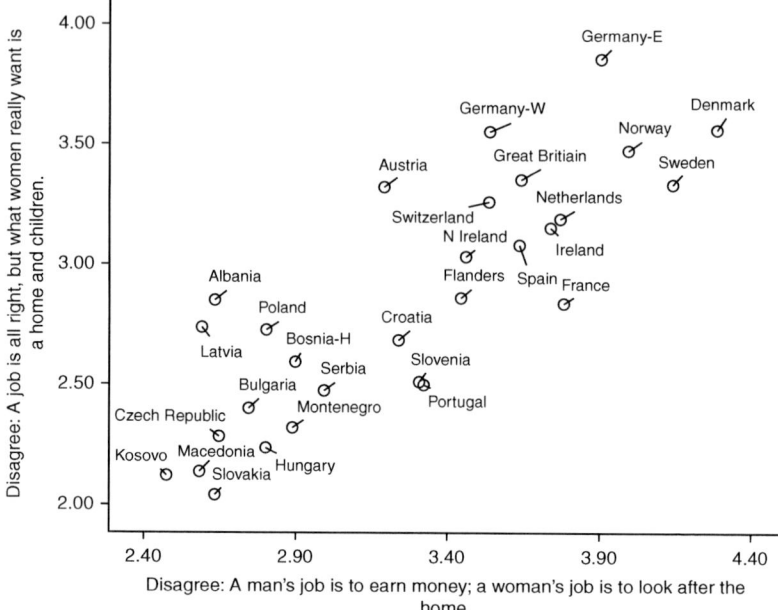

*Figure 17.6*   Questionnaire responses on items regarding traditional gender attitudes for European countries

*Source*: Author, on the basis of merged data for countries from the 2003 International Social Survey Project (ISSP) and the 2003–04 SEESSP. The measures are the average values for each country for responses two survey items: 'A man's job is to earn money; a woman's job is to look after the home'; and 'A job is all right, but women really want is a home and children.' Possible responses to the items involved five categories, from 'strongly agree' through to 'strongly disagree', with codes ranging from 1 to 5. Here high values reflect disagreement with the statements.

of specific questions related to gender role attitudes than are available for comparisons between these countries and South East Europe more broadly. The questions used in this figure are those that also allow wider comparisons with other South East European countries.

## Attitudes towards marriage

Figures 17.8 and 17.9 display average answers to questions regarding marriage. These figures are based on combined data from the ISSP surveys of 2003 and from the SEESSP data for 2003–04. The first statement is: 'Divorce is the best solution if there are problems in the marriage.' The second statement is: 'A bad marriage is better than no marriage at all.' Responses to both questions are coded in such a way that higher values

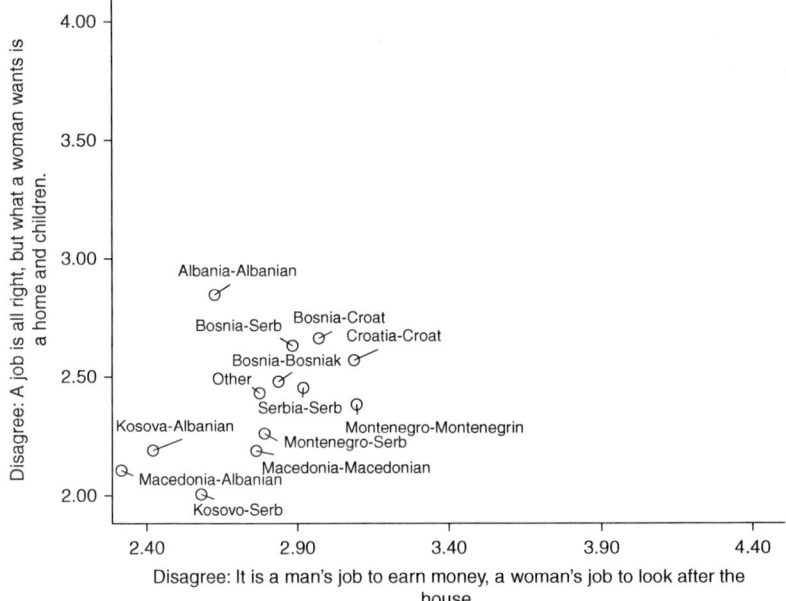

*Figure 17.7* Questionnaire responses on items regarding traditional gender attitudes for major ethnic groups in the countries of the Western Balkans
Source: Author, on the basis of data from the 2003–04 SEESSP. The measures are the average values for each major ethnic group by country for the same two survey items as in Figure 17.6, coded in the same way and plotted on the same scale. The labels identify first the country, then the ethnicity of respondents.

indicate less traditional values concerning marriage. Figure 17.8 clearly shows that there is much more national variation regarding 'A bad marriage is better than no marriage at all.' than for 'Divorce is the best solution if there are problems in the marriage.' On both scales, Albania is the most traditional country, and obviously the countries of South East Europe are generally most traditional in Europe, being joined perhaps by Poland, Latvia and the Czech Republic.

Figure 17.9 shows the differences between groups within the Western Balkans. Albanians in Albania and Macedonia are the most traditional, while Croats in Croatia, Montenegrins, Serbs in Bosnia and Herzegovina and perhaps Albanians in Kosovo are the least traditional in this generally relatively traditional set of countries. Of course, these comparisons are complicated by being based only on individual questions, each with different nuances of meaning. Comparing Figure 17.9 with Figure 17.8, the countries and groups of the Western Balkans are not very different

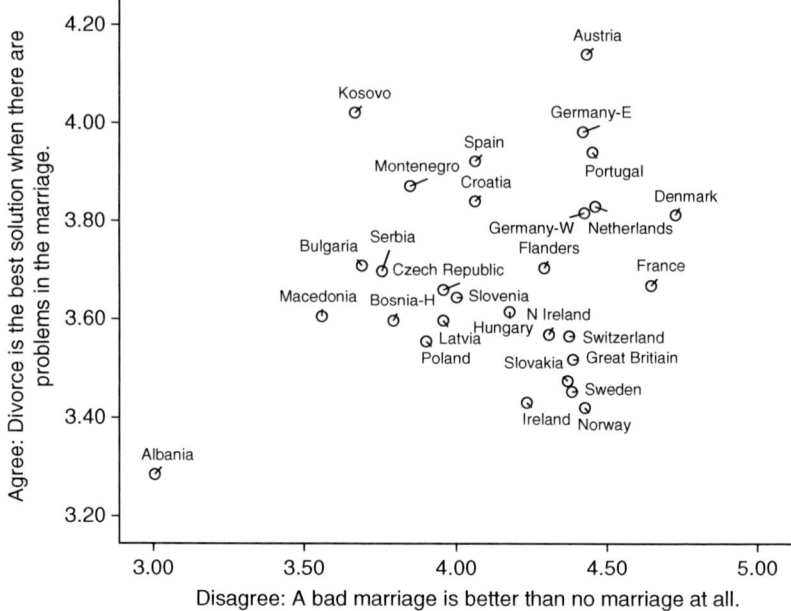

*Figure 17.8* Average responses on survey items regarding traditional values regarding marriage and divorce for European countries

*Source:* Author, on the basis of combined data for countries from the 2003 International Social Survey Project (ISSP) and the 2003–04 SEESSP. The measures are the average values for each country for responses to the two survey items: 'A bad marriage is better than no marriage at all.'; and 'Divorce is the best solution when there are problems in the marriage.' Possible responses to the items involved five categories, from 'strongly agree' to 'strongly disagree', with codes ranging from 1 to 5. The responses have been coded here such that higher values reflect less traditional responses, specifically being more open to the value of divorce or no marriage.

on the vertical dimension, but clearly more traditional on the horizontal dimension – that is, the 'A bad marriage is better than no marriage at all' dimension.

### Attitudes towards ethnic relations in the Western Balkans

For this dimension of attitudes, it is simply not possible to compare survey questions across the whole of South East Europe and Europe. Given the importance of ethnic conflict in the Western Balkans, the SEESSP surveys included regionally specific questions. Matching questions are not available in the ESS, ISSP and WVS, and, even if they were, the different national contexts would make comparisons meaningless.

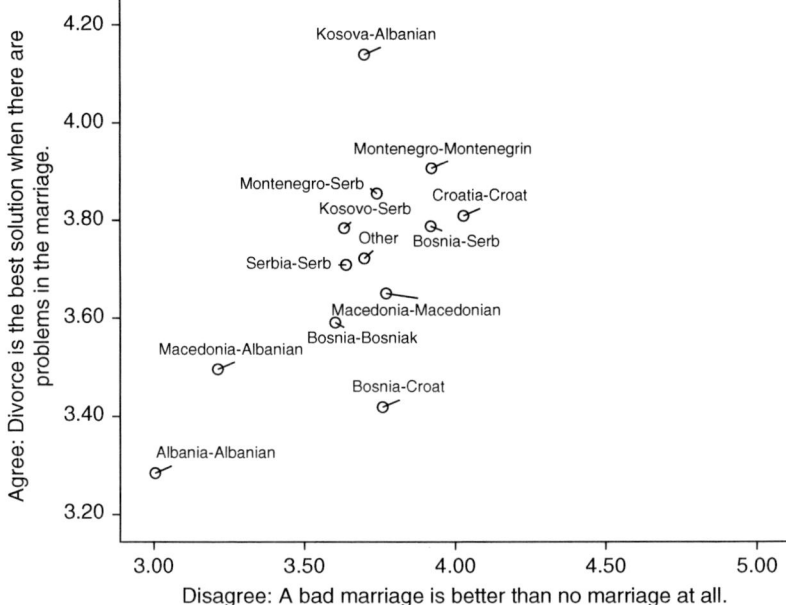

*Figure 17.9* Average responses on survey items regarding traditional values regarding marriage and divorce among major ethnic groups, by country, for the Western Balkans

*Source*: Author, on the basis of data from the 2003–04 SEESSP. The measures are the average values for each major ethnic group by country for the same two survey items as in Figure 17.8. The labels identify first the country, then the ethnicity of respondents. The values and coding of the items are as in Figure 17.8.

Therefore only comparisons within the Western Balkans are presented here. For the purposes of this book, perhaps these are also the most important ones. There is now a fairly large published or about to be published literature about indices of what is variously labeled 'ethnic intolerance' or 'ethnic exclusionism'. These analyses are based on scales including three to seven questionnaire items. Here we want to show differences on the basis of two crucial statements: 'People can only feel safe when they are of the national majority'; and 'It is best that villages and towns be composed of only one nationality.'

Figure 17.10 shows differences among groups and countries in the Western Balkans. The correlation between the two statements is relatively strong. Undoubtedly the highest level of mistrust about ethnic cooperation is among the Albanians of Kosovo, Macedonia and Albania, and this is nearly matched by the mistrust of Serbs in Kosovo

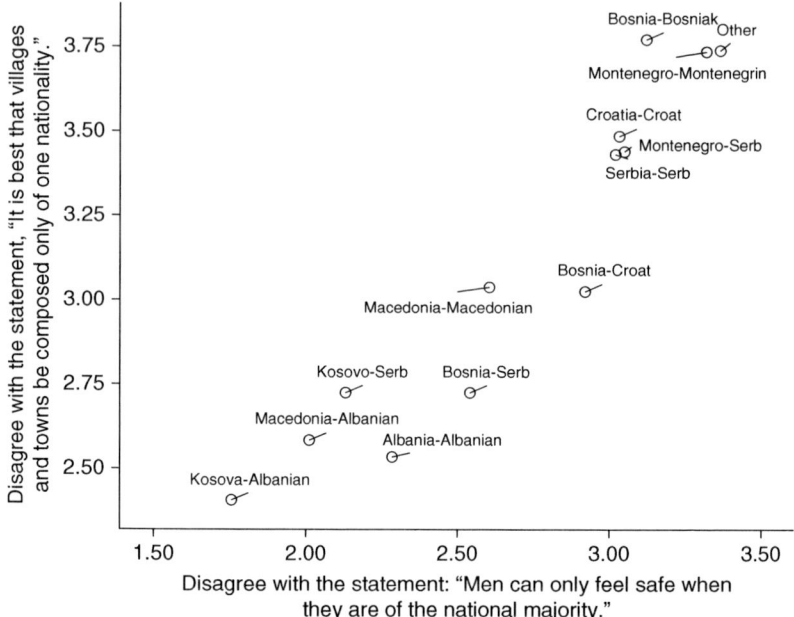

*Figure 17.10*   Average responses to survey items related to ethnic exclusionism for major ethnic groups by country in the Western Balkans

*Source*: Author, on the vasis of data from the 2003–04 SEESSP surveys. Possible responses to the items involved five categories, from 'strongly agree' to 'strongly disagree', with attached codes ranging from 1 to 5. Values here are coded such that higher values indicate higher levels of disagreement with the statements.

and Bosnia and Herzegovina. At the other end of this regional spectrum are Bosniaks in Bosnia and Herzegovina as well as with members of the other smallest ethnic groups – Montenegrins, Croats in Croatia and Serbs in Serbia.

## Conclusion

Although outside this region it is common to hear people talk about South East Europe as if it were one homogeneous place, it is obviously not. Those living within the region recognize and act upon a huge number of cultural distinctions – far more than we have even been able to enumerate here. The basic starting point for understanding the ethnic diversity in the region is recognizing the intersections among the twelve countries, ten major ethnic groups, four major language groups and four major religious groups.

This task is simplified somewhat by the fact that only two of the countries – Bosnia and Herzegovina, and Macedonia – have individual ethnic minorities and language groups which comprise more than 10 per cent of the population. The populations of these countries, as well as major ethnic minorities in other countries of the region, differ in key aspects of traditionalism in values. They differ among each other and they differ, on average, from the populations of the more North Western countries of Europe. A considerable body of cross-national social survey research illustrates the existence of these differences. Explanations of the differences range from ethnographic discussions of particular ethnic groups in certain countries to the general influence of economic development and modernization.

At least over very short periods, one can live and work in one part of South East Europe at a time. In each of these parts, one encounters richer and richer complexities of local diversity, some of which have been elaborated upon here. There is, however, much more to learn.

## Notes

1. A marvellous and classic travel-ethnographic description of the countries of former Yugoslavia just before the First World War is West (1941).
2. Obviously this is related to the use of 'Serbo-Croatian' as lingua franca in the former Republic of Yugoslavia.
3. Ironically, the name 'Hoxha' means 'priest'.
4. For details, see http://www.europeanvaluesstudy.eu/and www.worldvalues survey.org, accessed 30 October 2010.
5. Further in this chapter referred to as SEESSP. For details, see http://www.svt. ntnu.no/iss/ringdalweb/SEESSP%20Surveys.html, accessed 30 October 2010.
6. For details, see http://www.europeansocialsurvey.org, accessed 30 October 2010.
7. For details, see http://www.issp.org, accessed 30 October 2010.
8. Wave 4 for 2008 of the ESS was chosen, rather than the ESS survey of 2004, which would have matched the survey year for SEESSP, because Romania was only included in the ESS surveys of 2008. Making cross-national comparisons such as the ones presented in this chapter demands balancing solutions among several different difficulties: the years in which the surveys were conducted, the quality of the surveys, the comparability of the survey questions and whether the sample sizes and designs allow comparisons of sub-groups within countries. The comparisons in this chapter involve kinds of behaviour and abstract attitudes that have generally been shown not to change quickly over time – nothing like the changes in the popularity of particular politicians or political parties. For this reason, we accept year differences in surveys of one to four years in favour of data quality, sample size and comparability of questions.

9. Additional sources of social survey data for South East Europe, on issues related to those discussed here, but not included in the discussion of this chapter, are Evans and Need (2002), Gallup (2010) and CSSP and the Paul Lazersfeld Society (2009).

10. We have survey data from a number of cross-national survey projects on how often people attend church or mosque, and on how often they pray. The precise categories for responses vary somewhat between projects, as does the assignment of numerical codes to the responses. Here we needed to make measures that are comparable across projects and not based on arbitrary category codes. Analyses of these data have been conducted to estimate the scores for categories of frequency of prayer, attendance and self-reported religiosity, which produce the maximum correlation among these three. It turns out that, for church attendance and prayer across the countries of the ESS and the SEESSP, the natural logarithm of the number of times per year is not logically arbitrary and results in the highest correlations among these variables and between these variables on a scale of self-rated religiosity ranging from 0 to 10 (self-reported religiosity is used for the horizontal axis in Figures 17.4 and 17.5).

# References

Ballinger, P. (1999) 'Definitional Dilemmas: Southeastern Europe as a "Culture Area"?', *Balkanologie*, 3 (2), http://balkanologie.revues.org/index745.html, accessed 12 November 2010.

Bracewell, W. and A. Drace-Frances (1999) 'South-Eastern Europe: History, Concepts, Boundaries', *Balkanologie*, 3 (2), http://balkanologie.revues.org/index741.html, accessed 12 November 2010.

Brajdić-Vuković, M., Birkelund, G. E. and Stulhofer, A. (2007) 'Between Tradition and Modernization: Attitudes toward Women's Employment and Gender Roles in Croatia', International *Journal of Sociology*, 37, 32–53.

Brajdić-Vuković, M. and Stulhofer, A. (under review) ' "The Whole Universe is Heterosexual!" Correlates of Homonegativity in Seven South-East European Countries', in Ringdal, K. and Simkus, A. (eds), *Aftermath of War: Experiences and Attitudes in the Western Balkans*.

Crompton, R. and Harris, F. (1997): 'Women's Employment and Gender Attitudes: A Comparative Analysis of Britain, Norway and Czech Republic', *Acta Sociologica*, 40, 183–202.

Ellingsen, T., Ringdal, K., Simkus, A. and Strabac, Z. (under review) 'Security Dilemmas and Ethnic Intolerance in the Western Balkans', in Ringdal, K. and Simkus, A. (eds), *Aftermath of War: Experiences and Attitudes in the Western Balkans*.

Evans, G. and Need, A. (2002) 'Explaining Ethnic Polarization over Minority Rights in Eastern Europe: A Multilevel Approach', *Social Science Research*, 31, 653–680.

Gallup (2010) *Gallup Balkan Monitor*, http://www.balkan-monitor.eu, accessed 20 October 2010.

GRIDA (2007) 'Population Groups in the Balkan Region and Eastern Europe' (map), designed by Philippe Rekacewicz, *Le Monde Diplomatique* and UNEP/GRIS-Ardenal, http://maps.grida.no/go/graphic/population-groups-in-the-balkan-region-and-eastern-europe, accessed 17 December 2010.

Hodson, R., Sekulić, D. and Massey, G. (1994) 'National Tolerance in Socialist Yugoslavia', *American Journal of Sociology*, 99, 1534–1558.

Inglehart, R. and Baker, W. (2000) 'Modernization, Cultural Change, and the Persistence of Traditional Values', *American Sociological Review*, 65, 19–51.

Inglehart, R. and Norris, P. (2003) *Rising Tide: Gender Equality and Cultural Change around the World* (Cambridge: Cambridge University Press).

Inglehart, R. and Norris, P. (2004) *Sacred and Secular: Reexamining the Secularization Thesis* (Cambridge: Cambridge University Press).

Norris, P. and Inglehart, R. (2009) *Sacred Cosmopolitan Communications: Cultural Diversity in a Globalized World* (New York: Cambridge University Press).

Listhaug, O., Ringdal, K. and Simkus, A. (under review, 2011) 'Serbian Civic Values in a European Context', in Listhaug, O., Ramet, S. and Dulić, D. (eds), *Civic and Uncivic Values in Serbia: The Post-Milošević Era* (Budapest: Central European Press), 51–75.

CSPP and Paul Lazersfeld Society (2009) 'South-East Europe Barometer Public Opinion Compared in 7 Countries', Centre for the Study of Public Policy SPP 407 (Aberdeen: CSPP Publications).

Pesić, J. (under review) 'Patriarchal Value Orientations in the Western Balkans', in Ringdal, K. and Simkus, A. (eds), *Aftermath of War: Experiences and Attitudes in the Western Balkans*.

Ringdal, K., Listhaug, O. and Simkus, A. (under review) 'Bosnian Civic Values in a European Context', in Listhaug, O. and Ramet, S. (eds), *Civic and Uncivic Values in Bosnia-Herzegovina: The Record Since Dayton*.

Schöpflin, G. (1999) 'Defining South-Eastern Europe', *Balkanologie*, 3 (2), http://balkanologie.revues.org/index743.html, accessed 12 November 2010.

Sekulić, D.,Massey, G. and Hodson, R. (2006) 'Ethnic Intolerance and Ethnic Conflict in the Dissolution of Yugoslavia', *Ethnic and Racial Studies*, 29, 797–827.

Simkus, A. (2007a) 'Guest Editor's Introduction', *International Journal of Sociology*, 37, 3–14.

Simkus, A. (2007b) 'Cross-National Differences in the Western Balkans in Three Dimensions of Attitudes', *International Journal of Sociology*, 37, 15–31.

Simkus, A. (under review a) 'Divisions within Bosnia and Herzegovina on Core Values: Effects of Nationality, Gender, Age, Education, and Size of Place of Residence', in Ramet, S. (ed.) *Civic Values in Bosnia and Herzegovina*.

Simkus, A. (under review b) 'Nationality, State, and Values in the Western Balkans', in Ringdal, K. and Simkus, A. (eds) *Aftermath of War: Experiences and Attitudes in the Western Balkans*.

Strabac, Z. and Ringdal, K. (2008) 'Individual and Contextual Influences of War on Ethnic Predjudice in Croatia', *Sociological Quarterly*, 49, 769–796.

Welzel, C., Inglehart, R. and Klingemann, H.-D. (2003) 'The Theory of Human Development: A Cross-Cultural Analysis', *European Journal of Political Research*, 42, 341–379.

West, R. (1941) *Black Lamb and Grey Falcon: A Journey through Yugoslavia* (New York: Viking Press).

# 18
# Work-Related Attitudes in the SEE Region

*Ágnes Borgulya*

## Introduction

When planning to start a business in a certain area, for example in SEE, one decisive factor of interest is whether the chosen area is characterized by economic growth. As human capital, according to human capital theory, is able to generate growth, productivity will depend to a very high degree on the quality and behaviour of employees. According to Glaser (2004, p. 2), '[t]he productive advantage that one area has over another is driven mostly by the people'. As work-related values and attitudes determine the behaviour of employees, this chapter will be concerned with a detailed examination of the characteristic features of these determinants in the context of SEE countries.

Both values and attitudes are deeply embedded in people's behaviour, leading them to act in certain ways. Values and attitudes are intertwined in such a way that values underlie attitudes. Values are integral components of the cultural set of a society, telling its members what is good, beneficial, useful, appropriate and desirable for them and for the whole community. Thus the values of a society provide an orientation for its members in decision-making.

According to Tosi and Mero (2003),

> Attitudes are propensities or tendencies to react in a favourable or unfavourable way toward an object. It makes sense to study and know about attitudes because strong attitudes will very likely affect a person's behaviour. Attitudes toward supervision, pay, benefits, promotion, or anything that might trigger positive or negative reactions. As a result, employee satisfaction and attitudes represent one of the key areas for measuring organizational effectiveness.

The first part of this chapter addresses the question why work-related values and attitudes play an important role in productivity and efficiency. The second part reviews those changes that have occurred in the world of work in the transition countries during the last two decades. Part three is concerned with work-related values and attitudes today and extends the analysis to other factors that might influence values and attitudes. It aims to explain what role work plays in the lives of South East Europeans, what aspects of work they regard as important and what groups of values are distinguishable with regard to the importance that South East Europeans attach to various job benefits. This part will present and analyse the latest findings of social surveys in Europe. The results reveal characteristics that countries have in common, as well as differences in work orientation in the SEE region. It also highlights potential pitfalls for human resource management and possibilities for effectively managing a workforce.

## The importance of work-related attitudes for productivity and efficiency

Work-related attitudes, such as emotional and cognitive relationships to work itself and to the complex world of regularly paid work, influence work performance in various ways.

- Attitudes towards work act as *engines of motivation*. If someone finds attractive positions with high freedom of decision, this positive attitude will function for them as a driving force to get a position in which they can realize their ambitions. Leaders and managers may utilize workers' different attitudes as motivating tools. Whether employees can be motivated with higher salaries and wages, with longer holidays or with flexible working hours depends on their attitudes towards the world of work.
- *Divergences in attitudes* as well as divergences in values are very often *sources of cultural conflicts*. Cultural conflicts arise when people interpret the same phenomenon in different ways, or when something is valuable for one person but not for another because of their different cultural backgrounds. Cultural conflicts cannot be solved easily and they often become persistent, exerting a negative influence on workplace climate and achievement (Jávor and Rozgonyi, 2005).
- If the phrase *work-related* is extended to include the 'human factor' in a working environment (as, for example, colleagues or superiors), *tolerance* appears as an attitude of outstanding importance.

Florida's theory states that human creativity is the ultimate source of economic growth. The main criteria of creativity are 'the 3Ts': technology, talent and tolerance. In his opinion, successfully developing regions are embedded in open and tolerant cultural environments, where people are tolerant, diverse and inclusive (Florida, 2002, 2004). If a company employs workers for whom tolerance, acceptance of diversity and inclusiveness are fundamental values, the company has a good chance to develop a supportive and open climate, in which people can generate and implement new ideas. Tolerance is a socio-cultural precondition for creativity. In this sense certain attitudes are doubtlessly pillars of economic growth. Thus, when we examine to what extent SEE countries can be characterized by tolerance, acceptance of diversity and inclusiveness, we can also draw conclusions about the potential growth capacity.

## Fundamental changes in the status of work in SEE countries during the last two decades

After the transition from centrally planned to market-based economies, SEE countries experienced significant changes in the world of work. Under the communist regime, work was a right and an obligation at the same time.

As the communist ideology promoted the value of work too aggressively, it was adversely devalued in real life. People learned to prefer components of work other than its prestige and their own achievements through formal labour. More often, primary importance was given to such features as the absence of any supervisory control or less strict working conditions, which permitted less of a work burden and more hours of leisure, allowing time to perform informal jobs or bricolage at home.

(Večernik, 2006, p. 1222)

After 1989, full employment, a fundamental feature of former centrally planned economies, disappeared. The transition led to radical changes in labour markets. During the 1990s labour market trends showed a high rate of long-term unemployment, accompanied by large regional disparities. Particularly hard-hit groups were the young, the disabled, low-skilled workers and certain ethnic minorities. The exodus of the workforce to foreign countries intensified, which resulted in 685,200 new member state nationals being employed in the EU-15 between 2004 and 2006 (Traser and Venables, 2008).

Borgulya and Hahn argue that these trends had two consequences. On the one hand, work-related values were affected by the appearance of unemployment in SEE countries. People had to face unemployment, job insecurity and the loss of regular income, which not only lowered living standards, but also made getting bank-loans more difficult. On the other hand, labour migration and new subsidiaries of multinational enterprises in the transition countries put an end to the monocultural feature of workplaces, thus causing cultural conflicts (Borgulya and Hahn, 2008).

The transformation also generated problems in people's expectations.

> There is a deep legacy of relaxed attitudes towards employment, which had previously been obligatory, while the expectations concerning social protections are high. The pressure put on the quality and intensity of work performance is weak [...] While the transformation of the external institutional framework is over, it is still going insofar as the intrinsic characteristics of work and job attitudes are concerned. (Večernik, 2006, p. 1220)

Večernik made these comments relating to the CEE countries, but they aptly characterize the SEE countries, too.

During the first half of the last decade (2000–05) there was a moderate increase in the amount of people in employment, and at the end of the decade these numbers increased considerably. However, labour market figures showed that job losses escalated by the end of 2009 (Unicredit Group, 2010). This probably caused a further shift in values and attitudes, which will presumably be reflected only in future survey findings.

At present, work-related values and attitudes are generation dependent: there are differences between *the over-45s and the younger generation*. At the beginning of their careers, those in the older group learned to regard the following work-related values as important: stability, long-term planning and mutual loyalty. This generation can be characterized as follows:

– It has experienced full employment and so called 'in-house unemployment' (that means that everyone had a job and some guaranteed income, but some people in a certain workplace actually had no work to do – they were kept there just to avoid unemployment).

- It has no experience of unemployment. Paid work is, on the one hand, the most important source of income, on the other hand, it creates social contacts and shapes personal identity. Working activity represents a value in itself: it is an instrument for the expression of human creative potential (Mareš, 2001). Losing this sphere of life causes painful breaks in individuals. Unemployment, for this generation, constitutes a personal financial crisis, but it also leads to a psychological crisis, particularly a crisis of self-evaluation.
- It still needs to cope with the feeling of decreasing mutual commitment and instability. While in the former system loyalty to a firm was rewarded, for example through the payment of loyalty bonuses at 10, 20, 30 and 40 years of employment, there are now new requirements in the world of work, such as dynamic attitudes, mobility and tolerance of change.

The generation under 45 started their careers at the beginning of the transition or later. They have the following characteristics in common:

- higher mobility;
- less fear of insecurity on the labour market;
- greater tolerance to constant change.

In addition, they have probably experienced situations in which a multinational company closes a subsidiary overnight and moves to another country, where production costs are lower. Mutual commitment is unknown.

Attitudes and behaviour can only be reliably interpreted if these aspects of the historical background are taken into consideration.

## Work-related values and attitudes today

There are authors who point out that employment relations are mostly influenced by economic and sociological variables, cultural backgrounds, some macro-economic factors and the institutional structure of labour markets, which, together, function as contexts of work processes (Kalleberg and Reve, 1992; Medgyesi and Róbert, 2000). However, historical and cultural characteristics of a society have as strong an influence on work-related values and attitudes as economic and sociological variables. These factors will be examined below.

## The determinants of value preferences and attitudes

Tosi and Mero point out that '[s]ocialization is one way to understand how people develop the values and beliefs that lead to a whole range of general and specific attitudes about work. It can also have significant influences on our behaviors' (Tosi and Mero, 2002, p. 44). At the same time, values develop under the influence of the natural and the human-made environment. They are dominated by psychological, economic, socio-cultural, ideological, political and technical factors acting as frameworks. Some factors affecting values are related to the environmental frames at macro (national) and organizational levels, others to the individual concerned. The model below shows the determinants of values and work-related attitudes for an individual (Figure 18.1).

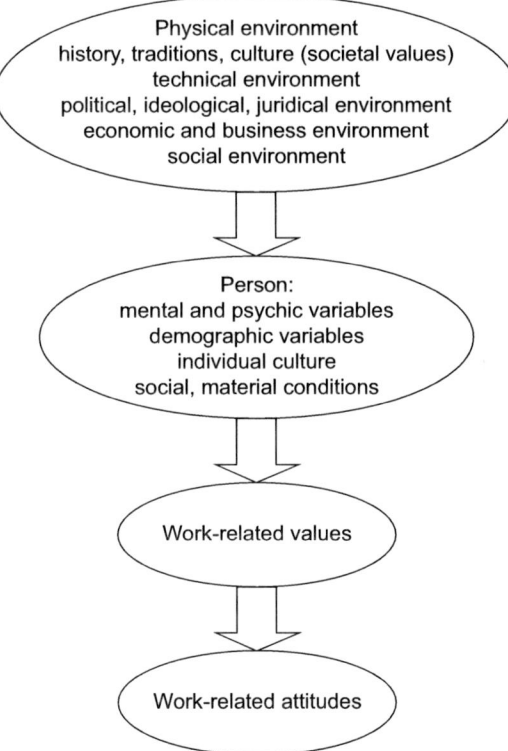

*Figure 18.1*   Determinants of work-related values and attitudes
*Source*: Author.

The *physical environment* in this model relates to the geographical and climatic conditions an individual lives and works in. The historical backgrounds of the nation or ethnical group the person belongs to, the traditions and general national societal or ethnical values all belong to the *historical and cultural determinants* that influence an individual living in this society.

The *technical development of a society* considerably determines infrastructure and work conditions. The *political, juridical and ideological environment* affects the institutional frameworks within which the individual can act. The *economic and business determinants* shape the labour market, and the *social environment* the well-being of individuals.

How a person evaluates his or her actual or desired job is mostly affected by personal, psychological and mental abilities, by demographic characteristics such as age or gender, by an individual's cultural background and education, by the social and material situation and by the position in the hierarchy of the workplace structure.

Some criteria play an outstandingly important role among the complex combinations of variables that shape work-related values and attitudes:

– The general standard of living, general security of livelihood and job security in the society the person lives in, as well as the personal standard of living and personal security of livelihood.
– General income levels in the country a person lives in, as well as the income level of the individual. It is important to note that the former socialist countries are at the bottom of the income scale in Europe. In Hungary, for example, 51 per cent of employees had an income of less than half of the EU median in 2005, while nearly 9 per cent of the country's population lived on an income of under five euros per day. Slovenia had a better situation, as only 0.5 percent had an income of less than five euros per day (Ward et al., 2009).
– Income distribution, poverty, financial deprivation and access to benefits and social services. SEE countries are not homogenous regarding the distribution of income.
– General competition on the labour market as well as individual competitiveness.
– The employment rate in the countries of origin and of residence of a person as well as the labour market status of the individual. In shaping work-related attitudes, it is crucial whether someone is employed or not.
– General level of workforce skills as well as education level, abilities and skills (for instance language skills, work skills, e-readiness and

so on) of the individual, which determine his or her position and competitiveness on the national and international labour markets.

- Individual socio-demographic, mental and psychological variables such as age, gender, ethnic status (member of ethnic majorities or minorities), immigration status, education, household size and structure, social role in the household (head of houshold); degree of urbanization.
- Personal attitudes such as devotion to entrepreneurship, competitiveness and innovation: these belong to the new requirements on the labour market. It was found that innovativeness, for example, is very weak in Croatia. New and small enterprises have limited access to international markets, which indicates a need for them to develop international competitiveness, personal devotion to entrepreneurship and innovation (Kušić and Grupe, 2006).
- Working conditions are also examined when people evaluate jobs. There are significant differences in working hours: in 2008 the average number of weekly hours of work in the EU-27 was 38 hours. In the EU countries in SEE people tended to spend more time at work: 40.5 hours in Hungary, 41.1 hours in Slovenia, 41.5 hours in Bulgaria and 41.8 hours in Romania (European Foundation for the Improvement of Living and Working Conditions, 2009).
- The role of trade unions and collective agreements determine the level of protection at work. As Kasahara and Makó (1996) point out, in Hungary, for example, '[t]rade unions have only a modest influence on wages, working conditions and employees lay-offs'.

The resulting complex interrelations between these dimensions shape the work-related attitudes of people in SEE countries.

### Work values and attitudes in SEE countries

As values and attitudes affect the performance of companies, it is no wonder that they have received a lot of attention in recent decades. Most information on attitudes in the field of employment is gathered by sociologists through opinion surveys. These surveys alone are not sufficient to obtain a realistic view of values or to draw conclusions on performance. However, with the help of their findings it is possible to get some orientation, and, combined with observations and studying the frameworks of values in a national economy, opinion surveys can be useful tools for making management decisions. The very few studies directly addressing work-related attitudes in transition countries include those of Sersic et al. (2005), Alas and Rees (2006), Večernik (2006) and Borgulya and Hahn (2008).

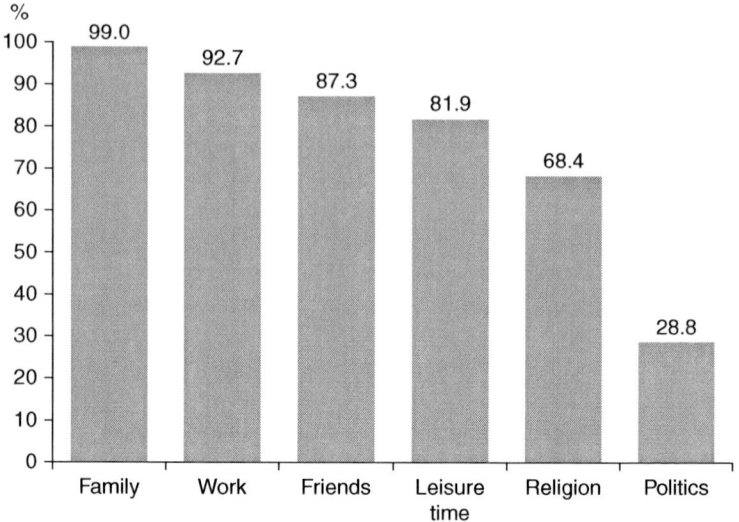

*Figure 18.2*   Importance of different spheres of life in SEE countries in 2008
*Source*: EVS Foundation/Tilburg University (2010).

For South East Europeans, as for all Europeans, *work is very important.* This fact is supported by findings of the 2008 wave of the European Values Study (EVS) social survey.[1] Comparing life spheres such as family, work and friends (among others), it was found that *work is the second* most important sphere, not only in SEE countries but also in the minds of Europeans generally (Figure 18.2). Closely behind family (SEE average: 99.0 per cent) and before friends (SEE average: 87.3 per cent), work takes a highly valued position in people's lives (SEE average: nearly 93 per cent of respondents consider work to be an important part of their lives) in South East European countries.[2] As we will see below, many different aspects of work are covered in the survey.[3]

If one looks at opinions about the importance of work in life on a country-by-country basis (Figure 18.3), over 89 per cent of respondents in each of the SEE countries think that work is either important or very important for them. In Albania, only 3.5 per cent of the respondents do not find work to be important in life. Even in EU-15 member countries such as Germany or Austria, which we use as reference countries throughout the following analysis, work is highly valued. Although the German rate lies about 10 per cent below the lowest SEE country level (Bulgaria), the approximately 80 per cent of 'important' and 'very important' answers are unquestionably high.

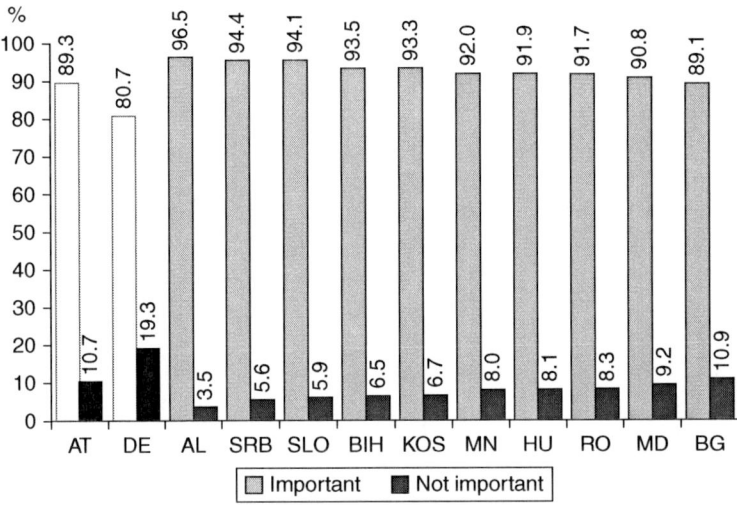

*Figure 18.3* Importance of work in life in Austria, Germany and SEE countries in 2008
*Source*: EVS Foundation/Tilburg University (2010).

No close association could be found between judgements about the importance of work and GDP per capita levels. In Albania, where 96.5 per cent of people think that work is important, GDP per capita is only about 26 per cent of the EU median. The indicator of importance of work lies only 2.5 per cent lower in Slovenia (with 94 per cent) than in Albania, while the GDP per capita is much higher, at a level of only 6 per cent lower than the EU average (17,105 EUR in 2009). Therefore, the conclusion cannot be drawn that there is a clear correlation between attitudes towards work and GDP or standard of living. The reasons why people in Albania and in Slovenia think work is important are likely to be different.

The importance of work is reflected in another fact as well: up to 61 per cent of people living in SEE countries believe that work comes first in their lives and that all other activities are secondary. Many parents bringing up children usually make it a rule that activities like playing, watching TV or doing sports should only be performed after completing school homework. While in Albania and in Kosovo two-thirds of respondents agree with the superior rank of work, in Slovenia, Bosnia and Herzegovina and Montenegro only about half of the population share this opinion. By comparison, in Germany, 60 per cent agree that work always comes first.

Why do South East Europeans think that they should work?

– A high proportion (74 per cent) feel that *people become lazy if they do not work.*
– Many (68 per cent) are of the opinion that *it is humiliating to receive money without working.*
– On average, more than half of the respondents (57 per cent) think that *work is a duty towards society.* However, this average also includes significant country-to-country deviations. While in Bulgaria 78 per cent of people agree with this statement, only 28 of Montenegrins share this opinion.
– Not even half (46 per cent) argue that *work is needed to develop talents.* There are, however, some very contrasting opinions in different SEE countries on this topic: while 56 per cent of Albanians agree with it, 64 per cent of Slovenians disagree.

If work-related values are grouped according to the importance that respondents in SEE countries place on them, a pyramid of groups of values emerges (Figure 18.4). It cannot be stated, however, that values

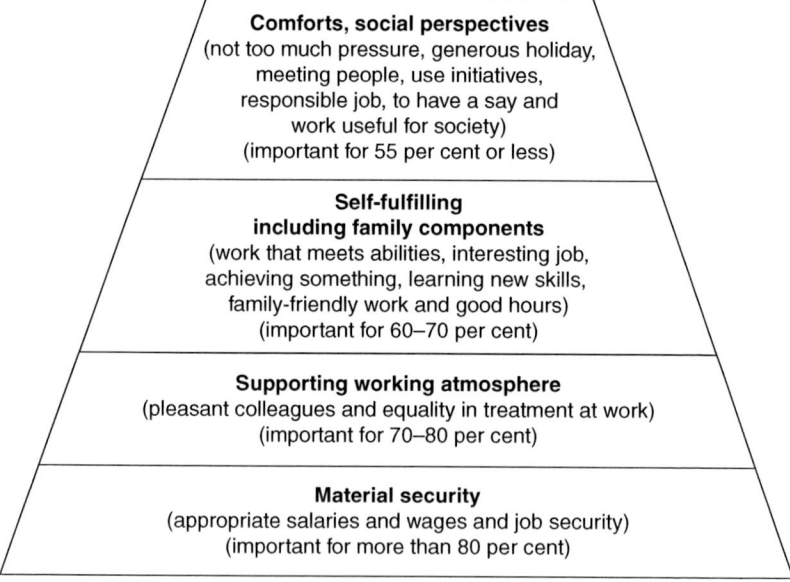

*Figure 18.4*   Order of work-related values in the SEE region
*Source*: Author.

selected by fewer respondents would only appear after satisfying the ones that were mentioned by more respondents: whether such a hierarchy (like Maslow's) exists or not could be investigated by further research.[4]

The first group of values, which can be labelled *financial security*, is composed of *appropriate salaries and wages*, and *job security*. The two aspects seem to be of fundamental importance to people in SEE countries, as between 80 and 90 per cent identify them as important.

The next category of values is associated with creating supporting psychological conditions of work and a good working environment. In this category we find, for instance, *pleasant colleagues*, or *equal treatment* of men and women and of different ethnic groups. This group can be labelled *supporting working atmosphere*. Between 70 and 80 per cent of SEE citizens consider these work characteristics as being important.

Other criteria contribute to *self-fulfilment*. Here we find aspects such as *work appropriate to one's abilities*, *having an interesting job*, *the opportunity to achieve something*, having a *work with family-friendly benefits* or having a job that makes it possible to *learn new skills*. As for most Europeans, it is family and work, together, that constitute the meaning of life. Family-friendly work conditions and good working hours contribute considerably to a meaningful life. About 60 to 70 per cent of all South East Europeans attach great importance to these benefits.

For a smaller proportion (50–60 per cent) of SEE citizens, criteria such as *generous holidays*, *not too much pressure*, *work useful for society* or *having responsibility at work* are also important. These can be called components of individual *comforts* and *social perspectives*. The *opportunity to use initiative* also has effects on society, as initiative is linked to creativity, which – as has already been pointed out – serves the whole society. Figure 18.4 provides an overview of the hierarchy of work-related values in SEE countries.

The individual factors in these four categories will be investigated in greater detail in the following sections of this chapter.

*Financial security*

Among the many aspects of work, the strongest preference, as mentioned above, is given to high *salaries and wages* in the SEE countries. The fact itself is not surprising. The connection between the leading job aspects good pay (considered important by an average of 92 per cent of the respondents in the ten SEE countries) and the next most important aspect job security (80 per cent of all respondents) is evident. Both of these aspects are linked to the most basic needs of people: having a safe

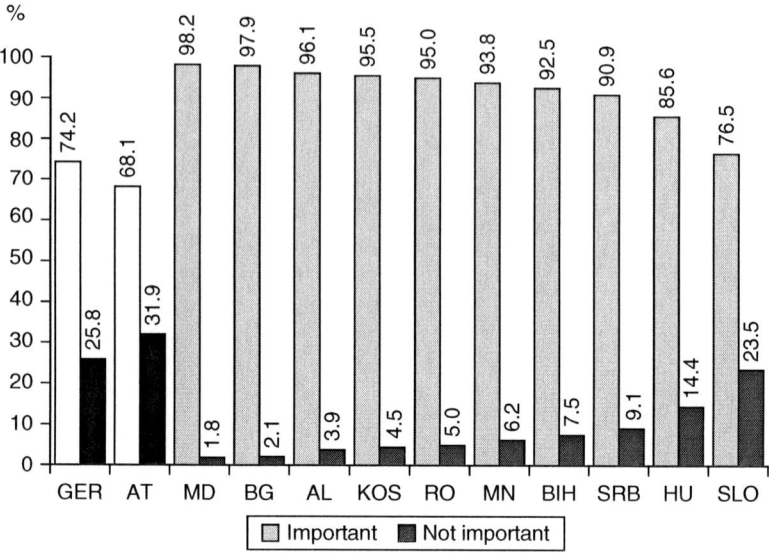

*Figure 18.5*   Importance of 'good pay' in Germany, Austria and SEE countries in 2008
*Source of data*: EVS Foundation/Tilburg University (2010).

job gives them purchasing power and guarantees good living conditions. The opinions of people living in different SEE countries do not show any great variations regarding salaries. The difference between the top end of the scale (98 per cent importance in Moldavia) and the bottom end (76.5 per cent in Slovenia) is 21.5 percentage points (Figure 18.5).

Higher salaries and job security, however, play a decisive role in immigration to Western countries from South East Europe.

The high average value obtained for *desire to have job security* (80 per cent) is probably a sign of fear of being unemployed or of having to give up familiar circumstances. When the EVS survey was completed in 2008–09, the first effects of the economic crisis had already reached many of these countries. In spite of this, there was no rise in the desire for a safe job between 1999/2000 (when the third wave of the EVS survey was completed) and 2008. On the contrary, the opposite can be observed: in the more prosperous EU-member SEE countries, Hungary and Slovenia, the figures show a decreasing tendency. It may be hypothesized that anxiety will increase in 2010, when families experience difficulties in paying off their loans following the effects of the global financial and economic crisis of 2008–09.

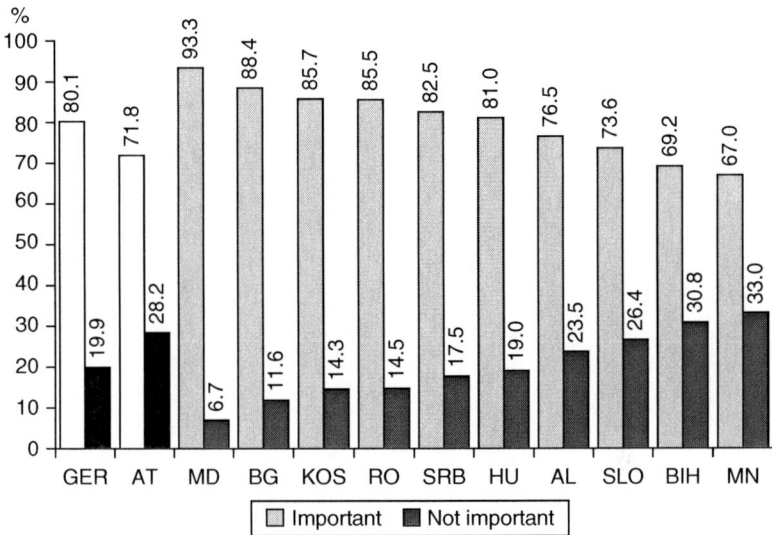

*Figure 18.6* Importance of job security in Germany, Austria and SEE countries in 2008

*Source*: EVS Foundation/Tilburg University (2010).

As Figure 18.6 shows, it is not only SEE people who identify a safe job as important, but also EU-15 citizens such as Germans and Austrians.

### Supporting working atmosphere

*Pleasant people at work* and the *desire to be given equal treatment at the workplace* were ranked high among the important aspects of work, both gaining between 70 and 80 per cent of agreement. These two factors contribute to mental balance and thus have a supporting influence on work.

Respondents in five out of ten SEE countries (FYR of Macedonia, Kosovo, Slovenia, Bulgaria and Romania) show an especially strong desire for jobs in which it is possible to work together with nice colleagues and superiors (Figure 18.7). An average of 77 per cent is a definite indication that human relations are essential for most SEE citizens. With the exception of Hungary, all SEE countries exceed Austria (68 per cent) and Germany (62 per cent) in valuing this aspect.

Other research has shown that human relations at the workplace are more important in former socialist countries than task orientation (Kainzbauer and Brück, 2000; Schroll-Machl and Nový, 2002,

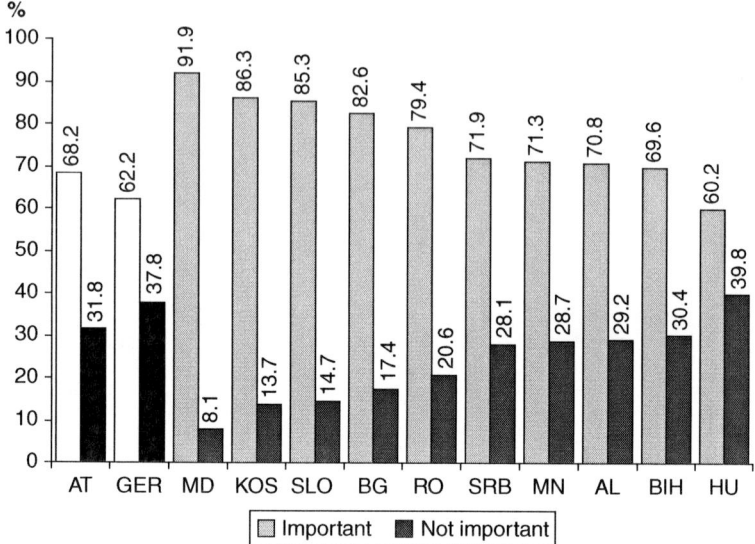

*Figure 18.7*    Importance of pleasant people at work in Austria, Germany and SEE countries in 2008
*Source*: EVS Foundation/Tilburg University (2010).

2003; Szalay, 2002). Maintaining human relationships was preferred to maintaining or increasing work performance. This attitude promoted a tendency to pass over deficiencies and had a negative effect on the quality of work (Borgulya, 2010).

Fink and Meierewert examined the results of cooperations with Eastern Europe from the perspective of Austrians and came to the conclusion that their work-related value standards are *risk aversion, priority setting by supervisors, working in collectives, harmony seeking* and '*saving one's own face*'. From these cultural standards, the authors derived a number of time management problems typical of Eastern Europeans. These are the slow speed of solving tasks, lengthy negotiations and decision-making processes and wasting the time of their colleague (Fink and Meierewert, 2004). According to the EVS data, risk aversion and harmony seeking may be typical of the SEE countries, too.

*Equal treatment* is a sensitive aspect of working conditions. Figure 18.8 demonstrates that more than 70 per cent of all people in SEE emphasise the importance of equality. There is a strong wish to eliminate differences in earnings among men and women in the same positions.

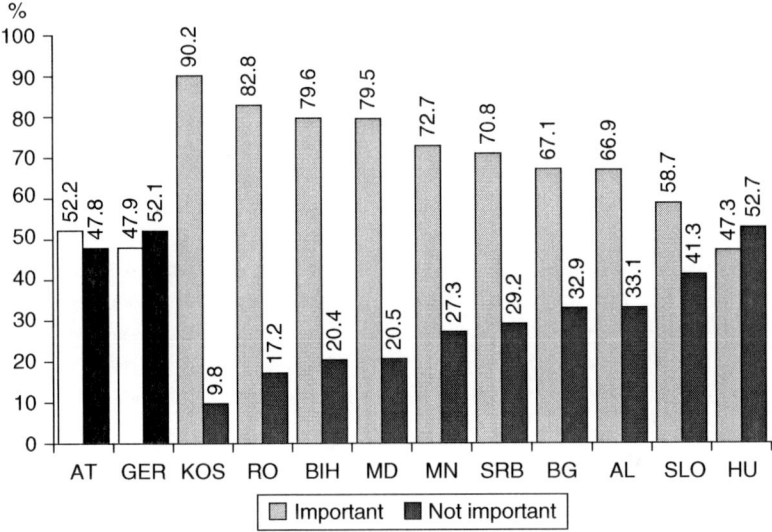

*Figure 18.8* Importance of equal treatment at work in Austria, Germany and SEE countries in 2008
*Source*: EVS Foundation/Tilburg University (2010).

One of the explanations could be that women's employment is also essential for a family's budget. In a study of CEE economies (among others Hungary, Slovenia and Romania), Lange (2008) points out that in both private and public sector services women's earnings in recent years were around 75–80 per cent of men's, a situation indicating men's continuing domination of better paid positions. The gender pay gap narrowed only marginally across CEE countries, and despite higher educational attainments, women are unable to move up in the occupational hierarchy. Although CEE women employees are more likely to hold university degrees than men, higher percentages of men than women hold managerial positions (Lange, 2008). Comparing findings on the importance of equality at work in SEE countries with those in Germany and Austria, with the exception of Hungary (nearly 47 per cent) all countries surpass Austria (52 per cent) and Germany (nearly 48 per cent) in the desire to be treated equally at work.

A study based on the ISSP (1999) survey also pointed out that people living in transition countries are very sensitive regarding inequality, and that they tolerate existing income differences to a significantly smaller extent than people in the West. This fact can be explained by the historical background, as 'inequality was the main issue proclaimed by the communist regime' (Večernik, 2006, p. 1222). Equality in treatment concerns not only income levels but also other benefits at work, for example the distribution of material and immaterial goods such as rooms, instruments, appreciations or distinctions.

Many conflicts at work have their origin in the *relationship between superiors and subordinates*. Where are the limits of an employee's freedom of action? Does s/he want to be instructed by his/her superior? Does the superior help him/her by giving clear instructions, or is the boss interested only in the outcome? The extent to which people in SEE countries are willing to follow instructions at work without questioning is also revealed by the EVS.

As Figure 18.9 shows, the highest rate of those who follow instructions even if they do not agree with them (37 per cent) is found in Romania. There are five among the ten SEE countries in which approximately one-third of all employees think in the same way. By contrast, only 6 per cent of German respondents would never question their superior's instructions. It can be assumed that this has something to do with a more authoritarian situation in the workplace in SEE countries. In a

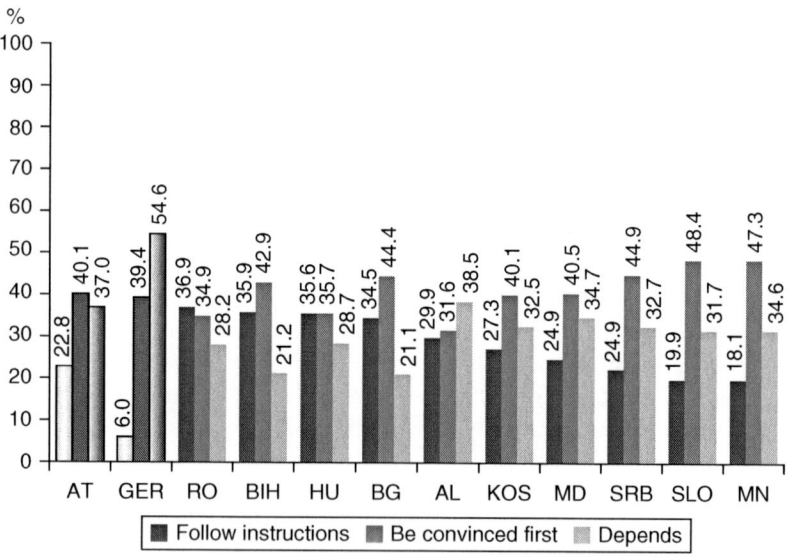

*Figure 18.9*   Following instructions at work in Austria, Germany and SEE countries in 2008

Source: EVS Foundation/Tilburg University (2010).

study of Danis and Parkhe (2002), the situation in Hungary is analysed by interviewed managers in the following way:

> Hungarian managers were generally more autocratic and more comfortable with the open use of power than their Western counterparts [...] [Hungarian] managers have a much more directive role, compared to Germany. [...] [In Hungary] if the managers say something, they follow that rule. The managers or shift leaders here have a much more powerful role with respect to telling the operators what they have to do [...] An Austrian characterized his Hungarian partner's parent company as a 'personality cult,' which revolved around the all-powerful chief executive officer.
>
> (Danis and Parkhe, 2002, p. 436)

Beside a more autocratic leadership style, Hungarian mentality in general also plays a role: there is a tendency towards *avoiding open confrontation*, which may be reflected in the high rate of those who do not question the instructions given by their superiors (close to 36 per cent). Beside this mentality, there are also pragmatic factors preventing employees from questioning their superiors: in Hungarian organizations it is still common for superiors to share only little or selected information (Danis and Parkhe, 2002). Thus employees are not mistaken when they believe that their superiors know more and are therefore more qualified to assess the situation and to decide what action should be taken.

### Self-fulfilment

The preconditions of well-being at work include, in addition to a supporting environment, the tasks and other duties that have to be carried out during working days. About 60 to 70 per cent of the population in the former communist societies think that those aspects of work that relate to self-fulfilment – having a work that meets their abilities and competences and having a job that offers other activities besides work – are important in their lives. This group of criteria, subsumed under the term *self-fulfilment*, includes the wish for a job that meets an individual's abilities, that is, interesting, and that allows an individual to achieve something and to learn new skills.

When the tasks *meet an individual's abilities*, skills can be improved, which is considered an achievement. The sense of achievement involved in performing such tasks might be the reason why this aspect ranks high on the scale of self-fulfilment. The SEE average of this category is 70 per cent, which is much higher than the figures for Austria and

Germany (58 and 56 per cent, respectively). With the exception of Hungary, the citizens of all SEE countries attach more importance to this aspect than the citizens of the Western countries included in the comparison. The figures relating to *abilities* correlate with those for *achieving something at work*. This might be regarded as evidence for the fact that South East Europeans are motivated by being able to make progress in their work.

*An interesting job* is on average as important for people in the SEE area as in Austria. For employees in Macedonia, Bulgaria, Slovenia, Kosovo, Serbia and Romania (93–69.5 per cent), however, an interesting job is more important than for their Austrian and German (69 and 63 per cent) counterparts.

As family life is, overall, the most important value in the SEE-region, the ideal workplace offers family-friendly conditions such as generous maternity leave, child-care benefits, kindergarten or nursery facilities provided by the workplace, supported family holidays. Good working hours are more important for South East Europeans than for Germans. The importance attached to meeting family or child-care responsibilities besides being a breadwinner is probably more typical for Macedonia, Bulgaria or Romania than for Germany, where many women take part-time jobs.

### Individual comforts and social perspectives

At the lower end of the importance scale (55 per cent or less) there are work-related criteria such as not having too much pressure, generous holidays and meeting people. The aspect *not too much pressure* is considered less important (20–30 per cent) by Austrians and Germans than by their Eastern counterparts, nearly half (or even more) of whom would like to work without too much stress. Hungarians seem to tolerate stress better, with only 18.5 per cent identifying *not too much pressure* as an important criterion in paid work.

Similar conclusions can be drawn relating to *generous holidays*, which take the second lowest place among the 17 aspects of work values ranked. Slovenians and Hungarians are at the bottom end of the scale, with figures similar to Germans (Hungarians 16 per cent compared to Germans 12 per cent). It is important to remember that German employees enjoy long holidays. The average leave entitlement across the EU-27 member states for which data are available is 25.2 days. The average collectively agreed annual paid leave in Germany is 30 days, while in Romania only 21 days (European Foundation for the Improvement of Living and Working Conditions, 2009).

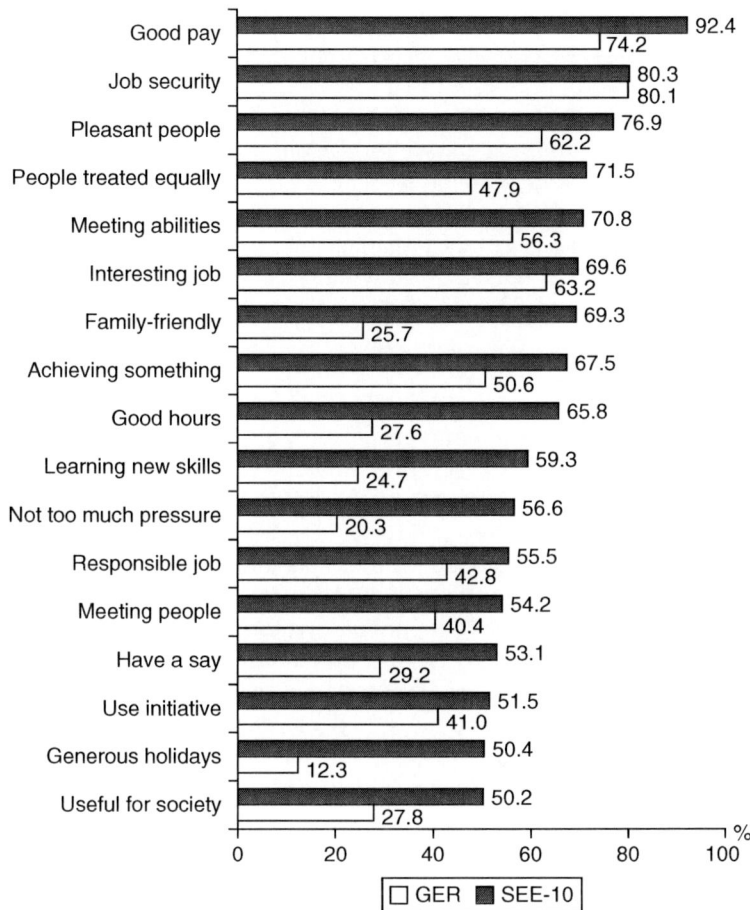

*Figure 18.10* Mean work values in SEE countries compared with Germany in 2008
*Source*: EVS Foundation/Tilburg University (2010).

There are four more aspects that rank at the lower end of the importance scale: *working in a responsible job, having freedom to make decisions in the job, opportunity for taking initiative* and *having a job useful for society.*

The explanation for these lower rankings may be the fact that in the socialist era personal responsibilities, individual ambitions and achievements, as well as risk-taking were traditionally considered incompatible with the socialist ideology and harmful to group harmony. Another reason may be that making decisions and initiating new solutions are linked with higher responsibility, which reduces comfort. Those people for whom a feeling of comfort is important may tend to refuse responsible jobs.

The findings show that *society* is the least important among the 17 aspects: having a job useful for society ranks at the bottom of the importance scale. On average, 50 per cent of SEE citizens think that serving the community while earning money is important, but this aspect is important only for 25 per cent of Hungarians and 27 per cent of Germans, which reflects a high degree of individualism in the thinking of these societies (Figure 18.10).

## Conclusion

Summing up recent trends in work-related values in the SEE region, it can be pointed out that the factors influencing values and attitudes have undergone radical changes after the reforms introduced in the economic and political systems.

There is still an older generation in the labour market whose cultural socialization dates back to the time of central planning in the economy. These people internalized the values of long-term employment, mutual loyalty, social protection, less pressure on quality and less intensive work performance. The younger generation started their careers after the transition to a market-based economy and has experienced the need for flexibility, tolerating higher pressures and having lower job security.

On the basis of findings from sociological surveys, it can be concluded that work plays a central role in the life of South East Europeans. It is the second most important sphere of life after the family.

This study has examined why South East Europeans think that work is important for them. A majority argues that people who do not work become lazy. Also, many respondents think that it is humiliating to receive money without working. An interesting aspect of the analysis is the difference of opinion on work as a social duty. In Albania, in Bosnia and Herzegovina and in Montenegro, less than half of the respondents said that work is a duty towards society. This proportion is noticeably higher in the old EU member states (about 70 per cent in Austria and Germany) and in Hungary, and even higher in Bulgaria and Slovenia.

Some of the various values connected with work, such as a high salary, long holidays or freedom of decision, are rated in a very similar ways across all the SEE countries, while, concerning other criteria, radical differences could be observed.

An analysis of work-related values reveals four groups of values. Within these groups the important percentages are close to each other and the values inside the groups also correspond to related attitudes: *financial security, supporting working atmosphere, self-fulfilment and family components, comforts and social perspectives.* Although an ordered grouping of values resembles Maslow's pyramid, only further research can determine whether the observed hierarchy of values means that some values are considered important only after more basic values have been satisfied.

High salaries constitute the most highly regarded aspect of work in SEE countries, being important for more than 90 per cent of the population in the region. Regarding the importance of 'good pay' and the aspect of job security, there is homogeneity among the different nations. The number of people who think that high salaries are important for them is higher than the number of those who attach great importance to job security. Job security ranks second on the scale of the most relevant work-related criteria, with more than 80 per cent of the population of the SEE region rating it as important. The two criteria 'good pay' and 'job security' embody the concept *financial security* in the SEE region.

We see evidence of a person-oriented culture in the fact that on average more than three-quarters of people in SEE declare that working together with pleasant colleagues is important to them. In other words, a pleasant working atmosphere is a highly valued asset in a good workplace. It may be surprising how many people in SEE countries wish to be treated equally at work. While in the reference countries Germany and Austria only about half of the respondents mentioned equal treatment as an important criterion, more than 70 per cent of South East Europeans picked equality as important. Likeable colleagues and equal treatment at the workplace create *a supporting working atmosphere.*

An interesting job seems to be important both in SEE and in the old EU member countries, although the average of 'it is important' answers is lower than that for the four most highly regarded criteria. There are also great variations in the way people in SEE countries rate different aspects within the group of *self-fulfilment, including family components.* Many people in Moldavia, Kosovo and Bulgaria, for example, think that it is important to learn new skills while working. In Hungary, as in Germany, this seems to be less of a motivator. Also, the criterion 'family-friendly conditions' is seen in different ways. While in Moldavia, Kosovo, Albania, Romania and Bulgaria more than 70 per cent emphasize family-friendly working conditions, in Hungary less than 40 per cent stress this aspect. In Germany the rate is even lower: only one-quarter marks this advantage of a workplace as important.

Even greater differences can be observed between some SEE countries such as Moldavia, Kosovo, Bulgaria and Romania and the old EU member Germany in terms of thinking about *good working hours*. Nearly three times as many people want to work at workplaces where working time is suitable for them than in Germany. In this respect, there are differences also across SEE countries. Approximately as many Hungarians and Slovenians as Austrians and Germans desire good working time conditions.

The most significant differences can be observed within the components of the group *comforts and social perspectives*. SEE people, for example, seek to avoid pressure more than their Austrian or German counterparts. There is a marked difference between Kosovo and Austria or Germany. Hungary also shows low stress avoidance.

*Generous holidays* are another example of huge differences: while in Moldavia or Kosovo there is a strong wish for long holidays, this is much weaker in Hungary and Slovenia, or in Germany and Austria.

The discussion above shows that the SEE countries share important common features in work-related values and attitudes, while there are also significant differences among them. On the basis of findings from the 2008 wave of the EVS, the highest differences can be observed between Moldavians and Hungarians. The citizens of three countries (Moldavia, Bulgaria and Kosovo), on the other hand, show many similarities regarding their work-related values and attitudes.

## Notes

1. The European Value Study (EVS), a large-scale cross-national and longitudinal research project on fundamental values in Western societies, was initiated by researchers at Tilburg University and Leuven Catholic University at the end of the 1970s. Their goal was to investigate empirically the main fundamental value patterns of Europeans. The first wave of surveys took place in 1981. When Ronald Inglehard, a researcher at Michigan University, joined, overseas institutes were also participating in the study. Thus the World Value Survey was born. In 1990 a new study was completed, to measure the changes that took place since then. This time all countries in the European Community, except for Greece, took part in the study, as well as some Eastern European and some Scandinavian countries. The third wave of surveys took place in 1999/2000, focusing on the same questions as before. These are the following: the importance of the most relevant spheres of life (as for example family, work or religion), social questions, politics, environmental awareness of society and other questions of morality. The attitudes towards other groups, such as immigrants and ethnic minorities, were also examined. This third wave of EVS took place in 32 European countries and analysed the questionnaires of 39,797 participants. Together with the results of the World Value Study, it encompasses the results of the whole world (Arts et al., 2003). In 2008, the

fourth wave of EVS was completed. The findings of this survey were published in July 2010. Some countries' data, such as those of Croatia and the FYR of Macedonia, are missed out in our analyses, because these data were not yet available at the time of writing this chapter.

2. As we are working on this book, EVS data about Croatia and Macedonia are still not avaible. So in the following analysis we compare the remaining ten SEE countries (Albania, Bosnia and Herzegovina, Bulgaria, Hungary, Kosovo, Moldavia, Montenegro, Romania, Slovenia and Serbia) with Austria and Germany. Rounded values will be used in the analysis of the survey results.

3. The EVS in its fourth wave 2008 listed 17 benefits of work and workplace on which the participants gave their opinions. These are (1) good pay, (2) pleasant people, (3) not too much pressure, (4) good job security, (5) good working hours, (6) opportunity to use initiative, (7) useful for society, (8) generous holidays, (9) meeting people, (10) achieve something, (11) responsible job, (12) interesting job, (13) meeting abilities, (14) learning new skills, (15) family-friendly job, (16) have a say, (17) people treated equally.

4. Analysing data of EVS 1999/2000, Mareš (2001) could identify three main groups of aspects of work typical for the Czech Republic: social aspects of work; material aspects of work; and self-fulfilling aspects of work. He identified not only *good pay* and *good job security*, but also *good working hours, generous holidays* and *not too much pressure* as material aspects. In examining 2008 EVS data it was reasonable to separate the latest three aspects in connection with the SEE countries, as the relevance of these aspects is quite different from that of good pay and job security.

## References

Alas, R. and Rees, C. (2006) 'Work-Related Attitudes, Values and Radical Change in Post-Socialist Context: A Comparative Study', *Journal of Business Ethics*, 68, 181–189.

Arts, W., Hagenaars, J. and Halman, L. (2003) *The Cultural Diversity of European Unity* (Leiden and Boston: Brill).

Borgulya, A. (2010) *Kommunikációmenedzsment a vállalati értékteremtésben* (Budapest: Akadémiai kiadó).

Borgulya, A. and Hahn, J. (2008) 'Work-Related Values and Attitudes in Central and Eastern Europe', *Journal for East European Management Studies*, 13, 216–239.

Danis, W. M. and Parkhe, A. (2002) 'Hungarian Western Partnerships: A Grounded Theoretical Model of Integration Processes and Outcomes', *Journal of International Business Studies*, 33, 423–455.

European Foundation for the Improvement of Living and Working Conditions (2009) *Working Time Developments 2008*, http://www.eurofound.europa.eu, date accessed 29 July 2010.

EVS Foundation/Tilburg University (2010) *European Values Study 2008*, 4th wave, Integrated Dataset, GESIS Cologne, Germany, ZA4800 Data File Version 1.0.0. (2010-06-30) DOI:10.4232/1.10059.

Fink, G. and Meierewert, S. (2004) 'Issues of Time in International, Intercultural Management: East and Central Europe from the Perspective of Austrian Managers', *Journal for East European Management Studies*, 1, 61–84.

Florida, R. (2002) *The Rise of the Creative Class* (New York: Basic Books).

Florida, R. (2004) 'The Great Creative Class Debate: Revenge of the Squelchers', *The Next American City*, Issue 5, July 2004, http://creativeclass.com/rfcgdb/articles/Revenge%20of%20the%20Squelchers.pdf, accessed 31 July 2010.

Glaser, E. L. (2004) 'Review of Richard Florida's *The Rise of the Creative Class*: The Capital of What?', *The New York Sun* [online], 19 February 2004, http://post.economics.harvard.edu/faculty/glaser/papers/Review_Florida.pdf, accessed 21 July 2007.

ISSP (1999) *ISSP Survey, 1999 Social Inequality III*, http://www.issp.org/page.php?pageId=4, accessed 31 July 2010.

Jávor, I. and Rozgonyi, T. (2005) *Hatalom, konfliktus, kultúra* (Budapest: KJK-KERSZÖV).

Kainzbauer, A. and Brück, F. (2000) 'Cultural Standards Austria–Hungary', *Journal of Cross-Cultural Competence & Management*, 2, 73–105.

Kalleberg, A. L. and Reve, T. (1992) 'Contracts and Commitment: Economic and Sociological Perspectives on Employment Relation', *Human Relations*, 45, 1103–1132.

Kasahara, K. and Makó, Cs. (1996) *Manpower and Skill use in the Transformation Process*, (Tokyo: Rikkyo University, Department of Social Relations and Budapest: Hungarian Academy of Sciences), p. 132.

Kušić, S. and Grupe, C. (2006) 'Croatian SMEs Between EU Integration and Intraregional Cooperation', *Osteuropa-Wirtschaft*, 51, 40–48.

Lange, T. (2008) 'Communist Legacies, Gender and the Impact on Job Satisfaction in Central and Eastern Europe', *European Journal of Industrial Relations*, 14, 327–346, http://ejd.sagepubl.com, accessed 25 July 2010.

Mareš, P. (2001) 'The Czechs: Jobs and Work', *Czech Sociological Review*, 9, 69–84.

Medgyesi, M. and Róbert, P. (2000) 'A munkával kapcsolatos elégedettség nemzetközi összehasonlításban' in Kolosi, T., Tóth, I. G. and Vukovics, G. (eds) *Társadalmi riport* (Budapest: TÁRKI), 591–616.

Schroll-Machl, S. and Nový, I. (2002) *Beruflich in Tschechien* (Göttingen: Vandenhoeck and Ruprecht).

Schroll-Machl, S. and Nový, I. (2003) *Perfekt geplant oder genial improvisiert?* (Mering: Rainer Hampp Verlag).

Sersic, D. M., Serko, B. and Galic, Z. (2005) 'Work Values and Job-related Attitudes in Croatia', *Journal of General Social Issues*, 14, 1039–54.

Szalay, G. (2002) *Arbeit und Kommunikation in deutsch-ungarischen Teams* (Budapest: Goethe Institut Inter Nationes).

Tosi, H. L. and Mero, N. P. (2003) *The Fundamentals of Organizational Behavior* (Malden: Blackwell Publishing).

Traser, U. and Venables, T. (2008) *Who's Afraid of the EU's Latest Enlargement* (Bruxelles, ECAS), http://www.ecas.org, accessed 10 May 2007.

UniCredit Group (2010) *CEE Quarterly*, 1Q 2010 (München: UniCredit Bank AG), http://www.unicreditgroup.eu, accessed 31 July 2010.

Večernik, J. (2006) 'Work Values and Job Attitudes in the Czech Republic between 1997 and 2005', *Czech Sociological Review*, 42, 1219–40, www.papers.ssrn.com, accessed 29 July 2010.

Ward, T., Lelkes, O., Sutherland, H. and Tóth, I. G. (eds) (2009) *European Inequalities: Social Inclusion and Income Distribution in the European Union* (Budapest: TÁRKI).

# 19
# Values and Trust in Business Relationships in Former Yugoslav Markets

*Maja Makovec Brenčič and Vesna Žabkar*

## Introduction

The former Yugoslavia has gone through turbulent political, economic and societal changes since 1990. After the 22-million market split into separate countries, numerous differences arose among them. War and political instability also led to many business and economic risks, and therefore slower economic growth. Yet, in the last few years, markets have stabilized and some of them have grown – as that of Slovenia, which also became a member of the European Union (EU). Croatia is expected to follow a similar path soon. These two countries show economic and political stability, as well as economic development and growth comparable to EU countries. This is not yet the case for the rest of the former Yugoslav countries, such as Macedonia, Serbia, Kosovo, Bosnia and Herzegovina and Montenegro. Nevertheless, the former 22-million market is interesting for investors and all those who would like to expand their businesses to this part of Europe, especially as it shows great potential for growth. To enter these markets and to create business relationships within them requires an understanding of the core elements and specifics of the local business culture. The acknowledgement of economic, political and cultural differences between different former Yugoslav markets is a precondition for successful business development, as is an understanding of the meaning of trust, values, commitment and cooperation when doing business with partners in these diversified markets. This is particularly important when companies want to position themselves in these markets over the long term.

In 2001 the Faculty of Economics, University of Ljubljana (FELU) conducted one of the biggest research projects to date about business relationships and their components, as well as about attitudes of Croatian,

Serbian, Montenegrin and Bosnian firms towards their suppliers, buyers and competitors (Prašnikar, 2001). The 200 largest firms of each country were included in the survey (producers of finished and semi-finished goods; total n = 613). Most of the respondents were either CEOs or marketing directors. At that time, the research showed that firms were (despite the consequences of the war and political turbulences) traditionally embedded in relationships with their partners from former Yugoslav republics, whom they trust and with whom they want to keep or renew business relationships. Most of these were business relationships in manufacturing, with high commitment and long-term orientation, as respondents claimed at the time of the research.

There has been no up-to-date renewal of the survey, yet it continues to serve as a good illustration of 'bonding' relationships that are built when several countries or markets develop in the same cultural and economic environment, as Yugoslavia used to be for decades. Despite the break-up, the war and a turbulent political situation in some former Yugoslav countries, through business a way has been found to continue certain relationships and to fulfil the demand of the market. As an illustration of this, the growth of international exchange between Slovenia as an EU member state and the rest of former Yugoslav countries since the early 1990s is shown in Tables 19.1 and 19.2.

## Values and trust as crucial elements of business

Despite the fact that many factors, contextual and non-contextual, collectivistic and personal, influence the success of business relationships, values, trust and commitment are those which 'produce outcomes that promote efficiency, productivity and effectiveness; and which lead directly to cooperative behaviors', as stated by Morgan and Hunt (1994, p. 22). Their relationship marketing view of commitment and trust has been the foundation for most of the research in the field of relationship components, especially in the business-to-business area. They point out that commitment must be explored as two interrelated and dependent variables when analysing relationships.

Values 'are held by individuals as well as by collectives; culture presupposes a collectivity' (Hofstede, 2001, p. 5). According to the socio-cultural view, values are 'an enduring belief that one mode of conduct of end-state of existence is preferable to an opposing mode of conduct or end-state of existence' (Rokeach, 1973, p. 5). Most of the sensitive yet crucial elements of relationships (cooperation, long-term attitude and so on) should be explored before creating relationships in different cultural

Table 19.1 Exports and foreign direct investment (FDI): Comparison of trade and investment entrance modes of Slovenian companies into the former Yugoslav markets from the early 1990s until 2009 (in million EUR)

| Markets | 1994 | 1995 | 2000 | 2001 | 2002 | 2003 | 2004 | 2005 | 2006 | 2007 | 2008 | 2009 |
|---|---|---|---|---|---|---|---|---|---|---|---|---|
| Total exports (in million EUR) | 5.772 | 6.437 | 9.483 | 10.346 | 10.962 | 11.284 | 12.783 | 14.397 | 16.757 | 19.385 | 19.808 | 16.054 |
| Exports to former Yugoslav countries | 880 | 935 | 1.480 | 1.748 | 1.950 | 1.965 | 2.249 | 2.476 | 2.735 | 3.101 | 3.413 | 2.608 |
| Croatia | 690 | 683 | 747 | 894 | 954 | 1.007 | 1.166 | 1.304 | 1.464 | 1.569 | 1.693 | 1.241 |
| BiH | 58 | 92 | 406 | 444 | 492 | 471 | 490 | 516 | 484 | 535 | 626 | 501 |
| Serbia* | 14 | 7 | 155 | 263 | 346 | 345 | 454 | 523 | 509 | 741 | 791 | 618 |
| Montenegro* | – | – | – | – | – | – | – | – | 79 | 111 | 120 | 87 |
| Macedonia | 184 | 146 | 172 | 147 | 158 | 142 | 139 | 134 | 125 | 144 | 181 | 161 |
| Outward FDI | 299 | 379 | 862 | 1.120 | 1.445 | 1.884 | 2.224 | 2.789 | 3.452 | 4.889 | 5.661 | NA |
| FDI – former Yugoslavia | 223 | 248 | 556 | 655 | 834 | 1,100 | 1.276 | 1.715 | 2.235 | 3.389 | 3.803 | NA |
| Croatia | 163 | 177 | 389 | 455 | 530 | 617 | 673 | 817 | 927 | 1.077 | 1.108 | NA |
| BiH | 13 | 13 | 67 | 98 | 148 | 188 | 216 | 277 | 343 | 565 | 690 | NA |
| Serbia* | 24 | 42 | 29 | 49 | 96 | 219 | 294 | 509 | 770 | 1.396 | 1.626 | NA |
| Montenegro* | – | – | – | – | – | – | – | – | 79 | 160 | 145 | NA |
| Macedonia | 13 | 16 | 51 | 53 | 60 | 76 | 92 | 112 | 116 | 193 | 235 | NA |

* Until 2006 Montenegro was included in the data for Serbia.
Sources: Pavlič Damijan (2001, pp. 108–122); Banka Slovenije (2008, p. 29; 2010, p. 4); Statistični urad Republike Slovenije (2010).

*Table 19.2*   Slovenian imports 2001–09 from former Yugoslav countries (in million EUR)

| Market | 2001 | 2002 | 2003 | 2004 | 2005 | 2006 | 2007 | 2008 | 2009 |
|---|---|---|---|---|---|---|---|---|---|
| Total imports | 11.344 | 11.574 | 12.238 | 14.143 | 15.804 | 18.340 | 21.508 | 23.045 | 17.066 |
| Imports from former Yugoslavia | 601 | 580 | 624 | 804 | 1.048 | 1.345 | 1.608 | 1.619 | 1.171 |
| Croatia | 453 | 427 | 455 | 514 | 609 | 736 | 849 | 835 | 630 |
| BiH | 70 | 69 | 79 | 151 | 208 | 313 | 321 | 311 | 235 |
| Serbia* | 51 | 60 | 69 | 113 | 188 | 239 | 357 | 386 | 264 |
| Montenegro* | – | – | – | – | 14 | 19 | 24 | 40 | 18 |
| Macedonia | 27 | 24 | 21 | 26 | 29 | 38 | 58 | 46 | 25 |

* Until 2006 Montenegro was included in the data for Serbia.
*Sources*: Banka Slovenije (2009, 2010); Statistični urad Republike Slovenije (2010).

environments. Morgan and Hunt (1994) claim that shared values in business (marketing) relationships are a 'direct precursor of relationship commitment and trust' (p. 25). They posit that values in business relationships are reflected by the extent to which partners share beliefs about relationship goals, policies and behaviours. According to De Mooij (1998), a value is a preference of one mode of behaviour over another mode of behaviour, and these modes are not only influenced by culture, but are also very diverse when different cultures are compared.

Spekman (1988, cited in Morgan and Hunt, 1994) sees trust as a building block for strategic partnership. Trust is also an important factor for the successful development of business relationships; it brings a feeling of security, reduces uncertainty and creates an atmosphere of support in relationships (Naudé and Buttle, 2000). Anderson and Narus (1990) define trust as a belief that the other party will act in a way that positively influences the company and will avoid any activities that might have negative consequences. Morgan and Hunt (1994) claim that trust exists when one can rely on a partner's integrity and reliability. An important part of understanding trust is that the partner is worthy of trust, which is related to a partner's knowledge, reliability or intentions (Moorman et al., 1992). Dwyer et al. (1987) assume that common values contribute to the development of trust. Therefore we will take a look into the link between values and trust in business relationships in former Yugoslav countries.

Since business relationships are influenced by culture (Kluckhohn, 1951, 1967; Rokeach, 1972; Trompenaars and Hampden Turner, 2000; Hofstede, 2001; Javidan and House, 2001among others), values and trust can be influenced by the collective and individual perception of culture. Therefore vital components of relationships, such as trust and commitment, also co-create the relationship value. Since business-to-business relationships tend to be long-term (Ford, 1997), it is of high importance that relationship values are developed, maintained and understood as common values of partners, enabling the creation of an intangible value of the relationship. For Ravald and Grönroos (1996), relationship value means safety, credibility and security, on which trust is based. According to Wimmer and Mandjak (2002), trust increases loyalty and can result in a mutually profitable relationship for suppliers and buyers. Trust is also defined as willingness to rely on an exchange partner in whom one has confidence (Ganesan, 1994, cited in Blois, 1999).

This means that specific values, as well as trust and commitment, are not only influenced by external culture (from a collectivistic point of view) embedded in the business relationships and in the business culture of a certain market, but are also created by the culture of the relationship itself.

Regardless of the values and of trust, the development of business (buyer–seller) relationships can be understood as a sequence of decisions that buyers and sellers make about whether they should enter a relationship, continue a relationship or enhance the scope of a relationship. There are different kinds of decision in which satisfaction and trust are likely to play different roles in risk reduction, depending on the nature of the decision to be made (Selnes, 1998). Former Yugoslav countries and business partners active in those markets were faced with exactly this challenge when the economic and political turbulences started and when, after the war, relationships needed to be revived. The results of our 2001 research show that most of the companies from other former Yugoslav countries were willing to renew and interested in renewing their business relationships with Slovenian companies despite political differences. This was mainly due to economic reasons, but also to the fact that Slovenia always used to be 'a window' to the Western world for these countries. Table 19.3 shows the relationship renewal perception of companies that did not yet cooperate with Slovenian companies at the time of the study.

From each of the markets except Montenegro, the 200 largest companies (with more than 200 employees) were included in the study. The final sample included 613 companies: 203 from Croatia, 216 from Serbia, 66 from Montenegro and 127 from Bosnia and Herzegovina. Telephone interviews were conducted, with the support of a professional

*Table 19.3*   Readiness to renew cooperation with Slovenian firms

|      | Croatia | Serbia | Montenegro | BiH | Total |
|------|---------|--------|------------|-----|-------|
| Yes  | 82%     | 94%    | 94%        | 97% | 93%   |
| No   | 18%     | 6%     | 6%         | 3%  | 7%    |
| Total| 100%    | 100%   | 100%       | 100%| 100%  |

*Source*: FELU (2001).

research agency, in each market, in order to assure that each respondent was contacted in their own language. The respondents were business managers responsible for relationships with buyers, mostly from manufacturing companies. The majority of companies had domestic owners and were, geographically, predominantly oriented towards the domestic market. The structure of the sample is provided in Tables 19.4, 19.5 and 19.6.

When asked about common values and norms, respondents evaluated the relationship with their most important buyer. Results show that companies from the former Yugoslav markets mostly recognize the

*Table 19.4*   Respondents categorized by industry

| Industry | Croatia | Serbia | Montenegro | BiH | Total |
|----------|---------|--------|------------|-----|-------|
| Agriculture, Forestry, Fisheries (%) | 3.9 | 3.7 | 0.0 | 3.9 | 3.4 |
| Mining (%) | 0.0 | 1.4 | 1.5 | 0.8 | 0.8 |
| Manufacturing (%) | 82.3 | 85.6 | 60.6 | 95.3 | 83.8 |
| Other (%) | 13.8 | 9.3 | 37.9 | 0.0 | 11.9 |
| Total | 100 | 100 | 100 | 100 | 100 |

*Source*: FELU (2001).

*Table 19.5*   Respondents categorized by share of foreign ownership (in %)

| Share of foreign ownership | Croatia | Serbia | Montenegro | BiH | Total |
|----------------------------|---------|--------|------------|-----|-------|
| 0% | 83.9 | 96.6 | 95.4 | 90.2 | 90.9 |
| 1% to 99% | 13.0 | 3.4 | 4.6 | 8.0 | 7.7 |
| 100% | 3.1 | 0 | 0 | 1.8 | 1.4 |
| Total | 100 | 100 | 100 | 100 | 100 |

*Source*: FELU (2001).

*Table 19.6*   Respondents categorized by geographic orientation of markets

| Geographic orientation | Croatia | Serbia | Montenegro | BiH | Total |
|---|---|---|---|---|---|
| Mostly domestic market (%) | 58.1 | 79.2 | 92.3 | 65.4 | 70.8 |
| Mostly foreign markets (%) | 41.9 | 20.8 | 7.7 | 34.6 | 29.2 |
| Total | 100 | 100 | 100 | 100 | 100 |

*Source: FELU* (2001).

importance of common values and norms, and that these norms are also present in their business relationships (see Table 19.7). They mostly agree that they treat jointly rather than individually problems that arise in the relationship. However, they do not share similar views on ethics in business behaviour, or they do not share them to the same degree. Respondents from Bosnia and Herzegovina mostly agreed with all the statements, while there was slightly less agreement among the respondents from Croatia. Additional analyses (analysis of variance, post hoc tests) showed that managerial views were significantly different in the different countries. Bosnian and Serbian companies supported their partners in achieving business results and treated problems in relationships together with their partner to a higher degree than their

*Table 19.7*   Evaluation of values in business relationships in former Yugoslav markets

| Statements | Country | Mean | Std. deviation |
|---|---|---|---|
| Your company supports your partner in achieving good business results. | Croatia | 5.75 | 1.41 |
| | Serbia | 6.16 | 1.24 |
| | Montenegro | 6.02 | 1.40 |
| | BiH | 6.27 | 1.31 |
| | Total | 6.03 | 1.34 |
| Problems that arise in this relationship are treated by the parties as joint responsibilities rather than as individual responsibilities. | Croatia | 6.18 | 1.18 |
| | Serbia | 6.54 | 0.99 |
| | Montenegro | 6.32 | 1.33 |
| | BiH | 6.65 | 0.89 |
| | Total | 6.42 | 1.09 |
| You and your partner respect the values of keeping promises and reliability. | Croatia | 6.17 | 1.26 |
| | Serbia | 6.51 | 1.06 |
| | Montenegro | 6.67 | 0.77 |
| | BiH | 6.76 | 0.71 |
| | Total | 6.47 | 1.06 |

*Table 19.7*  (Continued)

| Statements | Country | Mean | Std. deviation |
|---|---|---|---|
| You and your partner support each other in reaching goals. | Croatia | 5.65 | 1.37 |
| | Serbia | 6.14 | 1.25 |
| | Montenegro | 5.91 | 1.45 |
| | BiH | 6.46 | 1.09 |
| | Total | 6.02 | 1.32 |
| You and your partner have similar views on ethics in business behaviour. | Croatia | 5.58 | 1.38 |
| | Serbia | 5.76 | 1.48 |
| | Montenegro | 5.88 | 1.63 |
| | BiH | 6.08 | 1.48 |
| | Total | 5.78 | 1.47 |

*Note*: Scale: 1 – completely disagree, 7 – completely agree.
*Source*: FELU (2001).

Croatian counterparts. Relatively speaking, there seemed to be less trust and reliability in the relationships of Croatian companies with their business partners than in the relationships of companies from other former Yugoslav markets. Also, the respect for common values was less present in the relationships of Serbian and Montenegrin companies by comparison with Bosnian companies.

Regarding trust in business relationships with the most important buyers, respondents at least partially agreed with all statements (see Table 19.8). They mostly agreed that trust is very important in relationships with their buyers. The highest agreement with this statement was expressed by companies from Montenegro, the relatively lowest agreement by companies from Croatia. Additional analyses (analysis of variance and post hoc tests) showed that the differences were significant. Croatian companies seemed to evaluate trust in business relationships lower than companies from the other three markets. It is possible that their experiences with the honesty of their business partners had been less favourable in the past. On the other hand, companies from Bosnia and Herzegovina seemed to have the most positive experiences with their buyers keeping their promises in the past, compared to companies from other former Yugoslav markets.

Finally, links were tested between common values and trust, for respondents from all former Yugoslav markets. In all markets except Bosnia, these links were positive and significant. However, they were not very strong, but of medium intensity for Croatian companies and low for Serbian and Montenegrin companies.

*Table 19.8* Evaluation of trust in business relationships in former Yugoslav markets

| Statements | Country | Mean | Std. deviation |
|---|---|---|---|
| Trust is very important in the relationship with your buyer. | Croatia | 6.68 | 0.77 |
| | Serbia | 6.88 | 0.53 |
| | Montenegro | 6.97 | 0.17 |
| | BiH | 6.88 | 0.45 |
| | Total | 6.82 | 0.59 |
| Your buyer has been honest with you so far. | Croatia | 5.46 | 1.36 |
| | Serbia | 5.85 | 1.29 |
| | Montenegro | 5.89 | 1.04 |
| | BiH | 6.17 | 1.19 |
| | Total | 5.79 | 1.29 |
| Your buyer keeps promises. | Croatia | 5.36 | 1.35 |
| | Serbia | 5.43 | 1.28 |
| | Montenegro | 5.26 | 1.40 |
| | BiH | 6.06 | 1.31 |
| | Total | 5.52 | 1.35 |

*Note*: Scale: 1 – completely disagree, 7 – completely agree.
*Source*: *FELU* (2001).

When comparing the outcome of the 2001 study with the total exports and imports, as well as with FDIs in former Yugoslav markets, from a Slovenian point of view (see Tables 19.1 and 19.2), we can interpret the results also through a business relationship perspective. The data indirectly show that trust and commitment have kept playing an important role since the business focus of Slovenian companies still stayed in the former Yugoslav markets, which account for 16–18 per cent of total Slovenian exports. Not only the geographic proximity, but also the cultural and psychographic understanding of business terms and behaviour helped Slovenian companies to keep their positions on these markets. Partners in former Yugoslav markets, especially in some industries such as the wood, textile, FMCG or software industry, have kept long-term relationships regardless of the differences in political or economic beliefs and attitudes. At the same time, these countries also opened their borders and economy to other foreign investments and experienced the entrance of international and global multinational companies (MNCs), since the supply had been severely diminished during the turbulent times. Yet Slovenian firms kept their position of being credible and value-creating partners, which shows how important it is to nourish and invest into crucial relationship components such as trust, commitment and common values.

When exploring current attitudes and perceptions about value and trust from the perspective of Slovenian firms that are experienced in doing business with former Yugoslav markets, some interesting points of view are revealed. For example, the Sales Director of Trimo, a proactive Slovenian international firm dealing with construction and development of new building materials, states:

> Risk of business cooperation is still much higher in former Yugoslav countries than in Western Europe markets. If you want to do business in this area you have to be very close to the customer. Business is still mostly based on trust. It is not so usual to get bank guarantees or any other quality payment insurance in this area, at least in our business [...] Therefore it is very important that you follow customer activities and that you are able to respond to any situation at the right time. You spend much more time with them than with other customers and you get to know them personally very well. There are a lot of emotions involved in the business so it is quite often that you become a real friend to your customer.
>
> (Interview by the authors with Mr Vovk, Sales
> Manager of Trimo, September 2010)

Another Slovenian multinational corporation, Gorenje, one of the largest producers of domestic appliances in Central and South Eastern Europe, has been present in former Yugoslav markets for decades, including during the war. Gorenje's Regional Sales Manager, Mrs Borkovič, evaluates relationships of the past and compares them with today's. In an interview with the authors in September 2010, she reported on difficult times during the war and on political turbulence, which also created a lot of operational and process obstacles, for instance with customs or distribution. But they managed to overcome these problems. Gorenje, she says, 'was actually growing together with the development on these markets. Therefore, the relationships were established differently and had different meaning than in other parts of the world. Somehow the products of Gorenje were "ours" from the Yugoslav perspective.' Regardless of the development and modernization of economies, changes of consumer behaviour and the influence of the globalization on these markets, she points out the importance of building on values and on trust from the beginning of a relationship. Like Mr Vovk from Trimo, she also claims that relationships 'in this part of the world are different than [*sic*] anywhere else', also due to the fact that 'we used to grow together as one country and one market'. For that reason, Gorenje invests a lot into understanding the changing habits, customers and distribution structures in former Yugoslav countries and works with their representatives and sales units on intensifying the long-term relationships with final customers through different channels.

As the two respondents reveal, understanding values and trust, as they are embedded in the specific cultural and political development, remains a crucial building block of business relationships. The turbulences of the past have left certain impacts, yet committed and long-term oriented partnerships still present an advantage for doing business in these markets. An understanding and knowledge of the history and culture is an important benefit when entering these markets, as it is in entering all markets. Certain relationship dimensions such as openness, friendship, flexibility, adjustment or commitment are important components of creating and maintaining values and trust in relationships.

## Conclusions

From the analysis of common values and norms among managers from former Yugoslav markets it is evident that the importance of relationships with buyers is widely recognized. There is respect for reliability and for trying to solve disagreements jointly with one's partners. Differences in the attitude of managers could be determined between Serbia and Bosnia on the one hand and Croatia on the other hand, the former placing a higher emphasis on common values and the mutual support of partners for achieving their goals. However, trust seems to continue to be essential in business relationships even today. Trust is evaluated more highly by Bosnian managers than by Serbian managers, and most of all by Croatian managers, although general trust levels in all countries are relatively high. Also from a current perspective, values and norms, showing dedication to partners with persistent personal investments into relationships and a flexible understanding of political and cultural market changes (including global influences) are important elements for gaining trust and confidence among business partners. Recent cultural and political developments in the region do play an important role. But with the entrance of new international capital, especially through MNCs, and with an advancing liberalization of these economies and development towards EU standards, business relationships in certain former Yugoslav markets are also getting the flavour of 'standard' business relationships.

## References

Anderson, J. C. and Narus, J. A. (1990) 'A Model of Distributor and Manufacturer Firm Working Partnerships', *Journal of Marketing*, 54, 42–58.

Banka Slovenije (2008) *Neposredne naložbe* (Ljubljana: Banka Slovenije).

Banka Slovenije (2009) *Neposredne naložbe* (Ljubljana: Banka Slovenije).

Banka Slovenije (2010) *Neposredne naložbe* (Ljubljana: Banka Slovenije).

Blois, K. (1999) 'Trust in Business to Business Relationships: An Evaluation of Its Status', *Journal of Management Studies*, 36, 197–215.

De Mooij, M. (1998) *Global Marketing and Advertising, Understanding Cultural Paradoxes* (Thousand Oaks: Sage Publications).

Dwyer, F. R., Schurr, P. H. and Oh, S. (1987) 'Developing Buyer–Seller Relationships', *Journal of Marketing*, 51, 11–27.

FELU (2001) *Research on Former Yugoslav markets*, Internal research data, Faculty of Economics, University of Ljubljana.

Ford, D. (ed.) (1997) *Understanding Business Markets: Interaction, Relationships and Networks* (London: The Dryden Press).

Ganesan, S. (1994) 'Determinants of Long-Term Orientation in Buyer–Seller Relationships', *Journal of Marketing*, 58, 1–19.

Hofstede, G. (2001) *Culture's Consequences: Comparing Values, Behaviours, Institutions, and Organizations Across Nations* (London: Sage Publications).

Javidan, M. and House, J. R. (2001) 'Cultural Acumen for the Global Manager: Lessons from Project GLOBE', *Organizational Dynamics*, 29, 289–305.

Kluckhohn, C. (1951) 'The Study of Culture', in Lerner, D. and Lasswell, H. D. (eds), *The Policy Sciences: Recent Developments in Scope and Method* (Stanford: Stanford University Press).

Kluckhohn, C. (1967) 'Values and Value-Orientations in the Theory of Action: An Exploration in Definition and Classification', in Parsons, T. and Shils, E. A. (eds), *Toward a General Theory of Action* (Cambridge, MA: Harvard University Press).

Moorman, C., Zaltman, G. and Deshpandé, R. (1992) 'Relationships between Providers and Users of Market Research: The Dynamics of Trust within and between Organizations', *Journal of Marketing Research*, 29, 314–329.

Morgan, R. M. and S. D. Hunt (1994) 'The Commitment-Trust Theory of Relationship Marketing', *Journal of Marketing*, 58, 20–38.

Naudé, P. and Buttle, F. (2000) 'Assessing Relationship Quality', *Industrial Marketing Management*, 29, 351–362.

Pavlič Damijan, J. (2001) 'Trgovinski vs. investicijski način vstopa na trge nekdanje Jugoslavije', in Prašnikar, J. (ed.), *Izzivi in priložnosti na trgih nekdanje Jugoslavije* (Ljubljana: Finance).

Prašnikar, J. (ed.) (2001) *Izzivi in priložnosti na trgih nekdanje Jugoslavije* [*Challenges and Opportunities on Former Yugoslav Markets*] (Ljubljana: Finance).

Ravald, A. and Grönroos, C. (1996) 'The Value Concept in Relationship Marketing', *European Journal of Marketing*, 30, 19–30.

Rokeach, M. (1972) *Beliefs, Attitudes and Values: A Theory of Organization and Change* (San Francisco: Jossey-Bass).

Rokeach, M. (1973) *The Nature of Human Values* (New York: Free Press).

Selnes, F. (1998) 'Antecedents and Consequences of Trust and Satisfaction in Buyer–Seller Relationships', *European Journal of Marketing*, 32, 20–30.

Spekman, R. (1988) 'Strategic Supplier Selection: Understanding Long-Term Buyer Relationships', *Business Horizons*, July/August, 75–81.

Statistični urad Republike Slovenije (2010) www.stat.si, accessed 20 June, 2010.

Trompenaars, F. and Hampden-Turner, C. (2000) *Riding the Waves of Culture* (London: Nicholas Brealey Publishing).

Wimmer, A. and Mandjak, T. (2002) 'Business Relationships as Value Drivers?', *Proceedings of 18th Annual IMP Conference*, ESC Dijon, Dijon, p. 154.

# Appendix: Country profiles

## Country profile ALBANIA

### Basic data

| | |
|---|---|
| Area in km² | 28,748 |
| Capital city | Tirana |
| Government type | Republic |
| Currency | Lek (ALL) |
| Main religions (percentages n. a.) | Muslim, Albanian Orthodox, Roman Catholic |
| Economic sectors (2009 estimate) (in % of GDP) | Agriculture 21.4%, Industry 19.4%, Services 59.2% |
| Illiteracy rate (in % of population) (2001 census) | 1.3% |
| Population in mn (2010) | 2.9 |
| Population age profile (2010 estm.) | 0–14: 23.1% 15–64: 67.1% 65+: 9.8% |
| Press freedom | partly free |

# Timeline

| | 1995 | 2000 | 2001 | 2002 | 2003 | 2004 | 2005 | 2006 | 2007 | 2008 | 2009 |
|---|---|---|---|---|---|---|---|---|---|---|---|
| Gross foreign debt in % of GDP | n.a. | n.a. | n.a. | n.a. | n.a. | n.a. | n.a. | n.a. | n.a. | 53.6% | 58.1% |
| GDP per capita (EUR)* | 559 | 914 | 1,014 | 1,100 | 1,393 | 1,832 | 2,048 | 2,226 | 2,631 | 3,141 | 2,896 |
| Export of goods and services (% of GDP) | 12,5% | 19.1% | 20.5% | 20.4% | 20.6% | 21.5% | 22.3% | 25.1% | 28.4% | 29.5% | 28.7% |
| Import of goods and services (% of GDP) | 34.5% | 37.5% | 38.7% | 46.7% | 45.9% | 43.3% | 46.3% | 49.2% | 54.3% | 56.1% | 54.4% |
| Unemployment rate | n.a. | 16.8% | 16.4% | 15.8% | 15.0% | 14.4% | 14.1% | 13.8% | 13.5% | 13.0% | 12.5% |
| Corruption perception index (0: highly corrupt; 10: highly clean) | n.a. | n.a. | n.a. | 2.5 | 2.5 | 2.5 | 2.4 | 2.6 | 2.9 | 3.4 | 3.2 |
| Foreign direct investment, net inflows (% of GDP) | 2.9% | 3.9% | 5.1% | 3.0% | 3.1% | 4.6% | 3.1% | 3.6% | 6.1% | 7.2% | 8.1% |

*Original current USD values converted as per 20 December 2010 (USD-EUR): 1.3147 (European Central Bank, URL: http://www.ecb.int/stats/exchange/eurofxref/html/index.en.html)

*Sources*: CIA World Factbook (2008, 2010); BBC News; The World Bank; Transparency international; Freedom House; National Labour Force Survey.

# Country profile BOSNIA AND HERZEGOVINA

## Basic data

| | |
|---|---|
| Area in km² | 51,209 |
| Capital city | Sarajevo |
| Government type | Emerging federal democratic republic |
| Currency | Convertible mark (BAM) |
| Main religions | Muslim 40%, Orthodox 31%, Roman Catholic 15% |
| Economic sectors (2010) (in % of GDP) | 19,7% Agriculture, 31,0% Industry, 49.3% Services |
| Illiteracy rate (in % of population) (2000 estimate) | 3.3% |
| Population in mn (2010) | 3.8 |
| Population age profile (2010) | 0–17: 20,9%; 18–64: 62,9%, 65+: 16,2% |
| Press freedom | partly free |

Timeline

| | 1995 | 2000 | 2001 | 2002 | 2003 | 2004 | 2005 | 2006 | 2007 | 2008 | 2009 |
|---|---|---|---|---|---|---|---|---|---|---|---|
| Gross public debt in % of GDP | n.a. | n.a. | n.a. | n.a. | n.a. | n.a. | n.a. | 29% | 24.5% | 39% | n.a. |
| GDP per capita (EUR)* | 426 | 1,134 | 1,167 | 1,339 | 1,683 | 2,016 | 2,166 | 2,465 | 3,065 | 3,732 | 3,442 |
| Export of goods and services (% of GDP) | 20.4% | 28.7% | 28.4% | 24.3% | 30.6% | 32.2% | 32.7% | 36.9% | 38.9% | 36.7% | 33.4% |
| Import of goods and services (% of GDP) | 71.5% | 75.5% | 75.9% | 70.9% | 83.2% | 77.5% | 73.9% | 67.1% | 73.3% | 69.4% | 58.0% |
| Unemployment rate | n.a. | 39.7% | 40.0% | 41.1% | 41.6% | 41.8% | 43.9% | 31.1% | 29.0% | 45.5% | 24.1% |
| Corruption perception index (0: highly corrupt; 10: highly clean) | n.a. | n.a. | n.a. | n.a. | 3.3 | 3.1 | 2.9 | 2.9 | 3.3 | 3.2 | 3.0 |
| Foreign direct investment, net inflows (% of GDP) | n.a. | 2.7% | 2.1% | 4.0% | 4.6% | 7.1% | 5.6% | 6.3% | 13.6% | 5.0% | 1.4% |

*Original current USD values converted as per 20 December 2010 (USD-EUR): 1.3147 (European Central Bank, URL: http://www.ecb.int/stats/exchange/eurofxref/html/index.en.html).

Sources: Agency for Statistics of Bosnia and Herzegovina; National Labour Force Survey; CIA World Factbook (2008, 2010); The World Bank; UniCredit Bank Austria AG; Transparency international; Freedom House.

## Country profile BULGARIA

### Basic data

| | |
|---|---|
| Area in km² | 110,879 |
| Capital city | Sofia |
| Government type | Parliamentary democracy |
| Currency | Bulgarian lev (BGN) |
| Main religions (2001 census) | Bulgarian Orthodox 82.6%, Muslim 12.2% |
| Economic sectors (2009) (share of total Gross Value Added) | Agriculture 7%, Industry 32%, Services 61% |
| Illiteracy rate (in % of population) (2001 census) | 1.8% |
| Population in mn (2010) | 7.6 |
| Population age profile (2010) | 0–14: 13.6% 15–64: 68.9% ab 65: 17.5% |
| Press freedom | partly free |

# Timeline

|  | 1995 | 2000 | 2001 | 2002 | 2003 | 2004 | 2005 | 2006 | 2007 | 2008 | 2009 |
|---|---|---|---|---|---|---|---|---|---|---|---|
| Gross foreign debt in % of GDP | n.a. | 86.5% | 76.7% | 70.1% | 65.6% | 63.0% | 69.0% | 78.4% | 100.2% | 108.7% | 111.3% |
| GDP per capita (EUR)* | 1,184 | 1,218 | 1,333 | 1,545 | 2,010 | 2,471 | 2,839 | 3,281 | 4,182 | 5,171 | 4,886 |
| Export of goods and services (% of GDP) | 51.9% | 50.5% | 48.7% | 47.4% | 48.5% | 51.9% | 40.5% | 61.2% | 59.5% | 58.2% | 47.8% |
| Import of goods and services (% of GDP) | 49.9% | 55.8% | 58.1% | 55.5% | 58.9% | 63.4% | 55.6% | 78.8% | 79.2% | 78.7% | 55.8% |
| Unemployment rate | 15.7% | 16.4% | 19.5% | 18.2% | 13.7% | 12.1% | 10.1% | 9.0% | 6.9% | 5.6% | 6.8% |
| Corruption perception index (0: highly corrupt; 10: highly clean) | n.a. | 3.5 | 3.9 | 4.0 | 3.9 | 4.1 | 4.0 | 4.0 | 4.1 | 3.6 | 3.8 |
| Foreign direct investment, net inflows (% of GDP) | 0.7% | 7.8% | 5.9% | 5.7% | 10.1% | 10.5% | 14.9% | 23.4% | 31.4% | 17.8% | 9.4% |

*Original current USD values converted as per 20 December 2010 (USD-EUR): 1.3147 (European Central Bank, URL: http://www.ecb.int/stats/exchange/eurofxref/html/index.en.html)

*Sources:* Eurostat; National Statistical Institute of Bulgaria; CIA World Factbook (2010); The Economist (online); Loman, H. (2009) Country update Bulgaria (Amsterdam: Rabobank Nederland); Eurostat; The World Bank; UniCredit Bank Austria AG; Transparency international; Freedom House.

## Country profile CROATIA

### Basic data

| | |
|---|---|
| Area in km² | 56,594 |
| Capital city | Zagreb |
| Government type | Presidential/parliamentary democracy |
| Currency | Croatian Kuna (HRK) |
| Main religions (2001 census) | Roman Catholic 87.8%, Orthodox 4.4% |
| Economic sectors (2009) (in % of GDP) | 4.6% Agriculture, 30.8% Industry, 64.6% Services |
| Illiteracy rate (in % of population) (2001 census) | 1.8% |
| Population in mn (2010) | 4.4 |
| Population age profile (2008) | 0–14: 15,4%; 15–64: 67,3%; 65+: 17,3% |
| Press freedom | partly free |

## Timeline

| | 1995 | 2000 | 2001 | 2002 | 2003 | 2004 | 2005 | 2006 | 2007 | 2008 | 2009 |
|---|---|---|---|---|---|---|---|---|---|---|---|
| Gross public debt in % of GDP | n.a. | n.a. | n.a. | n.a. | n.a. | 69.1% | 41.7% | 49.7% | 56.2% | 45.6% | n.a. |
| GDP per capita (EUR)* | 3,603 | 3,664 | 3,919 | 4,532 | 5,800 | 6,973 | 7,609 | 8,403 | 10,041 | 11,894 | 10,818 |
| Export of goods and services (% of GDP) | 33.0% | 42.0% | 43.8% | 41.0% | 42.9% | 43.3% | 42.6% | 43.4% | 42.8% | 41.9% | 36.1% |
| Import of goods and services (% of GDP) | 41.4% | 45.3% | 47.6% | 49.4% | 50.8% | 49.6% | 49.1% | 50.4% | 50.4% | 50.3% | 39.4% |
| Unemployment rate | n.a. | 17.0% | 16.3% | 14.7% | 14.1% | 13.6% | 12.6% | 11.1% | 9.6% | 8.4% | 9.1% |
| Corruption perception index (0: highly corrupt; 10: highly clean) | n.a. | 3.7 | 3.9 | 3.8 | 3.7 | 3.5 | 3.4 | 3.4 | 4.1 | 4.4 | 4.1 |
| Foreign direct investment, net inflows (% of GDP) | 0.5% | 5.2% | 6.9% | 4.2% | 6.1% | 2.7% | 4.0% | 7.0% | 8.5% | 8.6% | 4.6% |

*Original current USD values converted as per 20 December 2010 (USD-EUR): 1.3147 (European Central Bank, URL: http://www.ecb.int/stats/exchange/eurofxref/html/index.en.html)

*Sources*: CIA World Factbook (2008, 2010); The Economist (online); Croatian Bureau of Statistics; Eurostat; National Labour Force Survey; The World Bank; Transparency International; Freedom House.

# Country profile FORMER YUGOSLAV REPUBLIC OF MACEDONIA

## Basic data

| | |
|---|---|
| Area in km² | 25,713 |
| Capital city | Skopje |
| Government type | Parliamentary democracy |
| Currency | Denar (MKD) |
| Main religions (2002 census) | Macedonian Orthodox 64.7%, Muslim 33.3% |
| Economic sectors (2009 estimate) (in % of GDP) | Agriculture 12.1%, Industry 29.5%, Services 58.4% |
| Illiteracy rate (in % of population) (2002 census) | 3.9% |
| Population in mn (2010) | 2.1 |
| Population age profile (2010 estimate) | 0–14: 19.2%, 15–64: 69.4%, 65+: 11.4% |
| Press freedom | partly free |

## Timeline

| | 1995 | 2000 | 2001 | 2002 | 2003 | 2004 | 2005 | 2006 | 2007 | 2008 | 2009 |
|---|---|---|---|---|---|---|---|---|---|---|---|
| Gross foreign debt in % of GDP | n.a. | n.a. | 43.1% | 43.4% | 38.9% | 38.2% | n.a. | n.a. | n.a. | n.a. | n.a. |
| GDP per capita (EUR)* | 1,724 | 1,356 | 1,295 | 1,425 | 1,736 | 2,010 | 2,173 | 2,378 | 2,954 | 3,547 | 3,434 |
| Export of goods and services (% of GDP) | 33,0% | 48.6% | 42.7% | 38.0% | 37.9% | 41.1% | 45.5% | 48.1% | 53.4% | 52.6% | 44,3% |
| Import of goods and services (% of GDP) | 42.8% | 63.5% | 56.6% | 58.2% | 54.8% | 61.9% | 62.8% | 66.8% | 72.3% | 78.6% | 67.3% |
| Unemployment rate | n.a. | 32.2% | 30.5% | 31.9% | 36.7% | 37.2% | 37.3% | 36.0% | 34.9% | 33.8% | 32.2% |
| Corruption perception index (0: highly corrupt; 10: highly clean) | n.a. | n.a. | n.a. | n.a. | n.a. | n.a. | n.a. | n.a. | 3.3 | 3.6 | 3.8 |
| Foreign direct investment, net inflows (% of GDP) | 0.2% | 6.0% | 13.0% | 2.8% | 2.5% | 6.0% | 1.7% | 6.7% | 8.8% | 6.2% | 2.7% |

*Original current USD values converted as per 20 December 2010 (USD-EUR): 1.3147 (European Central Bank, URL: http://www.ecb.int/stats/exchange/eurofxref/html/index.en.html)

*Sources:* CIA World Factbook (2010); BBC News; Eurostat; The World Bank; UniCredit Bank Austria AG; Transparency international; Freedom House.

# Country profile HUNGARY

## Basic data

| | |
|---|---|
| Area in km$^2$ | 93,030 |
| Capital city | Budapest |
| Government type | Parliamentary democracy |
| Currency | Hungarian forint (HUF) |
| Main religions (2001 census) | Roman Catholic 51.9%, Calvinist 15.9%, Lutheran 3% |
| Economic sectors (2009) (in % of GDP) | Agriculture 2,5%, Industry 25,3%, Services 72,2% |
| Illiteracy rate (in % of population) (2003 estm.) | 0.6% |
| Population in mn (2010) | 10,0 |
| Population age profile (2010 estm.) | 0–14: 15%, 15–64: 69.3%, 65+: 15.8% |
| Press freedom | free |

# Timeline

| | 1995 | 2000 | 2001 | 2002 | 2003 | 2004 | 2005 | 2006 | 2007 | 2008 | 2009 |
|---|---|---|---|---|---|---|---|---|---|---|---|
| Gross foreign debt in % of GDP | n.a. | 67.3% | 65.5% | 55.8% | 62.3% | 70.3% | 78.4% | 89.1% | 99.3% | 122.6% | 135.2% |
| GDP per capita (EUR)* | 3,288 | 3,567 | 3,971 | 4,979 | 6,332 | 7,682 | 8,309 | 8,535 | 10,496 | 11,720 | 9,788 |
| Export of goods and services (% of GDP) | 46.1% | 72.2% | 71.2% | 63.1% | 60.8% | 63.2% | 66.0% | 77.1% | 80.4% | 81.4% | n.a. |
| Import of goods and services (% of GDP) | 45.8% | 75.8% | 72.5% | 65.1% | 64.7% | 66.5% | 67.8% | 77.8% | 78.8% | 80.2% | n.a. |
| Unemployment rate | 10.2% | 6.4% | 5.7% | 5.8% | 5.9% | 6.1% | 7.2% | 7.5% | 7.4% | 7.8% | 9.8% |
| Corruption perception index (0: highly corrupt; 10: highly clean) | 4.1 | 5.2 | 5.3 | 4.9 | 4.8 | 4.8 | 5.0 | 5.2 | 5.3 | 5.1 | 5.1 |
| Foreign direct investment, net inflows (% of GDP) | 10.8% | 5.8% | 7.4% | 4.5% | 2.6% | 4.4% | 6.9% | 17.5% | 52.1% | 41.0% | −4.5% |

*Original current USD values converted as per 20 December 2010 (USD-EUR): 1.3147 (European Central Bank, URL: http://www.ecb.int/stats/exchange/eurofxref/html/index.en.html)

*Sources*: CIA World Factbook (2010); BBC News; The Economist (online); UniCredit Bank Austria AG; Eurostat; The World Bank; Transparency international; Freedom House.

# Country profile KOSOVO

## Basic data

| | |
|---|---|
| Area in km² | 10,887 |
| Capital city | Priština |
| Government type | Republic |
| Currency | Euro (EUR) |
| Main religions (percentages n. a.) | Muslim, Serbian Orthodox, Roman Catholic |
| Economic sectors (2009 estimate) (in % of GDP) | Agriculture 12.9%, Industry 22.6%, Services 64.5% |
| Illiteracy rate (in % of population) (2007 census) | 8.1% |
| Population in mn (2010) | 2.2 |
| Population age profile (2010) | 0–14: 33%, 15–64: 61%, 65+: 6% |
| Press freedom | n.a. |

# Timeline

| | 1995 | 2000 | 2001 | 2002 | 2003 | 2004 | 2005 | 2006 | 2007 | 2008 | 2009 |
|---|---|---|---|---|---|---|---|---|---|---|---|
| Gross foreign debt in % of GDP | n.a. | n.a. | n.a. | n.a. | n.a. | n.a. | n.a. | n.a. | n.a. | n.a. | n.a. |
| GDP per capita (EUR)* | n.a. | 828 | 1,120 | 1,184 | 1,460 | 1,576 | 1,611 | 1,676 | 1,993 | 2,401 | 2,270 |
| Export of goods and services (% of GDP) | n.a. | n.a. | n.a. | n.a. | n.a. | n.a. | n.a. | 14.1% | 15.1% | 14.9% | 14.1% |
| Import of goods and services (% of GDP) | n.a. | n.a. | n.a. | n.a. | n.a. | n.a. | n.a. | 50.8% | 53.7% | 56.4% | 54.4% |
| Unemployment rate | n.a. | n.a. | 57.1% | 55.0% | 49.7% | 39.7% | 41.4% | 44.9% | 43.6% | 47.5% | 45.4% |
| Corruption perception index (0: highly corrupt; 10: highly clean) | n.a. | n.a. | n.a. | n.a. | n.a. | n.a. | n.a. | n.a. | n.a. | n.a. | n.a. |
| Foreign direct investment, net inflows (% of GDP) | n.a. | n.a. | n.a. | n.a. | n.a. | n.a. | n.a. | n.a. | n.a. | n.a. | n.a. |

*Original current USD values converted as per 20 December 2010 (USD-EUR): 1.3147 (European Central Bank, URL: http://www.ecb.int/stats/exchange/eurofxref/html/index.en.html)

*Sources:* CIA World Factbook 2010; The World Bank; Transparency international; Republic of Kosovo – Ministry of Public Administration, Statistical Office of Kosovo; Freedom House.

# Country profile MOLDOVA

## Basic data

| | |
|---|---|
| Area in km$^2$ | 33,846 |
| Capital city | Chişinău |
| Government type | Republic |
| Currency | Leu (MDL) |
| Main religions (2004 census) | Eastern Orthodox 93,3%, Baptist 1,0% |
| Economic sectors (2009 estimate) (in % of GDP) | Agriculture 10.7%, Industry 16.9%, Services 72.4% |
| Illiteracy rate (in % of population) (2004 census) | 1.1 |
| Population in mn (2009) | 3.6 |
| Population age profile (2009) | 0–14: 16.9%, 15–64: 72.9%, 65+: 10.2% |
| Press freedom | not free |

Timeline

| | 1995 | 2000 | 2001 | 2002 | 2003 | 2004 | 2005 | 2006 | 2007 | 2008 | 2009 |
|---|---|---|---|---|---|---|---|---|---|---|---|
| Gross public debt in % of GDP | n.a. | n.a. | n.a. | n.a. | n.a. | 88.4% | 63.4% | 79.6% | 84.5% | 24.6% | n.a. |
| GDP per capita (EUR)* | 364 | 269 | 310 | 349 | 417 | 548 | 632 | 723 | 936 | 1,290 | 1,153 |
| Export of goods and services (% of GDP) | 49.3% | 49.8% | 49.9% | 52.7% | 53.5% | 50.7% | 51.1% | 45.3% | 47.5% | 40.8% | 36.8% |
| Import of goods and services (% of GDP) | 58.0% | 75.4% | 73.5% | 77.9% | 87.2% | 82.0% | 91.7% | 91.9% | 97.1% | 93.6% | 73.4% |
| Unemployment rate | n.a. | 8.5% | 7.3% | 6.8% | 8.0% | 8.1% | 7.3% | 7.4% | 5.1% | 4.0% | 6.4% |
| Corruption perception index (0: highly corrupt; 10: highly clean) | n.a. | 2.6 | 3.1 | 2.1 | 2.4 | 2.3 | 2.9 | 3.2 | 2.8 | 2.9 | 3.3 |
| Foreign direct investment, net inflows (% of GDP) | 1.5% | 9.9% | 3.7% | 5.1% | 3.7% | 3.4% | 6.4% | 6.8% | 12.3% | 11.8% | 2.4% |

*Original current USD values converted as per 20 December 2010 (USD-EUR): 1.3147 (European Central Bank, URL: http://www.ecb.int/stats/exchange/eurofxref/html/index.en.html)

*Sources:* National Bureau of Statistics of the Republic of Moldova; CIA World Factbook (2008, 2010); BBC News; Eurostat; Transparency international; The World Bank; Freedom House.

## Country profile MONTENEGRO

### Basic data

| | |
|---|---|
| Area in km$^2$ | 13,812 |
| Capital city | Podgorica |
| Government type | Republic |
| Currency | Euro (EUR) |
| Main religions (2003 census) | Orthodox 74.2%, Muslim 17.7% |
| Economic sectors (2009) (share of total Gross Value Added) | Agriculture 10%, Industries (NACE C, D, E) 13.5%, Construction 6.5%, Services 70% |
| Illiteracy rate (in % of population) (2003 census) | 2.4% |
| Population in mn (2009 estm.) | 0.6 |
| Population age profile (2003 census) | 0–14: 20.7%, 15–64: 67.2%, 65+: 12.1% |
| Press freedom | partly free |

# Timeline

| | 1995 | 2000 | 2001 | 2002 | 2003 | 2004 | 2005 | 2006 | 2007 | 2008 | 2009 |
|---|---|---|---|---|---|---|---|---|---|---|---|
| Gross public debt in % of GDP | n.a. | n.a. | n.a. | n.a. | n.a. | n.a. | n.a. | n.a. | n.a. | 38% | n.a. |
| GDP per capita (EUR)* | n.a. | 1,133 | 1,342 | 1,503 | 2,029 | 2,499 | 2,749 | 3,300 | 4,495 | 5,524 | 5,047 |
| Export of goods and services (% of GDP) | n.a. | 36.8% | 38.4% | 35.4% | 30.6% | 42.0% | 43.5% | 49.6% | 44.4% | 39.5% | 32.8% |
| Import of goods and services (% of GDP) | n.a. | 51.1% | 62.0% | 59.9% | 47.0% | 58.1% | 61.1% | 80.0% | 86.7% | 94.0% | 65.9% |
| Unemployment rate | n.a. | 19.3% | 21.2% | 20.7% | 22.7% | 27.7% | 30.3% | 29.6% | 19.3% | 16.8% | 19.1% |
| Corruption perception index (0: highly corrupt; 10: highly clean) | n.a | n.a | n.a | n.a | 2.3 (data for Serbia & Montenegro) | 2.7 (data for Serbia & Montenegro) | 2.8 (data for Serbia & Montenegro) | n.a | 3.3 | 3.4 | 3.9 |
| Foreign direct investment, net inflows (% of GDP) | n.a | n.a | n.a | n.a | n.a | n.a | n.a | n.a | 25.3% | 19.6% | 32.3% |

*Original current USD values converted as per 20 December 2010 (USD-EUR): 1.3147 (European Central Bank, URL: http://www.ecb.int/stats/exchange/eurofxref/html/index.en.html)

*Sources:* Statistical Office of Montenegro – MONSTAT; Eurostat; BBC News; CIA World Factbook (2008, 2010); The World Bank; Transparency international; Amnesty International; Employment Agency of Montenegro; Freedom House.

# Country profile ROMANIA

## Basic data

| | |
|---|---|
| Area in km$^2$ | 238,391 |
| Capital city | Bucharest |
| Government type | Republic |
| Currency | Romanian leu (RON) |
| Main religions (2002 census) | Eastern Orthodox 86.8%, Protestant 7.5%, Roman Catholic 4.7% |
| Economic sectors (2009) (share of total Gross Value Added) | Agriculture 6.5%, Industry 37.8%, Services 55.7% |
| Illiteracy rate (in % of population) (2002 census) | 2.7% |
| Population in mn (2010) | 21.5 |
| Population age profile (2010) | 0–14: 15.1%, 15–64: 70.0%, 65+: 14.9% |
| Press freedom | partly free |

# Timeline

| | 1995 | 2000 | 2001 | 2002 | 2003 | 2004 | 2005 | 2006 | 2007 | 2008 | 2009 |
|---|---|---|---|---|---|---|---|---|---|---|---|
| Gross foreign debt in % of GDP | 19.0% | 30.4% | 32.0% | 36.8% | 37.8% | 38.8% | 36.9% | 44.2% | 50.9% | 50.8% | 72.5% |
| GDP per capita (EUR)* | 1,190 | 1,256 | 1,381 | 1,599 | 2,082 | 2,648 | 3,478 | 4,321 | 5,976 | 7,074 | 5,705 |
| Export of goods and services (% of GDP) | 27.6% | 32.7% | 33.4% | 35.4% | 34.7% | 35.9% | 32.9% | 29.6% | 30.7% | 31.0% | 33.3% |
| Import of goods and services (% of GDP) | 33.2% | 37.9% | 41.1% | 41.1% | 42.2% | 45.0% | 43.3% | 38.6% | 42.9% | 43.8% | 40.2% |
| Unemployment rate | n.a. | 7.3% | 6.8% | 8.6% | 7.0% | 8.1% | 7.2% | 7.3% | 6.4% | 5.8% | 6.9% |
| Corruption perception index (0: highly corrupt; 10: highly clean) | n.a. | 2.9 | 2.8 | 2.6 | 2.8 | 2.9 | 3.0 | 3.1 | 3.7 | 3.8 | 3.8 |
| Foreign direct investment, net inflows (% of GDP) | 1.2% | 2.8% | 2.9% | 2.5% | 3.1% | 8.5% | 6.6% | 9.3% | 5.9% | 6.9% | 3.9% |

*Original current USD values converted as per 20 December 2010 (USD-EUR): 1.3147 (European Central Bank, URL: http://www.ecb.int/stats/exchange/eurofxref/html/index.en.html)

*Sources*: National Institute of Statistics of Romania; National Labour Force Survey; CIA – World Factbook (2010); BBC News; The Economist (online), Transparency international; Freedom House.

# Country profile SERBIA

## Basic data

| | |
|---|---|
| Area in km$^2$ | 77,474 (Kosovo excluded) |
| Capital city | Belgrade |
| Government type | Republic |
| Currency | Serbian Dinar (RSD) |
| Main religions (2002 census) | Serbian Orthodox 85%, Catholic 5.5%, Muslim 3.2% |
| Economic sectors (2007) (in % of GDP) | Agriculture 13.3%, Industry 29.1%, Services 57.7% |
| Illiteracy rate (in % of population) (2003 census) | 3.6% |
| Population in mn (2010) | 7.3 |
| Population age profile (2009) | 0–15: 16,4%, 16–64: 66,6%, 65+: 17,1% |
| Press freedom | Free |

487

# Timeline

| | 1995 | 2000 | 2001 | 2002 | 2003 | 2004 | 2005 | 2006 | 2007 | 2008 | 2009 |
|---|---|---|---|---|---|---|---|---|---|---|---|
| Gross public debt in % of GDP | n.a. | n.a. | n.a. | n.a. | n.a. | n.a. | 53.1% | 53.1% | 37.0% | n.a. | n.a. |
| GDP per capita (EUR)* | n.a. | 615 | 1,155 | 1,532 | 2,000 | 2,417 | 2,579 | 2,998 | 4,059 | 5,056 | 4,466 |
| Export of goods and services (% of GDP) | n.a. | 23.9% | 21.3% | 19.6% | 22.2% | 23.4% | 26.2% | 29.9% | 30.2% | 30.4% | 27.5% |
| Import of goods and services (% of GDP) | n.a. | 40.5% | 39.4% | 40.1% | 41.6% | 50.0% | 47.2% | 51.4% | 54.1% | 53.7% | 43.9% |
| Unemployment rate | n.a. | 13.3% | 13.3% | 14.5% | 16.0% | 18.7% | 21.1% | 21.0% | 18.3% | 13.6% | 16.1% |
| Corruption perception index (0: highly corrupt; 10: highly clean) | n.a. | n.a. | n.a. | n.a. | 2.3 (data for Serbia & Montenegro) | 2.7 (data for Serbia & Montenegro) | 2.8 (data for Serbia & Montenegro) | 3.0 | 3.4 | 3.4 | 3.5 |
| Foreign direct investment, net inflows (% of GDP) | n.a. | 0.9% | 1.6% | 3.8% | 7.1% | 4.3% | 8.1% | 17.0% | 8.8% | 6.1% | 4.5% |

*Original current USD values converted as per 20 December 2010 (USD-EUR): 1.3147 (European Central Bank, URL: http://www.ecb.int/stats/exchange/eurofxref/html/index.en.html)

*Sources:* CIA World Factbook (2008, 2010); The Economist (online); The World Bank; Transparency international; Statistical Office of the Republic of Serbia; National Labour Force Survey; Federal Statistical Office of Germany; Freedom House.

## Country profile SLOVENIA

### Basic data

| | |
|---|---|
| Area in km² | 20,273 |
| Capital city | Ljubljana |
| Government type | Parliamentary republic |
| Currency | Euro (EUR) |
| Main religions (2002 census) | Catholic 57.8%, Muslim 2.4%, Orthodox 2.3% |
| Economic sectors (2009) (in % of GDP) | Agriculture 2.1%, Industry 30%, Services 67.9% |
| Illiteracy rate (in % of population) | 0.3% |
| Population in mn (2010) | 2.0 |
| Population age profile (2010 estm.) | 0–14: 13.5%, 15–64: 69.9%, 65+: 16.5% |
| Press freedom | Free |

## Timeline

| | 1995 | 2000 | 2001 | 2002 | 2003 | 2004 | 2005 | 2006 | 2007 | 2008 | 2009 |
|---|---|---|---|---|---|---|---|---|---|---|---|
| Gross foreign debt in % of GDP | n.a. | 34.3% | 35.8% | 48.9% | 52.8% | 58.7% | 69.4% | 78.5% | 100.7% | 105.1% | 115% |
| GDP per capita (EUR)* | 7,956 | 7,606 | 7.785 | 8,800 | 11,075 | 12,845 | 13,593 | 14,763 | 17,833 | 20,469 | 18,047 |
| Export of goods and services (% of GDP) | 49.9% | 53.9% | 55.5% | 55.2% | 54.0% | 58.0% | 62.1% | 66.5% | 69.5% | 67.7% | 58.9% |
| Import of goods and services (% of GDP) | 51.8% | 57.4% | 56.3% | 54.1% | 54.2% | 59.3% | 62.5% | 67.0% | 71.3% | 70.7% | 57.4% |
| Unemployment rate | 7.2% | 6.7% | 6.2% | 6.3% | 6.7% | 6.3% | 6.5% | 6.0% | 4.9% | 4.4% | 5.9% |
| Corruption perception index (0: highly corrupt; 10: highly clean) | n.a. | 5.5 | 5.2 | 6.0 | 5.9 | 6.0 | 6.1 | 6.4 | 6.6 | 6.7 | 6.6 |
| Foreign direct investment, net inflows (% of GDP) | 0.7% | 0.7% | 2.5% | 7.2% | 1.0% | 2.5% | 1.5% | 1.7% | 3.2% | 3.6% | -1.2% |

*Original current USD values converted as per 20 December 2010 (USD-EUR): 1.3147 (European Central Bank, URL: http://www.ecb.int/stats/exchange/eurofxref/html/index.en.html)

*Sources:* UniCredit Bank Austria AG; CIA World Factbook (2010); The Economist (online); Eurostat; The World Bank; Transparency international; Freedom House.

# Index